Rude & Barbarous Kingdom Revisited

Essays in Russian History and Culture
in Honor of Robert O. Crummey

RUDE & BARBAROUS KINGDOM REVISITED

ESSAYS IN RUSSIAN HISTORY AND CULTURE IN HONOR OF ROBERT O. CRUMMEY

EDITED BY

CHESTER S. L. DUNNING

RUSSELL E. MARTIN

DANIEL ROWLAND

Bloomington, Indiana, 2008

SLAVICA

ISBN 978-0-89357-359-1

Library of Congress Cataloging-in-Publication Data

Rude & barbarous kingdom revisited : essays in Russian history and culture
in honor of Robert O. Crummey / edited by Chester S. L. Dunning, Russell E.
Martin, Daniel Rowland.
     p. cm.
  Includes bibliographical references.
  ISBN 978-0-89357-359-1
  1. Russia--History. I. Crummey, Robert O. II. Dunning, Chester S. L., 1949-
III. Martin, Russell, 1963- IV. Rowland, Daniel B. (Daniel Bruce), 1941- V.
Title: Rude and barbarous kingdom revisited.

DK4.R83 2009
947--dc22

2008040701

Slavica Publishers
Indiana University
2611 E. 10th St.
Bloomington, IN 47408-2603
USA

[Tel.] 1-812-856-4186
[Toll-free] 1-877-SLAVICA
[Fax] 1-812-856-4187
[Email] slavica@indiana.edu
[www] http://www.slavica.com/

Contents

Rulers and Ruling Elites

Monks and Old Believers

Rude & Barbarous Kingdom

Culture, Law, Women, and War

Introduction

We the contributors and editors gratefully dedicate this volume to Robert. O. Crummey, mentor, scholar, and friend. In his long career, Bob has enriched the field of Russian and Muscovite history in diverse ways, each characterized by his trademark intelligence, hard work, honesty, and great sense of humor. Each of the editors has benefited from his friendship and direct mentorship. One was his official Ph.D. student at Yale, while the two others had a more informal, but no less important, apprenticeship during and after the completion of their dissertations. For all of us, Bob has been a constant supporter, always ready with encouragement and sound advice, year in and year out. We have depended on his knowledge of Muscovite history to guide our own work for decades; we have basked in a friendship that knows no limits of time or space; and we have admired Bob's own continuing scholarship, which seems to get ever better as the years pass.

We have chosen the occasion of the 40th anniversary of the publication of Professor Crummey's famous compilation *Rude & Barbarous Kingdom: Russia in the Accounts of Sixteenth-Century English Voyagers* to celebrate his life and work. That volume, with its provocative and controversial title, excellent textual work (by Lloyd Berry), and remarkably full annotation, has proved the most popular and useful collection of texts by English visitors to Muscovy ever published. It enunciated no grand theories, but has served as an invaluable guide to a crucial set of sources for the interpretation of early modern Russia for generations of students and scholars, including, no doubt, every contributor to this volume. It was also Prof. Crummey's first major publication. We happily celebrate the anniversary of this publication, which launched both the career of Prof. Crummey and a passionate interest in Muscovy in many of us.

Professor Crummey was born in Nova Scotia and raised in Nova Scotia and Toronto. He received his B.A. from Victoria College in Toronto in 1958. He immediately proceeded to the University of Chicago, where he earned both his M.A. (1959) and, working with the legendary Michael Cherniavsky, his Ph.D. (1964). After one year teaching at the University of Illinois at Champaign/Urbana, he was hired by Yale University, serving both as an assistant professor (1965–71) and associate professor (1971–74). As a result of a university decision to abolish his position (discussed below in the two personal introductions), Prof. Crummey moved to the University of California, Davis, where he had a highly successful career. He was granted tenure upon his appointment in 1974, was made full professor in 1979, and served as

Rude & Barbarous Kingdom Revisited: Essays in Russian History and Culture in Honor of Robert O. Crummey. Chester S. L. Dunning, Russell E. Martin, and Daniel Rowland, eds. Bloomington, IN: Slavica Publishers, 2008, 1–2.

Associate Dean (1986–88), Acting Dean (1988–90), and Dean (1990–94) of the College of Letters and Science at Davis.

After nearly a decade of work in administration, Prof. Crummey retired from his official duties at Davis, but held a series of short-term appointments at some of America's most prominent universities. He was Visiting Adjunct Professor at Columbia University and Visiting Professor at the University of California, Berkeley in 1995. The following year, he was the Union Pacific Visiting Professor at the Early Modern History Center, University of Minnesota. He won many prestigious fellowships and honors over his long career, including awards from the Canada Council (1968–69), the American Council of Learned Societies (1973 and 1976), the Kennan Institute for Advanced Russian Studies (1988), and the Harriman Institute at Columbia University, where he was Senior Fellow in 1995. In 1989, he won both a National Endowment for the Humanities Fellowship and a University of California President's Fellowship in the Humanities, but had to decline both in order to take up his duties as Dean of Letters and Science.

A number of individuals and institutions have helped us assemble and publish this volume. It is our great pleasure to recognize them here. Our greatest debt is to our contributors, who have produced a series of truly remarkable essays, and have done so in a timely manner, allowing us to keep to our tight schedule. They have responded with alacrity to our editorial pestering and have taken our suggestions to heart. Administrative assistance for the volume was gladly and ably provided by Lori Shaffer, secretary of the Department of Religion, History, Philosophy, and Classics at Westminster College, who oversaw the initial invitations to contributors and all other correspondence. Anatoli Dorosh, a research assistant also at Westminster College, provided essential help with administrative matters as well, and with copy editing and tracking down sources and bibliography. Arnold Krammer of Texas A&M University offered us his expertise on modern Europe. David Hudson, also of Texas A&M University, provided expertise in historical geography. Elsie Kersten helped us in a myriad ways using new technology and software. We are grateful to Slavica Publishers for undertaking a type of publication that few other presses are prepared to support, and for fine editorial work on the completed manuscript. George Fowler and Vicki Polansky of Slavica have been invaluable sources of advice and admonitions. There would surely be no book without the help of these colleagues, staff, and students.

Chester S. L. Dunning
Russell E. Martin
Daniel Rowland

An Appreciation of Robert O. Crummey

Daniel Rowland

Bob Crummey belongs to a generation of American scholars of Muscovy that has made a truly extraordinary contribution to our knowledge of early modern Russia. Prof. Crummey's remarkable corpus of published work, as well as his profound influence on his own students and on many others not officially under his academic care, clearly places him at the forefront of this remarkable generation. These short comments cannot do justice to his contributions, but they can provide a short overview, and some personal memories from one of his Ph.D. students at Yale in the late 1960s and early 1970s.

Robert Crummey has revolutionized two of the most important subfields within Muscovite history: studies of the Old Belief and studies of the Muscovite elite. He has also written more general studies that place the history of Muscovy in the broader contexts of Russian history, European history, and world history.

Bob is recognized worldwide as one of the greatest scholars of the Old Belief. His dissertation at Chicago concentrated on Old Believers in the Olonets region, chiefly the famous Vyg community there, and his first monograph (1970), now regarded as a classic, was on the same subject. Given the restraints on Old Believer studies under the Russian Empire, as well as the vicissitudes of the historical profession in the Soviet period, Bob was among a small group of scholars, including important Russian specialists with whom he has collaborated closely, who elevated Old Believer studies to a new academic level and may almost be said to have founded the subject on a modern scholarly basis. Over time, however, Bob's emphasis has changed somewhat, from the study of the "social and economic development" of the Chicago thesis (even then an overly narrow description) to the broad cultural approach to the Old Belief that particularly characterizes his work in the 1990s and beyond. He has been remarkably successful, perhaps uniquely so, in giving his readers a view of how Old Believers, over a remarkably long span of time and in many places, looked at their world—the cultural and spiritual convictions that motivated them to do what they did.

His study of the boyar elite is no less impressive, and perhaps even more respected. In a series of prosopographical studies in the 1970s, Bob surveyed the composition of the Boyar Duma from the time of Ivan the IV through the reign of Peter the Great, summing up and developing his conclusions in his 1983 classic, *Aristocrats and Servitors*. Again, he developed a three-dimensional

Rude & Barbarous Kingdom Revisited: Essays in Russian History and Culture in Honor of Robert O. Crummey. Chester S. L. Dunning, Russell E. Martin, and Daniel Rowland, eds. Bloomington, IN: Slavica Publishers, 2008, 3–7.

picture of these crucially important players in Muscovite politics, tracing their
military and court careers, their economic interests and connections, and, as
far as possible, their religious and other belief systems. He also compared
these aristocrats with their counterparts in Western Europe. *Aristocrats and
Servitors* and his earlier essays on continuity and change within the boyar
aristocracy are still our best source for a full picture of this all-important
group of people, particularly in the 17th century.

   Prof. Crummey has put his pioneering detailed knowledge to work to
give a wider group of readers a more general view of Muscovy. His most
important contribution under this rubric is, of course, his *The Formation of
Muscovy, 1304–1613*, a period, we should note in passing, that ends just as the
17th century, the century at the center of most of Bob's other research, begins.
This slender volume has become the first stop for students and scholars alike
in finding a quick answer to a question or seeking a balanced view of a
historiographic dispute. It remains the best overall textbook for that period,
not only in English, but in any language. His 1989 edited book on what
"reform" has meant at various periods in Russian history not only illuminates
a crucial subject often misunderstood, but places reforms under Ivan the
Terrible and projects during the Time of Troubles into the overall context of
reform throughout Russian history. In several incisive articles Bob has
explored the degree to which ideas from the historiography of Western
Europe ("absolutism," "the general crisis of the seventeenth century") apply
(or don't) to the case of early modern Russia. His more general works have
often been published appropriately in venues not specifically devoted to
Russia, ranging from his seminal article in the *Journal of Modern History* on
absolutism to his reflections on modernization and reform in Russia for the
Newsletter for Modern Chinese History published in Taipei.

   Finally, we come to the book whose title is reflected in *our* title, *Rude &
Barbarous Kingdom*. This book was startlingly successful in bringing some of
the most important and accessible (and controversial) primary sources on
16th-century Muscovy to a broad audience, particularly of university
students. A quick check of the Library of Congress database reveals that some
849 libraries worldwide hold one or more copies of the book, with many
libraries holding multiple copies. Doubtless, the database missed many copies
in non-U.S. libraries. The book is so successful partly, no doubt, because of the
editing of the texts done by Lloyd Berry, but largely because of the extensive
notes provided by Bob, notes which verify or challenge virtually every statement by the English visitors on the basis of Bob's exhaustive knowledge of
the scholarship in Russian as well as in Western languages. The result is that
the volume's notes constitute a kind of summary of academic knowledge on
16th-century Russia, and thus provide an essential context to help students
and other readers to put the visitors' often one-sided statements into context.
Many generations of students, including many at my own university, have

first become acquainted with Muscovy, and the fascinating challenges its interpretation presents, by reading this wonderful book.

Among the many qualities that have enabled Bob to create such a large body of impressive work, I would like to single out four. First, Bob was (and is) an exceptionally hard worker. I remember calling him around Labor Day one year when I was his student at Yale, and he told me that he was planning to take that holiday off from work, his first day off since Christmas. Everything he has done bears the stamp of his amazing energy and thoroughness. Second, Bob has focused much effort on languages. His Russian is excellent, allowing not only close and regular collaboration with Russian colleagues now for many decades and participation in conferences and seminars in Russia, but also a number of publications in Russian. Unusually, he also knows Finnish well, having published an early article in that language. Most important, he has developed a knowledge of German and a deep respect for German scholars of Muscovite affairs. While for many of us American scholars of Muscovy, the German language is something of an Achilles' heel, Bob has made a major point of bringing German and North American scholars together, by regularly reviewing books by German scholars, by organizing the participation of German scholars in American conferences, and by happily returning the favor by traveling to Germany to present his own work. Third, Bob has developed a well-deserved reputation for scrupulous fairness and evenhandedness in a field that, by nature of the dynamic scholarship in it, is often contentious. In his reviews and his comments at conferences, he always considers all sides of a controversy, and offers his typical judicious evaluation on whatever question is at hand. Finally, Bob has a wry, a very wry, sense of humor, that appears sometimes in his published work, but more often in person, when a particularly apt and humorous metaphor draws the poison from a potentially confrontational discussion and restores a healthy perspective.

Given his scholarly achievements, one would think that Bob Crummey would have had little time to spare for his students. Nothing could be further from the truth. I arrived at Yale shortly after Bob did, and thus my time with him as my mentor coincided with his attempts to achieve the almost impossible goal (in those days) of getting tenure from within at Yale. In spite of the tenure pressure that I saw devastate other junior faculty members at Yale, Bob was always available to help me and his other students, literally at any hour of the day or night, and on any subject, whether personal or professional. I simply can't remember a single occasion when he was too busy to see me or answer a question. (Like most graduate students, I was not well trained to wait for the proper time and place.) He remained remarkably cheerful and upbeat, again in spite of great professional and personal stress. Here again, his wonderful sense of humor came into play, for he used humorous irony to great advantage to diffuse his students' concerns, both about our own careers and his own. His ability to laugh at problems always seemed to make them smaller in our minds.

Alexis Pogorelskin has written in detail about Bob's departure from Yale, putting it in a perspective that we at the time only dimly perceived. What we did perceive was how unjust, and how disastrous for us, that departure was. Unaware of the real forces at work, which had little or nothing to do with Bob's qualifications, we all did everything lowly graduate students could do to persuade Yale to keep Bob (though much of that effort occurred after I had left New Haven). What I remember most from that painful episode is Bob's remarkable lack of bitterness. I had seen other junior faculty members be badly and permanently scarred by just this experience, but Bob emerged from it seemingly stronger and happier than before. He threw himself into his new life at U. C. Davis with gusto, and with the remarkable success attested to by his impressive achievements there.

Alexis has also written about Bob's exceptional skill as a seminar leader. My recollections parallel hers: in a department with a number of frighteningly impressive faculty members, Bob stood out for his thoroughly unpretentious manner and his genuine respect for each of his students, in spite of the diversity of their backgrounds and degrees of preparation. He was unusual in the department in concentrating on our virtues rather than our demerits. I know that I was a frustrating student. I had a good record coming in, but I was too often distracted by non-academic matters, particularly the Yale Russian Chorus. An enthusiast for both singing and Russia, Bob indulged me in this interest, something I remain profoundly grateful for.

I was also particularly impressed by Bob's undergraduate lectures in Russian history. Like his published work, they were beautifully crafted and based on a remarkably complete knowledge of the evolving scholarship. He used quotations from primary sources with great frequency, bringing such characters as Peter the Great and Catherine the Great to life through primary-source anecdotes about their personalities. More important, he was consistent in stressing the large themes of Russian history, many illuminated by his own research: the nature of the autocracy, the meaning and function of reform, the nature and limits of the government, and so on. And, of course, they were often very funny, again in the wry way so typical of Bob.

Years later, I had a chance to see these lectures in a new light. I was hired at the University of Kentucky before I had completed my dissertation, and Bob, in a typically generous gesture, send me a photocopy of his entire set of lectures, so that I could concentrate on finishing my thesis. As a result, I have looked virtually every year at Bob's notes as I prepare my own lectures, and I am ever more impressed by them. At first, he wrote out every word of every lecture, but then developed shorter outlines that allowed him to speak more spontaneously while still having precise wording to fall back on. In both versions, I can now appreciate, as I could not when I was listening as a graduate student, the incredible care that he put into these lectures. Each was a carefully polished piece of prose, each covered the subject thoroughly in just the right amount of time, and each has stood the test of time since I first received them from Bob.

Looking back on my 41 years of work with Bob since I arrived at Yale in 1966, the one word that comes to mind is "supportive." I had not learned Russian as an undergraduate, and had to pick it up as I went. Bob was patient with me, while insisting that I buckle down and get the requisite knowledge of both Russian and Church Slavonic. My interest in cultural, rather than social or economic, history was unfashionable, but Bob obviously shared that interest and encouraged me at every turn. He was a constant help as I sought a job in an extremely tight job market, providing both wise advice and endless letters of recommendation. Once I had the job, he continued to help, not only by taking the extraordinary step of sending all of his lectures, beautifully typed, but by keeping in touch, helping with the dissertation, and giving advice about academic life. He took me under his wing at my first convention of the American Association for the Advancement of Slavic Studies, introducing a quivering newcomer to the major lights of the profession with exaggerated claims about my talents. Ever since, he has been a one-man cheering section for my work, offering generous praise as well as hard-headed advice on publishing, fellowships, and other essential topics.

Although it is impossible to repay the debt that I owe to Bob Crummey, I try to do so by attempting to treat my own students with the care and consideration that Bob showed to me. Like the other editors, I hope that this volume will be a token of my appreciation, in my case for over 40 years of inspired mentorship.

Remembering Bob Crummey at Yale

Alexis E. Pogorelskin

I first met Bob Crummey at Yale, where I pursued a doctorate in Russian history. Although the modern period attracted me, I studied with Bob at every opportunity and taught sections in his undergraduate surveys. He has had a profound influence on me as a scholar and a teacher.

The reader of this collection will readily discern Bob's influence on my work. I have contributed a prosopographical study of Lenin's possible successors at the critical moment when his health had failed and the Bolshevik elite stood on display at the Twelfth Party Congress in April 1923. Bob was just beginning work on the prosopographical study of the members of the Boyar Duma of the 17th century that would become his masterful *Aristocrats and Servitors* when I began graduate study with him.

As my contribution suggests, I owe to Bob a deep sense of the continuities of Russian history. The crown, for example, has always found a way to control the regions. In Russia, power resides at the center. Bob has written that the Boyar elite depended "on the crown for rank and service assignments that brought power, economic prosperity, and social standing...."[1] I study a latter-day tsar who used the Secretariat and the *nomenklatura* to control the state and its empire in the same way. Kamenev and Zinov'ev would have been well served to realize that their regional power bases in Moscow and Leningrad, respectively, made them vulnerable to Stalin's pervasive control which radiated from the hub of the party in the Secretariat. By the same token, swift was the rise of those who comprehended in 1920–23 the significance of the power of appointment which the Secretariat of the party monopolized. Regional patrons such as Kamenev and Zinov'ev could not hope to wield power for long. As a student of the Soviet 1920s, I have found that Bob's instruction in the rude and barbarous kingdom has served me well.

Bob came to Yale in 1967, two years before I did. Those were good years in American higher education, especially so at Yale. Kingman Brewster, president of Yale since 1963, had launched an academic renaissance of the institution. Between 1963 and 1969 "the ladder faculty — assistant, associate, and full professors — jumped by eighty percent...."[2] History was among the blessed. Not only had Yale seen the potential in a brilliant first-year academic at Illinois in Muscovite history, in 1969 alone the department had lured R. R.

---

[1] Robert O. Crummey, *Aristocrats and Servitors: The Boyar Elite in Russia, 1613–1689* (Princeton, NJ: Princeton University Press, 1983), 168.

[2] Geoffrey Kabaservice, *The Guardians: Kingman Brewster, His Circle, and the Rise of the Liberal Establishment* (New York: Henry Holt and Co., Inc., 2004), 198.

Rude & Barbarous Kingdom Revisited: Essays in Russian History and Culture in Honor of Robert O. Crummey. Chester S. L. Dunning, Russell E. Martin, and Daniel Rowland, eds. Bloomington, IN: Slavica Publishers, 2008, 9–12.

Palmer from Princeton and Peter Gay from Columbia. As a first-year Ph.D. candidate, I had an embarrassment of riches from which to choose.

Few of us realized how significant the changes at Yale were. Brewster sought to undo past mistakes that had cost the institution dearly. Yale had, in an earlier day, managed its money poorly; and, unlike Harvard, suffered significant losses in the stock market crash of 1929. When brilliant European academics sought refuge in this country in the 1930s, Yale was not among the institutions that hastened to take them in. It had little money for expansion and new equipment. Worse still, anti-Semitism besmirched both hiring decisions and admissions. Brewster, who graduated from Yale in 1941, has referred to the "subliminal anti-Semitism" that permeated Yale in that era.[3] It did not end there. A Jewish quota in admissions existed until 1960. Anti-Semitism also discouraged Yale from hiring from among the flood of brilliant scientists on the job market after the Manhattan Project shut down.

Brewster came to the Yale presidency determined to do two things: rejuvenate the university through new faculty ("even by 1960, almost half the faculty were Yale products")[4] and to make Yale competitive in the sciences. He succeeded brilliantly in both regards. Among other achievements, he established the first computer science department in the Ivy League.[5] Those among the "old Blue" aristocrats who joined him in creating a new Yale flourished. George Pierson, who chaired the History Department, expanded instruction in non-Western societies.[6] The renowned Eurasianist George Vernadsky, who established Russian history at Yale, may have encouraged Pierson in those innovations. Brewster, at first, certainly supported them. The Russian pattern in the exercise of power came to prevail. Comfortable academic fiefdoms disappeared as Brewster used the power of the presidency to re-make the institution.

They were heady times for those of us in Russian history. Firuz Kazemzadeh imparted his fascination with the empire to us. Bob guided us into Muscovite historiography with diligence and respect, not only for the texts before us, but for our ability to comprehend them. He encouraged us to converse as equals with those whose work we read. In Bob's classes we steeped ourselves in the work of Zimin, Skrynnikov, Veselovskii, Lur'e, Likhachev, and Platonov. We argued over the essays in *Kritika*, then the work of Harvard faculty and graduate students. We talked of starting a similar publication of our own. When I took Bob's seminar on Muscovite history, he would arrive to find the group already in earnest discussion of the week's reading. He simply joined in.

Bob's own work had taken a new direction at that time. He had begun to collect meticulous data on the 17th-century Boyar Duma. We joined in the new project and analyzed the data along with him. Bob generously shared his

---

[3] Dan A. Oren, *Joining the Club: A History of Jews at Yale* (New Haven: Yale University Press, 1982), 82, quoted in Kabaservice, *The Guardians*, 66.

[4] Kabaservice, *The Guardians*, 190.

[5] Ibid., 194.

[6] Ibid., 191.

work, initiating us into new methodologies, which as noted above, I still employ.

In the early 1970s Muscovite history was hot. Had there been a Chosen Council? Was Ivan IV literate? Ivan III intrigued me. I encouraged my younger brother to re-name his rock band Nil Sorskii and the Judaizers, to no avail. We poured over Keenan's *Kurbskii-Groznyi Apocrypha*, "the magic circle," Bob dubbed it. The field itself seemed a magic circle.

Bob in those days was an Associate Professor without tenure, a peculiar place within the academic hierarchy. The department supported and promoted him. The university itself waited to grant him tenure. I must now return to the larger picture of the university to explain why it did not.

Kingman Brewster's success at rebuilding Yale had come at a price. The bill for the expansion of the 1960s came due in the 1970s. As early as 1967, Brewster had confided in his close friend, McGeorge Bundy, "Yale is ... excellent [at last] and broke."[7] By the mid-1970s there were numerous reasons why the university's resources had not improved.[8] Yale's decision to go co-ed in 1969, one of the jewels in the crown of change, cost the university dearly. The Ford Foundation withdrew its generous subventions, and the Vietnam war had drained funds that might have gone to higher education. Yale, in particular, faced a challenge unbeknownst to the institution. Kingman Brewster, for his opposition to the war, had made President Nixon's notorious enemies list. In practice, John Dean later explained, membership on the list meant "how best can we screw them."[9] For the institution that Brewster represented, it resulted in fewer grants and contracts; litigations and prosecutions increased.[10] Brewster's program of expansion contracted.

Yale's president could not face making the cuts that were now necessary. He turned, in 1972, to Richard Cooper, whom he plucked from the Economics Department to serve as Provost. "Some departments suffered only minor pruning, while the budgets of others were slashed 25 percent or more."[11] In the midst of Cooper's two years as Provost, Bob came up for tenure. He had left for Moscow in mid-year on an IREX, having been told by a senior member of the department, "It's in the bag." The senior members, as predicted, unanimously voted him appointment without term; but the days were long gone when as Brewster had proclaimed, "Ultimately the faculty must decide who the faculty shall be."[12]

Cooper decided to cut in the field of Russian history, and Brewster backed him up. We rallied. Kazemzadeh went to the president to argue the

---

[7] Kingman Brewster, Jr. to McGeorge Bundy, 2 May 1967, Brewster Presidential Records, RU ii I-98: 8, quoted in Kabaservice, *The Guardians*, 325.

[8] See discussion in Kabaservice, *The Guardians*, 324–25.

[9] John Dean to H. R. Haldeman, Nixon Presidential Materials, Haldeman Files, box 270, quoted in Kabaservice, *The Guardians*, 439.

[10] Kabaservice, *The Guardians*, 439.

[11] Ibid., 429.

[12] Yale University News Bureau, News Release #302, 8 March 1965, Brewster Presidential Records, RU ii I-44: 2, quoted in Kabaservice, *The Guardians*, 226.

case for Bob. Brewster seemed to take a dim view of Muscovite history. In the parlance of the time, it was not "relevant." The History Department's rapid growth now made it vulnerable. Bob's students joined the effort to keep him. We wrote the administration of his extraordinary contribution to the life of the university. We praised his "mental agility" in the classroom, that is, his ability to fine tune discussion or take it in an entirely different direction. He possessed an innate sensitivity to the intellectual rhythms of his students and brought out the best in all of us. I had won a Graduate Prize Teaching Fellowship, in part, because of the classroom atmosphere that Bob created and imparted to his T.A.s.

To no avail. Bob returned from Moscow to complete a terminal year. But that year the sun rose in the West. First, the University of California at Davis called to tell Bob that the History Department had hired him. Several weeks later, I had just finished teaching a class on the Witte System to find Bob waiting on the landing outside the classroom, grinning from ear to ear. He told me that the Chair of the History Department at Davis had called the night before to inform him that he had been granted tenure. He would leave for California unburdened by the anxieties that had plagued him (and his graduate students) at Yale.

A year later I left for England to take up a Rhodes Visiting Fellowship at St. Hilda's College, Oxford. We had all landed on our feet. While at Oxford I regularly went down to London to have lunch with Leonard Schapiro. One morning I arrived early and decided to spend a leisurely hour strolling through the Tate. As I paused before a painting, I realized that someone else had been as intrigued by the piece as I. Glancing to my right, I caught the unmistakable chiseled features of Yale's former president, now our ambassador to the court of St. James. He too, it seemed, was catching a brief respite from the day's schedule. I let go the moment to ask him of past decisions. It was his morning of escape as well as my own.

Later, over lunch, Leonard said, "Alexis, you may not know this. I am the primary advisor to her majesty's government on Russia." Leonard paused, and the moment filled with weariness. Sighing, he added, "You cannot know how ignorant are those responsible for our fates." Yes, I thought, I do; but we had after all landed on our feet.[13]

---

[13] In the interests of fairness, I would like to make one more point about Kingman Brewster and Russian history at Yale. Leonard Schapiro told me that Brewster had invited him to Yale on any terms he chose—a semester each year or teaching every other year. Leonard turned him down on the grounds that he could not leave London. The President of Yale at least got it half right.

Bibliography of Robert O. Crummey

Chester S. L. Dunning

1959

"The Society for Christian Morality, 1821–1825." Master's thesis, University of Chicago.

1963

"Kappale Karjalan historiaa ja sen lähteitä." *Historiallinen Aikakauskirja* (1963): 271–83.

1964

"The Old Believers and the World of Antichrist: The Social and Economic Development of the Raskol in the Olonets region, 1654–1744." Ph.D. diss., University of Chicago.

1965

Review of *The Life of the Archpriest Avvakum by Himself*, translated by Jane Harrison and Hope Mirrlees with a preface by Prince D. S. Mirsky. Hamden, CT: Archon Books, 1963. *Slavic and East European Journal* 9: 463–64.

1968

Lloyd E. Berry and Robert O. Crummey, eds. *Rude & Barbarous Kingdom: Russia in the Accounts of Sixteenth-Century English Voyagers.* Madison: University of Wisconsin Press. xxiii + 391 pp.
Review of I. U. Budovnits, *Monastyri na Rusi i bor'ba s nimi krest'ian v XIV–XVI vekakh (po "zhitiiam sviatykh").* Moscow: Nauka, 1966. *The American Historical Review* 74: 667–68.

1970

The Old Believers and the World of Antichrist: The Vyg Community and the Russian State, 1694–1855. Madison: University of Wisconsin Press. xix + 258 pp.
Review of Harry W. Nerhood, ed., *To Russia and Return: An Annotated Bibliography of Travellers' English-Language Accounts of Russia from the Ninth Cen-*

Rude & Barbarous Kingdom Revisited: Essays in Russian History and Culture in Honor of Robert O. Crummey. Chester S. L. Dunning, Russell E. Martin, and Daniel Rowland, eds. Bloomington, IN: Slavica Publishers, 2008, 13–20.

tury to the Present. Columbus: Ohio State University Press, 1969. *Slavic Review* 29: 500–01.

1971

Review of V. I. Buganov *Moskovskie vosstanija konca XVII veka.* Moscow: Nauka, 1969. *Jahrbücher für Geschichte Osteuropas* 19: 292–93.
Review of S. B. Veselovskii, *Issledovaniia po istorii klassa sluzhilykh zemlevladel'tsev.* Moscow: Nauka, 1969. *Slavic Review* 30: 388–89.
Review of Osmo Jussila. *Suomen perustuslait: Venäläisten ja suomalaisten tulkintojen mukaan, 1808–1863.* Helsinki: Suomen Historiallinen Seura, 1969. *The American Historical Review* 76: 1560.

1972

"Crown and Boiars under Fedor Ivanovich and Michael Romanov." *Canadian-American Slavic Studies* 6: 549–74.
"The Kurbskii Controversy." *Canadian Slavonic Papers* 14: 684–89.

1973

"The Reconstitution of the Boiar Aristocracy, 1613–1645." *Forschungen zur osteuropäischen Geschichte* 18: 187–200.

1974

"Peter and the Boiar Aristocracy, 1689–1700." *Canadian-American Slavic Studies* 8: 274–87.
"George Vernadsky (1887–1973)." *Jahrbücher für Geschichte Osteuropas* 22: 479–80.
Review of Peter Nitsche, *Grossfürst und Thronfolger; die Nachfolgepolitik der Moskauer Herrscher bis zum Ende des Rjurikidenhauses.* Cologne: Böhlau Verlag, 1979. *Slavic Review* 33: 533–34.

1975

Review of John Fennell, Ludolf Müller, and Andrzej Poppe, eds. *Russia Mediaevalis*, Vol. 1. Munich: Fink, 1973. *Canadian Slavonic Papers* 17: 524–35.
Review of B. N. Floria, Russko-pol'skie otnosheniia i baltiiskii vopros v kontse XVI–nachale XVII v. Moscow: Nauka, 1973. *The American Historical Review* 80: 434–35.

1976

"Ivan the Terrible." In Samuel H. Baron and Nancy W. Heer, eds., *Windows on the Russian Past: Essays on Soviet Historiography since Stalin,* 57–74.

Columbus, OH: The American Association for the Advancement of Slavic Studies.

"Aleksei Petrovich (1690–1718)." In Joseph L. Wieczynski, ed., *The Modern Encyclopedia of Russian and Soviet History*, 55 vols. (Gulf Breeze, FL: Academic International Press, 1976–93) [cited hereafter as *MERSH*], 1: 120–23.

"Arsenii Glukhov (?–1643)." *MERSH* 2: 113–15.

Review of Robert Payne and Nikita Romanoff, *Ivan the Terrible*. New York: Crowell, 1975. *Canadian Slavonic Papers* 18: 94–95.

Review of N. I. Pavlenko, L. A. Nikiforov, and M. Ia. Volkov, eds. *Rossiia v period reform Petra I: Sbornik statei*. Moscow: Nauka, 1973. *The Russian Review* 35: 339–41.

Review of Hans-Joachim Torke, *Die staatsbedingte Gesellschaft im moskauer Reich: Zar und Zemlja in der altrussischen Herrschaftsverfassung 1613–1689*. Leiden: Brill, 1974. *Slavic Review* 35: 529–30.

1977

"Russian Absolutism and the Nobility." *The Journal of Modern History* 49: 456–67.

"Basmanov, Petr Fedorovich (?–1606)." *MERSH* 3: 156.

"Belokrinitsk Hierarchy (Belokrinitskaia Ierarkhiia)." *MERSH* 3: 230–31.

"Bezpopovtsy." *MERSH* 4: 120–23.

"Boiar." *MERSH* 5: 49–51.

Review of V. I. Koretskii, *Formirovanie krepostnogo prava i pervaia krest'ianskaia voina v Rossii*. Moscow: Nauka, 1975. *The Russian Review* 36: 352–53.

1978

"Court Groupings and Politics in Russia, 1645–1649." *Forschungen zur osteuropäischen Geschichte* 24: 203–21.

"Chosen Council." *MERSH* 7: 77–78.

"Council of 1666–1667." *MERSH* 8: 78–79.

"Denisov, Andrei and Denisov, Semen." *MERSH* 9: 67–70.

1979

"C. Bickford O'Brien, 1909–1979." *Slavic Review* 38: 549–50.

"Fedoseevtsy." *MERSH* 11: 94–96.

"Filippovtsy." *MERSH* 11: 134–35.

Review of Antonio Possevino, *The Moscovia of Antonio Possevino, S.J.*, translated by Hugh Graham. Pittsburgh: University Center for International Studies, University of Pittsburgh, 1977. *The Russian Review* 38: 83–84.

Review of R. E. F. Smith, *Peasant Farming in Muscovy*. Cambridge: Cambridge University Press, 1977. *Jahrbücher für Geschichte Osteuropas* 27: 283–84.

1980

"The Origins of the Noble Official: The Boiar Elite, 1613–89." In *Russian Officialdom: The Bureaucratization of Russian Society from the Seventeenth to the Twentieth Century*, edited by Walter McKenzie Pinter and Don Karl Rowney, 46–75. Chapel Hill: University of North Carolina Press.
"Reflections on Mestnichestvo in the 17th Century." *Forschungen zur osteuropäischen Geschichte* 27: 269–81.
"Kurbskii-Groznyi Controversy." *MERSH* 18: 174–77.
Review of R. G. Skrynnikov, *Boris Godunov*. Moscow: Nauka, 1978. *The American Historical Review* 85: 431.

1982

Review of Samuel H. Baron, *Muscovite Russia: Collected Essays*. London: Variorium, 1980. *Slavic Review* 41: 326.
Review of Henrik Birnbaum, *Lord Novgorod the Great: Essays in the History and Culture of a Medieval City-State*, Part One, *The Historical Background*. Columbus, OH: Slavica Publishers, 1981. *Canadian Slavonic Papers* 24: 429.

1983

Aristocrats and Servitors: The Boyar Elite in Russia, 1613–1689. Princeton, NJ: Princeton University Press. xvi + 315 pp.
Review of Richard Hellie, *Slavery in Russia, 1450–1725*. Chicago: University of Chicago Press, 1983. *Slavic Review* 42: 684–87.

1984

"Periodizing 'Feudal' Russian History." In *Russian and Eastern European History: Selected Papers from the Second World Congress for Soviet and East European Studies*, edited by Ralph C. Elwood, 17–42. Berkeley, CA: Berkeley Slavic Specialties.

1985

"Court Spectacles in Seventeenth-Century Russia: Illusion and Reality." In *Essays in Honor of A. A. Zimin*, edited by Daniel C. Waugh, 130–58. Columbus, OH: Slavica Publishers.

1986

"The Fate of Boyar Clans, 1565–1613." *Forschungen zur osteuropäischen Geschichte* 38: 241–56.
"Kliuchevskii's Portrait of the Boyars." *Canadian-American Slavic Studies* 10: 341–56.

Review of Manfred Hellmann, Klaus Zernack, and Gottfried Schramm, eds., *Handbuch der Geschichte Russlands*, Band 2, Lfg. 1–4. Stuttgart: Anton Hiersemann, 1981–83. *Jahrbücher für Geschichte Osteuropas* 34: 263–65.
Review of Charles Halperin, *Russia and the Golden Horde.* Bloomington: Indiana University Press, 1985. *Slavic Review* 45: 314–15.

1987

The Formation of Muscovy, 1304–1613. London and New York: Longman Group. xv + 275 pp.
"New Wine in Old Bottles? Ivan IV and Novgorod." *Russian History/Histoire Russe* 15: 61–76.
"The Silence of Muscovy." *The Russian Review* 46: 121–28.

1988

Review of Nancy Shields Kollmann, *Kinship and Politics: The Making of the Muscovite Political System, 1345–1547.* Stanford, CA: Stanford University Press, 1987. *Slavic Review* 47: 111–12.

1989

Robert O. Crummey, ed. *Reform in Russia and the U.S.S.R.: Past and Prospects.* DeKalb: Northern Illinois University Press.
"Introduction," 1–11;
"Reform under Ivan IV: Gradualism and Terror," 12–27;
"'Constitutional' Reform during the Time of Troubles," 28–44.
Review of Λ. L. Shapiro, *Russkoe krest'ianstvo pered zakreposhcheniem (XIV–XVI vv.).* Leningrad: Leningradskii gosudarstvennyi universitet, 1987. *The American Historical Review* 94: 183–84.

1990

"Istochniki boiarskoi vlasti v XVII veke: Potomki sluzhilykh kniazei sverkhov'ev Oki." *Nash radavod* (Grodno: Belorusskii fond kul'tury): 91–106. [Unauthorized translation of an article published in *Cahiers du monde russe et soviétique* in 1993.]
Review of Maureen Perrie, *The Image of Ivan the Terrible in Russian Folklore.* Cambridge: Cambridge University Press, 1987. *The English Historical Review* 105: 729.
Review of Ruslan G. Skrynnikov, *The Time of Troubles: Russia in Crisis, 1604–1618,* translated by Hugh Graham. Gulf Breeze, FL: Academic International Press, 1988. *The American Historical Review* 95: 1586.

1991

"The Spirituality of the Vyg Fathers." In *Church, Nation and State in Russia and Ukraine*, edited by Geoffrey A. Hosking, 23–37. New York: St. Martin's Press.

Review of Abby Smith and Vladimir Budaragin, eds. *Living Traditions of Russian Faith: Books and Manuscripts of the Old Believers. An Exhibition at The Library of Congress, May 31–June 29, 1990*. Washington, DC: Library of Congress, 1990. *Russian History/Histoire Russe* 18: 202–04.

1992

"Religious Radicalism in Seventeenth-Century Russia: Reexamining the Kapiton Movement." *Forschungen zur osteuropäischen Geschichte* 46: 172–85.

"Istoricheskaia skhema 'vygoretskikh bol'shakov.'" In *Traditsionnaia dukhovnaia i material'naia kul'tura russkikh staroobriadcheskikh poselenii v stranakh Evropy, Azii i Ameriki. Sbornik nauchnykh trudov*, edited by N. N. Pokrovskii and Richard A. Morris, 90–96. Novosibirsk: Nauka, Sibirskoe otdelenie.

"Russian Historical Traditions in the Perspective of Modernization and Reform." *Newsletter for Modern Chinese History* (Institute of Modern History, Academia Sinica, Taipei) 14: 28–46.

Review of Lindsey Hughes, *Sophia, Regent of Russia 1657–1704*. New Haven: Yale University Press, 1990. *The American Historical Review* 97: 250–50.

1993

"Old Belief as Popular Religion: New Approaches." *Slavic Review* 52: 700–12.

"Sources of Boyar Power in the Seventeenth Century: The Descendants of the Upper Oka Serving Princes." *Cahiers du monde russe et soviétique* 34: 107–18.

"Interpreting the Fate of Old Believer Communities in the Eighteenth and Nineteenth Centuries." In *Seeking God: The Recovery of Religious Identity in Orthodox Russia, Ukraine, and Georgia*, edited by Stephen K. Batalden, 144–59. DeKalb: Northern Illinois University Press.

1994

N. S. Gur'ianova and R. O. Crummey. "Istoricheskaia skhema v sochineniiakh pisatelei vygovskoi literaturnoi shkoly." In *Staroobriadchestvo v Rossii (XVII–XVIII vv.)*, edited by E. M. Iukhimenko, 120–38. Moscow: Arkheograficheskii tsentr.

Review of Evgenii V. Anisimov, *The Reforms of Peter the Great: Progress through Coercion in Russia*, translated by John T. Alexander. Armonk, NY: M. E. Sharpe, 1993. *The American Historical Review* 99: 1361.

1995

"The Origins of the Old Believer Cultural Systems: The Works of Avraamii." *Forschungen zur osteuropäischen Geschichte* 50: 121–38.

1997

"The Miracle of Martyrdom: Reflections on Early Old Believer Hagiography." In *Religion and Culture in Early Modern Russia and Ukraine*, edited by Samuel H. Baron and Nancy Shields Kollmann, 132–45. DeKalb: Northern Illinois University Press.

Review of Valerie Kivelson, *Autocracy in the Provinces: The Muscovite Gentry and Political Culture in the Seventeenth Century*. Stanford, CA: Stanford University Press, 1996. *Slavic Review* 56: 777–78.

Review of Maureen Perrie, *Pretenders and Popular Monarchism in Early Modern Russia: The False Tsars of the Time of Troubles*. Cambridge: Cambridge University Press, 1995. *The American Historical Review* 102: 1528–29.

1998

"The Cultural Worlds of Andrei Borisov." *Forschungen zur osteuropäischen Geschichte* 54: 135–57.

"Muscovy and 'The General Crisis of the Seventeenth Century.'" *Journal of Early Modern History* 2: 156–80.

Review of James Cracraft, *The Petrine Revolution in Russian Imagery*. Chicago: University of Chicago Press, 1997. *Slavic Review* 57: 913–14.

1999

Review of Janet Martin, *Medieval Russia, 980–1584*. Cambridge: Cambridge University Press, 1995. *Speculum* 74: 792–94.

2000

"Seventeenth-Century Russia: Theories and Models." *Forschungen zur osteuropäischen Geschichte* 56: 113–32.

2001

Robert O. Crummey, Holm Sundhaussen, and Ricarda Vulpius, eds. *Russische und Ukrainische Geschichte vom 16.–18. Jahrhundert*. Wiesbaden: Harrassowitz Verlag. [*Forschungen zur osteuropäischen Geschichte* 58.]

"Die staatsbedingte Gesellschaft Revisited." *Forschungen zur osteuropäischen Geschichte* 58: 21–28.

"The Latest from Muscovy." *The Russian Review* 60: 474–86.

"'Konstitutsionnaia Reforma' v Smutnom vremeni." In *Amerikanskaia rusistika: Vekhi istoriografii poslednikh let, period Kievskoi i Moskovskoi Rusi. Antologiia,* edited by George P. Majeska, 240–58. Samara: Izd-vo Samarskogo universiteta.

"In Memoriam: Hans-Joachim Torke, 1938–2000." *Kritika* 2: 3 (Summer): 1–7.

"Tom Noonan: An Appreciation." *Russian History/Histoire Russe* 28: 3–7.

2003

"Propovedi Andrei Borisova." In *Vygovskaia pomorskaia pustyn' i ee znachenie v istorii Rossii: Sbornik nauchnykh statei i materialov,* edited by A. M. Pashkov, 40–51. St. Petersburg: Dmitrii Bulanin.

2004

"Ecclesiastical Elites and Popular Belief and Practice in Seventeenth-Century Russia." In *Religion and the Early Modern State: Views from China, Russia and the West,* edited by James Tracy and Marguerite Ragnow, 52–79. Cambridge: Cambridge University Press.

2006

"The Orthodox Church and the Schism." In *Cambridge History of Russia,* Vol. 1, *From Early Rus' to 1689,* edited by Maureen Perrie, 618–39. Cambridge: Cambridge University Press.

"Eastern Orthodoxy in Russia and Ukraine in the Age of the Counter-Reformation." In *Cambridge History of Christianity,* Vol. 5, *Eastern Christianity,* edited by Michael Angold, 302–24. Cambridge: Cambridge University Press.

Review of Nicholas B. Breyfogle, *Heretics and Colonizers: Forging Russia's Empire in the South Caucasus.* Ithaca, NY: Cornell University Press, 2005. *The Russian Review* 65: 324–25.

Rulers and Ruling Elites

Redating the *Life of Alexander Nevskii*

Donald Ostrowski

The time of composition of the *Life of Alexander Nevskii* has been generally accepted as the late 13th century, but the reasons for that acceptance need to be reexamined.[1] Establishing the date of composition of the First Redaction of the *Life* is dependent on determining the relationship of it to chronicle accounts; in particular, whether or not the Older Redaction of the Novgorod I Chronicle (Novg. I-OR) served as a source for the *Life*. In addition, I explore the possibility that the *Life* is the reworking of a chronicle tale about Alexander Nevskii. My contention is that the *Life* is indeed based on a no-longer-extant *Tale of Alexander Nevskii*, and that it borrows from the Novg. I-OR. In contrast, the Younger Redaction of the Novgorod I Chronicle (Novg. 1-YR) incorporates parts of the *Life* into its account (for the relationship of these texts, see figure 1, below).

Begunov identified three main redactions of the *Life of Alexander Nevskii* that existed by the 15th century. The First Redaction of the *Life* is extant in full in eleven MS copies (one of which dates to the end of the 15th century, the other ten to the 16th and 17th centuries) and in part in two MS copies (one of which dates to 1377, the other to the end of the 15th century).[2]

---

[1] The composition that is usually referred to in the scholarly literature as the *Life of Alexander Nevskii* is titled in most MS copies the *Tale about the Life of the Brave, Blessed, and Great Prince Alexander Nevskii*. But the earliest MS copy of the First Redaction of the *Life*, which appears in the Laurentian Chronicle (*Лв*), merely begins: "That same year Grand Prince Alexander, son of Iaroslav, passed away. We speak [about] his bravery and life...." Five other MS copies (*A, B, M, Ap*, and *O*) of the first redaction amplify the first sentence by adding a date and specific year, November 23, 1263, but repeat the "skazhem muzhestvo i zhit'e ego" part. See "Zhitie Aleksandra Nevskogo (pervaia redaktsiia)," in Iu. K. Begunov, *Pamiatnik russkoi literatury XIII veka "Slovo o pogibeli Russkoi zemli"* (Moscow: Nauka, 1965), 159. For reasons that should become clear below, I continue the practice of calling the First Redaction the *Life of Alexander Nevskii*.

[2] The MSS that contain the full *Life*, according to Begunov's listing, are: Gosudarstvennyi arkhiv Arkhangel'skoi oblasti (GAAO), sobranie ruskopisnykh knig, no. 18 (*Ap*); Gosudarstvennyi istoricheskii muzei (GIM), sobranie E. V. Barsova, no. 1413 (*Б*); GIM, Muzeiskoe sobranie, no. 1706 (*M*); GIM, Sinodal'noe sobranie, no. 154, fols. 156–162v (*Пс*); GIM, sobranie A. S. Uvarova, no. 279 (*У*); Institut russkoi literatury (Push-kinskii dom) (IRL-PD), R. IV, op. 24, no. 26 (*Л*); Rossiiskaia gosudarstvennaia biblio-teka (RGB), sobranie Iosifo-Volokolamskogo monastyria, f. 113, no. 523 (*В*); RGB,

Rude & Barbarous Kingdom Revisited: Essays in Russian History and Culture in Honor of Robert O. Crummey. Chester S. L. Dunning, Russell E. Martin, and Daniel Rowland, eds. Bloomington, IN: Slavica Publishers, 2008, 23–39.

M. D. Priselkov proposed in 1939 that the original redaction of the *Life* appears in the Laurentian Chronicle (*Лв*) and was composed shortly after Alexander's death in 1263.[3] Priselkov did not analyze the relationship of the Life to the chronicle accounts. In 1947, D. S. Likhachev pointed out what he considered to be parallels in motifs, style, and words between the Galician Chronicle (GC) and the *Life of Alexander Nevskii*. He attributed the common source of these parallels to the Galician literary tradition, and he saw Metropolitan Kirill as the link between them, either as the author or more probably in commissioning both of them.[4] As further evidence, Likhachev cited the words from the Pskovo-Pecherskii copy of the *Life*: "This was preached by the holy metropolitan Kirill and by his cellarer Sebastian."[5] If Metropolitan Kirill did have something to do with the composition of the *Life*, then that would place the date of its composition sometime between 1263, the year of death of Alexander Nevskii, and 1280, the year of death of Kirill.

It is difficult to see, however, in the version of the quotation that Likhachev cited, which is limited to two (*П* and *Л*) copies of the First Redaction (as reported by Begunov), any evidence of Kirill's writing or commissioning the *Life* to be written. Even less so is there such evidence in this passage with the readings attested to by the other MS copies. Four copies (*Пс, Б, Р,* and *У*) do not mention the metropolitan by name and indicate the source of the author's information about the funeral: "This was heard from the lord metropolitan and from his cellarer Sebastian."[6] The other six copies (*A, B, M, O, Ap,* and *Пг*) that are extant to the end of the *Life* do not mention the metropolitan or his cellarer at all. Begunov thought that *Пс, У, Б,* and *Р* best represent the archetype, while he considered *П* and *Л* closer to the archetype than *A, B, M, O, Ap,* and *Пг*. Instead, I consider *Лв*, in the part of the *Life* that it has, to best represent the archetype. I then give priority to *Пг* (and *A, B, M, O, Ap* insofar as they support it). In this case, the null reading that they carry (*Лв* being non-

---

sobranie Moskovskoi dukhovnoi akademii, f. 173, no. 208 (*A*); RGB, sobranie A. N. Ovchinnikova, f. 209, no. 281 (*O*); RGB, sobranie Olonetskoi seminarii, f. 212, no. 15 (*P*); Rossiiskaia natsional'naia biblioteka (RNB), sobranie M. P. Pogodina, no. 641 (*Пг*). The MS that contains only the beginning part of the *Life* is: RNB, F. IV., no. 2, fols. 168–169v (*Лв*). The MS that contains the beginning and end parts of the *Life* is: Gosudarstvennyi arkhiv Pskovskoi oblasti (GAPO), sobranie Pskovo-Pecherskogo monastyria, f. 449, no. 60 (*П*). Begunov, *Pamiatnik*, 159.

[3] M. D. Priselkov, "Lavrent'evskaia letopis': Istoriia teksta," *Uchenye zapiski Leningradskogo gosudarstvennogo universiteta*, no. 32: *Seriia istoricheskikh nauk* 2 (1939): 130.

[4] D. S. Likhachev, "Galitskaia literaturnaia traditsiia v zhitii Aleksandra Nevskogo," *Trudy Otdela drevnerusskoi literatury* (*TODRL*) 5 (1947): 52. Cherepnin had previously proposed that Kirill had some relationship to the composition of the Galician Chronicle. L. V. Cherepnin, "Letopisets Daniila Galitskogo," *Istoricheskie zapiski*, no. 12 (1941): 245–52.

[5] Begunov, *Pamiatnik*, 180.

[6] Ibid., 180.

extant here) is primary. The copies Б, Р, Пс, and У add the reference to information being obtained from the metropolitan and his cellarer Sebastian. Finally, at the last stage, П and Л add *Kirill* as the name of the metropolitan and change *слышано от* (heard from) to *проповедано* (preached). In any case, the phrase "this was preached" refers to comments at Alexander's funeral, not to the entire text of the *Life*.

In addition, the stylistic similarities that Likhachev pointed out between the GC and the *Life* are not compelling evidence of single authorship, but only suggestive of possible familiarity of one work by the author of the other or of other comon sources. But all of these "parallels" are commonplaces of Rus' literature that could have derived from other texts. Nor would a common commissioner of both works necessarily have a stylistic or word-borrowing effect on either work.[7]

Begunov dated the First (i.e., the earliest) Redaction of the *Life of Alexander Nevskii* to 1282–83 and placed its composition in the Rozhdestvenskii Monastery in Vladimir. His conclusion is based on his observation that "the author of the *Life* devotes special attention to the personality of Dmitrii Aleksandrovich and the basis of his right to the grand-princely throne."[8] As support for the 1282–83 dating, Begunov pointed to what he called "one curious fact"; that is, the *Life* "does not mention the town that the Germans constructed in the fatherland of Alexander in the winter of 1240/41." Since the Synodal copy of the Novgorod I Chronicle does mention the name of the town, Kopor'e, "it is obvious," according to Begunov, "that this naming was consciously dropped by the compiler of the *Life*" because he did not want to allude to the feud that Dmitrii had with the Novgorodians "over the construction of this fort, the taking into captivity by the Novgorodians of two of Dmitrii's daughters and boyars, and the insulting words of the Novgorodians spoken to the prince: 'if your men leave Kopor'e, then we will release them.'"[9] The feud involving Kopor'e was reported in the Novg. I-OR under the entry for 1282/83 (6790).[10] If the *Life* "consciously dropped" the name of the town that appears

---

[7] All of which I have argued in "The Galician Chronicle, the *Life of Alexander Nevskii*, and the 13th-Century Military Tale," *Palaeoslavica* 15 (2007): 307–24.

[8] Begunov, *Pamiatnik*, 61. See also Iu. K. Begunov, I. È. Kleinenberg, and I. P. Shaskol'skii, "Pis'mennye istochniki o ledovom poboishche," in *Ledovoe poboishche 1242 g. Trudy kompleksnoi èkspeditsii po utochneniiu mesta ledovogo poboishcha*, ed. G. N. Karaev (Moscow and Leningrad: Nauka, 1966), 183; cf. drawing 2 following p. 192 "Skhema vzaimootnosheniia tekstov izvestii o Ledovom poboishche russkikh letopisei"; and Jurij Biegunow [Iu. K. Begunov], "Itwory literackie o Aleksandrze Newskim w składzie latopisów ruskich," *Slavia Orientalis* 18 (1969): 309.

[9] Begunov, *Pamiatnik*, 61.

[10] *Novgorodskaia Pervaia letopis': Starshego i mladshego izvodov*, ed. A. N. Nasonov (Moscow-Leningrad: Akademiia nauk SSSR, 1950), reprinted in *Polnoe sobranie russkikh letopisei* (*PSRL*), 41 vols. (St. Petersburg/Petrograd/Leningrad and Moscow: Arkheogra-

in Novg. I-OR, then that would seem to imply the *Life* was secondary in relationship to the Novg. I-OR, but Begunov concluded there was no relationship between the two. He did recognize, however, that the Novg. I-OR influenced the editing of the Second Redaction of the *Life*.

Norman Ingham saw the *Life of Alexander Nevskii* as indicative of "a new trend" in Rus' literature. He stated that "[t]he frame of a hagiographical *Life* is present, with a customary opening (modesty topos; reason for writing; biblical quote; prayer for assistance) and close (the hero becomes a monk; report of his death and burial; lament; a miracle as sign of sainthood)." What he finds "interesting" are "that the central portions (*praxeis*) are distinctly secular in substance and style." In addition, the "[e]vents of Aleksandr's life (almost exclusively military) are related in the pure manner of the *voinski povest* and with few pious motifs." Ingham found the "hypothesis" proposed by some scholars "that a monkish hagiographer had borrowed from a secular work" to be "superfluous." He pointed out that "there was a tendency always to treat military campaigns in this familiar style." Since "[t]he author simply had no model for a purely secular *Life*," he "let subject-matter dictate style."[11]

According to S. A. Zenkovsky, writing in 1974, "[t]he original version of this *vita* was apparently written as a 'military tale' by one of the warriors of his [Alexander's] household who witnessed Alexander's last years of life." Zenkovsky pointed to the title of the work: "Tale of the Life and Courage of Prince Alexander" as being "unusual for a *vita*." He also saw in the author's words upon Alexander's death, "A man may leave the house of his father but he cannot leave the house of his good lord; and if he has to, he should share the coffin with him," evidence of "the fealty of a feudal warrior to his lord." A third piece of evidence that Zenkovsky mentions is the author's describing "[t]he details of the deeds of some warriors of Alexander's army," which indicates that the author "[p]robably … knew many of the prince's warriors …." Zenkovsky concluded that "[t]he original *Tale* … was rewritten later, around 1280, by some ecclesiastic from the city of Vladimir." That ecclesiastic, according to Zenkovsky, "added some deeds, quotations, and motifs from the Bible and, especially, from the Psalms, the First, Second, and Fourth Books of Kings, First and Second Chronicles, Isaiah, and the Apocryphal book of The Wisdom of Solomon." In Zenkovsky's view, "In most cases this second writer drastically rephrased the words of these quotations, as well as the original contents, often replacing the names of heroes from antiquity and Byzantine history with those from biblical sources." Zenkovsky claimed to have de-

---

ficheskaia komissiia, Nauka, and Arkheograficheskii tsentr, 1843–2002), vol. 3 (Moscow: Iazyki russkoi kul'tury, 2000), 324.

[11] Norman Ingham, "The Limits of Secular Biography in Medieval Slavic Literature, Particularly Old Russian," in *American Contributions to the Sixth International Congress of Slavists, Prague, 1968, August 7–13*, 2 vols., ed. William E. Harkins (The Hague: Mouton, 1968), 1: 193–194.

tected evidence of "[t]his reworking ... in the text that has reached us, for in some places it destroyed the *Tale's* narrative and stylistic unity and resulted in an unsystematic rearrangement of the source material."[12] Thus, as Zenkovsky saw it, the original form of the *vita* was a military tale written by someone who knew Alexander personally; yet all we have to go on is the reworking of it around 1280 by a Vladimir ecclesiastic. Zenkovsky made no guess as to when the original *Tale* was written, although it would have been written between 1263 and 1280. Nor did he state whether he thought the Vladimir ecclesiastic added any eyewitness testimony.

Also in 1974, the Oxford University scholar John Fennell wrote that he found Begunov's argument for the dating of the composition of the *Life* to the 1280s in the Rozhdestvenskii Monastery to be "convincing." Fennell's reasons for accepting Begunov's conclusion about the place and time of composition are these:

1. "the earliest version (*izvod*) is concerned only with Vladimir-Suzdal' information—there is no specifically Novgorodian news";
2. "Aleksandr is portrayed primarily as a Suzdalian ruler, rather than [as] the Novgorodian prince....";
3. the *Life* mentions the Rozhdestvenskii Monastery "as the place of Aleksandr's burial";
4. "the author is clearly connected with" the Rozhdestvenskii Monastery;
5. "this particular monastery was the seat of the metropolitan from the mid-thirteenth century to 1323";
6. "Metropolitan Kirill II, who plays a large role in the *Zhitie*, was closely linked with its writing";
7. "evidence [exists] that the Rozhdestvensky Monastery was the centre of the cult of Aleksandr up to the mid-sixteenth century";
8. "it seems very probable that this local worship of the prince was started by the metropolitan and the monastic authorities";
9. the fact that "the earliest version contains, sandwiched between Aleksandr's final trip to the Horde and his death, the information that Aleksandr 'sent his son Dmitry [nine years old at the time] to the western lands' and that Dmitry 'captured the German land [i.e., Livonia] and took the city of Yur'ev' points to the 1280s as the time of writing";
10. "Dmitry was a patron of the monastery."[13]

---

[12] Serge A. Zenkovsky, ed., *Medieval Russia's Epics, Chronicles, and Tales*, rev. ed. (New York: E. P. Dutton, 1974), 224–225.

[13] John Fennell, "Literature of the Tatar Period (13th–15th Centuries)," in John Fennell and Anthony Stokes, *Early Russian Literature* (London: Faber and Faber, 1974), 108–09.

In 1984, Fennell added that "the *Life* was written ... or commissioned by a man who had every reason to be antagonistic to the West, particularly to the Catholic West—Metropolitan Kirill."[14] In 1995, Fennell stated merely that the *Life* was "written in all probability by Metropolitan Kirill II...."[15] Fennell was apparently under the impression that Kirill had died in 1287, not 1280. It might still have been possible, nonetheless, for Kirill to have commissioned a work, which then someone else wrote later, in 1282–83.

Fennell, like Zenkovsky, also claimed to have detected two kinds of writing in the *Life*: "the hagiographical passages are distinct from the annalistic episodes, but sometimes religious sentiments are tacked on to purely military clichés."[16] The first example he cited of this adding on of "religious sentiments" is when the *Life* describes Alexander's "returning victorious (*vozvratisya s pobedoyu*)" after the battle on the Neva, which Fennell called "a stock ending to any military campaign." Then the author of the *Life* tacks on the phrase "praising and glorifying the name of his Creator."[17] The second example he cited is Alexander's treatment of the enemy after he razed the fortress the Livonian knights had built "on Alexander's land": "some he killed, others he took with him, and others he pardoned and let go." The author of the *Life* adds, "for he was merciful beyond measure."[18] Fennell commented that "the reader is not allowed to forget that this is, after all, the Life of a saint."[19]

Fennell saw "the style of the 'secular' passages" as being "entirely typical of early chronicle battle descriptions" and "[t]he structure of the 'battle piece' or 'campaign piece' "as being "traditional." He pointed to "the so-called 'Paroemia' reading in honour of Boris and Gleb, which contains a vivid description of the Al'a battle (1019), or the same episode in the *Povest' vremennykh let* (s.a. 1019)" as being "the model for the" battle piece.[20] In addition, he termed the phrasing "conventional (*byst' secha zla*: there was a violent battle; *s"stupishasya oboi*: both sides clashed; *poverva i pozhzhe*: he destroyed and burned; *polona vzya bes chisla*: he took innumerable prisoners; *v sile velitse*: in great strength...)."[21] Fennell referred to as "typical not only of folklore but of annalistic battle descriptions" what he called "the epic exaggeration of the

---

[14] John Fennell, *The Crisis of Medieval Russia 1200–1304* (London: Longman, 1984), 103.

[15] John Fennell, *A History of the Russian Church to 1448* (London: Longman, 1995), 198.

[16] Fennell, "Literature of the Tatar Period," 113.

[17] Begunov, *Pamiatnik*, 168.

[18] Ibid., 169.

[19] Fennell, "Literature of the Tatar Period," 113.

[20] Ibid., 113. Cf. A. S. Orlov, "Ob osobennostiakh formy russkoi voinskoi povesti (konchaia XVII v.)," *Chteniia v Imperatorskom obshchestve istorii i drevnostei rossiiskikh pri Moskovskom universitete (ChOIDR)*, bk. 4 (1902): 8–11.

[21] Fennell, "Literature of the Tatar Period," 113–114. Cf. Orlov, "Ob osobennostiakh," 11–49.

battles (the 'innumerable multitudes' of participants and killed, the covering of all 1356 square miles of Lake Chudskoe 'with the multitude of soldiers', etc.)."[22] He cited examples of the "chronicle formulas" in the *Life*: "*byst' zhe v to vremya*: and there was at that time; *po pobeded zhe Oleksandrove*: and after the victory of Aleksandr; *v vtoroe zhe leto*: and in the second year; *po plenii zhe Nevrueve*: and after the invasion of Nevryuy...."[23] Finally, he said, "the syntax is identical to that of the chronicle *voinskaya povest'*—short clauses joined together by the conjunction *i* (and), absence of subordination except for the occasional participle/gerund used to relieve the monotony." He cited as "[a] good example of this bald, unadorned impartial military style ... the laconic description of" Dmitrii Aleksandrovich's campaign against Iur'ev that appears toward the end of the *Life*:

> Prince Dmitrii went in great strength
> and invaded the German land,
> and took the town of Iur'ev
> And returned to Novgorod with many
> prisoners and with great booty.[24]

Nonetheless, Fennell, like Ingham, did not see evidence of two authors at work, only one: "There can be little doubt that all the secular passages were written by the same person who wrote the introduction and the end: the differences are not so great as to warrant the assumption of different authors."[25] He asserted that "the author is simply using the conventional language of the *voinskaia povest'* in its basic, crudest form, a technique which could have been assimilated by any writer capable of manipulating the greater subtleties of the hagiographical style" and that "[t]here, then, seems to be no reason why we should not assume that this was an attempt by a cleric to write the Life of a layman." The author, according to Fennell, merely "fitted the purely secular episodes" into a "hagiographic framework [that] is [already] there." In the end, the author created something that "can only be called semi-secular hagiography or semi-clerical biography, a new departure in the history of Russian biography."[26]

Although Fennell is correct that a cleric could fairly easily learn the style of a military tale, I find that I cannot agree with Fennell's assessment that the "hagiographic framework is there" for the author to insert military tale-like episodes. Although the work is, as Ingham pointed out, "framed" as a *vita*,

---

[22] Fennell, "Literature of the Tatar Period," 114.

[23] Ibid.

[24] Begunov, *Pamiatnik*, 177.

[25] Fennell, "Literature of the Tatar Period," 110.

[26] Ibid., 111.

the structure of the *Life of Alexander* does not conform to the standard "frame-work" of a saint's *vita*.[27] Instead, Fennell's observation that the author is tacking on, sometimes in a rather gratuitous way, religious comments is a more accurate way of describing the composition process. This work does indeed appear to be "a new departure."

If we accept the testimony of the *Life*, then we have to rule out Metropolitan Kirill as the author. The *Life* states that the author is recounting "what I heard from my father and I am an eyewitness to [while] growing up."[28] He would appear to have been a younger man than Kirill was in the 1260s or 1270s. Kirill had been metropolitan of Rus' since 1242. Instead, it sounds very much like someone who was no older than 15 or 20 years when Alexander died in 1263.

The suggestion that the *Life* was based on an earlier military tale to which religious elements were later added has its appeal.[29] It would explain the statement that the author grew up at the court of Alexander Nevskii as well as the author's going into some detail about military aspects of the battles on the Neva and on Lake Chud. When reworking the *Tale* into the *Life*, the ecclesiastical reviser decided to keep the introductory testimony of the *Tale*'s author. It is unlikely Metropolitan Kirill would have commissioned the writing of a military tale about Alexander. Evidence of textual relationships also rules out the possibility that Kirill commissioned the rewriting of the *Tale* into the *Life* because, if such a reworking of a military tale into a saint's life occurred, then it was done, as I discuss below, not earlier than the middle of the 14th century, some 70 to 90 years after Kirill's death.

The relationship of the *Life* to the chronicle accounts is key to dating the probable time of its composition. I argued elsewhere that in regard to the 1242 Lake Chud battle, Novg. I-OR derived from the Laurentian and Suzdal' chronicles, and that the *Life* derived from the chronicles, and was not a source of them.[30] The Laurentian MS (dated to 1377) contains an account of Alexander's battle against the Livonian knights in 1242 (col. 470).[31] This account is

---

[27] For a description of the standard framework of a saint's *vita*, see Ihor Ševčenko, *Three Byzantine Literatures: A Layman's Guide* (Brookline, MA: Hellenic College Press, 1985), 16.

[28] Begunov, *Pamiatnik*, 159.

[29] It should be mentioned that there are those who, like Zhivov, believe "military tales as a genre are a fictitious invention of literary scholars." Viktor Zhivov, review of Frithjof Benjamin Schenck, *Aleksandr Nevskij: Heiliger—Fürst—Nationalheld. Ein Erinnerungsfigur im russischen kulturellen Gedächtnis (1263–2000)*, in *Kritika* 8: 3 (2007): 664n5.

[30] See my "Alexander Nevskii's 'Battle on the Ice': The Creation of a Legend," *Russian History* 33 (2006): 298–99.

[31] According to Shakhmatov, the Laurentian Chronicle was compiled between 1305 and 1308, or possibly 1316. A. A. Shakhmatov, "'Povest' vremennykh let' i ee istochniki," *TODRL* 4 (1940): 14. Priselkov dated it to the Compilation of 1305. M. D. Prisel-

minimal, more concerned with the actions of Grand Prince Iaroslav in Vladimir than with Prince Alexander in Novgorod:

> Grand Prince Iaroslav sent his son Andrei to Great
> Novgorod in aid of Alexander against the Germans and
> defeated them beyond Pskov at the lake and took many
> prisoners. Andrei returned to his father with honor.[32]

The Suzdal' Chronicle also contains an account of the battle.[33] It mentions Lake Chud and Raven's Rock specifically as the location of the battle as well as a chase along or across the ice:

> Alexander Iaroslavich went with Novgorodians against the Germans
> and fought with them at Lake Chud by Raven's Rock. Alexander defeated them and they chased them across the ice for 7 versts.[34]

The Novgorod I Chronicle is extant in two redactions—an Older Redaction and a Younger Redaction. The Novg. I-OR is maintained in a single copy, the Synodal. Shakhmatov and Likhachev dated the Synodal copy to the first half of the 14th century.[35] Kloss dated the first part of the Synodal copy, including part of the entry for 1234 (fols. 1–118ᵛ), to the second half of the 13th century on the basis of the handwriting.[36] A second handwriting fills most of

---

kov, *Istoriia russkogo letopisaniia XI–XV vv.* (Leningrad: Izdatel'stvo Leningradskogo gosudarstvennogo universiteta, 1940), 96–106. The last entry for the Laurentian Chronicle is 1305. In *PSRL* 1 (1926), cols. 290–487, where the section of the Laurentian Chronicle that runs from 1111 to 1305 is called the "Suzdal' Chronicle according to the Laurentian Copy."

[32] *PSRL* 1: col. 470.

[33] The Suzdal' Chronicle is also contained in the Moscow Academy copy (MAk), which dates to ca. 1500. According to Lur'e, MAk represents "the Rostov or Suzdal'-Rostov compilation .... from 6747 [1239] to 6927 [1419]." Ia. S. Lur'e, *Obshcherusskie letopisi XIV–XV vv.* (Leningrad: Nauka, 1976), 97. Priselkov dated the composition of this entry to the 1260s–70s. Priselkov, *Istoriia russkogo letopisaniia*, 98. The Suzdal' Chronicle is published in *PSRL*, vol. 1 (1928), 490–539, where it is called the "Continuation of the Suzdal' Chronicle according to the Academy Copy."

[34] *PSRL*, vol. 1: col. 523. A verst is usually equivalent to 1.067 km.

[35] A. A. Shakhmatov, *Obozrenie russkikh letopisnykh svodov XIV–XVI vv.* (Moscow and Leningrad: Akademiia nauk SSSR, 1938), 128–32; D. S. Likhachev, *Russkie letopisi i ikh kul'turno-istoricheskoe znachenie* (Moscow and Leningrad: Akademiia nauk SSSR, 1947), 440–43.

[36] B. M. Kloss, "Predislovie k izdaniiu 2000 g.," in *PSRL* 3 (2000), v. It was previously thought the first part of the MS contained two handwritings, but Gippius identified them as a single hand. A. A. Gippius, "Novye dannye o ponomare Timofee—nov-

the second part of the Synodal MS, from the entry for 1234 to the entry for 1330 (fols. 119–66ᵛ). Then four different hands in turn write the entries for 1331–33, 1337, 1345, and 1352 (fols. 167–69).[37] The Synodal copy ends with the entry for 1352, but Kloss, Gimon, and Gippius have proposed that the compilation (*svod*) was made in 1330, since it is after this entry that a change from hand no. 1 to hand no. 2 occurs (fol. 167).[38] Yet, changes in hand are not necessarily sufficient enough evidence for dating when a compilation was made. Another explanation to be considered is that the Synodal copy was compiled in 1352 at the earliest and that the chronicle-copying project that constituted the Novg. I-OR may have been intended to go to at least 1352, perhaps to coincide with the reign of Archbishop Vasilii (1330–52). The Black Death could have led to changes concerning which monks were copying the chronicle, especially toward the end of the project. My difference in views with Kloss, Gimon, and Gippius, however, does not significantly affect the argument I present here. So we can set that issue aside for the moment.

The Synodal copy includes the information testified to in the Laurentian Chronicle that Alexander's brother Andrei was at the battle. And it coincides with the testimony of the Suzdal' Chronicle about the chase being across the ice. But it also adds that the chase went to the Subol shore (understood to mean the western shore of Lake Chud). It adds *Uzmen* as the name of the area near Raven's Rock where the battle was fought and includes a plea by Boris and Gleb on behalf of Alexander Nevskii to God during the battle:

> In the year 1242 [6750] Prince Alexander with the Novgorodians and with his brother Andrei and the low country men to the Chud land went against the Germans.... Prince Alexander and the Novgorodians drew up their forces at Lake Chud at Uzmen by Raven's Rock. The army of the Germans and Chuds rode at them driving themselves like a wedge through their army, and there was a great battle with the Germans and Chuds. God and Holy Sophia and the Holy Martyrs Boris and Gleb, for whose sake the Novgorodians shed their blood, by the great prayers of those saints, God helped Prince Alexander. The Germans fell there and the Chuds gave shoulder [fled], and pursuing them they fought them for seven versts across the ice to

gorodskom knizhnike serediny XIII veka," *Informatsionnyi biulleten' MAIRSK* 25 (1992): 59–86.

[37] *Novgorodskaia kharateinaia letopis'*, ed. M. N. Tikhomirov (Moscow: Nauka, 1964), 339–41.

[38] Kloss, "Predislovie k izdaniiu 2000 g.," v; G. V. Gimon, "Pripiski na dopolnitel'nykh listakh v Sinodal'nom spiske Novgorodskoi I letopisi," in *Norna u istochnika: Sbornik statei v chest' Eleny Aleksandrovny Melnikovoi*, ed. T. N. Dzhakson, G. V. Glazyrina, I. G. Konovalova, S. L. Nikol'skii, and V. Ia. Petrukhin (Moscow: Indrik, 2001), 59. My thanks to Aleksei Gippius for bringing Gimon's article to my attention.

the Subol shore. There fell a countless number of Chuds, and of the Germans 400. They captured 50 and brought [them] to Novgorod. They fought on April 5, the Commemoration Day of the Holy Martyr Claudian, to the glory of the Holy Mother of God, on a Saturday.[39]

Begunov concluded that "a comparison of the Synodal copy with the three copies of Novgorod I Chronicle of the Younger Redaction ... shows that neither the chronicle information of the Synodal copy served as a source for the *Life of Prince Alexander* nor was the information of the *Life* a source of information of the Synodal copy."[40] He went on to point out that "totally absent in the *Life of Alexander Nevskii* is any Novgorodian information of 1238–1263, concerning the marriage of the prince, the arrangement of towns along the Shelon River, the feuds and arguments of Prince Alexander with the Novgorodians, his leaving from Novgorod for the Suzdal' land, details about the Battle on the Ice known to the Novgorod chronicler, no discussion concerning the German embassy after the Battle on the Ice, concerning the approach of Alexander to them in 1256, concerning the dispute of Alexander with his son Vasilii and his druzhiniki, [and] concerning the Tatar treaty."[41] While all this may pertain to the *Tale of Alexander Nevskii*, the redactor of the *Life of Alexander Nevskii* is indeed aware of the Novg. I-OR and manages, it seems to me, to incorporate passages from it into the basic structure of the *Life* in at least three places, one in its description of the battle on the Neva and two in its description of the battle on Lake Chud. First, in describing the day when the battle on the Neva took place, both the Novg. I-OR and the *Life* use the same formula:

Novg. I-OR	Life of Alexander Nevskii
On July 15th, *on the commemoration day of Holy Kiurik and Ulita, on the Sunday [neděliu] of the Council of the 630 Holy Fathers in Chalcedon*[42]	On Sunday [vskresen'ia], *on the commemoration day* when *630 Holy Fathers* who were at the *Council in Chalcedon*, as well as the *holy* martyrs, *Kiurik and Ulita* and holy Prince Volodimer who baptized the Rus' land....*[43]

---

[39] *PSRL* 3: 78.

[40] Iu. K. Begunov, "Zhitie Aleksandra Nevskogo v sostave Novgorodskoi 1-oi i Sofiiskoi 1-oi letopisei," *Novgorodskii istoricheskii sbornik* 9 (1959): 230.

[41] Begunov, "Zhitie Aleksandra Nevskogo v sostave Novgorodskoi 1-oi i Sofiiskoi 1-oi letopisei," 230.

[42] *PSRL* 3: 77.

[43] Begunov, *Pamiatnik,* 164. Note: I have created my own text from the evidence of the critical apparatus that Begunov provides for his edition of the *Life*. See my "Dressing a Wolf in Sheep's Clothing: Toward Understanding the Composition of the *Life of Alexander Nevskii,* in *Centers and Peripheries in the Christian East: Papers from the Second Bien-*

Although, at first glance, the similar phrasing may appear to be only a topos in identifying particular days in their religious context, the combining of mention of the commemoration days of both the 630 Holy Fathers of Chalcedon and the martyrs Kiurik and Ulita is unusual. This formula does not appear in either the Laurentian or Suzdal′ Chronicles. I propose that the coincidence of this combination is an indication of direct textual borrowing. If borrowing between the Novg. I-OR and the *Life* occurred, then the direction of that borrowing would more likely have been from Novg. I-OR to the *Life* than vice versa because if the Novg. I-OR borrowed from the *Life*, then it is unlikely the phrase "and holy Prince Volodimer who baptized Rus′" would have been dropped.

A second textual borrowing by the author of the *Life* from the Novg. I-OR occurs when the hagiographer has Alexander going against the Germans as the Novg. I-OR or the *Tale* does. Then he tells us Iaroslav sent Andrei to help Alexander as the Laurentian Chronicle does. He incorporates the information about the place of battle that the Suzdal′ Chronicle and the Novg. I-OR have. Finally, he incorporates the account of the Novg. I-OR or the *Tale* with Alexander's appeal to God and the pursuit. In particular the following passage indicates a probable textual borrowing:

Novg. I-OR   *Life of Alexander Nevskii*

The Germans fell there and the   And they defeated them with the help
Chuds *gave shoulder and chasing*   of God, and the warriors *gave* their
them they fought them for seven   *shoulder and they fought them, chasing* as
versts across the ice....[44]   through the air....[45]

The similar phrasing of "gave shoulder and chasing them they fought them" in Novg. I-OR and of "gave their shoulder and they fought them, chasing" in the *Life* is striking. It seems unlikely, if the Novg. I-OR borrowed from the *Life* that the phrase "with the help of God" would have been dropped. Instead that phrase seems to be an addition to a textual borrowing from the Novg. I-OR.

A third case of textual borrowing from the Novg. I-OR occurs in the description of the death of Alexander Nevskii:

---

nial Conference of the Association for the Study of Eastern Christian History and Culture, ed. Eugene Clay, Russell Martin, and Barbara Skinner, vol. 3 of *Eastern Christian Studies*, ed. Jennifer Spock (Columbus, OH: Center for Slavic and East European Studies, forthcoming). For my translation of passages from the *Life* into English, I consulted Zenkovsky's translation in his *Medieval Russia's Epics, Chronicles, and Tales*, 225–36.

[44] *PSRL* 3: 78.

[45] Begunov, *Pamiatnik*, 171.

Novg. I-OR	Life of Alexander Nevskii
and he came to Gorodets and was shorn *on November 14, the commemoration day of the Holy Apostle Philip. He died* the same night and they took him to *Volodimir* and laid him in the monastery of the *Nativity of the Holy Mother of God*. And the bishops and hegumens *having come together with the Metropolitan* Kiuril and *with all* the hierarchical *rank* and monks and with *all* the Suzdal′ians, they buried him honorably on the *23rd* of the same month, Friday, [the day] of *Holy Amfilokhii*[46]	Great Prince Alexander Iaroslavich, who was always firm in his faith in the Lord God, giving up this worldly kingdom and desiring the heavenly kingdom adopted the angelic form of a monk's life…. And then *he* gave up his soul to the Lord and *died* in peace *on November 14, on the commemoration day of the holy Apostle Philip….* His holy body was carried to *Volodimer*. The *Metropolitan with the rank*, the princes and boyars and all the people…. His body was laid in the *Nativity of the Holy Mother of God* in the Great Abbey, on November *23rd*, the commemoration day of *Holy Father Amfilokhii*.[47]

Although the formulas regarding November 14 as the commemoration day of Philip and November 23 as the commemoration day of Amfilokhii can be regarded as religious topoi, the juxtaposition of these two topoi with the descriptions of the taking of Alexander's body to Vladimir, of the presence of the metropolitan with the prelates, and of the placing of the body in the Nativity of the Holy Mother of God monastery suggests that the author of one text used the other as a source. Since the wording in the Novg. I-OR is less expansive than the wording in the *Life*, it is more likely the Novg. I-OR was the source text. These formulas do not appear in either the Laurentian or Suzdal′ chronicle accounts.

Thus, the account in the *Life*, in addition to being based on the *Tale*, appears to include interpolative passages from earlier chronicle accounts, specifically those found in the Laurentian Chronicle and the Novg. I-OR. In contrast, the information in the Novg. 1-YR interpolates a passage from the *Life*.

The Novg. 1-YR is extant in three MS copies: (1) Commission (dated to ca. 1450);[48] (2) Academy (dated to ca. 1445);[49] and (3) Tolstoi (dated to the 1720s).[50] It was probably compiled in the mid-15th century. I base this conclu-

---

[46] *PSRL* 3: 83–84.

[47] Begunov, *Pamiatnik*, 178–79.

[48] Kloss "Predislovie k izdaniiu 2000 g.," vi.

[49] Ibid.

[50] Ibid., vi–vii.

sion on two pieces of evidence. First, the last entry for the Commission copy is 1447. Second, Novg. I-YR contains derogatory epithets to describe the Tatars that the Novg. I-OR does not have. This second point indicates that its composition occurred in the post-1448 period. The Novg. 1-YR increases the number of "Germans" killed from 400 to 500, and changes the name of the saint commemorated on that day from Claudian to Feodul, who also is commemorated on April 5. In addition, after the words "Raven's Rock" and before the sentence that begins "The army of the Germans and Chuds ...," the Novg. 1-YR interpolates a passage that contains three components: a comparison of Alexander with the biblical David in that both of them had "brave warriors"; a declaration by Alexander's soldiers, after the chronicler compares their hearts to those of lions, that they were ready to put their lives on the line for him; and a plea by Alexander Nevskii to God just before the battle in which he asks for the same help that God provided Moses against the Amalekites as well as Iaroslav against Sviatopolk:

> And they gathered at Lake Chud: there were many soldiers of both sides. Prince Alexander had as many brave warriors; as of old during the time King David had strong and mighty ones. Also Alexander's men were filled with the spirit of courage, for their hearts were like those of lions, and they said, "O, our honored *and worthy* Prince, now is the time to place our heads [on the line] for you." And Prince Alexander raising his hands to the sky, said, "Judge, my God, and deliver me from this haughty people, and help me, my Lord, as in the ancient times you helped Moses to defeat the Amalekites, and as you helped my forefather, Iaroslav, against accursed Sviatopolk." On Saturday when the sun rose....[51]

This interpolated passage in the Novg. 1-YR also appears in the *Life*, and I propose below that the compiler of the Novg. 1-YR borrowed this passage from the *Life*. The words *and worthy* appear in the Novg. 1-YR, but not in the *Life*:

Life of Alexander Nevskii	Younger Redaction of Novg. I
"O, our honored Prince, now is the time....	"O, our honored *and worthy* Prince, now is the time....

---

[51] *PSRL* 3: 295–96.

These words were more likely to have been added in the Novg. 1-YR than dropped in the *Life* since both works seek to extoll Alexander.[52] I suggest, then, the following relationship among these texts (see figure 1).

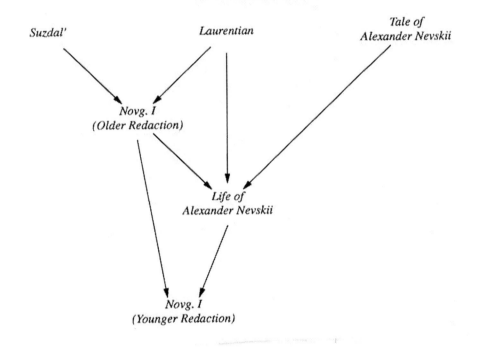

Figure 1: Relationship of Chronicle Accounts and *Tale of Alexander Nevskii* to *Life of Alexander Nevskii*

If this relationship is accurate, then it brings into question the assertion that the *Life* was written in the 1280s. It could not have been written before the account in the Novg. I-OR, which as I indicate above most likely was compiled in the middle of the 14th century. Even if one accepts the argument that the change in hand in the entry for 1330 represents a compilation, that still places its composition no earlier than 1330. Since we have only a partial copy of the *Life* from 1377, one must at least consider the possibility that parts of the rest of the *Life* were not composed before the late 15th century, the date of the earliest copy of the full first redaction.[53] One key to the dating of the *Life* is

---

[52] For a discussion of the relationship of the *Life* to the Novg. I-OR and the Novg. I-YR, see Begunov, "Zhitie Aleksandra Nevskogo v sostave Novgorodskoi 1-oi i Sofiiskoi 1-oi letopisei," 229–38.

[53] Begunov, *Pamiatnik*, 16–17 and 195–212: *Лв* (1377); *Пс* (ca. 1486); *П* (end of 15th century); *Л* (mid-16th century); *А* (mid-16th century); *Б* (3rd quarter of 16th century); *М*

its general treatment of the Mongols in a neutral way and without demeaning slurs. Fennell pointed out that the author of the *Life* tends "to stress the 'divine' role of the Tatars...." In addition, Fennell wrote: "Baty, in his encounter with Aleksandr, is shown in an almost chivalrous light. There are none of the derogatory epithets—'foul', 'thrice-accursed', 'evil', etc.—which in later literature were fastened to the Tatars. The 'tsar' and the Tatars are portrayed as some sort of benevolent force in the background...."[54]

While Fennell's observation is mostly accurate, I did find two passages in the full First Redaction of the *Life* that can be identified as interpolations of the second half of the 15th century. The first of these is the sentence: "And the women of the Moabites began to frighten their children, saying: 'Alexander is coming.'"[55] The second is: "And there was at that time great violence from foreign peoples: they oppressed the Christians, forcing them to campaign in the ranks of the army; but Great Prince Alexander went to the Khan and beseeched him not to drive his people into misery."[56] Neither the reference to Tatars as "Moabites" nor any allusion to Christians being oppressed by the Tatar khan is likely to have appeared in a source written in northeastern Rus' between 1252 and 1448.[57] Without these interpolations, the full version of the *Life* could have been composed before 1448.[58] If, however, the Laurentian copy of the *Life* constituted a full version of the First Redaction (with lost folios accounting for the missing second part), then we can place its composition (or reworking of the secular military *Tale*) between 1352 (or 1330, at the earliest) and 1377.

Scholars, like Fennell, have pointed out the chronicle-like format in the *Life*, such as sentences beginning with the phrase "In that same year." Although such phrases appear already in the *Tale* (as I have reconstructed it), which (if my reconstruction is correct) indicates the *Tale* was intended for in-

---

(3rd quarter of 16th century); *Ap* (3rd quarter of 16th century); *Пг* (3rd quarter of 16th century); *Б* (end of 16th–beginning of 17th century); *P* (2nd quarter of 17th century); *O* (mid-17th century); *У* (3rd quarter of 17th century).

[54] Fennell, "Literature of the Tatar Period," 119.

[55] Begunov, *Pamiatnik*, 174.

[56] Ibid., 177.

[57] For the argument that a change in Russian ecclesiastical writing toward the Mongol/Tatars occurred around 1448, see my *Muscovy and the Mongols: Cross-Cultural Influences on the Steppe Frontier* (Cambridge: Cambridge University Press, 1998), 144–67.

[58] The appearance of these statements in the *Life* along with the absence of a full version of the *Life* before the 2nd half of the 15th century led me to hypothesize that the first full version of the *Life* was composed after the middle of the 15th century. See my article "Alexander Nevskii's 'Battle on the Ice': The Creation of a Legend," 298n24 and 299. Shortly after the article appeared in print, I realized that a better explanation was available.

clusion in a chronicle, I suggest the revision of it into the saint's tale was also intended for a chronicle. If the military tale[59] was reworked into the saint's tale for inclusion in the Laurentian Chronicle, where it first appears, then we can explain the interest in the saint's tale in Suzdal' and in the Rozhdestven-skii Monastery since the Laurentian Chronicle was copied in the Rozhdest-venskii Monastery in Suzdal'.

If the author of the *Tale* was around 20 years old in 1263 when Alexander died, then he would have been around 50 years old in 1293, which would put him at the upper range of normal life expectancy in the 13th century. Some people did live into their 60s, 70s, and 80s, but if the author had been any older than his 50s, one might expect some reference by him to his age. Thus, we can tentatively place the composition of the military tale about Alexander Nevskii between 1263 and the early 1290s. We might speculate a little further and propose that the author of that tale was someone who indeed did grow up at the court of Alexander Nevskii (as the *Tale* suggests) and may have been the son of one of Alexander's military servitors. Since the *Tale* was intended for inclusion in a chronicle, we can further surmise that at some point the author was tonsured and, at the time of writing the *Tale*, was a monastic scribe. The attempt at reworking a military tale into a saint's tale probably occurred some time between 1352 (or 1330) and 1377. In my view, it could well have been as late as the 1370s and the reworking may specifically have been for in-clusion in the Laurentian Chronicle. Only in the second half of the 15th cen-tury did the text assume the form of what we now call the First Redaction.

---

[59] Charles J. Halperin has suggested "chronicle tale" in place of "military tale" as a bet-ter description of the genre of the *Tale of Alexander Nevskii*.

The Minority of Ivan IV*

Charles Halperin

Ivan IV was born on August 25, 1530 (7038). His father, Vasilii III, died on December 3, 1533 (7042). Thus Ivan was three years and three months old when he became grand prince of Muscovy. Ivan's minority lasted approximately fourteen years, ending no earlier than 1547 with his coronation as tsar and marriage when he was sixteen.

Nancy Shields Kollmann has noted an anomaly in the narrative accounts of these years: governmental decisions are improbably credited to Ivan despite the obvious fact that he "was too young to have performed most of the acts which the chronicles blithely attribute" to an "underage sovereign," which she considers a characteristic of the "genre" of the depiction of the ruler.[1] However, this pattern was not confined to narrative sources; all government documents—such as charters, military registers, and diplomatic records—derived their legitimacy from the minor grand prince.

The degree to which the Muscovites were guilty of cognitive dissonance in their perception of the minor Ivan need not be gauged by inference alone. There is considerable evidence, both indirect and direct, that the Muscovites "knew" that the boy Ivan was not in charge. The indirect evidence is found in their treatment of Ivan's widowed mother, Grand Princess Elena Glinskaia; the direct evidence is found in numerous explicit references to Ivan's youth.

With stultifying monotony, the very same annals which identified decisions as emanating directly and only from Ivan also depicted him as acting in concert with his mother. The phrase "Grand Prince Ivan Vasil'evich of all Rus' and his mother, Grand Princess Elena" appeared ubiquitously on the pages of

---

* An earlier version of this article was presented at the annual convention of the American Association for the Advancement of Slavic Studies, Arlington (Crystal City), VA, 17 November 2001.

[1] Nancy Shields Kollmann, "The Grand Prince in Muscovite Politics: The Problem of Genre in Sources of Ivan's Minority," *Russian History/Histoire russe* 14 (1987): 298, 305. Mikhail Markovich Krom, "'Mne sirotvuiushchu, a tsarstvu vdovstvuiushchu': Krizis vlasti i mekhanizm priniatiia reshenii v period 'boiarskogo pravleniia' (30–40 gody XVI veka)," in *Rossiiskaia monarkhiia: Voprosy istorii i teorii. Mezhvuzovskii sbornik statei, posviashchennyi 450-letiiu uchrezhdeniia tsarstva v Rossii (1547–1997)*, ed. Mikhail D. Karpachev (Voronezh: Izd-vo "Istoki," 1998), 46, concurs.

Rude & Barbarous Kingdom Revisited: Essays in Russian History and Culture in Honor of Robert O. Crummey. Chester S. L. Dunning, Russell E. Martin, and Daniel Rowland, eds. Bloomington, IN: Slavica Publishers, 2008, 41–52.

all the early chronicles, the Resurrection Chronicle (*Voskresenskaia letopis'*), the Obolenskii manuscript of the Nikon Chronicle, the separate tale of the arrest of Prince Andrei Ivanovich, the Vologodsko-Perm' Chronicle, short chronicles from the Kirillo-Belozerskii and Iosifo-Volokolamsk monasteries, the Continuation of the 1512 Chronograph (*Khronograf*), and others. Ivan and his mother consulted the boyars, received congratulations from Archbishop Makarii from *their* patrimony of Novgorod and Pskov, ordered arrests, deployed troops, enhanced urban fortifications, reformed the currency, and attended church services. According to these narratives the dying Grand Prince Vasilii III entrusted Ivan until his majority (*vozmuzhanie*) to his widow.[2] Inconsistently the same passages sometimes attributed actions both to Ivan alone, and to Ivan and Elena jointly.[3]

In his redaction of the vita of Mikhail Klopskii, Vasilii Tuchkov wrote that Ivan and his Christ-loving mother Elena ordered troops gathered in Novgorod in 1537 to fight the Tatars. Elena was referred to as *samoderzhitsa* (the feminine form of *samoderzhets*, autocrat) because Ivan was only seven years

---

[2] *Polnoe sobranie russkikh letopisei* (hereafter *PSRL*), vol. 8 (*Voskresenskaia letopis'*) (St. Petersburg: Tip. Eduarda Pratsa, 1859), 285–90 (7042–46 [1534–38]); *PSRL*, vol. 13, pt. 1 (Nikon Chronicle) (1904; repr., Moscow: Nauka, 1965), 76–98, right columns (7042–46); Mikhail Nikolaevich Tikhomirov, "Maloizvestnye letopisnye pamiatniki XVI veka," *Istoricheskie zapiski*, no. 10 (1941): 84–87; *PSRL*, vol. 26 (Vologodsko-Perm' Chronicle, starting only with the Andrei Ivanovich episode) (Moscow: Akademiia nauk SSSR, 1959), 317–18 (7045/1537); Aleksandr Aleksandrovich Zimin, "Kratkie letopistsy XV–XVI vv.," *Istoricheskii arkhiv*, no. 5 (1950): 12–13 (early 1550s short chronicle of Mark Levkeinskoi from the Iosifo-Volokolamsk monastery); ibid., 38–39 (1536–37 chronicle from the Kirillo-Belozerskii monastery); Sigurt Ottovich Shmidt, "Prodolzhenie khronografa 1512 goda," *Istoricheskii arkhiv*, no. 7 (1951): 85; Arsenii Nikolaevich Nasonov, ed., *Pskovskie letopisi*, vypusk 1 (Moscow-Leningrad: Izd-vo AN SSSR, 1941), 107–08 (Pskov I, continuation of Pogodin manuscript, [7044/1536]); *PSRL*, vol. 4, pt. 1, vypusk 3 (Rostov Chronicle) (Leningrad: Akademiia nauk, 1929), 573 (7044). Consequently, Sergei Bogatyrev oversimplified when he observed that only uninformed local, provincial chronicles attributed decisions to the minor Ivan IV. See Bogatyrev, *The Sovereign and His Counsellors: Ritualised Consultations in Muscovite Political Culture, 1350s–1570s*, Suomalaissen Tiedeakatemian toimituksia/Annales Academiae Scientiarum Fennicae, Humaniora series, vol. 307 (Saarijervi: Gummerus, 2000), 82. Kollmann documents the depiction of Ivan's "improbable" actions by citing the admittedly later Alexander Nevskii Chronicle (*Aleksandro-Nevskaia letopis'*), which appears to be derivative of the "Tsar's Book" (*Tsarstvennaia kniga*), though nonetheless often conjoins Ivan to Elena (Kollmann, "The Grand Prince in Muscovite Politics," 298n18).

[3] For example, in the Sofia II chronicle, Vasilii did not entrust Ivan to Elena until his majority, but the elite still swore a loyalty oath to them both. *PSRL*, vol. 3 (St. Petersburg: Tip. Eduarda Pratsa, 1853), 267–76.

old and was only in the fourth year of his holding the scepter of his realm (*tsarstvo*).[4] Ivan was still young and had not yet fully grown up.[5]

Non-chronicle sources reproduced this practice. An imprisoned informer claimed in a petition for mercy to have saved both Ivan's and Elena's lives.[6] The 1475–1598 official Muster Book (*Razriadnaia kniga*) twice attributed assignments and decisions to the inseparable pair—Ivan and his mother "agreed" (*prigovorili*)—while the private 1475–1605 Redactions did so more often.[7] A Nogai mirza in 1537 petitioned not only Ivan, but also "the prince's mother."[8] The inventory for the royal archive referred to a copy of a 1533 (7042) oath of Prince Andrei Ivanovich Staritskii to Grand Prince Ivan Vasil'evich of all Rus' and his mother Grand Princess Elena.[9] In an extant "agreement charter" (*dokonchal'naia gramota*), perhaps from 1537, Prince Andrei Ivanovich Staritskii kissed the cross to his elder, "lord" (*gospodin*) Grand Prince Ivan and to his mother Grand Princess Elena; this loyalty oath repeated the well-worn phrase no fewer than 15 times.[10] In his May 1537 "admonitory speech" (*nakaznaia rech'*) Metropolitan Daniil threatened Prince Andrei Ivanovich Staritskii with excommunication if he did not return to Moscow, for betraying the love of Grand Prince Vasilii III, "our mother" Grand Princess Elena, and the metropolitan himself.[11]

---

[4] This term might be considered an anachronism, since Ivan was not crowned tsar until 1547.

[5] Lev Aleksandrovich Dmitriev, ed, *Povest' o zhitii Mikhaila Klopskogo* (Moscow-Leningrad: Akademiia nauk SSSR, 1958), 166–67.

[6] *Akty istoricheskie, sobrannye i izdannye Arkheograficheskoiu komissieiu* (hereafter *AI*), vol. 1 (1841), 197–98 (no. 136), translated in *Russian Private Law in the XIV–XVII Centuries*, ed. Horace W. Dewey and Ann M. Kleimola, Michigan Slavic Materials, no. 9 (Ann Arbor: Department of Slavic Languages and Literatures, 1973), 7–8 (no. 1).

[7] *Razriadnaia kniga 1474–1598*, ed. Viktor Ivanovich Buganov (Moscow: Nauka, 1966), 83 (7042/1533–34), 93 (7046/1537–38); *Razriadnaia kniga 1475–1605 gg.*, ed. N. G. Savich, vol. 1, pt. 2 (Moscow: Akademiia nauk SSSR, 1977), 243, 244, 249, 252, 253, 271. The redaction names utilized here reflect Iurii Vladimirovich Ankhimiuk, *Chastnye Razriadnye knigi s zapisiami za posledniuiu chetvert' XV – nachalo XVII vekov* (Moscow: Drevnekhranilishche, 2005). I wish to express my sincerest appreciation to Russell E. Martin for calling Ankhimiuk's work to my attention.

[8] *Prodolzhenie drevnei Rossisskoi vivliofiki* (hereafter *PDRV*), pt. 7 (St. Petersburg: Imperatorskaia Akademiia nauk, 1791; repr., Slavistic Printings and Reprintings, no. 251/7; The Hague: Mouton, 1970), 259.

[9] Sigurt Ottovich Shmidt, ed., *Opisi tsarskogo arkhiva XVI v. i arkhiva Posol'skogo prikaza 1614 g.* (Moscow: Izd-vo Vostochnoi literatury, 1960), 61.

[10] *PDRV*, pt. 6 (St. Petersburg: Imperatorskaia Akademiia nauk, 1790; repr., Slavistic Printings and Reprintings, no. 251/6; The Hague: Mouton, 1970), 28–33 (no. 182).

[11] *AI*, 1: 201 (no. 139).

The precise nature of Elena's role, its formal or juridical status, is a separate matter. Elena might have been receiving no more than the ceremonial deference due a Queen Mother, who exercised effective power behind the scenes. However, there is no ambiguity whatsoever in passages in the "Brief Chronicle of the Beginning of the Empire" (*Letopisets nachala tsarstva*), the Academy manuscript of the Nikon Chronicle, the "Book of Degrees" (*Stepennaia kniga*), and the "Tsar's Book" (*Tsarstvennaia kniga*), all of later provenance, which characterized Elena as *gosudarynia* (the feminine form of *gosudar'*, sovereign, an even more potent title than *samoderzhitsa*). Iurganov has comprehensively traced such usages.[12] According to these chronicles, on his deathbed Vasilii III granted Elena governance (*pravlenie*), the scepter of the realm (*derzhava*). Elena was likened to Grand Princess Ol'ga, and even to the mother of Emperor Constantine I, the sainted Helena. She received the disgraced Muscovite client Chingissid Shah Ali (Shigalei) and his wife, Fatma Saltan, in her own quarters in the Kremlin when Shah Ali sought restoration to the grand prince's good graces. In her obituary, the *Letopisets nachala tsarstva* summarized that after her husband's death, Elena "held authority" (*vlastodr"-zhavstvovala*) for four years and four months, and the *Stepennaia kniga* notes that Elena "reigned" (*derzhatstvova*) beginning with Vasilii III's death.[13]

Naturally there were still ambiguities. These chronicles did not always label Elena *gosudarynia*; both in passages from earlier chronicles and in new entries she was still sometimes referred to as "grand princess" alone. An intriguing passage from the Academy manuscript of the Nikon Chronicle suggests the inconsistencies in Elena's elevation to *gosudarynia*. In January 1536 (7044) the autocrat (*samoderzhavets*) Grand Prince Ivan and his mother, Grand Princess and *gosudarynia* Elena, in the third year of *his* "reign" (*gosudarstvo*), ordered the relocation of the city of Temnikov, for which the grand princess, not called *gosudarynia* in this clause, ordered new fortifications.[14]

These passages cannot be dismissed as anachronistic rhetorical excesses by chroniclers craving favor with Ivan IV by extolling the virtues of his deceased mother. While there are no state charters (*gramoty*) issued by Ivan and his mother jointly, let alone one in which she was described as *gosudarynia*, there is incontrovertible evidence of the title's contemporaneousness. Disgraced boyar Prince Andrei Shuiskii petitioned Makarii, archbishop of Nov-

---

[12] Andrei L'vovich Iurganov, "Politicheskaia bor'ba v 30-e gody XVI veka," *Istoriia SSSR*, no. 2 (1988): 101–12.

[13] *PSRL*, vol. 29 (Moscow: Nauka, 1965), 9–32, esp. at 9–10, 12, 14, 16, 20–23, 23–24, 25, 32 (7042–46/1533–38); *PSRL*, vol. 13, pt. 2, 76–123 left column, esp. 76, 80, 85, 87 (*tsaritsa vtoraia Elena*), 92, 102–07, 109–11, 112, 123 (7042–46/1533–38); *PSRL*, vol. 21, pt. 2 (St. Petersburg: Tip. M. A. Aleksandrova, 1913; repr., Slavica-Reprint no. 67/2, Dusseldorf: Brücken Verlag; Valduz: Europe-Printing, 1970), 630, 634 (both *derzhatstvova*); *PSRL*, vol. 13, pt. 2, 416 (as wise as Ol'ga), 425–27.

[14] *PSRL*, vol. 13, pt. 1, 109–10, left column; *PSRL*, vol. 29, 25.

gorod, to intercede with *gosudar'* Ivan Vasil'evich and his mother *gosudarynia* Grand Princess Elena on his behalf.[15] In September 1534 the Trinity-St. Sergius Monastery successfully petitioned Grand Prince, not *gosudar'*, Ivan and his mother, *gosudarynia* Grand Princess Elena, for restoration of the full eight *dengi* (small silver coins) customs from the sale of each Nogai horse in Moscow.[16] According to the collected diplomatic papers dealing with Polish affairs, on September 22, 1535, Prince Ivan Fedorovich Ovchin Telepnev Obolenskii wrote Prince Fedor Vasil'evich Ovchin Telepnev Obolenskii, who was being held in Lithuanian captivity, that he had petitioned Grand Prince Ivan and his mother, the great *gosudarynia* Elena, to protect his wife, family, and property, which *they* had granted (*pozhalovali*).[17] In his will, written in 1534 or 1535 (7043), Prince Mikhail Vasil'evich Gorbatyi left an icon and 100 pieces of gold to Ivan, and another icon with a like sum of money to his "mother," *gosudarynia* Elena.[18] A letter from the captive Prince Fedor Obolenskii's servitor Andrei Gorbatyi to his lord's sons accorded Elena that title,[19] as did documents from the negotiations with appanage Prince Andrei Ivanovich Staritskii in 1537.[20]

---

[15] *Dopolneniia k Aktam istoricheskim, sobrannye i izdannye Arkheograficheskoiu Komissieiu* (St. Petersburg: Tip. II otd. Sobstvennoi Ego Imperatorskago Velichestva kantseliarii, 1846), 27 (no. 27), dated only approximately 1533–38.

[16] Published in Sergei Mikhailovich Kashtanov, *Ocherki russkoi diplomatiki* (Moscow: Nauka, 1970), 437–38. Elena carried this title only once in the extract from the books of "secretary" (*d'iak*) Timofei Kazakov; elsewhere she was merely "grand princess."

[17] *Sbornik [imperatorskogo] russkogo istoricheskogo obshchestva* [hereafter *SbIRIO*], vol. 59, entitled: *Pamiatniki diplomaticheskikh snoshenii drevnei Rossii s derzhavami inostrannymi*; additional title: *Pamiatniki diplomaticheskikh otnoshenii moskovskogo gosudarstva s Pol'sko-litovskim*, vol. 2 (1533–60), ed. G. Karpov (St. Petersburg, 1887), 14–15 (no. 3); *Akty, otnosiashchiesia k istorii Zapadnoi Rossii, sobrannye i izdannye Arkheograficheskoiu Komissieiu*, vol. 2 (1506–44) (hereafter *AZR*) (St. Petersburg: Tip. II otd. Sobstvennoi Ego Imperatorskago Velichestva kantseliarii, 1848; Slavistic Printings and Reprintings 261/2, The Hague-Paris: Mouton, 1971), 232–35 (no. 175).

[18] *Akty Suzdal'skogo Spaso-Efim'eva monastyria, 1506–1608 gg.* (Moscow: Pamiatniki istoricheskoi mysli, RGADA, Akty russkikh monastyrei, 1988), 90–93 (no. 35). Iurganov did not refer to this document, available to him in Nikolai Tikhonravov, comp., *Vladimirskii sbornik: Materialy dlia statistiki, etnografii, istorii i arkheologii Vladimirskoi gubernii* (Moscow, 1857), 128–30, which is cited in *Akty Suzdal'skogo Spaso-Efim'eva monastyria*, 93. I wish to thank Mikhail Krom for calling this earlier publication to my attention and confirming the reference.

[19] *AZR*, 2: 340–41 (no. 188).

[20] *Sobranie gosudarstvennykh gramot i dogovorov* (hereafter *SGGD*) (Moscow: Tip. N. S. Vsevolozhskago, 1819), pt. 2, 37–38 (no. 30), 38–39 (no. 31), unlike *SGGD*, pt. 1 (Moscow: Tip. N. S. Vsevolozhskago, 1813), 451–52 (no. 163).

One need not agree with Iurganov that as *gosudarynia* Elena was her young son Ivan's co-ruler[21] to conclude that calling Elena *gosudarynia* made sense only if her son, *gosudar'* Ivan, were a minor or otherwise incompetent to rule on his own. Regardless of her title, the Muscovites were hardly likely to misconstrue who actually made decisions attributed to Ivan and his mother.[22] The Muscovite chroniclers must have understood that an adult and mentally competent ruler would not have required his mother's assistance in performing the functions of his office.[23] Repeated allusions to Elena's role attest to an implicit recognition that Ivan did not yet rule.

In addition to this circumstantial evidence of Muscovite consciousness of, indeed, sensitivity to, Ivan's tender years during his minority, there are sources which directly state more than once that Ivan was a child during this time. Allusions to Ivan's youth during his minority did not originate only after he became an adult; they began contemporaneously. The *Voskresenskaia letopis'* and Obolenskii manuscript of the Nikon Chronicle described how Vasilii III summoned to his deathbed his eldest son, Ivan, who was still young (*mlad*), "in his fourth year from birth."[24] The *Tsarstvennaia kniga* modified Vasilii III's admonition to Elena to include a more specific reference to Ivan's age, urging her protect Ivan during his youth (*mladenstvo*) and until his maturity (*vsmuzhanie*).[25] The *Tsarstvennaia kniga* contained a story, echoed in the "unofficial" or "private" Postnikov Chronicle, of Vasilii III's deathbed blessing of Ivan. Vasilii did not want to see his son because Ivan was still young, three going on four, and Vasilii was afraid his illness would frighten the boy. Ivan had to be carried in, because he was a child. Vasilii admonished Elena to

---

[21] Iurganov asserts that references to Elena as *gosudarynia* were absent in the foreign-policy papers and in public and legal sources (i.e., government-issued documents). Although no charters seem to have been issued in Elena's name, she certainly appears in foreign-policy papers, albeit not as a sole policy initiator. Iurganov's use of artistic evidence, miniatures, is very intriguing (Iurganov, "Politicheskaia bor'ba v 30-e gody XVI veka," 103–04, 111). It is possible Elena waged the same kind of legitimacy campaign as Sofiia Alekseevna. See Lindsey Hughes, "Sophia, 'Autocrat of all the Russias': Titles, Ritual and Eulogy in the Regency of Sophia Alekseevna," *Canadian Slavonic Papers/Revue canadienne des slavistes* 28: 3 (September 1986): 266–86; and Isolde Thyrêt, *Between God and Tsar: Religious Symbolism and the Royal Women of Muscovite Russia* (DeKalb: Northern Illinois University Press, 2001), 139–69.

[22] Krom concludes that Vasilii III intended a regency council to run the government during Ivan's minority, but Elena outmaneuvered its members and soon assumed control. See Krom, "Sud'ba regentskogo soveta pri maloletnem Ivane IV," *Otechestvennaia istoriia*, no. 5 (1996): 34–49.

[23] Elena Glinskaia's role is to be distinguished from the grand prince's traditional consultation with his mother, especially on family matters, during the 14th and 15th centuries (Thyrêt, *Between God and Tsar*, 19).

[24] *PSRL*, vol. 8, 285; *PSRL*, vol. 13, pt. 1, 75 (1533/7042).

[25] *PSRL*, vol. 13, pt. 2, 416.

take care of Ivan, because of his youth (*mladenstvo*), until he attained his man-
hood (*vsmuzhanie*).[26] The *Stepennaia kniga* declared still more precisely that
Ivan was still young, three years and three months old, when Vasilii died.[27]
The Pskov I chronicle (Pogodin manuscript) opined that Vasilii III ordered his
boyars to protect Ivan until he was fifteen (the standard age at which *deti
boiarskie* ["gentry"] became liable for military service), and in an entry for 1535
noted that the five-year-old Ivan dispatched Pskov contingents to the Lithuanian border.[28] The chroniclers were hardly ignorant of Ivan's age.

The *Voskrenskaia letopis'* and Obolenskii manuscript of the Nikon Chronicle *sub anno* 1537 (7045), when Ivan was seven, conveyed the contents of
Prince Andrei Ivanovich's appeal for support from Novgorodian conditional-
land holders (*pomeshchiki*) against Grand Prince Ivan and his mother Elena:
"[t]he grand prince is young [*mal*], the boyars run the state [*gosudarstvo*]."[29]
Outside the confines of the Court and Moscow, the Pskov I chronicle praised
the anti-brigandage (*guba*) reform in 1541 (7049), attributed entirely to Ivan,
observing that although the eleven-year-old Ivan was still young (*mlada vozrastom*), he was "old in wisdom."[30]

According to these same narratives, when a Crimean incursion threatened Moscow in May 1541 (7049), Ivan, who was eleven, and his younger
brother Iurii prayed to the sainted Metropolitan Aleksei: "Have mercy on us
orphans! We have been separated from the bosom of our father and from our
mother's skirts [literally: waist (*chresl*)] while still young, and cannot find consolation from anyone on earth." The boyars debated whether to evacuate Ivan
from the city. Some said that if the *gosudari* were not "small children" (*malye
deti*), then they could leave Moscow. "But now the grand prince is young and
his brother younger still, and where can we flee with young children?" They
could not ride horses quickly, they would soon get tired; how quickly can one
ride with little children? It would be difficult to provide (*promyshliati*) for
young children without advance preparations. Ultimately Metropolitan Ioasaf
and the boyars agreed that if they evacuated the young children, soon it
would be difficult to take care of them. Prince Dmitrii Fedorovich Bel'skii and
the military commanders (*voevody*) in the field received a charter from Ivan
urging them to impede the khan from crossing the Oka River. Their response
was: "The time has not yet come for our sovereign, Grand Prince Ivan, to arm

---

[26] *PSRL*, vol. 13, pt. 1, 412–16; *PSRL*, vol. 34 (Moscow: Nauka, 1978), 22ff. Tikhomirov,
"Zapiski o regenstve Eleny Glinskoi i boiarskom pravlenii 1533–1547," *Istoricheskie
zapiski*, no. 46 (1954): 283ff (the earlier partial publication of the Postnikov Chronicle
begins its excerpts after this passage).

[27] *PSRL*, vol. 21, 629.

[28] *Pskovskie letopisi*, 1: 105–06, 107.

[29] *PSRL*, vol. 8, 286; *PSRL*, vol. 13, pt. 1, 95, right column.

[30] *Pskovksie letopisi*, 1, continuation of Pogodin manuscript, 110 (the word *guba* does
not appear in the passage).

himself and stand against the khans, he has not yet attained his majority (*nes"vr"shen eshche lety*), so let us serve the young grand prince."[31] Here not only was Ivan's age recognized, but particular sensitivity was expressed for the exigencies of travel with a young child; Ivan's age played a significant role in deciding policy.

The later *Letopisets nachala tsarstva* and the Academy manuscript of the Nikon Chronicle blamed the arrest of Prince Iurii Ivanovich in 1534 (7042) on evil boyars who believed that the three-year-old Ivan could not run the state firmly (*krepko*) against his mature uncle. Prince Andrei Shuiskii tried to lure Prince Boris Gorbatyi into supporting Iurii by observing that the grand prince was still young. The *Stepennaia kniga* interpolated the comment that the boyars seized Iurii because they were afraid of civil unrest caused by the "sovereign's youth" (*iunoshch"stvo gosudarskoe*), while Metropolitan Ioasaf prayed that God would protect the realm (*tsarstvo*) during the youth of the autocratic sovereign.[32] Hence Ivan's age lay at the root of court intrigues.

Obituaries for Elena in the *Letopisets nachala tsarstva*, Academy manuscript of the Nikon Chronicle, and the *Stepennaia kniga* all justified her authority after Vasilii III's death by pointing out that Ivan was young; the latter noted that Ivan was only eight when Elena died, and boyar misdeeds continued until he reached maturity (*vozrast'*).[33] The Academy manuscript of the Nikon Chronicle interpolated a reference to Ivan's youth into the *Letopisets nachala tsarstva* story of boyar feuding which led to the execution of secretary (*d'iak*) Fedor Mishurin on September 22, 1538 (7047).[34] Archbishop Feodosii of Novgorod described Ivan as "young" much later, in an epistle to him from before 1547, perhaps 1545, wishing him well on his forthcoming spring campaign against Kazan. Feodosii lauded Ivan as "still young but ruling his patrimony (*otechestvo*) in complete wisdom."[35] Therefore, chronicle references to Ivan's youth, from the time of his father's death until close to his coronation, are totally consistent with documentary sources which attest to Muscovite consciousness of Ivan's age.

The youth of Muscovy's ruler could hardly be kept a secret from her neighbors. There is direct confirmation of foreign knowledge of Ivan's youth. In an epistle to King Sigismund the Muscovite émigré Prince Semen Bel'skii urged attacking Moscow "while the grand prince is growing up" (*dorostet let*

---

[31] *PSRL*, vol. 8, 295–301; *PSRL*, vol. 13, pt. 1, 103–07, right column.

[32] *PSRL*, vol. 29, 10–11; *PSRL*, vol. 13, pt. 1, 77–78, left column (the two versions are not identical; *krepko* appears only in Nikon); *PSRL*, vol. 21, 630.

[33] *PSRL*, vol. 29, 32; *PSRL*, vol. 13, pt. 2, 123, left column; *PSRL*, vol. 21, 634.

[34] Cf. *PSRL*, vol. 13, pt. 1, 126–27, left column with *PSRL*, vol. 29, 34.

[35] *Drevniaia Rossisskaia Vivliofika*, pt. 14, 2nd ed. (Moscow: Novikov, 1790; Slavistic Printings and Reprintings, no. 250/14, The Hague-Paris: Mouton, 1970), 260–62 (no. 29).

svoikh?).[36] The Crimean Khan Saip Girei referred to Ivan as "a great sovereign but still young in years" (*gosudar' velikoi a lety eshche mlad*).[37] The Muscovite diplomatic corps had no choice but to address the issue head-on, but it was well-prepared for that endeavor.

Dealing with serving Tatars constituted both domestic and foreign policy. Grand Princess Elena consulted the boyars on the propriety of her receiving Shah Ali in October 1535 (7044) because "the great sovereign is still young."[38] Perhaps the advisability of letting a Chingissid vassal learn first-hand of Ivan's age was a factor in this consultation.

Invocations of Ivan's youth were not confined to narrative sources such as chronicles. The issue came up repeatedly in Muscovite-Lithuanian relations. According to the diplomatic papers, King Sigismund of Poland-Lithuania referred to Ivan as "in his youth" (*v molodosti*), and Lithuanian envoys argued that because Sigismund was "in his senior years" (*v starykh letekh*) but Ivan "in his youthful years" (*v molodykh letekh*), Ivan should send envoys to Lithuania, or at least the border, treating Sigismund as a son treats his father, rather than the reverse, requiring Polish-Lithuanian envoys to come to Moscow. To this the Muscovites replied, after Ivan had spoken to his mother and the boyars, that although Ivan was young, his state (*gosudarstvo*), inherited from his grandfather Ivan III and father Vasilii III, was mature, and therefore traditional protocol should be observed.[39] Sigismund's envoy in 1536, Nikodim Tekhonovskii, after his initial reception, was informed by Prince Vasilii Vasil'evich Shuiskii on Ivan's behalf that Ivan would not be inviting the envoy to dinner (literally: "to the table") since he was "still immature" (*v letekh nesovershennye*), and a formal dinner or banquet would weary him (*v istomu*). Shuiskii informed Tekhonovskii that Ivan would instead send him food (this entire explanation was repeated when the food was delivered). Muscovite personnel explained that Ivan did not yet give banquets.[40] The Lithuanian envoys brought up Ivan's immaturity again on January 11, 1537, sarcastically implying that it explained the lack of sense (*razum*) in a Muscovite proposal to grant Lithuania territories it already possessed.[41] In 1543 a

---

[36] *AZR*, vol. 2, 375 (no. 211).

[37] Iurganov, "Politicheskaia bor'ba," 112, citing *Krymskie dela*, RGADA f. 123, op. 1, no. 8, fol. 485 (February 1538).

[38] *PSRL*, vol. 13, pt. 1, 102, left column.

[39] *SbIRIO*, 59: 10–13 (no. 2, 24 February 1534); and 33, 34, 37 (no. 4, 8 May–11 June 1536); *AZR*, vol. 2, 246–48 (no. 175). Krom interprets this last passage to mean that Ivan could be considered adult despite his age. I believe the meaning of *gosudarstvo* here is more abstract, that Muscovite sovereignty has antiquity on its side. See Krom, "Politicheskii krizis 30–40-kh godov XVI veka (Postanovka problemy)," *Otechestvennaia istoriia*, no. 5 (1998): 7.

[40] *SbIRIO*, 59: 43–45 (no. 5, 31 June–11 November 1536); *AZR*, pt. 2, 253, 269 (no. 175).

[41] *SbIRIO*, 59: 66–67, 95 (no. 6, 12 December 1536–22 March 1537).

memorandum (*pamiat'*) to Privy Courtier (*blizhnyi dvorianin*) Boris Ivanovich Sukin instructed him on how to reply if the Lithuanians asked how big (*velik*) Ivan was and if Ivan intended to marry. The memorandum states that Ivan, who was 13, is "of a manly age, already the height of a mature man (*muzheskii vozrast', rostov sovershennogo cheloveka uzh est'*)" and was thinking about marriage—this four years before Ivan supposedly surprised the Court by expressing himself on the subject.[42] The Muscovite diplomatic establishment became old hands at dealing with Ivan's youth, which they could neither deny nor ignore.

❧ ☙

Muscovite sources substantiate the conclusion that the Muscovites knew that the boy Ivan was not making political decisions, indirectly by invoking the role of his mother, Grand Princess Elena, and directly by making quite specific reference to Ivan's youth and actual age. These patterns also hold for Court and Church, official and unofficial (that is, public and private) chronicles, and for narrative and documentary sources alike. In short, the Muscovites understood the difference between myth and reality, theory and practice. The Muscovite elite was not so rigid as to censor from their written sources all details which detracted from their ideal image of the ruler's role in government.[43]

And yet the Muscovites did not stop attributing all political decisions to the minor Ivan. It was just as much a conceit to declare that Ivan consulted his mother or acted jointly with her as to attribute actions to him alone. It would

---

[42] Ibid., 228 (no. 15, 16 September 1543–June 1544).

[43] Krom argues that the political crisis of the 1530s and 1540s was caused by the "organic weakness" of the Muscovite political structure in dealing with a minor or incapacitated ruler. The Muscovites were incapable of dealing with the "collision of ideology and life" this caused, producing ideological, psychological, and social instability (Krom, "Politicheskii krizis," 3–19, at 10, 15). Muscovy certainly lacked any constitutional structures for dealing with a minor ruler, but the situation in 1533 could not have come as a total shock to the Muscovites if they had any institutional memory of the minorities of Dmitrii Donskoi in the 14th century or Vasilii II in the 15th. See Iurganov, "Politicheskaia bor'ba v 30-e gody XVI veka," 109–10. After all, Vasilii III, according to Krom's own account, thought he had dealt with the institutional problem by creating a regency council. The territorial expansion, centralization, and more sophisticated bureaucratic structure of mid-16th-century Muscovy compared to the periods of earlier minorities should not have invalidated the lessons of those experiences. During Ivan's minority no attempt was made to provide a permanent solution to the problem of minor rulers, since the "problem" itself was temporary: minor rulers grew up. The "crisis" of Ivan's minority was real, but it was political and practical, not ideological or psychological. On the miniatures of the Radziwill Chronicle depicting minors, including Iaropolk Rostislavovich of Vladimir in the late 12th century, surrounded by feuding boyars, see Bogatyrev, *The Sovereign and His Counsellors*, 71, 72, 94 (plate 5).

seem that only a chronicler who was not paying attention could record Ivan's date of birth and date of accession and still pretend that "Grand Prince Ivan" was running the Muscovite government, yet nearly all chroniclers did, even in the face of passages which described Ivan as "young." The only attempt to reconcile these seemingly irreconcilable propositions was the cliché that Ivan was wise beyond his years, which, even if true, was still disingenuous, since for all his wisdom, Ivan was not yet making policy.

The Muscovites were not divorced from reality by ideological blinders. What the Muscovites wrote was not meant literally.[44] Attributing all government actions to the ruler was much more than a genre, a legal fiction, literary etiquette, political protocol, or social mores. It was a reflection of one aspect of the central element of Muscovite ideology, the ruler cult, the monopolization of legitimate authority in the person of the monarch.[45] The Muscovites intended such statements symbolically. What looks like an "anomaly" in Russian narrative and documentary sources actually reflects a profound application of deep-seated Muscovite ideological perceptions; far from "strange," this pattern of usages is perfectly understandable.

The conclusion of this essay also has implications for evaluating Ivan's writings and biography. First, it suggests the need to reevaluate those vivid and famous passages in Ivan the Terrible's First Epistle to the defector Prince Andrei Kurbskii of July 5, 1564 (7072), in which Ivan, just shy of his 34th birthday, described his childhood. After the death of Ivan's mother Elena in 1537, according to Ivan, he and his younger brother Iurii received "no human care from any quarter" and were not deemed "worthy of any loving care" (*promyshlenie*) by those responsible for their maintenance. Various boyars "began to feed us as though we were foreigners or the most wretched menials. What sufferings did I [not] endure through [lack of] clothing and through hunger! Everything was contrary to my will and unbefitting my tender years.... Many a time did I eat late, not in accordance with my will." This con-

[44] In the same way, Marshall Poe has persuasively shown that the Muscovites declared Muscovy the patrimony (*otchina*) of the ruler, although his subjects also owned *otchiny*; or the Muscovite elite the slaves (*kholopy*) of the ruler, although its members also owned *kholopy*. Marshall Poe, "What Did Russians Mean When They Called Themselves 'Slaves of the Tsar'?" *Slavic Review* 57: 3 (Fall 1998): 585–608.

[45] On the multiple layers of the ruler cult during the reign of Ivan IV, consult Michael Cherniavsky, "Khan or Basileus: An Aspect of Russian Medieval Political Theory," *Journal of the History of Ideas* 20 (1959): 459–76, reprinted in Cherniavsky, ed., *The Structure of Russian History* (New York: Random House, 1970), 65–79; idem, *Tsar and People* (New Haven: Yale University Press, 1961), 44–53; idem, "Ivan the Terrible as a Renaissance Prince," *Slavic Review* 27 (1968): 195–211; idem, "Ivan the Terrible and the Iconography of the Kremlin Cathedral of Archangel Michael," *Russian History/Histoire russe* 2 (1975): 3–28.

tinued until Ivan physically grew up (*mne vozrastom telom prespevaiushche*).[46]
Ivan attached no year to the termination of his neglect, which could have been
as early as 1543, if Ivan really were responsible for the execution of Prince Andrei Mikhailovich Shuiskii then, or as late as 1547. The considerable evidence
adduced in this article suggests that Ivan's autobiographical depiction of his
childhood and adolescence was not accurate.[47] Muscovite consciousness of
Ivan's youth and the conscientiousness with which Ivan's minority was
treated make it highly unlikely that Ivan was neglected or abused as a child.
Doubts about Ivan's mistreatment as a child in turn suggest, secondly, that
the fairly widespread view that Ivan's misbehavior as an adult can be explained by his childhood neglect, present already in Karamzin, also needs to
be reconsidered. Therefore, examination of Ivan the Terrible's minority not
only addresses questions about Muscovite sources, regencies in Muscovy, and
the Muscovite political system, but also raises additional questions about
Ivan's self-image and historians' interpretations of the process of character
formation that made Ivan the man and ruler he became.

---

[46] John L. I. Fennell, trans., *The Correspondence of Prince A. M. Kurbsky and Tsar Ivan IV
of Russia 1564–1579* (Cambridge: Cambridge University Press, 1963), 72–77. Brackets
are from Fennell's translation. I find Keenan's objections to the authenticity of this text
unconvincing; see Charles J. Halperin, "Edward Keenan and the Kurbskii-Groznyi
Correspondence in Hindsight," *Jahrbücher für Geschichte Osteuropas*, N. F., 46 (1998):
376–403.

[47] Isabel de Madariaga writes that these passages in Ivan's First Epistle to Kurbskii are
"the only existing evidence on the years between 1533 and 1547" about Ivan's treatment during his minority. De Madariaga, *Ivan the Terrible: First Tsar of Russia* (New
Haven: Yale University Press, 2005), 164. This article has contested that assertion.

Architecture, Image, and Ritual in the Throne Rooms of Muscovy, 1550–1650: A Preliminary Survey

Daniel Rowland

This paper attempts to build on Robert Crummey's work by exploring two themes that he has written about: rituals and the secular elite of Muscovy.[1] As the title indicates, it is more of a quick survey than a scholarly discussion of a complex but important set of problems presented by Muscovy's two main throne rooms, the Hall of Facets (*Granovitaia palata*) and the Golden Hall (*Zolotaia palata*). Professor Crummey has examined in great detail the composition of the elite over time, and the various ties that bound elite and monarch together. Professor Crummey and other scholars[2] have argued that the health and prosperity, even the very survival, of the Muscovite state throughout all of its life depended on the maintenance of a consensus among members of the ruling elite and between the elite and the monarch, and have uncovered many of the details of this relationship over both time and space. Less attention has been paid to the symbolic expression of this consensus, to the images used to portray the state, its elite, and its ruler to the elite itself (the court), to other residents of Muscovy, and to foreigners. The history of other premodern states would lead us to believe that this type of symbolic action could serve as a powerful cohesive force for political organisms like the Muscovite state that lacked the wealth, bureaucratic reach, and military power to compel obedience from all subjects. This essay will concentrate on two places where this symbolic action was especially densely concentrated: the two throne rooms of the Moscow Kremlin.

---

[1] Robert O. Crummey, *Aristocrats and Servitors: The Boyar Elite in Russia, 1613–1689* (Princeton, NJ: Princeton University Press, 1983), together with related essays listed in this volume's bibliography. On rituals, see idem, "Court Spectacles in Seventeenth-Century Russia: Illusion and Reality," in *Essays in Honor of A. A. Zimin*, ed. Daniel C. Waugh (Columbus, OH: Slavica Publishers, 1985), 130–58.

[2] In addition to the works cited in n. 1 above, see Edward L. Keenan, "Muscovite Political Folkways," *The Russian Review* 45 (1986): 115–81; Nancy Shields Kollmann, *Kinship and Politics: The Making of the Muscovite Political System, 1345–1547* (Stanford, CA: Stanford University Press, 1987); Valerie A. Kivelson, *Autocracy in the Provinces: The Muscovite Gentry and Political Culture in the Seventeenth Century* (Stanford, CA: Stanford University Press, 1996).

Rude & Barbarous Kingdom Revisited: Essays in Russian History and Culture in Honor of Robert O. Crummey. Chester S. L. Dunning, Russell E. Martin, and Daniel Rowland, eds. Bloomington, IN: Slavica Publishers, 2008, 53–71.

These two halls of state are ideal examples of "glowing centers" as defined by Clifford Geertz. According to Geertz, such centers are "concentrated loci of serious acts; they consist in the point or points in a society where the leading ideas come together with the leading institutions to create an arena in which the events that most vitally affect its members' lives take place."[3] It is precisely this coincidence of political institutions and symbolic display that gave these throne rooms their power for contemporaries then and constitute their importance for historians now. The tsar and the members of his court spent many hours in these chambers, making (or enunciating) important decisions or, through their persons and their dress, the costly furnishings of the rooms and rituals of unity and devotion, displaying to foreign visitors the power and wealth of the state and the unanimity of the court. The walls of each palace were covered with elaborate murals, those in the Golden Hall originating in the period right after the Moscow fire of 1547, and those in the Hall of Facets in the reign of Boris Godunov. More than any text, these mural cycles displayed the basic ideology of rulership in Muscovy. By depicting the governance of state in the context of Christian salvation history, they elevated the tsar and courtiers sitting immediately below to world historical significance and connected their decisions to the will of God. This conviction that the tsar's will reflected God's will, reinforced in countless other ways and attested by the observations of many foreign observers, was surely as vital a tool of statecraft as the army or the bureaucracy, and was, besides, a whole lot cheaper.

The mural cycles are important to the historian for another reason. In the West, there was a long tradition of sustained, disciplined discussion of politics and political theory that went back at least to Aristotle's *Politics* and was structured according to the rules of Aristotle's logic. This tradition was vigorous in the Middle Ages and flourished even more robustly in the early modern period. In Muscovy, this tradition was almost completely absent. This relative absence of formal political discourse is not surprising when we realize that the works translated from Greek that made their way into Kiev or Moscow offered no literary models for political philosophizing that went much beyond the tags and aphorisms of Agapetus or the Pseudo-Basil, texts that Ihor Sevcenko has aptly called "rather second-rate compendia."[4] No serious classical works of political theory were known in Rus', and Aristotle's Logic was not available until the end of the 17th century to provide the intellectual framework which supported much of Western political theorizing.

---

[3] Clifford Geertz, "Centers, Kings, and Charisma: Reflections on the Symbolics of Power," in *Rites of Power: Symbolism, Ritual, and Politics since the Middle Ages*, ed. Sean Wilentz (Philadelphia: University of Pennsylvania Press, 1985), 14.

[4] Ihor Sevcenko, "A Neglected Source of Muscovite Political Ideology," *Harvard Slavic Studies* 2 (1954), reprinted in Michael Cherniavsky, ed., *The Structure of Russian History* (New York: Random House, 1970), 99.

Political ideas are certainly present in many kinds of Muscovite texts, but they are not connected through logic into a coherent set of principles; rather they lie as unconnected distinct ideas in various historical, polemical, or other texts. Architecture and painting together address, if not solve, this problem, since they operated in a quite distinct tradition which provided an organizational principle based, as we will see, on space rather than logic.

If we are to capture within the short compass of an essay the significance of these throne rooms and the rituals that took place within them, we must at least attempt to bring all three elements into focus—architecture, images, and ritual.

A useful, if unconventional, place to begin our discussion is with a memory board (*lukasa*) from the Luba people of central Africa, in present-day Zaire (see fig. 1 following p. 72). A recent exhibit of Luba political art at the Museum for African Art in New York and the excellent catalogue produced in connection with it show that the *lukasa* stands simultaneously (among other things) for the body of the tortoise, the animal form of the founding ancestress of the society of historians (and royal advisers) whose job it is to "read" the *lukasa*, and for the territory of the kingdom, with sacred sites and rulers represented by beads, shells, and nails. Created specifically for a particular ruler, the *lukasa* conveys in esoteric signs the principles upon which Luba politics are founded. The Luba are useful to our inquiry because they have little connection with the tradition of Christian rulership of which the Muscovite throne rooms are part. Nevertheless, their "memory" art—memory boards, and closely related objects like staffs, stools, statues, and murals, together with dances, songs, and body decoration, which together constitute "the theater of Luba royal experience"—asks many of the same basic questions that the art and rituals of our throne rooms do. These ceremonial objects tell the history of Luba kings against the background of Luba geography, epic tales, and spirit worship; they are produced by a society of court historians/advisers (the Mbudye) whose job it is to interpret their multilayered and ambiguous symbols to suit the present time and place. They provide legitimacy for the monarch, but at the same time furnish standards for proper etiquette and behavior by which the monarch's actions may be (and are) judged. Used together, they explain the history of Luba kings starting with the legendary founder of kingship (appointed by a goddess or spirit in the form of a turtle), they describe the special divine wisdom by which the king and his advisors make judgments (spirit possession by Mbudye members), they map the social hierarchy of the society, they demonstrate the solidarity of the state, and they associate the power of the king with the forces of nature, the sun, moon, stars, trees, etc.[5] These functions are strikingly similar to the functions performed,

---

[5] Mary Nooter Roberts and Allen F. Roberts, eds., *Memory: Luba Art and the Making of History* (Munich: Prestel, for the Museum for African Art, New York, 1996), esp. chap. 4.

as we shall see, by Russian throne rooms. This similarity, in turn, underlines the basic nature of the questions that Muscovy's throne rooms set out to answer and helps us put the Muscovite answers in a comparative perspective.

There are three differences that stand out, however. The first is that knowledge of political principles is for the Luba esoteric knowledge, available to a few initiates and accessed by spirit possession; for early modern Russians, the principles of Christian rulership were at least in theory available to the public, though of course the way those principles were applied in practice was not. In both cultures, however, the production of state ideology was a monopoly of the court. A second difference is that the Luba have a more richly complex ideology of rulership than the Musocvites had, more ambiguous because unwritten, more coherently described in a variety of media from body decoration to implements to statues to dance to architecture to murals. The other difference revealed by the comparison is the comparative lack of concern with geography in Muscovite ideology; the Luba, like the Balinese of Clifford Geertz's descriptions, saw the landscape as inhabited by spirits that embodied the state on the spiritual level in the way that local officials embodied the state on a mundane level, so that the landscape in potential form *was* the state, even if no governing apparatus existed. Christianity obviously did not permit the veneration of local spirits. In Muscovite ideology, therefore, the geographical dimension in the core definition of the state was left largely blank; this disadvantage made it both all the more difficult and all the more imperative to extend the symbolic reach of the state out into the rapidly growing provinces.

The churchmen who developed and elaborated the image of rulership in Muscovy, like contemporary Luba historians, were working in a well-developed tradition whose general precepts had to be interpreted for specific circumstances. In both the Christian East and the Christian West, there was a long tradition of palace architecture and art that provided the basic vocabulary within which the Muscovites could work. The prototype of the imperial palace seems to have been the residence (*palatium*) of the Emperor Domition (A.D. 81–96) on the Palatine Hill. This residence was approached across an open square, had an impressive façade with colonnades and pediment, and contained three separate halls for audiences, justice, and eating. In the West, Charlemagne built a *Sacrum Palatium* in Aachen, which in turn served as the prototype for a whole series of medieval halls of state, some, like the gigantic hall built by William II at Westminster (20 x 72 meters) built for monarchs, some, especially in Italy, built for republican regimes.[6] In the East, important palaces were built both in Constantinople and in the provinces. Typically, they contained images of the current ruler and/or his ancestors, and de-

---

[6] This brief discussion is based on Randolph Starn and Loren Partridge's inspiring *Arts of Power: Three Halls of State in Italy, 1300–1600* (Berkeley: University of California Press, 1992), 1–3.

pictions of their victories. In individual palaces, images of the personified virtues, the Genesis creation story, or images of the Mother of God as guardian were also included.[7] The epic of Digenes Akritas contains a fairly lengthy description of Digenes' palace, "a big square house of cut stone, having stately columns and windows up above," containing halls whose ceilings were decorated with gold mosaics depicting Old Testament heroes, Samson, David, Moses, and Joshua, together with other heroes from Greek classical history.[8] Rus' chronicles frequently mention royal palaces, but we know almost nothing about their decoration. They probably followed Byzantine models, at least at first. Theophanes the Greek apparently executed paintings in both the residence of the Grand Prince in Moscow and in the palace of Prince Vladimir Andreevich of Serpukhov.[9]

Architecture

Compared to the complex source problems relating to the murals in Muscovy's throne rooms, their architectural history is relatively straightforward. Figure 2 shows the two throne rooms as they appeared in the 1672–73 *Book about the Election of Mikhail Fedorovich*. On the right (nos. 17 and 18 on the plan in fig. 3) is the Hall of Facets, begun in 1487 by Marco Friazin ("the Italian") who laid out the basic plan of the building, including its main hall (22.1 by 22.4 by 9 meters) supported by one massive central pillar. The Milanese Pietro Antonio Solari, who was also active in the design of parts of the Kremlin wall, took over the project in 1490, and may have added the finish details, especially the faceted limestone façade that gave the building its name, and the original paired gothic windows clearly seen in this drawing. Note the "Great Beautiful Golden Stair," the elaborate entrance stair with two landings (no. 16 in fig. 3). Recent scholarship indicates that it was originally open, but at some point before the date of this drawing, an elaborate copper tent roof was added with a gilded grille to guard the entry. Some sources say that the roof was also gilded. An elaborate portal, possibly designed by Alevisio Novyi, led from the "Boyars' Porch" at the top of the stair into the vestibule of the palace

---

[7] Cyril Mango, *The Art of the Byzantine Empire, 312–1453* (Englewood Cliffs, NJ: Prentice-Hall, 1972), 15, 224, 197, 184, 247, 235, 252–53. The acts of the Seventh Ecumenical Council condemn emperors for being depicted with the attributes of Christ: "They ought instead to have recounted their manly deeds, their victories over the foe, the subjugation of barbarians which many have portrayed on panels and on walls so as to consign their narration to memory and to arouse the love and zeal of spectators" (ibid., 154).

[8] Ibid., 215–16.

[9] The evidence comes from a letter from Epiphanius the Wise to Kiril of Tver': O. I. Podobedova, *Moskovskaia shkola zhivopisi* (Moscow: Izdatel'stvo Nauka, 1972), 59–60; I. Grabar', "Feofan Grek," in idem, ed., *O drevnerusskom iskusstve* (Moscow: Nauka, 1966), 78.

(no. 11 in fig. 3). Note also that the faceted limestone blocks originally covered the whole façade, and the first story was considerably higher. During the restoration of the building that was carried out in 1968, traces of colored paint (red, yellow, light blue, green) were found on pieces of limestone from the building's exterior. Exactly where these pieces came from and what color patterns they imply has not been discussed in print, as far as I know. I also cannot find any clear evidence of when this color was first applied, though documentary evidence from 1667 indicates that the building was *repainted* at that time, and that a considerable amount of paint was used. We do know that the building's side walls were painted a dark red.[10] At least by the middle of the 17th century then, the hall's exterior was characterized by considerable color contrasts: the red side wall with the white limestone of the façade and the original window frames, the other colors, wherever they were, and the steep copper roof, possibly gilded. Considerable evidence also exists that down to 1684 an inscription ran around the building just below the cornice.[11]

The history of the Golden Palace is a little simpler, largely because it is (unfortunately) shorter. The two rooms (vestibule and throne room, nos. l and 2 on the plan in fig. 3) were built as part of the royal residence from 1499–1508 by Alevizio Novyi. Figure 2 shows what seems to have been the basic form of the façade, approached by three sets of stairs leading to a balcony (the Boyars' Porch or Front Passages, no. 11 in fig. 3), from which in turn one entered through a portal into the vestibule and finally into the throne room. Barberino states that the palace had a golden roof; around the cornice ran an inscription (dated 1561 and seemingly proclaiming the palace built by order of Ivan IV and his sons!) that survived until the building was pulled down in 1752, to be replaced by Rastrelli's Kremlin palace. Inside, the dimensions of both the throne room (12 meters square and about 12 meters in height) and the vestibule (about 12 by 8 meters) were quite modest, compared to either the Hall of Facets or to Western European palaces. Like the floor of the Hall of Facets, the floor of the Golden Hall was stepped down near the middle, leaving an ele-

---

[10] The best straightforward description of the Hall of Facets is A. I. Komech and V. I. Pluzhnikov, eds., *Pamiatniki arkhitektury Moskvy: Kreml', Kitai-gorod, Tsentral'nye ploshchadi* (Moscow: Iskusstvo, 1982), 330–31. Vital documentary evidence is discussed by E. M. Kozlitina, "Dokumenty XVII veka po isotorii Granovitoi Palaty Moskovskogo Kremlia," *Gosudarstvennye muzei Moskovskogo Kremlia: Materialy i issledovaniia* 1 (1973): 95–110.

[11] Major renovations carried out by Osip Startsev in 1682 substituted large baroque windows for Solari's late-gothic paired openings. A fire in 1696 caused the original copper peaked roof to be replaced by a flatter roof. The removal of the first-floor limestone blocks on the main facade to create a smooth stuccoed surface and the alteration of the original first-floor openings were carried out in the 18th and 19th centuries. The elaborate entrance stair that, with its original three landings, was an essential part of the approach to the throne hall has also been removed, replaced in the 1930s by the low building seen to the viewer's left in most contemporary photographs.

vated platform around the wall for benches from which courtiers could watch various court rituals, including the reception of foreigner diplomats, from above (fig. 7). Unless the lower center space was very small, this platform would probably have been about two meters wide.[12]

These two throne rooms present a fascinating contrast one with the other. The Faceted Hall projected itself out into Cathedral Square, where it boldly took its place among the other, largely religious, buildings there. Like them, its placement and design ensured that it would be seen as a three-dimensional object standing in space. It loudly proclaims its Italian origins, as can be seen by a quick comparison with Ferrara's Palazzo dei Diamanti (fig. 4), and its placement in Cathedral Square is, at least to some extent, typical of how a Renaissance palace might be placed in a piazza.

As can be seen in figure 2, the Golden Hall, by contrast, was not really an independent structure, but rather a part of the royal residence as a whole. Seen from Cathedral square, neither the hall nor the whole residence of which it was a part could be seen as clear and understandable three-dimensional objects. There was no attempt to create a front facade or to express the mass of the building. Rather, the front of the Golden Hall is concealed from an observer standing down at the level of Cathedral Square by the wide Boyars' Porch, revealing behind the balustrade only the roofs and tantalizing top parts of the building behind. If the Faceted Hall plainly represented an import from the Renaissance West, the Golden Hall and its surrounding palace harked back to an older and more complex ancestry going back both to the Great Palace of Constantinople and to a series of Islamic palaces whose central planning concept originated with the placement of tents in the Mongol court and reached its fullest development in the Topkapi Palace of Sultan Mehmed II, built about the same time as Ivan III carried out his rebuilding of the Kremlin, and, like the Kremlin, self-consciously using Italian architects (and, for the Ottomans, other foreign architects) in addition to the local talent. The tsar's palace had no apparent axial organization and consisted largely of comparatively low structures grouped around courtyards and passages. The verticality that was seen as appropriate for church architecture is here replaced by horizontal extension over space. Like the Topkapi as described by Gulru Necipoglu, the Kremlin was impressive as seen from a distance behind its walls and towers, but from inside the royal residence itself, the architecture appeared much more modest, and was characterized by "the repetitive use of elementary forms acting as surfaces for decoration applied with varying de-

---

[12] K. K. Lopialo, "K primernoi rekonstruktsii Zolotoi palaty Kremlevskogo dvortsa i ee monumental'noi zhivopisi," in Podobedova, *Moskovskaia shkola*, 193–98.

grees of elaboration." The integration of nature in the form of gardens was also an important ingredient for both residences.[13]

The sprawling spaces of the Topkapi were held together by the "glue" of court ceremonies in which the official visitor moved by carefully articulated stages through a series of ever more restricted spaces (restricted spatially and socially) toward the secluded monarch. Whether this is true of the royal palace as a whole I do not know, but it seems to have been true, on a small scale at least, of our throne rooms. The Golden Hall is the most obvious example, since the visitor, after moving from the open spaces of Red Square through the massive Spasskii gates and the narrow street next to the Voznesenskii Monastery to Cathedral Square, experienced the building in stages, starting in the square, rising according to status on one of three stairways (14, 15, 16 in fig. 3) to the porch (there were grilles protecting the stairways), from which the palace complex was much more visible, and proceeding to the vestibule and into the throne room itself. The same sequence also applied, surprisingly, to the Faceted Hall. Instead of entering the building directly from the square through a central doorway, as one would expect (and as was done in the Palazzo dei Diamanti; the central door opens onto the street), the visitor climbed to the porch via one of the ceremonial staircases, and then entered the building from the back of the south wall, continuing on through the vestibule to the throne room. Thus the Faceted Hall, although it actually stood prominently in the square itself, was experienced ceremonially as if, like the Golden Hall, it receded away from the square into a hidden, privileged realm. The effect was to mark the space of the two halls off from the more public space of Cathedral Square, which itself was even more clearly separated from the truly public space of Red Square by the walls and intervening spaces of the Kremlin. Even a high-ranking boyar, who might live in the Kremlin and be familiar with most of its spaces, was made to feel the privileged nature of the throne halls and the exalted social status of those who frequented them. The space of the Kremlin as a whole, and the royal palace in particular, was thus encoded to display rank: the closer you got to the center of power, the tsar and his residence, the higher your rank. The distance from Red Square to the throne rooms mirrored the social distance from the lowliest commoner to the court, consisting of the highest nobles and ruler. Having access to "the bright eyes of the tsar" had a spatial as well as a symbolic meaning.

The increasing *social* restrictions of the Kremlin spaces were echoed by spaces that were meant to be experienced as increasingly restricted *physically*. Participants in throne-room ceremonies must have felt these restrictions bodily. This progressive tightening of spaces was felt as one progressed from the vast open space of Red Square and its bustling and freely moving market

---

[13] Gulru Necipoglu, *Architecture, Ceremonial, and Power: The Topkapi Palace in the Fifteenth and Sixteenth Centuries* (Cambridge, MA: MIT Press, 1991), passim, quotation on p. 243.

into the Kremlin to the more sedate and controlled space of Cathedral Square, up to the much smaller and narrower space of the Boyars' Porch. Spatial and physical restriction reached its height on the comparatively narrow steps on which courtiers sat on benches, restricted largely to movement in the two dimensions created by benches and the narrow space of the raised platform on which they sat. (See Fig. 7.) This same progression of spaces reflected a sharply changing degree of freedom of action, from the free-wheeling hurly-burly of Red Square to the carefully choreographed movements and stiff rituals of the two throne rooms.[14] This feeling of physical restriction would have been amplified by the heavy and elaborately embroidered costumes (with lavish use of gold thread) worn by courtiers on state occasions, discussed below.

The architecture of the two halls suggests two other points, one about the nature of the ruler and the other about Russia and the West. Necipoglu has perceptively observed that the architecture of the Topkapi, characterized by movement toward an aloof, receding ruler implies, just that: a ruler who is more icon than actor, a semidivine part of the natural order whose government governs but who personally is seldom or never seen to act. She sees this description as particularly appropriate to later 16th-century rulers who were depicted by an increasingly ossified ceremonial in just this way. This image is the one conveyed by the Golden Hall. The Faceted Hall, on the other hand, implies just the opposite: the self-conscious active ruler who strides confidently into the public square and boldly governs. Literary portraits of Russian rulers reflect both types of ruler.[15] Tsar Fedor Ivanovich, mentally defective and almost totally inactive in government as far as we can tell, plays the first role, contemporary sources complementing him on his ritual success in interceding with God for Muscovy. Tsar Ivan IV himself might also fall into this category, particularly in his later years. Literary depictions of his son, Ivan Ivanovich, would place him in the second category; he was not shown as a Renaissance prince, certainly, but he was portrayed as forceful and active, both on the battlefield and off. Ivan III and Boris Godunov are two other rulers who could be put in this latter category. The fascinating thing is that in

---

[14] These comments were inspired in part by reading the stimulating essay by Dell Upton on the occasion of the 25th anniversary of the Vernacular Architecture Forum, an American organization devoted to the study and interpretation of vernacular buildings: Upton, "The VAF at 25: What Now?" *Perspectives in Vernacular Architecture* (hereafter, *VAF*) 13: 2 (2007), 7–13, and derive from the work of LeFebvre, de Certeau, Gibson, and Bordieu. The work of these seminal theoreticians is clearly relevant to our study, and could be applied profitably in much greater detail than is possible here.

[15] On these portraits, see Daniel Rowland, "Did Muscovite Literary Ideology Place Limits on the Power of the Tsar (1540s–1660s)?" *The Russian Review* 49 (1990): 125–55, esp. 131–42.

throne-room architecture, in literary texts, and in political practice, both images of the ruler remained active and acceptable.

Another surprising point is that both throne rooms were built by Italian architects at roughly the same time for the same ruler (though Ivan III did not live to occupy his new palace). What we see here is something slightly more complex than the mere aping of Italian renaissance forms. The interplay between the two throne rooms suggests the desire to incorporate the Italian technology and elegance that so captivated the rest of Europe, to integrate it into a larger vision of the state, but not to be overwhelmed by it. What now seems to us a balancing of native with foreign elements, so characteristic also of the Archangel Michael and the Dormition Cathedrals, bespeaks a surprising cultural self-confidence that inspired the sophisticated team of Italians to make their remarkable contributions to Russian culture, rather than making mere copies of what they built at home. The best way to explain this evidence, it seems to me, is to suppose that neither the tsar nor his architects perceived the Russia/West dichotomy that so pervades our own view; rather, they held a premodern universalistic view which encouraged the borrowing of whatever was useful without worrying about its cultural identity.

Images

Architecturally, then, the Golden Hall and the Hall of Facets were based on very different, even opposing, principles, but the Faceted Hall was linked ceremonially and by the addition of decorative elements (colors, roofs, possibly an inscription) to the Golden Hall into one coherent system. The mural programs for the two halls were more closely related to start off with, and more explicit in their messages. But first, a few words about the sources. The Faceted Hall was first furnished with murals in the 1590s under Boris Godunov. The Golden Hall was decorated under Vasilii III, but these murals were apparently destroyed in the great fire of 1547, requiring the repainting of the hall shortly thereafter. The new murals were mentioned in a complaint by I. M. Viskovatyi, head of the Foreign Office, about new developments in iconography. Almost all of our information about the murals in both halls, however, comes from very detailed and systematic descriptions made in March 1672, by the famous icon painter Simon Ushakov and the *pod"iachii* Nikita Klement'ev.[16] To summarize a lot of confusing evidence, I think that the best

---

[16] The question is: what precisely were the murals that Ushakov and Klement'ev described? The answer for the Hall of Facets now seems fairly straightforward. The murals described were old enough that the need for their repair had been clear for some time. They might well have been repainted in the early decades of the century, but the presence of Fedor Ivanovich and Boris Godunov in a mural immediately next the throne suggests that later painters tried hard to follow the original program, as was the custom at least from the 1630s on. The question of the origin of the Golden Hall murals described in 1672 is so murky that I am not sure it can ever be resolved.

we can do is to date the murals of Ushakov's description to the long period between 1547 and the 1630s. I am inclined toward the 1550s as the most likely date, however.

The diagrams in figures 5 (for the Golden Hall murals[17]) and 6 (for the Hall of Facets murals) allow us an overview of the fairly complex set of images in each throne room and its associated vestibule. To oversimplify considerably, the upper domed spaces in the Golden Hall are dominated by the theme of Wisdom (throne room) and godly governance (vestibule), while the corresponding spaces in the Faceted Hall contain images of the Creation of the Universe (throne room) and miscellaneous scenes, some from the Old Testament (vestibule). Military and historical scenes from the Old Testament and from Rus' history occupy the lower vaults and walls. In the Golden Hall, Old Testament scenes in the vestibule are seen as prefigurations of scenes from Rus' history in the throne room.

There are plainly many levels on which these complex mural programs can be read. There is space here to touch on only a few of them. On a basic level, they answer many of the questions that Luba objects answered: they explain the founding of kingship in Christian terms by emphasizing the connection between the current ruler of Muscovy and Old Testament rulers who in the Christian tradition were the first rulers to be chosen and protected by God. Both halls trace the ancestors of the current ruler in some detail; in the Faceted Hall, a long list of ancestor portraits were found starting with the illustrations from the Tale of the Vladimir Princes on the east wall and then continuing in the window embrasures of the east, south, and north walls. In the Golden Hall, Riurikide ancestors were placed in the squinches of the throne room in parallel with the Old Testament rulers on the squinches of the vestibule. Royal ancestors also appeared in illustrations to the Tale of Vladi-

---

For further information on the Golden Hall, see Lopialo, "K premernoi rekonstruktsii..."; Michael Flier, "K semioticheskomu analizu Zolotoi palaty Moskovskogo Kremlia," in *Drevnerusskoe iskusstvo: Russkoe iskusstvo pozdnego Srednevekov'ia. Shestnadtsatyi vek*, ed. Andrei Batalov et al. (St. Petersburg: Dmitrii Bulanin, 2003), 178–87 (by far the best analysis of the meaning of the murals); and Daniel Rowland, "Biblical Military Imagery in the Political Culture of Early Modern Russia: The Blessed Host of the Heavenly Tsar," in *Medieval Russian Culture, Vol. II*, ed. Michael Flier and Daniel Rowland (Berkeley: University of California Press, 1994), 194–95, and 194 n. 29. The Ushakov and Klement'ev descriptions have been twice published: S. P. Bartenev, *Moskovskii kreml' v starinu i teper'* (Moscow, 1916), 183–93; and I. E. Zabelin, *Materialy dlia istorii, arkheologii, i statistiki goroda Moskvy*, 2 vols. (Moscow, 1884), 1: 1238–55. The Hall of Facets murals were redone in the late 19th century closely following the notes of Ushakov, and were recently restored, with impressive results. See Aida Nasibova and B. Groshnikov, *Granovitaia palata Moskovskogo Kremlia* (Leningrad: Aurora, 1978) for color illustrations and full information on the mural scheme.

[17] I am deeply grateful, as always, to Michael Flier for permission to reproduce this diagram.

mir Princes and in the window embrasures. As the Luba associated the ruler with the natural order of the universe, the throne rooms of Muscovy (like many of their predecessors and successors) made the creation of the world a major theme, complete with the sun, moon, stars, and other natural features of the universe. The theme of the creation was found on the southern section of the dome of the Golden Hall throne room, as part of the larger theme of Holy Wisdom, through which God created the universe and the tsar now rules his *tsarstvo*. In the Faceted Hall, the creation of the world occupies virtually the entire ceiling surfaces of the throne room. It begins with an impressive composition (Cr. 0 in fig. 5) above the southern wall depicting the creation of the Heavenly Host as a kind of heavenly court, arranged in nine ranks, reflecting the social hierarchy of the court below, and continues with the seven days of creation followed by the Fall and the Expulsion from Eden. In both halls, as for the Luba, kingship is associated with the established order of the universe and thus imagined as both natural and immutable. On an even larger scale, the purpose of the murals in both halls is to place the Muscovite state within salvation history, starting with the creation and stretching out to the Apocalypse, an event very present in the Golden Hall but largely absent in the Hall of Facets.

Within this larger context, there are a number of themes common to both halls, most of which would have been quite understandable, because of their straightforward presentation, to an illiterate courtier or a foreigner. In an earlier paper,[18] I listed 7 themes that were elaborated in the Golden Hall, all of which in slightly variant forms can also be found in the Hall of Facets. These themes included 1) the descent of political power from God; 2) Holy Wisdom (largely absent in the Hall of Facets); 3) the protection of Rus' by the Mother of God; 4) the glorification of the clan of the ruler; 5) divine protection and aid in battle; 6) the obligations of the ruler to be merciful and just and to maintain his own piety and righteousness; and 7) advice and the relationship between the ruler and his courtiers. Particularly striking is the emphasis on the ruler's obligations and the importance of royal advisers. ("Boyars," "vel'mozhi," "mudrye skazateli" were listed by Ushakov and his assistant in almost every image of Godly rule.)

This emphasis on the tsar's obligation to choose the righteous path is significant. If for the general public the identity of God's will with the tsar's will was, it was hoped, axiomatic, for the elite in the throne rooms, it was conditional. The great emphasis on moral choice, especially in the Golden Hall, clearly brought with it the possibility of a wrong choice. Not only the salvation of the tsar, but God's blessing on the *tsarstvo* and, ultimately, the legiti-

[18] Daniel Rowland, "Two Cultures, One Throne Room: Secular Courtiers and Orthodox Culture in the Golden Hall of the Moscow Kremlin," in *Orthodox Russia: Belief and Practice under the Tsars*, ed. Valerie A. Kivelson and Robert H. Greene (University Park: Pennsylvania State University Press, 2003), 32–57.

macy of the whole political system depended on the "good soil" of the tsar's soul. This evidence shows how far Russia was from the automatic and unquestionable identification of the ruler's will with God's will that was such an important part of Western European absolutist thought in the 17th century.

The Hall of Facets, as well as the Golden Hall, placed a major emphasis on advisers, not surprisingly in view of Boris Godunov's role as chief adviser to Tsar Fedor, and as chief patron, presumably, of the Hall of Facets murals. "Premudrye skazateli" appear as a part of Pharaoh's court in the story of Joseph, as "vel'mozhi" in the parables about just and unjust judges, and, most significantly, as part of Tsar Fedor Ivanovich's court with Boris Godunov prominently at their head on the south wall next to the throne. Of the nine creation scenes, three (0, 4, and 7 in fig. 6) show God with His heavenly court of angels and archangels, images that I believe were meant as heavenly analogues of the tsar's earthly court meeting immediately below.[19] Whereas in the tales about the Time of Troubles, advisers were important chiefly as the most convenient means to correct an erring or sinful tsar, in both throne rooms wise advisers are shown as part of the normal running of a pious tsar's court. The consistency with which Ushakov and Klement'ev mention them indicates that the authors of the mural programs in both throne rooms considered boyar advisers an essential part of the tsar's court and made a point of including them in the murals' depiction of Christian governance. Indeed, "advice" may not be the right rubric for our discussion here; "boyars" or "grandees" are more accurately depicted as partners of the tsar in governance.

Ritual

We now turn to the rituals that took place in and around the throne rooms, chiefly, for the purposes of this essay, the rituals connected with the greeting and feeding of foreign ambassadors. Ritual, of course, is what knit together architecture and image, activating each in the context of ceremonies in which the actors—tsar, court, and foreign visitors—were also the chief audience. The importance of this dual role is crucial in convincing those present of the power and glory of the kingdom, and the importance of their own role within it: a ritual may look impressive from the outside, but it is often far more moving for those who take part in it, because, by taking part, those involved affirm by their own bodily actions the values implicit in the ritual. There were two important audiences, then, for these rituals, the foreign outsiders and the court itself, including the tsar. Although ostensibly the rituals were designed to impress the first, I believe that they also had a powerful effect on the second.

---

[19] On Joseph, see Zabelin, *Materialy*, cols. 1265–66; on parables, ibid., cols. 1269–71. On other scenes with "boyars": St. Vladimir and Sons, east wall, ibid., col. 1266; Constantine Monomakh and his "sanovniki," south wall, ibid., cols. 1266–67.

There were three chief types of ceremony carefully reported on by foreign
ambassadors:[20] the procession by which the foreign delegation and its presents were conveyed to the throne rooms, the greeting of the delegation by the
tsar and court and the accompanying exchange of gifts, and, finally, an elaborate and lengthy feast, which usually took place in the Hall of Facets, but
which was sometimes replaced, probably to save time, by the sending of a
large number of dishes to the ambassador's lodgings.

Our sources for these rituals are remarkably rich and reliable. The most
important by far are the accounts of foreign diplomats who took part in the
ceremonies and whose official duties included reporting a description of
them. These accounts present far fewer source problems than most of our
other sources on Muscovite history; their publishing history and/or archival
location usually make it clear by whom they were written and, roughly, when
they were written. There are also substantial Russian records (the *posol'skie
knigi*) about these ceremonies, well described recently by Iuzefovich.[21] A third
type of record is far less reliable: the illustrations that sometimes graced the
pages of the published versions of various foreigners' accounts (see fig. 7).
These images are compelling and are very useful in registering those things
that the diplomat-authors thought were important, like the arrangement of
the room and the placement of the various actors (tsar, courtiers, diplomats),
but they were often drawn up after the event, in some cases after the author
had returned home. For that reason, details in the images concerning subjects
like architecture and painting, which were not of such interest to the diplomats, are far less reliable.

Read together, these accounts eloquently testify to the extraordinary ef-
fectiveness of Muscovite rituals in displaying the wealth and political power
of the state. The 16th century was an age of great diplomatic display, as anyone familiar with the meeting between Henry VIII and Francis I on the "Field
of the Cloth of Gold" will know.[22] Several of the diplomats who visited Russia were exceptionally experienced and sophisticated men, yet virtually every
one was impressed by Muscovite ritual. Richard Chancellor was typical when
he worried about his audience with the tsar, that "this so honorable an assem-

---

[20] Michael S. Flier, "Political Ideas and Rituals," in *The Cambridge History of Russia*, 3
vols., vol. 1, *From Early Rus' to 1689*, ed. Maureen Perrie (Cambridge: Cambridge University Press, 2006), 387–408.

[21] L. A. Iuzefovich, *Kak v posol'skikh obychaiakh vedetsia* (Moscow: Mezhdunarodnye otnosheniia, 1988).

[22] See, for example, Joycelyne Gledhill Russell, *The Field of Cloth of Gold: Men and Manners in 1520* (New York: Barnes and Noble, 1969). I gladly thank Marshall Poe for this
reference.

bly, so great a majesty of the emperor and the place, might very well have amazed our men and dashed them out of countenance...."[23]

One major tool to this end was the lavish and unceasing use of luxury goods, descriptions of which appear in almost every foreign account. The gifts brought and received by the ambassadors, the clothing of the tsar and his court, the tsar's regalia—all were described with a kind a breathless materialist devotion worthy of the voice-over on "The Wheel of Fortune." We unfortunately do not have time to enumerate these splendors, but the mountains of plate and the endless cloth of gold costumes were clearly effective in impressing foreigners. They cannot have failed also to have impressed Muscovites. The gifts brought by ambassadors were carefully displayed during the initial procession to the Kremlin, and the foreigners tell us that the common people crowded around to look at them. More important, the courtiers cannot have been insensitive to the obvious message of wealth and power conveyed by all of these goods.[24]

These deluxe objects also reinforce our earlier impressions about the "Russia and the West" problem: they were not entirely or even mainly Russian, but were drawn freely from all of the countries with which Russia had relations. Textiles came from Russia, Poland, and Western Europe; of the hatchets that the tsar's ceremonial body guards (*ryndy*) carried, some were of Russian manufacture and others were made in Turkey. Even the thrones themselves were of international origin. Of surviving thrones of this period that I have run across, one was made in Western Europe, one was Russian, another was Persian, and yet another was a gift from Armenian merchants trading in Persia.[25] Olearius tells us of another that was being crafted jointly

---

[23] Lloyd E. Berry and Robert O. Crummey, eds., *Rude and Barbarous Kingdom: Russia in the Accounts of Sixteenth-Century English Voyagers* (Madison: University of Wisconsin, 1968), 25.

[24] See the display of silver and gold plate around the central pillar in the Hall of Facets in fig. 8. For the unique collection of pre-Civil-War English silver still preserved in the Kremlin, see the remarkable *Britannia & Muscovy: English Plate to the Court of the Tsars*, ed. Ol'ga Dmitrievna and Natalya Abramova (New Haven: Yale University Press, 2006).

[25] For Russian hatchets, see *Gosudarstvennaia Oruzheinaia Palata* (Moscow: Gosudarstvennoe izdatel'stvo izobrazitel'nogo iskusstva, 1958), plates 98–99; on Turkish (?) hatchets, see *Treasures of the Czars from the State Museums of the Moscow Kremlin*, ed. A. F. Boldov and N. S. Vladimirskaia (London: Booth-Clibborn Editions, 1995), 117. For textiles, see Tsar Peter's caftan, made in Kremlin workshops with materials from Venice and Western Europe: Irina Polynina, N. N. Rakhmanov, and G. Mekhova, *The Regalia of the Russian Empire* (Moscow: Red Square, 1994), 100, plate 81. On caftan of Italian velvet, see *Treasures*, 114; formal caftan *terlik* made from Polish and Italian velvet, ibid., 115. On thrones, see *Regalia*, 38, plate 25 (Western Europe); ibid., 71, plate 56 (Russia and "orient"); ibid., 46, plate 32 (Iran); ibid., 84, plate 69 (Armenian merchants).

by Russian craftsmen and a German from Nuremberg named Esaias Zink-graf.[26] Again, objects were acquired wherever necessary, without much trace of national or ethnic awareness.

A second effective element of the ritual was the skillful use of space, sound, and personnel to impress the observer and to map out social divisions. In our discussion of architecture, we have already seen how visually impressive was the progression from Red Square to the throne rooms, and the social distinctions that were reflected in this progression of spaces, from public to highly restricted. The foreigners' accounts allow us to add more details. The ceremonial entrance really began while the envoys were still a short distance outside of Moscow, whence they were conducted to their residence by noble courtiers and a large procession. Long rows of musketeers are often mentioned, through whose serried ranks the procession wound its way both into Moscow and, later, from the ambassador's residence to the Kremlin. Behind and above the soldiers clamored the common people, anxious for a look at the spectacle. Olearius[27] mentions the ringing of huge bell cast by Boris Godunov (356 hundredweight, requiring "24 or more" people standing below to ring it), which, when added to other Kremlin bells, must have made the air fairly vibrate as the party entered Cathedral Square, dismounted, and then proceeded up the appropriate set of stairs to the large porch giving onto the two throne rooms. As the diplomats entered the vestibule of one of the throne rooms, they report seeing some 100 or more courtiers lavishly dressed (in outfits borrowed from the royal treasury) to do honor to the occasion. They then progressed, sometimes after a delay, into the throne room itself, which was full of splendidly arrayed courtiers, carefully arranged, as we know, according to rank, with the tsar on his throne in the southeast corner. Here, the foreign diplomats were architectually put on the defensive, since, as Olearius' drawing shows (fig. 7), they stood below in the center, while the tsar and his court sat around the periphery of the room on benches elevated several steps above the diplomats.

The spatial mapping of social relations inherent in this progression of spaces was reinforced by a culinary mapping of society. (Fig. 8 shows an illustration from 1672 of the coronation banquet of Mikhail Fedorovich in 1613.) The number and quality of dishes provided to diplomats, either in a throne room or later at their residences, was carefully recorded and seems now quite amazing, in the 30 to 100 range, usually, starting, in the Kremlin at least, with roast swan. In the Faceted Palace, where banquets seem usually to have been held, the tsar himself took an active role as provider of nourishment, personally giving bread and other dishes both to diplomats and Russian courtiers, calling each by name, a feat that impressed several observers. The tsar was

---

[26] Samuel H. Baron, ed. and trans., *The Travels of Olearius in Seventeenth-Century Russia* (Stanford, CA: Stanford University Press, 1967), 62.

[27] Ibid., 144.

able to display a finely graduated scale of royal favor by the order of presentation and the dishes presented. He also emphasized the personal protective relationship that bound him to his courtiers. Then there were the toasts. Again, there is not time, and probably no need, to go into details. Herberstein was probably not the first foreigner, and certainly not the last, to pretend inebriation and exhaustion as a desperate excuse to avoid further toasts *do kontsa*. For our purposes, however, two points are important: the toasts gave another opportunity for the court system to express finely graduated preferences and the process took up a lot of everyone's time, probably a reason for what seems to be a change over time from ceremonial dinners in the Faceted Hall to take out-dinners, also very elaborate, sent to the ambassadorial residence so that the diplomats and their Russian friends and caretakers could, like the hunters in court entertainments who killed a bear, drink "bravely" and "merrily" to the sovereign's health without keeping everyone else up all night.

Conclusion

So far, our attention has been fixed on the impressions made on foreign visitors. Here one has to admire the skill displayed by the Muscovite state, with very slender financial resources as compared to those of many Western European states and a culture that Western Europeans looked on as backward, in impressing its sometimes quite sophisticated visitors with its wealth and power. These ceremonies also conveyed a carefully calculated image of unity and social order by mapping out the social order spatially, gastronomically, and choreographically, and depicting the great boyars of the realm and the rest of the court as harmonious partners in godly governance. (Why many of these same visitors concluded that the government was "plain tyrannical" was not, I submit, the fault of these ceremonies.)

More important, however, was the effect made on the domestic audience, the courtiers of various ranks who were both the actors and a major audience for these dramas. These courtiers seem to have spent an inordinate amount of time at these diplomatic rituals, not counting weddings, church ceremonies, and trials.[28] The historical record (and Marshall Poe's excellent bibliography[29]) has made the writings of Western travelers particularly accessible, but there were waves of other diplomats from virtually every point of the compass, each of whom had to be received and entertained by basically the same *dramatis personae*. This meant that courtiers experienced these cere-

---

[28] See Valerie Kivelson's essay in this volume for a trial that took place in the Golden Hall. On royal weddings, see Russell Edward Martin, "Dynastic Marriage in Muscovy" (Ph.D. diss., Harvard University, 1996).

[29] Marshall Poe, ed., *Foreign Descriptions of Muscovy: An Analytic Bibliography of Primary and Secondary Sources* (Columbus, OH: Slavica Publishers, 1995). I am indebted to Marshall Poe for excellent and painstaking advice on these sources, the results of which, for the most part, await further publication.

monies over and over again, with what must have been a mind-numbing repetition. Forced to sit in their borrowed stiff cloth-of-gold court dress, perhaps with the added burden of wearing a tall fur hat, for hours on end while formal questions were asked and toasts proposed, even disinterested courtiers must have been forced to look at the surrounding mural cycles, if only the way one looks at the Readers Digest in the dentist's office. Others, it seems safe to assume, took a more genuine interest in court symbolism. Although both mural programs that we have briefly examined were subtle and designed to communicate some quite complex messages, a courtier need not have been a theological whiz kid to take away some basic messages. These messages were repeated many times in the murals, reinforced by the rituals we have discussed, and elaborated at some length in both texts and images unconnected with the throne rooms.

What were these messages? Basically, they answered the same questions that the Luba asked through their art and ritual. They explained the origin of Christian kingship in the Old Testament, and traced the connections of the current court back to those origins and forward to the apocalypse. These historical connections gave people a reason to believe under normal circumstances that the tsar's will reflected God's will. They also made the welfare of the Muscovite state, at least by implication, crucial to salvation history. The architecture and the rituals within it served to mark off the social divisions of the realm, and so contributed to maintaining the social hierarchy, an essential goal for any premodern state. The pomp and circumstance that so impressed foreigners must also have impressed the locals with the wealth and power of the state. More important, the very courtiers on whose consensus and cooperation the realm depended were forced to act out over and over again rituals of agreement and unity under the gaze of the monarch. These rituals gave an important role to the court as a whole and to occasional individual courtiers, a message reinforced by the strong emphasis on courtier-advisors in both cycles of murals. These benefits came with a cost, however; the logic of Christian rulership meant that the ruler had to be perceived as personally pious and as following God's will in order for his power to be valid. The Golden Hall murals in particular emphasized these responsibilities of the tsar.

Richard Wortman has recently argued that the monarch was presented in Muscovite "scenarios of power" as a foreign, here Byzantine, hero ruling a Slavic state.[30] The evidence of the throne rooms indicates that this assertion rests on an anachronistic ethnic orientation to a later question of national identity. The Muscovites, with their willingness happily to borrow architecture or luxury goods from any source available seem not to have been overly worried about such things. In the Kremlin, the nation-state was obviously not relevant, and notions of "foreign" may have been only marginally more use-

---

[30] Richard S. Wortman, *Scenarios of Power: Myth and Ceremony in Russian Monarchy* (Princeton, NJ: Princeton University Press, 1995), chap. 1.

ful. Instead, Muscovites borrowed the best from the world of jewelers, silver-smiths, armorers, and other international professions, regardless of national origin. Similarly, as the artists who designed the program for the Hall of Facets represented history, God's choice of sacred states jumped over ethnic boundaries starting with Moses and the burning bush, passing through Byzantium, and ending with Tsar Fedor Ivanovich and Boris Godunov.

A more useful approach to understanding our throne rooms was sug-gested by Dell Upton on the occasion of the 25th anniversary of the Vernacu-lar Architecture Forum. In urging his listeners to consider new approaches to the interpretation of architecture, he proposed thinking of a given building as reflecting a number of "circles of knowledge," each of which contributed to the creation and the meaning of a particular building: the architect(s) and their design philosophy and vision, the craftsmen who constructed the build-ing, other buildings with similar programs and uses, the engineers who made the building stand up, and so on. To this we might add the human actions and rituals performed in the building, performances which "create shared meaning through use."[31] The Kremlin throne rooms reflected widely different circles of knowledge: Italian architectural practice, Byzantine and Rus' (even Ottoman?) traditions of throne rooms, the rituals of diplomatic practice, bor-rowed both from Western Europe and the Eurasian steppe, international con-noisseurship of the individual arts so necessary for throne-room rituals: jewel-lery, armor, gold- and silversmithing, and textiles, to name a few. The mural programs brought in a further circle: the long tradition of monumental mural painting, secular as well as religious, again going back to Byzantium, and practiced by Greek and Armenian as well as Rus' painters. All of these were brought into focus by the political and social structure of the Muscovite state. The rulers who paid the not inconsiderable sums to keep these theaters of Muscovite political culture running, together with the powerful courtiers who spent so much time there, fashioned spaces, images and rituals to reflect their values. The finely graded social divisions, marked spatially and ritually, re-flected the preoccupation with rank embodied legally in the *mestnichestvo* sys-tem as well as in literary texts that placed a high value on the ruler's mainte-nance of the social order. The power of the ruler was shown as derived both from God and from powerful ancestors. Courtiers as symbolic advisors were given a prominent role, but severely restricted by the architectural spaces of the throne rooms in the way that they could give it. In these ways, the throne rooms reflected many of the themes and tensions in Muscovite political cul-ture uncovered or elaborated upon by the pioneering work of Robert Crummey.

---

[31] Upton, "What Now?" esp. 10–11. On performance, see Susan Garfinkel, "Recovering Performance for Vernacular Architecture Studies," *VAF* 13: 2 (2007): 100–14, quotation on 106.

The Privy Domain of Ivan Vasil'evich

Edward L. Keenan

> What we might call the character of Charles I is
> the product of powerful ideologies of rule and of
> church governance, but also of the emotions of a
> small boy who spent his childhood alternately ne-
> glected and plagued by his father and brother,
> always in pain, and deformed because of his
> chronic rickets. The latter is just as well docu-
> mented as the former.
> —Diane Purkiss, "What We Leave Out," *TLS*, 13
> October 2006, p. 11.

I am happy on this occasion to offer to our honorand a tribute based upon observations stimulated in part by two of his own publications in our field.[1]

❧ 1 ❧

Colorful prose has been written, since Ivan's own time, to describe his alleged creation, in December 1564, of "a state within a state," commonly designated in English by the untranslated Russian term *oprichnina*. This ungraceful diction, like so much of our perception of Ivan, originated with the reports of early or contemporary European adventurers: Heinrich von Staden (b. 1542), who had a good ear and a rough-and-ready Middle-German phonetic spelling, usually wrote "*aprisna*" or "*aprisnuy*"—a remarkably faithful German (s = <š>) rendering of how the word *oprichnyi* probably sounded in the Moscow dialect;[2] Richard James (1592–1638) heard it similarly

---

[1] I.e., Lloyd E. Berry and Robert O. Crummey, eds., *Rude and Barbarous Kingdom: Russia in the Accounts of Sixteenth-Century English Voyagers* (Madison: University of Wisconsin Press, 1968). His earlier work was in another field: Robert O. Crummey, "The Society for Christian Morality, 1821–25" (M.A. thesis, University of Chicago, 1959).

[2] Ivan Ivanovich Polosin, ed. and trans., *O Moskve Ivana Groznogo: Zapiski nemtsa oprichnika* (Leningrad: Izdanie M. i S. Sabashnikovykh, 1925), 136, available at http://www.vostlit.info/Texts/rus6/Staden/text4 (accessed September 2008). Cf. Fritz Theodor Epstein, ed., [Heinrich von Staden], *Aufzeichnungen über den Moskauer Staat: Nach der Handschrift des Preussischen Staatsarchivs in Hannover*, 2nd ed. (Hamburg: Cram, De Gruyter, 1964). A revised reprint of same title (Hamburg: Friederichsen, De Gruyter, 1930 = Hamburgische Universität. Abhandlungen aus dem Gebiet der Auslandskunde,

Rude & Barbarous Kingdom Revisited: Essays in Russian History and Culture in Honor of Robert O. Crummey. Chester S. L. Dunning, Russell E. Martin, and Daniel Rowland, eds. Bloomington, IN: Slavica Publishers, 2008, 73–88.

("*aprïshnoí*");[3] the more educated Giles Fletcher (1549–1611) recorded "*oppressini*," an evocative compound of Russian sound, Slavonic orthography, and (mistaken) Latin etymology.[4]

---

vol. 34. Series A: Rechts- und Staatswissenschaften, vol. 5: 20ff). Note that Thomas Esper calls Staden's text "semiliterate and incredibly disjointed." Thomas Esper, trans. and ed., *The Land and Government of Muscovy: A Sixteenth-Century Account* (Stanford, CA: Stanford University Press, 1967). v. A translation from Epstein's 1964 edition of Staden. Al'shits quoted Veselovskii's evaluation of the man: "neobrazovannyi i nekul'- turnyi avantiurist." Daniil Natanovich Al'shits [Daniil Al'], "Zapiski Genrikha Shta- dena o Moskve Ivana Groznogo kak istoricheskii istochnik," *Vspomogatel'nye istoriche- skie istochniki* 16 (1985): 135. Crummey notes that Turberville and Randolph, who visited Muscovy during the *oprichnina*, do not mention it (*Rude and Barbarous Kingdom*, xv).

[3] Boris Aleksandrovich Larin, ed., *Russko-angliiskii slovar'-dnevnik Richarda Dzhemsa, 1618–1619* (Leningrad: Izd-vo Leningradskogo universiteta, 1959), 188, 414. Cf. Boris Aleksandrovich Larin, *Tri inostrannykh istochnika po razgovornoi rechi Moskovskoi Rusi XVI–XVII vekov* (St. Petersburg: Izd-vo S.-Peterburgskogo universiteta, 2002), 304, 471. James apparently used the diarisis to indicate word stress.

[4] Giles Fletcher, *Of the Russe Commonwealth*. Facsimile edition with variants. With an introduction by Richard Pipes and a glossary-index by John V. A. Fine, Jr. (Cambridge: Harvard University Press, 1966), 25v–26ff. of text. Facsimile of Giles Fletcher, *Of The Russe Common Wealth. Or, Maner of Gouernement by the Russe Emperour, (commonly called the Emperour of Moskouia) with the manners, and fashions of the people of the Countrey* (Lon- don: Printed by T.D. for Thomas Charde, 1591), collated with the variations found in several other MSS of the author's book. Note that Fletcher arrived in Moscow in November 1588, i.e., almost three decades after the events dealt with here. One younger contemporary, Mark Ridley, had the sense right: "*oprishnoi*"—"othere." Ridley MS, Bodlean Library, Oxford, Ms. Laud misc., f. 47b. As we shall see, the narra- tive germ of later accounts seems to originate with a contemporary eyewitness, Albert Schlichting. Schlichting's original account survives only in a Latin version, however. It usesp an Italo-Latin transliteration, *opricina*, and translates the term as *siccarii* (i.e., sicarii = bodyguards) or *celeres* (= the same). Graham's "Swiftmen," perhaps influenced by Malein's "*provornye*" seems mistakenly etymological: Albert Schlichting, "De Moribus et Imperandi Crudelitate Basilij Moschoviae Tyranni Brevis Enarratio" (written 1571); translated by Hugh F. Graham as "A Brief Account of the Character and Brutal Rule of Vasil'evich, Tyrant of Muscovy (Albert Schlichting on Ivan Groznyi)," *Canadian-American Slavic Studies* 9 (1975): 210n30, 217n48; Aleksandr Iustinovich Malein, trans. and ed., *Novoe izvestie o Rossii vremeni Ivana Groznogo: "Skazanie" Al'berta Slichtinga*, 3rd ed. (Leningrad: AN SSSR, 1934), 18. Cf. also E. A. Andrews and William Freund, *A Latin dictionary founded on Andrews' edition of Freund's Latin dictionary*, rev. and enl. Charlton T. Lewis and Charles Short (1879; repr., Oxford: Clarendon Press, 1969), s.v. *celeres*. Note that one redaction of the *Vita* of Metropolitan Filipp says that Ivan "*nazyvashe ikh oprishnitsami, sirech' dvorovymi*." Stepan Grigor'evich Barkhudarov et al., eds., *Slovar' russkogo iazyka XI–XVII vv.* (Moscow: Nauka, 1975–), 13: 45.

The Western convention of using the transliteration, *oprichnina*, probably originated with these accounts, but it may owe its durability to the fact that it permits authors to demonstrate a familiarity with Russian terminology while simultaneously concealing an inconvenient detail: most could not translate it even if they wished. So long as the term remains untranslated, moreover, it serves as a convenient surrogate for whatever an author thinks Ivan created, or intended, or unwittingly caused, in December 1564: a political program; a legal-administrative entity; perhaps a territory.[5]

Educated native speakers are in only slightly better position: there being few non-obsolete cognates in Russian, the word and its derivatives are learnéd historical reminiscences.[6] In consequence most Russians today find themselves "understanding" the word roughly as in the Oxford definition: "the thing that Ivan IV introduced in 1564—whatever that was."[7]

The word itself was apparently somewhat uncommon even in Ivan's time, but our sources do permit us to investigate what it meant then, and *before* 1564.

In simplest morphological terms, *oprichnina* is an abstract noun formed by the addition of the desinence *-ina* to the adjectival stem *oprich-n-*, itself derived from a preposition/adverb *oprich'* = "other than, except, apart from, besides." Etymologically, the Slavic root *-pri-* is related to Latin *privus*, "alone, apart," and to English "private" and "privy."[8]

But Ivan was no etymologist, nor could those who advised him have thought in these terms. Why did that somewhat obsolescent word come to designate whatever it was that they were establishing in 1564? The answer

---

[5] Marcus Wheeler's *Oxford Russian-English Dictionary* (Oxford: Clarendon, 1972), 452, is unhelpful, but typical: "опри*чнин|а, ы, f. (*hist.*) oprichnina (*special administrative élite established in Russia by Ivan IV, also the territory assigned to this élite*)."

[6] See Sergei Aleksandrovich Kuznetsov, ed., *Bol'shoi tolkovyi slovar' russkogo iazyka* (St. Petersburg: "Norint," 2003), 720. Dal' correctly groups the word with forms and derivatives of "*oprich'*" (see below), but gets his interpretation from the historical literature: "Особое войско, телохранители и каратели, при Грозном ‖ Часть государства при Грозном; подчиненная дворцовому правлению...." Vladimir Ivanovich Dal', comp., *Tolkovyi slovar' zhivogo velikorusskogo iazyka* (Moscow: Gos. izd-vo inostrannykh i natsional'nykh slovarei, 1956). A reprint—with some significant editorial intervention—of the 2nd ed. (St. Petersburg-Moscow: M. O. Vol'f, 1880), 2: 685.

[7] I.e., as in n. 5, above. It was apparently such circular reasoning that prompted Ivan Ivanovich Polosin to entitle his otherwise thoughtful essay "Chto takoe Oprichnina?" Polosin, "Chto takoe Oprichnina?" (1955–56), in *Sotsial'no-politicheskaia istoriia Rossii XVI – nachala XVII v.*, ed. I. A. Golubtsov et al. (Moscow: Izd-vo Akademii nauk, 1963), 124–55.

[8] Maksimilian Romanovich Fasmer [Max Julius Friedrich Vasmer], *Etimologicheskii slovar' russkogo iazyka*, 4 vols. (Moscow: Progress, 1964–73). A translation, revised by Oleg Nikolaevich Trubachev, of Vasmer's *Russisches etymologisches Wörterbuch* (Heidelberg: C. Winter, Universitätsverlag, 1950–58), 3: 146.

seems clear: the term had for some time been used as a technical term in Muscovite legal and chancery language to designate property we would readily call "private" were it not for the widespread belief that notions of private property and personal possession were somewhat attenuated in Muscovy.[9]

Muscovite scribes, however, regularly used *oprichnina* and its cognates to designate, for example, private property generally,[10] and—most relevantly for our purposes—service land set aside for the support of widows and orphans—that is, not taken back into service upon the death of the holder.[11] Ivan's *oprichnyi dvor* was a private household or privy court—as was clear even to foreigners. Von Staden writes, "[T]he Aprisna were his own people, the 'Semsky' the commonalty";[12] Fletcher observes: "[T]he *Oppressini* ... were such of the nobilities and gentrie as he tooke to his owne part...."[13]

In fact the 16th-century meaning of the term seems so transparent and prosaic that it becomes hard to understand how it could have been thought mysterious. One can readily identify at least three possible causes for this terminological muddle.

First, the word *oprich'* and its cognates would go out of use (dialect and historical allusion excepted) within a generation or so after Ivan's time, slowly displaced by the Slavonic *krome* and derivatives, which displacement

---

[9] See the debate in *Slavic Review* between Richard Pipes and George G. Weickhardt: Weickhardt, "The Pre-Petrine Law of Property," *Slavic Review* 52: 4 (Winter 1993): 663–79; Pipes, "Was There Private Property in Muscovite Russia?" *Slavic Review* 53: 2 (Summer 1994): 524–30; Weickhardt, "Was There Private Property in Muscovite Russia?" *Slavic Review* 53:2 (Summer 1994): 531–38.

[10] "А у того, государь, Василья Угрюмова сына Корслина да у ево брата у Никиты опришенная духовная прадеда их ... на треть того села Николского...." *Akty sluzhilykh zemlevladel'tsev XV – nachala XVII veka* (Moscow: Arkheograficheskii tsentr, 1997), 1: 89.

[11] Cf. the discussion in Polosin, "Chto takoe Oprichnina?" 132ff. He points out that as late as Turgenev's time an *uchastok vdovii* was known as "*opridchii*" [sic] (134). See also Aleksandr L'vovich Diuvernua, *Materialy dlia slovaria drevne-russkogo iazyka* (Moscow: Universitetskaia tip., 1894), 122: "Да к тому ей даю вопришнину 2 села" (from *Sobranie gosudarstvennykh gramot i dogovorov, khraniashchikhsia v Gosudarstvennoi kollegii inostrannykh del* [hereafter *SGGD*], 5 vols. [Moscow: V Tip. N. S. Vsevolozhskago, 1813–94], 1: 73), now also Lev Vladimirovich Cherepnin and Sergei Vladimirovich Bakhrushin, eds., *Dukhovnye i dogovornye gramoty velikikh i udel'nykh kniazei XIV–XVI vv.* (Moscow: Izd-vo Akademii nauk SSSR, 1950), 56 (1407). I am grateful to Aleksandr Strakhov for this reference—his letter of February 21, 1993. Numerous other examples are to be found in Barkhudarov et al., *Slovar' russkogo iazyka XI–XVII vv.*, 13: 43ff.

[12] "Aprisna sind gewesen die seinen, Semsky aber das gemaine volk" (Staden, *Aufzeichnungen über den Moskauer Staat* [1964], 20–21).

[13] Fletcher, *Of the Russe Commonwealth* (1966), f. 25v. of facsimile.

permitted—and perhaps prompted—the punning use of *kromeshniki* for *oprichniki* by "Andrei Kurbskii" in the mid-17th century.[14]

Second, the foreign adventurers—especially Schlichting, upon whose texts later interpretations depend so heavily[15]—provided such vivid descriptions of the violence that ensued after 1564 that their own understanding of the term itself was obscured.

Finally, Russian authors—beginning with Godunov's generation and culminating in Karamzin's most recent imitators—have been at pains to "load" descriptions of this period with the polemical baggage of their own times.[16]

⮞ 2 ⮜

How and why did Ivan decide to establish a Privy Household in late 1564?

We must preface any discussion of this matter with a word or two about the culture in which Ivan found himself.[17] He was a member—the most emblemic and, in consequence, culture-bound member—of a hereditary caste of

---

[14] The phrase was probably intended to mean "a man of/from the outer darkness"; cf. "*kromeshniaia t'ma.*" The text is in Georgii Zakharovich Kuntsevich, ed., *Sochineniia kniazia Kurbskago*, vol. 1, *Sochineniia original'nye* (St. Petersburg: Imp. Arkheograficheskaia komissiia, 1914) (= *Russkaia istoricheskaia Biblioteka*, vol. 31.), 269. NB: apparently complete proofs of a planned second volume, *Sochineniia perevodnye*, ready in 1917 but never published, are to be found in the archive of the St. Petersburg branch of the Russian Academy of Sciences, f. 276, no. 30. *Oprich'* already required a gloss (*krome*) for Russian readers in the early 18th century. Aleksandra Petrovna Aver'ianova and Boris Aleksandrovich Larin, eds., *Rukopisnyi leksikon pervoi poloviny XVIII veka* (Leningrad: Leningradskii gosudarstvennyi universitet, 1964), 244.

[15] As we have seen (above, n. 4), Schlichting called the *oprichniki* "fautores tirannidis suae quasi siccarii" (Schlichting, Graham ed., 217n48).

[16] Cf. Stalin's reported reproach to Sergei Eizenshtein: "You have shown the *oprichnina* incorrectly. The *oprichnina* was the army of the king. It was different from the feudal army which could remove its banner and leave the battleground at any moment—the regular army, the progressive army was formed. You have shown this *oprichnina* to be like the Ku-Klux-Klan." Grigorii Borisovich Mar'iamov, "Zapis' besedy s S. M. Eizenshteinom i N. K. Cherkasovym po povudu fil'ma *Ivan Groznyi*, 26 fevralia 1947," in Mar'iamov, *Kremlevskii tsenzor: Stalin smotrit kino* (Moscow: Konfederatsiia soiuzov kinematografistov "Kinotsentr," 1992), 84–86. It bears mentioning, however, as will be seen below, that the later Muscovite chronicles, which will be cited repeatedly below, are strikingly "documentary," or convey other biases. The earliest known definition of the *oprichnina* known to me is to be found in the Piskarevskaia letopis': "*uchinisha* [*sic*!] *oprishninu: razdelenie zemli i gradom.*" *Polnoe sobranie russkikh letopisei* (hereafter, *PSRL*), 41 vols. to date (St. Petersburg-Petrograd-Leningrad-Moscow: Arkheograficheskaia komissiia, Nauka, and Arkheograficheskii tsentr, 1841–1995), 34: 190.

[17] Readers of my "Muscovite Political Folkways" (*The Russian Review* 45 [1986]: 115–81) or participants in the Ivan Groznyi International Quatracentenary Conference organized by Prof. Richard Hellie at the University of Chicago in March 1984 may find that some of what follows is familiar.

cavalrymen who in the 14th and 15th centuries constructed a uniquely successful military-political, clan-based, "shame-and-honor" society in the midst of a sea of culturally quite different communal agriculturalists. Much of the success of their system lay in those warriors' ability to suppress open warfare among themselves by means of a number of forms of obligatory behavior: rigid observance of kinship relations, especially birth order; laboriously contrived marriage relations; and ritual murder.[18]

Ivan, however, was trapped in the one Muscovite lineage that had come to practice strict primogeniture, rather than the more common shared (collateral) inheritance—that is, only one (the oldest living) son of a reigning Grand Prince could succeed him on the throne. In consequence, Ivan was in some important human respects the least autonomous individual in his realm. When he succeeded his father (1533) he was all of three, and he spent some unknown number of years under the tutelage of his kinsmen: at first relatives of his mother, Elena Glinskaia (d. April 3, 1538),[19] later the allies of the Iur'ev-Zakhar'ins, whose niece and daughter, Anastasiia Romanovna (1531?–60), eventually became his first wife. Ivan was decidedly a family man, for better or for worse.[20]

By 1560 or so, he faced another predicament: pain. Numerous contemporary accounts and the modern study of his remains lead one to conclude that Ivan suffered a good deal, either from the pain of his ankylosing spondelitis ("Maria-Strümpell's disease") or from the ministrations of his doctors, whichever was for the moment more pernicious.[21]

But, presumably because his courtiers (largely related to him and to one another by blood or marriage) were loath to countenance a renewal of the

---

[18] For descriptions of analogous practices, see Gideon M. Kressel, "Soroicide/filiacide: Homicide for Family Honour," *Current Anthropology* 22 (1981): 141–58; and John Kennedy Campbell, *Honour, Family and Patronage: A Study of Institutions and Moral Values in a Greek Mountain Community* (Oxford: Clarendon Press, 1964; 2nd. ed., New York : Oxford University Press, 1974), passim.

[19] Here and below all dates are Old Style.

[20] For a sketch of Ivan's family ties, consult Russell E. Martin, "Dynastic Marriage in Muscovy, 1500–1729" (Ph.D. diss., Harvard University, 1996).

[21] For literature on his health based on forensic study of his remains in 1963–65, see Edward L. Keenan, "Ivan IV and the Kings' Evil: *Ni maka li to budet?*" *Festschrift for Nicholas Valentine Riasanovsky = Russian History/Histoire russe* 20: 1–4 (1993): 5–13, esp. the literature cited in nn. 22–28. Cf. Donald J. Ortner, *Identification of Pathological Conditions in Human Skeletal Remains*, 2nd ed. (Amsterdam: Academic Press, 2003), 571; and Arthur C. Aufderheide and Conrado Rodríguez-Martín, eds., *The Cambridge Encyclopedia of Human Paleopathology* (Cambridge: Cambridge University Press, 1998), 102. I thank Prof. John Verano for the latter two references. Ivan's search for Western medical specialists seems to have begun in 1548 with the ill-fated mission of Hans Schlitte; see documents in the Danish archives at http://www.vostlit.info/Texts/Dokumenty/ Russ/XVI/Datsk_arhiv/text1.htm (accessed 7 September 2008).

bloody struggle among themselves that would (and ultimately did) result, Ivan could not shirk his duties either as arbiter of their competition and fulcrum of their power, or as progenitor of a viable son.

Consideration of this dual predicament permits us to understand two central—and, in my view, closely related—events: Ivan's marriage to Anastasiia (February 3, 1547); and the introduction of the *oprichnina* (December 1564). The first resolved the clan conflicts[22] of Ivan's childhood and adolescence; the second, triggered in large measure by Anastasiia's death, rekindled them, leading first to the open warfare of the *oprichnina* and ultimately to the so-called Time of Troubles.

We cannot know whether Ivan's marriage to Anastasiia was "happy"— the concept itself is probably anachronistic—but it *was* successful, in the most crucial, dynastic, sense: over the next decade Anastasiia bore Ivan six children. (We know nothing of miscarriages; probability would indicate at least one.) Having endured such procreative exertions, Anastasiia took to her bed—alone, presumably—and died, just short of her 30th birthday, on August 7, 1560.[23]

Anastasiia's death, like the births of her two sons, was a major political event—not, probably, because of any affective impact upon Ivan (he had actually left her alone to die),[24] but because it threatened to undo the painstakingly crafted political kinship arrangements that the Iur'ev-Zakhar'ins and others had constructed, which had brought Muscovy the first decade in memory relatively free from clan violence. The possibility of issue from a second marriage (Ivan himself was only 29), always a disruptive event in the Muscovite court,[25] threatened to drive the Zakhar'ins—six of whom were "uncles"

---

[22] For details, see Nancy Shields Kollmann, *Kinship and Politics: The Making of the Muscovite Political System, 1345–1547* (Stanford, CA: Stanford University Press, 1987), 161ff.; and Mikhail Markovich Krom, "Sud'ba regentskogo soveta pri maloletnem Ivane IV: Novye dannye o vnutripoliticheskoi bor'be kontsa 1533–1534 goda," *Voprosy istorii*, no. 5 (1996): 32–49, passim.

[23] *PSRL* 29: 287. Veselovskii, who thinks Anastasiia was 15 or 16 in 1547, blames her fatal illness on the trials of Ivan's frequent "progresses" (*ob"ezdy*). Stepan Borisovich Veselovskii, *Issledovaniia po istorii oprichniny* (Moscow: Izd-vo Akademii nauk SSSR, 1963), 92–93.

[24] He had returned to Moscow a day earlier, perhaps because of a fire in the city. See *PSRL* 29: 287 (17.VII.60). It appears that the myth of Ivan's love of Anastasiia, closely associated with the notion of a "good period" in his reign, derives from later, pro-Romanov, propaganda.

[25] Second marriages had for generations been fraught with political consequences in Muscovite court politics; Ivan's father and grandfather had both taken second wives— both foreigners—with dramatic results. See John Lister Illingworth Fennell, *Ivan the Great of Moscow* (London: Macmillan; New York: St. Martin's Press, 1962); and Aleksandr Aleksandrovich Zimin, *Rossiia na poroge novogo vremeni: Ocherki politicheskoi istorii Rossii pervoi treti XVI v.* (Moscow: Mysl', 1972).

of Anastasiia's two young sons, Ivan and Fedor—and their allies (including several more "uncles") out of the Kremlin.

Steps were taken—even before Anastasiia died—to preserve the integrity and fortunes of this big happy family. One day *before* her death—on the day when Ivan returned to Moscow—it was announced that private households, or separate courts (*osobnye dvory*), were to be created for little Ivan and Fedor, each of which was complete with a *duma* (headed by an "uncle") and court ranks modeled on those of their father's court. (These posts were filled, of course, by allies of the Zakhar'ins.)[26] Within days it was announced that Ivan, who had allegedly briefly considered not remarrying (presumably because his male children had survived infancy), had heeded the advice of religious and secular advisors and would seek a wife, but *"v ynykh zemliakh"* that is, someone with few allies among competing Muscovite clans.[27]

Matchmaking delegations were sent to the court of King Sigismund (*"v Litvu koroliu o sestre"*), to Sweden, where the court was in mourning for King Gustav Vasa (d. September 29, 1560) and not interested in matchmaking, and to the Caucasus.[28] Presumably because of the numerous kinship links between Muscovite and "Lithuanian" families,[29] it was decided to marry Ivan to Kuchenei, a daughter of Temriuk, a "Kabardinian" prince. Kuchenei arrived

---

[26] *PSRL* 29: 288 (6 August 1560). Matters of such consequence and complexity were obviously planned well in advance. *Osobnye dvory* were also created for Ivan's brother Iurii Vasil'evich and for Aleksandr (Utemish] Safagireevich, both of whom had previously lived in Ivan's household, and are collectively called his *"deti."* (Utemish/ Aleksandr was roughly 10; Iurii 17.) Iurii moved to his new quarters on November 21, 1560; Ivan was there for his brother's *novosel'e* (*PSRL* 29: 290).

[27] "[O]н детеи для своих возрасту мыслил был не женитися, да для митрополича прошения и земли для хочет то дело о женитве совершити, а искати бы ему невесты в ыных землях" (*PSRL* 29: 288 [16 August 1560]). The decision, presumably, was made by his "uncles;" the appearance of a benchling could lead to chaos ("занеже он, государь, во юноством возрасте, тех еще лет не дошел, чтобы ему мошно без супружества быти"). Note that the perspicacious Iur'ev-Zakhar'ins had apparently taken the precaution of marrying a daughter of Anastasiia's first cousin, Vasilii Mikhailovich Iur'ev, to a brother of the eventual bride, Saltankul/Mikhail Temriukovich (Veselovskii, *Issledovaniia*, 297–98).

[28] *PSRL* 29: 290.

[29] In addition to the Glinskiis (Ivan's own maternal clan), the Mstislavskiis, Odoevskiis, Vorotynskiis, Bel'skiis, Trubetskois and others. Cf. Aleksandr Aleksandrovich Zimin, *Formirovanie boiarskoi aristokratsii v Rossii vo vtoroi polovine XV– pervoi treti XVI v.* (Moscow: Nauka, 1988), 122–53; Nikolai Vladimorovich (occasionally erroneously "N. K.") Miatlev, "K rodosloviiu kn. Mstislavskikh," *Letopis' istoriko-genealogicheskogo obshchestva*, nos. 1–4 (= *Sbornik v chest' L. M. Saveleva*) (Moscow, 1915): 300–12. Note that the chronicle says that the talks with the "Lithuanians" broke down over territorial issues (*PSRL* 29: 290).

in Moscow on June 15, 1561, was hurriedly (July 6) renamed "Mariia Magda-
lena," baptized (July 20), and married to Ivan on August 21.[30]

Eventually, oaths (*prisiagi*) were taken from individuals and groups to
guarantee both loyalty to Ivan's new wife and—more pointedly—the succession of Fedor and Ivan Ivanovich.[31]

The newlyweds set out for the Trinity Monastery of St. Sergius within a
month, accompanied by Anastasiia's sons and Ivan's brother, Iurii. From
there, Ivan and Kuchenei (now Mariia) departed on a combination of honey-
moon trip and royal "progress" (*ob"ezd*), but the children were sent back to
Moscow, with instructions that Ivan Ivanovich should perform various sovereign functions in his father's absence, which was to last two and a half
months.[32] The tsar would have his older son stand in for him again some
months later during another, longer, absence from the Kremlin (May–November 1562), during which a son, who would be named Vasilii, was conceived.

Vasilii Ivanovich was born in late March 1563, but lived only 43 days.[33]
Aleksandr Zimin follows the report of his death with the phrase "buria razra-
zilas' vskore," and goes on to describe a complex series of savage measures
traditionally attributed to Ivan by a large number of authors, beginning with

---

[30] *PSRL* 29: 291–92. The text calls Kuchenei the daughter of a prince of Kabarda, but it
would appear that she was a Turkic-speaking "Cherkess." Her sister Altynchach was
married to Bekbulat, a son of Shigalei, the erstwhile Khan of Kazan. It is noteworthy
that even in their haste the matchmakers did not fail, it would appear, to assure themselves of the menstrual regularity of the bride-to-be, as was customary. The odd mention of the choice of a Christian name for her well before the baptism may have had to
do with the oath-taking mentioned below.

[31] Even before the wedding, for example, Vasilii Mikhailovich Glinskii, an uncle of
Ivan's mother Elena and competitor of the Zakhar'ins, was required to sign an oath
(*poruka*) to the effect that he would be loyal to the young princes (i.e., the grandchil-
dren of Roman Zakhar'in) in the first instance, and only secondarily to "such children
as God may send" to Ivan and Mariia (*SGGD* 1: 470–73 [no. 172]). Cf. A. A. Zimin,
Oprichnina Ivan Groznogo (Moscow: Mysl', 1964), 90ff. Both Ivan and his father Vasilii
III had in fact been children of second wives who introduced at court their allies and
relatives—i.e., Zoe Paleogue (the Trakhaniotovs and other Greeks) and Elena
Glinskaia (Glinskiis and other "Lithuanian" families).

[32] "[П]риказал царевичю Ивану на Москве быть в свое место и о всяких делех о
воинских и о земских во все его государство велел ему писати грамоты от себя"
(*PSRL* 29: 297). That young Ivan Ivanovich was only seven and three-quarters at the
time should not startle us; his father had taken up his title (and at least nominally his
duties) in 1533 at half that age, under the tutelage of some of the same boyar families.
Even less surprising should be the fact that young Ivan Ivanovich was left in the care
of five Iur'ev "uncles:" Anastasiia's brothers Daniil (Danilo) and Nikita, her first cousin Vasilii Mikhailovich, her second cousin Vasilii Petrovich Iakovlev, and her sister's
husband Vasilii Sitskii.

[33] *PSRL* 29: 320.

contemporary foreigners.[34] His narrative, like those of almost all specialists, conveys the well-established historiographic tradition, an accretion of reasonable but flawed deductions based upon several fundamental misconceptions: that the so-called "Kurbskii" materials are authentic, relatively trustworthy, and contemporary; that the so-called *sinodiki opal'nykh* are in fact what the term implies; and that the later Muscovite chronicles convey the biases of one or the other of the contemporary palace factions—or even of Ivan himself.[35]

In fact, during much of the time when various plots and murders are alleged to have taken place, Ivan was on long trips out of Moscow.[36]

Moreover, if there was a *buria*, its cause may lie elsewhere. Many people who had been important to Ivan were dying—of natural causes, apparently. His younger brother and constant companion Iurii, who is often described as "retarded,"[37] had been allowed to marry once Ivan and Anastasiia had done

---

[34] Zimin, *Oprichnina*, 104 ff. Zimin and others also make much of a series of indemnity charters (*poruchnye gramoty*) composed about this time. That such documents were important to contemporaries seems to be indicated by their survival in Romanov archives, and their importance to historians derives in some measure from their early publication, but it is not at all clear what one is to make of them as sources. For a summary view, see Horace W. Dewey, "Political Poruka in Muscovite Rus'," *Russian Review* 46 (1987): 117–34.

[35] Consult, respectively, Edward L. Keenan, *The Kurbskii-Groznyi Apocrypha: The Seventeenth-Century Genesis of the "Correspondence" Attributed to Prince A. M. Kurbskii and Tsar Ivan IV* (Cambridge, MA: Harvard University Press, 1972); Ruslan Grigor'evich Skrynnikov, *Nachalo Oprichniny* (Leningrad: Izd-vo Leningradskogo universiteta, 1966) (= *Uchenye zapiski Leningradskogo gosudarstvennogo pedagogicheskogo instituta im. A. I. Gertsena*, vol. 294; idem, *Oprichnyi terror* (Leningrad: Izd-vo Leningradskogo universiteta, 1969) (=*Uchenye zapiski Leningradskogo gosudarstvennogo pedagogicheskogo instituta im. A. I. Gertsena*, vol. 374); reprinted (with indexes) together as *Tsarstvo terrora* (St. Petersburg: Nauka, 1992); Nikolay Andreyev, "Interpolations in the 16th-Century Muscovite Chronicles," *Slavonic and East European Review* 35 (84) (1956): 95–115, and Daniil Natanovich Al'shits, "Ivan Groznyi i pripiski k litsevym svodam ego vremeni," *Istoricheskie zapiski* 23 (1947): 251–89 (the last now largely discredited). The broader tendency of treating Russian chronicles as tendentious or polemical texts probably originates with 17th-century historians, but was given new impetus in the works of Shakhmatov and his admirers. See esp. Aleksei Aleksandrovich Shakhmatov, *Istoriia russkogo letopisaniia* (St. Petersburg: Nauka, 2002); Iakov Solomonovich Lur'e, *Dve istorii Rusi XV veka: Rannie i pozdnie, nezavisimye i ofitsial'nye letopisi ob obrazovanii Moskovskogo gosudarstv*a (St. Petersburg: Éditions D. Bulanin; Paris: Institut d'études slaves, 1994); and the sober and balanced, but unfinished, discussion in Aleksandr Aleksandrovich Amosov, *Litsevoi letopisnyi svod Ivana Groznogo: Kompleksnoe kodikologicheskoe issledovanie* (Moscow: Editorial URSS, 1998).

[36] For example, from May 9–July 20 and September 21–November 1, 1563; May 7–July 8 and November 8–November 14, 1564. *PSRL* 29: 320ff.

[37] Although the mental deficiencies of Ivan's son Fedor seem to be well attested, I know of no documentary foundation for the widespread view concerning Iurii, who is

so,[38] had lost an infant son of that marriage (also Vasilii) and died without known issue in November 1563, assuring the unchallenged succession of Fedor and Ivan Ivanovichi. Iurii's death also ensured the prosperity of the grand coalition that had formed around the expectation of such a succession—including Ivan Fedorovich Mstislavskii, Ivan Dmitrievich Bel'skii, and some other members of the Iur'ev-Zakhar'in group[39]—who could now turn their political energies to competition amongst themselves, within the established system, for power and treasure.

❧ 3 ❧

Within a year, however, something very disruptive of all parties' plans occurred: Ivan attempted to retire, effectively, to private life. Why?

Let us reconsider his family situation—crucial in Muscovite court politics—first: the death of Ivan's brother Iurii Vasil'evich had apparently not only assured the succession of Ivan's sons by Anastasiia under the tutelage of his in-laws and their cousins, but had significantly changed and diminished Ivan's role in the Kremlin.

While it is unclear to what extent Ivan actually ruled or that others ruled in his name during this period,[40] it is quite apparent that there were two major functions for which he could not delegate responsibility: to serve as a fulcrum and ultimate umpire in the competition among his relatives; and to produce an heir.

The first of these Ivan could no longer accomplish, for several reasons: the political center of gravity had shifted to his sons, now, at 10 and 7, both beyond childhood mortality, and to their "uncles," who were again fighting among themselves, as they had done in Ivan's own childhood. Now married to a woman who had been chosen precisely because she and her most significant male relations were relative political outsiders, Ivan had little support from a traditionally influential quarter, the in-laws of the Grand Prince. Moreover, death had removed, in late October 1564, his most significant relative in

---

almost always called *"slaboumnyi."* Consult the indexes of Zimin, *Oprichnina*; Veselovskii, *Issledovaniia*; and Skrynnikov, *Tsarstvo terrora*. (NB: there is no index in Skrynnikov, *Nachalo Oprichniny*, or his *Oprichnyi terror*.)

[38] I.e., on September 18, 1547. The wedding protocol appears in Vladimir Ivanovich Buganov, ed., *Razriadnaia kniga 1475–1598 gg.* (Moscow: Nauka, 1966), 11–12.

[39] Note that Bel'skii was married to Mstislavskii's first cousin, Marfa Shuiskaia, and his sister Anastasiia was married to Vasilii Mikhailovich Iur'ev. Mstislavskii also had a very significant relationship with Nikita Romanovich Iur'ev-Zakhar'in: they were married to sisters, daughters of Aleksandr Gorbatyi. Mikhail Nikolaevich Tikhomirov, "Zapiski o regentstve Eleny Glinskoi i boiarskom pravlenii 1533–1547gg.," *Istoricheskie zapiski* 46 (1954): 287.

[40] As we have seen, Ivan spent a great deal of time away from Moscow on his various "progresses."

the earlier, Iur'ev-Zakhar'in group, Daniil (Danilo) Romanovich, Anastasiia's brother.[41]

As we have seen, there had been other recent significant deaths in the family: Ivan's only son by Mariia Temriukovna, Vasilii, died on May 3, 1563; Ivan's younger brother Iurii died at 31 in November of the same year, with Ivan at his deathbed. Two days later (November 26) Ivan and his first cousin Vladimir Andreevich of Staritsa exchanged properties inherited from their grandfather; they clearly were putting family matters in order. Finally, Archbishop Makarii, too sick to administer last rites to Iurii Vasil'evich, died five weeks later.[42]

Whether or not one accepts the historiographic tradition that Makarii was an important ally for Ivan, certainly Daniil Romanovich had been, and all these deaths must not only have made it difficult for Ivan to manage politics within his seniority-conscious court, but have prompted him as well to consider his own mortality. And as we have noted, he was himself suffering from a painful affliction, the usual onset of which lies between 15 and 25 years of age.[43]

As to the second indispensible function—provision of an heir—he had accomplished it, as the hasty actions of his in-laws on the eve of Anastasiia's death had confirmed. Either Ivan (now ten and a half) or Fedor (more than seven and a half) could continue the dynasty—as Ivan himself had, from the age of three. (Fedor's mental defectiveness, whatever may have been its cause or symptoms, was not a factor in the eyes of Muscovite courtiers, as subsequent events were to show.)

Having thus done his procreative duty and lost control—once again—of his courtiers, in December of 1564 Ivan handed the throne over to his sons, as Schlichting and others say, and went into a kind of semi-retirement in the Aleksandrovskaia Sloboda.[44]

---

[41] Skrynnikov (*Tsartsvo terrora*) says "27 October 1564" (205) or "nezadolgo do oprichniny" (225); Zimin says "November 1564" (*Oprichnina*, 372). Neither refers directly to his source, but Skrynnikov appears to refer to a note in a manuscript muster book.

[42] PSRL 29: 320, 325, 327. That Ivan and Vladimir of Staritsa were both present at Makarii's funeral is probably indicative of their maintaining familial relationships.

[43] Aufderheide and Rodriguez-Martin, *Cambridge Encyclopedia of Human Paleopathology*, 102. Ortner's view is congruent: "The disease usually begins in the second or third decade of life" (Ortner, *Identification of Pathological Conditions*, 571).

[44] In the remarkably well annotated translation of Hugh F. Graham: "Ivan pretended that he had grown tired of power and wished to lay aside his responsibilities.... Here are my sons, whose age and capacities fit them for rule.... I commend them to you as my heirs in merit and power.... Let them dispense justice and lead you in war" (Schlichting/Graham, "A Brief Account," 218). Schlichting, an unsympathetic but well-informed observer, had apparently just arrived in Moscow (ibid., 206). As Graham (ibid.) and Andreas Kapeller have pointed out, Schlichting's account was widely plagiarized by later authors, especially Guagnini and Oderborn. Kapeller, *Ivan Groznyj*

The chronicle account here is quite unadorned and, in my view, reliable; its cinnabar caption reads, "[Ivan's] Grand Progress" (*Poezd" bolshoi—sic.*" The chronicler specifies that the departure preparations (*pod"em*) were not similar to those of previous trips, as Ivan took with him pretty much everything of value in the Kremlin.[45] Moreover, he ordered those boyars and courtiers who were setting out with him to take their wives and children, and lesser ranks to take servants and whatever they needed for their continued service (*so vsem sluzhebnym nariadom*). The chronicler concludes that Ivan's courtiers and administrators were allegedly "confused and despondent" (*v nedoumenii i vo unynii*), not knowing where he was going.

Within a few days, the account continues, Ivan sent a document to those dignitaries who had remained in Moscow, enumerating the larcenous iniquities of all involved during his minority: the looting of his treasury and misappropriation of lands, etc. And, he allegedly wrote, he had abandoned his kingship (*ostavil svoe gosudar'stvo—sic*) and gone off to settle "wherever God tells him to."[46]

Thus the account of Schlichting and others is supported by the Muscovite court chronicle, which for the 1560s is quite "documentary," being—aside from extensive passages of Slavonicized exhortations attributed to Makarii and other churchmen—largely a compilation of summaries of diplomatic and other documentary texts.[47] From this account, we also learn that Ivan was setting up for himself an *osobnyi dvor*, one described in almost precisely the same terms as that set up for his sons before Anastasiia's death. The account of the establishment of the *oprichnina* is different, however, in its repeated— even redundant—stress of the fact that Ivan is setting up a *private* court, and privy incomes, for himself. The crucial passage reads: "учинити ему на своем государьстве себе опришнину, двор ему себе и на весь свой обиход учинити особной а бояр и окольничих и дворецкого и казначеев …

---

im *Spiegel der ausländischen Druckschriften seiner Zeit; ein Beitrag zur Geschichte des westlichen Russlandbildes* [Bern: H. Lang, 1972]). Cf. Hieronim Grala,"Arcyszpieg i Renegaci," at www.mowiawieki.pl/artykul (accessed 7 September 2008).

[45] "...взял же с собою святость, иконы и кресты, златом и камением драгим украшенные и суды золотые и серебрянные, и поставцы все всяких судов, золотое и серебряное, и платье и денги и всю свою казну повеле взяти с собою..." (*PSRL* 29: 341).

[46] *PSRL* 29: 342: "Оставил свое государьство и поехал где вселитися, иде же его государя богъ наставит." Note the change in linguistic texture just below, marked by a cinnabar letter, followed by patches of Slavonic. For another alternation, see p. 343: "Государь же им повеле…. пожаловал, очи свои видети им велел."

[47] I leave aside here the so-called "interpolations," which represent quite a different kind of text. For them, see *PSRL* 13: 210ff. and Al'shits, "Ivan Groznyi i prispiski," 251–89.

учинити себе особно...."[48] In the same passage, Ivan is quoted as accusing the boyars of squandering and pillaging *his* treasury, and as listing the income-producing properties that he will henceforth have as his own.

The private or familial nature of the *oprichnyi dvor* is particularly evident from the earliest known administrative listing of its members, where we find Ivan's maternal first cousin, Ivan Mikhailovich Glinskii, and his new wife's brother's father-in-law near the head, followed by the exceptional mention (the only woman in the list) of Glinskii's mother-in-law, Mar'ia, widow of the much-maligned Grigorii ("Maliuta") Skuratov.[49]

There follows a list of the properties taken by the tsar *na svoi obikhod*, with a specification that owners of patrimonial and service lands who are not themselves part of the *oprichnina* are to be given lands elsewhere, because Ivan has ordered his privy estate to be his alone: "понеже опришнину по-веле учинити себе особно."[50]

In the Muscovite kingship system, of course, Ivan could not abdicate — and he made arrangements for the court and palace to operate as usual (*po starine*), under the watchful eyes of Bel'skii, Mstislavskii, and "all the boyars." All functionaries were to operate as before, but to refer major (*bol'shie*) decisions to the boyars, and they the most important to him ("а ратные каковы будут вести или земские великие дела, и бояром о тех делех приходити к государю"[51]).

Almost as an afterthought, Ivan proclaimed that 100,000 rubles — an enormous sum at the time — be allocated for his trip (*za pod"em*).

It is not necessarily paradoxical that the most powerful and, in a sense, wealthiest man in the land should worry about such matters: in Muscovy,

---

[48] *PSRL* 29: 344.

[49] Al'shits, *Spisok oprichnikov*, 55. Glinskii was married to Anna Grigor'evna, Maliuta's daughter, and Boris Tulupov to the niece of Ivan's wife of the time, Anna Koltovskaia. Maliuta's nephew Bogdan-Andrei is also high on the list. Veselovskii, *Issledovaniia*, 301, 397, 203. The familial nature of Ivan's privy court is further indicated by the number of so-called *oprichniki* who occupied prominent places in the wedding musters of Ivan's time. One could go on: another daughter of Maliuta Skuratov, also Mar'ia, was married to Boris Godunov; a third to Dmitrii Shuiskii, brother of the future tsar Vasilii (Veselovskii, *Issledovaniia*, 298). Despite their absolutely fundamental importance in Muscovite politics, kinship — and especially marriage — relations have generally not been stressed by students of Muscovite politics, with the exception of Veselovskii (*Issledovaniia*), Kollmann (*Kinship and Politics*), and Martin ("Dynastic Marriage in Muscovy"). Marriage ties seem not even to be mentioned, for example, in Al'shits's biographical register (*Spisok oprichnikov*, 112 ff.), although he does point out the large number of *oprichniki* from the same families (11).

[50] *PSRL* 29: 344. Note that in the copy of the chronicle known as the Prodolzhenie Aleksandro-Nevskoi letopisi, the word *Oprishnina* is repeatedly accompanied by "*zri*" in the margin. *PSRL* 29: 344, note a (which refers to several places in the text).

[51] *PSRL* 29: 344–45.

where the notional and legal separation of what Ernst Kantorowicz once called "the two bodies of the king" had not occurred, Ivan may have owned everything "in body politic," and owned nothing "in body natural."[52] In choosing to withdraw, he needed to create a privy estate for himself, and an *oprichnyi dvor* was the form that his culture provided: as we have seen, the term designated a portion of a service estate set aside for the widows and orphans of the former holder *without the obligation of service*: Ivan was taking himself out of service.

∾ 4 ∾

Such an interpretation is supported by consideration of Ivan's later behavior: if he displayed any continuing and consistent objective after 1560, it was to flee: he abdicated in favor of his son, and of the Tatar Simon Bekbulatovich; he apparently conspired to flee to England; he turned on the Muscovite kinship system itself by making a mockery of the marriage politics that bound the clans in a chain of mutual strangleholds; he eventually murdered his son and heir.

But Ivan could not escape the web of culture woven by his courtiers, until death — the only event that the system would credit — gave him his freedom. Until that point, the boyars — his cousins and in-laws — could not permit it, because they found that, with two courts and a still unbetrothed heir, they simply could not compose their differences well enough to avoid the internecine strife they all feared most. Eventually they forced him back into the center of their jostling scrum.

The establishment of the *oprichnina*, then, was at first little more than Ivan's first, unsuccessful, attempt to escape from the prisonhouse of his kingship. It was not a devious plan to divide and conquer, nor a part of any grand design for Muscovy. It was an attempt by a sick man, who had done his job as procreator, and had become increasingly unable to perform as referee among his quarreling kinsmen, to flee.

Particularly nonsensical, in my view, is the notion that Ivan set out to "destroy" the class of great hereditary boyars who were allegedly impeding his putative drive towards the modernization of Muscovy. To begin, the old boyar clans were not destroyed, as any study of the following decades will reveal. Second, their "interests" were not — and could not be — significantly divergent from his own. Ivan was not a Hanoverian king: these were his in-laws, his cousins, his tutors, and his cronies. He was — and had been since childhood — their creature. The Zakhar'ins and Mstislavskiis and Bel'skiis

---

[52] For the distinction, see Ernst Hartwig Kantorowicz, *The King's Two Bodies: A Study in Mediaeval Political Theology* (Princeton, NJ: Princeton University Press, 1957), passim.

who ran things as Ivan came of age—and organized his marriage to Anastasiia—were still running things long after he left the scene.[53]

To be sure, the period we now call the *oprichnina* was one of heightened
mortality among courtiers, but that was largely because they were murdering
one another. And it is true that the emergence of the Godunovs and their
allies after Ivan's death changed the configuration of the ruling circle—
although not its rules. This change came about, however, largely as a result of
the fact that Ivan had murdered his elder son and heir, around whom all
major political expectations and alliances had come to revolve. (Fedor Ivanovich having died without issue, the dynasty came to an end.)

Thus in establishing his *oprichnina* Ivan was simply seeking to retire into
private life—a rather grand life, to be sure, and only partially private (grand
princes simply did not abdicate)—and he was taking proper and conventional
steps to accomplish this withdrawal. That he created a monster by failing to
anticipate strife between his "handlers" in the old court and his servants in
the new—all of whom were armed—is another matter.[54]

---

[53] See Andrei Pavlovich Pavlov, *Gosudarev dvor i politicheskaia bor'ba pri Borise Godunove*
(St. Petersburg: Nauka, 1992).

[54] It appears that such a conclusion renders moot the much-disputed question of
whether and when the *oprichnina* was "abolished" (See Al'shits, *Spisok oprichnikov*, 17–
53, esp. 43.) Ivan's private household was not abolished, and in a certain sense it could
not be. In the end, however, the traditional political and military forces he had left behind in the Kremlin defeated and re-absorbed those of his rag-tag "privy household."

Gifts for Kith and Kin: Gift Exchanges and Social Integration in Muscovite Royal Weddings

Russell E. Martin

As Tsar Mikhail Fedorovich's first wedding on September 19, 1624, was still being celebrated, a tableman (*stol'nik*) crossed the Kremlin's Cathedral Square to Voznesenskii Convent, where the former wife of Tsar Vasilii Shuiskii (ruled 1606–10), Ekaterina/Mariia Petrovna Buinosova-Rostovskaia, had been living for the past 14 years as the nun Elena.[1] The unnamed *stol'nik* brought wedding gifts with him, sent directly from the tsar and his bride: an oblong ornamental nuptial cloth (*ubrusets*), richly made of taffeta with pearls sewn into the fabric; and an ornamental kerchief (*shirinka*), also of taffeta, with rich gold-thread embroidery and gold fringe along its edges. At presumably the same time, the *stol'nik* Prince Danil Grigor'evich Gagarin was dispatched from the wedding to Tikhvin Convent, about 300 miles north of Moscow, bearing the same gifts, these intended for the nun Dar'ia, formerly Anna Alekseevna Koltovskaia, the fourth wife of Tsar Ivan IV.[2] The marriage commemorated in

Funding for this research was provided in part by the International Research Exchanges Board (IREX) and by the Ruth and George Watto Faculty Research Award from Westminster College, to whom I extend my sincere thanks. I also wish to thank Ideia Andreevna Balakaeva, Deputy Director of the Russian State Archive of Ancient Acts (hereafter, RGADA) for providing me open and unstinting access to rare manuscript materials essential for this study. I am indebted to Donald Ostrowski and to Chester Dunning, who offered useful suggestions on an early draft of this article that improved it in innumerable ways. Finally, I wish to thank Dr. Sheryl Simon and Dr. Kenneth Foon, during whose care this project was completed.

[1] RGADA f. 135, section IV, rubric II, number 14, folios 7–8. Tsar Vasilii Shuiskii's bride was born Ekaterina, but took the name Mariia shortly before the wedding. She then took the monastic name Elena at the time of her tonsuring. See S. A. Belokurov, ed., *Razriadnye zapisi za Smutnoe vremia (7113–7121 gg.)* (Moscow, 1907), 248. On royal brides changing names, see Ivan Egorovich Zabelin, *Domashnii byt russkogo naroda v XVI i XVII stoletiiakh*, vol. 2, *Domashnii byt russkikh tsarits* (Moscow: Tip. Gracheva, 1869; repr., Moscow: Iazyki slavianskoi kul'tury, 2001), 221; and Russell E. Martin, "Dynastic Marriage in Muscovy, 1500–1727" (Ph.D. diss., Harvard University, 1996), 68–72.

[2] RGADA f. 135, sec. IV, rub. II, no. 14, fols. 7–8. The task of sending these gifts to the nun Dar'ia from Tsar Mikhail's first wedding was originally given to her kinsman, Dmitrii Koltovskii. His name on one extant gift list (RGADA f. 135, sec. IV, rub. II, no.

Rude & Barbarous Kingdom Revisited: Essays in Russian History and Culture in Honor of Robert O. Crummey. Chester S. L. Dunning, Russell E. Martin, and Daniel Rowland, eds. Bloomington, IN: Slavica Publishers, 2008, 89–108.

these gifts was short-lived. Tsar Mikhail's bride, Mariia Vladimirovna Dolgorukova, was dead 4 months after the wedding. When Tsar Mikhail married
for a second time, on February 5, 1626, the nun Elena was already by then
dead too, but Prince Danil was sent yet again with another *ubrusets* and *shirinka* for the ex-tsaritsa Dar'ia.[3]

Written instructions (*pamiat'*) given to Prince Danil for this second trip fill
in some of the details for his, and probably the other *stol'nik*'s, missions. On
arrival at the Tikhvin Convent, he was to go immediately to Dar'ia and inform her that he had been sent to her "by the Sovereign, Tsar and Grand
Prince Mikhail Fedorovich of all Rus' and by his consort, Tsaritsa and Grand
Princess Evdokiia Luk'ianovna of all Rus', directly from their wedding" with
these gifts for her.[4] Prince Danil was then to present the gifts on two separate
platters to the nun Dar'ia, along with a letter from Tsar Mikhail (*gosudareva
gramota*), now lost but probably containing a text describing and formally be-
stowing these gifts on Dar'ia. The nun Dar'ia was then to offer Prince Danil
something to eat and to give him a return letter (*otpiska*) and a blessing to de-
part to Moscow, where, according to his instructions, Prince Danil was to report immediately to Council Secretary Ivan Gramotin at the Foreign Office
(*Posol'skii prikaz*) and deliver her *otpiska* to him. Dar'ia's letter would probably
later be read aloud publicly to the tsar and tsaritsa, and perhaps to many
others attending at court.[5]

The *ubrustsy* given to the nun Elena and nun Dar'ia were a type of gift
reserved exclusively for members of the ruling dynasty and for the patriarch.
At Tsar Mikhail Fedorovich's two weddings, *ubrustsy* were given only to the
tsar (the groom), to the patriarch (the groom's father), the nun Marfa Ivanovna (the groom's mother), and to the two ex-tsaritsy. Similarly, at Tsar Aleksei Mikhailovich's first wedding, *ubrustsy* were given only to the tsar, his

---

15, fol. 2) is crossed out and replaced with Prince Danil Gagarin's. Prince Danil may
have been the *stol'nik* sent to the nun Elena as well. The documentation for gifts at Tsar
Mikhail Fedorovich's and Tsar Aleksei Mikhailovich's weddings indicates that a *stol'-
nik* might be dispatched with commemorative gifts to more than one destination.

[3] RGADA f. 135, sec. IV, rub. II, no. 19, fols. 1, 2–3. The nun Elena died in 1624, shortly
after the wedding. Zabelin, *Domashnii byt russkogo naroda v XVI i XVII stoletiiakh*, vol. 3,
Domashnii byt russkikh tsarei i tsarits v XVI i XVII stoletiiakh. Materialy, "Materialy k tomu
II 'Domashnii byt russkikh tsarits v XVI i XVII stoletiiakh'" (repr., Moscow: Iazyki slavianskoi kul'tury, 2003), 576; *Polnoe sobranie russkikh letopisei*, 43 vols. to date, *Novyi letopisets* (Moscow: Nauka, 1965), 14: 152. The nun Dar'ia died in April 1626. N. de Baum-
garten, "Généalogies des branches régnantes de Rurikides du XIIIe au XVIe siècle,"
Orientalia Christiana 35: 94 (June 1934): 18–19 (Table 3), 24.

[4] RGADA f. 135, sec. IV, rub. II, no. 19, fol. 2.

[5] Inscriptions in many of the gift-related documents for Tsar Mikhail's and Tsar Aleksei's weddings indicate that the letters to and from the tsars were to be read aloud:
"*napisano v doklad*," "*chtenie v stolp*," "*v stolp*," and so on.

sisters (Irina, Anna, and Tat'iana), and Patriarch Iosif.[6] The ostensible giver of the gifts was the bride-to-be, who distributed the gifts just before the wedding service usually through her first best man (*bol'shoi druzhka s tsaritsynoi storony*), though the gifts likely derived from the tsar's own workshops. The *shirinki* given to the royal nuns were, from the extant descriptions available of them, more richly ornamented and luxuriantly crafted than the hundreds of other *shirinki* distributed to those who held honorific posts or otherwise served at these royal weddings. By their exclusiveness and the richness of their adornments, these gifts at once served to identify, maintain, and proclaim the recipients' status as members of Muscovy's royalty.

These missions to ex-tsaritsy from two previous dynasties (Danilovich and Shuiskii), living in separate monasteries, and who had not actually attended the wedding, are but the tip of the iceberg. Gifts and gift exchanges served a prominent ritual function at the weddings of Tsar Mikhail Fedorovich, and, in fact, at all Muscovite royal nuptials in the 16th and 17th centuries. Gift exchanges involved not just members of the dynasty but the entire court. Gifts were exchanged between the bride and members of the dynasty into which she was marrying and with courtiers of every rank who served at the wedding; church hierarchs sent and received gifts; boyars and other important servitors gave and received gifts; even, as we have seen, prominent members of the court who were not in attendance at the wedding for one reason or another were sent a *shirinka* to commemorate the wedding. No one was left out—not ex-tsaritsy living in remote monasteries, not even the guard who manned one of the Kremlin's gates during the three days of wedding celebrations. To be sure, the gifts were very different in quality and cost, but they all served the same function: to introduce and integrate the new bride and her family into her new political and social environs at court, including the highest ranking boyar to the lowest ranking Kremlin guard—the tsar's kith and kin.

Marcel Mauss, the great pioneer in gift theory, offered insights that can be useful for interpreting the meaning and importance of data on gift giving at Muscovite royal weddings. Mauss suggested that there were "three themes of the gift, the obligation to give, the obligation to receive and reciprocate," and that "generosity and self-interest...are linked in giving."[7] For Mauss, gift giving—what he called a "system of total services"[8]—was a fundamental attribute of human society: as foundational as economic class to Marxists or kinship to structuralists or the state to national-statist historians. Human society, including its religious beliefs and notions of the sacred, is, at its core, about exchange; and gifts both facilitated and symbolized the social, political,

---

[6] RGADA f. 135, sec. IV, rub. II, no. 25, fols. 1, 37, 39, 43.

[7] Marcel Mauss, *The Gift: The Form and Reason for Exchange in Archaic Societies*, trans. W. D. Halls (New York: W. W. Norton, 1990), 39, 68.

[8] Ibid., 6.

and economic interactions of groups of humans. Mauss has not gone unchallenged in the last century. Claude Lévi-Strauss, Annette Weiner, Maurice Godelier and others have all stretched and pulled on Mauss' original thesis in various ways, emphasizing kinship (the exchange of women in the marriage market), or objecting to Mauss's religious component in gifts (the insistence that objects exchanged are endowed with a spirit that calls for circulating the gift between givers and receivers), or introducing exceptions to the gift-giving ethic (the notion that some objects are too important or sacred to be exchanged).[9] But none of these corrections to Mauss' arguments have challenged his original contention that gifts and gift exchanges lay behind the formation and maintenance of increasingly elaborated social structures.

Of particular interest is Mauss's insight that gift giving simultaneously creates both solidarity and hierarchy.[10] The exchange of gifts fosters social solidarity and integration while at the same time reinforcing the hierarchical structures already in place in society. The giver of a gift forms a bond with the receiver inasmuch as the gift signifies that the two parties belong to the same social world or both embrace the same religious and social assumptions and rules. As Mary Douglas put it, "[a] gift that does nothing to enhance solidarity is a contradiction."[11] At the same time, a gift obliges one party to the other. One side may be required socially to offer gifts, but the other side is obliged equally to accept them and the "burden" that comes along with them: a responsibility to reciprocate—either literally or through patronage or other means of social and political support.

This study borrows Mauss's conceptual framework and examines gift exchanges over the course of more than two centuries of Muscovite royal weddings. It is based on unpublished gift ledgers, correspondence, and other chancellery documentation from 17th-century weddings, and on the descriptions of gifts and gift exchanges in wedding descriptions (*svadebnye chiny*), many of which are also unpublished, from the reigns of Grand Prince Ivan III (ruled 1462–1505) to Tsar Aleksei Mikhailovich (ruled 1645–76). Many of these sources have never been seriously studied, and gift exchange in general

---

[9] See Claude Lévi-Strauss, "Introduction à l'œuvre de Mauss," in *Sociologie et anthropologie* (Paris: Presses universitaires de France, 1950). In English, see *Introduction to the Work of Marcel Mauss*, trans. Felicity Baker (London: Routledge and Kegan Paul, 1987); Annette Weiner, *Inalienable Possessions: The Paradox of Keeping-while-Giving* (Berkeley: University of California Press, 1992); Maurice Godelier, *The Enigma of the Gift*, trans. Nora Scott (Chicago: University of Chicago Press, 1999); Aafke E. Komter, *Social Solidarity and the Gift* (Cambridge: Cambridge University Press, 2005). For a good and recent survey of the anthropological literature on gifts, see Godelier, *Enigma of the Gift*, 10–41.

[10] Mauss, *The Gift*, 33–42; Godelier, *Enigma of the Gift*, 12.

[11] Mary Douglas, "Forward: No Free Gifts," in Mauss, *The Gift*, vii.

remains a fallow field.[12] Like the sacramental bonds of matrimony itself that bound the tsar to his bride and to his in-laws, gifts and gift exchanges played a key integrating role at these weddings by uniting ritually—and thereby in fact—the entire court around the new tsaritsa in the new configuration of power that the royal marriage represented in each generation, not unlike the way Mauss describes in his own work.[13] And the political system needed to devise ways like gift exchanges at weddings to accomplish this integration since so often the bride came from outside the inner circle of servitors at court—an outsider whose lack of connections to the great boyar clans was one of her desirable features to the tsar and to the boyar oligarchy. As Robert Crummey has put it, "[n]o one doubted that the Streshnevs, Miloslavskiis, Naryshkins, Apraksins, Grushevskiis, and Lopukhins were upstarts."[14]

So central was gift exchange to weddings that one of the first forms of documentation that the grand princely scriptorium devised to record a royal wedding was the dowry inventory (spisok pridannykh). Three survive today: from the weddings of Elena Ivanovna, daughter of Ivan III, and Grand Duke Alexander of Lithuania (in 1495); of Evdokiia Ivanovna, another daughter of Ivan III, and Tsarevich Peter/Kudai Kul (in 1506); and of Mariia Saburova, Vasilii III's sister-in-law, and Prince Vasilii Semenovich Starodubskii (also in 1506).[15] These inventories provide extensive lists and descriptions of gifts

---

[12] Besides the several publications of the texts of wedding descriptions, there have been few dedicated studies of royal weddings or their component parts. For an early treatment of the various ranks and rituals involved, see Ivan Petrovich Sakharov, ed., *Skazaniia russkogo naroda*, 2 vols. (St. Petersburg, 1841–49).

[13] On the role of royal weddings in Muscovite political culture, see Russell F. Martin, "Choreographing the 'Tsar's Happy Occasion': Tradition, Change, and Dynastic Legitimacy in the Weddings of Tsar Mikhail Romanov," *Slavic Review* 63: 4 (Winter 2004): 794–817; Nancy Shields Kollmann, *Kinship and Politics: The Making of the Muscovite Political System, 1345–1547* (Stanford, CA: Stanford University Press, 1987); Edward L. Keenan, "Muscovite Political Folkways," *Russian Review* 45: 2 (1986): 115–81.

[14] Robert O. Crummey, *Aristocrats and Servitors: The Boyar Elite in Russia, 1613–1689* (Princeton, NJ: Princeton University Press, 1983), 77.

[15] Elena and Alexander: Biblioteka Rossiiskoi akademii nauk (hereafter, BAN), 16.15.15, fols. 1–26v; BAN 32.4.21, fols. 6–23v; and also Nikolai [Ivanovich] Novikov, ed., *Drevniaia rossiiskaia vivliofika. Soderzhashchaia v sebe sobranie drevnostei rossiiskikh, do istorii, geografii, i genealogii rossiiskoi kasaiushchikhsia* (hereafter, DRV), 2nd ed., 20 vols. (Moscow, 1788–1791), 14: 1–4, 4–21; *Sbornik Imperatorskogo russkogo istoricheskogo obshchestva*, 148 vols. (St. Petersburg, 1867–1916), 35: 71–192; and *Razriadnaia kniga 1475–1605 gg.*, ed. V. I. Buganov, 3 vols. (Moscow: Institut Istorii Akademii nauk, 1977–89) (hereafter, *RK 1475–1605*), 1: 40–42. Evdokiia Ivanovna and Tsarevich Peter: BAN 16.15.15, fols. 30v–47; BAN 32.4.21, fols. 27–37v; and also *RK 1475–1605*, 1: 91. Mariia Saburova and Starodubskii: BAN 16.15.15, fols. 47v–63v; BAN 32.4.21, fols. 38–48; and also *RK 1475–1605*, 1: 91; and *Razriadnaia kniga 1475–1598 gg.*, ed. V. I. Buganov (Moscow: Nauka, 1966), 16. The BAN manuscript compilations of royal wedding

exchanged between the grand prince (Ivan III or Vasilii III) and his consort (Sofiia Paleologa or Solomonida Saburova), on the one hand, and the bride and groom, on the other.

Rich as these inventories are for insights and data on Muscovite material culture, they are not genuine dowry inventories, despite the name given them (by later archivists, evidently). These are chronologically arranged (by day of the wedding) descriptions of the gifts that changed hands during the wedding celebrations; and in the case of Elena Ivanovna and Alexander, the inventory lists objects given to the groom as well as to the bride. Moreover, the gift exchanges described in the texts are limited to the immediate royal family and the new in-laws; they do not show how gifts moved back and forth between all the courtiers present and serving at the wedding, or, for that matter, those high-ranking servitors who were not in attendance.[16]

With the development by the scribes working in the grand princely chancellery of the wedding ceremonial (*svadebnyi chin*), the potential to describe gift exchanges grew enormously. The ceremonial is essentially a blow-by-blow description of the main ritual components of a wedding that extended, in the 16th century, over three days, and, in the 17th century, over four days. The first extant (and, very likely, the first ever) ceremonial was for Vasilii III's wedding to Elena Glinskaia in 1526, but it is rudimentary and contains no mention of gift exchanges, though one might safely assume that they took place.[17] The next wedding of a Muscovite dynast, Prince Andrei Staritskii, in 1533, does contain brief notes about gift exchanges, as do seven other wedding ceremonials down to 1671.[18] Gift ledgers for the first and second wed-

---

descriptions date from the second quarter of the 17th century (16.15.15) and the second quarter of the 18th century (32.4.21). On these manuscripts, see Martin, "Dynastic Marriage," 468–74.

[16] On these so-called dowry inventories, see Martin, "Gifts for the Bride: Dowries, Diplomacy, and Marriage Politics in Muscovy," *Journal of Medieval and Early Modern Studies* 38: 1 (Winter 2008): 119–45.

[17] On the ceremonial for Vasilii III's 1526 wedding, see Martin, "Choreographing the 'Tsar's Happy Occasion,'" 801–02. The wedding ceremonial is published in *DRV*, 13: 5–19. Fragments of the original survive: RGADA f. 135, sec. IV, rub. II, no. 2, fols. 1–5; no. 8, fols. 2–3.

[18] Andrei Staritskii and Evfrosiniia Khovanskaia: RGADA f. 135, sec. IV, rub. II, no. 4; Russell E. Martin, "Royal Weddings and Crimean Diplomacy: New Sources on Muscovite Chancellery Practice during the Reign of Vasilii III," *Harvard Ukrainian Studies* 19 (1995): 389–427; *DRV*, 13: 19–29. Iurii Vasil'evich and Ul'iana Paletskaia: RGADA f. 135, sec. IV, rub. II, no. 8, fol. 7 (fragment); *DRV*, 13: 36–46. Vladimir Staritskii and Evdokiia Nogaia: RGADA f. 135, sec. IV, rub. II, no. 9, fols. 1–1v (fragment); *DRV*, 13: 46–57. Tsar Semeon Kasaevich and Mariia Kutuzova-Kleopina: *DRV*, 13: 57–73. Ivan Dmitreevich Bel'skii and Marfa Vasil'evna Shuiskaia: *DRV*, 13: 73–79. Mikhail Romanov and Evdokiia Streshneva: RGADA f. 135, sec. IV, rub. II, nos. 16 and 17; *DRV*, 13: 144–74. Aleksei Mikhailovich and Mariia Miloslavskaia: RGADA f. 135, sec.

dings of Tsar Mikhail Fedorovich and the first wedding of Tsar Aleksei Mikhailovich also survive and can be used to fill in some gaps in the official record of these weddings.[19] Table 1 presents an overview of these progressively more extensive descriptions of gift exchanges in wedding ceremonials. The table shows the centrality of gift exchanges at weddings, and considerable change over time in how these exchanges were performed and who was involved in them over the course of the three (or more) days of celebrations.

Day 1

The distribution of gifts on the first day of a Muscovite royal wedding was the key exchange of gifts for the purposes of integrating the entire court around the newly-married royal couple. It was on this day that gifts were distributed to those who held the most important honorific duties at the wedding, in the 16th century, and to the entire wedding party, in the 17th—from the thousandman, to the bride's and groom's best men, to guards at Kremlin gates and trelliseworks, even to musicians and other entertainers of various sorts.

Day 1 was all about the bride. In each of the weddings for which we have data, the disbursal of gifts on the first day took place at the same moment in the sequence of rituals: at the time when the bride-to-be and the groom had gathered together in the principal venue (usually the Golden Palace or, later, the Palace of Facets) where most of the banqueting, speeches, and many other nuptial rituals would take place. It was at this moment that the bride's hair was braided, her face was veiled, she and her groom were sprinkled with hops (osypalo), and bread and cheese were cut and distributed among all those present. This crucial moment, laden with ancient and earthy fertility symbolism, was also the moment when the bride—sometimes through her best man—distributed gifts (shirinki) on platters to all those present (along with the bread and cheese). At the weddings of Prince Iurii Vasil'evich (Ivan IV's brother), the bride herself performed this ritual bestowal of gifts.[20] At the weddings of Andrei Staritskii, his son Vladimir Staritskii, and Tsar Semeon Kasaevich, the task was performed by the ruler's consort (Elena Glinskaia and

---

IV, rub. II, no. 24; DRV, 13: 174–232. Aleksei Mikhailovich and Natal'ia Naryshkina: RGADA f. 135, sec. IV, rub. II, nos. 28, 29, 30.

[19] Gift ledgers (plus correspondence, memoranda and other related documentation) include the following: Mikhail Romanov and Mariia Dolgorukova: RGADA f. 135, sec. IV, rub. II, no. 15. Mikhail Romanov and Evdokiia Streshneva: RGADA f. 135, sec. IV, rub. II, no. 19. Aleksei Mikhailovich and Mariia Miloslavskaia: RGADA f. 135, sec. IV, rub. II, nos. 25, 26, 27. For descriptions of these unpublished sources, see Russell E. Martin, "Muscovite Royal Weddings: A Descriptive Inventory of Manuscript Holdings in the Treasure Room of the Russian State Archive of Ancient Acts, Moscow," Manuscripta 50: 1 (June 2006): 77–198 (at 138–41, 151–53, and 167–80).

[20] DRV, 13: 41.

Table 1. Gift Exchanges at Muscovite Royal Weddings, 1533–1671

Wedding	First Day	Second Day	Third Day	Fourth Day	Other
Andrei Staritskii and Evfrosiniia Khovanskaia 2 Feb. 1533	GPr→GP, groom, "boyars and princes," *poezd*	groom→GP, GPr; groom←GP			
Iurii Vasil'evich and Ul'iana Paletskaia 3 Nov. 1547	bride→T, Ts, groom, boyars and *deti boiarskie, poezd*	groom→T, Ts; groom←T			
Vladimir Staritskii and Evdokiia Nagaia 31 May 1549	Ts→T, groom, boyars and *deti boiarskie, poezd*	groom→T, Ts, Tsarevna, Iurii, Ul'iana	T→mother of groom, groom, bride; Ts→groom, bride		
Tsar Simeon Kasaevich and Mariia Kutuzova-Kleopina 5 Nov. 1554	Ts→T, Iurii, groom, boyars and *deti boiarskie, poezd*	T→groom; groom→T, Ts, Iurii, Ul'iana; groom←T, Ts, Ul'iana			
Ivan Dm. Bel'skii and Marfa Vasil'evna Shuiskaia 8 Nov. 1555	bride's druzhki gives *shirinki*	groom→T, Ts, Iurii, Ul'iana, Simeon; T→Vladimir Staritskii; Tysiatskii→Vasilii Vladimirovich; Ts→bride; Iurii→groom; Ul'iana→bride	T→groom; Ts←bride; T→groom		
Mikhail Fedorovich and Evdokiia Streshneva 5 Feb. 1626	bride's bol'shoi druzhka→groom, patriarch/father, Marfa Ivanovna;				hierarchs→groom; boyars, courtiers merchants→groom (gifts not accepted);

Aleksei Mikhailovich and Mariia Miloslavskaia 16 January 1648	bride→Dar'ia; bride's second best man→proxy parents, tysiatskii, boyars and other senior attendants; Bride's first best man→groom, Irina M., Anna M., Tat'iana M., patriarch Iosif; bride's second best man→proxy parents, tysiatskii, boyars, and other senior attendants	hierarchs→bride; boyars, courtiers, merchants→bride; Patriarch and hierarchs→groom and bride; boyars, courtiers merchants→groom
Aleksei Mikhailovich and Natalia Naryshkina 22 January 1671	Groom's first best man→sons and daughters of groom, to patriarch, to other senior church figures; Groom's first best man→those holding honorific posts at wedding	February 7: patriarch→groom; patriarch→bride; boyars and other leading courtiers, merchants→groom and bride; Gifts from lesser servitors returned to them; groom→hierarchs: goblet (kubok)

GP =grand prince
GPr=grand princess

T=tsar
Ts=tsaritsa

↑ Indicates direction
↓ of the gift

Anastasiia Iur'eva), probably because these weddings of appanage princes and a converted Chinghisid were hosted by and, therefore, under the tight control of, the Muscovite ruler.[21] At the weddings of the Prince Ivan Bel'skii (a prominent boyar whose bride was descended from the ruling family) and the first two Romanovs, it was performed on the bride's behalf by her first best man, though at Tsar Aleksei's second wedding he had his own first best man do the job.[22]

The gifts disbursed at this moment and shortly thereafter were, as the sources unanimously indicate, *shirinki*, and they were given in large numbers. Details exist only for 17th-century weddings, but the overall pattern and purpose may have been the same throughout the period. The totals are impressive: for Mikhail Romanov's first wedding in 1624, 818 *shirinki* of four different classes were distributed.[23] The most richly decorated examples went to those who held the most important honorific posts at the wedding, and less luxurious examples went to the lower ranks of servitors, including scribes and clerks at the chancelleries whose workshops produced many of the accoutrements for the wedding (including the *shirinki* themselves), palace guards, *zhil'tsy* who served food and drink, and musicians. At the first wedding of Tsar Aleksei Mikhailovich in 1648, 345 *shirinki* were distributed.[24] Most of these gifts, certainly those for the most prominent attendants at the wedding, appear to have been distributed at this moment, but *shirinki* given to lower-ranking servitors—such as those who served food and drink at the banquets—were sent the next day, presumably also in the bride's name.[25]

---

[21] *DRV*, 13: 23, 50, 64.

[22] Bel'skii: BAN 16.15.15, fol. 137v. Mikhail Fedorovich: RGADA f. 135, sec. IV. rub. II, no. 14, fols. 7–8 (first wedding); *DRV*, 13: 157 (second wedding). Aleksei Mikhailovich: *DRV*, 13: 197–98 (first wedding); RGADA f. 135, sec. IV. rub. II, no. 30, fols. 23–23v, 36–36v (second wedding).

[23] RGADA f. 135, sec. IV. rub. II, no. 15, fol. 30. Three hundred ninety-seven *shirinki* of taffeta with gold fringe were given to the metropolitans, bishops, proxy parents, thousandman, best men, seated boyars and *boiaryni*, boyars and *boiaryni* at the nuptial bed or attending the bride, servitors who walked in procession, the officiating priest, and other officiating clergy and ranks of servitors holding high honorific posts at the wedding. One hundred sixteen *shirinki* of taffeta with fringe of gold silk were given to chancellery scribes who held honorific posts at the wedding and to commanders of guards at doors, trellisworks, and gates. One hundred ninety-one *shirinki* of calico, muslin, or linen, with fringe of gold silk were given to *zhil'tsy* who served food and drink, cupbearers, chancellery scribes and clerks, artisans in the tsar's workshops, clergy, commanders of *strel'tsy* units, and guards at trellisworks and gates. And finally one hundred fourteen *shirinki* of muslin or linen, with fringe of silk without gold were given to clergy, chancellery clerks, artisans in the tsar's workshops, singers, and performing musicians.

[24] RGADA f. 135, sec. IV. rub. II, no. 25, fols. 43–51.

[25] RGADA f. 135, sec. IV, rub. II, no. 25, fol. 50.

Gifts were given far and wide, but there is change in the range of gift exchanges between 16th-century weddings and Romanov weddings of the 17th century. According to the ceremonial for Prince Andrei Staritskii, Grand Princess Elena gave *shirinki* to "the grand prince and Prince Iurii Ivanovich [his brother], and to the boyars and *deti boiarskie* on the grand prince's side, and to the entire wedding train [*poezd*]."[26] The same formula appears in the wedding ceremonials for the other 16th-century weddings.[27] Thus, 16th-century weddings mention gifts given in the bride's name only to the most senior members of the wedding entourage. Seventeenth-century wedding ceremonials, however, mention more ranks of servitors receiving gifts on the first day. According to the ceremonial for Tsar Mikhail Fedorovich's second wedding, the bride's second best man, Roman Pozharskii, "gave in the tsarevna's and grand princess's name, *shirinki* and bread and cheese to the proxy mother and father, to the thousandman, and to the seated boyars and boiaryni, and to the other boyars and boiaryni who attended the wedding bed."[28] The ceremonial for Tsar Aleksei Mikhailovich's first wedding similarly points out that the bride's first best man brought gifts to the tsar, his sisters, and the patriarch. At the same time, the second best man took *shirinki*, bread, and cheese in the bride's name to the "proxy mother and father, the thousandman, to the seated boyars and boiaryni, and to the boyars and okol'nichie who served in ranks [*v chinekh*] and to the wedding train," as well as to the "*boiaryni* who were in the bride's room [*v komnate*] and to the boyars and *boiaryni* who attended the wedding bed."[29] Even those not in attendance were included, as we have seen. It was at this time when the bride was preparing to have her hair braided and sprinkled with hops that the *stol'nik* Prince Danil Gagarin was dispatched to the nun Dar'ia at Tsar Mikhail's two weddings, and it was at this moment in other weddings that *shirinki* were sent to others not in attendance but whose station or rank required a gift of the first class: such as boyar Prince Ivan Mikhailovich Vorotynskii and his wife, who may have been too elderly to attend Tsar Mikhail's first wedding;[30] or the elderly boyars Nikita Ivanovich Romanov, Dmitrii Mamstriukovich Cherkasskii, and Fedor Ivanovich Sheremetev, who did not attend Tsar Aleksei's first wedding;[31] or the

[26] RGADA f. 135, sec. IV, rub. II, no. 4, fol. 5; *DRV*, 13: 23.

[27] The exception is the Bel'skii-Shuiskaia wedding, which merely reports that "the bride's best men gave out (*podali*) *shirinki*" without specifying to whom (*DRV*, 13: 72).

[28] RGADA f. 135, sec. IV, rub. II, no. 16, fols. 22–23.

[29] RGADA f. 135, sec. IV, rub. II, no. 24, fols. 26v–27v.

[30] RGADA f. 135, sec. IV, rub. II, no. 15, fol. 18.

[31] RGADA f. 135, sec. IV, rub. II, no. 25, fol. 40.

large number of Orthodox hierarchs and monastic authorities whose duties kept them from attending any of these weddings.[32]

It appears that, for all the careful planning, sometimes there were not enough *shirinki* to go around. Just after the first wedding of Tsar Mikhail Romanov, 100 rubles were requisitioned from the Great Court (*Bol'shoi Dvor*) to give to *zhil'tsy* who "served food and drink at the [banquet] tables and who were stationed at the court on various duties [*u del*]" during the wedding. They were to be given 1 ruble each in place of a *shirinka* (*za shirinku*). Seventy *zhil'tsy* were paid (leaving 30 rubles to be returned, presumably, to the Treasury).[33] Similarly, seven priests, six deacons, and six readers (*d'iachki*) who evidently served in some unspecified capacity at the wedding never received their *shirinki*, and petitioned the tsar for them. An investigation ensued, in part by examining the records reporting what *shirinki* other clergy who served at the wedding had received. The text is truncated, so we do not know how the petition was resolved or if the clergy received rubles instead of *shirinki*, as the *zhil'tsy* did.[34]

Shortages of gifts also occurred at Tsar Aleksei Mikhailovich's first wedding. Once again, it was the *zhil'tsy* who were shortchanged. A petition survives from *zhil'tsy* who "served food [*est' stavit'*]" at the wedding, requesting "*shirinki* or money instead of *shirinki*."[35] The tsar complied with the request; a note in Council Secretary Nazaryi Chistyi's hand records that on January 26 (10 days after the wedding), the tsar ordered the men to be given 2 rubles each.[36] (Note that the money value substituted for a *shirinka* had doubled between 1624 and 1648.) To fulfill the tsar's order, the Keeper of the Seal (*Pechatnik*) Fedor Fedorovich Likhachev was commanded to send 40 rubles to Chistyi at the Foreign Office for disbursal to the 20 *zhil'tsy*. The only problem was that the list of *zhil'tsy* sent to Chistyi contained 24 names, not 20.[37] Four still had received nothing. As a result, one of the four, Denis Timofeev syn Ul'ianov, petitioned again.[38] Chistyi and other scribes evidently went back and looked over the list of *zhil'tsy* in the first petition, saw that they needed more money, and took action to get the tsar to approve the disbursal of rubles, 2 each, for the men. But the careless scribes in either the office of the Keeper of the Seal or in the Foreign Office misread the list (two brothers were

[32] RGADA f. 135, sec. IV, rub. II, no. 15, fols. 2, 3, 18, 25–28, 31–41; no. 19; no. 25, fols. 1–2, 39, 44, 50; and no. 26.

[33] RGADA f. 135, sec. IV, rub. II, no. 15, fol. 29.

[34] RGADA f. 135, sec. IV, rub. II, no. 15, fols. 31–33.

[35] RGADA f. 135, sec. IV, rub. II, no. 25, fol. 33.

[36] RGADA f. 135, sec. IV, rub. II, no. 25, fol. 33v. On the identification of Chistyi's hand, see fol. 55. The petition was evidently made on January 26, the date it was acted upon by the tsar (fol. 55).

[37] RGADA f. 135, sec. IV, rub. II, no. 25, fols. 34–35.

[38] RGADA f. 135, sec. IV, rub. II, no. 25, fols. 53–53v.

listed together but counted, evidently, only as one name) and so money was procured for only three additional *zhil'tsy*.[39] The surviving documentation does not tell us if the last poor man on the list ever got his rubles.

But it is a safe bet that he did. It is clear that these petitions and payments were not fees for service, but gifts. In the case of the vast majority who received *shirinki*, the object likely functioned not just as a reminder of their service at the wedding but also as token of honor—a tangible link between the servitor (and his family) and the court—indeed, a link even with the royal couple. These ceremonial objects could be displayed prominently in the household, or worn at important functions, or, for the practical minded, perhaps donated to a church or monastery or even sold. The objects became part of the wealth and honor of the recipient's family. For those who received money—whether 1 or 2 rubles (in some cases more)—the opportunity to put their honor on display was lost, but money could otherwise be used to enhance the family's comfort and honor. What is vital to note here is that enormous efforts were made to include everyone who served at the wedding. Missing even one servitor would diminish or negate the very social integration the gifts on Day 1 of the wedding were intended to foster.

While one must be cautious when drawing conclusions about the content of any ritual over time when the textual descriptions of these rituals are, generally, becoming more and more detailed, it nonetheless appears that the Romanov weddings spread *shirinki* to a larger group than was the case in 16th-century weddings. It may very well be the case that gift exchanges on the first day served a double purpose: to integrate the bride into her new milieu, as we have seen, and to solidify the power and status of the fledgling Romanov dynasty, especially at Tsar Mikhail Romanov's first wedding, where the number of *shirinki* distributed was so high. More so than any dowry, these gifts introduced the bride into her new milieu in the broadest way possible. The gifts given in her name served as a means to insinuate herself into (and, perhaps, ingratiate herself to) the ranks of servitors at court; and the fact that gifts in her name went to all ranks of servitors, dipping down even to palace guards, could only help to facilitate her membership in the social world of the court.

Days 2 and 3

The next exchange of gifts on Days 2 and, sometimes, on Day 3, appear to be all about the groom, and, again, we note some evolution in the practice between the 16th and 17th centuries. In each of the 16th-century weddings, the

---

[39] A summary of the entire episode up to this point is provided in a brief memorandum: RGADA f. 135, sec. IV, rub. II, no. 25, fols. 55–56v. Other petitions are extant as well, such as one from Borisko Fedorov syn Sukochev, a hundredman (*sotnik*) of the Moscow *strel'tsy*, who had manned Kolymazhnyi Gate during the wedding (RGADA f. 135, sec. IV, rub. II, no. 25, fols. 54–54v).

groom is not the ruler; these are weddings of collateral members of the dynasty (a younger brother and a cousin), a cognatic descendant of the dynasty (Bel'skii-Shuiskii), or a converted Chinghisid. Thus we do not know how the exchanges would have worked had the groom been the grand prince or tsar. Still, Days 2 and 3 are true gift exchanges (rather than the giving of gifts without receiving any in return, as on Day 1); and these exchanges all involve the groom, on the one hand, and other members of the dynasty, on the other. Thus, we know that Prince Andrei Staritskii gave unnamed gifts to his older brother, Grand Prince Vasilii III, and to his sister-in-law, Grand Princess Elena, and that the grand prince gave Prince Andrei in return a fur coat (*shuba*).[40] The pattern of exchanges is the same at Prince Iurii Vasil'evich's wedding (groom gave unspecified gifts to the tsar and tsaritsa, the tsar gave a fur coat to the groom).[41] The other wedding ceremonials for the 16th century likewise describe exchanges between the groom and sometimes the bride, and members of the immediate royal family; and in two cases, Day 3 is used as an additional opportunity for an exchange of gifts between the groom, the bride, the ruler, the ruler's consort, and, in the case of Vladimir Staritskii's wedding, the groom's mother-in-law (see Table 1). Gift exchanges on Days 2 and 3 shifted the focus from the bride to the groom as both the giver and receiver of gifts. It also focuses narrowly on the new family created by the marriage: the newlywed couple and their extended relatives and in-laws. The setting for these exchanges is more intimate—not the public audience for Day 1—and the purpose more familial and private.

This more intimate gift exchange disappeared in the 17th century. Day 2 was not used for a gift exchange at Tsar Mikhail Romanov's second wedding or at Tsar Aleksei Mikhailovich's first wedding. The gift exchanges between the members of the royal family seems to have been subsumed into the activities on Day 1 (see Table 1) and are no longer separated from the larger and more public bestowal of gifts at that time. Day 2 does, however, contain a gift exchange at the second wedding of Tsar Aleksei, but this is because gifts normally given on the first day were divided between Days 1 and 2: the members of the dynasty and the senior servitors receiving gifts on Day 1, and the rest of the servitors at the wedding receiving them on Day 2. Again, these gifts on either day may no longer have been symbolically from the bride since it is the groom's best men who bestowed the gifts, not the bride's. Why the intimate gift exchange between the newlywed couple and the royal family should disappear in the 17th century is never explained in the sources, though one cannot help but note the greater emphasis that the new Romanov dynasty was placing on the larger, more public gift exchanges (on Day 1 and, as shown below, Day 4), probably both as a means to solidify its legitimacy among the court elite—the givers and recipients of wedding gifts—and, more practically,

---

[40] RGADA f. 135, sec. IV, rub. II, no. 4, fol. 10.

[41] *DRV*, 13: 44.

as a means to refill the coffers of the royal treasury, which had been so deci-
mated during the Time of Troubles.[42]

Day 4

Perhaps the biggest innovation in gift exchanges at Muscovite royal weddings
falls on Day 4, which had not been part of 16th-century antecedents. It was
probably at Tsar Mikhail Fedorovich's first wedding in 1624 that gift exchanges were reconceptualized and that the fourth day of the wedding was
added specifically, it appears, to provide for a banquet with Church hierarchs
and for a final gift exchange. Archival manuscripts surviving from this wedding show correspondence between Church hierarchs and the tsar, expressing
thanks for the gifts dispatched to them and offering prayers for the health of
the couple and for a fruitful union: "heirs for the succession of the realm."[43]

On this fourth day, it was the bride and groom that received gifts from
the entire court and from Muscovite elite society, starting with the hierarchs
and monastic authorities, down even to lower ranking servitors and to merchants. This audience both reversed the direction that gifts flowed as compared with the first day (from bride to groom and members of the court on
Day 1; members of the court and society to the bride and groom on Day 4),
and it included the leadership of the Orthodox clergy, who went unmen-
tioned in 16th-century wedding ceremonials. The ceremonial for Tsar Mikhail
Fedorovich's second wedding describes this ritual in detail:

> And on the fourth day, at the third hour, the sovereign ordered the
> Lesser Golden Palace [*Zolotaia polata menshaia*] be prepared, and he
> sent for his father, the Great Sovereign Patriarch Filaret Nikitich ...
> and Prince Aleksei Lvov presented to the sovereign and to the Patri-
> arch gifts inscribed on a list, and what these gifts were is written
> down at the Royal Treasury [*na Kazennom dvore*]. And the metropoli-
> tan of Krutitsa and Bishop Iosif blessed the sovereign with icons, and
> archimandrites and hegumens [did so as well], and they brought gifts
> to the sovereign by rank [*po chinu*]: silver cups [*kubki serebrianye*], and
> bowls [*stopy*] and gold satin [*otlas zolotnye*] and sables. And after that,
> boyars and those in Duma ranks [*dumnye liudi*] approached the sover-
> eign with gifts, and after the boyars, the ranks of merchants [*gosti,
> and gostinye* and *sukonnye* and *chornye sotni*] presented gifts, and the
> sovereign accepted none of these gifts. And after that, the tsar and
> grand prince and the great sovereign the patriarch walked together to

---

[42] On the situation in the royal treasury, see L. E. Morozova, *Rossiia na puti iz Smuty:
Izbranie na tsarstvo Mikhaila Fedorovicha* (Moscow: Nauka, 2005), 152–210.

[43] RGADA f. 135, sec. IV, rub. II, no. 15.

the tsaritsa's apartments, and gifts were brought to her in the same manner as they had been brought to the tsar.[44]

This audience was performed generally the same way at Tsar Aleksei Mikhailovich's two weddings, though, at his first wedding the gifts were given to the tsar and tsaritsa together (not in separate audiences), and at the second wedding the joint audience was held 15 days after the wedding, not on the fourth day (see Table 1).[45] The ceremonial for the second wedding also points out that Tsar Aleksei ordered the gifts from the lesser ranks returned, just as Tsar Mikhail had done.[46] Majesty and magnanimity were expressed together when the tsar received then returned the gifts of the lower ranks and merchants.

This audience must have been a sight to behold. Processions of robed clergy with carts bearing luxurious presents for the sovereign and his consort, rows of boyars and other senior servitors dressed in their finest costumes and bearing gifts of their own, and representatives of all the lower ranks of servitors and merchants in Moscow, many of whom, very likely, had on this occasion their first peek inside the palace complex. There was also a rigid ritual observed, as the ceremonial for Tsar Aleksei's second wedding (the most descriptive ceremonial for a traditional Muscovite royal wedding) points out. While the clergy was allowed to enter the Palace of Facets, where the audience was held, and to approach the tsar, even to kiss his hand, lesser ranks were not allowed to approach as near, and the merchants, who were represented by only two or three from each rank, were received only at the doorway to the room and not allowed to enter.

The gifts that the tsar received were rich and varied. A remarkable ledger of gifts brought to Tsar Aleksei on the fourth day of his first wedding in 1648 survives. The text is fragmentary: the first lines are missing, but the text declares itself to be a list of gifts brought to the royal couple from the patriarch and other clergy and from the monasteries, from boyars and others in Duma ranks, from stol'niki and chancellery scribes and clerks, and from merchants of various ranks.[47] Unfortunately, the only part of the text that survives contains a list of the gifts from Church hierarchs and from monasteries.[48] The list is

---

[44] RGADA f. 135, sec. IV, rub. II, no. 16, fols. 41v–43v.

[45] For Tsar Aleksei's first wedding, see RGADA f. 135, sec. IV, rub. II, no. 24, fols. 56–61. For his second, see: RGADA f. 135, sec. IV, rub. II, no. 30, fols. 39v–41, 49–49v, 51v–61v.

[46] RGADA f. 135, sec. IV, rub. II, no. 30, fol. 61.

[47] RGADA f. 135, sec. IV, rub. II, no. 27, fol. 1.

[48] Tsar Aleksei Mikhailovich and his bride received gifts from the following (listed in the order they appear in the ledger): Patriarch Iosif, Metropolitan Varlam of Rostov, Metropolitan Serapion of Krutitsa, Archbishop Serapion of Suzdal', Archbishop Moisei of Riazan', Archbishop Iona of Tver', Bishop Rafael of Kolomna, the "authorities" of Holy Trinity-St. Sergius Monastery, Nativity Monastery in Vladimir, Simonov Mon-

systematic and organized, including gifts from 7 hierarchs and 19 monasteries and gives a glimpse of the ritual and wealth being exchanged. It reports, for example, that Patriarch Iosif give 3 richly inlaid and engraved silver goblets with lids, 6 bolts of Turkish velvet of varying sorts and colors, 4 bolts of satin, one bolt of moire, 3 bolts of damask, sables (grouped in forties, but the manuscript is frayed here and so does not show how many), and 100 zolotykh (ducats).[49] The patriarch similarly gave the tsaritsa 3 goblets, 6 bolts of Turkish and Persian velvet, 4 bolts of satin, 1 bolt of moire, 3 bolts of damask, 3 forties of sables, and 100 zolotykh.[50] The total value of these gifts was 982 rubles, 2 altyn, 1 den'ga.[51] The text also reports that the authorities (*vlasti*) at Holy Trinity-St. Sergius Monastery gave to the tsar 3 silver engraved goblets, a small engraved wash basin, 3 bolts of Venetian and Turkish velvet, 7 bolts of various kinds of satin, 3 bolts of moire, 4 bolts of damask, 2 forties of sables, and 100 zolotykh. Holy Trinity-St. Sergius gave the tsaritsa 3 similar silver engraved goblets, a silver cup, 3 bolts of Venetian and Turkish velvet, 9 bolts of satin, 1 bolt of moire, 3 bolts of damask, 2 forties of sables, and 100 zolotykh. To total value for these gifts (excluding the zolotykh) was 1,238 rubles, 27 altyn, 4.5 den'gi (the largest single amount given).[52] Nativity Monastery in Vladimir gave to the tsar a silver cup with a lid, 1 bolt of Persian velvet with stripes, and 40 sables, and the tsaritsa a similar cup and lid, 1 bolt of gold satin, and 40 sables, all valued at 128 rubles, 3 den'gi.[53] Adding together the values included in the ledger for all the gifts from hierarchs and monasteries, the tsar and his bride collected 5,282 rubles, 2 altyn, 3 den'gi, plus the 200 zolotykh from Holy Trinity-St. Sergius Monastery. Remembering that this is a mere fragment of the total brought in (boyars and Duma ranks are missing from the surviving ledger, as are the lesser ranking servitors and merchants),

---

astery, New Savior Monastery, Chudov Monastery, Kirillov Monastery, Savior Monastery in Yaroslavl', Pafnut'ev Monastery in Borovsk, Solovetskii Monastery, Bogoiavlenskii Monastery in Kolomna, Savior-St. Evfimii Monastery in Suzdal', Iosif-Volokolamskii Monastery, Znamenskii Monastery, Andronnikov Monastery, Savior Khutynia Monastery, Tikhvin Monastery, Holy Trinity-St. Paul Monastery, Makar'ev Monastery in Galitskii district, and Nikol Ugreshskii Monastery. RGADA f. 135, sec. IV, rub. II, no. 27.

[49] These ducats, or gold coins, were common gifts at weddings. According to Jacques Margeret, "Ducats become very valuable when an emperor is crowned or marries and [when there is an imperial] baptism, for everyone comes to offer him presents.... Among these presents there are customarily a number of ducats." See Jacques Margeret, *The Russian Empire and Grand Duchy of Muscovy: A 17th-Century French Account*, trans. and ed. Chester S. L. Dunning (Pittsburgh: University of Pittsburgh Press, 1983), 40. I thank Chester Dunning for this reference.

[50] RGADA f. 135, sec. IV, rub. II, no. 27, fols. 1–3.

[51] RGADA f. 135, sec. IV, rub. II, no. 27, fol. 17.

[52] RGADA f. 135, sec. IV, rub. II, no. 27, fol. 19.

[53] RGADA f. 135, sec. IV, rub. II, no. 27, fols. 8–12, 19.

the exchange in valuables that day between the tsar, his bride, and his servitors—sacred and secular—must have involved a staggering sum.

Day 4 extended the boundaries of gift exchange past the servitors in the wedding party of Day 1, and past the royal family and in-laws of Days 2 and 3, to the entire secular and spiritual elites of the realm, and, consequently, to the farthest reaches of Muscovy. Day 4 linked the entire ruling classes with the tsar and tsaritsa as a ruling couple, a point underscored by the separate audiences (one for the tsar, the other for the tsaritsa) in the earliest performances of this ritual in the 17th century. Through the tribute of gifts, the entire society, with the exception of peasants and the unfree, showed its acceptance and approval of the royal match.

The structure and purpose of gift giving and exchange as seen in royal wedding ceremonials (*chiny*) is mirrored in the descriptions of Muscovite royal weddings both in chapter 67 of the *Domostroi* and in Grigorii Kotoshikhin's *O Rossii v tsarstvovanie Alekseia Mikhailovicha* (*Russia in the Reign of Tsar Aleksei Mikhailovich*)—both 17th-century texts.[54] That the first day's events were centered around the bride and her family is substantiated in the *Domostroi*. The four wedding rituals in chapter 67 all mention *shirinki* (and sometimes also bread and cheese) being given by the bride at precisely the same moment in the ritual as the official wedding ceremonials—at the time of the braiding of the bride's hair, veiling, and sprinkling. *Shirinki* were at this time also sent to "any relatives who could not attend the ceremony," just like the ex-tsaritsy in the cases discussed above.[55] Kotoshikhin's account of royal weddings also centers the action on the first day of the wedding on the bride, reporting, as do the ceremonials, that the bride's best man distributed "bread, cheese and gifts."[56] The intimate nature of the exchanges on Day 2 is likewise supported by the *Domostroi* and by Kotoshikhin, both of which mention that the bride's father sent "bathing gifts"—a fine new set of clothes for the groom that he is to put on after his ritual bath on the morning of Day 2. The *Domostroi* furthermore mentions land that is given to the couple on the second day, and that other gifts were distributed only among family members, the text emphasizing the intimacy of the moment by pointing out that "no gifts are

---

[54] The wedding chapter (chapter 67) of the *Domostroi* is almost certainly an addition from the first third of the 17th century. See Carolyn Johnston Pouncy, "The Origins of the *Domostroi*: An Essay in Manuscript History," *Russian Review* 46 (1987): 357–73; and Martin, "Dynastic Marriage," 337–40.

[55] Carolyn Pouncy, ed. and trans., *The* Domostroi: *Rules for Russian Households in the Time of Ivan the Terrible* (Ithaca, NY: Cornell University Press, 1994), 206, 209, 210–11, 220, 225–27, 229, 230, 232–37. The fifth element of this chapter contains only notes about separate elements of the wedding ritual, and does not include any commentary on gifts.

[56] Grigorii K. Kotoshikhin, *O Rossii v carstvovanie Alekseia Mikhailovicha*, ed. A. E. Pennington (Oxford: Clarendon Press, 1980), 23 (fols. 13–13v).

given to the retainers."[57] Finally, the descriptions of gift exchanges on the last day of wedding celebrations in the *Domostroi* and Kotoshikhin are remarkably similar to the gift exchanges on Day 4 described in the official ceremonials. The *Domostroi* describes how the bride was given rings and crosses by attendants, and Kotoshikhin, who is clearly describing a 17th-century wedding (with which he had personal experience as a scribe working in the Foreign Office), not a 16th-century model, reports that gifts were brought to the tsar and his tsaritsa from the entire court, and that it was on the fourth day of celebrations that Church hierarchs brought the couple gifts.[58] The similarities in the descriptions in the *Domostroi*, Kotoshikhin, and official ceremonials suggest that gift exchanges were, as we have suggested, a central and stable component of the wedding ritual over these two centuries. These texts also highlight the social and familial solidarity that these gift exchanges were supposed to engender. In the *Domostroi*, as the best man distributes gifts in the bride's name on the first day of the wedding, he is scripted to say to each person "the bride, N., shows her respect for you with this bread, cheese, and cloth."[59]

Gifts exchanges fulfilled a number of functions simultaneously. First, following Mauss's argument, gift exchanges reinforced and maintained social solidarity. Much of the gift exchange activity was centered around the bride, who bestowed gifts on the entire court elite, represented for the most part by those tapped to fill honorific posts at the wedding (but also including, as we have seen, those not able to attend the wedding for one or another reason). Given the middling social origins of most brides in the 16th and 17th centuries, it is hard not to imagine that the gifts given on day one of the wedding were contrived specifically in response to—and as social compensation for—the relatively low social status of so many of the rulers' brides. If so, these gifts did their job well, providing a ritually rich and meaningful opportunity for the bride and her family to join the highest ranks of the elite through the act of gift giving, which, as Mauss would remind us, necessitates reciprocity on the part of those receiving the gift, whether in the form of gifts given back or, more likely in this case, social support and loyalty.

Second, and again following Mauss, gift exchanges also underscored and strengthened the existing social hierarchy at court and in Muscovite elite society at large. The marriage of a Muscovite ruler was the event that created a new configuration of power—a new regime—that, it was hoped, would last for a generation. The parade on Day 4 of boyars, courtiers of various ranks, bishops, priests, chancellery clerks, and merchants before the ruler and his

---

[57] *Domostroi*, 226–28, 236; Kotoshikhin, *O Rossii*, 26 (fols. 17–18). It was on Day 2 that "villages in Pereslavl': Romanovo and Petrishchovo" were given in 1506 by Grand Prince Vasilii III to his daughter Evdokiia Ivanovna, who had married Kudai Kul/ Tsarevich Peter. See BAN 16.15.15, fols. 42v.

[58] *Domostroi*, 237; Kotoshikhin, *O Rossii*, 27 (fols. 18–19v).

[59] *Domostroi*, 220.

consort, all bearing rich and costly gifts, was a spectacle that must have rivaled the ostentation of all the other rituals filling the three or four days of wedding celebrations. And for good reason. The gifts served to enfranchise the higher strata of elite society into the new political arrangement that would take shape around the new bride and, just as importantly, her family, which would be elevated to the highest ranks at court in the days and weeks after the wedding. Gifts thus opened to the royal in-laws the doors of membership into the ruling oligarchy of royal in-laws (and in-laws of in-laws) while they simultaneously elevated the bride to the singular heights of royalty. Gifts were, in a word, the ties the bind.

Finally, this study of gift exchanges casts light on the role of marriage and kinship in the Muscovite political system. Weddings were perhaps more than any other ritual, including coronations, a formative moment. Weddings were unique spectacles of grandeur, majesty, and social cohesion. They were hopeful moments in often troubled times. Though highly formulaic and prescribed by custom and Orthodox liturgical rubrics, weddings were surprisingly flexible rituals that provided the means and opportunity for mending rifts, healing wounds, and reconciling former foes. Gifts and gift exchanges were a centerpiece of the ritual activities performed at weddings. They were a means for transforming what was, in essence, a ritual that pertained necessarily and exclusively to two persons (the bride and groom) into a broadly social and political affair. The stunning amounts spent on gifts, the broad participation of courtiers of every rank, the energies expended to include everyone in the bestowal or exchange of gifts—all this should retrain our focus on weddings as the chief constituting device in every generation in Muscovy: a moment of renewal, an opportunity to add new blood into the elite, a prize in the game of politics.

Marfa Ivanovna and the Expansion of the Role of the Tsar's Mother in the 17th Century

Isolde Thyrêt

Amongst the royal women of Muscovite Russia in the late 16th and early 17th centuries, Marfa Ivanovna, the mother of the first Romanov tsar, Mikhail Fedorovich, stands out for her harsh treatment in historical literature. Previous tsaritsy, such as Mariia Grigor'evna Skuratova-Bel'skaia and Mariia Fedorovna Nagaia, understandably received bad publicity because of their association with unpopular or controversial blood lines during the Time of Troubles.[1] One would expect, however, a positive characterization of Marfa Ivanovna, who after all was the matriarch of Russia's new legitimate dynasty after the Time of Troubles. Nevertheless, prominent scholars of the early Romanov dynasty have few good words for the tsar mother. V. O. Kliuchevskii calls Marfa "a capricious intriguer who kept a tight hold on her son," and S. V. Bakhrushin depicts her as "a power-loving, very mean, but by far not intelligent woman."[2] The scholarly prejudice reflects the tone of 17th-century sources, notably the *Pskov Chronicle*, which expresses resentment about the rise of some of Marfa's kinsmen into leading positions at the Romanov court.[3] Inquest records concerning treasonous activities against the royal family also contain mean-spirited comments about Marfa Ivanovna. In one case from July 1626, a prison guard in Mozhaisk allegedly blamed Marfa Ivanovna for Tsar Mikhail's failed wedding to Mariia Khlopova and lamented that the tsar was oblivious of the intrigues of his meddlesome mother and did not have her sewn into a bearskin and then hunted down by dogs, as previous lords would

---

[1] Isolde Thyrêt, *Between God and Tsar: Religious Symbolism and the Royal Women of Muscovite Russia* (DeKalb: Northern Illinois University Press, 2001), 103–17.

[2] V. O. Kliuchevskii, *A Course in Russian History: The Seventeenth Century*, trans. Natalie Duddington (Armonk, NY: M. E. Sharpe, 1994), 82; S. V. Bakhrushin, "Politicheskie tolki v tsarstvovanie Mikhaila Fedorovicha," in *Trudy po istochnikovedeniiu, istoriografii i istorii Rossii epokhi feodalizma (nauchnoe nasledie)*, ed. B. V. Levshin (Moscow: Nauka, 1987), 95.

[3] *Pskovskie letopisi* (hereafter, *PL*), 2 vols. (Moscow: Izdatel'stvo Akademii nauk SSSR, 1941–55), 1: 132–33; Bakhrushin, "Politicheskie tolki," 98.

Rude & Barbarous Kingdom Revisited: Essays in Russian History and Culture in Honor of Robert O. Crummey. Chester S. L. Dunning, Russell E. Martin, and Daniel Rowland, eds. Bloomington, IN: Slavica Publishers, 2008, 109–29.

have done.[4] In another incident, a retainer of the governor of Tobolsk was accused of rejoicing at Marfa Ivanovna's death in 1631, saying that Russians had escaped the first evil and now only had to get rid of her husband, Patriarch Filaret.[5]

The negative attitude toward the Romanov matriarch results from the fact that Marfa Ivanovna, who had never been a tsar's wife and therefore could not claim having the blessed womb of a tsar mother, met the challenge of defining her unique role head on.[6] An examination of Marfa Ivanovna's role in the events leading up to Mikhail Fedorovich's coronation in 1613 shows that in order to appropriate the role of a tsaritsa, the Romanov matriarch carefully manipulated a Muscovite political ritual of pleading with a tsar candidate to assume the throne. Marfa Ivanovna was conscious of the fact that the delegation of the Muscovite Assembly of the Land to Mikhail Fedorovich in Kostroma in 1613 followed the protocol a previous assembly had applied to Boris Godunov and his sister Irina in the succession crisis of 1598. Using this knowledge, she inserted herself into the pleading ritual in such a way that she expanded on Irina's role and set herself up to assume a much more visible position at the future royal court than previous tsaritsy had enjoyed.

Marfa Ivanovna's potential dynastic significance became apparent shortly after the death of the last Rurikide tsar, Fedor Ivanovich, in 1598. Boris Godunov's subsequent ascendance to power was accompanied by reprisals against the Romanov clan, which had risen to political prominence after Ivan IV had married Anastasiia Romanova in 1547. In order to forestall a rival claim to the throne by Anastasiia's influential and well-liked nephew, Fedor Nikitich Romanov, Boris Godunov forced him and his relatives to take monastic vows in 1600. Fedor's wife, Kseniia Ivanovna Shestova, who later took the monastic name Marfa, was forced to share his fate.[7] The forced tonsure of Kseniia supports the contention that in Muscovite Russia women related to the Rurikide clan by marriage were intrinsically linked to the issue of succession. This notion is underscored by a rumor recorded by Isaac Massa that on the day Boris was elected tsar, Kseniia started a domestic dispute with her husband. Kseniia, who supposedly had never aroused her spouse's wrath, reproached him with harsh words for not putting up a fight for the throne that belonged

[4] N. Novombergskii, ed., *Slovo i delo gosudarevy: Protsessy do izdaniia Ulozheniia Alekseia Mikhailovicha 1649 goda*, vol. 1 (hereafter, *Slovo i delo*) (Moscow, 1911), no. 30, pp. 36–40; Bakhrushin, "Politicheskie tolki," 96.

[5] Several people seem to have been accused of such a remark; see Bakhrushin, "Politicheskie tolki," 96.

[6] Isolde Thyrêt, "'Blessed is the Tsaritsa's Womb': The Myth of Miraculous Birth and Royal Motherhood in Muscovite Russia," *Russian Review* 53: 4 (October 1994): 479–96; and Thyrêt, *Between God and Tsar*, 16–46.

[7] *Akty istoricheskie, sobrannye i izdannye Arkheograficheskoi komissiei* (hereafter, *AI*), 5 vols. (St. Petersburg, 1841–42), vol. 2, no. 38, VI, p. 36.

to their family. Her words supposedly angered her husband so much that he struck her on the chin. Whether Kseniia actually conspired with her husband's brothers to have the Godunovs assassinated, as another rumor seemed to suggest, or whether Massa was correct in his conviction that Boris and his supporters circulated these rumors to eliminate her, the very existence of such tales suggests that regardless of their political tendencies, Muscovites saw Kseniia as a defender of the Romanov clan's rights to the throne.[8]

By 1613 Marfa Ivanovna used her reputation to play a prominent role in the negotiations surrounding Mikhail Fedorovich's ascendance to the throne. Most scholars who study the mission of the delegation of the Muscovite Assembly of the Land to Kostroma on March 13, 1613, designed to inform Marfa and her son of its election of Mikhail Fedorovich mention his mother's involvement in the act. Nevertheless, the actual role of Marfa Ivanovna, both perceived and real, in the circumstances leading up to her son's coronation and its implication for the position of royal women in the Romanov dynasty have yet remained unstudied.[9] The lack of interest in Marfa's role is surprising since her participation in the reception of the envoys is recorded in virtually all 17th-century chronicles and political tales that deal with the event.[10] In addition, a series of letters composed shortly before and after the meeting in Kostroma by the Assembly of the Land, its delegation, Mikhail Fedorovich, and Marfa Ivanovna, and Avraamii Palitsyn's eyewitness account of the Kostroma mission provide valuable insight into the Romanov matriarch's political maneuverings. Taken together, these documents show that Marfa Ivanovna represented more than a figurehead to the noble elite that governed Muscovy at the time. The mother of the future tsar was quite aware of both the political predicament the Assembly of the Land faced and the prestigious position the mothers of Muscovite rulers traditionally held. She also was familiar with the 1598 precedent of Muscovites petitioning for another ruler in the absence of direct royal offspring. This knowledge gave her the opportunity to manipulate this ritual to bargain for the most advantageous

---

[8] Isaac Massa, *A Short History of the Beginnings and Origins of These Present Wars in Moscow under the Reign of Various Sovereigns down to the Year 1610*, trans. G. Edward Orchard (Toronto: University of Toronto Press, 1982), 41.

[9] See, for example, Robert O. Crummey, *The Formation of Muscovy, 1304–1613* (London: Longman, 1987), 232; R. G. Skrynnikov, *The Time of Troubles: Russia in Crisis 1604–1618*, trans. and ed. Hugh F. Graham (Gulf Breeze, FL: Academic International Press, 1988), 277–78; and Kliuchevskii, *Course in Russian History*, 82.

[10] See, for example, *Polnoe sobranie russkikh letopisei* (hereafter, *PSRL*), 41 vols. to date (St. Petersburg-Petrograd-Leningrad-Moscow: Arkheograficheskaia komissiia, Nauka, and Arkheograficheskii tsentr, 1841–1995), 34: 219 *(Piskarev Chronicle)*; 14, pt. 1: 129 *(Novyi letopisets)*; *Russkaia istoricheskaia biblioteka* (hereafter, *RIB*), 39 vols. (St. Petersburg-Leningrad, 1872–1927), 13 (2nd ed.): 1319–20 *(1617 Khronograf)* and 124 *(Inoe Skazanie)*; also see *Dvortsovye razriady po vysochaishemu poveleniiu izdannye II-em otdeleniem velichestva kantseliarii* (hereafter, *DR*), 4 vols. (St. Petersburg, 1850–55), 1: 8–18.

political position for her son and to carve out an indispensable role for herself in the new political order.

The behavior of the delegation and the response of Marfa Ivanovna and her son show that the Kostroma mission of 1613 was carefully choreographed. The meeting between the two parties followed the protocol of the events leading up to Boris Godunov's ascendance to the throne in 1598 documented by the so-called *Charter of Confirmation*.[11] After Tsar Fedor Ivanovich's death on January 6, 1598, his wife and designated successor, Irina Godunova, refused the throne and took the tonsure in the Novodevichii Monastery. Patriarch Iov called an Assembly of the Land, which unanimously decided to offer the reins of government to Irina's brother, Boris Godunov. After several failed attempts to gain the approval of both sister and brother, on February 21, 1598 Patriarch Iov organized a procession by members of the assembly and common people to the Novodevichii Monastery to press their demand. Following a service for the monastery's patron icon, the Virgin Hodegetria, the procession set out, taking with it crosses and icons, amongst them the miracle-working icons of the Virgin of Vladimir (Muscovite Russia's state icon), the Virgin of the Don, the Virgin painted by Metropolitan Petr of Moscow, the image of the Virgin Hodegetria from the Monastery of the Ascension in the Kremlin, and icons of the Muscovite metropolitan saints Petr, Aleksii, and Iona. Upon their arrival at the Novodevichii Monastery, the nuns came out to meet their visitors at the gate, carrying their own miracle-working image of the Virgin of Smolensk (another Hodegetria icon). Boris Godunov, who resided in the monastery at the time, followed the monastery's patron icon. When he reached the icon of the Virgin of Vladimir, Boris, shedding tears and kneeling before the image, asked why the Virgin had come to the monastery. Blessing him with the life-giving cross, Patriarch Iov told him that the Virgin herself had come to make sure that Boris would listen to the will of God, the Virgin, and the miracle-

---

[11] The *Charter of Confirmation* survives in two copies, dating from July and August 1598 respectively. The July version is published in *Drevniaia Rossiiskaia Vivliofika* (hereafter, *DRV*), ed. Nikolai Novikov, 2nd ed., vol. 7 (Moscow, 1788), III, pp. 36–127. For the August version, see *Akty sobrannye v bibliotekakh i arkhivakh Rossiiskoi imperii Arkheograficheskoiiu ekspeditsieiu Akademii nauk* (hereafter, *AAE*), 4 vols. (St. Petersburg, 1836), vol. 2, no. 7, pp. 16–54. For the dating of the two versions and their differences, see R. G. Skrynnikov, "Zemskii sobor 1598 goda i izbranie Borisa Godunova na tron," *Istoriia SSSR*, no. 3 (1977): 141–57; V. O. Kliuchevskii, *Sochineniia v deviati tomakh*, ed. V. L. Ianin, 9 vols. (Moscow: Mysl', 1990), 8: 323–36; M. N. Tikhomirov, *Rossiiskoe gosudarstvo XV–XVII vekov* (Moscow: Nauka, 1973), 42–69; S. P. Mordovina, "K istorii utverzhdennoi gramoty 1598 g.," *Arkheograficheskii ezhegodnik za 1968 god* (Moscow: Izdatel'stvo Akademii nauk SSSR, 1970), 127–41; L. E. Morozova, *Dva tsaria: Fedor i Boris* (Moscow: Russkoe Slovo, 2001), 238–50; A. A. Zimin, *V kanun groznykh potriasenii: Predposylki pervoi krest'ianskoi voiny v Rossii* (Moscow: Mysl', 1986), 220–33.

workers. The procession then moved to the church of the Virgin Hodegetria in the monastery where the patriarch celebrated the Divine Liturgy.[12]

Following the service the visitors petitioned Boris to become their tsar, but Boris refused and joined his sister in her cell. Taking the true and life-giving cross and the icon of the Virgin painted by Metropolitan Petr with them, Iov and select members of the assembly followed him. They beseeched Irina to allow her brother to become tsar and pressured Boris to assent to their request. After hours of fruitless pleading, the group finally kneeled before Irina and with great wailing implored her not to despise the icons that had come to her in support of the petitioners' request. Unable to withstand the will of these supernatural intercessors, Irina then blessed her brother with the Muscovite tsardom and asked him to abide by her decision. When Boris still refused, Irina turned herself into an intercessor for the delegation, insisting that he obey her wish since it represented God's blessing. This remark finally forced Godunov to comply with the assembly's wishes. The patriarch blessed the future ruler with the life-giving cross and the icon painted by Petr. After a final service in the monastery's church during which Boris once more was blessed with the rule of the entire Muscovite state in the presence of all the miracle-working icons, the procession returned to Moscow.[13]

Five days later, on February 26, Boris made his entry into Moscow. He was met by the people with the traditional honors outside town and accompanied to the Cathedral of the Dormition, where the icon of the Virgin of Vladimir and the relics of Metropolitans Petr, Aleksii, and Iona were housed. After Patriarch Iov celebrated the Divine Liturgy there, and the *polichronion* was sung to Boris, his wife, and children, Boris visited the Cathedral of the Archangel Michael where he kneeled before the coffins of the previous tsars, asking their forgiveness. Then the new tsar moved on to the Cathedral of the Annunciation to venerate the icons there. Following a private meeting with Iov in the Patriarch's Palace during which he received absolution and a meeting with the ecclesiastical hierarchy, Boris returned to his sister in the Novodevichii Monastery where he stayed until Easter. On March 9, at Patriarch Iov's instigation, the assembly agreed to establish the annual veneration of the Virgin Hodegetria because of her assistance in persuading Boris Godunov to accept the throne. The new feast day was supposed to be celebrated with an annual procession with crosses and icons to the Novodevichii Monastery. The patriarch then admonished the members of the assembly to serve the new tsar and his family faithfully and to refrain from any plots or betrayals against them.[14]

---

[12] *DRV*, vol. 7, III, pp. 39–74; *AAE*, vol. 2, no. 7, pp. 19–31.

[13] *DRV*, vol. 7, III, pp. 74–80; *AAE*, vol. 2, no. 7, pp. 31–35.

[14] *DRV*, vol. 7, III, pp. 80–93; *AAE*, vol. 2, no. 7, pp. 35–41. The information in the *Charter of Conformation* is corroborated by a number of contemporary sources; see, for example, *RIB*, vol. 13, 2nd ed.: 13–16 (*Inoe Skazanie*); A. N. Shemakin, ed. "Donesenie o

The protocol of 1598 that directed all petitions regarding a new tsar to both Boris Godunov and his sister provided the framework for the pleading ritual at Kostroma in 1613, which affirmed Russia's commitment to another new ruling dynasty. As in 1598, when Irina figured prominently in Boris Godunov's election to the throne, the Assembly of the Land included Marfa Ivanovna in its plans for a new ruling dynasty from the very outset. The assembly announced its unanimous election of Mikhail Fedorovich in two letters dating from February 1613 to the tsar and "the great mistress, the nun Marfa Ivanovna."[15] This title, "great mistress" (*velikaia gosudarynia*), a female equivalent of the tsar's title "great lord" (*velikii gosudar'*), was applied to a tsaritsa for the first time in the Charter of Confirmation of 1598 to denote Irina Godunova's inherent capacity to rule.[16] Irina herself used the title in charters she issued shortly after her husband's death.[17] The title was later claimed by Mariia Grigor'evna during her regency for her son Fedor Borisovich.[18] By associating this title with Mikhail Fedorovich's mother, the Assembly of the Land in 1613 opened the door for Marfa to assume the position of a royal mother at the Muscovite court endowed with legitimate political rights.

---

poezdke v Moskvu pridvornago Rimskago imperatora Mikhaila Shilia v 1598 godu," *Chteniia v Imperatorskom obshchestve istorii i drevnostei rossiiskikh pri Moskovskom universitete* (hereafter, *ChOIDR*) (1875), bk. 2, sec. IV, pp. 12–16; *Vremennik Ivana Timofeeva* (hereafter, *Vremennik*), ed. V. P. Adrianova-Peretts (Moscow-Leningrad: Izdatel'stvo Akademii nauk SSSR, 1951), 53–60 (original), 219–26 (modern Russian translation); *PSRL*, 14: 50 (*Novyi letopisets*); Massa, *Short History*, 38–42; Konrad Bussow, *Moskovskaia khronika 1584–1613* (Moscow-Leningrad: Izdatel'stvo Akademii nauk SSSR, 1961), 81–83 (Russian translation), 205–07 (German original).

[15] The letters are published in *Sobranie gosudarstvennykh gramot i dogovorov khraniashchikhsia v Gosudarstvennoi kollegii inostrannykh del* (hereafter, *SGGD*), 5 vols. (Moscow, 1813–94), vol. 3, no. 3, pp. 5–11, 10 (formal address to Marfa Ivanovna); also see *DR* 1: 18–31.

[16] The title is used throughout the charter; see for example *DRV*, vol. 7, III, pp. 38, 41, 61, 64, 78; *AAE*, vol. 2, no. 7, pp.19, 25, 28, 29, 30, 32, 33, 34; During Fedor Ivanovich's lifetime Irina only bore the title "tsaritsa"; see, for example, *Dopolneniia k aktam istoricheskim sobrannye i izdannye Arkheograficheskoiu komissieiu*, 12 vols. (St. Petersburg, 1846–72), 1: 235; no. 143, pp. 236–37; V. I. Buganov and M. P. Lukichev, *Posol'skaia kniga po sviaziam Rossii s Gretsiei (pravoslavnymi ierarkhami i monastyriami) 1588–1594 gg.* (Moscow: Institut istorii SSSR AN SSSR, 1988), 53, 54, 58, 59, 83, 92, 135–41. During Fedor Ivanovich's reign Irina was occasionally called "mistress"; see *Posol'skaia kniga*, 89, 133–34.

[17] See, for example, S. P. Mordovina, "Ukaz ob amnistii 1598 goda," *Sovetskie arkhivy*, no. 4 (1970): 86.

[18] G. N. Anpilogov, *Novye dokumenty o Rossii kontsa XVI–nachala XVII v.* (Moscow: Izdatel'stvo Moskovskogo universiteta, 1967), 439, 441, 442–45; *SGGD*, vol. 2, no. 83, pp. 187–88; no. 85, pp. 191–95. Even Mariia Nagaia, the alleged mother of the first False Dmitrii, was addressed as "mistress." See Thyrêt, *Between God and Tsar*, 112.

The fact that the Assembly of the Land in 1613 perceived Marfa's role to be equivalent to that of Irina Godunova in 1598 is also evident in its expectation that the royal mother would act as a facilitator of its request. While the letter to Mikhail Fedorovich tries to persuade him to come to Moscow and to accept the loyalty oath from his subjects, the equivalent note to Marfa pleads with her to have mercy on all Orthodox Christians in the Russian realm and to give her blessing to her son's new position.[19]

The letter to Marfa Ivanovna makes clear that in the eyes of the various social ranks represented in the Assembly of the Land, Mikhail's mother enjoyed tremendous respect. They recognized her personal suffering on account of her family's dynastic position and for her son's sake. Forced to take the veil, she had been separated from her last surviving son when he was four years old.[20] Moreover, the letter reveals that the assembly recognized Marfa Ivanovna's influence in all political decisions concerning her son and appealed to her capacity as a mediator. Significantly, it extended a separate invitation to her to accompany her son to Moscow where she could pursue her spiritual commitment (*podvig*) as a nun in the presence of her son, the new tsar.[21] In the absence of Mikhail's father, Filaret, who was still in Polish captivity, Marfa's cooperation with the assembly was crucial to the successful

---

[19] *SGGD*, vol. 3, no. 3, pp. 5–8; *DR*, 1: 22–23, 29.

[20] Reunited by the first False Dmitrii, Mikhail and Marfa returned to the Kremlin and stayed there until 1612, thus witnessing and possibly acquiescing in the siege of Moscow by the Poles during this time. The fact that Mikhail's father and uncle Ivan had at one point collaborated with the Poles required the Romanovs to distance Mikhail from his physical and political environment in 1612 to assure his viability as a candidate for the Russian throne; see Chester L. Dunning, *Russia's First Civil War: The Time of Troubles and the Founding of the Romanov Dynasty* (University Park: Pennsylvania State University Press, 2001), 441, 445, 453. Mikhail's and Marfa's pilgrimage to Kostroma that year fulfilled this purpose. Kostroma, a participant in the Russian national liberation movement, the seat of which was located in nearby Iaroslavl', lent the young Romanov candidate the correct political aura. Moreover, the pilgrimage fostered the view promoted by the Romanovs that the boy and his mother suffered from the turmoil of the Time of Troubles and were forced to flee from their enemies and lead a peripatetic life. For this myth, see W. Bruce Lincoln, *The Romanovs: Autocrats of All the Russias* (New York: The Dial Press, 1981), 28–29. The correspondence of the Assembly of the Land with Marfa from February 1613 clearly reflects this myth.

The movements of Mikhail Romanov and his mother in 1612/13 are difficult to reconstruct because in the 1620s the Romanovs ordered the purging of embarrassing records and fostered the creation of new historical works that gave the Time of Troubles a new interpretation; on this point, see L. E. Morozova, *Smuta nachala VII v. glazami sovremennikov* (Moscow: RAN, 2000), 263–446. I wish to thank Chester Dunning for sharing with me his insights concerning Marfa's and Mikhail's whereabouts before Mikhail's accession to the throne.

[21] *SGGD*, vol. 3, no. 3, p. 5–10; *DR*, 1: 29.

establishment of a new Muscovite ruling house since the still adolescent candidate for the throne needed to be presented to the realm with the proper genealogical connections. This would legitimize his position and put an end to all dynastic strife for good. The letter to Marfa points out that Mikhail had been elected the next ruler of Russia since he also had kinship ties to the last Rurikide tsar.[22]

All these considerations induced the members of the Assembly of the Land to view Marfa Ivanovna as an integral part of the negotiations surrounding Mikhail Fedorovich's ascendance to the throne. This is further reflected in the assembly's instructions to the delegation to Kostroma dated March 2, 1613, which contain specific details about how and by whom Marfa was to be addressed.[23] The provisions direct both the secular and spiritual leaders of the expedition, Boyar Fedor Ivanovich Sheremetev and the archbishop of Riazan', Feodorit, to make individual appearances before her. Sheremetev was charged with conveying to Marfa the greetings of all social ranks of the Muscovite state and with persuading her son to become tsar to allay his subjects' fears. Moreover, he was to invite her to come to Moscow as well. The archbishop was supposed to point out to Marfa the danger the Orthodox flock in Russia faced if she refused. These stipulations suggest that in the eyes of the Assembly of the Land, Marfa Ivanovna assumed the traditional role of the tsaritsa as dynastic mediator and defender of the Orthodox faith.[24]

The numerous descriptions of the visit of the delegation to Kostroma on March 13–14, 1613, confirm that Marfa Ivanovna was treated with all the privileges of and expectations associated with a traditional tsar mother. Moreover, a study of the ritual of the negotiations suggests that both sides exploited the symbolic aspects of the event to guarantee the most favorable outcome for themselves. For Marfa Ivanovna, the Kostroma delegation represented both an opportunity and a challenge. Kliuchevskii and Platonov, who treat the outcome of the Kostroma visit as a foregone conclusion, are undoubtedly right about Marfa's ambitions for Mikhail Fedorovich. They do not consider, however, that Mikhail's mother, who was very protective of her son, also had to weigh the possible dangers she and Mikhail Fedorovich faced if he accepted the government of a realm that had been rocked by a bloody civil war.[25]

---

[22] *SGGD*, vol. 3, no. 3, p. 10; *DR*, 1: 29; also see *RIB*, 13, 2nd ed.: 129 (*Inoe Skazanie*).

[23] *SGGD*, vol. 3, no. 6, pp. 19–22; *DR*, 1: 38–43.

[24] On this role of the tsaritsy, see Thyrêt, *Between God and Tsar*, 80–117.

[25] Kliuchevskii, *Course in Russian History*, 63–66; S. F. Platonov, *The Time of Troubles: A Historical Study of the Internal Crisis and Social Struggle in Sixteenth- and Seventeenth-Century Muscovy*, trans. John T. Alexander (Lawrence: University Press of Kansas, 1970), 158–61. Skrynnikov takes a more cautious view; see Skrynnikov, *The Time of Troubles*, 271–78. Marfa Ivanovna's protectiveness of her son is understandable insofar as Mikhail Romanov (born in 1596) was her only surviving child out of five boys and

Therefore the negotiations on March 14 represented a ritual that aimed not only to reflect but also to transform the political reality.[26]

The delegation's preparations for its first meeting with the future tsar and his mother after its arrival in Kostroma on March 13 show that the assembly relied on the same principles as its 1598 counterpart to assure the successful outcome of its mission. According to the cellarer of the Trinity-Sergius Monastery, Avraamii Palitsyn, who was amongst the envoys, the delegation had brought from Moscow some of the same icons used in the procession to the Novodevichii Monastery in 1598, namely the icon of the Virgin painted by Metropolitan Petr and the images of the traditional Muscovite protector saints, Metropolitans Peter, Aleksii, and Iona.[27] The presence of these prestigious icons in Kostroma clearly lent the assembly's decision the aura of religious sanction. As in 1598, the delegation's members represented all social groups from various parts of Russia in order to impress on Marfa and her son the wide-ranging approval of Mikhail's election.[28] Moreover, in order to give the meeting a public context, the envoys sought to reenact the 1598 procession to the Novodevichii Monastery. They gathered the local dignitaries of Kostroma and ordered them to accompany them in a religious procession on March 14 to the Ipat'ev Monastery, where Marfa Ivanovna and Mikhail Fedorovich were staying.[29]

The first contact between the delegation of the Assembly of the Land and the chosen tsar's family was crucial insofar as it defined the relationship between subject and ruler in the future. The murder of the first False Dmitrii in 1606 and the forced tonsure of Tsar Vasilii Shuiskii in 1610 had shown that disloyalty on the part of the subjects could endanger the entire Russian political system. This explains the noticeable anxiety in the assembly's instructions to its envoys that all communication with Marfa Ivanovna and her son had to

one daughter. For Marfa's children, see P. Kh. Grebel'skii and A. B. Mirvis, *Dom Romanovykh* (St. Petersburg: GPP imeni Ivana Fedorova Ministerstva pechati i informatsii Rossii, 1992), insert "Rodoslovnoe drevo predkov Romanovykh."

[26] I am using the term "ritual" here in the sense developed by Kay F. Turner; see Kay F. Turner, "Contemporary Feminist Rituals," in *The Politics of Women's Spirituality*, ed. Charlene Spretnak (Garden City, NY: Anchor Press, 1982), 221.

[27] *Skazanie Avraamiia Palitsyna* (hereafter, *Skazanie Avraamiia*), ed. L. V. Cherepnin (Moscow-Leningrad: Izdatel'stvo Akademii nauk SSSR, 1955), 233; also see *DR*, 1: 53. For the icons used in 1598, see *DRV*, vol. 7, III, pp. 66–67, 71; *AAE*, vol. 2, no. 7, pp. 29, 30.

[28] *RIB*, 13, 2nd ed: 129 (*Inoe Skazanie*); *DR* 1: 17–18. The *Charter of Confirmation* mentions the participation of all social ranks in the procession to the Novodevichii Monastery as well; see *DRV*, vol. 7, III, pp. 67, 72; *AAE*, vol. 2, no. 7, pp. 29, 30.

[29] *SGGD*, vol. 3, no. 10, p. 39; *DR*, 1: 53. Avraamii mentions the participation of many local men, women, and children in the procession; see *Skazanie Avraamiia*, 234. The presence of women and children in 1598 is attested in *DRV*, vol. 7, III, p. 67; *AAE*, vol. 2, no. 7, p. 37.

proceed according to previously determined rules. In order to avoid any suspicion of disrespect, the messengers applied the pleading ritual of 1598 to Mikhail Fedorovich and his mother.

As in 1598, the ritual proceeded in stages starting with Mikhail and Marfa meeting the crowd that had come with icons and crosses to the monastic gate. After politely inquiring about Mikhail's and Marfa's health, the delegation presented the decision of the Assembly of the Land and petitioned Marfa and her son to accept it. According to the delegation's report to the assembly regarding Mikhail Fedorovich's acceptance of the throne, Marfa and her son initially refused to consider the petition "with anger and with tears" and rejected the messengers' repeated pleas to follow the procession to the Cathedral of the Life-Giving Trinity. Mikhail insisted that he never wanted to be tsar, and his mother refused to give her blessing to the assembly's plan.[30] After many attempts the two eventually agreed for decorum's sake to follow the procession into the cathedral after receiving the blessing of the archpriest and crossing themselves before the icons.[31]

The initial phase of the Kostroma ritual by and large copied its 1598 counterpart. The procession with icons and crosses, the encounter at the monastic gate, the initial refusal by the royal candidate and his insistence that he never had thought of being tsar, and the transfer of the scene of the action to the monastery's church are all formal elements of the pleading ritual.[32] The striking exception is Marfa Ivanovna's appearance in the early stage of the ritual. While Irina Godunova stayed hidden in the confines of her monastic cell, the nun Marfa assumed a much more public role by taking part in the welcoming ceremony.[33]

Marfa Ivanova's desire to expand the ritual role assigned to her at Kostroma becomes even more evident in the following stage. After the church service the messengers delivered the letters and oral addresses of the assembly and resumed their pleading. Following Mikhail's renewed refusal to become tsar, the delegation implored his mother to have mercy on the Russian subjects and come to Moscow so that their enemies would be intimidated. Another angry refusal by mother and son was accompanied by declarations that they had no designs on the Russian tsardom and by references to the recent political troubles. Marfa's reply in particular was designed to impress on

---

[30] *SGGD*, vol. 3, no. 10, p. 40; *DR*, 1: 53–54; *Skazanie Avraamiia*, 234. A detailed description of the event is also given in *SGGD*, vol. 1, no. 203, pp. 618–30 (*Charter confirming Mikhail Fedorovich's Election* from May 1613).

[31] *SGGD*, vol. 3, no. 10, p. 40; *DR*, 1: 54; *RIB*, 13, 2nd ed.: 1240 (*Skazanie Avraamiia*).

[32] *DRV*, vol. 7, III, pp. 71–73; *AAE*, vol. 2, no. 7, pp. 30–31. In 1598, Boris's declaration that he never dreamed of becoming tsar occurred soon after Irina's tonsure; see *DRV*, vol. 7, III, p. 43; *AAE*, vol. 2, no. 7, p. 21.

[33] On Irina's confinement to her cell, see *DRV*, vol. 7, III, pp. 74–75; *AAE*, vol. 2, no. 7, p. 31.

those assembled the extent of the sacrifice she and her son would be making were they to comply with their request. Marfa told the petitioners that the turmoil in Russia was their own fault because they had broken their loyalty oaths to the previous tsar, Vasilii Shuiskii. Questioning how anybody could be tsar under these circumstances, she pointed out that her approval of her son's accession to the throne would be synonymous with his destruction.[34]

After her frank expression of displeasure Marfa at least allowed the possibility that she eventually might consider the assembly's decision. But since her ex-husband Filaret was still in a Polish prison, she claimed she was unable to act at the present time since such a step might endanger his life, and, in any case, required his blessing.[35] Realizing the opening in the negotiations, the messengers renewed their pleas and promised that all Muscovites were ready to swear their loyalty to Mikhail Fedorovich and to give their lives for him. They pointed out that in contrast to Tsar Vasilii Shuiskii's selection, Mikhail Fedorovich's choice as ruler had been unanimous.[36] With regard to Marfa's concerns about Filaret, they brought the news that envoys had already been sent to the King of Poland to negotiate his release from prison. In spite of all these assurances, however, Marfa and her son remained unmoved.[37]

Marfa's role in the second stage of the pleading ritual finds no counterpart in 1598. Irina did not participate in the exchange between the petitioners and the royal candidate immediately after the church service. Moreover, if she was concerned about Boris Godunov's future, as is implied in the first version of the *Charter of Confirmation*, she never openly expressed it.[38] Marfa, on the

---

[34] *SGGD*, vol. 3, no. 10, p. 41; *DR*, 1: 54–58; *Skazanie Avraamiia*, 234. The *Charter confirming Mikhail Fedorovich Romanov's Election*, which was drawn up two months after the Kostroma events and thus expressed the official Romanov position, adds that Marfa was also concerned about her son's youth and the destruction of resources in the Russian land; see *SGGD*, vol. 1, no. 203, p. 621. While the official version of the Kostroma mission elevated Marfa's prestige as tsar mother by ascribing to her the traditional traits of a tsaritsa—care for the wellbeing of royal children and the realm at large—sources dated more closely to the event depict Marfa as primarily concerned with the political risks associated with her son's ascendance to the throne. Mikhail Fedorovich's age and the economic situation of Muscovy were less a concern for her than the loyalty of her son's future subjects. On the association of the tsaritsy with the wellbeing of royal children and the realm, see Thyrêt, *Between God and Tsar*, 39–45, 47–79.

[35] *SGGD*, vol. 3, no. 10, p. 42; *DR*, 1: 58.

[36] G. Edward Orchard, who notes the validity of other candidates to the Russian throne, such as the Swedish Prince Karl Philipp, points out that the election result was not as unanimous as claimed in later sources associated with the Romanov court; see G. Edward Orchard, "The Election of Michael Romanov," *Slavonic and East European Review* 67: 3 (July 1989): 378–402.

[37] *SGGD*, vol. 3, no. 10, p. 43; *DR*, 1: 58–61.

[38] *DRV*, vol. 7, III, p. 86.

other hand, did not spare words pointing out the magnitude of the sacrifice the delegation expected both from her and her son. This heightened sense of sacrifice explains the expressions of anger absent in the 1598 protocol. Marfa's frankness regarding the past treasonous activities of her future subjects and her bold assertion of their untrustworthiness are without precedent. On the whole, Marfa's flamboyant behavior in the second stage of the pleading ritual attests to her desire to assume a much more visible role in political life than Irina and other previous tsaritsy had enjoyed.

As in 1598, the delegation conducted the final stage of the pleading process in private. Moving to Marfa's and Mikhail's living quarters, it repeated promises that the Muscovites would welcome Mikhail and Marfa with icons and crosses for many hours. Unable to persuade the pair, the messengers played their final card by appealing to Marfa's obligation as a tsar mother to act as a spiritual intercessor for the realm and a defender of the faith. They entreated mother and son to consider that if they continued to refuse their request, they would be responsible for the destruction of the realm and the eclipse of the Orthodox faith in Russia by Latinism, a reference to the threat of Polish interests in Russia. Conjuring up images of how relics and icons would be cursed, the envoys made it impossible for the royal mother and son to insist on their position.[39] According to Avraamii Palitsyn, Marfa Ivanovna still persisted in her view, though. In his last desperate attempt to move her, Avraamii and the archbishop of Riazan' raised the icons of the Virgin and saints Petr, Aleksii, and Iona before Marfa's eyes. They then reminded Marfa that these icons had come all the way from Moscow to petition that Mikhail Fedorovich become tsar. He and his mother ought to understand that God himself had chosen Mikhail Fedorovich as the next ruler of Russia and that with their refusal they offended these religious images. These words finally are said to have softened Marfa's stance. She led her son to the icon of the Virgin and placed his fate into her hands. After she had given her blessing to her son's accession to the throne, the delegation invested him with the life-giving cross and the scepter. Following a liturgical service in which the assembled sang the *polichronion* to the new tsar, he gave his first audience in which he announced his and his mother's imminent arrival in Moscow.[40]

Although Marfa's role in the final stage of the pleading ritual imitates that of Irina Godunova in 1598, it deviated from that of the latter in several respects. Like Irina, Marfa was sensitive to the mediation of supernatural powers, which caused her to offer up her son to the Virgin on behalf of the delega-

---

[39] *SGGD*, vol. 3, no. 10, p. 44; *DR*, 1: 61–64; also see *PSRL*,14, pt. 1: 129 (*Novyi letopisets*). For the final stage of the pleading ritual in 1598, see *DRV*, vol. 7, III, pp. 73–79; *AAE*, vol. 2, no. 7, pp. 31–34.

[40] *Skazanie Avraamiia*, 234–35; *SGGD*, vol. 3, no. 10, pp. 44–45; *DR*, 1: 64–66. Avraamii's statement is corroborated by Mikhail Fedorovich's letter to the authorities in Moscow from Iaroslavl' dating from March 23, 1613; see *DR*, 1: 76–77.

tion.[41] But the reference to the threat of the defamation of icons and relics in 1613 places a burden of responsibility for the wellbeing of the realm on the future tsar mother that was not associated with Irina. Moreover, Mikhail Fedorovich's acquiescence in his mother's final decision contrasts starkly with Boris Godunov's initial refusal to accept the changed mind of his sister and shows that Marfa was much more in charge of the events than her female counterpart in 1598.[42]

The prominent role Marfa Ivanovna assumed in the Kostroma negotiations foreshadowed the significance the future Romanov regime attributed to her status as tsar mother. Chronicles and court records from the period of the first two Romanov tsars identify "the great mistress, nun Marfa Ivanovna" as the focal point of the Kostroma mission.[43] The eyewitness account of Avraamii Palitsyn states that in its ritual entreaties to Mikhail and his mother, the delegation addressed Marfa first and that the delegation had a harder time persuading the royal mother than Mikhail Fedorovich to agree to the assembly's decision. [44] *The Charter confirming Mikhail Fedorovich Romanov's Election* also stresses that the success of the delegation's mission depended on its ability to enlist the tsar mother's support first. The charter, which contains direct appeals by Fedor Ivanovich Sheremetev and his companions and by the crowd participating in the ritual, notes that Marfa reluctantly granted the messengers' petition after their appeal to the holy icons. Marfa is said to have demanded that the Muscovites pray for the future tsar and swear not to recognize another ruler, especially one of Polish descent.[45] After receiving the required assurances, Marfa herself interceded on the assembly's behalf with her son and eventually convinced him that he must obey the will of God.[46]

In view of the fact that the charter was drawn up after Mikhail Fedorovich's accession to the throne and thus expressed the official Romanov version of the event, the discrepancy with Avraamii's eyewitness account can be explained by the Romanovs' desire to make the tsar mother's role even more

---

[41] *DRV*, vol. 7, III, pp. 76–77; *AAE*, vol. 2, no. 7, pp. 33–34.

[42] *DRV*, vol. 7, III, p. 78; *AAE*, vol. 2, no. 7, p. 34.

[43] See, for example, the *Novyi letopisets* (*PSRL*, 14, pt. 1: 129) and the so-called *Book of State* (*Gosudarstvennaia kniga*) in *SGGD*, vol. 3, no. 1, p. 4; *DR*, 1: 64–65. Letters from the Assembly of the Land to Mikhail Fedorovich and the leaders of the Kostroma delegation written sometime after March 23, 1613 give Mikhail's mother credit for the successful negotiations; see *DR*, 1, Prilozheniia, no. 8, cols. 1057–64; no. 9, cols. 1065–71. Similar statements are included in letters by the Assembly of the Land to Mikhail Fedorovich and Marfa Ivanovna in Iaroslavl'; see *DR*, 1, Prilozheniia, nos. 10–11, cols. 1071–82.

[44] *Skazanie Avraamiia*, 235.

[45] *SGGD*, vol. 1, no. 203, pp. 621, 626 (appeals to Marfa); vol. 1, no. 203, pp. 628–29 (assurances for Marfa).

[46] *SGGD*, vol. 1, no. 203, pp. 629–30.

explicit. Strikingly, the charter achieves this purpose by attributing to Marfa Ivanovna Patriarch Iov's admonition to the elite in the 1598 protocol to swear loyalty to the new Russian ruler and disregard any other candidates for the throne.[47] The charter also borrows the theme of Marfa pleading with her son on behalf of the delegation from the 1598 precedent, resulting in a more active image of both the tsar candidate and his mother.[48] The tendency to heighten Marfa's role as intercessor is also expressed in other later renditions of the event, such as in the *1617 Khronograf*, the *Inoe Skazanie*, and the *Novyi letopisets*, which hold that during the pleading ritual the petitioners kneeled before Marfa Ivanovna and shed tears.[49]

The interpretation of the Kostroma mission in the sources dating from a time after Mikhail Romanov's accession to the throne suggests that the pleading ritual was viewed from different perspectives by the Muscovite delegation and the Romanov party. The representatives of the Assembly of the Land used the negotiations primarily as a means to convey to Marfa and her son the latest political decision of the country. Through their ritual self-humiliation and invocation of God's will, they merely reasserted the major principles of the Muscovite autocracy, the tsar's complete power over his subjects and the religious sanction of his position. While for the messengers the pleading ritual represented Muscovite political reality, its meaning for Marfa Ivanovna (and her son) was much more complex. Aware that the messengers' speeches had been determined and rehearsed before their arrival in Kostroma, Marfa approached the pleading ritual as a means to gain leverage for her son and to assure her own inclusion in the new political order. If she was pleased that her years of suffering would finally pay off, the dynastic instability caused by the Time of Troubles must have filled her with caution about the assembly's decision. A letter she sent in the aftermath of the Kostroma mission from Iaroslavl' to the Assembly of the Land reinforces this notion. In the letter, dated March 23, 1613, Marfa insisted on guarantees that the treasonous activities resulting in the forced tonsure of Tsar Vasilii Shuiskii and his wife, the murder of Tsar Fedor Borisovich Godunov and his mother, Mariia Grigor'evna, and the shameful treatment of Fedor's sister Kseniia never were to repeat themselves.[50] In order to impress on the Muscovites the seriousness of her concerns, Marfa inserted into the pleading ritual reproaches and demands that forced the delegation to come face to face with the failures of the Muscovite political elite during the Time of Troubles and to affirm its commitment to the new dynasty. At every stage of the petitioning process, her stipulations

---

[47] *DRV*, vol. 7, III, pp. 89–93; *AAE*, vol. 2, no. 7, pp. 38–41.

[48] *DRV*, vol. 7, III, pp. 78–79; *AAE*, vol. 2, no. 7, p. 34.

[49] *RIB*, 13, 2nd ed.: 1319–20 (*Khronograf*), 129 (*Inoe skazanie*); *PSRL*, 14, pt. 1: 130 (*Novyi letopisets*).

[50] *SGGD*, vol. 3, no. 11, p. 53; *DR*, 1: 83–84; on Fedor Borisovich and his mother, see Thyrêt, *Between God and Tsar*, 103–07.

became more specific. In the end she not only gained assurances concerning the Muscovites' loyalty to her son and efforts to set her husband free, but she also made sure that the new dynasty would share in the religious sanction of the Rurikides.

By representing her son's interests in the Kostroma negotiations, Marfa Ivanovna availed herself of an opportunity to formulate her own role in the new royal family. As a nun she would never receive the title "tsaritsa" that was reserved for the wives of Muscovite rulers. Nevertheless, she had all intentions to claim the privileges and prestige of a tsar mother. The pleading ritual enabled her to style herself as a mediator between the Muscovite subjects and their future tsar. Symbolically her consent guaranteed the restoration of traditional autocratic rule and dynastic cohesion. At the same time, the envoys' insistence on the religious implications of her decision also provided Marfa with an opportunity to assume the role of defender of the Orthodox faith traditionally accorded to the Muscovite tsaritsy.

Marfa Ivanovna's intentions to assume a visible role at her son's side in the new Muscovite political order are also evident in her letter from Iaroslavl' to the Assembly of the Land on March 23, 1613. By greeting all ranks of the assembly and recounting the details of the Kostroma mission, she affirmed her new position as "mistress of the realm."[51] In particular she pointed to the fact that the delegation had come to her with icons and had petitioned her to bless her son's accession to the royal throne. Reminding the Muscovites of the huge sacrifice she had made for their sake, she again stated her expectation that they would kiss the cross to her son honestly, reject any pretenders, and stop violence in Moscow and other cities of the realm. The letter concludes with specific information concerning her trip to Moscow.[52]

The journey of the newly elected tsar and his mother from Kostroma to Moscow served to underscore Marfa Ivanovna's significance as "mistress of all Russia." According to Avraamii Palitsyn, who accompanied mother and son, Marfa participated in the ritual greeting by the inhabitants of Iaroslavl', who thereby expressed their acceptance of Mikhail Fedorovich as tsar. Members of all ranks, accompanied by their wives and children, met the new lord and mistress with crosses and icons and offered them the traditional bread and gifts as a sign of their hospitality.[53] From Iaroslavl' Marfa and her son pilgrimaged to monasteries in Rostov and Pereslavl-Zalesskii in order to venerate icons and miracle-working relics there. They eventually proceeded to the Trinity-Sergius Monastery, where Avraamii Palitsyn with Arkhimandrite Dionisii and their brothers received the tsar and his mother at the monastic gate. Marfa attended the liturgy in the Cathedral of the Holy Trinity and crossed herself before the famous icon of the Trinity and the relics of the

---

[51] *SGGD*, vol. 3, no. 12, pp. 50–51; *DR*, 1: 78.

[52] *SGGD*, vol. 3, no. 12, pp. 53–54; *DR*, 1: 87–88.

[53] *RIB*, 13, 2nd ed.: 1243; *PSRL*, 14, pt. 1: 130 (*Novyi letopisets*).

traditional protector saints of the Muscovite tsars, Sergius and Nikon. Following a week's stay in the monastery where mother and son demonstrated their royal generosity through alms-giving, the two set out for the final stretch of their trip, which was frequently interrupted by further ceremonial receptions.[54]

Marfa and her son finally arrived in Moscow on the second Sunday after Easter.[55] As in Iaroslavl', people of all ranks met Marfa Ivanovna and Mikhail Fedorovich outside the city gate and led them into the Kremlin in a procession.[56] According to the memoirs of Archbishop Arsenios Elasonis, Marfa Ivanovna received the same treatment during the ritual welcome as her son. Arsenios recalled that the archpriests approached her with holy icons and blessed her, and that the people bowed to her.[57] When, as a sign of his introduction to the political and spiritual center of power, Mikhail Fedorovich was led into the Kremlin cathedrals, Marfa stayed by her son's side. In the Cathedral of the Dormition the two kissed miracle-working icons and the relics of the traditional protector saints of the Russian tsars, saints Peter and Iona.[58] From there they proceeded to the Cathedral of the Archangel Michael to greet the new tsar's Rurikide relatives who lay buried there. Again Marfa participated in the ritual acquaintance of her son with his ancestors by embracing the images and tombs of the previous Muscovite rulers. The procession concluded with a visit by Marfa and Mikhail to the Cathedral of the Annunciation, where they worshipped the icons housed there.[59]

Marfa Ivanovna's participation in the Muscovites' welcoming ceremony for the new tsar created the impression that the new royal mother of the realm would be a force to reckon with. Marfa's decision to accompany her son to Moscow and share in the welcoming rituals stands in stark contrast to the 1598 precedent where Boris left his sister in the Novodevichii Monastery and visited Moscow on his own.[60] The *Pskov Chronicle* explains Marfa's active

[54] *Skazanie Avraamiia*, 236.

[55] *PSRL*, 14, pt. 1: 130 (*Novyi letopisets*); also see *DR*, 1: 89.

[56] *PSRL*, 14, pt. 1: 131 (*Novyi letopisets*), 34: 219 (*Piskarev Chronicle*); *DR*, 1: 89; *RIB*, 13, 2nd ed.: 1245.

[57] A. Dmitrievskii, *Arkhiepiskop Elasonskii Arsenii i memuary ego iz russkoi istorii po rukopisi trapezuntskago sumeliiskago monastyria* (Kiev, 1899), 176.

[58] Dmitrievskii, *Arkhiepiskop*, 176; *Skazanie Avraamiia*, 237. The Cathedral of the Dormition housed the most famous of Russia's miracle-working icons, the image of the Virgin of Vladimir. Already Ivan IV had prayed to this icon before his Kazan campaign in 1552; see *PSRL*, 29: 78–80 (*Letopisets nachala tsarstva*).

[59] Dmitrievskii, *Arkhiepiskop*, 176; *Skazanie Avraamiia*, 237.

[60] Boris made his first appearance in the Kremlin as a ruler on February 26, 1598. On April 1, 1598 he settled there permanently with his wife, Mariia Grigor'eva, and his children Fedor and Kseniia; see *DRV*, vol. 7, III, pp. 80–86; 100–03; *AAE*, vol. 2, no. 7, pp. 36–37.

involvement in the affairs of the realm, noting that due to the tsar's youth and lack of experience, "his God-loving mother, the great nun Marfa, governed under him and maintained the realm with her kin because his father was still in the captivity of the Polish king."[61]

Marfa's perceived prominence in the political arena seems to have continued even after her ex-husband's return to Moscow, although possibly Filaret curtailed the influence of Marfa's natal kinsmen.[62] The 17th-century government official Ivan Timofeev mentions that God, who had entrusted the autocracy to Mikhail Fedorovich, intended both his father and mother to be part of the reconstruction of Russia because of their piety and nobility.[63] The "great petitioner," as Timofeev calls her, lost no time to take advantage of the opportunity the Assembly of the Land offered her when it invited her to come to Moscow.[64] In Timofeev's words, she manipulated her close attachment to her son to gain dominance over him "by ruling with him, even if it is strange, but she is his mother."[65] The tsar's filial loyalty to his mother manifested itself in a number of political favors to people who had supported her during the Time of Troubles.[66]

Marfa Ivanovna seems to have expanded the role of tsar mother at court by engaging in a variety of both private and public administrative activities. Like some of Ivan IV's ex-wives and daughters-in-law, who after their tonsure managed and maintained large holdings, Marfa Ivanovna owned lands of her own and exercised rights of justice over the peasants living on them.[67] Charters she issued to the Monastery of the Epiphany in Uglich in 1629 and 1630 show that she owned patrimonial lands and freely donated them to assist the reconstruction of the monastery after the Time of Troubles.[68] The tsar mother also had her own governor (*voevoda*) in the town of Meshchovsk, who handled disturbances amongst her peasants.[69] At the same time Marfa Ivan-

---

[61] *PL*, 1: 131.

[62] Bakhrushin, "Politicheskie tolki," 95.

[63] *Vremennik*, 165 (original), 344 (modern translation).

[64] *Vremennik*, 166 (original), 345 (modern translation).

[65] *Vremennik*, 161 (original) 339 (modern translation).

[66] *AI*, vol. 3, no. 151, pp. 245–49.

[67] On Ivan's ex-wives and daughters-in-law, see Isolde Thyrêt, "The Royal Women of Ivan IV's Family and the Meaning of Forced Tonsure," in *Servants of the Dynasty: Palace Women in World History*, ed. Anne Walthall (Berkeley: University of California Press, 2008), 159–71.

[68] "Uglichskii Bogoiavlenskii zhenskii monastyr'," *Iaroslavskiia eparkhial'nyia vedomosti*, no. 12, 21 March 1873, unofficial part, 100–02; no. 10, 7 March 1873, unofficial part, 79–81. In return for her contribution Marfa Ivanovna asked the nuns to pray for the tsar and his family and to place her daughter Tat'iana's name into the memorial registers of their institution. On Marfa's land holding, also see *Slovo i delo*, vol. 1, no. 6, p. 7.

[69] *Slovo i delo*, vol. 1, no. 26, pp. 27–28.

ovna maintained an official correspondence much like the previous "great mistresses" Irina Godunova and Mariia Grigor'evna. Marfa even used her own seal. One of her letters dating from 1614, which still shows black wax remnants in the place where the seal was attached, contains the note: "The mistress and great nun Marfa Ivanovna ordered that her seal be affixed to this charter."[70] In the document Marfa granted the return of two new settlers to the Paisiev Monastery. In another instance she settled a property dispute to bolster the interests of the Romanov dynasty. Rather than returning the land in question to its legitimate owners, whose loyalty to the Romanovs was dubious, she gave it to the Novospasskii Monastery, which later became a final resting place for members of the Romanov family.[71]

The Romanov matriarch also increased her visibility by involving herself in public pious activities that were meant to proclaim God's approval of the Romanov dynasty and therefore strengthen its legitimacy. Like previous tsaritsy, she accompanied Mikhail Fedorovich on numerous pilgrimages to the shrines of the Russian tsars' traditional protector saints and thus acted as a spiritual intercessor for the well-being of her son and of the realm at large.[72] Moreover, Marfa Ivanovna participated in the generous alms-giving of her family to leaders of the Eastern Orthodox church.[73] She developed a particularly close relationship with Feofan, Patriarch of Jerusalem.[74]

Marfa's desire to increase the visibility of her role as tsar mother is also evident in the inclusion of her name in the liturgical commemoration of the Romanov dynasty. The practice of mentioning a royal woman in the *polichronion* and the litanies had only been established in 1598 with the "great mistress" Irina Godunova.[75] Similarly, after Mikhail Fedorovich's marriage to Mariia Dolgorukaia on September 19, 1624, Marfa Ivanovna's name was

[70] *AI*, vol. 3, no. 45, p. 40. Similar notes can be found in Marfa Ivanovna's charters to the Monastery of the Epiphany in Uglich dating from 1629 and 1630; see "Uglichskii Bogoiavlenskii zhenskii monastyr'," *Iaroslavskiia eparkhial'nyia vedomosti*, no. 12, 21 March 1873, unofficial part, 100–02; no. 10, 7 March 1873, unofficial part, 101, 102.

[71] Mikhail Fedorovich and Aleksei Mikhailovich both upheld Marfa's decision. See *ChOIDR*, 1915, no. 2, section I, no. 124, pp. 381–82; and no. 125, p. 382. For Marfa Ivanovna's patronage of the Novospasskii Monastery, see Arkhimandrit Leonid, "Vkladnaia kniga Moskovskago Novospasskago monastyria," *Pamiatniki drevnei pis'mennosti i iskusstva* 39 (1883): 19–23.

[72] Arkheograficheskaia komissiia, ed., *Pis'ma russkikh gosudarei i drugikh osob tsarskago semeistva*, vol. 1 (Moscow, 1848), no. 8, p. 11; no. 10, p. 12; no. 76, p. 73; no. 79, pp. 74–75; no. 91, p. 82; no. 124, pp. 103–4; no. 37, p. 47; no. 63, pp. 63–64.

[73] N. F. Kapterev, "Snosheniia ierusalimskikh patriarkhov s russkim pravitel'stvom s poloviny XVI do kontsa XVIII stoletiia," *Pravoslavnyi palestinskii sbornik* 15, no. 1 (1895): 53–55.

[74] Kapterev, "Snosheniia," 58–59.

[75] *AAE*, vol. 2, no. 1, pp. 1–6.

inscribed into the prayer lists along with the names of the tsar and his new wife. In a letter to the clergy of Velikii Ustiug, the metropolitan of Rostov, Varlaam, noted the stipulation of Filaret, who had become Patriarch of Russia in 1619, that Marfa's name be mentioned in the Great Litany during vespers after those of the patriarch, Metropolitan Varlaam, and the tsar, and his wife Mariia. During compline and vigils she was to be commemorated in the liturgy after prayers for the tsar, tsaritsa, all Orthodox princes, Filaret, Varlaam, and all church servants, and in the Divine Liturgy her name was to be mentioned after the tsaritsa's.[76] The inclusion of Marfa Ivanovna in the liturgical prayers together with the tsar, his wife, and his father, the patriarch, created the impression of a sanctified dynasty in which both the male and female sides bore the signs of distinction. At the same time it also elevated Marfa's status as tsar mother, disregarding the fact that she never had been a royal spouse.

Marfa Ivanovna's efforts to strengthen her family's dynastic claims by stressing its pious and God-pleasing aspects is also reflected in her involvement in the establishment of the cult of several "national" icons. The contemporary *Novyi letopisets* ascribes to the Romanov matriarch the leading role in instituting the feast day of the icon of the Virgin Fedorovskaia, which was traditionally kept in the Church of the Dormition of the Virgin in Kostroma. According to the chronicle, the delegation of the Assembly of the Land took this icon to the Ipat'ev Monastery on March 14, 1613. The icon is said to have been influential in swaying the tsar mother's opinion. For this reason those involved in the Kostroma negotiations instituted the feast of this miracle-working icon after the royal mother and her son accepted the assembly's decision.[77] After Mikhail Fedorovich's accession to the throne, a copy of the Fedorovskaia icon was brought to Moscow. There it was kept in the Church of the Birth of the Virgin in the Kremlin and celebrated by the royal family every year on March 13, in commemoration of the delegation's arrival in Kostroma.[78] During a visit to Kostroma in September 1619, Mikhail Fedorovich

---

[76] *AAE*, vol. 3, no. 157, pp. 222–24.

[77] *PSRL*, 14, pt. 1: 130.

[78] For the cult of this icon, see Andreas Ebbinghaus, *Die altrussischen Marienikonen-Legenden*, Veröffentlichungen der Abteilung für slavische Sprachen und Literaturen des Osteuropa-Instituts [Slavisches Seminar] an der Freien Universität Berlin, vol. 70 (Berlin: Otto Harrassowitz, 1990), 22. The Romanov tsars celebrated the feast day of this image regularly; see Arkheograficheskaia komissia, ed., *Vykhody gosudarei tsarei i velikikh kniazei, Mikhaila Feodorovicha, Aleksiia Mikhailovicha, Feodora Aleksievicha, vseia Rusii samoderzhtsev (s 1632 po 1682 god)* (Moscow, 1844), 11, 28, 46, 60, 91, 100, 118, 127, 152, 202, 225, 239, 255, 178, 309, 325, 349, 372, 391, 414, 435, 456, 475, 488, 511, 545, 568, 592, 652. For a detailed description of a copy of the "Virgin Fedorovskaia" from the tsar's school of icon painting, see V. I. Antonova and N. E. Mneva, *Katalog drevnerusskoi zhivopisi XI – nachala XVIII vv.*, 2 vols. (Moscow: Iskusstvo, 1963), 2: 364–65, no. 855.

and his mother attended an all-night service in honor of the Fedorovskaia icon.[79] The *Novyi letopisets* also credits Marfa Ivanovna with instituting the veneration of the image of the Virgin of Kazan', which according to popular belief helped Dmitrii Mikhailovich Pozharskii retake the Kremlin from the Poles in 1612. According to the chronicle, Marfa Ivanovna and her son ordered the yearly celebration of the icon on July 8, to commemorate the appearance of the miracle-working image in Kazan', and on October 22, the day of Moscow's liberation.[80]

Marfa's association with the establishment of feast days of patron icons of the Romanov dynasty served as yet another example of the royal mother's conscious exploitation of opportunities presented by the events of 1598 to expand her own role in the process. In particular, the new cult of the Virgin Fedorovskaia parallels that of the Virgin Hodegetria established in the aftermath of the 1598 procession to the Novodevichii Monastery to celebrate Boris Godunov's acceptance of the Russian throne.[81] While the institution of the latter cult came at the suggestion of the Patriarch Iov, Marfa appropriated the role of the spiritual head of the Russian Orthodox Church in the former.

An examination of Marfa Ivanovna's function in the accession of her son Mikhail Fedorovich to the throne and thereafter at the Romanov court suggests that the matriarch of the new royal dynasty consciously expanded her role as tsar mother. The findings clearly provide a corrective to the demonization of the Romanov matriarch in the historical literature as an unintelligent woman in love with intrigue and power. Nevertheless, Marfa's expansion of the traditional role of the tsar mother helps explain her negative image. Aware of the fact that the Muscovite political elite modeled the events around the tsar's election in 1613 after those leading to Boris Godunov's elevation to tsar in 1598, Marfa Ivanovna, who lacked the credentials of a tsar's wife, used the opportunity not only to claim the status Tsaritsa Irina Godunova had enjoyed in 1598 but to improve on it. The pleading ritual of Kostroma, modeled after its antecedent of February 21, 1598, at the Novodevichii Monastery, shows that Marfa was granted and accepted the title "great mistress" assigned to Irina Godunova to indicate her status as legitimate successor to her late husband, Fedor Ivanovich. Like Irina, Marfa Ivanovna appeared as a defendant of the royal candidate's interests and a mediator between him and the petitioning party. At the same time Marfa interpreted Irina's ritual role in 1598 in a way that increased her visibility both physically and politically. Marfa refused to be confined in her private quarters and preferred to be at her son's side during all the stages of the ritual. Moreover, during the negotia-

[79] *Pis'ma russkikh gosudarei*, vol. 1, nos. 23–24, pp. 32–33.

[80] *PSRL*, 14, pt. 1: 132–33. Processions in honor of the Virgin of Kazan' took place first in 1621. Aleksei Mikhailovich decreed the celebration of this icon in the entire Russian realm in 1649; see Ebbinghaus, *Marienikonenlegenden*, 40–41; *AAE*, vol. 4, no. 40, p. 61.

[81] *DRV*, vol. 7, III, p. 88; *AAE*, vol. 2, no. 7, p. 38.

tions Marfa went far beyond the mediating role of Irina Godunova by blaming the political elite for Russia's political crisis and rebuking it for its lack of loyalty to past rulers. As a result, the Romanov matriarch appears as a visible defender of the interests of the new dynasty and of the realm as a whole.

The expansion of the tsar mother's role is also evident in the events leading up to Mikhail Fedorovich's coronation and beyond. Throughout Mikhail Fedorovich's reign, Marfa Ivanovna carefully manipulated the country's need for a stable government to negotiate a strong position for her son and to increase her own visibility in the new political landscape. On the one hand she achieved this by appropriating the traditional role of the tsaritsa sanctioned by religious ritual and myth. Like previous tsars' wives, Marfa Ivanovna helped foster the creation of a pious image for the tsar's family by undertaking arduous pilgrimages, engaging in charitable activities, and having her name inscribed into the prayer books. But the matriarch of the Romanov dynasty did not merely aspire to the accepted status of a tsaritsa but rather used her prestige to enhance her role as tsar mother. In contrast to Irina Godunova, who remained in her monastic cell after her brother's ascendance to the throne, Marfa Ivanovna accompanied her son to Moscow and participated in all the rituals associated with the welcoming of a new ruler. Following the examples of previous "great mistresses" and royal women subjected to the tonsure just like herself, Marfa claimed administrative and economic freedoms in the emerging Romanov regime. She even went as far as claiming the moral authority of the patriarch of the Russian church, as her insistence on the Muscovites' loyalty to her son displayed in the pleading ritual at Kostroma and her promotion of several icons associated with Russia's revival under the Romanovs shows. In all these instances Marfa coupled her efforts for the sake of the autocracy with her own goal to be viewed as a visible, integral part of the Romanovs' dynastic scheme and thus shaped the role of the future Romanov tsar mothers in the 17th century and beyond.

Служебная деятельность бояр в XVII веке[1]

О.Е. Кошелева и Б.Н. Морозов

Основной обязанностью и одновременно привилегией лиц, имевших думный чин, являлось их участие в царском совете. Кроме того, они несли военную и гражданскую службы, совмещение которых было характерным для управленческого аппарата феодального государства. Бояре, как первый думный чин, занимали места высшего руководства, считавшиеся наиболее престижными. Они осуществляли командование армией, во главу Большого, Передового и Сторожевого полков воеводами ставились только бояре и наиболее знатные из окольничих. Их деятельность контролировалась Разрядным и Тайным приказами, куда они должны были присылать подробнейшие отписки о ходе военных кампаний. Планы крупных военных манёвров обсуждались всей Думой,

---

[1] Этот текст начал готовиться еще в начале 1980-х гг., но темы, связанные с изучением российской элиты XVII в., были «неактуальны» для того времени, и он остался неопубликованным. Данный пробел во многом был заполнен вышедшей в 1983 г. книгой Р. Крамми «Aristocrats and Servitors. The Boyar Elite in Russia. 1613–1689». Волею судьбы идеи Р. Крамми по исследованию персонального состава Боярской думы на основе архивных документов смогли осуществляться в России с 1991 г., когда авторы этих строк совместно с Р. Мартином и М. По начали работу над проектом «Биографический банк данных Российского государства XIV–XVII вв.» (Muscovite Biographical Database). Результаты этой работы были обобщены в справочнике: «The Russian Elite in the Seventeenth Century» (Helsinki, 2004. Vol. 1) и в исследовании М. По (ibid., vol. 2). Большое значение для изучения данной темы имеет справочник Ю.М. Эскина «Местничество в России XVI–XVII вв.» (М., 1994). Близка к данной теме и диссертация Г.В. Талиной «Государственная власть и системы регулирования социально-служебного положения представителей высшего общества в начальный период становления абсолютизма в России (1645–1682 гг.)» (М., 2001). Наконец, недавно вышли книги, прямо освещающие историю высших слоев русского общества в XVII в.: Правящая элита Русского государства IX – начала XVIII вв.: Очерки истории / Е.А. Анисимов, В.Г. Вовина, Л.И. Ивина и др. Отв. ред. А.П. Павлов. СПб., 2006 (XVII в. посвящен наиболее значительный раздел); Седов П.В. Закат Московского царства. Царский двор конца XVII в. СПб., 2006. Однако, авторы полагают, что и данный текст имеет не только историографический интерес.

Rude & Barbarous Kingdom Revisited: Essays in Russian History and Culture in Honor of Robert O. Crummey. Chester S. L. Dunning, Russell E. Martin, and Daniel Rowland, eds. Bloomington, IN: Slavica Publishers, 2008, 131–53.

таковы, например, решения Думы о военных действиях перед Конотопским сражением 1659 г.[2] или о Чигиринском походе 1677 г.[3]

Самостоятельные действия воеводам как правило возбранялись, так кн. И.А. Хованский[4] получил выговор от царя за самовольный приступ к г. Ляховичам[5], окольничий кн. П.А. Долгорукий за Копысский приступ[6] и т.д. Строгий контроль за воеводами был во многом обусловлен тем, что воевода прежде всего избирался по принципу родовитости и мог быть человеком совершенно неспособным к военной службе. Часто стольник, посланный из Тайного приказа в полк с каким-либо поручением, имел еще тайный наказ выяснить, что делается в полку и как проявляет себя воевода. Таков наказ стольнику Ф. Колтовскому, посланному в полк к кн. И.А. Хованскому[7], или И. Колычеву, посланному к кн. И.И. Лобанову-Ростовскому. Выполняя поручение, Колычев выяснил, что воевода сообщает царю заниженные цифры «урона ратных людей», им было проведено следствие в полку по этому делу.

Иногда Тайному приказу приходилось действовать за спиною воеводы через его помощников. Показательным представляется тайный наказ, полученный стрелецким головой, доверенным лицом царя А.С. Матвеевым, который был послан в полк к кн. И.И. Лобанову-Ростовскому. Он должен был спросить о здоровье воеводы, проведать, что делается в полку, а главное, передать царский указ взять город Быхов. Но сомневаясь в возможности осуществить этот приказ, царь велел Матвееву сначала узнать втайне у товарища воеводы стольника С. Змеева его мнение о приступе к городу. В то же время Матвеев должен был «не доезжая полков оставить стряпчего конюха, где мочно, и учётчи дни, велеть ему за собой пригнать, будто с Москвы гонец к нему, Артемону». Если Змеев «скажет, что самыми скорыми днями на Быхов промыслу учинить никак не мочно», то приедет конюх, как-будто бы с грамотой из Москвы и «ему, Артемону, тое государеву грамоту отдавать окольничему и воеводе князю Ивану Ивановичу Лобанову-Ростовскому, смотря по тамошнему делу»[8]. Так, важные вопросы могли быть решены за спиной воеводы низ-

[2] РГАДА. Ф. 210. Севский стол. Д. 192. Л. 32.

[3] Приговор бояр относительно Чигиринского похода 185 г. / Публ. Е.И. Забелина. М., б/г. С. 5–6.

[4] Почти все лица деятельность которых рассмотрена, имели высший думный чин (то есть были боярами в прямом смысле), но каждый раз он не называется, отмечаются лишь другие чины.

[5] РГАДА.Ф. 27. Д. 166. Л. 31.

[6] РГАДА. Ф. 210. Московский стол. Записные книги. Д. 12. Л. 44–44 об.

[7] РГАДА. Ф. 210. Новгородский стол. Д. 148. Л. 41 об. – 42 об.

[8] РГАДА. Ф. 27. Д. 166. Л. 121–139, 202, 204–205. См. также: Записки отделения русской и славянской археологии Русского археологического общества (Далее: ЗОРСА РАО). СПб., 1861. Т. 2. С. 742–743.

шими чинами, но все формальности в отношении боярина точно соблюдались.

Полковой воевода имел много обязанностей. Одной из главных была забота о состоянии дворянского войска. Воеводы проводили сборы и смотры ратных людей, оружия и полковых припасов; организовывали своевременную раздачу денежного и хлебного жалования; составляли и посылали в Разряд годовые сметы по своему полку и книги обозного строя; производили сыск беглых солдат; организовывали заставы в случаях морового поветрия; вылавливали вражеских лазутчиков; осуществляли ремонт старых и постройку новых фортификационных укреплений. В пограничных районах страны в XVII в. были образованы военные территориальные округа – "разряды"[9]. На юго-западном рубеже, входившем в Белгородский и Севский разряды, городами, где сосредоточивались основные военные силы, являлись Белгород, Яблонов, Севск и Путивль; по черте на северо-западных рубежах, входивших в Новгородский разряд — Новгород и Псков. Воеводы этих крупнейших полков, находившиеся в боярском чине, имели и некоторые административные полномочия, им подчинялись воеводы городов их округа. Боярин иногда сам мог поставить в подчинённый его полку город воеводу и дать ему наказ[10]. Главной судебной инстанцией в этих городах также бывал боярин-воевода, например, отошедшие к России в 1644—1645 гг. города, ранее принадлежавшие Речи Посполитой, царским указом стали подсудны Яблоновскому воеводе кн. Б.А. Репнину. Над воеводами этих городов суд творил сам Репнин[11]. Воевода следил за состоянием городов и находившихся в них войск; городовые воеводы регулярно посылали ему отписки, чертежи и отписные книги своих городов. На их основе боярином составлялись донесения в Москву[12]. В случае военной опасности воеводы городов шли «в сход» к главному полку своего разряда.

Бояре служили и городовыми воеводами, но согласно своей «чести» только в особо значимых городах – центрах «царств» и «государств»: по перечню Г. Котошихина это – «Великий Новгород, царства Казанское, Астраханское, Сибирское, государство Псковское, княжество Смоленское, и тех государств в первые городы посылаются первые воеводы,

---

[9] Чернов А.В. Вооруженные силы Русского государства в XV–XVII вв. М., 1954. С. 170–171.

[10] См., например, назначение С. Степанова воеводой в г. Ковно и дачу ему воеводского наказа боярином кн. Я.К. Черкасским (Акты Московского государства. СПб., 1894. Т. 2. С. 301).

[11] РГАДА. Ф. 210. Севский стол. Д. 129. Л. 565–566, 695–699.

[12] См., например, донесение в Разрядный приказ воеводы Новгородского полка кн. Б.А. Репнина с приложением отписок городовых воевод (РГАДА. Ф. 210. Новгородский стол. Д. 148).

бояре и окольничие»[13]. К таким городам относились ещё Киев и Вильна (в недолгий период ее захвата русскими войсками). Большинство этих областей не находилось в ведомстве Разряда, а подчинялось самостоятельным приказам: Сибирскому, Казанского дворца, Малороссийскому, Литовскому, Смоленскому, эти земли рассматривались в какой-то степени как вассальные государства, наместниками в которых сидели бояре. Воеводы осуществляли на местах административную, судебную и полицейскую власть, из центра их деятельность строго контролировалась приказами[14], особенно следили за своевременной присылкой различных сборов. Эти воеводы осуществляли судебную власть также над городовыми воеводами своего «царства» и отчасти контролировали их деятельность. Если в Новгороде и Пскове военные обязанности лежали на воеводе Новгородского полка, то в Астрахани, Казани, Сибири их во многом осуществлял городовой воевода; они следили за тем, чтобы нерусские народности, жившие на подведомственной им территории, не выходили из повиновения.

Смены воевод в полках и городах происходили очень часто и отрицательно сказывались на службе. Определённую роль в этом играло местничество, вносившее сложности при распределении должностей, и смена одного воеводы вызывала за собой целую цепь других замен. Кроме того, правительство опасалось, что воевода мог пустить слишком глубокие корни в подвластном ему районе, стать там своим «царьком». Сами бояре не считали городовую службу почётной, достойной их высокого чина, и часто рассматривали её как опалу, как отсылку от двора в места, куда ссылают преступников. Так, когда кн. А.А. Голицын узнал, что его посылают воеводой в Киев, то бил царю челом «что он и так ему, великому государю, в Казани будучи, служил, и будет какая его вина… есть, и вместо опалы указал (бы) его великий государь послать и на смерть, и великий бы государь велел ему сказать его вину»[15]. Киевский воевода В.Б. Шереметев был отозван в Москву, но с полпути возвращен опять в Киев, так как там требовался опытный воевода в связи с напряженной обстановкой на Украине в 1660 г. Но Шереметев расценил указ как опалу, и царь вынужден был послать ему два письма, в которых увещевал воеводу «не оскорбляться»[16].

Бояре постоянно добивались себе перемены, и отставка с воеводского места воспринималась как милость, писалось «государь *пожаловал*, велел отставить». Боярские книги, в которых фиксировались пожалования

---

[13] Котошихин Г.К. О России в царствование Алексея Михайловича. СПб., 1906. С. 124.

[14] См. Андреевский И. О наместниках, воеводах и губернаторах. СПб., 1864; Очерки русской культуры XVII в. М., 1979. Ч. 1. Гл. «Государственный строй».

[15] Дворцовые разряды. СПб., 1852. Т. 3. Стб. 1144, 1145.

[16] ЗОРСА РАО. Т. 2. С. 749–755.

чинов, служебные назначения, оклады, награды и опалы[17], не отмечают наград и увеличения жалования за городовую службу за исключением одного случая: астраханский воевода кн. В.Г. Ромодановский получил то, что «ево службою таймыцкие тайши, и калмыки, и улусные мурзы, и татары учинились под государевою рукою и, будучи в Астрахани, в государевой казне учинили прибыль и устроили каменное и деревянное и многое строение — придачи — 100 рублёв»[18].

Организация во второй половине XVII в. крупных военно-административных округов под руководством боярина-воеводы создавала основу для проекта о наместничествах 1681 г.[19]. Проект предусматривал прекращение практики постоянной смены воевод и устанавливал пожизненное пребывание боярина в наместничестве. Вопреки мнению, высказанному В.О. Ключевским и утвердившемуся в литературе, о том, что проект был создан «реакционным боярством» для упрочения своей власти, представляется, что большинство бояр выступало против этого проекта[20]. Ключевский исходил из умозрительно представлявшихся ему жизненных ценностей людей того времени, в то время как для боярства удаление в наместничество означало неучастие в деятельности Думы и в придворной жизни и могло расцениваться только как опала, как умаление роли бояр, попавших в наместники, поэтому каждый боялся оказаться в этой категории. М. Я. Волков, исследовавший историю создания проекта, справедливо отметил, что одной из целей творца проекта кн. В.В. Голицына как раз и являлось удаление из Москвы враждебных ему бояр.

Дипломатическая служба издавна была для бояр одной из основных. Внешнеполитический курс страны вырабатывался царём совместно с думой и особенно с ближними боярами. Наиболее важные политические акции, такие как удержание за Россией Азова или присоединение Украины, вносились Думой на обсуждение Земским собором. Посольский приказ находился в подчинении Думы и являлся не столько творцом, сколько проводником внешней политики государства.

---

[17] О боярских книгах см.: *Лукичев М.П.* Боярские книги XVII века. Труды по истории и источниковедению. М., 2004. Все сведения о служебной деятельности бояр по боярским книгам и боярским спискам включены в Биографический банк данных Российского государства – Muscovite Biographical Database и отражены в указанном выше справочнике.

[18] РГАДА. Ф. 210. Оп. 1. Кн. 5. Л. 5.

[19] Проект Устава о служебном старшинстве бояр, окольничих и думных людей по 43 степеням, составленный при Федоре Алексеевиче / Публ. М.А. Оболенского. М.,1850; РГАДА. Ф. 210. Оп. 2. Д. 18. Л. 1–9.

[20] Впервые точку зрения, противоположную мнению В.О. Ключевского, высказал *Волков М.Я.* в статье «Об отмене местничества в России» (История СССР. 1977. № 2).

Глава боярского правительства мог заниматься некоторыми внешне-политическими делами единолично, не ставя в известность Посольский приказ. Так, например, к кн. И.Б. Черкасскому из-за рубежа с известиями приезжал гонец, «а с какими делы приехал и что речью наказал, и о тех о всех делех ведомо боярину князю И.Б. Черкасскому, а в Посольском приказе про те дела неведомо»[21]. Ф.И. Шереметев, а после него Б.И. Морозов, лично руководили разведывательной деятельностью русских агентов за границей[22], чьи сведения доставлялись непосредственно в их руки. Так, шифровки А.Л. Нащокина из Молдавии, куда он был послан в качестве агента, поступив в Посольский приказ нераспечатанными, передавались Ф.И. Шерметеву[23]. Уже в них Нащокин высказывал недоверие к дьякам этого приказа, а в дальнейшем, став видным дипломатом, постоянно враждовал с ними и писал царю только через Тайный приказ.

Между боярами и служащими приказа часто возникали конфликты. В историографии было распространено мнение, что бояре в посольских делах являлись людьми некомпетентными, что боярин — «глава посольства обычно был для дипломатического ведомства человеком случайным, в делах дипломатии "не навычен", чаще всего фигурой для представительства»[24]. Безусловно, могли встречаться люди неспособные, но в целом боярство было постоянно втянуто в круг дипломатической деятельности. Даже полковым воеводам в отписках из Москвы всегда сообщались политические новости. Воеводе Новгородского полка кн. И.А. Хованскому, например, были посланы статьи мирного договора, чтобы использовать их в случае согласия Польши на мир[25].

Большая дипломатическая работа возлагалась на новгородского городового воеводу в Новгородской посольской палате. Он должен был заранее «проведывать всякими мерами накрепко» все возможные сведения о приближающихся к русским границам посольствах, посланниках и проч. Для доставки этих и других известий воевода организовывал разведывательную деятельность, лично осуществляя связь со своими агентами за рубежом[26]. Боярин организовывал встречу посольств, прибывающих с запада, инструктировал приставов, обеспечивал

[21] Цит. по: Сташевский Е.Д. Очерки по истории царствования Михаила Федоровича. Киев, 1913. Ч. 1. С. 360.

[22] Джинчарадзе В.З. Борьба с иностранным шпионажем в России // Исторические записки. М., 1952. Т. 39. С. 240, 248–249.

[23] Галактионов И.В. Ранняя переписка А.Л. Ордина-Нащекина. Саратов, 1968. С. 61.

[24] См., например: Алпатов М.А. Русская историческая мысль и западная Европа XII–XVII вв. М., 1973. С. 325.

[25] РГАДА. Ф. 27. Д. 166. Л. 245–252.

[26] Архив СПб Института истории. Ф. 109. Д. 176, 179, 819 и др.

кормом, давал проезжие грамоты, устраивал послам приёмы[27]. Очевидно, в связи с деятельностью в Посольской палате новгородскому воеводе давался наместнический титул, так кн. Г.С. Куракин именовался «боярин и воевода и наместник Псковский»[28].

Постоянным видом службы бояр являлся приём посольств иностранных держав и проведение с ними переговоров, происходивших в ответной палате, где «у бояр и у послов о делех бывают разговоры и споры многие»[29]. Чем представительнее было посольство, тем более знатные лица назначались "быть в ответе" с послами. Для придания боярам еще большего весу на политической арене им давались звания наместников, для чего велись специальные книги о наместнических титулах[30]. Знатность лица должна была сочетаться со знатностью города или района, наместником которого оно фиктивно назначалось. Наивысшим рангом считался наместник Владимирский.

Уже в раннем возрасте знатные юноши знакомились с дипломатической службой, присутствуя на посольских приёмах в качестве рынд, в чине стольника они бывали приставами у послов, а также ездили с посольствами за границу. Бояре же и окольничие выезжали за рубеж только в особых случаях, возглавляя посольства самого высокого ранга. Бояре ездили великими послами только в Польшу на сеймы (таковы посольства кн. А.М. Львова в 1644 г., Г.Г. Пушкина в 1650 г., Б.И. Стрешнева в 1645 г., кн. Б.А. Репнина в 1653 г.), иногда в Польшу же посылались окольничие «которые бывают в боярех», в Швецию уже посылались только окольничие. Причём этими послами могли быть только бояре, недавно получившие чин или не самых знатных родов. Во все другие страны посылались стольники, стряпчие или московские дворяне «добрых родов», при этом обязательно учитывалось происхождение, так в Англию, например, посылались только «стольники первые статьи родов, которые из стольничества бывают в боярех». Самые знатные бояре назначались великими послами на съезды с комиссарами Польши и Швеции для заключения мирных договоров и решения других международных проблем, к ним в товарищи ставились также бояре или окольничие, имевшие ранг, согласно которому они могли быть послами в Польшу или Швецию[31].

---

[27] См. например, о приеме кн. Г.С. Куракиным шведского посольства Бента Горна (Архив СПб Института истории. Ф. 109. Д. 161, 162, 176 и др.).

[28] Такой титул новгородского воеводы появился, очевидно, с середины XVII в. Так в грамоте 1623 г., сообщающей полный титул новгородского воеводы, наместником он не назван (Архив СПб Института истории. Ф. 109. Д. 231).

[29] Котошихин Г.К. О России в царствование Алексея Михайловича. С. 65.

[30] РГАДА. Ф. 166 (Дела и сочинения о титулах). Д. 3–5, 9.

[31] Котошихин Г.К. О России в царствование Алексея Михайловича. С. 41.

За удачно выполненную посольскую миссию послам повышали оклады, давали дары[32], жаловали «милостивым словом» и повышали чином[33]. В посольской службе очень часто были случаи местничества.

Среди придворных должностей бояре занимали две высших должности — дворецкого и оружничего. Эти места считались одними из самых почётных. Котошихин писал, что дворецкий считался вторым лицом после конюшего[34], то есть после премьера боярского правительства, который правда в XVII в. уже не имел этого звания: должность конюшего была упразднена и заменена ясельничим, имевшим чин думного дворянина. Дворецкий и оружничий имели почётное право на особый вид жалования — путь. Дворецкий стоял во главе приказа Большого дворца, в его же ведомстве до 1653 г. находился приказ Печатного дела; оружничий возглавлял Оружейную палату.

При Алексее Михайловиче эти должности занимали бояре не самых знатных родов: князя А.М. Львова в 1652 г. на должности дворецкого сменил В.В. Бутурлин. Потом дворецким был назначен Ф.М. Ртищев, не имевший боярского чина, но практически стоявший наравне с боярами — он получал оклад, равный боярскому, а в Житие Ртищева говорится о том, что он сам отказался принять предложенный ему царём боярский чин[35]. После Ртищева дворецким стал Б.М. Хитрово, много лет носивший звание оружничего, до него оружничим был Г.Г. Пушкин, а после него — А.С. Матвеев. Очевидно, царь стремился давать высшие придворные должности фаворитам незнатного происхождения и захудавших родов, чтобы таким образом уравнять их со знатью. Вполне уместно замечание Покровского: «антиномия феодального общества, где король не мог посадить маркиза ниже графа, но где и граф, и маркиз низко кланялись королевскому камердинеру, целиком воспроизводилась московским придворным обществом времён царя Алексея»[36].

Ещё одной придворной должностью, возложенной на бояр, являлось выполнение обязанностей дядьки царевичей, который следил за их здоровьем и воспитанием. Близость к наследнику престола в дальнейшем сулила большие выгоды, примером чему являлась карьера Б.И. Морозова, дядьки Алексея Михайловича. Придворной, вероятно, являлась и должность дворового воеводы, возглавлявшего государев полк во время

[32] См. Выпись из дел Посольского приказа о пожаловании даров за выполнение наиболее важных посольских миссий XVII в. // Временник ОИДР. Кн. 5. Смесь. С. 1–10.

[33] Например, были пожалованы в бояре: кн. А.М. Львов за участие в заключении Поляновского договора, Г.Г. Пушкин за посольство в Швецию в 1646 г. для подтверждение Столбовского мира, Б.И. Стрешнев в 1645 г. за посольство в Польшу.

[34] Котошихин Г.К. О России в царствование Алексея Михайловича. С. 88.

[35] Архив СПб Института истории. Ф. 66. Д. 168. Л. 19 об.

[36] Покровский М.Н. Русская история с древнейших времен. М., 1933. Т. 2. С. 33.

царских выездов из Москвы. На неё назначались наиболее близкие к царю лица — дворовыми воеводами были Б.И. Морозов и И.Д. Милославский, их сменили кн. Ю.А. Долгорукий и К.П. Нарышкин[37]. В периоды отъездов царя из Москвы несколько знатнейших бояр назначались «ведать» столицу. Их задачей было сообщать царю обо всех событиях и выполнять присылаемые царские указы.

Бояре ставились во главе специальных комиссий, создаваемых для проведения особых государственных мероприятий (часто они именовались «приказами») — например, для создания Соборного уложения образован был приказ во главе с кн. Н.И. Одоевским, для осуществления посадской реформы – Сыскной приказ во главе с кн. Ю.А. Долгоруким, для постройки Засечной черты, которую возглавляли кн. И.Б. Черкасский, а потом кн. Н.И. Одоевский — приказ Городового дела, а для поиска полезных ископаемых — приказ Рудного сыска во главе с кн. Б.А. Репниным. Он же, а потом Г.Г. Пушкин занимались ремонтом соборов Кремля. Специальная комиссия, возглавляемая кн. Н.И. Одоевским, разбирала документы приказа Тайных дел после его упразднения. Особые комиссии создавались для проведения расследований после окончания всех народных восстаний; они же чинили жестокую расправу над восставшими. Боярская комиссия занималась делом патриарха Никона.

В московских приказах бояре занимали должности приказных судей[38]. Если в XVI в. «премьером» боярского правительства являлся боярин в должности конюшего, то в XVII в. отличием такого лица стало право сосредоточения в своих руках управления 4—мя приказами: Большой казны, Стрелецким, Иноземским, Аптекарским[39]. Впервые эти четыре приказа возглавил двоюродный брат царя Михаила Фёдоровича кн. И.Б. Черкасский, выдвинутый патриархом Филаретом в число первых лиц правительства. Вероятно, таким образом был создан прецедент и возглавивший после смерти Черкасского в 1642 г боярское правительство Ф.И. Шереметев также взял руководство этими приказами в свои руки. В 1646 г. место Шереметева в правительстве занял Б.И. Морозов, и руководство вышеуказанными приказами перешло к нему. Но уже в 1648 г. в

---

[37] Дворцовые разряды. Т. 3. Стб. 1380.

[38] В тексте все сведения о приказной службе боярства основаны на справочнике С.К. Богоявленского «Приказные судьи XVII в.» (первое издание вышло в 1940 г., второе исправленное – в сборнике трудов С.К. Богоявленского «Московский приказной аппарат и делопроизводство XVI–XVII веков», подготовлено в 2006 г. А.В. Топычкановым под ред. С.О. Шмидта)

[39] Впервые этот факт был отмечен С.В. Бахрушиным в работе «Московское восстание 1648 г.» (Научные труды. М., 1954. Т. 2. С. 61), но в эту четверку он не включил Аптекарский приказ, а вместо него указал на Новую четь. Но последний приказ из всех «премьеров» возглавляли только Ф.И. Шереметев, Б.И. Морозов и И.Д. Милославский, а Аптекарский приказ – все.

результате Московского восстания Морозову пришлось оставить все государственные посты. Его падением сразу же воспользовались противники, которыми на место Морозова был выдвинут кн Я.К. Черкасский, заменивший Морозова в тех же приказах. Черкасский удерживал в своих руках власть всего несколько месяцев: первенство опять перешло к «партии» Морозова, но сам Морозов после событий 1648 г. опасался открыто стоять во главе правительства и правил через своего шурина И.М. Милославского[40], который и возглавлял в 1649 г. 4 приказа, а также вновь созданный Рейтарский приказ и руководил ими до 1666—1667 гг. Уж в 1665 г. Милославский был очень тяжело болен[41], но хотя на его место не было сделано новых назначений, царь его имя ставить в грамотах не велел, и в приказах всем ведали дьяки. После Милославского управление Большой казной, Иноземским и Рейтарским приказами перешло к кн. Н.И. Одоевскому (1667–1670 гг.), позднее, (в 1676 г.) он возглавил Аптеку. С этого времени уже видно некоторое нарушение традиции, а после 1670 г. приказы, ранее сосредоточенные в одних руках, перешли к разным лицам, но в 1677 г. Большая казна, Иноземский и Рейтарский приказы опять, уже в последний раз, встали под начало главы боярского правительства И.Л. Милославского. С 1682 г. правительство возглавил фаворит царевны Софьи кн. В.В. Голицын, но в его управлении из традиционных приказов остались только Иноземский и Рейтарский, однако после Милославского вместо Большой казны к Голицыну перешли другие приказы финансового ведомства — чети (Владимирская, Галицкая, Новгородская, Устюжская).

Служба в приказах, так же, как и городовое воеводство, не считалась боярством престижной: за неё не давали денежных и поместных придач, не объявляли «милостивое слово». В своих родословных знать отмечала приказную службу предков в редких случаях и местничество в приказной области также не было распространено[42]. Исключение составлял Владимирский судный приказ: должность судьи этого приказа (так же, как и звание Владимирского наместника в посольствах) считалась почётной и давалась только боярину и редко — окольничему. Это объясняется тем, что приказ имел право судить думных людей[43]. Бояре добивались назначения во Владимирский судный приказ, и редко кто из них не побывал судьёй этого приказа, поэтому судьи сменялись в нём чрезвы-

[40] См.: Состояние России в 1650-1655 гг. по донесению И. де Родеса / Публ. Б.Г. Курца. М., 1915. С. 93.

[41] Коллинс С. Нынешнее состояние России. М., 1846.С. 33.

[42] См.: Морозов Б.Н. Служебные и родословные документы в частных архивах XVII в. // Исследования по источниковедению истории СССР дооктябрьского периода. М., 1982. С. 70–98; Эскин Ю.М. Указ соч.

[43] См.: Князьков С.Е. Судные приказы в конце XVI – первой половине XVII в. // Исторические записки. М., 1987. Т. 115. С. 273–275.

чайно часто. Вторыми судьями во Владимирский приказ назначались окольничие и стольники, также самых знатных фамилий. Из других приказов, имевших судебные функции, бояре и окольничие назначались в Московский судный приказ, Разбойный, Челобитный и приказ Сыскных дел. Особое место занимает приказ «Что на сильных бьют челом», который был создан по решению Земского собора 1619 г.[44] Право судить «сильных» получал глава боярского правительства, стоявший выше других бояр. На место судьи этого приказа были назначены кн. И.Б. Черкасский, после него — Ф.И. Шереметев, на эту же должность прочили Б.И. Морозова[45]. Но как самостоятельное ведомство приказ, очевидно, практически не действовал, слившись с Сыскным приказом, который возглавляли кн. И.Б. Черкасский и Ф.И. Шереметев, а также дворецкий кн. А.М. Львов, которого современники по влиятельности ставили рядом с последним[46]. В правительстве Б.И. Морозова этот приказ недолго возглавлялся кн. А.Н. Трубецким[47] – одним из знатнейших бояр и правой рукой Морозова. Назначение после этих лиц в Сыскной приказ в 1649 г. кн. Ю.А. Долгорукова, происходившего не из «первостатейной» фамилии и только что получившего боярский чин, но занявшегося в приказе именно притеснением «сильных» и согласно посадской реформе возвращавшего закладчиков за боярами и духовенством, являлось фактом примечательным[48].

Остальные приказы не имели иерархии с местнической точки зрения, но в некоторые из них всё же чаще назначались бояре, а в другие – бояре не назначались никогда. Из областных приказов бояре бывали судьями в Казанском и Сибирском, из военных — в Стрелецком, Иноземском, Пушкарском, Рейтарском, Сбора ратных людей, Оружейном и Аптекарском. В приказах, ведавших финансами, бояре возглавляли Большую казну, Большой приход и чети — Новгородскую,

---

[44] ААЭ. СПб., 1836. Т. 3. № 105.

[45] В челобитной, поданой царю Алексею Михайловичу во время восстания 2 июня 1648 г. говорилось о том, что как при отце его знатнейшим боярам кн. И.Б. Черкасскому и Ф.И. Шереметеву был поручен суд над теми боярами, которые «над простым народом твоего царского величества подданными мошейничества и преступления учиняли», то и теперь эту миссию надо возложить на Б.И. Морозова (См.: Базилевич К.В. Городские восстания в Московском государстве, М.; Л., 1936. С. 46).

[46] Известие о поездке в Россию Вальдемара Христиана Гильденлеве // ЧОИДР. 1867. № 4. С. 35–36.

[47] Сведения об этом отсутствуют в справочнике С.К. Богоявленского. См.: Соколова А.А., фон Мекк А.К. Расходные книги и столпы Поместного приказа. М., 1910. Кн. 1. С. 123; РГАДА. Ф. 6. Д. 3 (Судное дело С.Л. Стрешнева).

[48] См.: Смирнов П.П. Посадские люди и их классовая борьба в первой половине XVII в. М.; Л., 1940. С. 254.

Устюжскую, Владимирскую, Костромскую и Новую. Из дворцовых приказов во главе Большого дворца всегда стоял дворецкий.

Три наиболее крупных приказа: Разрядный, Поместный и Посольский возглавлялись думными дьяками. С.А. Белокуров писал, что за весь XVII в. только в течение 20 лет во главе Посольского приказа стояли бояре[49], но очевидно, что все эти 20 лет приходятся на 2-ую половину XVII в.: 1667—1671 гг. — во главе приказа А.Л. Ордин-Нащокин, 1671—1676 гг. — А.С. Матвеев, 1680—1681 — В.С. Волынский, 1682–1689 — кн. В.В. Голицын. Таким образом, в этот период наблюдается явная тенденция вытеснения дьяков из Посольского приказа, прервавшаяся только с падением правительства Софьи, когда в приказ был назначен дьяк Е.И. Украинцев (1689–1699 гг.). Во главе Поместного приказа в это время также встречаются бояре — кн. И.Б. Репнин (1676–1679 гг.), кн. И.Б. Троекуров (1682–1690 гг.), П.В. Шереметев (1690–1697гг.), а во главе Разрядного — кн. М.Ю. Долгорукий (1681–1682 гг.), Т.К. Стрешнев (1690–1699). В Конюшенном приказе в конце века был вместо ясельничего не боярина вновь поставлен боярин – Т.Н. Стрешнев (1690–1699 гг.). В последней четверти XVII в. приказы, близкие по своим функциям, объединяются под руководством одного лица[50].

Дети бояр, как правило, назначались на службу в те же приказы, что и их отцы. Например, в 1638 г. во Владимирском судном приказе и приказе Сбора ратных людей служили кн. А.А. Голицын и его сын кн. И.А. Голицын, оба бояре; в 1687 г. сын кн. В.В. Голицына Андрей получил боярский чин и был назначен в те же 10 приказов, которые возглавлял его отец; в 1682 г. в Сыскном приказе был кн. И.А. Хованский с братом кн. С.А. Хованским и сыновьями Андреем и Петром. Такие семейные назначения помогали частично избежать обычных распрей на службе между боярином и его помощниками, так как сын или младший брат должен безусловно подчиняться отцу или другому старшему родственнику.

Некоторые из бояр никогда не имели назначений в приказные судьи[51]. Возможно предположить, что проект устава 1681 г. кн. В.В. Голицына предусматривал назначение на руководящие должности в при-

---

[49] Белокуров С.А. О Посольском приказе. М., 1906.

[50] Устюгов Н.В. Эволюция приказного строя Русского государства в XVII в. // Абсолютизм в России (XVII–XVIII в.). М., 1964.

[51] Князья Ю.Н. Барятинский, И.А. Воротынский, И.П. Пронский, Г.Г. Ромодановский, А.С. Урусов, Г.С. Черкасский, а также Ф.Б. Долматов-Карпов, Н.И. Романов. Очень мало служили в приказах князья Ю.П. Буйносов-Ростовский, М.М. Темкин-Ростовский, Ф.Ю. Хворостинин, И.Н. Хованский, Я.К. Черкасский, а также И.И. Салтыков и В.И. Стрешнев.

казах только окольничих (они должны были «у челобитчиков челобитные принимать»)[52].

Уже в правление Алексея Михайловича среди думных людей начали появляться деятели «петровского» типа: энергичные, улавливавшие всё убыстряющийся с уходом средневековья темп времени[53], не чуждавшиеся Запада, имевшие интерес к государственным делам и разбиравшиеся в них. «Самым замечательным из московских государственных людей XVII в.», по определению Ключевского[54], являлся А.Л. Ордин-Нащокин, анализ деятельности которого занял большое место в исторической литературе. Но было бы неверно полагать, что Нащокин был единственным лицом среди бояр, способным к государственной деятельности и радевшим о пользе государства. Находясь во главе наиболее крупных военных и административных предприятий, бояре не могли ограничиваться только указаниями из центра, но всегда вынуждены были проявлять и собственную активность. Даже кн. А.И. Хованский, которого Нащокин справедливо обвинял в отсутствии государственного мышления, самостоятельно разрабатывал и присылал в Тайный приказ свои предложения о том, как над врагами лучшим образом «промысл учинить»[55]. Пример организации строительства Белгородской засечной черты кн. Н.И. Одоевским показывает, какие сложные и разнообразные проблемы призван был решать воевода. Он лично руководил работой по снятию чертежей с местности и выбирал места для постройки сторожевых городков. В процессе этих работ Одоевским было предложено перенести г. Белгород на стратегически более выгодное место, что и было осуществлено в дальнейшем[56]. Для создания макета вала Одоевским были приглашены «горододельцы немцы»[57]. Трудности встретились при организации рабочей силы для строительства, т.к. дворяне полка и белгородцы отказывались в нём участвовать и «заводили бунт». Но работы на участке, за который Одоевский отвечал непосредственно: от заложенного им г. Болхового (или Болховца) до Карпова, строившегося под руководством товарща Одоевского В.П. Шереметева, были закончены «в семь недель безо всякие мешкоты»[58]. Сложность представлял вопрос о заселении новых городов:

---

[52] Проект Устава о служебном старшинстве бояр, окольничих и думных людей. С. 10.

[53] См.: Демин А.С. Русская литература второй половины XVII – начала XVIII в. М., 1977. Глава «Стиль работы практических деятелей второй половины XVII в. и литература».

[54] Ключевский В.О. Сочинения. М., 1957. Т. 3. С. 334.

[55] АМГ. Т. 3. С. 236. № 236.

[56] Загоровский В.П. Белгородская черта. Воронеж. 1969. С. 136.

[57] РГАДА. Ф. 159. Оп. 1. Д. 869. Л. 29, 52.

[58] РГАДА. Ф. 141. 1647 г. Д. 25. Л. 1.

первоначально Одоевский предлагал записывать «на вечное житье» в Карпов и Болховой служилых людей из близлежащих городов (Мценска, Новосиля, Ливен и др.), но их жители переезжать отказывались, да и в этих городах их было немного. Тогда Одоевским был издан указ о приборе «на вечное житьё» в новые города московских стрельцов с сохранением за ними московских окладов. Боярин давал указания поставленному им воеводе в Болховом и присланным туда же из Белгорода дьякам о размерах дворов и пашен, которыми наделялись прибывшие на житьё драгуны, о подготовке фуража и саней для зимних походов на татар, о составлении росписи «пороховой свинцовой казны и всяких пушечных запасов», об устройстве безместных попов, приехавших искать работу в новые города, о присылке из Курска церковной утвари для новых церквей и т.д.[59]

Проблема формирования и размещения полков на южном рубеже России постоянно вставала и перед другими воеводами, предлагавшими свои проекты. Так кн. Ю.Н. Борятинским была разработана схема расположения командного состава полков на южной границе, отражавшая особенности расселения различных социальных групп из служилых людей[60]. Большую работу по укреплению южной границы проводил Яблоновский воевода кн. Г.С. Куракин[61].

Боярство в целом тяготилось государственной службой и рассматривало её как источник дополнительного дохода: воеводы занимались поборами с населения, во время войн процветал грабёж, приказные судьи брали взятки, послы занимались за рубежом торговыми операциями. В литературе фигура своекорыстного боярина, не радеющего о государстве, является типичной, но представляется, что подобная психология в данном случае имела свои исторические корни. Несмотря на образование единого централизованного государства, психологически знать ещё долго не могла перестроиться, воспринимала себя потомками свободных вассалов, не служивших за государственное жалование в городах воеводами и в приказах, а помогавшее своему сюзерену войском и советом в Думе. В XVII в. понятия службы государству, государственного долга, государственного деятеля только — только начинали зарождаться, знать не находила никакого высокого смысла в гражданской службе и воспринимала свое положение как унизительное по сравнению с предками. Не понятие служения государству, а понятие служения православной вере, защита от нашествия иноверцев и служба лично государю — вот что воспринималось боярством. Отсутствие понятия гражданственности ярче всего проявлялось в местничестве, когда интер-

[59] РГАДА. Ф. 210. Белгородский стол. Д. 1412.

[60] Загоровский В.П. Изюмская черта. Воронеж. 1980. С. 35.

[61] РГАДА. Ф. 210. Белгородский стол. Д. 335. Л. 51–58, 271–272.

есы собственной чести открыто и демонстративно ставились выше интересов государства.

В период складывания централизованной монархии занять высокое место при Московском дворе означало не только получить личную честь, но и не уронить престиж своей земли. В XVII в. эти соображения уж не имели места.

Укрепление русского государства, превращение его в могущественную Российскую империю, усиление его международного значения, переход от Средневековья к Новому времени и окончательное утверждение абсолютизма создали объективные условия для появления идеи служения государству, активным проповедником которой явился Петр I, сам считавший себя первым слугой государству. Пётр указывал, что, царствуя, он одновременно и служит, переходя из чина в чин, начиная с чина бомбардира, принятого им во время первого Азовского похода[62], подавая пример своим подданным.

Царь Алексей Михайлович также считал себя первым слугой, но не государства, а Бога и через эту идею давал идеологическое обоснование боярской службы. В грамотках боярам он не уставал повторять, что боярская «честь» даётся «не просто» и должна быть «не в туне»: «государевы и родословные люди», в отличие от «обышных людишек», поставлены во главе государства от Бога и должны расценивать свою службу как исполнение Божественной воли, которую на Богоизбранной земле осуществляет непосредственно сам Алексей Михайлович – «царь тленный». Держать ответ за свою службу бояре должны перед Богом, и царь постоянно напоминал им об этом: «Молю же ся вам, — писал он, — не разленяйтесь, ниже унывайте, понеже суд велий бывает на великих, менший убо прощён будет и достоин помилованию есть. Силнии жь крепко истязани будут… и истязает наши дала Господь и советы изыскает, яко работницы суще царствию его: не сохранихом закона, ниже судихом по правде, ниже по воли Божии ходихом, и скоро и страшно придет на вас»[63].

Алексею Михайловичу приходилось прибегать не только к увещеванию бояр, но иногда и к прямому рукоприкладству: царевичем, он хватал за грудки и выставлял своего дядьку Б.И. Морозова с официального приёма королевича Вольдемара[64]. По рассказу Мейерберга, царём был выдран за бороду и выгнан пинком из Думы тесть И.Д. Милославский[65]. А. Роде сообщает о том, как был оттаскан за бороду кн. Ю.И.

[62] Павленко Н.И. Петр I. (к изучению социально-политических взглядов) // Россия в период реформ Петра I. М., 1973. С. 41–48.

[63] ЗОРСА РАО. Т. 2. С. 743–744, 751–755, 773.

[64] Известие о поездке в Россию Вольдемара Христиана Гильденлеве // ЧОИДР. М., 1867. Т. 4. С. 27.

[65] Мейерберг А. Путешествие в Московию. М., 1874. С. 169.

Ромодановский[66]. Павлу Алеппскому даже рассказали, что за взяточничество Алексей Михайлович «убил собственною рукою одного из вельмож среди дивана»[67].

Характерно, что все эти скандальные случаи попали под перо иностранцев, постоянно подчёркивавших, что русская знать, по сравнению с европейской, находится в бесправном и униженном положении. Иностранцев удивляла непривычная для западного человека атмосфера раболепия и обожествления персоны самодержца, царившая при русском дворе и напоминавшая дворы восточных деспотов. Ю. Крижаничем был даже предложен проект реформ, по его мнению, необходимых для поднятия престижа и значимости в государстве высших сословий. Причину городских восстаний, свидетелем которых он явился, Крижанич видел в том, «что у боляр несть тоя силы, нить крепости, кая бы могла чёрное людство на вузде держать и от бешеных поступков возпящать»[68]. Жалким представлялось положение русского боярства и Я. Рейтенфельсу: «У поляков всё направлено к свободе знати, в Москве же, вообще говоря, всё находится в жалком, рабском подчинении. Некоторые высшие должности, когда-то обладавшие некоторым подобием свободы, либо совершенно отменены царями или же власть и могущество их до того ограничены, что даже сами бояре, именовавшиеся правителями государств, ныне едва-едва могут считаться наравне с частными, простыми советниками»[69].

У иностранных авторов можно даже встретить сообщение о том, что бояре подвергались битью кнутом. «Кнут и дубины… общеупотребительны и знакомы даже боярам, — писал тот же Рейтенфельс, — Так, несколько лет тому назад покойная царица приказала всенародно наказать одного боярина знаменитым ужасным кнутом за то, что он изнасиловал сенную девушку; не говорю уже… о некоторых, недавно тем же награждённых»[70]. И. Лиллиенталь следующим образом описывает наказание обвинённого во взяточничестве кн. Ф. Хилкова и его товарища: «Их, полунагих, обвешали мешками золота и соболями и вели по улицам, не взирая на большой холод, сзади следовал палач, наносивший им удары кнутом»[71]. Такие примеры являются явным преувеличением:

[66] Описание 2-го посольства в Россию датского посланника Ганса Ольделанда 1659 г., составленное посольским секретарём А.Роде // Голос минувшего. 1916. № 7–8. С. 374.

[67] Павел Алеппский. Путешествие антиохийского патриарха Макария в Россию. М., 1898. Вып. 3. С. 95.

[68] Крижанич Ю. Русское государство в половине XVII в. М., 1859. С. 312.

[69] Рейтенфельс Я. Сказание светлейшему герцогу тосканскому Козьме Третьему о Московии. М., 1906. С. 110.

[70] Там же. С. 117.

[71] Форстен Г.В. Сношения Швеции с Россией // ЖМНП. 1898. № 6. 331.

случаи наказания кнутом представителей высшего думного чина в русских источниках не встречаются, но более низкие чины действительно ему подвергались: например, сохранился список стольников и стряпчих, битых батогами перед Разрядным приказом и посланных в тюрьму «за челобитье: они в походе били челом государю об отпуске с челобитною гурьбою»[72].

Мало кто из иностранцев за внешней видимостью полного бесправия русской знати сумел разглядеть её действительное могущество. Пожалуй, наиболее проницательным оказался А. Мейерберг, который замечал, что Алексей Михайлович правит самодержавно, «распоряжаясь всем по своему произволу, или лучше, думая распоряжаться, потому, что осаждаемый и проводимый своими любимцами, либо совсем не знает положения дел, либо видит его под прикрытием обмана тех же любимцев»[73].

Русские источники хорошо показывают, что думные чины, в особенности бояре, редко несли какую—либо судебную ответственность за преступления по службе. Государственная деятельность бояр оставалась практически бесконтрольной и давала широкие возможности для самых различных злоупотреблений. Отсутствие самого понятия «службы государству» вызывало и отсутствие законодательства о наказаниях за государственные преступления по службе. Соборное уложение впервые оговаривает только один вид таких преступлений – взяточничество должностных лиц судебных органов. Судебную деятельность приказных судей и воевод должна была контролировать Дума, которая во главе с царём рассматривалась как высшая апелляционная инстанция[74]. В случае предвзятого решения судьи, согласно Соборному уложению, у него отнималась «честь», а судья, не имевший думного чина, подвергался торговой казни (X, 5). В случае ложного челобитья на представителей думных чинов челобитчику полагалось битьё кнутом (X, 14).

Полковую воеводскую деятельность думных людей контролировал сам царь с помощью Тайного и Разрядного приказов. Во всяком случае, Дума в Соборном уложении в этих случаях не упоминается (см. гл. VII, 10, 12). Дипломатическая служба, вообще не фигурировавшая в Уложении, контролировалась Тайным и Посольским приказами.

И всё же дела Тайного приказа дают представление о некоторых случаях расследования служебных злоупотреблений бояр и воевод. Так, например, воевода кн. Г.Г. Ромодановский должен был по указу отпустить из своего полка ратных людей в полк воеводы С. Змеева, что он и сделал, но ратные люди «пять верст отшедчи», опять вернулись к Ромоданов-

---

[72] РГАДА. Ф. 199. Портфель 385. Ч. 1. Л. 2.

[73] Мейерберг А. Путешествие в Московию. С. 166.

[74] Маньков Г.А. Уложение 1649 г. кодекс феодального права в России. Л., 1980. С. 165.

скому. «И ты, — писал ему лично царь, — не токмо не отослал их.., куда им идти велено, и с собой их взял, прельщаючи их нашим государевым большим жалованьем и обещаючися тайно отпускать их по домам». По Соборному уложению за такой проступок боярину и воеводе полагалось "чинить жестокое наказание, что государь укажет" (VIII, 11). Царь ограничился разгромным письмом Ромодановскому с обещанием Божьей кары, в заключении которого писал: «а буде ты желаешь впредь… в нашем государеве жалованьи быти по—прежнему, и тебе б, оставя всякое своё упрямство, учинить по сему нашего великого государя указу». В то же время о каком—то помощнике Ромодановского, который «то дело ухищрённым и злопронырливым умыслом учинил», царь написал: «а страдника Климку велим повесить»[75].

Другой воевода окольничий кн. И.И. Лобанов—Ростовский был виноват в том, что утаил истинное число убитых, раненых и взятых в плен во время стычки с неприятелем, а также в том, что самовольно хотел взять приступом город Мстиславль, но плохо подготовив операцию, потерпел неудачу. В грамоте Лобанову царь писал, что «указали было тебя… с нашей, великого государя, службы переменить», но по случаю праздника и по просьбе царевича велено ему быть на службе «по-прежнему» и «служить ныне и впредь, наипаче мимошедшего, и прежняя своя непристойная воля и нераденье покрыть нынешнею службой и радением от всего сердца и всякую высость оставить и смирить себя»[76].

Воевода кн. Ю.А. Долгорукий в 1657 г. одержал большую победу над литовским гетманом Гонсевским и захватил его в плен, но не сумел закрепить свой успех и без указа отступил из—под Вильны. Царь был очень этим недоволен, а также тем, что Долгорукий ничего обо всём этом не сообщал в Москву. Но и в этом случае Алексей Михайлович ограничился выговором в личном письме, которое заключил так: «А мы и ныне за твою усердную веру к Богу, а нам верную службу, всяким милостивым жалованьем жаловать тебя хотим»[77].

Показательны статьи, данные из Тайного приказа стольнику, посланному к воеводе В.П. Шереметеву, взявшему 1655 г Витебск. При ратных людях он должен был передать боярину милостивое слово и спросить о здоровье. В личной же беседе «на него, Василия, пошуметь гораздо» за то, что выпустил из взятого города всю шляхту вместе с имуществом, в то время как Боярская дума постановила всех жителей сослать в Казань, а имущество раздать солдатам[78]. Подобные наказы, с одной стороны,

---

[75] ЗОРСА РАО. Т. 2. С. 771, 774, 775.

[76] Там же. С. 747, 749.

[77] Цит. по: С.М. Соловьев. История России с древнейших времен. М., 1961. Кн. 6. Т. 11. С. 47.

[78] ЗОРСА РАО. Т. 2. С. 736–737.

объявляющие «милостивое слово», а с другой, велящие «шуметь гораздо» на воеводу, встречаются часто.

Государство старалось строго блюсти перед народом престиж думных людей. Воевода кн. А.П. Трубецкой в 1659 г. потерпел под г. Конотопом страшное поражение от объединившихся войск гетмана И. Выговского и крымского хана. В Москве уже стали готовить оборонительные сооружения, опасаясь подхода врагов к столице, но ханское войско, без которого Выговский был бессилен, вернулось в Крым. Таким образом, неудача под Конотопом не привела к катастрофическим результатам и в официальных документах расценивалась как победа. Трубецкого, который «за Конотопскую службу 1659 и 1660 году и за большой бой с крымским ханом, и что обрал Юрия Хмельницкого» получил к окладу огромную прибавку — 200 рублей[79]. За Конотопский бой получили прибавку к жалованью и все ратные люди полка Трубецкого[80]. Но правду о Конотопском поражении нельзя было утаить: Новгородский летописец прямо говорит о поражении и обвиняет кн. А.Н. Трубецкого в том, что он не прислал подкрепления передовому отряду конницы под руководством его товарища кн. С. Пожарского, успешно сражавшегося с татарами[81]. Аналогичен и вышеупомянутый случай, когда воевода кн. В.В. Голицын, не подошедший во—время со своим полком во время Чигиринского похода, также получил прибавку к жалованию за Чигиринский бой.

В дворцовых разрядах зафиксировано много случаев государевой опалы на думных и ближних людей; наиболее частая их причина — упорство в местничестве, но встречаются случаи должностных и других преступлений. Например, 4 июня 1675 г. вернулся из Киева воевода кн. Ю.П. Трубецкой, и тут же на него поступил извет от стольника Ф. Колтовского в том, что он в Киеве расходовал государеву казну не так, как следовало, давая стрельцам и их головам огромные оклады, вплоть до ста рублей. Была назначена специальная комиссия по расследованию, которая работала 3 дня, и уже 8 июня Трубецкой был «у государевой руки», а «свой гнев государь положил на стольников Колтовских», а ещё через 5 дней «пожаловал государь к руке стольника Фёдора Иванова Колтовского»[82]. Также недолго продолжалась и опала кн. А.А. Голицына, посланного в Киев на смену кн. Ю.Г. Трубецкому.

Вопросы о наказании воевод за их противозаконные действия царь ставил на обсуждение бояр, как это видно из продиктованного им

---

[79] РГАДА. Ф. 210. Боярские книги. Д. 5. Л. 2.

[80] АМГ. Т. 3. № 30. С. 34.

[81] Тихомиров М.Н. Русское летописание. М., 1979. С. 304–306. Сражение кн. С. Пожарского с татарами нашло отражение в русской народной песне «Под Кронотопом под городом» (Сборник Кирши Данилова. М., 1977. С. 153).

[82] Дворцовые разряды. Т. 3. Стб. 1436–1437, 1449, 1463.

наброска с собственноручными пометами «о каких делех говорить бояром» (1657 г.?), в котором даны тезисы его речи на совместном заседании с боярами (всей Думы или только «комнаты» — неясно). Один из пунктов — обсуждение вины астраханского воеводы кн. В.Г. Ромодановского и его товарища И. Колтовского, каким—то образом «солгавших» и не сумевших выручить православных пленников у калмыков. Этот документ единственный в своём роде и представляет особый интерес[83]. Кн. В.Г. Ромодановский, судя по всему, полностью оправдался, и, как указывалось выше, в этом же году получил большую прибавку к окладу за астраханскую службу.

В источниках все же встречаются некоторые сведения о наказаниях бояр за служебные злоупотребления. По сообщению Коллинса в 1667 г. подвергся опале П.М. Салтыков, так как до царя дошли жалобы на него о неуплате служилым людям жалования и о других злоупотреблениях. Царь «сделал ему строгий выговор, удалил от двора и, назначив великого министра Нащокина на его место, препоручил ему разыскать и рассмотреть злоупотребления Салтыкова… Говорили об этом шёпотом и под великой опасностью лишиться языка»[84]. В дальнейшем Салтыков продолжал занимать при дворе одно из ведущих мест.

И де Родес сообщал, что 16 марта 1652 г. у путивльского воеводы кн. С.В. Прозоровского было отнято боярство, и он был брошен в тюрьму, а его товарищи — биты кнутом: «им предъявляется тяжёлое обвинение, что они задержали несколько греков, которые отправлялись в Иерусалим, и не хотели пустить их через границы, прежде чем они им не дали… «посула» или подарков». Родес объяснял такое тяжёлое наказание дворцовыми интригами: «так как если бы все, — писал он, — которые берут здесь «посулы» наказывались, то очень мало от высших до низших лиц освободились бы от такого наказания»[85]. В боярском списке 1652 г. зафиксирована опала Прозоровского: «за вину в боярех писать не велено», но уже в июле этого же года сказано «ему быть в боярех по—прежнему»[86].

Наказание взяточников было выгодно для казны, поскольку с них взыскивались крупные суммы денег. Так, с астраханского воеводы И.Ф. Волынского требовалось взыскать 7 тысяч рублей; сразу с него была получена 1 тысяча и «те деньги посланы на Чёрный Яр для дачи государева жалованья черноярским всяких чинов служилым людям»[87].

[83] ЗОРСА РАО. Т. 2. С. 333–335.

[84] Коллинс С. Нынешнее состояние России. С. 35.

[85] Состояние России в 1650-1655 гг. по донесению И. де Родеса. С. 103.

[86] РГАДА. Ф. 210. Московский стол. Д. 245/1. Л. 6 об.; The Russian elite in the seventeenth century. Vol. 1. P. 161.

[87] РГАДА. Ф. 210. Новгородский стол. Д. 788. Л. 1.

Преступления против царской персоны карались наиболее сурово. Братья боярин Б.М. и окольничий М.М. Салтыковы, расстроившие свадьбу царя Михаила Федоровича с Хлоповой, были сосланы в 1625/1626 г. «невозвввратно» и находились в изгнании около 10 лет. Помимо того, что они «государской радости учинили промешку», им в приговоре припомнили и то, что они «только и делали, что себя богатили, и домы свои и племя своё полнили, и земли крали, и во всяких делах делали неправду и промышляли тем, чтобы, при государской милости, кроме себя, никого не видети, доброхотства есте и службы ко государю не показывали»[88]. Но после смерти патриарха Филарете Салтыковы были возвращены ко двору и в дальнейшем оба получили боярский чин. Наиболее строго был наказан Н.А. Зюзин, лишенный по делу патриарха Никона боярского чина и сосланный в конце 1664 г. (или в начале 1665 г.[89]) в Казань, где находился под стражей. Все его земли были конфискованы. Впоследствии он был ненадолго переведён в Саранск, а потом опять возвращён в Казань[90]. О дальнейшей его судьбе сведений не сохранилось. Известно, что во время следствия Зюзин был подвергнут пыткам, возможно, он вскоре умер.

За весь XVII в. до Петра I известны только две боярские казни: М.Б. Шеина в 1634 г. за потерю Россией Смоленска (его товарищ кн. С. Прозоровский, первоначально также приговорённый Думой к смертной казни, был отправлен в ссылку)[91] и кн. И.А. Хованского с сыном Андреем за руководство стрелецким мятежом 1682 г.[92] По настоянию патриарха, несмотря на сопротивление боярства, за активное участие в движении раскола были казнены боярыни Ф.П. Морозова и кнг. Е.П. Урусова[93]. В целом же бояре, сочувствовавшие расколу, репрессиям не подвергались. Существовавшая в литературе, в том числе и советской, версия о том, что боярин кн. А.М. Львов, возглавлявший Печатный двор, был сослан за отказ печатать новоисправленные книги в Соловки и там стал одним из главных зачинщиков восстания[94], основана на явном недоразумении и была опровергнута ещё в конце XIX в.[95].

---

[88] СГГД. М., 1822. Ч. 3. № 64.

[89] The Russian elite in the seventeenth century. Vol. 1. P. 199.

[90] РИБ. СПб., 1907. Т. 21. Ч. 1. Стб. 1222.

[91] См.: Поршнев Б.Ф. Социально-политическая обстановка в России во время Смоленской войны // История СССР. 1957. № 5.

[92] Восстание в Москве 1682 г. Сб. документов. М., 1976. № 86.

[93] См.: Панченко А.М. Боярыня Морозова – символ и личность // Повесть о боярыне Морозовой. Л., 1979. С. 3–14 и новейшее исследование о политических аспектах осуждения Морозовой: Седов П.В. Закат Московского царства. С. 155–174.

[94] См.: Филарет. История русской церкви. М., 1862. Т. 4. С. 145; Сырцов И. Возмущение соловецких монахов-старообрядцев в XVII в. // Православный

Самые серьёзные политические обвинения часто оставались для бояр без последствий. Характерно, что после восстания 1648 г., во время следствия, проводившегося группировкой Морозова, была выяснена некоторая причастность к подстрекательству восставших Н.И. Романова и кн. Я.К. Черкасского, но Дума замяла все эти обвинения, хотя они были очевидны. «В эти дни много народу подверглось жестоким пыткам: умирают у Морозова, Ильи Даниловича (Милославского), Пушкина, — писал Поммеренинг, — кроме них присутствовали ещё только по 14 и 17 больших бояр, они желали расследовать, какая была причина смятения. Но на Романова и князя Якова (Черкасского) они не хотели возводить обвинений»[96].

Для народа была очевидна безнаказанность боярства. Известны случаи челобитья крестьян и холопов на своих господ, но, как правило, они кончались плохо для челобитчиков. Так, человек боярина кн. С.В. Прозоровского жаловался, что князь хотел пытать своих дворовых, узнав о побегах, и что в боярском доме развешены «листы литовские» (т.е. гравюры), а на тех де листах печатаны всякие скаредные и непристойные блудные статьи». Челобитчик был бит кнутом и отдан боярину «для того, что он то всё затеял, избегая холопства»[97]. Ссылкою в Томск закончилась попытка человека боярина кн. А.Н. Трубецкого К. Курбатова обвинить его «в духовном деле». Патриарх счёл обвинение ложным, так как Курбатов не смог представить доказательств.

Истинно религиозный и следующий далеко не формально христианским догматам, Алексей Михайлович не чужд был идеям всепрощения и милосердия, но распространялось оно, как правило, на лиц высших чинов. Оставляя без наказания вину кн. Г.Г. Ромодановскому, он в том же письме писал о его помощнике: «а страдника Климку велим повесить» (см. выше). Прощая неумелым воеводам бездарные военные действия, приводившие к бессмысленной гибели сотен людей, царь велел отрубить руку и ногу и сослать в Сибирь дворового юношу боярина Морозова за то, что тот на территории Кремля стрелял из ружья по воронам[98]. В 1688 г. были повешены люди стольника кн. Я.И. Лобанова—Ростовского (сына боярина), принимавшие вместе с ним участие в ограблении обоза с государевой казной (тяжкое преступление, карающееся смертью), сам

собеседник. 1880. № 2. С. 150–151; Колчин М. Ссыльные и заточенные в острог Соловецкого монастыря. М., 1908. С. 56; Барсуков Н.А. Соловецкое восстание. Петрозаводск, 1954.

[95] Николаевский П. Московский Печатный двор при патриархе Никоне // Христианские чтения. 1890. № 1–2. С. 121–122.

[96] Якубов К. Россия и Швеция в первой половине XVII в. М., 1879. С. 439.

[97] РИБ. СПб., 1907. Т. 21. Ч. 1. Стб. 98.

[98] РИБ. Т. 21. Ч. 1. Стб. 1156.

же он «по упросу» дальней родственницы кнг. А.Н. Лобановой-Ростовской – «верховой боярыни» отделался битьем кнутом[99].

Поскольку самоуправство и другие преступления бояр фактически оставлялись государством без последствий, народ сам брал их наказание в свои руки: недаром все восстания XVII в. носили антибоярскую направленность. Достаточно вспомнить ликвидацию в 1648 г. восставшим народом всей верхушки московской администрации и требования казни Б.И. Морозова, которого царю удалось с трудом спасти. В 1662 г. восставшие требовали наказания за «изменническую» деятельность И.Д. Милославского, Ф.М. Ртищева и др. Горячо призывал расправиться с боярством Разин. Но наиболее страшным для бояр оказались стрелецкие мятежи, в которых нашли свою гибель многие виднейшие представители Думы.

---

[99] Желябужский И.А. Дневные записки // Рождение империи. М., 1997. С. 268.

The Roman Empire in the Era of Peter the Great

Paul Bushkovitch

In the reign of Peter the Great Russian conceptions of the nature of monarchical rule and the manner of presentation of the tsar to the elite and the common people changed fundamentally. The tsar had been a component in a fundamentally religious view of the world. Russians had not asked: is he bound by law? Is he absolute? What is sovereignty and what is his part in it? Should the state be a monarchy? These are the terms of Western political thought, and most of them could not even be expressed in Russian before the end of the 17th century. The Russians who compiled the known texts that reflect their understanding of the tsar had asked one question: is the tsar a good and faithful Orthodox Christian? Or does he violate God's commandments? Peter changed all that, and by the end of his reign all the "Western" questions could be formulated and various answers given, at least among the ruling elite and a small number of educated gentry.[1]

The new idea of the state and the monarch implied new forms of presentation of the ruler, and as Russia was now undergoing what we call "Westernization," there were a number of sets of images available in Europe. The older forms of presentation, the rituals of the court, the pilgrimages, and the events of the "private" life of the tsar took place in a religious framework. In the new secular and European world, one of the most obvious possibilities was to present the monarch in Roman terms by referring to the history of the Roman

---

[1] Daniel Rowland, "The Problem of Advice in Muscovite Tales about the Time of Troubles," *Russian History* 6: 2 (1979): 259–83; idem, "Did Muscovite Literary Ideology Place Limits on the Power of the Tsar (1540's–1660's)," *Russian Review* 49 (1990): 125–55; idem, "Moscow—the Third Rome or the New Israel?" *Russian Review* 55 (1996): 591–614; Joel Raba, "Moscow—the Third Rome or the New Jerusalem," *Forschungen zur osteuropäischen Geschichte* 50 (1995): 297–308; Robert O. Crummey, "Court Spectacles in Seventeenth-Century Russia: Illusion and Reality," in *Essays in Honor of A. A. Zimin*, ed. Daniel Waugh (Columbus, OH: Slavica, 1985), 130–58; Paul Bushkovitch, "The Epiphany Ceremony of the Russian Court in the Sixteenth and Seventeenth Centuries," *Russian Review* 49 (1990): 1–17. On political ideas in Peter's time, see, among others, Georgii Gurvich, "'Pravda voli monarshei' Feofana Prokopovicha i ee zapadnoevropeiskie istochniki," *Uchenye zapiski imp. Iur'evskogo universiteta* 11 (1915); Lindsey Hughes, *Russia in the Age of Peter the Great* (New Haven: Yale University Press, 1998), 248–97, 378–89; James Cracraft, *The Petrine Revolution in Russian Culture* (Cambridge, MA: Harvard University Press, 2004), 181–92.

Rude & Barbarous Kingdom Revisited: Essays in Russian History and Culture in Honor of Robert O. Crummey. Chester S. L. Dunning, Russell E. Martin, and Daniel Rowland, eds. Bloomington, IN: Slavica Publishers, 2008, 155–72.

emperors, world-conquerors (it seemed), enactors of law codes, and endlessly glorious and powerful. For the Europeans, Rome was a cliché. European noblemen kept whole galleries of real and imaginary portraits of Roman emperors, and visual images derived from Rome, like the many statues of Louis XIV in Roman armor on horseback, were commonplace. One would think that Peter would avail himself of this possibility, and some historians have claimed that he did. Richard Wortman wrote of the "shift from a Byzantine to a Roman imperial model." Some Russian historians of culture have preferred either to resurrect the Third Rome (Lotman and Uspenskii) or to assert that Peter's model was Christian Rome (Zhivov). Lindsey Hughes described the Romanization of the tsar's image, though she also noted the European Baroque elements in the new image.[2]

Two aspects of Peter's presentation of monarchy seem to give support to a Roman model. One is the triumphal processions that marked his victories and the other is the adoption of the new title, *imperator*, in 1721. The processions with their triumphal arches are part of the visual culture of Peter's state, and are certainly relevant to the examination of Roman themes. They have recently been the object of considerable attention on the part of Russian art historians, who have found little Roman in them beyond the general idea of a triumphal procession. The pseudo-Roman triumph was a feature of virtually every European state of Peter's time, and even republican Holland celebrated the victories of its *stadhouder*, William III of England, with Roman arches and processions. The Russians imitated these processions, and thus the art historians have found that Peter's triumphs echoed those of contemporary Europe, not ancient Rome unmediated. To complicate matters more, Peter's triumphs rarely displayed images of Peter himself and normally presented him by an allegorical image of Hercules or Mars. William III and his fellow Europeans, by contrast, appeared in person in pictures or statues over the triumphal arches. Peter made no attempt to show himself as the successor to Augustus and rarely even alluded to the more appropriate Constantine.[3] Zhivov has

---

[2] Hughes, *Russia*, 206–08; Richard Wortman, *Scenarios of Power*, 2 vols. (Princeton, NJ: Princeton University Press, 1995–2000), 1: 43; Iu. M. Lotman and B. A. Uspenskii, "Otzvuki kontseptsii 'Moskva—Tretii Rim' v ideologii Petra Pervogo (K probleme srednevekovoi traditsii v kul'ture Barokko," in *Khudozhestvennyi iazyk Srednevekov'ia*, ed. V. A. Karpushchin (Moscow: Nauka, 1982), 236–49; V. M. Zhivov, "Kul'turnye reformy v sisteme preobrazovanii Petra I," in *Iz istorii russkoi kul'tury*, ed. A. D. Koshelev, 5 vols. (Moscow: Iazyki russkoi kul'tury, 1996), 3: 543–51.

[3] E. A. Tiukhmeneva, *Iskusstvo triumfal'nykh vrat v Rossii pervoi poloviny XVIII veka* (Moscow: Progress-Traditsiia, 2005), 89–90, 145; D. D. Zelov, *Ofitsial'nye svetskie prazdniki: Istoriia triumfov i feierverkov ot Petra Velikogo do ego docheri Elizavety* (Moscow: URSS, 2002), and V. N. Vasil'ev, *Starinnye feierverki v Rossii (XVII – pervaia chetvert' XVIII veka)* (Leningrad: Izd-vo Gosudarstvennogo Ermitazha, 1960) (useful illustrations). Some European examples: D. P. Snoep, *Praal en Propaganda: Triumfalia in de Noordsche Nederlanden in de 16de en 17de eeuw* (Alphen aan den Rijn: Canaletto, 1975);

also recently recognized that the triumphs were reflections of the practice of Baroque Europe, not ancient Rome.[4] These triumphal processions do, however, reveal to some extent the image of ancient Rome on the part of Peter and his contemporaries, and thus will be examined later.

It is the new title, *imperator*, that seems most "Roman," but that conception is fundamentally a misunderstanding. At the conclusion of the treaty of Nystad in 1721, the treaty that put an end to the great war with Sweden, the Russian Senate voted to offer the tsar new titles, "отец отечества (Pater patriae), император всероссийский, Петр Великий." The first two titles were certainly Roman, though neither specifically imperial. The Romans granted the first two to consuls and generals under the republic as well as to later emperors. *Imperator* signified a military commander under the republic and only came to form part of the emperor's title under Vespasian (69–79). The addition of "Great" was also a Roman usage, applied by the Romans, not the Greeks, to Alexander of Macedon and to many Roman emperors. It was also a quasi-official title of Louis XIV, who followed Roman images in many of his public ceremonies and monuments. "Pater patriae" had a similar history, first granted to Roman heroes and then from the time of Augustus onwards, to the emperors.[5]

Even the best read of Russians in Peter's time did not know these details established by modern scholars. The crucial figure in the new titles seems to have been Feofan Prokopovich, who already called Peter "otets otechestva" in his 1709 sermon on the victory at Poltava. Prokopovich was also the probable author of the Senate's decree in 1721, for the initiative seems to have come from the Synod, not the Senate itself. The Synod's proposal was to call Peter Father of the Fatherland because his glorious deeds brought Russia from nonexistence into being, to call him Great because "the ancient Roman and Greek цесари, Julius and others, were called Great," and to use the title "emperor" because Maximilian, the Holy Roman Emperor had already applied it to the ruler of Russia.[6] Thus the reference was not specifically to Rome, but more

Peter Burke, *The Fabrication of Louis XIV* (New Haven: Yale University Press, 1992), 43–44, 74, 78, 156, and illustrations 4, 29, 30.

[4] Viktor Zhivov, *Iz tserkovnoi istorii vremen Petra Velikogo: Issledovaniia i materialy* (Moscow: Novoe literaturnoe obozrenie, 2004), 38.

[5] Robert Combès, *Imperator: Recherches sur l'emploi et la signification du titre d'imperator dans la Rome républicaine* (Paris: Presses universitaires de France, 1966), 132–54; Andreas Alföldi, *Der Vater des Vaterlandes im römischen Denken* (Darmstadt: Wissenschaftliche Buchgesellschaft, 1978), 27–39; Diana Spencer, *The Roman Alexander* (Exeter, UK: University of Exeter Press, 2002), 1, 165, 184–85; Burke, *Fabrication*, 192–98. In the 18th century no one knew that Alexander's epithet dated only from Roman times.

[6] Feofan Prokopovich, "Panegirikos, ili pokhvalnoe o preslavnoi nad voiskami sveiskimi pobede...," in *Panegiricheskaia literatura petrovskogo vremeni*, ed. V. P. Grebeniuk, *Russkaia staropechatnaia literatura XVI – pervaia chetvert' XVIII vv.*, vol. 4 (Moscow:

generally to antiquity, as well as to the Habsburgs. The remark about Maximilian demonstrates that Prokopovich was scarcely a pioneer in this proposal.
Long ago Reinhard Wittram traced the conversations that Russian diplomats
had over this issue with the Habsburg representatives, conversations that
went back at least to 1710 and involved the Russian archival discovery of the
1514 letter of Emperor Maximilian to Vasilii III calling him *imperator* in Latin.[7]

If the title and the triumphs came out of imitation and rivalry with the
Habsburgs and other contemporary European monarchies, then it would
seem that the Roman idea was simply irrelevant to Peter's time. Some aspects
of Roman heritage did penetrate to Moscow and St. Petersburg, but not an
"imperial" image such as that foremost in the minds of modern historians.
The Russian image of ancient Rome inherited from earlier times did not
change immediately when Peter ascended the throne, and that image was
very different from that of post-Renaissance Europe and modern times.[8]

The Russians of the Middle Ages and after, until about 1660, took their
knowledge of ancient Rome from the Byzantines in the form of the translated
world histories that eventually made up the Russian *Khronograf*. As is well

---

Nauka, 1979), 187; Elena Pogosian, *Petr I – arkhitektor russkoi istorii* (St. Petersburg:
Iskusstvo-SPb, 2001), 220–43, esp. 221–22.

[7] Reinhard Wittram, *Peter der Grosse: Czar und Kaiser*, 2 vols. (Göttingen: Vandenhoeck
and Ruprecht, 1964), 2: 250–52, 462–74. Pogosian (above) concludes as well that the reference in the title was to the Habsburgs, not Rome (Pogosian, *Petr I*, 243). The rivalry
with the Habsburgs was also an element in the adoption of the title *tsar'* earlier on; see
W. Vodoff, "Remarques sur la valeur du terme 'tsar'" appliqué aux princes russes
avant le milieu du XVe siècle," *Oxford Slavonic Papers*, New Series, 11 (1978), 1–41;
Gustave Alef, "The Adoption of the Muscovite Two-Headed Eagle: A Discordant
View," *Speculum* 41 (1966): 1–2; Marc Szeftel, "The Title of the Muscovite Monarch up
to the End of the Seventeenth Century," *Canadian/American Slavic Studies* 13 (1979): 59–
81; A. I. Filiushkin, *Tituly russkikh gosudarei* (Moscow: Alians-Arkheo, 2006). A more
"Byzantine" view is to be found in Boris Uspenskii, *Tsar' i Patriarkh: Kharizma vlasti v
Rossii* (Moscow: Iazyki russkoi kul'tury, 1998); and idem, *Tsar' i imperator: Pomazanie na
tsarstvo i semantika monarshikh titulov* (Moscow: Iazyki russkoi kul'tury, 2000). Another
element in the picture was the use of the term *tsar'* for the titles of the Ottoman sultan,
the Tatar khans, and the kings of ancient Israel. The usage of the title *tsar'* was both a
response to the need for international prestige and to continue biblical usage.

[8] In spite of the prominence of the "Third Rome" in the historiography, there is very
little writing on the image of Rome or antiquity in general in Russia before Peter's
time. See Jaroslav N. Scapov and Nina V. Sinicyna, "La Rome antique et médiévale
dans les textes russes du IXe au XVIes.: Etude sur le sens des mots russes Rim, rimskij
et rimljanin," in *La nozione de "Romano" tra cittadinanza e universalita* (Napoli: Edizioni
scientifiche italiane, 1984), 481–503; and D. M. Bulanin, *Antichnye traditsii v Drevnerusskoi literature XI – XVI vv.* (Munich: Otto Sagner, 1991). Though they address other
issues, see also Francis J. Thomson, *The Reception of Byzantine Culture in Mediaeval Russia* (Aldershot: Variorum, 1999); and Max J. Okenfuss, *The Rise and Decline of Latin
Humanism in Early Modern Russia* (Leiden: E. J. Brill, 1995).

known, these histories did not constitute the totality of Byzantine knowledge of history, rather the more ecclesiastical variety that flourished in the monasteries. From Kievan times the works of the sixth–century Syrian Ioannes Malalas and the ninth-century Greek Georgios Amartolos formed the backbone of history, supplemented later by Constantine Manasses (ca. 1130–ca. 1187), the last major Byzantine world chronicler. This history was the story of ancient Israel, the four empires from the prophecy of Daniel VII in Christian interpretation (Persia, Babylon, the empire of Alexander the Great, and Rome) and the early history of Byzantium. Malalas skipped the Roman republic, as did later writers, but he devoted several books of his narrative to the pagan emperors of Rome. Georgios covered the years from Augustus to Constantine but gave most of his attention to Christian history and various theological excursions, with little space left for the emperors. These two texts formed the basis of the 11th century and later versions of the *Khronograf* among the eastern Slavs, and in coverage of the Roman empire followed the model of Georgios, not that of Malalas: the pre-Christian Roman emperors received short shrift.[9]

---

[9] O. V. Tvorogov, *Drevnerusskie khronografy* (Leningrad: Nauka, 1975); Evgenii G. Vodolazkin, *Vsemirnaia istoriia i literatura Drevnei Rusi* (Munich: Otto Sagner, 2000). In the schema of the *Khronograf* ancient Athens and Sparta, the Greek history we know, does not exist. Byzantine scholars knew a great deal about that history, for they read Thucydides and even imitated his style, but that knowledge did not penetrate the monastic chronicles. Similarly the scholars knew the history of the Roman republic from Polybius, Cassius Dio, and other writers. The monastic world chronicles cover the Roman kings from Romulus to the establishment of the republic (of the consuls, in their conception) and then skip the actual history of the republic until they get to Julius Caesar. The result is a Rome that is an empire plain and simple, as the prophecy of Daniel is about kingdoms, *tsarstva*, not just states in general. The republic had no part in the scheme of Christian salvation. E. M. Jeffreys, "The Attitudes of Byzantine Chroniclers towards Ancient History," *Byzantion* 49 (1979): 199–238; Bulanin, *Antichnye traditsii*, 35–54. On Daniel, see Klaus Koch, *Europa, Rom und der Kaiser von dem Hintergrund von zwei Jahrtausenden Rezeption des Buches Daniel*, Berichte aus den Sitzungen der Joachim-Jungius-Gesellschaft der Wissenschaften e. V. Hamburg, Jg. 15, H. 1 (Hamburg: Joachim Jungius-Gesellschaft der Wissenschaften; Göttingen: Vandenhoeck & Ruprecht, 1997); and Mariano Delgado, Klaus Koch, and Edgar Marsch, *Europa, Tausendjähriges Reich und Neue Welt: Zwei Jahrtausende Geschichte und Utopie in der Rezeption des Danielbuches*, Studien zur christlichen Religions- und Kulturgeschichte (Freiburg/Schweiz: Universitätsverlag; Stuttgart: Kohlhammer, 2003). Warren Treadgold, *The Early Byzantine Historians* (Basingstoke: Palgrave Macmillan, 2007), 235–56; idem, "The Byzantine World Histories of John Malalas and Eustathius of Epiphania," *International History Review* 29: 4 (December 2007): 709–45; Gerhard Podskalsky, *Byzantinische Reichseschatologie: Die Periodisierung der Weltgeschichted in den Vier Grossreichen (Daniel 2 und 7) und dem tausendjährigen Friedensreiche (Apok. 20): Eine motivgeschichtliche Untersuchung*. Münchener Universitäts-schriften, Reihe der philosophischen Fakultät 9

This is exactly the version of Roman history that appears in the Russian *Khronograf* of 1512. This history is related as part of the history of the four monarchies, Rome being the last. In spite of the prophetic base and a long exposition of Daniel, the text does not indulge in apocalyptic speculation. It moves from the Hellenistic "monarchy" to Rome via Romulus and Remus and skips the republic but does provide brief notices of the Roman emperors amidst a long narrative of the life of Christ, the Mother of God, and the deeds of the apostles and martyrs.[10] These notices say almost nothing about the greatness and power of Rome, instead they are brief moral portraits of the caesars. Thus Titus was "добродетельный и кротькый моужь и даролюби-вый, раздоваяй имениа и власти." In contrast Domentian "желаа имениа и крови," chopped people in pieces and "по всему блудень с женами и съ мужи, яко же Неронъ."[11]

Julius Caesar himself is a bit more complicated. The republic he replaced, as we noted, essentially did not exist. The brief notice at the end of the tidbits on the Roman kings, however, is revealing. The last king Tarquin is a bad king, who kills many and whose son rapes Lucretia. Brutus then, to revenge the persecution of this father, first plays the loyal courtier, and goes to Delphi on behalf of Tarquin. The oracle tells him that the first to kiss his mother on return will rule in Rome, and that turns out to be Brutus. Brutus then "созва народъ и словесы вооруживъ, разрушение навести возможе мучителемъ, Тарквинию глаголю и его чадомъ. По разрушению оубо царской власти, ипатъ перьвый бысть в Римлянехъ Врутъ, таже Каталинъ, а по нихъ друзии. Такава же сила и дръжава Римськаа ипаты правима леть 400 и 61 до Иоулиа кесаря." The uninitiated Slavic reader might well understand the "ipaty" (Gk. hypatoi = Lat. consules) as some new type of monarchs. Julius Caesar then comes to power when he "izbisha ipaty," defeated Pompey, and "единъ облада Римьскыми скыпетры со многою гордынею и буестию." He receives the title of "dictator." His successes at war and conquests aroused envy, and the envious killed him. In his place "поставиша болярe Римстии сестричища Кесарева Августа" and Antony, but Antony together with Cleo-patra rebelled against Rome and Augustus defeated him. Augustus then con-quered many lands (a few lines) but then has to suffer the reproaches of his wise teacher (оучитель премудръ) Athenodorus before he learns to control his lust (a whole story). The story of Athenodorus shifts the focus from the conqueror to the moral portrait of the emperor.[12] The story lacks the myth so

---

(Munich: Wilhelm Fink Verlag, 1972), 57–61. Manasses did not follow the four mon-archies scheme.

[10] *Polnoe sobranie russkikh letopisei*, 42 vols. (St. Petersburg-Leningrad-Moscow: Imp. Akademiia nauk-Nauka, 1841–1994) [hereafter cited as *PSRL*], vol. 22, pt. 1, 224–61.

[11] *PSRL* 22/1, 253–54.

[12] The Stoic Athenodorus of Tarsus was in fact a philosopher at the court of Augustus, though the story here is a later invention.

prominent in medieval Western accounts of Julius Caesar, that he assumed the imperial title and throne, but does explain how the successors of Augustus came to have the title "tsar." The *Khronograf* presented Caesar as a military hero, a proto-monarch, not as a medieval knight or as the ruler of a feudal monarchy as in the West. The Byzantine model shows here, but with the curious detail that it is the *"boiars"* of ancient Rome that elected Augustus emperor.[13] Finally, the world power of Rome serves as a background for the birth of Christ, showing it to be an event of cosmic significance.[14]

These brief notices appear to be all that the Russians knew of ancient Rome: nothing of the republic, a brief series of moral portraits of the pagan emperors, and then an increasingly detailed history from Constantine through the Byzantine era. The emphasis on the virtue of the emperors or lack thereof completely overshadows any account of imperial power and grandeur. It contrasts sharply with some 18 pages devoted to Alexander the Great, the longest and most detailed portrait of any ruler in the *Khronograf*, about the same length as the section on David and Solomon combined. Both of them got far more space than any Roman ruler other than Constantine.[15]

There are no other Old Russian texts with any substantial information about the Romans. The *Tale of the Vladimir Princes*, the object of so much attention by historians, certainly had a Roman base in that one of its legends presents Augustus as the ancestor of Riurik. The story, however, also had a firm biblical base as it begins with Noah and the division of the earth among his sons. The story of Augustus comes from the *Khronograf* and thus adds little to its information. Augustus appears as the ruler of the whole universe (reunited after the postdiluvian division) who assigns various parts to his relatives, Prussia going to the legendary Prus, ancestor of Riurik. This story has nothing to do with Roman grandeur in the Renaissance understanding; its purpose is to provide a glorious ancestor, internationally recognized as such, to substantiate the territorial claims of the Moscow dynasty, and that is how it was used

---

[13] *PSRL* 22/1, 228–30. The image of Caesar in West European poetry and prose romance is strikingly "medieval." See Jeannette M. A. Beer, *A Medieval Caesar* (Geneva: Droz, 1976), 22–28, 129–54; Joachim Leeker, "Die Darstellung Cäsars in den romanischen Literaturen des Mittelalters," *Analecta Romanica*, H. 50 (Frankfurt am Main, 1986). Any story about Caesar or imperial Rome played very little part in medieval literature, for the main themes were the Arthurian legends, the story of Troy, and the legends of Alexander the Great. Caesar was a very distant fourth in popularity.

[14] *PSRL* 22/1, 231–35. "Tsarstvovanie Avgusta – eto uzhe 'sviashchennaia istoriia'" (Vodolazkin, *Vsemirnaia istoriia*, 168).

[15] Though educated Byzantines certainly knew more Roman history than was found in the world chroniclers, their use of it in political contexts seems to have been limited. Authors of panegyrics on the emperors, at least after 1204, most often compared the Byzantine emperors to Alexander the Great, David, and Solomon, rarely to any Roman emperor. Dimiter Angelov, *Imperial Ideology and Political Thought in Byzantium 1204–1330* (Cambridge: Cambridge University Press, 2007), 85–101.

in the *Sovereign's Genealogy* and practical diplomacy. In other references to the tale, such as that of the *Book of Degrees,* the importance of Augustus is that he ruled the world at the time of the birth of Christ. The frescoes of the Hall of Facets in the Kremlin palace also placed the story of Augustan descent in a religious context, not one of Roman glory. As it was painted in the reign of Tsar Fedor, the Hall was completed at the last moment that the legend had any relevance, as the dynasty then came to an end.[16]

The first Russian reading and translation of new historical texts from outside of Russia did not change things. Part of the reason for this lack of challenge from the West was the persistence of the four monarchies scheme in parts of Europe. Widely circulated until the 13th century, it remained important afterwards in Germany and other lands of the empire.[17] In Germany the four monarchies persisted partly because the scheme fitted the claims of the Holy Roman Emperors and partly because Phillip Melanchton and especially the Protestant historian Johannes Sleidanus gave it new life in his *De quattuor monarchiis* (1556).

Italian humanists generally ignored this scheme and concentrated on Italian cities, but they did not bother to refute it. That was left to Jean Bodin in his *Methodus ad facilem scribendum historiae* (1566). For Bodin the four monarchies were an absurdity precisely because of the claim that the Holy Roman Empire was still the Roman empire. Germany was not Rome. One might think that outside of Germany Christianity might keep the scheme alive, but it did not.

---

[16] R. P. Dmitrieva, *Skazanie o kniaz'iakh vladimirskikh* (Moscow-Leningrad: Akademiia nauk SSSR, 1955), 123–29, 145–51; *Stepennaia kniga, PSRL* 21: 7, 20; Andrei Batalov, *Moskovskoe kamennoe zodchestvo kontsa XVI veka* (Moscow: Rossiiskaia akademiia khudozhestv, 1996), 249–57.

[17] Early Western medieval historians based their image of Rome on the scheme of the six ages of man as well as Daniel. Here the turning point of the last age is the incarnation of Christ, so Rome starts with Augustus. Both versions eliminated the Roman republic from the story as well as Greece before Alexander. By the 12th century the pagan Latin historians were becoming known again, so some Western medieval chroniclers such as Otto of Freising filled out the four monarchies with a more detailed account of Alexander the Great and ancient Rome, including the republic. They stuck to the scheme of the four monarchies, however, in which the republic was the prologue to the really important event, the transferral of the monarchy from the descendants of Alexander to the Roman emperors. The much more widely circulated vernacular *Kaiserchronik,* in contrast, starts with Julius Caesar and portrays good and bad emperors to Constantine, then leaving the Byzantines and recounting the story of the Western emperors. See Bernard Guenée, *Histoire et culture historique dans l'occident medieval* (Paris: Aubier Montaigne, 1980), 148–54, 258–70; Adolf Hofmeister, ed., Otto of Freising, *Chronicon sive de duabus civitatibus,* Monumenta Germaniae Historica, Scriptores rerum germanicarum in usum scholarum (Hannover-Berlin: Hahn, 1912), 5; and Hans Ferdinand Massmann, ed., *Der kaiser und der kunige buoch oder die sogenannte Kaiserchronik,* 3 vols. (Quedlinburg-Leipzig: G. Basse, 1849–54).

Bossuet's *Discours sur l'histoire universelle* (1679) is certainly theistic and follows scripture and Catholic tradition, but omits the four monarchies.[18] Nevertheless, there were plenty of old-fashioned texts from the Middle Ages printed and circulating in the West right up to Peter's time, as well as those of later German world historians.[19]

An example of these more traditional histories is one of the earliest Western texts to make its way to Russia, the 1584 translation of the Polish chronicler Marcin Bielski's 1564 *Kronika* of world history. In his original text Bielski, right on the title page, advertised that his work would describe the six ages of man and the four monarchies (explicitly from Sleidanus), that is to say, he stuck to the medieval scheme. At the same time he knew and quoted various classical authors, like the Western medieval chroniclers, and thus gave more space to Roman history than the Russian *Khronograf*. He gives a much fuller account of the end of the kings and the republic, noting that the consuls were elected and clearly describing the Roman state as a republic. His account of the empire is also much fuller that that of the *Khronograf*, though closer in substance if not detail: a series of moral portraits of the emperors (mostly negative).[20] The Russians had a translation of Bielski by 1584, and used it extensively in their versions of the *Khronograf* from 1617, but when they borrowed texts from the Polish chronicle they did not choose Roman history. Instead they copied and added to the *Khronograf* many stories from classical mythology and other miscellaneous subjects.[21]

The Russians lacked any sense of the Roman grandeur and greatness so dear to the Renaissance. In Russia Rome was the fourth of the *tsarstva* ordained by God, a part of His scheme for man's salvation. On this level it belonged in the realm of the spirit, not of this world. The Rome of this world was certainly a large, important, state ruled by a series of emperors, some

---

[18] Sir Walter Raleigh's attempt at a world history ignores Daniel and merely presents the Bible history combined with Greece and Rome: Sir Walter Raleigh, *History of the World* (London: Printed [by Humphrey Lownes] for H. Lownes, G. Lathum, and R. Young, 1628).

[19] Edgar Marsch, *Biblische Prophetie und chronographische Dichtung: Stoff- und Wirkungsgeschichte der Vision des Propheten Daniel nach Dan. VII* (Berlin: E. Schmidt, 1972), 125–58.

[20] Marcin Bielski, *Kronika to esth Historya Swiata* (Krakow: Matteusz Siebeneycher, 1564; repr. Warsaw: Wydawnictwa Artystyczne i Filmowe, 1976), 9v–10, 100–30, 140–49v. Though Bielski never joined the Reformation, he was one of many Polish Catholics then sympathetic to the movement and its writers: I. Chrzanowski, *Marcin Bielski: Studium historyczno-literackie* (Lwow and Warsaw: Książnica-Atlas, 1926), 12–14, 43–100.

[21] Andrei Popov, *Obzor khronografov russkoi redaktsii*, 2 vols. (Moscow, 1866–69, repr., Osnabrück: Otto Zeller, 1968) 2: 87–111; O. V. Tvorogov, "Khronika Martina Bel'skogo," *Slovar' knizhnikov i knizhnosti Drevnei Rusi*, vyp. 2, pt. 2 (Leningrad: Nauka, 1989), 496–97.

wise and some wicked, until the conversion of Constantine, after which it gradually turned into the *grecheskoe tsarstvo* of the *Khronograf*. It was a central part of history, but it was not the faithful *tsarstvo* of ancient Israel, reborn in Orthodox Russia.

New information about the Romans began to seep into Russia starting in the 1650s. Starting about 1650 the Russians also began to read translations of post-1453 Greek historical texts, Pseudo-Dorotheos of Monemvasia and Matthaios Kigalas. The work of Arsenii and Dionisii Grek, these translations did not change the situation, and for reasons similar to the case of the Bielski chronicle: the authors followed the old scheme of the four monarchies plus ancient Israel. They covered the Roman kings but provided only a few lines on the Roman republic ("demokratia" = "народодержание") started again with Julius Caesar (already "basileus" = "царь"), and moved on quickly to Constantine. Both Greeks continued the story of Rome on to the Ottoman Empire, ending in the later 16th century. They gave the Russians a better idea of late Byzantium and the Ottomans, but not of ancient Rome.[22]

In the 1660s the first generation of Russians began to learn Latin and Polish and there was a wave of translations for those who remained monolingual, but wanted access to the new currents.[23] This generation was also the same as the audience of the new trends in Orthodoxy, the work of the Kievan monks Epifanii Slavinetskii, Simeon Polotskii, and some lesser figures. The establishment of the Slavo-Greco-Latin Academy, with its Jesuit, Western (not Byzantine) curriculum further increased this audience. This audience was the younger generation of the boyars, the court elite broadly defined, and the clergy in Moscow and a few other centers.[24]

Knowledge of the cultural interests of the court elite is limited, but there was some interest in ancient history. Boris Morozov, the tutor of Tsar Aleksei, possessed a translation of Justin's abridgement of Pompeius Trogus, a still common introduction to what the Romans knew of Babylon, Persia, Egypt,

[22] Curiously both texts are extremely brief on Alexander the Great. I. N. Lebedeva, "Pozdnie grecheskie khroniki i ikh russkie i vostochnye perevody," *Palestinskii sbornik* 18 (81) (Leningrad: Nauka, 1968): 35; Rossiiskii gosudarstvennyi arkhiv Drevnikh Aktov (RGADA) f. 181, d. 2 (translation of Pseudo-Dorotheos), fols. 105v–106; and d. 579/1081 (translation of Kigalas).

[23] Paul Bushkovitch, "Cultural Change among the Russian Boyars 1650–1680: New Sources and Old Problems," *Von Moskau nach St. Petersburg: Das russische Reich im 17. Jahrhundert,* published as *Forschungen zur osteuropäischen Geschichte* 56 (Wiesbaden: Harrassowitz Verlag, 2000), 91–112.

[24] Paul Bushkovitch, *Religion and Society in Russia: The Sixteenth and Seventeenth Centuries* (New York: Oxford University Press, 1992): 128–75; Nikolaos Chrissidis, "A Jesuit Aristotle in Seventeenth-Century Russia: Cosmology and the Planetary System in the Slavo-Greco-Latin Academy," in *Modernizing Muscovy, Reform and Social Change in Seventeenth Century Russia,* ed. Jarmo Kotilaine and Marshall Poe (London: RoutledgeCurzon, 2004), 391–416.

and the Hellenistic world (ending with Romulus, however, and not covering Roman history). He presented the book to his pupil, and it remained in the library of the tsars.[25]

Another person with similar but more extensive interests was Artamon Matveev the head of the Posol'skii Prikaz and the tsar's favorite in the last years of the reign of Aleksei Mikhailovich.[26] It is probably from his library and perhaps literally from his son's pen that we have one of the early manuscript translations of the *Annales ecclesiastici* of Cardinal Cesare Baronio. Usually ignored as yet another religious writer in an age of dawning secularization, Baronio's massive tome in defense of the Catholic view of the first millennium of Christianity provided the Russian reader with a mass of information about imperial Rome. Arranged by years, it presented for each year not only the main events of Christian history (the names and deeds of the Popes, the main saints and martyrs, the fathers and their writings), it also told the story of Rome from Augustus onward (thereby omitting the republic) into the Middle Ages, for in Baronio's understanding the Holy Roman Empire continued ancient Rome. Baronio also did not bother to compose a wholly new narrative, he summarized the classical writers and indicated his sources. Thus the Russians heard for the first time of Tacitus and other classical writers, and had a detailed account of the emperors. Most of the account is fairly negative, not just because of the use of Tacitus but also because Baronio was, after all, a propagandist, and his story was one of the triumph of faith in spite of persecution by the wicked, depraved, and despotic Roman emperors. The translation of Baronio was rather widely read among the elite. The surviving

---

[25] I. N. Lebedeva, *Biblioteka Petra I: Opisanie rukupisnykh knig* (St. Petersburg: Biblioteka Akademii nauk, 2003), 36. The translation (from Polish) of Pompeius Trogus did not even include the brief chapters of the original on the Roman kings: Biblioteka akademii nauk, Otdel rukopisei, P.I.A. 15.

[26] Under Artamon Matveev in the Posol'skii Prikaz was the Moldavian exile Nicolae Spatharie Milescu, translator of the *Chrysmologion* (1672) and author of the *Vasiliologion* (1673–74). The former, which exists in many manuscripts, was an account of the prophecies of Daniel, probably based on an earlier work of Paisios Ligarides. It contains a short account of the Roman empire including Byzantium and the Holy Roman Empire up to his own time. The *Chrysmologion* clearly recounts that Caesar abolished the republic (*rech' pospolitaia*) and established *edinovlastie* (Gosudarstvennyi istoricheskii muzei, Otdel rukopisei, Patriarshaia biblioteka, Sobranie slavianskoe 192, op. 259, fols. 290v–93). These details appear in an otherwise highly traditional view of Rome within the context of Daniel's prophecies, and there is no sense of Roman grandeur or power. The *Vasiliologion* is a collection of brief lives of successful and virtuous monarchs, including Julius and Augustus Caesar, Constantine, and Theodosius. The monarchs come from the traditional four monarchies plus Israel and Russia. Again Constantine is the most important of the Roman rulers, though Julius Caesar does receive praise for his wisdom and writings (Biblioteka Akademii nauk, f. Arkhangel'skoi seminarii S 129, f. 274).

MSS include several we can connect with boyars or important people at court.[27] We also know that Tsarevich Aleksei read it, it was printed in 1719, and Peter had it in his library.[28]

There were few other sources on Rome available to Peter and the educated elite, judging from the printed books of the time. Some information came from newer sources on Julius Caesar. In 1711 Peter's press produced a Russian translation of the work of Duke Henri de Rohan on warfare. This 1636 work (*Le parfaict capitaine*) of the French Huguenot general consisted of brief excerpts from Caesar's commentaries with his own comments, an abridgement of a larger work that included a full translation of Caesar. There was information on Caesar, but not much compared to Rohan's larger work, which was less well known both in Europe and Russia. *Le parfaict capitaine* was more Rohan than Caesar, and perhaps for that reason Peter wanted a translation of Caesar's full text, but it never appeared.[29]

For all these hints of a new approach, the only modern work of history published in Russia in Peter's time that touched on the Romans was the late 17th-century world history of Wilhelm Stratemann, the *Theatrum historicum* (*Феатрон или Позор исторический*) of 1724. Peter owned the Latin original (Leipzig, 1694), a manuscript of the Russian translation by Gavriil Buzhinskii and a printed copy, so he may have used it before its actual publication. Buzhinskii thought it a good antidote to Baronio, and that it was. Stratemann, a Lutheran bishop, was violently anti-papal. He also followed the old scheme of the four monarchies, combined with that a version of the late medieval chronicles of the (Western) emperors and the popes, but appended to it a long history of Luther and the Lutheran church in Germany. The sections on Rome are almost as brief as in the Russian *Khronograf*, lack any clear account of the Republic, but include a bit more detail about the emperors, little on Byzantium and a very pro-imperial history of the Holy Roman Empire. In Stratemann, like Sleidanus, the inheritor of ancient Rome was the Holy Roman Empire, not Byzantium. He also claimed that the Byzantine church

---

[27] Of the several copies of this massive text, see Rossiiskaia gosudarstvennaia biblioteka, Otdel rukopisei, f. 256, d. 15 (Baronius Russian translation, possibly by Matveev), d. 16 (another copy); RGADA f. 381, dd. 341–43 (copy for the printer), 344 (another translation from 1695/6). The Polish original of these translations was *Roczne dzieje…Cesara Baroniusza* (Krakow, 1607), translated by Piotr Skarga, who worked from the abridgement of the multi-volume version published 1588–1607.

[28] E. I. Bobrova, *Biblioteka Petra I: Ukazatel'-spravochnik* (Leningrad: Biblioteka akademii nauk, 1978), 59. A manuscript translation from 1706–23 was also among Peter's books, though it may have come from someone else (Lebedeva, *Biblioteka*, 46).

[29] P. Pekarskii, *Nauka i literatura pri Petre Velikom*, 2 vols. (St. Petersburg: Tovarishchestva "Obshchestvennaia pol'za," 1862), 2: 259–61.

was in error in 1054, in spite of his hostility to the Pope.[30] Stratemann's Byzantium was not the second Rome, as the first had not fallen, even if it deviated from the true faith. There could be no Third Rome.

We know for sure that Peter read only one work of Roman literature, Ovid's *Metamorphoses*, which includes at the end a short account of Aeneas, the founding of Rome, and an apotheosis of Julius Caesar. That is in the last book, and strictly speaking we only know that Peter read the first half of Ovid (he had to get his mythology somewhere). If he read the last book, he finally found a positive account of Roman imperial magnificence. It is hard to believe that he did not read another work, the history of Alexander the Great by Quintus Curtius Rufus, as there were five editions printed in his lifetime, three of which he owned. Peter's library also included manuscripts of both Ovid and Quintus Rufus in translation.[31] Peter seems to have preferred Alexander to Caesar.

The tsar was not the only person in Russia with such books; indeed some of his court and government elite far surpassed him in classical reading, as we can see from the libraries of Andrei Matveev, the owner and probable youthful translator of Baronio, and that of Prince Dmitrii Golitsyn. The two also were leading figures in the ruling elite, Matveev being Peter's supporter and Golitsyn his opponent. Matveev had learned Polish and Latin in his youth from the tutor whom his father Artamon Matveev hired. Matveev's library was stuffed with works on classical antiquity as well as the books of the historians and writers of ancient Rome (Livy, Suetonius, Seneca, and others). He also had modern textbooks of world history from the 16th century onward, both the German ones that stuck to the four monarchies (Johannes Clüver) and those that abandoned the medieval schemes and presented a full account of the Romans (Louis Moreri).[32] He presumably read them, since he communicated with both the Dutch and English governments in Latin and seems to have learned French. The library of Prince Golitsyn was no different: Golitsyn too knew his ancient history from the works of Livy, Tacitus, Suetonius, and some modern textbooks: Baronio, Sleidanus, Pufendorff, and others.[33] These

---

[30] Wilhelm Stratemann, *Featron ili Pozor istoricheskii* (St. Petersburg, 1724), 61, 66, 71, 78–79v, 80v, 99v–100. 111–13v, 164–65v, 193–95, 254–59, 294v–95.

[31] Bobrova, *Biblioteka*, 75; Lebedeva, *Biblioteka*, 198; *Pis'ma i bumagi Petra Velikogo*, 13 vols. (St. Petersburg-Moscow: Gos. Tipografiia-Nauka-Drevlekhranilishche, 1887–2003), 3: 601 (letter of F. A. Golovin to Peter, 4 March, 1704).

[32] I. M. Polonskaia et al., *Biblioteka A. A. Matveeva: Katalog* (Moscow: Gos. Biblioteka SSSR im. V. I. Lenina, 1985), 82, 136, 147–48, 171–72, 177.

[33] B. A. Gradova, B. M. Kloss, and V. I. Koretskii, "K istorii Arkhangel'skoi biblioteki D. M. Golitsyna," *Arkheograficheskii ezhegodnik za 1978 god* (Moscow: Akademiia nauk, 1979), 242–43, 245–46; Isabel de Madariaga, "Portrait of an Eighteenth-Century Russian Statesman: Prince Dmiitry Mikhaylovich Golitsyn," *Slavonic and East European Review* 61: 1 (January 1984): 36–60.

were highly unusual accomplishments in the Russia of 1721, but the point is that these people, the few who knew about the ancient world, had power second only to the tsar himself.

In the very extensive library of Peter himself there were no modern works devoted to Roman history, and other than Caesar and Quintus Curtius, none of the other classical historians. Peter's cultural interests were quite real but they did not run to history and literature. An anonymous English work on Peter of 1723 described him as possessing a "mathematical mind," which in the terminology of the time did not mean someone addicted to abstract calculation with numbers.[34] Western mathematical textbooks of 1700 included not just pure mathematics but also surveying, fortification, hydraulics, architecture, ballistics, and mechanics, all of them absorbing interests of Peter's.

Peter knew little about Rome other than Julius Caesar's military accomplishments, and he did not care about Roman magnificence. In any case, the establishment of a great empire had nothing to do with the title of the emperor or one-man rule. If Matveev and Golitsyn were paying attention when they read their classical texts and their modern commentators, they would observe that the great, magnificent, powerful, world-encompassing Roman power was the work of the Republic. It was free republican Rome, not despotic imperial Rome, that enslaved the world. If Peter wanted to be a world conqueror, the Roman lesson would be: turn Russia into a republic. His beloved Dutch republic offered the same example, as did constitutional England. The absolute King of France, Louis XIV, did well in Europe (at first), but his overseas empire was far behind its rivals and soon to end in failure.

For most of Peter's reign the only Roman references in his public ceremonies came in the triumphal processions he staged after his victories. These triumphs, as Tiukhmeneva and other art historians have emphasized were imitations of Baroque Europe. This was a conscious choice, for Peter actually did have the right books in his library (though when, we do not know). The most relevant series of ancient Roman images in his collection were the works of Giovanni Pietro Berolli, the most important antiquarian of papal Rome in the later 17th century. Berolli produced a number of books with engravings by Pietro Santi Bartoli in order to capture and reproduce for scholars the images on the ruins still standing in Rome, the most famous work of this type being his book of the column of Trajan. Peter possessed several of Berolli's works, the most relevant being his 1690 *Veteres arcus triumphis insignes*, a series of plates of the triumphal arches of Rome. Berolli accompanied his plates with a detailed explication of the imagery, and in Peter's copies the text was accurately rendered into Russian. Here Peter could find prototypes for

---

[34] *A true, authentick, and impartial history of the life and glorious actions of the czar of Muscovy from his birth to his death: … the whole compiled from the Russian, High Dutch and French languages, state papers, and other publick authorities* (London [1725]), 5–6. The work was formerly attributed to Daniel Defoe.

his triumphal entries into Moscow, if he wanted them. The three arches in Rome, those of Titus, Septimius Severus, and Constantine, had each an inscription and scenes of battle in which the emperor figured, as well as the goddess of Victory. As was typical of Roman arches, they lacked the Baroque depictions of virtues, allegories, or gods other than Mars.[35]

Peter's first "Roman" triumph was on the return from Azov. On August 20, 1696, he wrote to Andrei Vinius, the Russo-Dutch official who seems to have been a sort of factotum for Peter in those years. He told Vinius that he wanted to honor the Generalissimus Aleksei Semenovich Shein with "триумфальные порты" on his entrance into Moscow.[36] The iconographic details he seems to have left up to Vinius, and the result honored Peter as much or more than Shein. On each side of the gates were statues of Hercules and Mars, and over the top "Приидохъ, Видехъ, Побѣдихъ," an Old Slavic version of the "veni, vidi, vici" of Julius Caesar. The rest of the decoration showed the events of Azov, a statue representing Fame, and biblical quotations to underline the triumph of Christianity, as did representation of the triumph of Constantine over Maxentius. The Roman allusions are only a small part of the imagery, and they are of military victory (the triumphal procession itself and Caesar) and the victory of faith under Constantine, not empire. Peter himself does not seem to have been depicted, though the Baroque arches showed the emperor leading the army. Note also that Peter called the structure a gate, using the Latin/Italian *"porta"* rather than *"arcus/arco."*[37]

A more "imperial," if not Roman, image appeared in the West, the engraving that Il'ia Kopievskii published in Holland to celebrate Peter's victory. That shows Peter seated on a throne between the two pillars of Hercules, as in the Habsburg device, and the connection is made obvious by the motto, "Plus ultra rosseanum," in place of Charles V's original and simpler "Plus oultre."[38] Again, the reference is the Habsburgs, not Rome.

The 1703 procession to celebrate the reconquest of Ingria, or the part of the procession that was the product of the Slavo-Greco-Latin Academy, consisted of masses of classical figures, Perseus, Jason, Neptune, Minerva, but no Roman emperors. At one point the images compare Tsar Aleksei to Philip of Macedon, the father of Alexander the Great, but the image of Peter does not

---

[35] Tiukhmeneva, *Iskusstvo*, 70. The translator gave "римляне" for "Quirites," and rendered Latin "imperator" by "император," "цесарь," or "правитель войска" according to context (Biblioteka Akademii nauk, Rukopisnyi otdel, P I B no. 109 [*Veteres arcus*], P I B no. 110 [*Admiranda...vestigia*], ff. 5, 17, 23, 25. In the Bobrova catalog Berolli's works are found under the name of his printer, de Rubeis (Rossi): Bobrova, *Biblioteka*, 147. Cf Lebedeva, *Biblioteka*, 221–22.

[36] *Pis'ma i bumagi*, 1: 122.

[37] M. M. Bogoslovskii, *Petr I: Materialy dlia biografii*, 5 vols. (Moscow: OGIZ, 1940–48), 1: 344–50; Tiukhmeneva, *Iskusstvo*, 63.

[38] Bogoslovskii, *Materialy dlia biografii*, 1: 345.

compare him to Alexander. That honor is reserved to Tsarevich Aleksei, then 12 years old.[39] The images for the 1709 triumphal procession after Poltava were a complex series. The report of the Danish ambassador Just Juel supplements the contemporary description from the Academy faculty. Juel reported a series of allegories, many directed at the Swedes, such as a lion in a cage, a lion knocking an eagle down a mountain, or Hercules in a lion skin. The imagery of the arch revolved around a depiction of Peter as Hercules, not Julius Caesar or any Roman emperor. The Hercules harked back to the 1696 engraving, which reminds us that Hercules could be both classical and a reference to equality with the Habsburgs. Much of this imagery returned in 1714 and 1721 and without Roman emperors.[40]

The arches were not just the work of the Slavo-Greco-Latin Academy, though theirs seems to have been the most elaborate as well as the most learned in their system of references. Menshikov, the Stroganovs, and the merchants of Moscow as a group also erected triumphal gates. E. A. Tiukhmeneva goes far in discovering the process of by which they were made, but the ultimate determination of the pictorial scheme remains unclear. It is difficult, however, to imagine that the schemes violated the tsar's wishes. Normally the representation of Peter was allegorical (Hercules or Mars). In 1709 the Stroganov gates featured a picture of Peter on horseback taking the Swedish surrender, as did the Menshikov gates. In 1721 the Menshikov gates displayed portraits of Peter and Catherine, but the others had only allegories of monarchical virtue. On the original triumphal arches that the Romans set up to memorialize such triumphs there were pictures of the emperors (e.g. the Arch of Titus), battle scenes and the occasional winged Victory. West European baroque arches commonly included an equestrian statue of the king at the summit. Peter's arches of triumph omitted the statue but were otherwise baroque, full of allegory and gods far more numerous than the real Romans ever included. Peter's arches and gates did not imitate actual Roman arches and settled for a less exuberant version of the Baroque of Paris and Vienna.[41]

The processions, however important, were nevertheless ephemeral. It was in Peter's palaces and gardens that he had a chance to show what he knew of ancient Rome, and architecture was one of his principal interests. This meant the decoration of the façades of his dwellings and well as the gardens, the latter primarily with sculpture. Besides the work of Berolli, he had many illustrated books of Roman ruins and statuary, such as that of Domenico Rossi

---

[39] "Torzhestvennaia vrata...," in Grebeniuk, *Panegiricheskaia literatura*, 135–49; Tiukhmeneva, *Iskusstvo*, 69.

[40] Tiukhmeneva, *Iskusstvo*, 69–92, 157–212; Just Juel, *En rejse til Rusland under tsar Peter* (Copenhagen: Gyldendal, 1893), 140–41.

[41] Tiukhmeneva, *Iskusstvo*, 70, 88–89, illustrations 24, 27, 43. Menshikov seems to have consistently managed to portray Peter in person. Judging by the 1696 gates, which we know Peter controlled, this was not his choice.

(1704). Other books illustrated modern buildings intended to convey the glory of a modern monarch with Roman means (Giacomo Barozzo da Vignola, Palladio). In 1717 he actually saw Versailles and the French palaces with their own Roman references, though he seems to have rather disliked the buildings if not the gardens.[42]

Peter's largest more or less public artistic product was the Summer Garden, whose mostly Venetian statuary survives in large part to this day. Of the first Summer Garden we know little, but it included allegorical statues as well as busts of King Jan Sobieski of Poland and his wife Maria Kazimiera. The rest of the Summer Garden statues and busts were purchased mainly in 1715–18 by Sava Vladislavich-Raguzinskii, Peter's agent in Venice. The tsar relied on the expertise of his agents, especially Vladislavich. In 1716 Peter asked for 11 statues with allegorical subjects (Dawn, Noon, Evening, Night, Fate, Nemesis) and gods (Saturn, Pomona, Nereis, and a Naiad). In response Vladislavich sent Peter a sort of handwritten catalog with drawings of some 124 statues and busts from Venice, one of them marked as showing statues typical of the princely and royal garden in Europe (Роспись, каковы статуи употребляют в наилутчих садах ц[еса]рских, кралевскых и протчых господ велможных). Peter ultimately chose 24 statues and 50 busts for the garden. The 24 statues were all allegories ("wisdom," "autumn") or ancient gods and goddesses, and formed the core of the ensemble. The 50 busts included representations of the first 12 Roman emperors (Augustus, Nero, Tiberius, and the others) and their wives. The choice of emperors is curious, that is, all 12 in order, good rulers and tyrants, and their mostly rather obscure wives—the better known being mostly rather dubious, like Messalina. These busts were not part of Peter's request, and in fact were an afterthought of Vladislavich, not in his original proposal to the tsar. The other busts depicted philosophers of antiquity and the Sybils. The result was more like a museum of antiquity than an image of glory, and in any case was an attempt to imitate European garden statuary: any Roman element was the result of imitating Europe, not of making Roman claims.[43] Peter did know about Roman equestrian statues of emperors. The Rossi book had a picture of the statue of Marcus Aurelius in Rome, and Peter asked the sculptor Niccolo Michetti to try to get him a reproduction, but he only wanted the horse, judging by his letter of October 1720. Nevertheless, he could not avoid recognizing that a civilized European people was supposed to put up huge statues of its kings in Roman dress, for he had seen Paris. In 1716 Carlo Bartolomeo Rastrelli (father of the architect) began to make a model of such an equestrian statue, and Peter approved it, but soon

---

[42] Wittram, *Peter der Grosse*, 2: 315–17; James Cracraft, *The Petrine Revolution in Russian Architecture* (Chicago: University of Chicago Press, 1988), 147–54.

[43] Another list headed "Последняя манера Европская" consisted of allegories of War, Peace, Harmony, and similar ideas: S. O. Androsov, *Ital'ianskaia skul'ptura v sobranii Petra Velikogo* (St. Petersburg: Dmitrii Bulanin, 1999), 13, 31, 32, 35, 38–39.

changed his mind and asked for a rearing horse. Rastrelli worked on it, but Peter seems to have still had doubts, for he commissioned another version from another Italian sculptor. By the time of Peter's death in 1725 neither project had advanced. Rastrelli's first model languished in a shed, and was not cast into bronze and put to use until Emperor Paul set it up in front of the Mikhailov Castle. The rather heavy and uninspiring result still stands there.[44] The statue does not seem to have had much priority with its subject.

In conclusion, it is important to remember that what Peter or even Matveev and Prince Golitsyn knew about Rome was much more limited than what modern historians know. Understanding of the meaning of their Roman references requires a careful reading of their statements and also the literature available to them and used by them. We cannot take any reference to ancient Rome to mean a reference to glory and empire. In practice, it was a reference to modern Europe, to the culture of the Baroque, to Peter's rivals. It was Vienna, Paris, and Europe generally that Peter and the Senate had in mind, and not only in 1721.

The triumphal processions, the few Romans in the Summer Garden, some decorative elements on buildings, and an unrealized plan for an equestrian statue are the sum total of Peter's "Roman" presentation of himself as ruler, and they do not add up to much. This should not be surprising. Peter did not know very much about ancient Rome, other than the military virtues of Julius Caesar, the story of Constantine, and its architecture. Among the ancient heroes, Alexander the Great loomed larger than Caesar. In building his new capital, his "paradise," he did not resort to Roman models. The few Roman elements that he commissioned came in response to the proposals of Vladislavich and Rastrelli, and they were not major elements of his public presentation in its architectural forms. The city that Peter built was not a monument to pseudo-Roman glory, instead it looked like a middle-sized north German port, with modest houses and unimpressive residences for the rulers. Modern Petersburg has plenty of classical magnificence, but it is the work of later rulers, who put Roman victory columns in front of Roman arches.

Peter's presentation of the monarchy to the public was a Russified version of the European Baroque tradition. His Romans were Baroque Romans, as were his allegories and his ancient gods. At the same time, all of his public ceremonies had the imprint of his own personal eccentricities. He was no Louis XIV, whose palaces were built to convey explicit grandeur and power. Peter was, after all, a monarch who lived in a six-room house, called it the Winter Palace, and spent most of his day in boat yards.

---

[44] Androsov, *Ital'ianskaia skul'ptura*, 16; Cracraft, *Revolution*; Alexander M. Schenker, *The Bronze Horseman: Falconet's Monument to Peter the Great* (New Haven: Yale University Press, 2003), 70–75.

Kamenev in Early NEP: The Twelfth Party Congress

Alexis E. Pogorelskin

In the spring of 1923, Lev Kamenev's position in the party appeared unassailable. As an intimate of Lenin in the years of exile, he had readily, despite early hesitations on his part in October and November 1917, moved into the highest echelons of power in the new Soviet state. By 1923 he was one of the triumvirs, along with Stalin and Zinov'ev, who had stepped in to rule as Lenin's health failed. Yet with extraordinary swiftness, in a mere two years, Kamenev existed on the fringes of power. In four years, at the Fifteenth Party Congress, his rout was complete.

To account for the swiftness of his fall, the Twelfth Party Congress held April 17–23, 1923, provides crucial information. Scholars have noted the importance of that congress for understanding the emerging succession struggle. N. I. Kapchenko called it "an important marker [*rubezh*] in the struggle for power."[1] Robert V. Daniels observed that it was "the last when individual delegates spoke their minds without prepared scripts."[2] Adam Ulam suggested that "it is possible that it was at the Twelfth Party Congress that Stalin was first seized with the idea of his personal dictatorship being ... feasible.[3] I would add that the Twelfth also provides remarkable evidence for understanding the paradox inherent in Kamenev's career during NEP, namely immense power coupled with precipitous decline. Kamenev, in that sense, experienced the fate of Trotskii and Zinov'ev. But they have something more in common. The careers of all three share the same hinge: the Twelfth Party Congress.

The Twelfth Congress was the first from which Lenin was absent since the Bolsheviks seized power. His deteriorating health meant not only that he would miss the congress, but that the party could never again count on his presence within the leadership. Yet as Kamenev noted, precisely at this time, the party faced overwhelming uncertainty and challenges that would determine the future course of Soviet power: "Before our congress stands the question of the proletariat and the peasantry ... the organization of industry, the decision on the nationality question, and the reorganization of the state and

[1] N. I. Kapchenko, *Politicheskaia biografiia Stalina* (Moscow: ROSSPEN, 2005), 688.

[2] Robert V. Daniels, *The Conscience of the Revolution* (Boulder, CO: Westview Press, 1988), 193.

[3] Adam B. Ulam, *Stalin* (New York: The Viking Press, 1973), 227.

Rude & Barbarous Kingdom Revisited: Essays in Russian History and Culture in Honor of Robert O. Crummey. Chester S. L. Dunning, Russell E. Martin, and Daniel Rowland, eds. Bloomington, IN: Slavica Publishers, 2008, 173–87.

party apparatus," Kamenev told the delegates, opening the conclave as chair of the congress.[4]

Some, if not all of those issues, raised the question of Stalin's position in the party. The Twelfth Congress was also the first to be held since Stalin had been appointed General Secretary of the party. In the year that he had occupied the position, the General Secretary had managed to turn the *Uchraspred*, the Account and Assignment Section of the Secretariat, into his lever to control the composition of the party.[5] Since the Eleventh Congress met in 1922, *Uchraspred* had made "10,000 assignments ... half ... involved so-called responsible officials."[6] As Robert Daniels has observed, Stalin may have possessed "effective control over a majority of the delegates"[7] thanks to his appointment of so many *gubkom* secretaries; but the Twelfth also witnessed a measure of independence on the part of delegates, who felt free to express themselves spontaneously in the give and take of debate.

The Twelfth Congress offered opportunities to the oligarchs as well. With Lenin absent they presented themselves to the party, vying in the political arena for allegiance and ultimately supremacy. Stalin, for example, may have taken control of party appointments; he had yet to convince the party to follow him. Kamenev had carefully cultivated a client group in the capital and its environs, but could his appeal extend beyond that region? Did he perceive that he might have to convince the party as a whole of his right to leadership? By the Thirteenth Congress, the first after Lenin's death, the oligarchs provided "a model of unanimity."[8] To lift the veil over the leadership struggle, we must turn back to the Twelfth Congress where Kamenev joined his fellow oligarchs on display for the first time with Lenin absent. Each stepped forward from Lenin's shadow to present himself in the glare of competition. Unspoken must have been the question, which of them could replace Vladimir Il'ich. The Twelfth Congress therefore offered a unique preview of the succession struggle to come.

The Twelfth Party Congress saw another first, namely the emerging cult of Lenin, as the real Lenin receded from view. Nina Tumarkin has stated that "at the Twelfth Congress ... the party's leaders ... cloaked ... the competition among them ... in a unified public reverence for Lenin and his ideas."[9] The

---

[4] *Dvenadtsatyi s"ezd RKP(b), 17–23 aprelia 1923 goda: Stenograficheskii otchet* (Moscow: Izd-vo politicheskoi literatury, 1968), 5. Henceforth *XII s"ezd*.

[5] See discussion in Merle Fainsod, *How Russia Is Ruled* (Cambridge, MA: Harvard University Press, 1963), 122.

[6] Ibid.

[7] Daniels, *Conscience of the Revolution*, 194.

[8] Leonard Schapiro, *The Communist Party of the Soviet Union* (New York: Vintage Books, 1960), 283.

[9] Nina Tumarkin, *Lenin Lives! The Lenin Cult in Soviet Russia* (Cambridge, MA: Harvard University Press, 1990), 122.

statement more accurately describes the Thirteenth Congress than the Twelfth. Reverence for Lenin in 1923 appeared far from unified. Distinct differences in attitudes to Lenin revealed both the status of the oligarchs as well as their relationship to each other.

Kamenev's invocation of Lenin was inextricably bound up with his support of NEP. Most delegates to the congress harbored serious reservations about the policy of concessions to the peasantry which Lenin had imposed on the barely willing party two years earlier. Kamenev, more than any other oligarch at the Twelfth Congress, assumed the role of NEP's defender.

He did so for political as well as economic reasons. His power base and the constituency that he represented lay in the Moscow region. The light industry and textiles of "calico Moscow," as the area was known before 1917, satisfied peasant hunger for consumer goods and therefore thrived under NEP. NEP had brought prosperity to Kamenev's Moscow's constituency. His arguments on behalf of "raising the buying power of the peasantry ... and the peasant market"[10] appeared self-serving. By the same token, Kamenev's use of Lenin to justify expansion of NEP diminished the authenticity of his fealty to the Leader. "Vladimir Il'ich," Kamenev told the congress, had in his teaching provided the antidote to any crisis.[11] Lenin had also insisted that "collaboration between the proletariat and revolutionary peasantry," the so-called *smychka*, "constitutes the basic, first idea of Bolshevism."[12] Moscow's continued prosperity lay with Kamenev's version of Lenin.

Kamenev's ardent defense of NEP also revealed his isolation in the leadership and the party as a whole, a harbinger of his fall. No one else wanted the role of defender of such controversial "unBolshevik" policies. Lenin's word repeatedly bolstered Kamenev's arguments for the unpopular compromise rather than the inherent soundness of NEP or Kamenev's own authority on economic matters. His repeated invocations of Lenin weakened rather than strengthened his arguments or his claim to leadership. While references to Lenin reminded Old Bolsheviks of Kamenev's long-standing closeness to the Leader, they also made him appear unable to lead on his own, incapable of conducting himself independently or of devising new and cogent economic reasons that would reconcile the party to NEP. He was unable to convince delegates as a whole to embrace the policy of "bias toward the peasantry."

Kamenev's relationship to the growing cult of Lenin proved to be his most paradoxical failing. He had good reason to invoke the man who had been both friend and mentor to him for decades. Lenin, in turn, trusted Kamenev. Lenin had made him his literary executor. He had chosen Kamenev to represent him during difficult negotiations with Bogdanov in 1908. At

---

[10] *XII s"ezd*, 447.

[11] Ibid., 5.

[12] Ibid., 425.

Lenin's urging Kamenev had taken up serious study of Chernyshevskii in 1913 which he would pursue for the rest of his life.[13] Kamenev's passing reference to Chernyshevskii in his opening address,[14] undecipherable to most delegates, in fact suggested his long-standing intimacy with Lenin. On the other hand, no delegate could miss Kamenev's endowing the dying Il'ich with infallible status. Many at the party congress hoped that NEP would be buried with Lenin. Kamenev's reliance on an expiring individual and a politically expedient cult in defense of an unpopular policy undermined his claim to leadership of party and state.

Zinov'ev's contribution to the Lenin cult proved even more damaging to his reputation. Isaac Deutscher has said of Zinov'ev at the Twelfth Congress that "his exaggerated and even ridiculous expressions of adoration of Lenin disgusted the sophisticated and critically minded..."[15] The damage, I would argue, went beyond the opinion of "the sophisticated and critically minded." While scholars generally agree that Zinov'ev did himself no good by assuming Lenin's role in delivering the political report to the congress "and paid the price for doing so,"[16] the very content of the speech may have proved more damaging than the fact that Zinov'ev appeared to replace Lenin in delivering it. Touching on every major issue before the assembly, Zinov'ev invoked Lenin as his authority on each one. The result was to make him look weak, incompetent, incapable of leadership save by reliance on a dying leader whose ideas might well have decreasing relevance. Zinov'ev had by his own hand made himself but a poor reflection of Lenin, rather than a usurper of Il'ich's role. In truth, both Kamenev and Zinov'ev had been personally closest to Lenin and could claim the longest and most intimate relationship with him. On the one hand they could most reasonably justify invoking him to support their views, because they knew Lenin best. On the other their attempts at times maudlin, compulsive, and inappropriate to turn personal closeness into political capital failed.

By the same token the cult of Lenin could be problematical for Trotskii. His perfunctory references to Lenin, and those few in number, communicated their own message. Trotskii appeared all too ready to go on without the Leader. His very defense of industry at the Twelfth Congress underscored his unwillingness to follow Lenin's directives, while offering alternatives of his own to NEP when it suited him. Trotskii's references to Lenin in his hard-hitting speech on industry also contrasted harshly with the almost tremulous invocations of Zinov'ev and Kamenev. In fact, Trotskii felt no need to deify

---

[13] L. B. Kamenev, *Chernyshevsky* (Moscow: Zhurnal'nogazetnoe ob"edinenie, 1913), iii.

[14] XII s"ezd, 4.

[15] Isaac Deutscher, *The Prophet Unarmed: Trotsky. 1921–1929* (London: Oxford University Press), 95.

[16] Philip Pomper, *Lenin, Trotsky, Stalin: The Intelligentsia in Power* (New York: Columbia University Press, 1990), 390.

Lenin. They had fought each other for over a decade and a half before aligning in 1917. To Trotskii, Lenin could be far from infallible. Most recently, he had charged him with confronting Stalin at the congress on the Georgian question, a burden, Lenin's erstwhile rival had chosen to relinquish.

In contrast, Stalin turned his very alienation from Lenin into an advantage at the Twelfth Congress. "The delegates knew that Lenin had fallen out with Stalin."[17] Many also knew that Lenin had broken with Stalin over the Georgian question. In that sense Stalin's prominence at the congress, whether speaking for the Central Committee on its expansion or his addressing the nationality question *ipso facto* belied the very integrity of the Lenin cult or at least showed it up for what it was: a malleable construct that revealed weakness as much as it imparted strength. In Stalin's case it could be irrelevant. Stalin barely mentioned Lenin in his speech on the nationality question. If Lenin condemned him on the Georgian question and even wanted him removed as General Secretary, Stalin would show his independence by disdaining Lenin in turn. For example, he cited Lenin only twice in his speech on the nationality question and on one of those occasions did so to emphasize that Lenin's view on the issue coincided with his own: Stalin very nearly appeared to confirm Lenin rather than the other way round.

Stalin had something else to impart in that speech. The medium was the message. While he paraded before the congress his disdain for the Georgian leadership, he also expressed contempt for his former homeland. Stalin mocked the Georgians for their "sense of superiority over other minorities,"[18] disparaging "the little piece [*kusochek*] of Soviet territory called Georgia..."[19] The General Secretary delivered those words in an accent redolent of the Caucasus. Though a Georgian, Stalin seemed to say, he had thrown off his past and his nationality. He belonged to the party alone.

Invoking the Georgian affair did something more. Lenin had broken with Stalin over it, as many delegates knew. Again, Stalin reiterated: he stood alone, without Lenin, without Georgia. He could confront Il'ich if he deemed it necessary. Such strength and independence qualified him to lead the party as well as administer it. The contrast between Kamenev's and Zinov'ev's almost tremulous reliance on Lenin could not be sharper.

Stalin's distancing himself from the emerging cult of Lenin at the Twelfth Congress made the oath sworn at Lenin's bier all the more dramatic. His pledge to Lenin at the founder's funeral had the appearance of both reconciliation and commitment. His obeisance to Lenin transcended the artificial and politically motivated invocations of his rivals on display the year before at the Twelfth Party Congress. In contrast, the eulogies of Kamenev and Zinov'ev remained tainted by the self-serving exaggerations of the Twelfth Congress.

---

[17] Daniels, *Conscience of the Revolution*, 205.

[18] *XII s"ezd*, 487

[19] Ibid., 204.

Stalin appeared to recognize how damaging the Lenin cult could be. Nina Tumarkin has observed Stalin's ambivalence regarding the cult. She writes "there is no doubt that Stalin played an important role in the development of the cult of Lenin." But she astutely questions "the contention" of "Western scholarship" that "Stalin was the architect of, and moving force behind, the Lenin cult."[20] I would refine the point.

The cult, that is the creation of an infallible Lenin, originated with Kamenev and Zinov'ev in their effusive speeches at the Twelfth Party Congress. They attempted to use Lenin to legitimize their own claim to leadership. Instead, they made themselves vulnerable to a shared past which included the "strike-breaker" episode of October 1917. Stalin's calm reserve and emotional restraint, in contrast, lay in political calculation. He could hardly affirm Lenin's infallibility when Il'ich sought his removal from responsibility for nationality policy and, *horrible dictum*, the Secretariat.

Stalin had only to wait. With Lenin safely dead even though infallible, Kamenev, Zinov'ev, and Trotskii, who all had a history of conflict with Lenin, would inevitably put themselves at odds with the cult. Zinov'ev saved Stalin from that fate in May 1924 on the eve of the Thirteenth Party Congress when he argued before the Central Committee that Lenin's warning about Stalin in his Testament had been unfounded. Only after Zinov'ev's miscalculated absolution would Stalin, as Leonard Schapiro has argued, become the prophet for a Lenin, who assumed the role of Allah.[21] But at the Twelfth and for over a year afterward, Stalin played a very different role. The ultimate paradox of the Lenin cult as it originated at the Twelfth Congress lay in the fact that it harmed those genuinely closest to Lenin and came to benefit the one whom Lenin considered "too rude" to lead the party.

Kamenev and Zinov'ev harmed themselves at the congress in another respect. Both attacked opposition in the party in a mocking and uncompromising fashion. Their words would come back to haunt them. Kamenev gave more attention to the presence at the congress of two oppositional groupings. One flourished inside the state apparatus as a "managerial opposition."[22] The other existed in the party as a new semi-underground Ultra Left movement, combining the Workers' Truth, Democratic Centralism, and the Workers' Opposition. The so-called "ultra left movement" had circulated an Anonymous Platform which called for uniting various dissident groups within the party and removing the triumvirs from power.[23] Kamenev opened the congress with a statement in which he entangled himself irrevocably with Lenin's uncompromising attitude to dissent: "[R]emember that ... as our greatest

---

[20] Tumarkin, *Lenin Lives*, 153.

[21] Schapiro, *Communist Party*, 286.

[22] Daniels, *Conscience of the Revolution*, 201.

[23] Ibid.

treasure ... we must regard the unity of our party ... here is what Lenin told us and here is the road along which our congress will go."[24]

Kamenev's statements on dissent at the Twelfth Congress, it should be noted, contrasted painfully with his actual role within the Soviet leadership. Just as in defending NEP, in denouncing the opposition, he appeared to fulfill a political obligation that the other oligarchs avoided. Kamenev, in fact, had long supported pluralism in Soviet society. He had joined Gor'kii to save Kadet professors arrested in the fall of 1920, assuring them that they could turn to him if they were again detained.[25] At the same time he collaborated with Gor'kii to promote world literature and European culture. Kamenev's statements on dissent, while consonant with the party's position on factions as already confirmed by the Tenth and Eleventh congresses, appeared out of character and unduly harsh coming from him. He now appeared two-faced. Kamenev lacked Stalin's talent to mask hypocrisy with what Kapchenko calls "transparent hints" (*prozrachnye nameki*)[26] and thus appear moderate rather than heavy-handed, deceiving with even the most hypocritical statements.

When speaking of dissent Kamenev did himself even more harm in the future than at the congress itself. He provided another justification for unity, reminding the delegates that "definite limits had to be maintained on our own internal party discussions ... [because] not only international enemies, but also petty bourgeois and NEP elements inside our country surround the proletariat and the Communist Party."[27] Delegates to the Fourteenth Congress might well recall those words spoken at the Twelfth two years before and ask what had changed to permit the dissent of Zinov'ev and Kamenev in 1925. By the same token, at the end of the Fourteenth, when Zinov'ev called on all opposition groups to join with him in producing a publication for the views of opponents of the General Line, no doubt many again recalled the Twelfth Congress where Kamenev had mocked just such a proposal. V. V. Osinskii and T. V. Sapronov had then urged "all honest proletarian elements grouped around Democratic Centralism, Workers' Truth, and ... the Workers' Opposition, both in the party and outside its ranks to join the founding manifesto of the Workers' Group RKP."[28] Kamenev asked why form a Workers' Group when "honest worker elements" had already "grouped around the Central Committee of our party."[29] In 1925 the opponents of Kamenev and Zinov'ev could themselves ask why the two had the right to

---

[24] *XII s"ezd*, 6.

[25] V. A. Keldysh et al., eds., *Neizvestnyi Gor'kii: K 125-letiiu so dnia rozhdeniia*, Gor'kii i ego epokha, vyp. 3 (Moscow: Nasledie, 1994), 49.

[26] Kapchenko, *Biografiia Stalina*, 692–93.

[27] *XII s"ezd*, 153.

[28] Ibid., 158.

[29] Ibid.

join with others and place themselves "in opposition to the Central Committee of our party...."[30] when Kamenev had denied the right to Sapronov and Osinskii, among others, to do just that two years earlier.

Arguably, Kamenev's finest moment in the party occurred when he told the Fourteenth Congress in unmistakable terms: "I have come to the conclusion that Comrade Stalin cannot fulfill the role of unifier of the Bolshevik general staff.... We are against the doctrine of one man rule, we are against the creation of a Leader."[31] Irony tempered heroism. At the Twelfth L. A. Lutovinov had engaged in a similar act of truth telling, observing that while the party demanded unity, it could only obtain it "by way of repression and shutting the mouths of those who wish to express themselves...."[32] Kamenev had responded that Lutovinov "reasoned like Kerensky."[33] Had Kamenev's courage at the Fourteenth, some delegates may have wondered, landed him among the ranks of Kerensky and a dissident like Lutovinov.

The question arises why Kamenev, who possessed the reputation of urbane and cultured pluralism—scholar, diplomat, and journalist who had written movingly on Herzen and Chernyshevskii—misused his power by bullying dissent and employed far too many arguments that ended with invoking Lenin. If this was the new role that Kamenev was to play in the party, it was a prelude to defeat even when he seemed part of a collective succession to Lenin. It is doubtful that he lacked the political imagination to perceive that his condemnation of the opposition could readily be turned against himself. He clearly found some advantages in defending an economic policy, no matter how unpopular elsewhere, that served the interests of the Moscow region. But what about his other tactical errors? Contributing to his inflexibility must have been awareness of Trotskii's genuine popularity and fear of a future without Lenin. Each member of the triumvirate possessed vulnerabilities. In addition, opposition groups that proliferated like mushrooms after rain, as Lutovinov observed, sought to remove the triumvirate from power.[34]

One of Kamenev's vulnerabilities revealed at the Twelfth Congress lay in his uncompromising defense of NEP. Only Sokolnikov, who elaborated on the new tax policy that Kamenev proposed, joined in consistent support of NEP. Trotskii and the other triumvirs, in contrast, all gave vent to the party's consternation over favoring the peasantry. Zinov'ev, as the head of the Leningrad delegation to the congress, represented a region whose economy depended on heavy industry. NEP had not encouraged Leningrad's prosper-

---

[30] Ibid.

[31] As cited in Schapiro, *Communist Party*, 295.

[32] *XII s"ezd*, 116.

[33] Ibid., 158.

[34] Ibid., 117; Daniels, *Conscience of the Revolution*, 204.

ity. Stalin blamed NEP for "nurturing Great Russian chauvinism,"[35] and Trotskii gave a much anticipated speech on how centralized planning and managerial accountability in industry could overcome NEP. For Trotskii the chance to speak in defense of industry outweighed the opportunity to confront Stalin on the Georgian question.[36] Few, it seemed, liked NEP.

Bukharin, interestingly enough, also figured among those at the Twelfth who avoided defending NEP. He reported on the Communist parties outside the Soviet Union and protested the attacks against Kamenev from the industrial managers whom he made his particular target at the congress.[37] He also made a brief but forceful defense of the Georgians, whose chauvinism, he insisted, did not present the dangers to the international communist movement that Russian chauvinism did.[38] But Bukharin did not take up serious defense of NEP until 1925 when he joined Stalin in partnership against the Left Opposition.[39]

Kamenev, alone among the oligarchs, shouldered the burden of defending a policy that at that time had so little genuine support in the party and rested on Lenin's waning and all too malleable authority. That authority was nonetheless sufficient to enable Kamenev to expand concessions to the peasantry. He made the case at the congress for combining the tax in kind on the peasantry with a monetary tax.[40] He argued that taxes should be consolidated, made direct, progressive, diminished to one-third of what they were, and they should be levied only once a year.[41] His final suggestion constituted more than a concession to the peasantry; it underscored the privileging of

---

[35] XII s"ezd, 481.

[36] Schapiro, Communist Party, 274–75.

[37] XII s"ezd, 250–305 and 186–93.

[38] Ibid., 611–15.

[39] Stephen F. Cohen, Bukharin and the Bolshevik Revolution: A Political Biography, 1888–1938 (New York: Vintage Books, 1973), 153–62. Cohen's account of the evolution of Bukharin's thinking in the early 1920s suggests consistent support for NEP. He writes that by "the latter part of 1922," Bukharin's "views on NEP were now similar" to those of Lenin (153). Just over a year later, shortly after Lenin's death, Bukharin's "acceptance of NEP" was "unequivocal" (159). By the first half of 1925, Bukharin had aligned with Stalin and become "identified as the architect" of an enhanced NEP (162). Given Bukharin's noticeable silence on NEP, which was embattled at the Twelfth Congress in Lenin's absence, another interpretation is possible. Bukharin, in fact, harbored ambivalence regarding NEP, becoming its "architect" only when he chose to commit himself to an alliance with Stalin as Kamenev, Zinov'ev, and Trotskii went down to defeat. The evidence encourages speculation that opportunism motivated Bukharin's evolving attitude toward NEP. Vladimir Glebov, Kamenev's son, in conversation with the author, concurred on Bukharin's opportunism regarding NEP.

[40] XII s"ezd, 440.

[41] Ibid., 442.

agriculture in the Soviet economy. He called for an additional *smychka*, that is the union between peasants and workers on which NEP was based. The new *smychka* would unite Russia's still largely agrarian economy with industrialized Germany. Bread must be exported abroad in return for German equipment to revitalize Russian heavy industry, Kamenev insisted. In other words industrial development would follow from the exportable wealth of agriculture. Kamenev later proclaimed that "no one else ... did as much as I did to explain the meaning of NEP..."[42] Certainly no one did as much as he did at the Twelfth Congress to defend it.

With regard to Kamenev's subsequent fate, it is instructive to examine the conduct at the Twelfth Congress of his future partner in opposition, G. E. Zinov'ev. Zinov'ev too condemned the various opposition groups lurking on the fringes of the congress. When they clamored for the right to present their platforms openly to the congress, Zinov'ev replied disdainfully, "[I]n our party there is [already] enough freedom for discussion of any opinion,"[43] words that would come back to haunt him, just as would Kamenev's criticism of the opposition. But Zinov'ev alone sniped at Trotskii and Stalin as though he could win the leadership contest by alienating his two most dangerous rivals.

Trotskii was an obvious target. The triumvirs worked "behind the scenes" at the congress, warning that Trotskii could usurp the revolution for his own ends. As Bonaparte had once been to the French revolution, Trotskii with his popularity and military following could become the "grave digger" of the Bolshevik revolution.[44] Zinov'ev and his fellow triumvirs had success with such tactics: "uttered in worried whispers, the hints by agents of the oligarchs made many a delegate apprehensive."[45] But Zinov'ev went further than the other oligarchs, going on the attack in public and alone. His target in this instance was not the Commissar of War, who stood on sand, but the exceedingly dangerous General Secretary. He referred to one of the most important departments in Stalin's personal bureaucratic domain, the *Uchraspred*, or Account and Assignment Section of the Secretariat, by which Stalin had been able to manipulate much of the delegate selection to the congress. Zinoviev pointed to a future shake-up there by calling for a member of the Central Committee to head *Uchraspred* to "diminish bureaucratism," i.e., Stalin's growing hold on appointments in the party.[46]

He did the same on the decision made unanimously by the Presidium not to publish "a certain letter" of Lenin on the nationality question. "In view of

---

[42] L. B. Kamenev, "Na ocheredi (16 okt. 1925g.)," in *Stat'i i rechi* (Moscow: Gos. izdatel'stvo, 1926), 12: 406.

[43] *XII s"ezd*, 220.

[44] Deutscher, *Prophet Unarmed*, 94.

[45] Ibid.

[46] *XII s"ezd*, 228.

the character of those instructions which Vladimir Il'ich gave," Zinov'ev hastened to explain, "the issue [not to publish] does not at all lie in personal attacks" contained in the document.[47] In fact such attacks, directed against Stalin, were precisely the issue; and Zinoviev had brought the threat to Stalin contained in Lenin's letter out into the open.

There is painful irony in Zinov'ev's admonition to the congress to heed Lenin and struggle against "anti-Semitism" and "strike-breaking [against unity]."[48] Stalin subsequently conducted his own whispering campaign against Zinov'ev and Kamenev about their being Jewish. "The man on horseback" found his revenge in attaching the label "strike-breaker" to them. In *Lessons of October*, published a year and a half after the Twelfth Congress, Trotskii publicized the failure of Zinov'ev and Kamenev to support Lenin's timing for the Bolshevik coup in 1917, labeling them "strike-breakers," a term that stuck with damaging effect.[49]

While Zinov'ev threatened Stalin from the podium and undermined Trotskii covertly, he defended Kamenev before the congress. When M. A. Larin, one of the "managerial dissidents" who opposed party interference in the work of industrial administrators,[50] accused Kamenev of being "the main representative" of "a right-wing deviation in the party," Zinoviev jumped to his defense. He refuted Larin's contention that Kamenev had committed "four of seven deadly economic sins," attesting that the head of Mossovet had the support of the Politburo on issues that Larin had misconstrued.[51] Zinov'ev's defense of Kamenev on economic matters was all the more striking in that each of them represented divergent constituencies. Heavy industry, such as the great Putilov factory in Leningrad, looked to Zinov'ev to argue for more attention to industrial recovery, just as "calico [light industry] Moscow" looked to Kamenev to defend its interests. The Twelfth Party Congress confirmed that while Kamenev and Zinov'ev relied on Lenin's talismanic authority, they also relied on each other.

Stalin could take the congress as a series of lessons in how his rivals could harm themselves. For example, they foolishly offered support, suppressing Lenin's criticisms of him. He learned then that victory might be his sooner from patience than from aggression. For the next four years he proved to be a master at letting his opponents defeat themselves. While rumors swirled around the congress that Trotskii might abuse his popularity to play the role of Napoleon, usurping all power for himself, the hero of the civil war

---

[47] Ibid., 601.

[48] Ibid., 607.

[49] See my discussion of the strike-breaker episode in "Kamenev and the Peasant Question: the Turn to Opposition, 1924–1925," *Russian History/Histoire Russe* 27: 4 (Winter 2000): 386–88.

[50] See Daniels, *Conscience of the Revolution*, 200, for more on this group.

[51] *XII s"ezd*, 216.

obligingly made repeated references to the Red Army and the importance of military accountability in industry. He went so far as to assert in the speech on industry that "hopes for the development of socialism in our country [rest] on strengthening the Red Army," second only to "the political strength of the party."[52] Trotsky's military analogies and references to the Red Army, natural enough, only encouraged the credibility of the rumors that he aspired to seize power like a latter-day Bonaparte.

Trotskii even appeared to abet the use of the French revolution against himself. According to Deutscher, "the agents of the triumvirate whispered" that he was not only "the Bonaparte of the Russian revolution" but "the potential Danton" as well.[53] Trotskii had "posed proudly next to a statue of Danton" shortly before the congress.[54] The photo may have circulated at the Twelfth Congress or otherwise have been made known to the delegates. Such an image would only embellish the whispers regarding Trotskii's ambitions.

The issue of rumor was no small matter. It provides a measure of Trotskii's position in the party at the time of the Twelfth Congress. If, as Philip Pomper maintains, Trotskii had lost all hope of power "in either the military or the economy"[55] as early as 1923, then, it is reasonable to argue (as Pomper does) that "all too much has been make of the dissemination of ... rumors" about Trotskii.[56] On the other hand, Robert Daniels argues that Trotskii on the eve of the Twelfth "had victory within his grasp..."[57] If Daniels is correct, then Trotskii's enemies out of fear of his influence might well have waged war furtively and aggressively to stop him. In fact, the very weaknesses of Trotskii's rivals made him a formidable opponent. To Stalin's relief, while Trotskii might have seized victory at the Twelfth, he failed to "lift a finger to secure it."[58] Instead, "Trotsky's defeat began to unfold" at the Twelfth Party Congress.[59] Rumor may have contributed to it and explain his resurrection of the "strike-breaker" episode in *Lessons of October* (November 1924) by way of revenge against Kamenev and Zinov'ev.

Stalin could observe another weakness in both Zinov'ev and Kamenev when they condemned dissent. Neither of them could hide their respect for L. B. Krasin, a renowned Soviet diplomat and one of the managerial dissidents

---

[52] *XII s"ezd*, 334.

[53] Isaac Deutscher, *Stalin: A Political Biography* (New York: Vintage Books, 1960), 273.

[54] Max Eastman, "Jacobinism and Bolshevism," *Queen's Quarterly* 31 (1923): 74, as cited in Jay Bergman, "The Perils of Historical Analogy: Leon Trotsky on the French Revolution," *Journal of the History of Ideas* 48: 1 (January–March 1987): 82.

[55] Pomper, *The Intelligentsia in Power*, 393.

[56] Ibid., 391.

[57] Daniels, *Conscience of the Revolution*, 206..

[58] Ibid., 206.

[59] Deutscher, *Prophet Unarmed*, 103.

at the congress. Kamenev, for example, praised Krasin's "bold and shining speech" even if it is "characterized by the deepest pessimism in relation to our internal strengths, yet the greatest optimism concerning the magnanimity of European capitalism."[60] Zinov'ev showed Krasin the same tolerance even though the managerial advocate had viewed "with horror" the merger of the Worker and Peasants' Inspectorate with the Central Control Commission, approved by the congress.[61] He forgave Krasin such failings because "an experienced administrator is after all worth his weight in gold," and they had been friends since 1905.[62] Stalin could see at the Twelfth Congress, if he had not known it before, that neither Kamenev nor Zinov'ev had his capacity to go for the jugular. They were softs in a world of hards. They would never fight him on the same terms that he would use against them.

The Twelfth Congress also revealed the potential for Kamenev and Zinov'ev to align with each other, not necessarily to their benefit. Kamenev had already begun to show a distinct political ineptitude seen in his solo defense of NEP and ill-considered language to attack opponents. Zinov'ev could perceive political danger in Stalin's accumulation of power, yet he addressed it ineffectually in a way sure to arouse Stalin's anger. Neither would employ their real weapons against Stalin, namely Lenin's Testament and the Georgian question. When Zinov'ev and Kamenev combined they paired mutual weaknesses, rather than complementary strengths.

The congress had opened by making all members of the leadership equals.[63] Kamenev explained that the Central Committee had already nominated 25 to serve on the congress Presidium. Ia. E. Rudzutak then proposed that they be listed alphabetically.[64] (At the last congress Lenin had come first with the rest of the Presidium listed in order of importance). By the end of the congress, the most important participants emerged from that undifferentiated alphabetical list. Stalin's rivals had proven their ineptitude to him as well as to observers in the hall. Early NEP revealed that neither high position nor closeness to Lenin could insulate the oligarchs of the party once they faced the cold competition for power on their own.

Early NEP saw the two most important party congresses for the founding of the Soviet Union. The Tenth, run by Lenin, launched NEP and gave Stalin one of his most potent weapons in the succession struggle, the ban on factionalism. The Twelfth provided the road map for the succession struggle itself. At the Eleventh, with Lenin at the helm, the enemy lay outside the leadership:

---

[60] *XII s"ezd*, 156–57.

[61] Ibid., 224. See also Daniels, *Conscience of the Revolution*, 200.

[62] *XII s"ezd*, 225–27.

[63] Ibid., 6.

[64] Ibid.

Aleksandr Shliapnikov and those who joined him in sending the Letter of the Twenty-two.[65] At the Twelfth conflict abounded within the leadership.

Kamenev's Moscow constituency demanded defense of NEP, however unpopular among the delegates at large. His defense of NEP may have had yet another source. In defending NEP, Kamenev did what he had failed to do consistently in 1917: support Lenin. Kamenev now made up for his previous sin. The *smychka*, the economic bond of trade between worker and peasant, city and countryside, provided the ideological underpinning of NEP. Kamenev adamantly argued for the *smychka*. The *smychka* of NEP, he maintained, was no recent expedient. It went back to the revolution of 1905 "when the collaboration of workers and peasants was the distinguishing mark of Bolshevism."[66] Kamenev might also have explained that the *smychka* emerged from Lenin's April Theses of 1917. The former youthful Populist of Simbirsk had called for Black Repartition, peasant seizure of the land, a basic tenet of Populism. To succeed, Lenin realized, the Rusian revolution had to be the result of a *smychka* binding the poorest peasants and the proletariat together. Unfortunately for Kamenev, many in the party by 1923 had grown restive over a *smychka* between an increasingly prosperous peasantry (hoarding grain) and a disgruntled and highly exploited proletariat.

The Twelfth unveiled to Stalin how short-sighted his rivals could be. Kamenev ably assisted Trotsky in keeping the lid on the Georgian question which would have disastrously, for Stalin, pitted him against Lenin.[67] Kamenev affirmed that Lenin's notes on the nationality question would not be published and that any charges that the Presidium [of the congress] delayed publication would be treated as "slander."[68] As Kapchenko has argued, "[f]or Stalin the central question at the congress was the nationality [Georgian] question."[69] Just as important for Stalin, Kamenev and Zinov'ev stood back while the General Secretary both expanded and packed the Central Committee (enlarged from 27 to 40) and the Central Control Commission (enlarged from 5 to 50). Small wonder, as Ulam observed, that Stalin might have begun to contemplate "the idea of his personal dictatorship." Not only were the tools of so much of the party bureaucracy now in his control, but his rivals had done nothing to stop him when it was easy to do so.

It did not end there. Kamenev's uncompromising defense of NEP made him appear an effective advocate of the Moscow region, but not of other groups and interests. His near isolation in defense of NEP revealed political

---

[65] See Barbara Allen, "Dissent Within the Party: Alexander Schliapnikov and the Letter of Twenty-two," *The NEP Era: Soviet Russia, 1921–1928* 1 (2007): 21–54.

[66] *XII s"ezd*, 425.

[67] Ibid., 821.

[68] In Robert Service's *Stalin, A Biography* (Cambridge, MA: Harvard University Press, 2004), he mistakenly claims (p. 213) that Kamenev referred to Lenin's Testament.

[69] Kapchenko, *Biografiia Stalina*, 693.

ineptitude as did his mocking condescension toward a broad range of opposition groups within the party. The more astute must have wondered if and when Kamenev's words would be used against him. They did not have long to wait.

However inept his rivals were, Stalin refrained from conflict. Aside from the Georgian leadership, he contented himself with one other victim, Christian Rakovsky.[70] As Kamenev subsequently observed, "'the exile' of Rakovsky [as ambassador to France] in 1923 was the first administrative repression of importance that Stalin utilized to remove an opponent from the political scene."[71] By 1927, when Kamenev shared diplomatic exile with him, Rakovsky had become one of his most important allies.[72] Both had acquired something in common even earlier. They had begun to go down to defeat at the Twelfth Party Congress.

Stalin took the measure of his rivals at the Twelfth, on display before the party for the first time without Lenin to determine their ranking. For Kamenev, on display were his allies in the looming struggle with Stalin. Alas, he failed to perceive that the battles were nearly lost before they had begun. The tactical errors that he and his confreres made at the Twelfth Party Congress meant that they were already beaten by the time that NEP was barely two years old.

[70] Ibid., 649–61.

[71] Houghton Library, Trotsky Archive, bMs. Russ 13, T3490b, "Notes of Trotsky on a Conversation with Kamenev," 1926.

[72] See my "Kamenev in Rome," *The NEP Era: Soviet Russia, 1921–1929* 1 (2007): 108.

Peter the Great in the Writings of Soviet Dissidents

Jay Bergman

In every nation's history there are figures who come to embody it. Whether because of their outsized personalities or the enormity of the actions they carried out, or through a combination of the two, such individuals transcend the period in which they lived and become timeless symbols of their country. In Russian history Peter the Great was such an individual. Virtually everyone of significance in Russian politics and culture who followed Peter expressed an opinion of him, and entire books have been written on how Russians over the centuries have explained not only the man himself, but the policies he pursued, the reforms he enacted, and the changes in Russian politics and culture he made or was unable to make because the forces opposing him were too strong and intransigent even for someone of Peter's will and seemingly inexhaustible energy to overcome.[1]

But there was a category of Soviet citizens for whom Peter had special significance, namely the critics of the Soviet Union in the Brezhnev era commonly referred to in the West, then and now, as dissidents. For them, determining what they thought of Peter was a way of clarifying the contours of their dissidence and also a means of situating their dissidence on the temporal expanse of Russian history. What is more, whether they realized it or not, the dissidents were the product in the Soviet era of the paradigm Peter introduced earlier into Russian history of a modernizing autocracy seeking simultaneously to perpetuate its monopoly of power.[2] Peter himself once stated that the Russian people were like children who "will not study the alphabet unless a master forces them to."[3] What is significant in this is not only that Peter thought little of the people he ruled, but that he did not exempt from his imputation of immaturity those of his subjects on whom he simultaneously conferred a semblance of adulthood by entrusting them to build the ships, command the armies, and collect the taxes he considered necessary for Russia to become a European power. Peter expected the educated elite he created, in

---

[1] See, for example, Nicholas V. Riasanovsky, *The Image of Peter the Great in Russian History and Thought* (New York: Oxford University Press, 1985).

[2] This is Marshall Shatz's thesis, which I find convincing, in *Soviet Dissent in Historical Perspective* (New York: Cambridge University Press, 1980), 12–38.

[3] Quoted in M. Bogoslavskii, *Oblastnaia reforma Petra Velikago: Provintsiia 1719–27 gg.* (Moscow: Universitetskaia tipografiia, 1902), 24.

Rude & Barbarous Kingdom Revisited: Essays in Russian History and Culture in Honor of Robert O. Crummey. Chester S. L. Dunning, Russell E. Martin, and Daniel Rowland, eds. Bloomington, IN: Slavica Publishers, 2008, 189–212.

other words, to support the tsar and the status quo politically, and to do so
with the same child-like deference he demanded of the uneducated masses.
The only autonomy this elite would enjoy would be vocational autonomy, because allowing this elite autonomy outside the workplace would be tanta-
mount to treating them as mature and responsible individuals—in short, as
adults—who might for that reason demand individual rights and political
freedom, neither of which Peter believed he could grant without losing power
himself.

In the Soviet Union a similar dynamic prevailed. Like Peter the Soviets allowed their educated elite a modicum of vocational autonomy, while simultaneously denying that elite any political freedom; since some members of
that elite—but by no means all of them—wanted freedom as well as autonomy, the inevitable result was Soviet dissidence, a particular form of opposition to the Soviet system emphasizing its violation of ethical principles, which
the dissidents called human rights and considered timeless, absolute, and
universal. Not surprisingly, the Soviet leadership recognized the challenge to
their moral legitimacy the dissidents posed, and did what they could, short of
reintroducing Stalinist terror, to silence them.

When they offered their opinion of Peter, the Soviets seemed instinctively
to feel a bond with him, not least because their objectives and Peter's, if one
excludes the whole matter of Marxist ideology, were so much alike: both the
Soviet Union and Peter's Russia were modernizing autocracies intent, at least
in domestic affairs, on perpetuating the political status quo. Indeed, by the
time the dissidents appeared in the late 1960s and early 1970s, the Soviet leadership had long ago incorporated Peter's reforms into a triumphant teleology
transcending the October Revolution in which Peter, in the words of Maksimilian Voloshin in 1921, was "the first Bolshevik."[4] Praise for Peter runs like a
thread through the writings and public statements of prominent Bolsheviks.
In 1918 Lenin analogized the Bolsheviks' adopting aspects of Germany's
economy in World War I to Peter's copying Western methods for the purpose
of overtaking the West; just a year later the historian M. N. Pokrovskii, despite his criticisms of Peter's personal character, acknowledged that Peter and
Lenin were both progressives fighting retrograde classes bent on stopping the
inexorable progress of history.[5] In a similar vein, Mikhail Kalinin saw Lenin
as Peter's successor, and Karl Radek proclaimed his belief in the veracity of a
wholly imaginary *Testament* Peter ostensibly wrote in justification of his policies, adding for good measure that his fellow Bolsheviks shared Peter's na-

---

[4] Quoted in Lev Kopelev, *Budushchee uzhe nachinaetsia* (Moscow: Dva veka, 1995), 98.

[5] V. I. Lenin, "'Left-Wing' Childishness and the Petty-Bourgeois Mentality," reprinted
in V. I. Lenin, *Collected Works* (Moscow: Progress Publishers, 1965), 27: 340; M. N. Pokrovskii, "Istoriia povtoriaetsia," *Narodnoe prosveshchenie*, no. 32 (26 April 1919): 3.

tionalism.[6] Even Leon Trotsky, who was perhaps the most cosmopolitan of the Bolsheviks and the one most mindful of the difficulties the Bolsheviks would have in building communism in the absence of communist governments elsewhere that could assist them, nonetheless saw nothing untoward in exploring Russia's history for useful precedents; the result was Trotsky in 1924 proclaiming Peter a forerunner of the current Soviet leadership in a number of the policies he pursued.[7]

Still, it was Stalin who fully incorporated Peter into the Bolshevik mythology he inherited when he came to power in the late 1920s. To be sure, in the last years of Stalin's rule Soviet historians criticized Peter for having gone too far in his reforms, for taking more from Western Europe than the Russian people, in their wisdom, were inclined to accept. Indeed Stalin himself, at a meeting in the Kremlin in 1947 at which Molotov, Zhdanov, Aleksei Fadeev, and Konstantin Simonov were present, allowed that while Peter "had some good ideas, too many Germans soon established themselves." According to Stalin, "this was a period of groveling before the Germans. First it was the Germans, then the French. There was much groveling before foreigners, before shits."[8]

Stalin's animadversions, however, were uttered privately, and whatever misgivings he may have harbored about Peter, his public pronouncements on the tsar were uniformly positive. In November 1928, for example, in a speech to the plenum of the Central Committee of the Communist Party, Stalin praised Peter for "feverishly building factories and mills to supply the army and to strengthen the defense of the country."[9] Peter's patriotism, his belief in the socially transformative possibilities of technology, and his willingness to use whatever means were necessary to achieve his goals regardless of the cost in human lives and happiness this entailed, all endeared Peter to Stalin, who was himself directing the even more disruptive endeavor of industrializing the Soviet Union rapidly; like Peter, Stalin recognized that economic growth

---

[6] Mikhail Agursky, *The Third Rome: National Bolshevism in the USSR* (Boulder, CO: Westview Press, 1987), 210; Ruth Fischer, *Stalin and German Communism* (Cambridge, MA: Harvard University Press, 1948), 267.

[7] Leon Trotsky, *Literature and Revolution* (Ann Arbor: University of Michigan Press, 1960), 94–96. It is entirely possible that the Bolsheviks, like the Russian people generally, were also favorably inclined to Peter from their knowledge of Pushkin, who did more than anyone else in Russian history and culture, including Peter himself, to foster a cult of Peter through his iconographic description of the tsar in his poem "The Bronze Horseman."

[8] Quoted in Konstantin Simonov, *Glazami cheloveka moego pokoleniia* (Moscow: Kniga, 1990), 111.

[9] J. V. Stalin, "Ob industrializatsii strany i o pravom uklone v vkp(b): Rech' na plenume tsk vkp(b) 19 noiabria 1928 g.," reprinted in J. V. Stalin, *Voprosy leninizma*, 9th ed. (Moscow: Partiinoe izdatel'stvo, 1933), 359.

was a prerequisite of political and military strength. [10] As a result, the image
of Peter as a proto-Bolshevik devoting his seemingly boundless energy to vast
projects of social engineering was an integral aspect of Stalinism. Aleksei Tolstoi's historical novel *Peter the First*, published in installments from 1929 to
1945, was especially effective in establishing in the public mind the Peter-
Stalin connection, and it is a measure of Stalin's ability to force writers to
write what he wanted them to write that Tolstoy's overwhelmingly positive
portrayal of Peter contrasted sharply with his depiction of the tsar as little
more than a cruel tyrant in a play he wrote on the same subject in 1929, before
this connection became part of the official Soviet mythology. [11]

Of course the dissidents were not the first group of oppositionists in Russian history to criticize Peter or to condemn the government that ruled them
for extolling him. The Old Believers, out of a conviction that Peter, in his
Western ways, was the Devil Incarnate, had done this while Peter was still
alive, and the Slavophiles of the 19th century, as well as Russians who considered blasphemous Peter's mockery of all matters Orthodox, did so as
well. [12] In all of these instances, opposition to Peter was primarily or exclusively philosophical or religious in its origins. But for the dissidents, attacking
Peter was inescapably a political act, a way of demonstrating that they opposed not just the philosophical and ethical assumptions of the Soviet regime,
but the regime itself. True, there were dissidents like Andrei Sakharov for
whom Peter was irrelevant because it mattered little to him that the Soviet
leadership found justification in Russia's prior history for the violations of
human rights it committed. [13] But for many other dissidents Peter was important because by clarifying his status in the larger context of Russian history,
they would likely shed some light on several of the questions about the Soviet
Union that concerned them: Was the Soviet Union an aberration in Russian
history or the logical consequence of it? What relationship did it have historically to the tsarist system and to the rulers this system produced, most
notably Peter the Great, whose objectives, and whose harsh methods for
achieving these objectives, were so similar to those of the Soviets? Were
Peter's reforms too much a reflection of Western ways for the Russian people

---

[10] Lindsey Hughes, in her article "Peter the Great and the Fall of Communism," *Irish
Slavonic Studies*, no. 17 (1996): 13, argues that the commitment to modernization Peter
and Stalin shared is traceable intellectually to the Enlightenment.

[11] Riasanovsky, *Image of Peter the Great*, 280.

[12] On how the Old Believers saw Peter, see Michael Cherniavsky, *Tsar and People:
Studies in Russian Myths* (New York: Random House, 1961), 72–100; and his "The Old
Believers and the New Religion," *Slavic Review* 25: 1 (March 1966): 1–39. On the Slavo-
philes, see Nicholas Riasanovsky, *Russia and the West in the Teachings of the Slavophiles*
(Gloucester, MA: Peter Smith, 1965).

[13] Jay Bergman, *An Intellectual Biography of Andrei Sakharov* (Ithaca, NY: Cornell University Press, forthcoming), passim.

to accept them completely and wholeheartedly, and if so, did their similarity to Soviet policies suggest that these policies will fail the way Peter's did? Indeed, did this similarity suggest that the Soviet Union itself might collapse sometime soon? Or did the relative ease with which Peter was able to impose his reforms on Russian society reflect in the Russian people a longstanding passivity in the face of political as well as religious authority that argued strongly against the dissidents enlisting them as partners in their effort to reform the Soviet Union? And if so, should the dissidents therefore adopt a "neo-Leninist" approach, in which acting for the Soviet people without their participation or even their expressed approval was not only morally justified but the only means by which beneficial change could come about? By answering these questions the dissidents could more easily determine how they should proceed against the Soviet regime, and what their chances of successfully reforming it might be.

As a dissident in the late 1960s and 1970s, Aleksandr Solzhenitsyn shared the view the Soviets held that Peter was one of their precursors in Russian history. But he inverted the moral value the Soviets placed on it. In Solzhenitsyn's jaundiced opinion, Peter and the Soviets were both evil, albeit to different degrees, and the moral depravity their actions revealed was a consequence of their both rejecting Orthodox Christianity for Western technology (in the case of Peter), and a secular ideology, Marxism-Leninism (in the case of the Soviets).

Significantly, Solzhenitsyn's disdain for Peter predated his hostility to Bolshevism and Communism. In an autobiographical poem he wrote sometime prior to becoming a dissident, Solzhenitsyn asked rhetorically whether "the cost of Poltava," Peter's decisive victory over the Swedes in 1709, was truly justified in light of "the two hundred years of conquest, conquest, conquest" that followed it.[14] Even in *The Gulag Archipelago*, a frontal assault on the whole Soviet system, Solzhenitsyn stated that Peter was in some ways the most brutal of the tsars, prescribing capital punishment for some 200 criminal acts—four times the number his father and predecessor, Aleksei Mikhailovich, prescribed. Indeed, Peter's daughter Elizabeth, while not changing or reversing the edicts requiring this particular kind of punishment, chose in most instances not to apply them, thereby making it possible for Catherine the Great, later in the 18th century, to limit this most extreme of punishments to political criminals, and for Paul, at the end of the century, actually to abolish it altogether, albeit only on paper.[15]

But Peter's transgressions had even more deleterious consequences, and they could not be undone very easily. In Solzhenitsyn's words, Peter's reign "did much to destroy the Russian way of life, its customs, consciousness and

---

[14] Quoted in Michael Scammell, *Solzhenitsyn* (London: Hutchinson, 1985), 104.

[15] Alexander Solzhenitsyn, *The Gulag Archipelago, 1918–1956: An Experiment in Literary Investigation*, 2 vols. (New York: HarperCollins, 1973), 1: 432–33.

national character."[16] In Solzhenitsyn's telling of it, Russian history prior to Peter was something of a golden age culturally and spiritually, a time when the Russian national spirit was strong, and "the gift of repentance irrigated a broad tract of the Russian character."[17] For this reason, the authoritarian order under which the Russian people lived "possessed a strong moral foundation," which Solzhenitsyn ascribed to Orthodox Christianity.[18] Under the impact of "the soulless reforms of Nikon and Peter the Great," however, this spirit withered, and the people's capacity for repentance diminished as well. The result, as Solzhenitsyn described it, was "the whole St. Petersburg period of our history [when] the external greatness of imperial conceit drew the Russian spirit even further from repentance."[19] And by looking westward to Protestant England, Sweden, and the Netherlands for his models, Peter failed to see the significance of the Russian Northeast, a vast frozen tundra inhospitable to human habitation that remained even in the 20th century largely untouched by the morally corrupting influences of Western rationalism and secularism.[20]

But it was with the ascension of the Bolsheviks to power in 1917 that the degeneration that Peter began reached its ultimate, and morally horrific, conclusion. Writing in 1974 in the *Vestnik Russkogo studencheskogo khristianskogo dvizheniia*, an émigré journal published in Paris from the 1960's through the 1990's, Solzhenitsyn located the origins of Russia's current predicament in the late 17th and early 18th century. To the two principal events of that period, the schism in the Church and Peter's persecution of the dissidents the schism created, could be traced the spiritual and ethical crisis in Russia that culminated in the 20th century in the October Revolution.[21] Indeed, for every respect in which Peter's reign and the Soviet system were similar—as in their simplifying the class structure, in Peter's case through the Table of Ranks, in that of the Soviets by reinstituting the internal passport system—there were aspects of the Soviet system that, in purely ethical terms, were much worse, such as the infliction of punishments that in Peter's time were still considered barbaric.[22] To be sure, in "The Courage to See," an article that appeared in

---

[16] Alexander Solzhenitsyn, "The Courage to See," *Foreign Affairs* 59, no. 1 (Fall 1980): 204.

[17] Alexander Solzhenitsyn, "Repentance and Self-Limitation in the Life of Nations," in Alexander Solzhenitsyn et al., *From Under the Rubble* (Boston: Little, Brown and Company, 1975), 114.

[18] Aleksandr I. Solzhenitsyn, *Letter to the Soviet Leaders* (New York: Harper and Row, 1975), 71.

[19] Solzhenitsyn, "Repentance and Self-Limitation," 114–15.

[20] Ibid., 140–41; Solzhenitsyn, *Letter to the Soviet Leaders*, esp. 32–40.

[21] "Pis'mo Aleksandra Solzhenitsyna tret'emu soboru zarubezhnoi russkoi tserkvi," *Vestnik Russkogo studencheskogo khristianskogo dvizheniia*, no. 112–13 (1974): 107–08.

[22] Solzhenitsyn, *Gulag Archipelago*, 1: 93–94.

Foreign Affairs in 1980, Solzhenitsyn seemed to qualify severely the resemblance between Peter and the Soviets he had previously affirmed. In the article Solzhenitsyn criticized the American historian of Russia, Robert Tucker, for "tracing the origins of the Gulag back to the practices of forced labor under Peter the Great"—which would seem to suggest that Solzhenitsyn was aware that at least in this respect the two regimes, Peter's and the Soviets', were different.[23] But this was not the case, for in the next sentence Solzhenitsyn explained that what Tucker had done was objectionable because it implied that forced labor was an exclusively Russian phenomenon, when in fact other countries, from ancient Egypt to England, France, and Holland, used forced labor as well.[24] What Solzhenitsyn abhorred in Tucker's formulation of the issue, in other words, was not that it was factually inaccurate, but that, by limiting his analysis to Russia, it was incomplete and misleading, leaving the reader with the false impression that other cultures and countries were not guilty of the crimes Peter and the Soviets committed, and that the moral depravity Peter and the Soviets revealed in their respective policies was uniquely Russian. This of course contradicted Solzhenitsyn's insistence, which pervades nearly all of his writings, that the Russian people are *sui generis* not in the bad things they did, but in their capacity, attributable to the Orthodox Christianity they professed, for repentance and redemption.

Five years after writing "The Courage to See," in an article entitled "Our Pluralists," Solzhenitsyn returned to Peter and his relationship to the communists.[25] In the context of equating intellectual and political pluralism with a kind of moral relativism incompatible with fundamental tenets of Christianity, he attacked both Russian as well as non-Russian critics of the Soviet Union for presenting a view of Russian history "in which Ivan the Terrible, Peter I, and Stalin stand up like three arches of a viaduct over centuries of Russian history, drained in the featureless bog below."[26] Implicit in Solzhenitsyn's analysis, once one factors into it what he had previously written about Peter and the Soviets, is the notion not displeasing to him that the Russian people, despite their abject failure to oppose Peter and the Soviets more energetically and effectively, are nevertheless preferable ethically to both of them.

In understanding Solzhenitsyn's attitude towards Peter, one must remember that while Solzhenitsyn considered Peter a precursor of the Soviets, in the final analysis it was from the Enlightenment, not Peter the Great or any other Russian ruler, that emerged the Marxism that Solzhenitsyn always believed was the ultimate progenitor of the Soviet Union and of all that was morally abhorrent about it. But drawing analogies and comparisons between

---

[23] Solzhenitsyn, "Courage to See," 203.

[24] Ibid.

[25] Alexander Solzhenitsyn, "Our Pluralists," *Crossroads* 29 (1985): 1–28.

[26] Ibid., 17.

.the Soviets and Peter was nonetheless useful to Solzhenitsyn. By doing so he was able to associate the Soviet Union with a tradition of Westernization in Russian history—a tradition beginning with Peter over a century before Marxism existed—that in his opinion robbed the Russian people of the moral discernment Orthodoxy provided, thereby making the Bolsheviks' seizure of power in 1917, and their holding onto it for the next 74 years, much easier.

Not surprisingly, Solzhenitsyn's view of Peter was shared in varying degrees by the other dissidents who contributed to the collection of articles, *Iz-pod glyb*, that Solzhenitsyn edited and that was published in the West in 1974. F. Korsakov, for example, saw Peter's inability to destroy the Russian Orthodox Church as proof of the Church's righteousness, while another contributor, Vadim Borisov, located the cause of the collapse of Russia's Christian consciousness in "the brutal reforms" of Peter the Great, whom Borisov bitterly castigated as "the first Russian nihilist."[27] While Korsakov and Borisov differed in their estimation of how successful Peter actually was in weakening Russian Orthodoxy, they agreed on the nefariousness of Peter's motives and intentions, which like Solzhenitsyn they ascribed to the tsar's not being, in some elemental and indefinable way, a real Russian.

Of course, Orthodox Christian dissidents would not be predisposed to anyone who preferred Western models to Russian ones, and for this reason the image of Peter that appears in the pages of the *Vestnik Russkogo studencheskogo khristianskogo dvizheniia* is an overwhelmingly negative one. O. Altaev, for example, wrote in 1970 that the tendency of the present-day intelligentsia to criticize the Soviet regime only perfunctorily and obliquely, and otherwise to support it in the name of a rationalism traceable historically to the Enlightenment, reminded him of the many Russians of earlier generations who saw in Peter's reforms a vindication of this same rationalism.[28] More directly than Altaev, V. Gorskii, also in 1970, argued that Peter so weakened the Church in the aftermath of the schism a half-century earlier that it could not oppose effectively the "skepticism" and "free thought" the intelligentsia fostered when it emerged in the early 19th century.[29] In fact, Gorskii grouped Peter, Pisarev, Lenin, and Metropolitan Filip at one end of the ideological spectrum he discerned in Russian intellectual history, while placing Tsar Aleksei,

---

[27] F. Korsakov, "Russian Destinies," in Solzhenitsyn, *From Under the Rubble*, 164; Vadim Borisov, "Personality and National Awareness," in Solzhenitsyn, *From Under the Rubble*, 212.

[28] O. Altaev, "The Dual Consciousness of the Intelligentsia and Pseudo-Culture," reprinted in Michael Meerson-Aksenov and Boris Shragin, eds., *The Political, Social and Religious Thought of Russian "Samizdat": An Anthology* (Belmont, MA: Nordland Publishing Company, 1977), 137.

[29] V. Gorskii, "Russian Messianism in the 19th and 20th Centuries," reprinted in Meerson-Aksenov and Shragin, *Political, Social and Religious Thought of Russian "Samizdat,"* 363.

Dostoevskii, Solov'ev, and Ivan the Terrible at the other end; it is obvious that
Gorskii preferred the latter to the former, and considered this spectrum an
ethical one as well as a political and intellectual one.[30] Finally, in language
similar to Gorskii's, yet another contributor to the *Vestnik*, Anatolii Skuratov,
praised the Slavophiles for their critique of Russian secularism, which Skuratov not surprisingly traced to Peter the Great.[31] But Altaev's, Gorskii's, and
Skuratov's animadversions on Peter cannot compare in their vitriol to those of
I. Dubrovskii, who in the *Vestnik* in 1978 drew up a bill of particulars against
the tsar in which he accused him of everything from usurping the spiritual
authority of the Church and subordinating it institutionally to the state to co-
ercing "with verve and cruelty" the Russian people as a whole, on behalf of
whose welfare he falsely claimed to be acting.[32]

All of the Christian dissidents who wrote about Peter in the *Vestnik*
viewed him unfavorably. But they differed significantly not only on his relationship historically to Bolshevism and communism, but also on how thoroughly his reforms constituted a reversal or a rejection of pre-existing trends
in Russian history, and on how much those reforms affected the history that
followed them. One suspects that if the October Revolution had never happened, Peter would have remained an object of opprobrium for Russians like
Dubrovskii and Skuratov, a historical figure impossible to ignore whose hostility to the Orthodox Church and whose mockery of certain of its shib-
boleths—but not all of them, since Peter throughout his life combined
contempt for the Church with a very real, if intermittent and idiosyncratic
piety[33]—would still be deserving of condemnation. I. Denisov, writing in the
Vestnik in 1971, called Peter's abolition of the patriarchate and its incorpora-
tion into the state bureaucracy "a fatal mistake," as a result of which the
Orthodox Church became effectively a prisoner of the state.[34] But other than
that, Peter reformed only "externally and artificially"—which is not to say his
reforms had no serious effects—because he took the wrong countries as his
models: instead of borrowing from the Protestant North—from England,
Holland, and Sweden—Peter should have followed Chaadaev's recommendation and tried to bring to Russia the Catholicism of Southern Europe—of Italy,

[30] Ibid., 382.

[31] Anatolii Skuratov, "At the Sources of Russian National Consciousness," reprinted in
Meerson-Aksenov and Shragin, *Political, Social and Religious Thought of Russian
"Samizdat,"* 404–13.

[32] I. Dubrovskii, "Novye intelligenty o Moskovskom tsarstve," *Vestnik Russkogo studencheskogo khristianskogo dvizheniia*, no. 125 (1978): 117.

[33] Lindsey Hughes, *Peter the Great: A Biography* (New Haven: Yale University Press,
2002), 150.

[34] I. Denisov, "Slovo otstupnikov," *Vestnik Russkogo studencheskogo khristianskogo dvizheniia*, no. 99 (1971): 109.

Spain, and France.[35] Although Denisov did not indicate what Peter's relationship to the Soviet Union was, his minimizing Peter's importance in Russian
history implies that for him the relationship would be tenuous or possibly
even non-existent; the Soviet Union, in other words, might have antecedents
in tsarist Russia or even in Muscovy and Kiev, but Peter's reign almost certainly would not be one of them.

E. Ternovskii, another dissident who wrote for the *Vestnik* in the early
1970s, argued that Peter's authoritarianism, however repressive, was too dissimilar to Stalin's totalitarianism to prefigure it. As a result, it could hardly be
cited as justification for the present-day Soviet Union.[36] From a slightly different perspective, P. Derzhavin, writing in 1975, left his readers with the same
impression of Peter's lack of historical responsibility for Soviet communism.
As Derzhavin explained it, a nation's culture was rarely if ever a reflection of
those who ruled it. For this reason the "statists" who claimed that Peter, by
virtue of his outsized personality and extensive reforms, left a permanent
mark on Russian culture were wrong. In fact, the few reforms Peter initiated
that had lasting consequences were foreshadowed in Muscovy; all Peter did
that was new was to invest his personal character in these reforms.[37]

In minimizing Peter's role as a forerunner of the Soviets, Derzhavin differed not only from the Christian dissidents who saw significant similarities
between Peter's regime and that of the Soviets. He differed as well from many
of the more secular dissidents, who no less than the Christian dissidents realized that Peter was a figure they had to reckon with in conceptualizing what
exactly it was about the Soviet Union they objected to. For example, 17 Latvian dissidents, none of them affiliated with any particular church, affirmed
in 1972 that the Soviet Union's acquisition of the Baltic states in the Nazi-
Soviet Pact in 1939 resembled Peter's absorption of the area these states comprised in the Great Northern War that ended in 1721. That this was also the
official Soviet view did not deter the Latvians from affirming it.[38] As opponents of the Soviet Union, they simply condemned what the Soviets praised.
Also among the more secular dissidents who found the two regimes comparable was Vasilii Grossman, who in his novel *Forever Flowing* claimed to see a
Promethean ethos in both Peter's reforms and Soviet communism. So sure
was Grossman of the correctness and relevance of this equivalence that his

[35] Ibid.

[36] E. Ternovskii, "Vzyskatel'nyi khudozhnik," *Vestnik Russkogo studencheskogo khristianskogo dvizheniia*, no. 114 (1974): 217.

[37] P. Derzhavin, "Zametki o natsional'nom vozrozhdenii," *Vestnik Russkogo studencheskogo khristianskogo dvizheniia*, no. 106 (1972): 262–64.

[38] "Against Russification," *Intercontinental Press* (3 July 1972), reprinted in *Samizdat:
Voices of the Soviet Opposition*, ed. George Saunders (New York: Pathfinder Press, 1974),
428.

description of it, as expressed by one of the characters in the novel, deserves to be quoted in full:

> [T]o Ivan Grigoryevich it seemed as if neither thirty years before nor one hundred and thirty years before, when Pushkin had brought his hero to this square, had the divine Peter been so mighty as today. There was no power in the world so immense as that which he had gathered unto himself and expressed—the majestic power of the divine state. It had grown and grown. It had come to reign over fields and factories, over the writing desks of poets and scientists, over the construction sites of dams and canals, over stone quarries, timber forests, sawmills. And it had the capacity in all its mighty power to establish its dominion not only over an area which was vast in its physical, geographical expanse, but also over the innermost, deepest heart of each hypnotized human being who was willing to offer up to it as a gift, in sacrifice, his freedom, and even his very wish for freedom.[39]

Having written this, however, Grossman was not about to let the matter of Peter's role in Russian history lapse. Later in the novel he faults the tsar for widening the abyss that already existed in Russia between freedom and non-freedom: while Peter may have "built the foundations of Russian scientific and military progress," the progress Russia achieved as a result of this was paid for in the suffering of the peasants.[40] In this case the ends were corrupted by the means used to achieve them, and as far as Grossman was concerned, the same thing could be said of the Soviets. Both they and Peter caused the Russian state to hypertrophy, and in doing so caused immeasurable suffering, the full horror of which was in no way vitiated by the fact that the purposes for which it was inflicted were progressive ones.

Other dissidents who shared Grossman's and the Christian dissidents' aversion to Peter focused less on the tsar's villainy than on the Soviets' embrace of him, and on what that required of Soviet historians and others who wrote about him. Mikhail Geller condemned Stalin in 1979 for forcing historians to extol the tsars and their adjutants, among them Peter, Ivan the Terrible, and the leader of Ivan's *oprichniki*, Maluta Skuratov, all of whom Geller described simply as "villains."[41] At greater length than Geller, Andrei Siniavskii decried the Soviets' appropriation of Peter for their own nefarious purposes not only because he was better, both in his policies and as a human being, than the Soviets, but because the Soviets' lying about Peter was emblematic of

---

[39] Vasily Grossman, *Forever Flowing* (New York: Harper and Row, 1972), 64.

[40] Ibid., 213–14.

[41] Mikhail Geller, "Pamiat' i 'Pamiat','" *Vestnik Russkogo studencheskogo khristianskogo dvizheniia*, no. 128 (1979): 194.

their lying about practically everything.[42] Indeed, Siniavskii considered the Soviets' claim to be Peter's logical and legitimate successor pernicious because it bespoke a utilitarian view of history that denied its inherent worth and validity. In the history Soviet historians wrote, figures like Peter the Great "did not know the word 'Communism', [but] they still knew quite well that our future will be brilliant."[43] If, for the Soviets and Soviet historians, Russian history was the present projected into the past, for Siniavskii the persons, the regimes, and everything else that comprises the past should not be used to validate the present or to demonstrate the inevitability and beneficence of the future. While differing with Solzhenitsyn on what should replace the Soviet system they both rejected, Siniavskii shared with him the conviction that the greatest crime the Soviets committed—the crime from which all the others they committed followed logically and inexorably—was their refusal, from the October Revolution to the Gorbachev era, to tell the truth.

Siniavskii was not the only dissident who tried to evaluate Peter without regard for any utility he may have had for the regimes and the rulers that followed him. Len Karpinskii, for example, rejected the view *de rigeur* among Soviet and Marxist historians that tsarist Russia was merely a prelude to Soviet Russia. Whatever similarities that may exist between tsarist and Soviet Russia, where the Soviets and the Marxists went astray, in Karpovskii's opinion, was in thinking that "lodged in the past is everything that now is and everything that shall be."[44] And although Karpinskii included Peter among "the special curses of Russian history ... whose work all went awry," Peter for him was less the representative of something larger and more generic than a human being *sui generis* in his ideas and personal attributes.[45] Similarly, Mikhail Agurskii argued that Peter should be evaluated by the criteria of his own time, not of any other, and that the glorification of Peter by Stalinist sycophants such as Aleksei Tolstoi linking communism and Russian nationalism was dangerous to the moral and spiritual well-being of the Russian people.[46] Finally, Evgenii Evtushenko, the perpetual weathervane of Soviet politics, evoked the Peter-Stalin analogy without either rejecting or affirming it. Instead Evtushenko equivocated. In an article on Andrei

---

[42] Abram Tertz [Andrei Siniavskii], "On Socialist Realism," reprinted in Abram Tertz [pseudo.], *"The Trial Begins" and "On Socialist Realism"* (Berkeley: University of California Press, 1960), 127–219.

[43] Ibid., 170–71.

[44] L. Okunev [Len Karpovskii], "Words are Also Deeds," *Political Diary*, no. 68 (May 1970), reprinted in *An End to Silence: Uncensored Opinion in the Soviet Union*, ed. Stephen F. Cohen (New York: W. W. Norton and Company, 1982), 301.

[45] Ibid.

[46] Mikhail Agursky, "Soviet Communism and Russian Nationalism: Amalgamation or Conflict?" in *The Soviet Union and the Challenge of the Future*, ed. Alexander Shtromas and Morton A. Kaplan (New York: Paragon House, 1989), 3: 152.

Platonov written in 1988, Evtushenko quoted Kliuchevskii on Peter's expanding the state at the expense of freedom and individual rights—which of course is what the Soviets did—while noting also that while Peter Westernized too much, Stalin feared the West and therefore Westernized too little. And while Stalin and Peter differed on how they treated their "boyars"—Peter cut their beards while Stalin created a whole new caste of them—Stalin nevertheless imitated Peter in how he dealt with his enemies.[47]

One finds a rather different view of Peter in what Igor Shafarevich wrote in the 1980s, after rejecting the liberal principles he had championed a decade earlier while serving with Sakharov and Valerii Chalidze on the Human Rights Committee they established to protest Soviet violations of human rights. In Shafarevich's best-known work, *Rusofobiia*, written in the early 1980s but not published legally in the Soviet Union until 1989, he defended Peter against the view that the October Revolution "flowed inexorably" from the tsarist system and everything else in Russia's history that preceded it, and that what specifically prefigured the atrocities the Soviets committed were those perpetrated earlier by Ivan the Terrible and Peter the Great.[48] For all of their faults, these rulers, in Shafarevich's taxonomy, were autocrats, not totalitarians, and thus not precursors of the Soviets. According to Shafarevich, only "Russophobes"—an amorphous term with antisemitic implications Shafarevich applied to persons who disagreed with him—would equate Ivan and Peter with Lenin and Stalin. But for Shafarevich the differences between these two sets of rulers were only a microcosmic reflection of a larger and more fundamental difference between the political systems these rulers led. Rejecting the charge Solzhenitsyn and other dissidents leveled against the Russian people that in Soviet communism they got what they deserved as a consequence of their spiritual degeneration, Shafarevich described the Soviet Union as *sui generis* in Russian history—thereby placing him in the camp of those dissidents who considered Peter within the mainstream of Russian history and culture, unlike the Soviets, who were outside of it. What followed logically from this was that any analogy between Peter and the Soviets in which the former prefigured the latter was false. In fact, in order to defend Peter against the charge that he prefigured the Bolsheviks, Shafarevich stated in *Rusofobiia* that the evil things Peter did monarchs in other countries did as well. With what one suspects was a certain relish, Shafarevich pointed out that monarchs in the supposedly more enlightened countries of Western Europe shared Peter's objective, which they all succeeded in achieving, of subordinating to the state the Christian church—be it Protestant, Catholic, or

[47] Yevgeny Yevtushenko, "The Proletariat Does Not Need Psychosis," reprinted in Yevgeny Yevtushenko, *Fatal Half-Measures: The Culture of Democracy in the Soviet Union* (Boston: Little, Brown and Company, 1991), 321–22.
[48] I. R. Shafarevich, *Rusofobiia* (Moscow: Tovarishchestvo russkikh khudozhnikov, 1991), 7.

Orthodox—to which their subjects evinced allegiance.[49] Similarly, Shafarevich claimed to hear in Feofan Prokopovich's justification of Peter's autocracy echoes of Hobbes' *Leviathan*.[50]

Alexander Yanov, a dissident who after leaving the Soviet Union composed lengthy critiques of it, resembled Shafarevich in that both men wrote about Peter in explicating a larger scheme of Russian history they believed explained how a people they admired and with whom they still identified could find itself living under a political system, the Soviet Union, they abhorred with every fiber of their being. Clearly, Yanov and Shafarevich hoped their respective theories of Russian history, in addition to explaining communism, would exonerate the Russian people of responsibility for it. But while Shafarevich endeavored to achieve this objective by essentially dividing Russian history at 1917, and claiming that what preceded the October Revolution had little or nothing to do with what followed it, Yanov, in his *The Origins of Autocracy*, published in 1981, argued instead that Russia's history was cyclical, and that the Russian people were very fortunate that it was: since one could find in Russian history before the Soviets the seeds of liberalism and democracy as well as of despotism and tyranny, not only were the Russian people as a whole not responsible for the catastrophe that was Soviet communism, but the Soviet system itself was destined to collapse and be followed by a more virtuous one no less rooted in the Russian past than the Soviet Union.[51] Yanov's conviction in the late 1970s and early 1980s, when the Soviet Union seemed impregnable, that its days were numbered stemmed not from any belief like Solzhenitsyn's that Marxism and communism were alien monstrosities imposed on the Russian people by a Westernized elite, but from the fact that Russian history was destined to repeat itself, so that what preceded the Soviet Union would eventually follow it.

What this meant for Peter the Great Yanov made clear in *The Origins of Autocracy*. There Yanov described Peter as a transitional figure in Russian history rather than as a transformative one.[52] In foreign affairs, Peter made Russia "a second-class power," which to Yanov hardly qualified as an achievement, since Russia before Peter, according to Yanov, was actually a first-class power.[53] Like Stalin, Peter reduced the fairly complex society he inherited by reducing it to two basic classes, the governors and the governed, whose interests were mutually exclusive. In addition, Peter resembled Stalin in that he greatly increased the power of the state over Russian society, and in so doing intervened in Russian society more or less to the same degree to

---

[49] Ibid., 7–12.

[50] Ibid., 14.

[51] Alexander Yanov, *The Origins of Autocracy: Ivan the Terrible in Russian History* (Berkeley: University of California Press, 1981), esp. 4–6, 59–66, 225–26.

[52] Ibid., 54–57, 69–70, 222–23.

[53] Ibid., 1, 6.

which Stalin did.[54] But according to Yanov, the roots of Stalin's regime, and of the Soviet Union as a whole, were traceable not to Peter but to Ivan the Terrible, who through his *oprichnina* turned the monarchy into an autocracy, and the subjects of this autocracy into slaves. Peter merely continued what Ivan began, refining the system Ivan created without changing it into something else. Moreover, since in Yanov's scheme of things history, or at least Russian history, was not linear but cyclical, the far more benevolent order that existed in Russia prior to Ivan reemerged, albeit briefly, in the 19th and early 20th century, only to be destroyed in 1917 as Russia, under the guise of Soviet communism, resumed the course it had begun to follow in the 16th century under Ivan, and continued to follow in the 18th century under Peter. According to Yanov, this more benevolent order that alternated in Russian history with more tyrannical ones was marked not only by a genuine concern for the individual and his welfare, but by a genuine, if embryonic capitalism, in which private property and the rudiments of a free market were emerging.[55]

A dissident who rejected Yanov's and Shafarevich's whole perspective on Russian history, while at the same time largely exonerating Peter of responsibility for Soviet communism, was Boris Shragin. In his major work, *The Challenge of the Spirit*, written in 1978, Shragin began by tracing to Peter the origins of the pre-revolutionary intelligentsia.[56] It was Peter, he wrote, who realized "that if Russia, half Byzantine and half Tatar, was to transform itself into a great European power, it would first have to be civilized. Only thus could the military pressure of Western Europe be resisted."[57] But according to Shragin, Peter, unlike Catherine the Great, was interested only in knowledge that was practical. For him, knowledge and education were not ends in themselves, but merely useful in achieving what was Peter's overarching goal, that of increasing his own power and that of the state. In this respect Peter was an "Oriental Despot," by which Shragin meant that, for all of Peter's admiration of Western technology, he was oblivious to the concepts of individual dignity and initiative that would emerge in the West in the Enlightenment, and only then come to Russia because of Catherine the Great. Peter, in other words, took only the first step in the creation of the intelligentsia: the educated persons his reforms created were not *intelligenty* but only a stratum of educated servitors, well-versed in practical matters but oblivious to humane and liberal values.[58]

For this reason Peter could be considered a precursor of the Soviets only indirectly: from the servitors Peter created came the leisured nobles of the late

---

[54] Ibid., 52–53.

[55] Ibid., esp. 3–4, 52–54, 67–70.

[56] Boris Shragin, *The Challenge of the Spirit* (New York: Random House, 1978), 86, 124–25.

[57] Ibid., 124.

[58] Ibid., 152–53.

18th century to whom Catherine allowed access to the ideas of the Enlightenment; from these leisured nobles came the intelligentsia; and from the intelligentsia there emerged the Bolsheviks, who created the Soviet Union while
simultaneously rejecting the belief in the primacy of the individual that was
the leitmotif of the intelligentsia from its inception; in fact it was Stalin who
destroyed the intelligentsia in the Great Terror. But even if one chose to consider Peter a precursor of the Soviets, in Shragin's opinion one still had to
explain why the Russian people were unable or unwilling, in all the years
Peter ruled them, to oppose the despotism he embodied; with the exception of
the Old Believers, whose dissent was primarily theological rather than political, the Russian people responded to Peter's tyranny with barely a murmur of
resistance, thus revealing a docility that Shragin insisted predated Peter. Shragin made this point, which clearly distinguished his view of Peter from
Yanov's and Shafarevich's, and from Solzhenitsyn's as well, in the following
way:

> It is generally held that the dualism in Russian life and consciousness
> [between the intelligentsia and the masses] dates from Peter the
> Great's reforms and the forcible introduction of alien elements from
> Western civilization. To some extent these reforms may indeed be
> blamed for the spiritual malady of the eighteenth and early nine-
> teenth centuries, as described by Klyuchevsky. But to understand
> fully the historical background of Russian doublethink, which so
> plagues us today, we cannot abruptly swing from a Westernizing to a
> Slavophile point of view and idealize everything in pre-Petrine
> Russia. It was precisely in old Muscovy that the seeds of dualism
> were first sown.[59]

The secular dissidents who tried to ascertain Peter's legacy were on the
whole not nearly as critical of Peter as the Christian ones were. To be sure,
their views varied. Some considered Peter a precursor of the Soviet Union.
Others did not. But because these secular dissidents did not have the same
investment in Russian Orthodoxy the Christian dissidents had (or the investment in Russian nationalism that Shafarevich had), they were more inclined
to credit Peter for many of his reforms, based as they were on Western models
that were therefore neither Russian nor Orthodox. Also, these secular dissidents were not as interested as the Christian dissidents (and also Shafarevich)
were in exonerating the Russian people of responsibility for the Soviet regime
that was ruling them. The reason for this was not that the secular dissidents
considered the Russian people morally deficient. Rather it was that they were
concerned with something else entirely, namely determining whether the
tradition Peter began in Russian history of looking to the West for models that

---

[59] Ibid., 148.

would facilitate technological progress in Russia could be considered responsible nevertheless for the moral disaster that was the Soviet Union. Could something good produce something that was bad? That was the question the dissidents who shared Peter's commitment to progress and modernization had to answer.

To Andrei Amalrik, Peter shared with the communists a desire to modernize Russia, but unlike the communists, Peter did not round up and force "the dregs of society" to work in factories. In contrast to the Soviets, there were limits to the amount of coercion Peter considered necessary to achieve his goals.[60] Similarly, Mikhail Heller and Aleksandr Nekrich, in their 1986 history of the Soviet Union, criticized Western historians who accepted the Soviet view that the current regime was prefigured in Russian history by rulers such as Peter the Great. To Nekrich and Heller, Peter's cruelties were real, but hardly of a magnitude and duration to warrant the equivalence Soviet historians claimed to see between the ruler who was responsible for them and the Soviet system as a whole.[61] For his part, the Ukrainian dissident Leonid Pliushch drew up a scathing indictment of Peter. In his estimation, Peter was a brutish and remorseless autocrat capable of building a new capital "on Ukrainian bones" that quickly became "the new center of the rapacious empire where thousands ... died from hunger and unceasing labor."[62] What was worse, Peter was guilty of "carnivalizing" Russian society and political life—by which Pliushch meant a mindless iconoclasm that Peter found useful in justifying the mass killings his henchmen carried out.[63] But while according to Pliushch all of the bad things Peter did the Soviets did as well three centuries later—which made the Soviet Union in his opinion "the logical consequence" of Peter's reign (as well as of the Mongol yoke and Ivan the Terrible's paranoia)—Peter did good things as well.[64] By "turning a barbaric state into a powerful country through concentration of forces and government involvement in the economy," Peter, in short, established a precedent the Soviets followed that explains their undeniable achievements in physics, mathematics, and space.[65]

Like Pliushch, Lev Kopelev harbored no illusions about Peter's brutality, and in responding in the mid-1970s to Solzhenitsyn's *Letter to the Soviet Leaders*, he stated flatly that Soviet foreign policy contained a tendency to

---

[60] Andrei Amalrik, *Involuntary Journey to Siberia* (New York: Harcourt Brace Jovanovich, 1970), 253.

[61] Mikhail Heller and Aleksandr Nekrich, *Utopia in Power: The History of the Soviet Union from 1917 to the Present* (New York: Summit Books, 1986), 10.

[62] Leonid Plyushch, *History's Carnival: A Dissident's Autobiography* (New York: Harcourt Brace Jovanovich, 1979), 175, 257.

[63] Ibid., 301.

[64] Ibid., 106.

[65] Ibid., 91.

expansion and aggression that was traceable to Peter the Great.[66] Kopelev's
aversion to the tsar resembled Solzhenitsyn's in that it predated his career as a
dissident. In his memoirs, Kopelev writes that in 1952, as he was being removed from a *sharashka* (the makeshift laboratories in the labor camps where
inmates who were scientists designed things the government needed) to an
ordinary camp, he considered what was happening to him analogous to
Peter's execution of the *strel'tsy* in 1698.[67] But in contrast to Solzhenitsyn, who
considered Peter's influence on Russian history wholly nefarious, so that
what followed Peter in Russian history was worse than what preceded him,
Kopelev's opinion was more balanced: the tsars did bad things before Peter as
well as after him; the Russian people were more receptive to the Western im-
provements Peter introduced than Solzhenitsyn is willing to admit; and not
everything for which Peter could be considered responsible, such as the emergence of the intelligentsia, was unreservedly evil; indeed, it was when Peter
and Aleksei Mikhailovich ruled Russia that "serious thinking regarding justice" first occurred in Russia.[68] As a physicist, Kopelev shared Peter's belief in
the utility of science and technology; perhaps for this reason he was able to
recognize that not everything Peter did was harmful to Russia, and that at
least some of what he did improved it.

Zhores Medvedev, as a gerontologist, was also inclined to view Peter
favorably. In a collection of *samizdat* materials published in 1971, he praised
Peter for allowing some of his subjects to go abroad, in contrast to the Soviets
who prevented theirs from doing so. In another document he took pains to
qualify his criticism of Peter's censorship by noting that it was limited to letters from Sweden, Russia's enemy in the Great Northern War.[69] As for Roy
Medvedev, Zhores's twin brother and by profession a historian, he went so
far as to argue, in a 1980 interview, that there ran through Russian history a
fundamental dichotomy between "clericalism and intolerance" on the one
hand, and a more praiseworthy "lay culture," for which Peter the Great was
responsible, on the other, that sought to increase Russia's ties with the West.[70]
What is clear from the interview, and from everything else the brothers have

---

[66] Lev Kopelev, "The Lie Can Be Defeated Only by Truth," reprinted in Meerson-
Aksenov and Shragin, *Political, Social and Religious Thought of Russian 'Samizdat,'* 311.

[67] Lev Kopelev, *Ease My Sorrows* (New York: Random House, 1983), 178. Kopelev mentions in this same memoir that he wrote a poem about his transfer shortly afterwards
entitled "The Morning of the Streltsy Execution."

[68] Kopelev, "The Lie Can be Defeated Only by Truth," 335.

[69] Zhores Medvedev, "The Soviet Citizen and His Passport, Internal and External," in
Medvedev, *The Medvedev Papers: Fruitful Meetings Between Scientists of the World* (London: Macmillan, 1971), 187; Zhores Medvedev, "Secrets of the 'Black Office,'" in ibid.,
368.

[70] Roy Medvedev, *On Soviet Dissent: Interviews with Piero Ostellino* (New York: Columbia University Press, 1980), 108–09.

written about Peter, is that they consider him among the most consequential modernizers and Westernizers in Russian history, a ruler who advanced rather than impeded Russia's development into a society significantly improved by the application of science and reason.

Somewhat different from the Medvedevs and several of the other secular dissidents in this respect was Grigorii Pomerants, who, quite possibly because he was not himself a scientist but rather a philosopher, was not as convinced as these dissidents were that science and technology were inherently benevolent, or that rulers who sought political advantage from their application, as Peter did, should be praised for doing so. In fact, Pomerants revealed in his writings an ambivalence about Peter that he never resolved. From the first works in which he tried to analyze Peter and to ascertain his place in Russian history, to those he wrote in the 1980s, Pomerants consistently considered the tsar an authoritarian modernizer not unlike the Soviets whose laudable intentions were vitiated by his trying to reform too much and too soon. But Pomerants also believed that Russia genuinely benefited from several of Peter's reforms, and as a result he seemed unsure of the extent to which the Soviets, in their policies, resembled Peter. At times when Pomerants was magnanimous toward the tsar, judging his good deeds more consequential than his bad ones, he would conclude that Peter was better than the Soviets, and thus only partly prefigured them. But on other occasions, when Pomerants was feeling less charitable, he would claim that Peter's reign for all practical purposes prefigured Stalinism and the Gulag Archipelago.

In 1985, for example, just prior to Gorbachev's ascension to power, Pomerants wrote that there was little either ethically or politically to distinguish Peter's regime from that of the Soviets:

> Like Peter, [the Soviet leaders] dream of pushing Russia forward through several centuries; like Peter, they want to create in it a new sensibility by surgical means; like Peter, they want to civilize it by the scourge and by torture. Between the Command Center in Preobrazhenskoe and the Secret Chancellery on the one hand, and the Extraordinary Commission [the Cheka] on the other, there are no substantial differences.[71]

Still, a good deal of what Peter did was progressive and therefore praiseworthy. In an article written in the early 1970s, Pomerants, in the context of comparing Peter's reforms to those of the Meiji Restoration in Japan, credited Peter with opening the closed society that was Muscovy.[72] In another article a

---

[71] Grigorii Pomerants, "Problema Volanda," reprinted in Pomerants, *Vykhod iz transa* (Moscow: Iurist, 1995), 169–70.

[72] Grigorii Pomerants, "Teoriia subekumen i problema svoeobraziia stykhovykh kul'tur," reprinted in ibid., 223.

few years later, he lauded Peter for having "cut through a window to Europe"—but hastened to add that Peter did this "[with] the same cruelty that became a tradition of Russian revolutions from above."[73] In yet another article, also written while the Soviet Union still existed, Pomerants noted the tendency among historians to claim to see in Russia's history examples of a generic category he called "dictatorships of development"; what was worse, these historians considered the paradigmatic expressions of these dictatorships to be Peter's and Stalin's.[74] To Pomerants, this was all wrong. While Peter and Stalin, as rulers and as human beings, may have shared certain characteristics, such as speaking bluntly and "cutting a wide swathe through brush as high as their shoulders" in the way they governed,[75] their objectives were not only different, but diametrically opposite:

> Peter pushed Russia towards Europe. He left in Russia the seeds of European culture, and a century later they sprouted. After Peter came Pushkin. After Stalin came winners of the Stalin Prize.... Not from Peter but from ourselves depends how we will live today.[76]

In a collection of articles published in Paris in 1984, Pomerants, in the flowery and highly rhetorical language he was prone to when writing on subjects about which he was passionate, tried to explain his position on Peter precisely.[77] He asked whether Peter was a reformer who, whatever the ultimate effects of his reforms, nevertheless meant well. Was he, in Pomerants's formulation of the question, "a devil who began with a song on the lips of an angel, who joined the battle for the holy and the ethical, for goodness, for truth, and for justice?"[78] Or was he inherently and relentlessly evil, the progenitor in Russian history of a tradition of using brute force to achieve one's objectives that would culminate in "Kolyma"—by which Pomerants meant Stalin's terror in its totality. Pomerants's answer was that Peter was both of these things simultaneously, a force for light as well as for darkness, and much else as well: "[Peter] was also a man, a new Russian type of man—a Russo-European pushing aside all that remained that was of Byzantine and Tatar origin."[79] Indeed, it was Peter, who through the sheer force of his will transformed "the Muscovite Tsardom into the Russian Empire," a feat of

---

[73] Grigorii Pomerants, "Rossiia na perekrestke kul'tur," reprinted in ibid., 232.

[74] Grigorii Pomerants, "Dolgaia doroga istorii," reprinted in ibid., 277.

[75] Ibid.

[76] Ibid., 277–78.

[77] Grigorii Pomerants, *Sny zemli* (Paris: Poiski, 1984).

[78] Ibid., 105.

[79] Ibid.

incalculable consequence for the history of Russia, and one for which he deserved considerable credit.[80]

Of the dissidents who evaluated Peter and judged the accuracy of the analogy Soviet historians posited between Peter and the Soviet state, Raissa Lert was one of only a few who evaluated this analogy without passing judgment on Peter himself. In an article she wrote in 1970 that appeared originally in Roy Medvedev's *Politicheskii dnevnik*, Lert began by exonerating Pokrovskii of the charge by the Stalinist historian Sergei Semanov that he condemned the tsars unreservedly and without exception, and that he saw in Peter specifically nothing but "drunkenness and syphilis."[81] This latter charge Lert branded a falsehood of the crudest sort, and suggested that a more nuanced view of Peter, one enumerating his virtues as well as his shortcomings, was preferable. But aside from a brief acknowledgment of how much Peter changed Russia, this was all she wrote about him. For this reason, one may venture the suggestion that for Lert Peter was a precedent not for any particular type of regime but for change itself. Peter changed the country he inherited from his father despite the inertial and countervailing tendencies so powerful in a society and political system as conservative as Russia was, and as Muscovy was before it. And if Peter could change tsarist Russia, and do so over opposition that was nothing if not persistent, then perhaps dissidents like Lert should not underestimate their own chances, two centuries later, of reforming Soviet Russia.

There was another, even more profound way in which Peter mattered to Lert. In the same context of defending Pokrovskii, Lert made clear her opinion that historical figures should not be sacralized the way Semanov sacralized Peter.[82] Instead, they should be treated as the complex and fallible human beings they were, neither damned nor idealized on the basis of patriotism, ideology, or any other reason having nothing to do with the period or the people being investigated. For Lert, Peter the Great did not "belong" to anyone, whether of his own time or of subsequent ones. Rather, he was autonomous, just the way Russian history and history in general were autonomous, in the sense that they should be studied for what they revealed about human existence, rather than for what they provided in the way of legitimacy or inspiration for persons of future generations with a particular agenda to advance. Regrettably, Lert did not always take her own advice. Peter was dear to her precisely for the inspiration his reforms provided. But this did not mean that people investigating the past should not also value it for its own sake, for the intrinsic worth it possesses. In her view, historians "should not make objects of worship even out of those who led the people's struggle for

---

[80] Ibid., 322.

[81] Raissa Lert, "The Charms of the Whip," reprinted in Cohen, *End to Silence*, 196.

[82] According to Lert, in contrast to Semanov, Pokrovskii "wrote history, not sacred scripture" (ibid., 195).

freedom and independence. Their duty is to describe and portray them truth-fully."[83] What the historian should strive for, above all else, is the truth, even if the truth, in some absolute sense, is never attainable. And what should determine whose interpretation of history is the most accurate, the one that is closest to the truth, is exactly the same thing dissidents like Lert claimed they used in formulating both their criticisms of the Soviet Union and the prescrip-tions they believed would make it more humane, namely reason and rational inquiry. At the philosophical core of Lert's dissidence, and of the dissidence of many others like her who found the Soviet Union ethically deficient and materially impoverished, was a core belief in the power of reason and rational inquiry, through the application of which human beings could improve not only the world around them, but themselves as well.

There were a number of reasons why the dissidents concerned them-selves with Peter the Great. Most obviously, by analyzing his reforms the dissidents could better understand the Soviet system they opposed: because the Soviet leadership never denied that Peter was one of the Soviet Union's progenitors, and at times affirmed his paternity enthusiastically (most notably in the Stalin era), it made sense for the dissidents to ascertain what it was about Peter the Soviet leadership found attractive, and whether the affinity it claimed with him was historically accurate. In fact, Peter *did* prefigure the Soviets by positing a paradigm of coercive modernization that the latter adapted to the changed circumstances of the twentieth century, when govern-ments had far more power than Peter did by virtue of the advances in science and technology that had occurred since the 18th century. But the assumptions the Soviets made that regimes like theirs had to modernize if they wished to survive, and that modernization, for all the political risks it entailed, could nevertheless be carried out without losing power, were, in fact, originally Peter's. For this reason alone, it made sense for the dissidents to study him.

But there were other reasons as well. For one thing, by ascertaining how easy or difficult it was for Peter to impose his reforms on the Russian people, the dissidents could gain a better sense, despite the two centuries that sepa-rated the Soviet Union temporally from Peter, of how receptive the Soviet people might be to the human rights the dissidents believed in. Because many of the dissidents originally thought that the Soviet leadership would be recep-tive to the reforms they recommended, when the KGB began repressing the dissident movement systematically in the early 1970s, it mattered even more to the dissidents whether the Soviet people would support them. What is more, by analyzing Peter as honestly and objectively as possible, the dissi-dents could underscore the comparable obligation they believed the Soviet leadership had to tell the truth about the history of the Soviet Union, and about the rest of Russian history as well. For it was only by doing this that the

---

[83] Ibid.

Soviet leadership could convince the Soviet people of its benevolent intentions, of its having given up the option of reinstating Stalinism.

Of course there was a contradiction in what the dissidents wrote and said
about Peter. Calling on historians, as the dissidents did, to value the past for
its own sake, to examine it irrespective of whatever justification it might provide for the actions and ideas of those who are examining it, is very different
from using history for contemporary political purposes, which is how not
only the Soviet Union used it, but also how some of the dissidents used it as
well, when by examining Peter they tried to "situate" themselves on the vast
temporal expanse that was Russia's past, and in so doing gain a better sense
of themselves and their chances of success. The dissidents, in other words,
did precisely what they condemned the Soviets for doing. Perhaps the best
gloss one can place on this is that for the dissidents, history had utility as well
as value. History was valuable for what it revealed about the absolute necessity, as the dissidents saw it, of simply telling the truth. But it was also useful
in the knowledge and comfort it provided people engaged in the extraordinarily risky endeavor of opposing a political system intent on silencing them
by virtually all the means that were available to it.

There was yet another reason for the dissidents to be concerned about history in general, and about Russian history and Peter in particular. While none
of the dissidents examined here identified the paradigm Peter established, in
which an educated elite gave rise to a revolutionary intelligentsia, as that
which in the Soviet Union caused the dissident movement itself to appear,
most of the dissidents seemed cognizant of Peter's paternalism—that he
viewed his subjects, the Russian people, as children. And this, in turn, made
any attempt to analyze Peter rationally and objectively, regardless of whether
it yielded a favorable opinion of him or an unfavorable one, itself an act of
defiance, a way of proclaiming that the persons carrying out this analysis
were not the children the Soviets, following in Peter's footsteps, considered
them to be, but rather adults, with the maturity and rationality to legitimize
the task they had established for themselves of changing the Soviet Union for
the better.

In the end, Peter's reforms, as most of the dissidents recognized, were
those of an autocrat with more than a streak of paternalism in his character
whose decision not to include the Russian people in his deliberations ensured
that these reforms could never yield the human rights the dissidents believed
in. Peter's penchant for treating his subjects as children limited the content of
his reforms, so that not even the best of them—not the Table of Ranks, not the
change from Ministries to Colleges in the government, not even the simplifi-
cation of the Cyrillic alphabet or the shaving of the boyars' beards—could
produce a society in which the worth and dignity of every individual human
being was assured. For the dissidents, this was the vision that energized their
opposition to the Soviet Union, and it was the same vision that animated their
examination of Peter. However laudable his objective of improving his sub-

jects and his country, and however praiseworthy his courage in challenging everyone and everything he believed was an obstacle to that endeavor, in the end Peter suffered from the serious flaw of not treating his subjects as mature and rational adults. In short, Peter's paternalism was his undoing. It was what prevented him from ruling humanely as well as effectively. This great and glorious figure Falconet sculpted and Pushkin wrote poetry about was incapable of creating a just society, a society based on human rights and a recognition of the inherent dignity and worth of the individual. In fact, he was probably not even capable of imagining it.

Monks and Old Believers

Nil Sorskii and *Prosvetitel'*

David M. Goldfrank

> Of the heretics who appeared in the first years,
> everyone knows, enlightened by the light of Or-
> thodoxy, and holds under a curse, having learned
> from the Divine Writings. But that now in our
> years, the devil has sown many heresies by means
> of the godless heretics, I have truthfully presumed
> to recount, so that we flee their doctrines and hate
> them with perfected hate.
>
> —Likely Author: Iosif Volotskii; Scribe of Earliest
> Extant Copy: Nil Sorskii[*]

Prosvetitel' (as it has come to be known)—Iosif Volotskii's *magnum opus*
against dissidents lumped together by him as the "Novgorod Heretics" and
commonly called "Judaizers"—stands out as Old Russia's most significant
original comprehensive religious treatise. Strangely, it has never been thor-

---

[*] Но яже в первых летех явльшаяся еретик, вси ведять, православиа светом про-
свещаемии, и под клятвою сих имуть, от божественных писаний научившиеся. А
еже ныне в наша лета многи ереси диавол безбожными еретики всеавь, праведно
непщевах сказати, яко учения их убежим, и съвершеною ненавистию възнена-
видим их. Text here as in Iosif Volotskii, *Prosvetitel'; ili, oblichenie eresi zhidovstvuiu-
shchikh*, 4th ed. (Kazan': Imperatorskii universitet, 1903; repr. Farnborough: Gregg International Publishers, 1972), 27–28; cf. N. A. Kazakova and Ia. S. Lur'e, *Antifeodal'nye
ereticheskie dvizheniia na Rusi XIV–nachala XVI v.* (hereafter *AfED*) (Moscow-Leningrad:
ANSSSR, 1955), 466. The potentially confusing translation at the top of the page attempts, in the words of the innovative stage director Roger Bensky, my long-standing
Georgetown colleague in French Theater, to "meet" and "encounter" the text, its rhetoric and poetics, rather than simply translate to the best of my ability using contemporary English phraseology, as here: *Everyone who is enlightened by the light of Orthodoxy
knows of the heretics who appeared in the first years, and, having learned from the Divine
Writings, holds [them] under a curse. I, though, have presumed truthfully to recount how now
in our years the devil has sown many heresies by means of the godless heretics, so that we flee
their doctrines and hate them with perfected hate.* The latter translation foregrounds "everyone" and the author. The author however, with his initial predicates, chose to fore-
ground the ancient and contemporary heretics.

*Rude & Barbarous Kingdom Revisited: Essays in Russian History and Culture in Honor of
Robert O. Crummey.* Chester S. L. Dunning, Russell E. Martin, and Daniel Rowland, eds.
Bloomington, IN: Slavica Publishers, 2008, 215–29.

oughly analyzed[1] or translated into another language.[2] Specialists, moreover, have known for 30 years that from Nil Sorskii's pen issued about 40 percent of the earliest extant copy of *Prosvetitel.*[3] Yet to my knowledge no one to date has attempted an analysis of that link. Leaving a full study of this work for monographic treatment, this essay will attempt to specify Nil's role or at least speculate on some reasonable possibilities—as consultant, editor, or even partial author—and to assess a few of the major scholarly judgments of Nil's activities regarding orthodoxy and dissidence. I shall touch briefly on redaction families, but devote more attention to comparisons of the structure, style, and content of the sections Nil copied with both the rest of the work and his other writings. Unfortunately, a festschrift essay of this type lacks the space for an adequate discussion of historical background and the structure and textological issues of this complex work, as we set the parameters of what we can know regarding Nil's place in its development and what this all means for our understanding of Nil as a historical and literary figure.

A response of the most forceful Russian monk of the day to the emergence, at least in the eyes of the Moscow-appointed Archbishop Gennadii

---

[1] Elements of such can be found in N. A. Bulgakov, *Prepodobnyi Iosif Volotskii* (St. Petersburg, 1865); Ivan Khrushchev, *Issledovanie o sochineniiakh Iosifa Sanina, Prep. Igumena Volotskogo* (St. Petersburg: Tip. Imperatorskoi Akademii Nauk, 1868); B. Vasil'ev, *"Prosvetitel'" Iosifa Volotskogo: Istoriko-literaturnoe issledovanie* (Kiev, 1912, MS, formerly GPB Ukr. SSR, Rukopisnyi otdel, no. 2181); Irene Holzwarth, *Der "Prosvetitel" des Joseph von Volokolamsk* (dissertation, typescript, Berlin, 1944); *AfED*, 305–523; Tomáš Špidlík, SJ, *Joseph de Volokolamsk: Un chapitre de la spiritualité russe,* Orientalia Christiana Analecta 146 (Rome: Pont. Institutum Orientalium Studiorum, 1956); Ia. S. Lur'e, *Ideologicheskaia bor'ba v russkoi publitsistike kontsa XV–nachala XVI veka* (Moscow-Leningrad: ANSSSR, 1960), 95–127, 261–66, 458–80; Thomas M. Seebohm, *Ratio und Charisma: Ansätze und Ausbildung eines philsophischen und wissenschaftlichen Weltverständnisses im Moskauer Russland,* Mainziger Philosophische Forschungen 17 (Bonn: Grundmann, 1977), 255–77, 484–86, 490–91, 493–505, 509–19.

[2] Contrast here with Nil Sorskii, for whom we have four solid translations of his genuine and sometimes spurious works: German (Fairy von Lilienfeld), modern Greek (Vasili Grolimund), modern Russian (Gelian Prokhorov), and English (Goldfrank), as well as one shaky and incomplete rendition (English) and four essentially phony translations of the treatise *Ustav* (modern Russian, French, Italian, also English). See David Goldfrank, "Preface to the Translations," in *Nil Sorsky: The Authentic Works* (Kalamazoo, MI: Cistercian Studies, 2008), 109–13. We also have a translation of both redactions of Iosif's Rule: David Goldfrank, *The Monastic Rule of Iosif Volotsky,* rev. ed. (Kalamazoo, MI: Cistercian Studies, 2000).

[3] B. M. Kloss, "Nil Sorskii i Nil Polev – 'spisateli knig,'" in *Drevnerusskoe iskusstvo: Rukopisnaia kniga* (Moscow: Nauka, 1974), 150–67; G. M. Prokhorov, "Avtografy Nila Sorskogo," in *Pamiatniki kul'tury: Novye otkrytiia. 1974 g.* (Leningrad: Nauka, 1975), 37–54.

Gonzov of Novgorod, of organized, Jewish-influenced heresy,[4] *Prosvetitel'*
comes down to us in about a hundred copies distributed among four textual
families. Two of these are brief (the initial, historical *Skazanie* and eleven
theological-polemical *slova*) and two are extended (adding four–five inquisitional *slova*). One set of the extended redaction is accompanied by three of
Iosif's pre-1504 synod inquisition-promoting epistles (sources for *Slova* 12–13
and 15), and one family of the brief redaction has both these epistles and earlier versions, in *slovo* or epistle form, of parts or all of *Slova* 13–16.[5]

If the orthographic analysis of at least six Russian scholars since the mid-
1970s is correct, then scribes based in Beloozero, rather than in Volokolamsk,
produced that earliest extant *Prosvetitel'*, a brief version, within the codex Sol.
346/326,[6] which, in its original form, the Iosifov elder Nil Polev donated to his
home cloister in 1513/14.[7] Nil Sorskii himself hand-wrote the first third of the
initial *Skazanie* text, the last five-eighths of the extensive *Slovo* 7, and all of
Slova 1–2 and 8–10.[8] The first of these contributions is not even a full 8-leaf

---

[4] Here the speculative literature is quite extensive, but no one, in my opinion, has yet
found the magical formula for pulling a convincing heretical rabbit out of the murky
hat of sources containing self-contradictory Orthodox polemical apologetics and
mainly Western-Rus' origin so-called "Judaizer literature." On the latter, as good as
any other place to start are Robert Romanchuk, "The Reception of the Judaizer Corpus
in Ruthenia and Muscovy: A Case Study of the Logic of Al-Ghazzali, the 'Cipher in
Squares,' and the 'Laocidean Epistle,'" in *Speculum Slaviae Orientalis: Muscovy, Ruthenia, and Lithuania in the Late Middle Ages*, ed. Viacheslav V. Ivanov and Julia Verkho-
lantsev (Moscow: Novoe izdatel'stvo, 2005), 144–65; and Moishe Taube, "The Fif-
teenth-Century Ruthenian Translations from Hebrew and the Heresy of the Judaizers:
Is There a Connection?" in ibid., 185–208.

[5] See Lur'e in *AfED*, 438–66, 486–88, 498–500, 503–05, 513–18; Lur'e, *Ideologicheskaia
bor'ba*, 95–127, 459–81.

[6] Russian National Library (hereafter RNB), f. Solovetskii Monastery Library (hereafter
Sol.), no. 346/326, fols. 47–337v; fols. 2–43v contain Iosif's Brief Rule, and fols. 339–411,
from the 17th century, *Slova* 13–16.

[7] Ia. S. Lur'e and A. A. Zimin, *Poslaniia Iosifa Volotskogo* (Moscow-Leningrad: ANSSSR,
1959), 298–99; Goldfrank, *Monastic Rule of Iosif Volotsky*, 117–19.

[8] In addition to Kloss and Prokhorov (n. 1), see Ia. S. Lur'e, "Unresolved Issues in the
History of the Ideological Movements of the Late Fifteenth Century," in *Medieval Russian Culture*, vol. 1, ed. Henrik Birnbaum and Michael S. Flier, California Slavic Studies
12 (Berkeley: University of California Press, 1984), 163–66; Andrei Pliguzov, "'Kniga
na eretikov' Iosifa Volotskogo," *Istoriia i paleografiia* 1–2, (1993): 93–138; Elena Romanenko, *Nil Sorskii i traditsii russkogo monashestva* (Moscow: Pamiatniki istoricheskoi
mysli, 2003), 85–96; Elena Shevchenko (co-author with Prokhorov of *Prepodobnyi Nil
Sorskii i Innokentii Komel'skii*), personal communication with author, July 2006. All accept Nil's Sorskii's pen here, even if they may differ concerning Nil as "non-
possessor," the alleged 1503 synod on monastic lands, and Nil's role in the repression
of dissidence.

fascicle, but, rather, six pages (folios 47–52v) which end with the narrated charge, associated with *Slovo* 10, that the "Novgorod Heretics" attacked the validity of the writings of Ephrem the Syrian. The accusation framing *Slovo* 11 picks up on the next page, but in a different hand, as if something else may have substituted for whatever Nil may have originally copied or intended to copy. At any rate, Nil, as far as we know for sure, had nothing at all to do with *Slovo* 11, although it is a lengthy scriptural and historic defense of monasticism, and, due to his redacting of monastic saints lives,[9] as well as his original compositions, he ought to have been Russia's leading expert on early monasticism. All of this strengthens the inviting hypothesis that a 10-*slovo* recension of *Prosvetitel'*, in some form or other, preceded the known, earliest, 11-*slovo* brief redaction.[10] This problem, however, is not terribly important, since *Prosvetitel'* was essentially a work in progress from the late 1480s or early 1490s through Iosif's life and well beyond, and most of it circulated in some form or other as distinct works or in separate bundles.

Overall, we need to be cautious in drawing conclusions from the little we know of Nil Sorskii's participation in the production of the 11-*slovo*, Sol. 346/326 recension. Indeed to characterize what Nil selected or was commissioned to copy is tricky, because not that much stands out in these pages in contrast to what other scribes copied. For example, both his and other sections of the initial *Skazanie* contain an emotive, invective, hyperbolic, and in places untruthful account of the "Novgorod Heretics." Both sets of sections fling insults at hypothetical opponents, who stand *ipso facto* condemned, the greatest number of such literary turns lying in sections copied by Nil.[11] And both

---

[9] Tamara Pavlovna Lënngren [Løngren], ed., *Sobornik Nila Sorskogo* (with an *Ukazatel' slov*), 5 vols., Studia philologica (Moscow: Iazyki russkoi kul'tury, 2000–05).

[10] Here lies an old debate, based on the fact that all brief redaction versions have 11 *slova*, but the table of contents lists only 10: it is covered well by Lur'e, most recently in one of his last articles, "Kogda byla napisana 'Kniga na novogorodskikh eretikov'?" *Trudy otdela drevnerusskoi literatury* (hereafter *TODRL*) 49 (1996): 78–98, where he notes that A. A. Zimin eventually agreed with him (Lur'e) on the primacy of a 1502–04 11-*slovo* version, represented by Sol. 346/326. In my opinion, Lur'e amply demonstrates that Pliguzov's above-cited article (n. 8) is unconvincing.

[11] For example, in *Slova* 1 and 9 (*Prosvetitel'*, 81, 89, 369; *AfED*, 405): "The heretical cadets reason contrary to this, for they say that God the Father Omnipotent has a spirit, which proceeds out of him and flows through the air. But look, inane and impudent ones! What is more inane than these words? And what is greater than this blasphemy?" or: "So that is how you opine, mindless ones, simply that being *in the image* means inalterable and like unto the one by whose image one is?" or: "O, what demonic enticement and inhumane boldness! This even the immaterial and eternal heavenly intellects do not dare to investigate, but completely submit and glorify the uninvestigable."

warn the reader/listener not to dare to second-guess God.[12] At the same time both sets of text explore some of the most profound theological problems;[13] both clarify their exegetical principles;[14] both touch on devotional issues;[15]

[12] For example, from Nil's copying, the last of the statements in the previous note, and an even stronger statement in *Slovo* 7 (*Prosvetitel'*, 303–04; *AfED*, 351): "And who dares, with his mucky tongue and his filthy flesh, to hypothesize on his own about the divine essence, and not from the holy Prophets' and Apostles' writings and from our holy and saintly and God-bearing Fathers, and to light a fire on his own head?" For other places, note in *Slovo* 6 concerning the veneration of holy objects (*AfED*, 327; *Prosvetitel'*, 127): "Did David really lie in saying this and prostrating himself [*poklianiaasia* = *worshipping*] toward the church [i.e., the Jerusalem temple]: 'I bow down toward your holy church.' [Ps 5:7 = LXX Ps 5:8] If David lies too, then who is truthful? For how can David himself say: 'You shall destroy all who tell lies'? [Ps 5:6 = LXX Ps 5:7; cf. Goldfrank, *Monastic Rule of Iosif Volotsky*, 2.16, p. 177]. And if David is truthful in saying, 'I bow down toward your holy church,' and he says it not just once, but many times, then who dares to say that it is not proper to bow down to a church?"

[13] Nil's share in *Slova* 1 (how, in the light of Ancient/patristic notions of natural philosophy, the Trinity actually works) and 8 (what can and cannot be known about God); others in *Slovo* 4 (the Christian notion of God's providential plan for human salvation): *Prosvetitel'*, 55–60, 88–93, 140–69, 333–34; *AfED*, 394–95.

[14] Nil's share in *Slova* 8–9; others in *Slovo* 5 (*Prosvetitel'*, 184–205, 345–48, 367–82; *AfED*, 364–69, 398–99, 404–06). One of Nil's copied passages states: "That which the Divine Writings teach us and legislate, it is proper exactly and unconcealedly to accept and guard. And that which they express in a hidden manner or in a parable or as destiny [*v priluchiai*], or they say with great wisdom, concerning these it is proper to pray to God with great labor and with the counsel of the experienced especially in the matter, and not to perceive by the word; and in no way seek out the concealed by the Divine Writings—for this is beastly" (*Prosvetitel'*, 346–46; *AfED*, 404). A similar passage not copied by Nil runs as follows (*Prosvetitel'*, 175–76; *AfED*, 364): "[T]hose who reason carnally, do not understand the Divine Writings by the Holy Spirit, but by carnal will. Therefore we struggle over this with fear of God, and we busy ourselves within the Divine Writings with humility, as the divine John Chrysostom says: 'It is for us to find out for any little chapter just as it lies, and to take it in its time and not untimely, and not as they discordantly appear to us, but greatly concordantly'" (source not yet identified).

[15] For a passage copied by Nil in favor of community over individual prayer, for example, in *Slovo* 7 (*Prosvetitel'*, 309; *AfED*): "If someone says, 'I can pray at home,' you fool yourself, man. For it is possible to pray at home, but it is impossible to pray as in the church, where there is a multitude of fathers, where unanimous chanting is sent up to God, and one thought and concord and union of love." A different scribe copied the following devotional passage from *Slovo* 6 (*Prosvetitel'*, 251; *AfED*, 334), which links object-veneration, individual mental prayer, and miracles: "See, how on account of these things honor is given to God, and not to a soulless item. In painting a depiction of saints on icons, we do not honor the thing, but as from this material seeing our intellect and thought flies up to divine desire and love, and on account of them divine grace operates ineffable miracles and healings."

and both implicitly assert opposition to state policies inconsistent with strict Orthodoxy and call for repression of heretics.[16]

The style of argumentation and some of the very arguments in *slova* sections copied by Nil and by others are the same.[17] Both sets of text make recourse to concrete history[18] and to scriptural and patristic authority. Both use rhetorical questions, "*if... then...*" constructions, and other logical devices.[19] Both may turn to the reader/listener at the end of an extended argument and

---

[16] Nil's share in *Slovo* 7 (*Prosvetitel'*, 282; *AfED*, 344–45), other copyists in the initial *Skazanie* (*Prosvetitel'*, 45–46; *AfED*, 474). Nil's section is, strictly speaking, accurate, only if "dishonoring the image of God" is the equivalent of apostasy, and then, as found in the *Kormchie knigi* (Orthodox Slavic collections of Church canons and relevant civil laws), the state laws stipulating death for certain apostates and active, anti-Christian Jews are "divine canons." The relevant passage in *Slovo* 7: "If someone dishonors the image of the king [*tsar*], he is tormented with capital punishment. How much more worthy—of these torments—is he who dishonors the likeness of the Heavenly King or his saints or churches? But here according to the divine canons he is punished with capital punishment and rendered an eternal anathema after death, with the Devil and the Judaeans, who crucified Christ and said: 'His blood is on us and our children'—condemned to the eternal fire." Cf. *Prosvetitel'*, 474–75; *AfED*, 491–92 (the relevant *Prosvetitel' Slovo* 13 passage), and its source, as in a 14th-century *Merilo pravednoe* (Russian State Library [RGB], f. Sviato-Troitskoi Sergievoi Lavry [hereafter Troits.], no 15, fols. 323–23v, http:// www.stsl.ru/manuscripts/index.php [this and other Troits. MSS accessed 2007]).

[17] For example, in *Slovo* 1, copied by Nil, concerning Abraham's hospitality ostensibly to three men or angels (Gen. 18:1–3; *Prosvetitel'*, 67): "That he indeed sees three men, he saw the Holy Trinity. And that he sees three and speaks to one, one Godhead appears, for he is one and three: one by nature and he has three constituents [*s"stav"* = the technical-theological Greek *hypostasis*]"; and in a different hand in *Slovo* 5 (*Prosvetitel'*, 181; *AfED*, 363): "And this means, and not simply from Abraham, but that to see three and to name by one Lord, this manifests the unity of the Godhead; but to speak to three, this manifests that the Godhead is tri-constituent and tri-personal."

[18] Text copied by Nil in *Skazanie* and *Slova* 2, 8; and by others in *Skazanie* and *Slova* 3, 4, 6, 11.

[19] For example, in *Slovo* 7, copied by Nil (*Prosvetitel'*, 294–95; *AfED*: "If Christ is God's Word and the Wisdom of God and is called 'Truth,' and He knows everything, as God, then who can say that He has spoken untruthfully, except for who does not confess our Lord Jesus Christ to be the true God? If someone calls Him the true God, he confesses as truth what is spoken by Him;" and, by another hand, in *Slovo* 5 (*Prosvetitel'*, 199; *AfED*, 368): "If, in every nation, he who fears God is pleasing to Him, then why didn't he [St. Peter—D.G.] leave Cornelius or those who were with him to remain in their own faith, he who feared God and did right more than all others, but commanded them to baptize in the name of Jesus Christ, even if they feared God and did right?" (cf. Acts 10, esp. 10:22, 48).

state *"See!...."* or: *"Do you see...?"*[20] Both employ three types of *refutatio*, that is, counters to objections by the imagined opponent or sceptic: the occasional *refutatio* within or at the end of the exposition of a major point;[21] a specific *refutatio* division towards the end of a discourse;[22] and an expository section constructed, as might befit a polemical work, in the form of what I term a "running *refutatio*."[23] In addition, each set of text turns to John of Damascus for theological principles;[24] each at least once strings a set of biblical citations with exegetical commentary;[25] and each may list a set of patristic authorities to prove a point.[26]

Nevertheless sometimes the text which Nil copied has a characteristic not found elsewhere in the brief *Prosvetitel'*. One, which might appear comparatively elementary and hence uncharacteristic for Nil, is the string of supportive biblical citations with hardly any commentary or exegesis.[27] Otherwise, though, the expected greater sophistication stands out, for example, in

---

[20] For example, in *Slovo* 8, copied by Nil (*Prosvetitel'*, 335; *AfED*, 394): "Do you see how He has most wisely made manifest and most usefully has concealed?"; for an example in another hand, see above, n. 15.

[21] In every *slovo* except for 10, 11b, 11d, these usually commence: "If someone says:..."

[22] Nil's share in *Slova* 8–10; others in *Slova* 4–6, 11a–11b; cf. Richard A. Lanham, *A Handlist of Rhetorical Terms: A Guide for Students of English Literature* (Berkeley: University of California Press, 1969), 112, on *dispositio/taxis*.

[23] For example, in Nil's part of *Slovo* 7, where refutations commence as well as conclude the section on the procession of Holy Spirit (*Prosvetitel'*, 293–304; *AfED*, 348–51); and where copied by others, almost all of *Slovo* 11c (*Prosvetitel'*, 449–53). This, technically speaking, would be a mode of creating the *amplificatio* (confirmation), which precedes the *refutatio* in one of the standard arrangements of a classical oration; see below, n. 52.

[24] Text copied by Nil in *Slovo* 8 concerning the knowable (see above, n. 13), and by another scribe in *Slova* 6 and 7 concerning veneration of holy objects (*Prosvetitel'*, 219–77; *AfED*, 325–43). Compare to John of Damascus's *Exact Exposition of the Orthodox Faith*, bk. 4, ch. 11–12, 15–16, in any edition, for example: *Saint John of Damascus. Writings*, trans. Frerderic H. Chase, Jr. (New York: Fathers of the Church, 1950), 349–54, 369–73; original in *Patrologiae cursus completus, series graecae* (hereafter *PG*), ed. Jacques-Paul Migne, 161 vols. in 166 (Paris: Migne, 1857–66), 94: 1117–34, 1163–76.

[25] Text copied by Nil in *Slovo* 1, with Old Testament prophesies purportedly of Christ (*Prosvetitel'*, 67–79); and by another in *Slovo* 3, on the nature of Old Testament worship (*Prosvetitel'*, 124–31).

[26] Text copied by Nil in *Slovo* 7, on the procession of the Holy Spirit only from the Father (*Prosvetitel'*, 298–300; *AfED*, 349–35; by others in *Slovo* 11, on the propriety of both the secular and monastic modes of life (*Prosvetitel'*, 417–18).

[27] *Prosvetitel'*, 108–19 and 385–96; *AfED*, 409–12, these being, from *Slovo* 2, examples of Old Testament dicta considered prophesies of Christ's crucifixion, resurrection, ascension, and second coming, and from *Slovo* 10, eschatological Old Testament and New Testament statements similar to those of Ephrem the Syrian.

the use of arguments, analogies, and explanations from natural science as then understood,[28] though such are not foreign to Iosif elsewhere, as in his Epistle to Archimandrite Vassian.[29] Where, moreover, I have so far identified patristic sources which the brief *Prosvetitel'* text modifies and adapts, an essential trait of Nil's monastic writings, he is the Sol. 346/326 copyist.[30]

Nil was also the only copyist of sections of this codex devoted to three subjects. One of these, namely, the Orthodox position on the procession of the Holy Spirit, directed here pointedly against the Western Church, might not be surprising.[31] After all the late Byzantino-Balkan cultural movement we associate with hesychasm, Nil's specialty, was defensively anti-Roman Catholic.[32] On the other hand, so far as we know, Nil directed all of his own writings, even the hagiography he redacted, exclusively to monks, yet the *Prosvetitel'* sections devoted essentially to lay morality in Sol. 346/326 are exclusively

---

[28] For example, from *Slovo* 1 (*Prosvetitel'*, 81–82): "And to what do you liken—wind? smoke? These flow through the air and come to non-being. If the Holy Spirit of God flows through the air, then how can the prophet Isaiah say of Him and call Him *Spirit of God, Spirit of wisdom,* Spirit *of knowledge, Spirit of light,* Spirit *of strength, Spirit of testimony, Spirit of piety, Spirit of fear of God*? [Isa. 11:1–3—actual citations in italics]. For a spirit flowing through the air does not grant wisdom, nor knowledge, nor light, nor strength, nor testimony, nor piety, nor fear of God, but when it occurs, it soon comes to non-being."

[29] *AfED*, 308–09; *Poslaniia Iosifa Volotskogo*, 143: Iosif's brief discussion of infinite divinity and finite creation, with his analogy of the "element," which appears simultaneously to be everywhere and nowhere, and God, without whose breath (i.e., Spirit), no living creature or inanimate creation could exist.

[30] Three such examples are: i) the above mentioned (n. 23) string of anti-Latin citations regarding the Holy Spirit in *Slovo* 7, based partially upon *Otveshtanie sviatago vselen'-skago patriarkha kйra Germana i sviashtennago s"bora ego*, in RNB, f. *Osnovnyi*, Q. XVII, no. 88, fols. 82–91v; ii) the *Slovo* 7 instructions for participatory, liturgical prayer in the church (*Prosvetitel'*, 305–19; *AfED*, 352–56), which constitutes the first version of similar instructions of both versions of Iosif's Rule (*Monastic Rule of Iosif Volotsky*, 1[B].18–25 and 1.13–18, 20–22, 27, 31: 125–29, 172–78, with sources, mainly John Chrysostom's sermons, indicated); iii) the above mentioned (nn. 13, 24) adaption from John of Damascus on the knowable and unknowable: cf. *Kniga o Boze, Slovo* 4 in RGB, f. Troits., no. 121, fol. 88v; original in PG 94: 797–800. On Nil's own source manipulation, see Goldfrank, *Nil Sorsky*, under chap. 3, "The Acolyte as Adapter," 80–83; David Goldfrank, "Nil Sorskii and Nikon of the Black Mountain," *Russian History/Histoire russe* 33: 2–4 (2006): 365–405, and "The Literary Nil Sorskii," *Harvard Ukrainian Studies* 28: 1–4 (2006): 99–102.

[31] See above, nn. 23, 26.

[32] John Meyendorff, *Byzantium and the Rise of Russia: A Study of Byzantine-Russian Relations in the Fourteenth Century* (Cambridge: Cambridge University Press, 1981), 124–25.

from Nil's pen.[33] And however much he may have opposed monks' or other peoples' attachment to material wealth or any aspect of fame, fortune, and public prestige,[34] he copied strictures calling for a tithe. He thereby commenced a brief section on memory of death and the Terrible Judgment with a quasi "Pay up or else!" command, and with no indication of how the churchmen, as custodians of God's property, might convert the huge property tithes from the super-rich into redistributions for needy, as a totally consistent "non-possessor" might demand.[35]

Nil is also the copyist of the celebrated *Slovo* 7 statements concerning the honoring of rulers, where, as with the preceding "bowing to each other," the negative follows the positive, but in the former case the negative is just "spurn the heretic," while for the latter the text contains a stinging paragraph on non-compliance with a blasphemous "tyrant," whose other pernicious traits are enumerated.[36] Perhaps Nil's hand is here in that the eight listed

---

[33] From *Slovo* 7, *Prosvetitel'*, 321–32; *AfED*, 356–60, to which one might add the section in *Slovo* 7 concerning prayer: *Prosvetitel'*, 304–21; *AfED*, 351–56.

[34] See, for example, Donald Ostrowski, "Loving Silence and Avoiding Pleasant Conversations: The Political Views of Nil Sorskii," *Harvard Ukrainian Studies* 19 (1995): 476–96. Nil's essential interest in the ethical-spiritual side of these matters, where material wealth is just one of several objects of improper attachment, is evident in Nil's *Ustav* 5.8.95 and 10.5 (my paragraph enumeration in *Nil Sorsky*): *Nila Sorskogo, Predanie i Ustav* (hereafter *NSPU*), ed. M. C. Borovkova-Maikova, *Pamiatniki drevnei pis'mennosti i iskusstva* 179 (1912): 59, 81; Gelian Prokhorov, *Prepodobnyi Nil Sorskii i Innokentii Komel'skii: Sochineniia* (hereafter *PNSIK*) (St. Petersburg: Oleg Abyshko, 2005), 158–61, 188–89; Goldfrank, *Nil Sorsky*, 186–87, 215.

[35] *Prosvetitel'*, 327; *AfED*, 359: "Whether you have a rich house or a poor, thank the Lord God for everything: for all is arranged by divine providence and his never-sleeping eye sees everything. Therefore endeavor to give a tenth of all of your property to God, who has given you life and promised you eternal life after death. For this world passes, and its glory perishes. The Lord shall come with the heavenly forces and place every human at judgment and render unto each according to his deeds. Therefore remember that tomorrow you shall see heavens splitting apart, and you shall gaze upon the angels, and stand before the terrible tribunal...."

[36] Sol. 326/346, fols. 218v–19; *AfED*, 346: "When you bow down to a king or prince or potentate, or serve, it is proper to bow down and serve, because it is well-pleasing to God to render submission and obedience to authorities: they have the care and planning for us. Yea it is written: 'Do not speak evil of the prince of your people' [Exod. 22:28]. And the Apostle says: 'Fear God and honor the king' [1 Pet 2:17)] and: 'Slaves, obey your lords in the flesh with fear and trembling' [Eph. 6:5], as men preferred by God and having received authority from Him, and able to be gracious and to torture bodily, but not the soul. Therefore it is proper to serve them with the body, but not with the soul, and to render unto them royal honor, but not divine, as the Lord says: 'Render Caesar's unto Caesar and God's unto God' [Matt. 22:21]. If you so bow down and serve, it is not unto the destruction of your soul, but rather you learn from this to

negative ruling passions parallel the eight classical *logismoi* or urges, which he analyzes in the extensive *Slovo* 5 of his spiritual treatise (*Ustav*), but Iosif too would have been independently familiar with them from "Nil the Ascetic/Sinaite" (really, Evagrius of Pontus), John Cassian, or a number of other monastic sources.[37] And if a few of the classic saints' lives, whose available Slavic versions Nil redacted, contained at least one such tyrant whom a monk upbraided,[38] Nil's own writings, in contrast to many of Iosif's other works,[39] did not address monarchial power as such.

To underscore the difficulty in identifying Nil Sorskii's share of the copying of *Prosvetitel'* with the specific tendencies of his original writings, we might note that the discourse with perhaps the greatest number and variety of clear affinities with his original compositions is *Slovo* 5 on the legitimacy of the OT Trinity icon. "Everything in its time is acceptable," *Prosvetitel'* allegedly cites John Climacus, similarly to Nil's "And Climacus, taking from Scripture, says: 'a time for everything under heaven' [Eccl 3:1]."[40] *Prosvetitel'* insists that all seemingly contradictory scriptural statements contain the same

---

fear God: 'For the King is God's servant' [Rom. 13:4], for mercy and punishment unto men."

"But is there is a king reigning over men, yet has, ruling over himself, passions and sins: avarice and anger, wickedness and injustice, pride and fury, and, worst of all, disbelief and blasphemy, such a king is not God's servant but the Devil's, and not a king but a tyrant. Such as king, on account of his wickedness, our Lord Jesus Christ did not call a king, but a fox: 'Go', he said, 'and tell that fox' [Luke 13:32, referencing Herod Antipas]. And the Prophet said: 'An arrogant king will perish, for his ways are dark [from Pss. 1:6 and/or Prov. 2:13, 32]. So you are not to obey such a king or prince, who leads you to impiety and wickedness, if he torments, if he threatens death. The Prophets and Apostles and all the Martyrs, who were killed by impious kings and did not submit to their command, bear witness to this." On this, see David M. Goldfrank, "The Deep Origins of *Tsar'-Muchitel'*: A Nagging Problem of Muscovite Political Theory," *Russian History/Histoire russe* 31: 3–4 (Fall–Winter 2005): 341–54.

[37] For example the Volokolamsk codices, State Historical Museum (hereafter GIM), f. Eparkhal'nyi (hereafter Eparkh.), nos. 315 and 369, from the 15th century contain, respectively, "Nil" (the Sinaite) and "Kassian the Italian" (*Rimlianin*) on the eight *pomysly*.

[38] Theodore of Sykeon, who dressed down the murderous tyrant-Emperor Phocas (r. 602–10). *Sobornik Nila Sorskogo*, 3: 341

[39] Virtually every piece Iosif wrote concerning the repression of heretics or his own conflicts with Ivan III, the local prince Fedor, and Archbishop Serapion of Novgorod, as well as several hortatory epistles to princes and four *Prosvetitel' slova*—that is, a total of 20 compositions—touched upon the monarch's power and responsibility and/or the monk's or subject's relation to it.

[40] *Prosvetitel'*, 186; *AfED*, 364; *NSPU*, 85; *PNSIK*, 192–95; Goldfrank, *Nil Sorsky, Ustav* 11.2; from *St. John Climacus, The Ladder of Divine Ascent*, trans. Archimandrite Lazarus Moore (London: Faber and Faber; New York: Harper, 1959), 26.87: 214; Slavic as in GIM f. Eparkh., no. 331, fol. 297v; original as in *PG* 88: 1032C.

thought and the same knowledge (*edinu mysl' i edin" razum" imut"*), while Nil writes concerning his heyschastic authorities, "just as each of them was instructed by God's grace with the same knowledge [*edinem zhe razumom*]."[41] In explaining who is privileged to interpret Scripture, *Prosvetitel'* states "But this word was said according to supreme wisdom and contains a certain secretiveness as Scripture says: 'my secret is for me and mine' [1 Cor. 2:7]," while Nil writes to two of his devotees, "I reveal my secrets to my own and to the *sons* of my *house*," and "I reveal my secret things to my beloved."[42] Additionally, *Prosvetitel'* illustrates a seeming contradiction among Church Fathers with two celebrated monk-theologian-hymnographers, Andrew of Crete (ca. 650–early 8th c.) and Joseph (of Sicily, 810–883/6), while Nil uses Andrew and several other such liturgists as sources for prayers of repentance and mourning.[43] Lest one imagine, however, that this section exhibited a peculiar orientation towards Nil, we ought note that here as well lay a crucial theological proposition, already used in Iosif's earlier theological Epistle to Archimandrite Vassian. This was John of Damascus's dictum that "the Holy, uniessential Trinity is invisible to bodily eyes," which needed reconciliation with the interpretation of Abraham's hospitality underlying that Trinity icon.[44] We certainly cannot argue from the evidence in this paragraph that Nil Sorskii had a hand in the initial authorship of this *slovo*, for which we have the unique notice, *spisok iosifove*, on an early, separate-fascicle copy with distinct paper within a complete extended redaction all of different paper.[45] Ultimately our problem here may be, as Seebohm concluded from his penetrating and thorough analysis of underlying principles, that "Nil ... *au fond* ... in proceeding from a monastic conception of philosophy, was in full agreement with Iosif."[46]

---

[41] *Prosvetitel'*, 206–07; *AfED*, 370; *NSPU*, 11; *PNSIK*, 96–97; Goldfrank, *Nil Sorsky, Ustav*, 126; Iosif says this somewhat similarly in his partial source for *Slovo* 5, the Epistle to Arkhimandrite Vassian: "[A]ll of them, say one truth and do not differ ... from long ago the Patriarchs and Prophets and Apostles and Holy Fathers—all confessed the Godhead, as if by the same lips, to be unknowable, inconceivable, and invisible..." (*AfED*, 308; *Poslaniia Iosifa Volotskogo*, 142).

[42] *Prosvetitel'*, 206; *AfED*, 370; Gelian Prokhorov, "Poslaniia Nila Sorskogo," *TODRL* 29 (1974): 141; *PNSIK*, 240–41, 236–37; Goldfrank, *Nil Sorsky*, "To German," 245, and "To Gurii," 243.

[43] *Prosvetitel'*, 206; *AfED*, 370; *NSPU* 69–70, 74; *PNSIK*, 172–79; Goldfrank, *Nil Sorsky*, *Ustav* 199–201, 205–07.

[44] *AfED*, 308; *Poslaniia Iosifa Volotskogo*, 142; see above, n. 17.

[45] GIM f. Eparkh., no. 339, fol. 113v.

[46] Seebohm, *Ratio und Charisma*, 486.

స్ర్ ~ఠ్

Returning to the problem of the genesis of Sol. 346/326, I can see the attraction of Lur'e's conclusion that the brief *Prosvetitel'* contained in Sol. 346/326 was produced in 1502–04 for use at the inquisitorial synod of 1504, which Iosif successfully masterminded. That date allows for the disappearance from public life of Fedor Kuritsyn, the powerful, third-named chief culprit in the opening section of most *Prosvetitel'* versions of the *slova*. But then why, after the 1504 synod, did this prize copy end up in the Sora-Beloozero region in the personal possession of Nil Sorskii's Iosifov assistant and co- (along with the Kirillov elder Gurii Tushin) literary executor Nil Polev, rather than in Moscow in the metropolitan's library or back at Iosifov? Could successful lobbying on Iosif's part and other inquisitorial events have overtaken the actual pre-editing and copying of these folios? Could the original of this Sol. 346/326, with an equally elaborate title page for the continuous 11 *slova* of Iosif's brief Rule (fols. 4–44v), one which makes no concessions whatsoever to personal possessions,[47] rather have served as his signature prestige work in a region where some people, if not Nil Sorskii himself, opposed the repression of heretics and talked non-possessor talk? This too is speculation.

We do know that by 1493–94 Iosif was complaining to Bishop Nifont of Suzdal that certain people considered it "a sin to condemn heretics," a position attributed to heretics in the *Skazanie* and *Slovo* 13.[48] Such thinking eventually attracted one of Nil Sorskii's long-standing Beloozero devotees, German Podol'nyi, and became a bone of the latter's contention with Nil Polev around 1509–10. Nil Polev in turn utilized either "To Nifont" or its *Slovo* 12 reworking to defend Iosif from the charge that he and his disciples had been validly excommunicated.[49] This means that not only the *Skazanie* and 11 *slova* of Sol. 346/326, but that some other purely inquisitional aspects of the other three types of *Prosvetitel'* were likely also to have been in Nil Polev's hands at the time he created the original codex (to fol. 337), which became Sol. 346/326. Thus the total absence of inquisitorial epistles and *slova* was a conscious editorial choice, not a sign that these did not simultaneously circulate. And the original codex, in contrast to Iosif's extended Rule and extended *Prosvetitel'*, was, in terms of quantity, rather short on regulations, administration, and punishments, and, in percentage terms, longer on ideals and didactic theology.

We come now to the final question concerning Nil Sorskii's role in the creation of *Prosvetitel'*, for which more than one hypothesis deserves consideration. Gelian Prokhorov has recently argued that Nil was not a proponent

---

[47] *Poslaniia Iosifa Volotskogo*, 307–09; *Monastic Rule of Iosif Volotsky*, 5ᴮ.

[48] *AfED*, 430; *Poslaniia Iosifa Volotskogo*, 164; *AfED*, 474.

[49] Lur'e, *Ideologicheskaia bor'ba*, 467; Goldfrank, *Nil Sorsky*, "The Loose Cannon" and "The Man in the Middle," 42–46.

of the execution of any heretics, merely the copyist of part of the text[50]—an expert's position, which we ought respect, although I do not see why Nil would have put his prestige as a teacher and authority on the line in copying anything with which he had a fundamental disagreement. On the other end of the spectrum is the possibility that Nil was chiefly responsible for part or all of what he copied and for crafting, with the help of available patristics, the defense and elucidation of the Trinity and the authenticity of Christ (*Slova* 1– 2), the ineffability of eschatological chronology and tenuousness of seven-age/century predictions (*Slova* 8–10), the Orthodox notion of the procession of the Holy Spirit, as well as outlining the essentials of lay social relations, morality, piety, and prayer (his share of *Slovo* 7), and even designing the initial polemical presentation of the Novgorod Heretics to the public (his share of the *Skazanie*)—in other words, that Nil served as a ghost-writer for Iosif. Against that proposition I would propose, from style, a modification of the proverbial "duck" paradigm: if *Prosvetitel'* flows and sounds very little like Nil's known writings, but, rather, like Iosif's argumentative epistles and the polemics within his monastic homiletics, then who else could have been its chief author?

The more modest possibility—that in response to Gennadii's appeal for calendrical consultation,[51] Nil (with or without aid from his oft presumed mentor Paisii) created the initial *skazania* underlying *Slova* 8–10—is inviting. Their overall construction or arrangement, if lacking the formulaic "*Slovo na novogorodskikh eretikov...*" or the specific name(s) *Aleksei glagoliu protopopa ... i vsekh takozhde mudr'stvuiushchtikh... ,*" conforms to the *Prosvetitel' slovo* model. It starts with a title followed by a positive statement of what one should believe, and then an elaboration of the position to be opposed with insults hurled at the adherents, all preceding the basic statement of what is to be demonstrated.[52] Hence these *skazaniia* could, in theory, be the earliest of all the pre-*Prosvetitel' slova* compositions, with Nil having even first created them

---

[50] Gelian Prokhorov, personal communication with author, 9 July 2007. Elena Romanenko noted that, of the Russian scholars, only Lur'e disputed the common opinion that Nil's (and his alleged "mentor" Paisi Iaroslavov's) role in the 1490 synod was to ensure "mild" punishments (*Nil Sorskii i traditsii russkogo monashestva,* 86). For a strong seconding of Lur'e's view, see Goldfrank, *Nil Sorsky,* "The Unexpected Bedfellow," 48–55.

[51] *AfED,* 320.

[52] *AfED,* 395, 401, 409: "[T]hey are the lips of their father, Satan. ... they ... manifest unforgivable mania and insanity and the latest mode of impiety and sign of pride and disbelief. ... they ... wish to introduce wicked doubt among men, ... and thereby demonstrate that all the writings of our holy Fathers are false." Even an amateur in Classical rhetoric will recognize in this construction a variant of entrance, precognition/narration, exposition/definition, and proposition, which precede the confirmation, confutation/refutation, and conclusion/epilogue of Cicero's arrangement of an oration. Lanham, *Handlist,* 112–13. See above, n. 23.

and then agreed to convert them into *slova* on Iosif's more developed model, as in the pre-existing *Slova* 5–6 and (probably) more recently created *Slova* 1–4. But would Nil have done all of that and then not been given any credit for the final product? Perhaps some future, more sophisticated rhetorical analysis will allow for a more concrete conclusion.

I would suggest, meanwhile, a slight modification of Lur'e's explanation. Nil's most likely role in the creation of the initial brief redaction of *Prosvetitel'* was that of reviewer, checker, and master-copier of what was intended to be an ornate initial version circulated among designated elite readers, all as part of the campaign to eradicate dissidence, but Nil's hand-written folios never served that purpose. Rather, the repressions of 1504–05 proceeded without that paper specifically playing any role, and it thus remained under the control of Nil Polev, just as did, at the end of Nil Sorskii's life (1508), his autograph copies of the *Predanie* with some addenda and of his three-volume hagiographic *sobornik*, if not his *Ustav* and epistles. In this regard we should note the marginality of any of Nil's peculiar additions or copyist's errors to *Prosvetitel'*. For example, he accidently or purposely added to a pair of sentences a second *myslenya* (mental), here within a citation from a Psalm, but such was not, so far as I can tell, reproduced in the other early recensions.[53]

Perhaps the codex Sof. 1474,[54] containing a ca. 1500 or early 16th-century separate copy of *Slovo* 6–7 and 5, and also kindred and possible source material for the brief redaction *Provetitel'*, can provide the clinching clue to Nil Sorskii's overall role here. This manuscript has on the front page, in what appears as the same handwriting as the subsequent text, *Sbornik Genada pustyn'* (Miscellany of Gennadii's Hermitage). This could have been the actual hermitage where the future Kornilii Komel'skii resided before 1497, and where he served as one of Archbishop Gennadii's Orthodox assistants.[55] Kornilii later became an exceedingly dynamic coenobiarch in the Vologda region (eight of his disciples founded their own monasteries), and he composed a rule by copying or adapting from both Nil Sorskii's *Predanie* (about 20 percent of text) and Iosif's Extended Rule (about 63 percent).[56]

---

[53] Compare the citation from Ps. 130:1 (LXX Ps. 129:1) in *Prosvetitel'*, 306 (reproducing Sol. 346/326 and noting the word's absence in three other copies, two of which, I would add, Sol. 347/327 and 351/331, stem from the Iosifov working copy, GIM f. Eparkh., no. 339); *AfED*, 352 (reproducing the earliest extant copy of the separate version of *Slovo* 7); RGB f. Troits., no. 187, fol. 225; and also the modified versions in Iosif's Rule, *Poslaniia Iosifa Volotskogo*, 301; *Monastic Rule of Iosif Volotsky*, 1ᴮ.22/1.17 (Nil's addition is in brackets): [T]ako i molitva, iz glubiny myslenya v"ssylaema, k vysote prostiraetsia. Sego radi prorok reche: iz glubiny [myslenya] v"zvakh k tebe, Gospodi.

[54] RNB f. Novgorod-Sofiiskaia Biblioteka, no. 474.

[55] D. S. Likhachev et al., eds., *Biblioteka literatury Drevnei Rusi* [v 20-ti tomakh], 15 vols. to date (St. Petersburg: Nauka, 1997–), 13: 308.

[56] See Goldfrank, *Nil Sorsky*, "The Colonizing Coenobite," 55–58.

Now would not Gennadii's Orthodox *pustynniki* have constituted some form of control commission over the work of his Roman Catholic consultants? And should we not envision the anti-Latin section in *Slovo* 7, copied and hence proofed by Nil, as a basic reminder to Orthodox Russians of the essential, salvific fault line separating them from all of those useful, necessary, and attractive Westerners residing and working in Moscow and Novgorod? Do we not then have further evidence from this fresh look at *Prosvetitel'*, that the active, alert, committed, monastic- and tradition-minded Orthodox of the time, be they located in Novgorod, Beloozero, Volokolamsk, or elsewhere in episcopal palaces, hermitages, or coenobia, were supporting each other's endeavors to combat and suppress dissidence and instruct the believers in the essentials of their faith? And does this not broaden our sense of Nil Sorskii from Old Russia's master-hesychast, whose essential concern was Orthodox monasticism, to a teacher-writer-editor who not only redacted hagiography and produced his own works in several established didactic genres—rule, testament, treatise, epistle—but also branched out, at least as a major copyist, most probably a reviewer, less likely as an active editor, yet even remotely possibly as a contributing writer, of pre-modern Russia's most significant original polemical-didactic treatise?

The ideals expressed in *Prosvetitel'* or, for that matter, Nil's monastic writings, like those of any sacred tradition, do not exactly square with our contemporary notions of knowledge, social equity, tolerance, or human rights. But the role of the historian, as Professor Crummey has shown us so well with Old Believers, Muscovite aristocrats, and other types from Russia's past, is to present our subjects at least partially in their own terms and to give credit where credit is due. As the 20 or so translated *Prosvetitel'* extracts in the notes demonstrate, its author(s) could ably marshal arguments and rhetoric in defense of Muscovite Orthodoxy. And some credit for this, maybe simply as a friendly and superb reader and copyist, or maybe more, was due to the expertise, support, and labor of Nil Sorskii, who, so far as we know, put his pen to the writings of only one Russia writer, past or contemporary, other than himself—Iosif Volotskii.

Realization vs. Standard: Commemorative Meals in the Iosif Volotskii Monastery in 1566/67

Ludwig Steindorff

Those who work on the history of the Iosif Volotskii monastery 75 miles northwest of Moscow know the *Eparkhial'noe sobranie* (the Diocesan Collection) in the manuscript depository of the State Historical Museum at Moscow as one of the most important collections of relevant sources since it forms a part of the former library of that monastery, which was founded by Iosif Sanin in 1479.[1] Beside readings from the Bible, liturgical books, and patristic literature, we find a number of memorial registers (*sinodiki*), Donation Books (*Vkladnye knigi*), and Books of Feasts (*Kormovye knigi*), i.e., those sources which refer to the role of the monastery as a receiver of donations and center of liturgical commemoration.[2] While some of these manuscripts were frequently used by researchers, one of them has hardly been taken into account so far.[3] Manuscript no. 417 (683) is described as "Rule for meals and the commemoration of the living and the dead, 1565, 8⁰ (15 cm x 10 cm), Russian cursive uncial. 38 folios. The ending is lost" ("Ustav o trapeze i pominanii zhivykh i umershikh, 1565 g., 8⁰ (15x10), russkii beglyi ustav. 38 l. Okonchanie utracheno").[4] The description of the contents is limited to the remark that feasts

---

[1] The latest monograph on the history of the monastery is by Tom E. Dykstra, *Russian Monastic Culture: "Josephism" and the Iosifo-Volokolamsk Monastery 1947–1607* (Munich: Otto Sagner, 2006 [=Slavistische Beiträge 450]). A table of all known monks from the monastery was published by him: "Inocheskie imena v Moskovskoi Rusi i problemy identifikatsii ikh obladatelei (na materiale istochnikov Iosifo-Volokolamskogo monastyria, 1479–1607)," in *Imenoslov: Istoricheskaia semantika imeni. Vypusk 2*, ed. Fedor Uspenskii (Moscow: Indrik, 2007), 238–98.

[2] For the typology of the whole complex of sources, see Ludwig Steindorff, "Commemoration and Administrative Techniques in Muscovite Monasteries," *Russian History/Histoire Russe* 22: 4 (1995): 433–54; L. Shtaindorf [Ludwig Steindorff], "Sravnenie istochnikov ob organizatsii pominaniia usopshikh v Iosifo-Volokolamskom i v Troitse-Sergievom monastyriakh v XVI v." *Arkheograficheskii ezhegodnik za 1996 god* (Moscow: Nauka, 1998), 65–78, esp. 67–69.

[3] Gosudarstvennyi istoricheskii muzei, Eparkhial'noe sobranie [hereafter GIM, Eparkh. sobr.], no. 417 (683).

[4] T. V. Dianova, L. M. Kostiukhina, and I. V. Pozdeeva, "Opisanie rukopisei biblioteki Iosifo-Volokolamskogo monastyria," *Knizhnye tsentry Drevnei Rusi: Iosifo-Volokolamskii*

Rude & Barbarous Kingdom Revisited: Essays in Russian History and Culture in Honor of Robert O. Crummey. Chester S. L. Dunning, Russell E. Martin, and Daniel Rowland, eds. Bloomington, IN: Slavica Publishers, 2008, 231–49.

and donations are enumerated in the order of the calendar, beginning from September 1. As pointed out in the description, all persons mentioned in the entries are closely linked to the monastery, and the entries offer information about the food.

So at first glance it looks as if the manuscript was an early variant of the extant *Kormovaia kniga* from the Iosif Volotskii monastery, which was composed in about 1581, and which, in the form of a calendar, indicates the dates of *kormy* (festive meals in memory of donors or their relatives), registers the donations on the basis of which the *kormy* were established, and contains instructions about food and beverage. The annual commemoration by a *korm* was normally bound to the donation of at least 100 rubles or corresponding real estate or movable goods.[5] But a more detailed analysis of the manuscript will prove that it is a unique example of a new source type, previously unknown, which supplies new information about the memorial practice in the monastery.

The book starts on folio 2:[6] "In the year 7075, on September 1, on the Feast of St. Semion, which fell on a Sunday. In the trapeze [refectory], the following food was served…" ("Leta 7000 sem'desiatogo piatogo mesiatsa sentiabria v 1, pamiat' prepodobna ottsa Semiona, prilochilos'[7] v nedeliu. V trapeze estva…"). A description of the food served for lunch follows: bread, *pirogi*, *shchi*, eggs, but, as explicitly noted, no *kolachi*. The brethren drank *kvas* which had been prepared from grain. Even from this short quotation it is obvious that the organization of the text is different from that of a Book of Feasts (*Kormovaia kniga*). The Book of Feasts is a normative text; it is not bound to a certain year, but it indicates the dates of commemorative meals as they fall every year. Here instead the manuscript refers exactly to the year 7075, which began on September 1, 1566.[8] While the day within the weekly cycle is indicated here, this could not occur in a *Kormovaia kniga*, of course, because the date falls on different days in different years. Moreover, from the past tense verb *prilochilos'* (and the past tense elsewhere in the text: *korm byl, tsar priekhal*, etc.),

---

monastyr' kak tsentr knizhnosti, ed. Dmitrii Sergeevich Likhachev (Leningrad: Nauka, Leningradskoe otdelenie, 1991), 122–414, at 409.

[5] *Das Speisungsbuch von Volokolamsk: Kormovaia kniga Iosifo-Volokolamskogo monastyria. Eine Quelle zur Sozialgeschichte russischer Klöster im 16. Jahrhundert*, ed. and trans. Ludwig Steindorff, in cooperation with Rüdiger Koke, Elena Kondrashkina, Ulrich Lang, and Nadja Pohlmann (Cologne: Böhlau, 1998) [=Bausteine zur Slavischen Philologie und Kulturgeschichte, NF, Reihe B, Editionen, Band 12], xxvii–xxxi [hereafter *Kormovaia kniga Ios. Vol. mon.*]. The edition is based on GIM, Sinodal Collection (Sinodal'noe sobranie), no. 403 (829).

[6] As for fol. 1, see below.

[7] Instead of *priluchilos'*.

[8] The obviously wrong dating of the manuscript derives probably exclusively from the dating of the watermarks from 1565 following Briquet.

it is obvious that, again unlike the Book of Feasts, the entries in this source do not record the food which should be served, but the food that had already been served on that day. Since the manuscript does not contain a self-designation, I propose the term *Godovaia kormovaia kniga*, or "Annual Feast Book."[9]

The manuscript is incomplete; it ends abruptly on Thursday, April 17, 1567 (fol. 24v). In addition, the order of the folios is disturbed, but thanks to the regular indication of the date in the month and the day in the week, it was not difficult to discover the mistake and to restore the correct order of folios (fols. 1–16, 25–38, 17–24). Of course, all important church feasts are noted, beginning from the Birth of the Mother of God on September 8, but the saint of the day is rarely recorded. No day during the year is omitted, even when no *korm* took place on that day. In this case the entry is limited to the food served. Sometimes we find only a hint: "as on Friday," "as last Wednesday," "drinking the same as for lunch," etc. Only the entry about the first day of the visit of Tsar Ivan IV and his family to the monastery on October 21–22, 1566 (fols. 9v–11) is a little more eloquent and detailed, reporting which services and meals the tsar attended.

The manuscript is written in a crude *ustav*, probably by one hand. But the flow differs depending on the quality of the quill and obviously also on the mood of the writer. Certainly the manuscript was written in sections, but as we can conclude from the partly continuous flow and also from one passage in the text (fol. 31),[10] the entries were not made day by day, but periodically. Probably the writer disposed of short notes on paper–or perhaps birch bark– and did not rely completely on his memory when he wrote down the entries after a certain period. Only the entry for supper on September 1 presumably follows a normative text, or it was written in advance, since it ends: "And if there are no *pirogi* left after lunch, then for dinner milk or cheese and eggs" ("a koli pirogov u obedu neustanettsa ino k uzhine moloko ili syr da iatsa") (fol. 2v). But this is an exception. I did not find any more alternative offers in other entries. Immediately, after this passage follows the entry for September 2.

Surprisingly, on folio 1 we meet another entry for September 1, again with the indication of the year 7075, with the same food for lunch, and only a slight variation in the formulation of the text. But supper is partly different.[11]

---

[9] I introduced this term in the introduction to *Kormovaia kniga Ios. Vol. mon.*, xix–xx.

[10] See below the discussion of the commemoration of Iona and Iev Sinitsyn.

[11] fol. 1: "For supper bread, cabbage soup, and milk, or instead, cheese or three eggs per brother, *kvas* from grain, and on midday they drink brewed *kvas*" ("Za uzhinoiu khleb da shti da maloko, abmena syr ili po tri eetsa na brata, da kvas zhitnai, da polden' kvas svarnoi p'iut"). (For the *poldennyi kvas*, see *Kormovaia kniga Ios. Vol. mon.*, 115); fols. 2–2v: "For supper bread and cabbage soup, and if there are *pirogi* left from lunch, half a *pirog* for each brother, or instead eggs, three eggs for each brother. But if there are no *pirogi* left from lunch, then milk or cheese and eggs" ("Za uzhinoiu khleb

The back of the folio (fol. 1v) is empty, on folio 2 starts the quoted entry for September 1. Of course, at first we may suspect that the entry on fol. 1 was written on another sheet of paper and bound to the complete calendar only later. But folio 1 and folio 8 form the first layer of the first fascicle of the manuscript, and folio 8 contains passages within the continuous text. So we have to suppose that the writer started on folio 1, but was not satisfied by his work and restarted now successfully on folio 2. The provisional character of the whole manuscript may justify such an explanation.

In analyzing the manuscript, I have so far paid less attention to the food and beverage than to the information concerning names and dates of *kormy*. I have compiled a complete list of all *kormy* mentioned in the manuscript and have verified if the persons to be commemorated by these *kormy* and the dates of these *kormy* are registered in the Donation Book which was composed in 1562/63,[12] or the Book of Feasts from 1581 or 1582. While both the Donation Book and the Book of Feasts offer information about the donations,[13] the *Godovaia kormovaia kniga* does not mention donations at all.

In the appendix the reader will find a table of all *kormy* not in chronological order as in the manuscript, but arranged in the same order as in the table in the appendix to the edition of the Book of Feasts: the family of the ruling dynasty, hierarchs, brethren, princely families, and then other families.[14] Within each group the order is alphabetical. If the family name of a hierarch is known, then he is registered within his family. If a name is crossed out in the manuscript, it appears in the table nevertheless.

As far as a monk or a nun is commemorated in the *Godovaia kormovaia kniga*, the entry indicates only the monastic and the family name and eventually the title "prince" or "princess." Since the Donation Book and the Book of Feasts normally indicate both Christian and monastic name, I was able to complete the entries in the table. Independent from the spelling of a name in the manuscript, the spelling in the table is normalized.

---

da shti, da u obedni zhe pirogov ostanetsia, po polupirogu na brata, a obmena itsa, po tri eitsa na brata. A koli pirogov u obeda ne ostanettsa ino k uzhine moloko ili syr da iatsa").

[12] *Vkladnaia kniga Iosifova Volokolamskago monastyria*, ed. A. A. Titov, Rukopisi slavianskie i russkie, prinadlezhashchie I. A. Vachromeevu (Moscow, 1906), 5: 1–79 [hereafter *Vkladnaia kniga Ios. Vol. Mon.*]. The edition is based on GIM, Eparkhial'noe sobranie, no. 419 (687).

[13] Information about donations is functionally not necessary in a Book of Feasts. As a result, many Books of Feasts from other monasteries omit it. See, for example, A. I. Alekseev, "Drevneishaia kormovaia kniga Kirillo-Belozerskogo monastyria," *Istoriia v rukopisiakh i rukopisi v istorii: Sbornik nauchnykh trudov k 200-letiiu Otdela rukopisei Rossiiskoi natsional'noi biblioteki* (St. Peterburg: Rossiiskaia natsional'naia biblioteka, 2006), 363–78, esp. 366–72.

[14] *Kormovaia kniga Ios. Vol. mon.*, 342–66.

The table contains 86 persons, 13 of them are commemorated twice, and once a whole family without indication of an individual name is registered (No. 25). If we want to estimate how many persons had gained the right for a *korm* in the Iosif Volotskii monastery in the given year, we have to take into account that a little more than a third of the year is missing in the manuscript, and that some persons mentioned in the extant part of the book were certainly commemorated another time between April 18 and the end of August. So certainly the figure for the whole year was probably not higher than 130, as compared to 219 persons whose commemoration by *korm* was registered in the Book of Feasts from about 1581.

As I demonstrated in previous studies, the memorial practice of Muscovite Russia was characterized by surprising regularity. The distribution of persons to be commemorated in the *Godovaia kormovaia kniga* is quite similar to the distribution found in other sources.

Book	Absolute figure	Percent women	Percent monks	Percent nobles
Godovaia kormovaia kniga	86[15]	16.3 % (14)	50.0 % (43)	38.4 % (33)
Korm. kn. Ios. Vol. mon.	219	22.8 %	46.9 %	36.2 %
Korm. kn. Kir. Bel. mon.[16]	378	21.2 %	36.8 %	33.6 %
Korm. kn. Tr. Serg. mon.[17]	59	22.3 %	17.7 %	43.9 %[18]

In this patriarchal society women were certainly less represented in the practice of donating and commemoration, but they were not excluded. In the

---

[15] The two cases of commemoration of living persons are taken into account too, the collective commemoration for the princes Khovanskie is omitted.

[16] *Kormovaia kniga Kirillo-Belozerskogo monastyria*, ed. I. P. Sacharov, in *Zapiski otdeleniia russkoi i slavianskoi arkheologii Imperatorskago arkheologicheskago obshchestva* 1 (1851), III, pp. 46–105.

[17] *Kormovaia kniga Troitse-Sergieva monastyria*, ed. Arkhimandrit Leonid, in A. V. Gorskii, *Istoricheskoe opisanie Sviato-troitskoi Sergievy lavry sostavlennoe po rukopisnym i pechatnym istochnikam v 1841 godu. S prilozheniiami arkhimandrita Leonida* (Moscow, 1890), pt. 2, pp. 45–64. This is in fact a Donation Book, but it is limited to donations on which *kormy* are based.

[18] The figures are taken from Liudvig Shtaindorf [Ludwig Steindorff], "Kto blizhnie moi? Individ i kul'tura pominoveniia v Rossii rannego novogo vremeni," in *Chelovek i ego blizkie na Zapade i Vostoke Evropy (do nachala novogo vremeni)*, ed. Iurii Bessmertnyi and Otto Gerhard Oexle (Moscow: Institut vseobshchei istorii, RAN, 2000), 208–39, esp. 213–14 ; Shtaindorf, "Sravnenie istochnikov," 72, 75–77.

Godovaia kniga and the other sources, the percentage of women donors is much higher within the group of nobles (12 out of 35) than in the group of non-nobles (2, both nuns, out of 47). The higher the status and the economic possibilities, the more likely it was that women participated in the highest forms of commemoration. The percentage of nobles who died as monks or nuns (10 out of 34) was still less than the percentage of non-nobles (33 out of 52), showing the reluctance among the nobles to be tonsured and the resistance of relatives to family members who wanted to leave the "world."[19] But there were only 2 nuns among the 28 non-noble monastic persons listed, while there were 5 nuns among the 12 noble women (never married or widows). This confirms again that the difference in the percentage of the genders was smaller among the nobles.

When we compile a chronological distribution of *kormy*, we obtain the following breakdown:

September	17 *kormy*
October	17 *kormy*
November	16 *kormy*
December	7 *kormy*
January	22 *kormy*
February	8 *kormy*
March	4 *kormy*
April	8 *kormy*
Total	99 *kormy*[20]

In evaluating this distribution over the months, we must of course take into account the popularity of certain names, such as Dmitrii or Ivan, and the probability of death cases in a certain month of the year, since normally the *kormy* took place on the saint's day or on the anniversary of death. But the most important factor causing this uneven distribution is certainly the periods of fast. One period of limited fasting starts six weeks before Christmas, on November 15. Great Lent started in 1567 on February 10, and Easter fell on March 30. During the periods of fast *kormy* could take place only on certain exceptional days, usually a Saturday since this day is reserved to the commemoration of the dead in the weekly cycle. Between March 15 and April 4 not a single *korm* was celebrated. As we will see later from the comparison of the prescribed dates in the Donation Book and the dates when *kormy* were

---

[19] Ludwig Steindorff, "Einstellungen zum Mönchtum im Spiegel altrussischer Quellen," *Archiv für Kulturgeschichte* 75: 1 (1993): 65–90.

[20] The total comprises 85 persons, 13 of them twice. The collective commemoration for the princes Khovanskie and those commemorations that are crossed out are not taken into account.

actually celebrated, the great number of *kormy* in January was at least partly due to the necessity to move celebrations to periods without fast restrictions.

As for the days in the week when the *kormy* took place, Tuesday, Thursday, and Saturday absolutely dominate. *Kormy* were prohibited on Wednesday and Friday because of fasting. Sunday is reserved to the commemoration of the living. So the only commemoration of a living donor, the *zazdravnyi korm* ("feast for the health") on the occasion of the name day (*imeniny*) of Ivan Vasil'ev men'shoi Sheremetev, took place on Sunday, March 2, 1567 (no. 76 in the table). Following the entry in the Donation Book, his saint's day was the Feast of the Discovery of the Head of Saint John the Baptist and Forerunner, on February 24. But this feast fell on Monday this year, so the celebration was moved to the next opportunity ahead. On the second day of the stay of the tsar's family in the monastery, on Tuesday, November 22, the monks enjoyed a *zazdravnyi korm* for the health of Tsarevich Ivan Ivanovich, the son of the tsar (no. 4).

The regular celebration of *kormy* for the deceased only on Tuesday, Thursday, and Saturday is in accordance with the *Obikhodnik* of the Iosif monastery,[21] which provides for *panikhidy* on Monday, Wednesday and Friday evening—that is, on the eve of Tuesday, Thursday, and Saturday.[22] I will demonstrate the interaction between the norms and the actual practice from the different books with only one example.[23]

According to the entry in the Donation Book from 1564 the commemoration of Nikita Grigor'ev Pleshcheev (no. 59 in the appendix) was fixed on September 15, his saint's day.[24] In 1566 this day fell on a Sunday, so the *korm* was moved to the following Tuesday, September 17. On Monday evening, during the *panikhida* on the eve of Tuesday, the deacons read the corresponding entry in the *kormovoi spisok*—a book in the order of the calendar which was obviously written for this purpose and contains entries for the whole family of the persons who were commemorated by a *korm*. The original entry for the Pleshcheevs consists of only four names, seven names were added later by different hands.[25] After the service the brethren would go to the grave of Nikita

---

[21] *Obikhodnik:* The special rules of a monastery, similar to the Western *consuetudines*.

[22] *Obikhod Iosifo-Volokolamskogo monastyria*, ed. partim E. E. Golubinskii, *Istoriia russkoi tserkvi*, vol. 2, pt. 2 (Moscow, 1910; repr., The Hague: Mouton, 1969), 577–82, at p. 577 (following Rossiiskaia gosudarstvennaia biblioteka, Otdel rukopisei, f. 113, d. 681, fol. 4). As for the other copies of the *Obikhodnik*, see the introduction to *Kormovaia kniga Ios. Vol. mon.*, xvi, xl.

[23] I presented another example, the case of the Tsarevna Anna (no. 5 in the appendix) in Ludwig Steindorff, "Mehr als eine Frage der Ehre: Zum Stifterverhalten Zar Ivans des Schrecklichen," *Jahrbücher für Geschichte Osteuropas* 51 (2003): 342–66, here 350–51.

[24] *Vkladnaia kniga Ios. Vol. mon.*, 62, no. 272.

[25] GIM, Eparkh. sobr., d. 415 (675), l. 5: (first hand:) inoka Guria. inoka Arseniia. Nikitu. Borisa. Grigoriia. (second hand:) Mariiu inoka Feodosiia (third hand:) Ioanna.

which, according to the entry in the Book of Feasts, was not far south from the crypt of the Church of the Dormition (Uspenskii sobor), where the founder, Iosif, was buried, in the direction of the gate.[26] On Tuesday after the Divine Liturgy the monks had the festive meal in the *trapeza*. In the *Godovaia kormovaia kniga* from 1666/67 is noted the following: "Pans, soup of smelts, in the pawns vendaces, half a slice [per person], both butter-baked [dishes, i.e., *pirogi* and pancakes], *kvas* from honey water" ("Skovorody, ukhi snetkovye, po skovorodam sigoviny, pol zvena, maslenoe oboe, kvas sychen"; ll. 5v–6). This is principally in correspondence with the entry in the younger normative Book of Feasts, which provides for a small *korm* and *kvas sychen*. A small *korm* is there defined under September 1 as a meal which comprises: "one whole cake per person, two sorts of fish, a butter-baked dish, fried *pirogi* with cheese, small pan cakes with honey, mead" ("kvas kolachi tselye odny, da ryba dvoa da maslenoe, pirogi s syrom priazheny da olad'i s medom, kvas medven").[27]

The very few cases when *kormy* in memory of deceased persons took place on other days in the week are easily explained by liturgical reasons. The commemoration of Iosif Sanin, the founder of the monastery, on Monday, September 9 (no. 74), served for the veneration of a saint, not for the salvation of his soul.

The *korm* for the Nashchokins on Monday, February 3, 1567 (nos. 55–56) was celebrated on the second day of the Meat Fare Week (*maslenitsa*) or Cheese Week (*syrnaia nedelia*), when fish and meat are normally already prohibited as part of the preparation for Great Lent. But following the normative Book of Feasts, on that day *kormy* were allowed, and fried fish could be served.[28] In 1567 the brethren received carp breams in pans.[29]

The monks celebrated the *korm* in memory of Aleksei Stupishin, former arkhimandrit of the Simonov monastery in Moscow, on Wednesday, April 16,

---

Varvaru. (first hand:) inoka Kirila. (fourth hand:) Fonasiia. Ioanna. I did not verify the entry in the other copy of this book: GIM, Eparkh. sobr., no. 1 (6). Cf. the description of the collection quoted in n. 4, here pp. 124–26. The classification as a *sinodik* is wrong.

[26] *Kormovaia kniga Ios. Vol. mon.*, 35: *bliz grobnitsy ot sviatykh vorot*. For a complete list of burial plots, see ibid., 367–74. As for the topography of the monastery, see the map on liv.

[27] *Kormovaia kniga Ios. Vol. mon.*, 5. On p. 9 it is noted that the description of the food under September 1 refers to all medium and small *kormy*. As for the behaviour of the brethren in the *trapeza*, see *The Monastic Rule of Iosif Volotsky*, ed. and trans. David Goldfrank, rev. ed. (Kalamazoo, MI: Cistercian Publications, 2000) [=Cistercian Studies Series 36], 186–88, 278–80 (Discourse II, 27–35, Tradition II, 1–11).

[28] *Kormovaia kniga Ios. Vol. mon.*, 131.

[29] Ll. 33–33v: "For the brethren pans with fresh smelts, and in each pan one fresh carp bream, fill of *kasha*, one butter-baked dish, *kvas* from honey water" ("Na bratiiu skovorody snetkov svezhikh, da po skovorodam po leshchu po svezhemu kasheiu nachininy, maslenoe odno, kvas sychen").

1567 (no. 80). During the weeks after Easter the fast regulations were less strict, and in accordance with the Book of Feasts of the monastery commemorative meals were allowed during these weeks also on Monday, Wednesday, and even Friday. Still, to serve fish depended on the special permission of the abbot,[30] which obviously was granted in 1667, since the *Godovaia kormovaia kniga* notes: "one butter-baked dish, two sorts of fish, mead" ("kvas maslenoe odno, ryba dvoia, kvas medvenoi").

How can it be explained that the commemoration of the monks Iona and Iev Sinitsyn took place on a Friday (January 24)? This week is the Week of the Tax Collector and the Pharisee, falling two weeks before *maslenitsa* and three weeks before the beginning of Great Lent. It is often called *sploshnaia*, "without interruptions," since it is without any restrictions concerning food.[31] This offered the opportunity to distribute the *kormy* over more days in the week than normally possible, and apart from this, helped to avoid problems because of the collusion of two feasts:

"Friday of *sploshnaia* week was the feast of St. Kseniia. They sang for Kseniia on the eve, but during the whole day they sang for Gregory the Theologian. [The feast] of Gregory fell on Saturday. [But] on that day they sang [the services of] the Orthodox Saturday, since on Saturday of the Cheese Week fell the eve of the feast of the Presentation of the Lord in the Temple. A *korm* took place in memory of the monk Iev and of the monk Iona Sinitsyn. Food and *kvas* as on Thursday" ("V piatok sploshnoi nedeli priluchilos' prepodobnoi Ksenii. Ksenii peli nakanune, a v tot den' peli Grigoriiu Bogoslovu. A Grigoriia priluchilos' v subotu na sploshnoi nedeli. V tot den' peli provoslavnuiu [sic!] subotu, tomu shto v miasopustnuiu subotu priklochilos' predprazdnestvo Sreteniia Gospodnia. Korm byl po inoke Ieve da po inoke Ione po Sinitsinykh. Pishcha i kvas i za uzhinoiu kak v chetverg"; l. 31).

The passage serves as a proof that entries were not written compulsorily day by day. The monks celebrated the anniversary of Saint Kseniia (January 24) only on the eve of that day;[32] the rest of the day was dedicated this year to Gregory the Theologian, whose commemoration should normally take place one day later, on January 25. So the monks could move forward the *pravoslavnaia subbota*, one of the Saturdays of general commemoration of the dead. This day normally coincides with *subbota miasopustnaia*, the last Saturday when meat is allowed. But in 1567 on that day, February 1,[33] an even more important feast had to be celebrated, the Eve of the Presentation of the Lord in the Temple on February 2. Indeed on Saturday, January 25, the entry reads: "A

---

[30] *Kormovaia kniga Ios. Vol. mon.*, 195.

[31] The commemoration of the nun Antonida Stupishina took place on Monday of this week (no. 83).

[32] The daily liturgical cycle starts on the eve of the day, not at midnight.

[33] At that same time, the *korm* in memory of bishop Akakii of Tver' was celebrated (no. 15 in the appendix).

korm was in memory of the princess nun Evfrosinia Bel'skaia and of all Orthodox [people]. Two sorts of fish, both butter-baked dishes, mead. For Supper
the same as on Friday" ("Korm byl po Bel'skoi po inoke kniagine Evfrasinie i
po vsekh provoslavnykh. Ryba dvoia, maslenoe oboe, kvas medvenyi. Za
uzhinoiu po tomu zhe kak v piatok"; l. 31v).[34]

We have already seen a number of cases when a *korm* was postponed or
moved forward to an earlier date because of conflicts between the Book of
Feasts and the Typicon (*Ustav*), the general liturgical rule. On the basis of the
entries in column G in the table we are able to analyze more systematically
how far the celebration of *kormy* was moved from the date which was fixed in
the Donation Book. In the event that the date of the *korm* is not indicated
there, and if the celebration in 1566/67 took place close to the fixed date in the
younger Book of Feasts, the difference between these dates is entered in the
table.

As is obvious from a comparison of the Donation Book and the Book of
Feasts, the fixed date of the commemoration of a person was sometimes replaced by another date, for instance by that of a relative of the person, or an
additional *korm* was introduced.[35] In the extant part of the *Godovaia kniga* we
encounter five cases in which the date of the commemoration in 1566/67 is not
based on the entry of the Donation Book, but corresponds to the Book of
Feasts (nos. 8, 10 [second *korm*], 20, 35, 65 [second *korm*] in the table). For instance the Donation book provides for *kormy* in remembrance of Prince
Andrei Fedorovich Golenin (the monk Afanasii) and his wife, Princess Mariia
(the nun Marfa), *kormy* on different dates—on May 12 and December 19. The
entry of Prince Andrei Golenin on January 4, 1567 (no. 20) obviously refers to
the date of the commemoration of his wife, who is not mentioned here at all.[36]
In the Book of Feasts, Andrei is registered on 19 December and 12 May, but
his wife is listed only on the original date.

Column G indicates the number of days for which a *korm* was postponed
or brought forward. The results are quite surprising:

---

[34] The entry on January 24 provides certain proof that the manuscript was not written
day by day, but at longer intervals.

[35] As for the Polevs (nos. 60–64 in the appendix), see in detail Ludwig Steindorff,
"Memorial Practice as a Means for Integrating the Muscovite State," *Jahrbücher für
Geschichte Osteuropas* 55 (2007): 517–33.

[36] Of course her name was mentioned when the entry for the Golenins was read from
the *Kormovoi spisok* during the *panikhida*. For the commemorations of this family, see in
detail Ludwig Steindorff, "Princess Mariia Golenina: Perpetuating Identity through
Care for the Deceased," in *Culture and Identity in Muscovy, 1359–1584//Moskovskaia Rus'
(1359–1584): Kul'tura i istoricheskoe samosoznanie*, ed. Ann M. Kleimola and Gail D.
Lenhoff (Moscow: ITZ-Garant 1997) [=UCLA Slavic Studies, New Series 3], 557–77.

Exact date	7 *kormy*
Postponed to a later date	48 *kormy*
Moved forward to an earlier date	26 *kormy*
No connection between the dates	7 *kormy*
No information about a fixed date	11 *kormy*
Total	99 *kormy*[37]

The chance of being able to commemorate a deceased person on the exact day prescribed for it was obviously quite small. Among the few cases when this was possible is the commemoration of the Metropolitan Daniil on Saturday of the second week of Great Lent, one of the rare examples where the fixed date of the commemoration is bound to the movable calendar depending on the Easter date (no. 13). Most of the commemorations were postponed not more than 8 days (28 out of 48), but three of them were postponed 24 days and two 57 days.[38] The date of the latter two *kormy*, February 17, fell that year on a Monday of the second week of Great Lent, and so the celebration took place only on Tuesday in the third week after Easter (nos. 41, 48). In slightly fewer cases (26 compared to 48) the celebration was moved forward, 18 times not more than 6 days, at the maximum 16 days.[39] The celebration of Fedor Al′ferev Nashchokin on 19 February would have fallen on Wednesday of the second week of Great Lent, so it was moved to Monday, February 3 (no. 56).

Even in our modern secular societies it is quite unusual and regarded as improper to celebrate anniversaries in advance, since we do not know if the person to whom we wish health will still be alive by that date. Maybe the monks from the Iosif monastery did not care about moving forward the celebration because the dates referred to deceased persons. As mentioned before, the only celebration of the saint's day of a living person in the whole manuscript was postponed, as we would expect also nowadays when the exact day is excluded for some reason (no. 76).

A detailed comparison of the food which should be served according to the Book of Feasts from about 1581 and the food which was served between September 1566 and the middle of April 1567 remains a future task. But at a first glance it seems that the table in the entries of the manuscript is sometimes more modest than in the Book of Feasts. Two explanations are possible:

---

[37] The total consists of 85 donors, the collective commemoration of the princes Khovanskie and the additional *kormy* for 13 persons. Crossed-out commemorations are omitted.

[38] Postponed for 1 day—4 times; 2 days—5 times; 3 days—3 times; 4 days—1 time; 5 days—5 times; 6 days—7 times; 8 days—3 times; 10, 12, or 13 days—1 time; 14 days—2 times; 16, 17, 20, 21, 22—1 time; 24 days—3 times; 25, 26, 32, 38, 49 days—1 time; 57 days—2 times.

[39] Moved forward for 1 day – 7 times; 2 days—2 times; 3 days—3 times; 4 days—2 times; 6 days—4 times; 7, 9, 10 days—1 time; 14 days—4 times; 16 day—1 time.

the standard rose within the 14 years between the dates of these sources, or, as seems to me more justified to suppose, the redaction of the Book of Feasts was based on a tradition established long ago. So we may conclude that the kitchen was not always able to offer the "standard food" which should correspond to the day in the year.

The now "deciphered" manuscript *GIM, Eparkh sobr. 417* allows us the answer to a question about which we could only guess up to now: How did the monks secure the fixed *kormy* without disrespecting the liturgical regulations in the *Ustav*, the Rule? As the analysis of the dates proves, they just moved the *kormy* to other days before or after the fixed date in a very generous way. But they took care that no name was forgotten.

This manuscript is unique within the whole complex of commemoration sources. While all other source types—Donation books, Books of Feasts, *sinodiki*, etc.—were written for use through an extended period of time, the *Godovaia kormovaia kniga* is bound to a specified period, the year 5075 (1566/67), and documents some aspects of life in the monastery precisely at that time. Maybe, looking at the tension between norm and realization, the book served for the preparation of a redaction of the normative *Kormovaia kniga,* the "Feast book."

The *Godovaia kormovaia kniga* fits perfectly in the system of regular commemoration of hundreds of persons through many decades. We can verify the smooth functioning of this hermetic system by many dozens of case studies. Accordingly, if we start from the name of a person in one of the relevant books, we are able to trace it in the whole set of books which refer to the administration of donations, the organization of commemorations, and food and beverage in the Iosif Volotskii monastery. And any changes or divergences from the expected dates are only very rarely attributable to a mistake; in most cases we are able to find convincing explanations within the logic of this system, which had developed since the end of the 15th century and declined at the beginning of the 17th century at the latest. The composition of the *Godovaia kormovaia kniga* in the Iosif Volotskii monastery was an apex during the perfection of this system, a system which was common with all important Muscovite monasteries at that time but nowhere was as consistently performed as here. Once again the statement by Aleksandr Aleksandrovich Zimin proves to be justified: "No other Russian monastery had as elaborated a system of commemorating the dead as the one at Volokolamsk."[40]

---

[40] A. A. Zimin, *Krupnaia feodal'naia votchina i sotsial'no-politicheskaia bor'ba v Rossii (konets XV–XVI v.)* (Moscow: Nauka, 1977), 103.

Appendix. Table of Persons Commemorated in the *Godovaia kormovaia kniga*

Column A:	Serial number within this table
Column B:	Title, family name, Christian name, patronymic, monastic name, status in the family
Column C–D:	Entry in the Donation book: *Vkladnaia kniga Ios. Vol. mon.*
Column C:	Original serial number in *Vkladnaia kniga Ios. Vol. mon.*
Column D:	Date of the *korm* (month / day)
Column E–F:	Entry in the *Godovaia kormovaia kniga* (GIM, *Eparkh. sobr.*, No. 417 (638))
Column E:	Folio
Column F:	Date of the korm in 5075 (1566/67) (year / month / day) ned = nedelia, etc., the day in the week
Column G:	For how many days was the korm brought forward to an earlier date or postponed compared to the fixed date in the Donation book (D)?
Column H–I:	Entry in the Feast book: *Vkladnaia kniga Ios. Vol. Mon.*
Column H	Serial number in the table at the end of: *Vkladnaia kniga Ios. Vol. mon.*, p. 342–66
Column I	Date of the *korm* (month / day)

Further explanations:

column A –	Bold numbers: women
	~ = second entry for the same person
column B –	kn. = kniaz'/kniagin'ija; in. – inok/inokin'ia
	* = monastic name.
column C –	Italics: The name is mentioned only in the table at the beginning of the book, the entry is missing
column G –	# = certainly no connection to the indicated date in D
	— = no information available
	§ = date taken from the Feast book (I) because of the lack of corresponding information in (D)

A	B: Commemorated person	C	D	E	F: Date	G	H	I
	The family of the ruling dynasty							
1	kn. vel. Vasilii, *Varlaam, in.	1	12 04	16v	1566, 12 03 vt	–01	2	12 04
~	kn. vel. Vasilii, *Varlaam, in.	1	03 26	23v–24	1567, 04 08 vt	+13	2	03 26
2	kn. vel. Georgii Vasil'evich, brat tsaria	5	11 03	12	1566, 11 02 sub	–01	3	11 03
~	kn. vel. Georgii Vasil'evich, brat tsaria	5	11 25	16	1566, 11 28 ch	+03	3	11 25
3	tsaritsa Anastasiia	241	10 02	7v	1566, 09 28 sub	–04	4	10 02
~	tsaritsa Anastasiia	241	10 29	11v	1566, 10 29 vt	0	4	10 29
~	tsaritsa Anastasiia	241	10 29	11v	1566, 11 02 sub (crossed out)	(+05)	4	10 29
4	tsarevich Ivan	—	—	11	1566, 10 22 vt zazdravnyi korm	—	—	—
5	tsarevna Anna	148	09 09	3v	1566, 09 07 sub	–02	9	09 09
6	tsarevna Mariia	149	12 08	26	1566, 12 14 sub	+06	10	12 08
~	tsarevna Mariia	149	03 18	24	1567, 04 12 sub	+25	10	03 18
7	kn. Dmitrovskii, Georgii Ivanovich (erroneously: Vasil'evich)	4 / 11	11 26 / 08 02	11v	1566, 11 02 sub (crossed out)	(–24)	11	11 26
~	kn. Dmitrovskii, Georgii Ivanovich	4	11 26	15v	1566, 11 16 vt	–10	11	11 26
~	kn. Dmitrovskii, Georgii Ivanovich	4	03 23 / 04 23	24v	1567, 04 17 ch	–06	11	04 23
8	kn. Staritskii, Andrei	2	08 19	26v	1566, 12 17 vt	+06 §	12	12 11
9	kn. Uglichskii, Dmitrii	10	10 26	11	1566, 10 26 sub	0	15	10 26
10	kn. Volotskaia, Iul'iana	6	11 04	12v	1566, 11 09 sub	+05	19	11 04
~	kn. Volotskaia, Iul'iana	7	11 28	18	1567, 03 08 sub	+04 §	19	03 04
11	kn. Volotskii, Ivan Borisovich	7	11 28	16	1566, 11 30 sub	+02	18	11 28
12	kn. Zvenigorodskii, Afanasii	—	—	33v	1567, 02 04 vt	—	—	—

A	B: Commemorated person	C	D	E	F: Date	G	H	I
	Hierarchs, brethren							
13	*mitropolit Daniil	71	2. sub. vel. p.	17	1567, 02 22 sub _2. sub. vel. posta_	0	25	2. sub. vel. p.[1]
14	*arkhiep. Feodosii novgorodskii	185	02 26	17	1567, 03 01 sub	+03	27	02 26
	*Trifon, arkhiep. Polotskij							
	see Stupishin							
15	*episkop Akakii tverskoi	154	01 15	32v	1567, 02 01 sub	+17	28	01 15
~	*episkop Akakii tverskoi	154	01 15	36	1567, 02 08 sub	+24	30	10 01
16	*episkop Gennadii Suzdal'skii	61	09 30	7	1566, 09 26 ch	–04		
	*episkop Gurii smolenskii							
	see Zabolotskii							
	*episkop Nifont Krutitskii							
	see Kormilitsyn							
	*episkop Savva Krutitskii							
	see Chernyi							
	*arkhimandrit Aleksei, Sim. mon.							
	see Stupishin							
	*igumen Iosif Vol.							
	see Sanin							
17	*Kassian bosoi, in.	186	02 11	19	1567, 03 15 sub	+32	32	02 11
~	*Kassian bosoi, in.	186	11 02	11	1566, 10 24 ch	–09		

1 Kormovaja kniga Ios. Vol. mon., p. 159. – The entry No. 25 in the table of the Kormovaia kniga is incomplete!

A	B: Commemorated person	C	D	E	F: Date	G	H	I
	Princely families							
18	kn. Bel'skaia, Kseniia, *Evfrosiniia, in.	224	01 24	31v	1567, 01 25 sub	+01	41	01 20
19	kn. Bel'skii, Semen	12	09 04	2v	1566, 09 03 vt	-01	42	09 01
20	kn. Golenin, Andrei, *Arsenii, in.	20	05 12	28	1567, 01 04 sub	+16 §	60	12 19
21	kn. Kholmskaia, Kseniia, zhena kn. Michaila	18	11 08	13v	1566, 11 14 ch	+06	44	11 08
22	kn. Kholmskii, Mikhail	18	11 08	13v	1566, 11 14 ch	+06	45	11 08
23	kn. Khovanskaia, *Evfrosiniia, in. (erroneously: *Evpraksiia), mat' Ivana Zherda Khovanskogo	159	11 13	25	1566, 12 07 sub	+24	48	11 13
24	kn. Khovanskaia, *Anna, in,, zhena Fedora	226	10 26	9	1566, 10 12 sub	-14	—	—
25	kn. Khovanskie	—	—	9	1566, 10 17 ch	—	—	—
26	kn. Khovanskii, Dmitrii Fedorovich	226	10 26	8v	1566, 10 12 sub	-14	47	10 26
27	kn. Khovanskii, Fedor	226	10 26	8v	1566, 10 12 sub	-14	49	10 26
28	kn. Khovanskii, Ivan Ivanovich	159	02 07	38	1567, 02 15 sub	+08	51	02 07
29	kn. Khovanskii, Ivan Ivanovich Zherd, *Iosif, in.	159	11 20	25v	*1. sub. vel. posta* 1566, 12 10 vt	+20	52	11 20
30	kn. Khovanskii, Ivan Vasil'evich	159	11 13	25	1566, 12 07 sub	+24	53	11 13
31	kn. Kubenskaia, *Aleksandra, in.	69	?	35	1567, 02 06 ch	+03 §	65	02 03
32	kn. Lopatin, Vasilii Fedorovich	175	12 19	29v	1567, 01 09 ch	+21	69	12 19
33	kn. Lopatina, *Marfa, in.	153	11 17	14v	1566, 11 19 vt	+02	68	10 02
34	kn. Obolenskaia Nemogo, Mariia, zhena Dmitriia Nemogo	292? 298?	?	8	1566, 10 03 ch	—	77	10 26

A	B: Commemorated person	C	D	E	F: Date	G	H	I
35	kn. Paletskii, David Fedorovich	221	03 07	4v	1566, 09 12 ch	+01 §	80	09 11
36	kn. Paletskii, Dmitrii Fedorovich, *Dionisii, in.	199	09 11	4v	1566, 09 12 ch	+01	81	09 11
37	kn. Serebrennyi, Semen Dmitrievich	67	?	7v-8	1566, 10 01 vt	−01 §	86	10 02
38	kn. Shcheniatev, Michail Danilovich	225	09 06	3	1566, 09 05 ch	−01	—	—
39	kn. Sitskaia, *Marfa, in.	94	?	24	1567, 04 10 ch	—	87	02 03
40	kn. Sitskii, Simeon Feodorovich, *Serapion, in.	94	?	24	1567, 04 10 ch	—	88	02 03
Non-princely families								
41	Chernyi, ep. *Savva Krutitskii	246	02 17	24v	1567, 04 15 vt	+57	110	02 17
42	El'chaninov, Afanasii, *Iosif, in.	36	12 13	12	1566, 11 05 vt	+38	119	10 26
43	Esipov Tiutchev, Vasilii Uskoi Petrov	141	10 08	8v	1566, 10 08 ch	0	122	10 15
44	Golovlenkov, Semen Nesyt Danilov	112	?	6v	1566, 09 21 sub	+06 §	126	09 15
45	Khvorostinin, Dmitrii Konstantinov	33	10 26	12v	1566, 11 07 ch	+12	113	10 26
46	Klokachev, *Petr, in.	53	10 08	9v	1566, 10 05 sub	−03	—	—
47	Klokachev, Samoil Petrov, *Savva, in.	53	10 08	8v	1566, 10 05 sub	−03	131	10 08
48	Kormilitsyn, ep. Nifont Krutitskii	246	02 17	24v	1567, 04 15 vt	+57	134	02 17
49	Kurchev, Dmitrii Istoma, *Dionisii, in.	239	10 26	12	1566, 11 05 vt	+10	139	07 21
50	Kutuzov-Kleopin, Andrei Michailov	96	11 24	15v	1566, 11 23 sub	−01	130	11 24
~	Kutuzov-Kleopin, Andrei Mikhailov			9	1566, 10 17 ch	−07	—	—
51	Levašev, *Damian, in.	—	—	13	1566, 11 12 vt	—	—	—
52	Mizhuev, Kliment Vasil'ev, *Kirill, in.	184	01 23	31	1567, 01 23 ch	0	153	02 01
53	Mizhuev, Vasilii, *Vassian, in.	184	01 23	31	1567, 01 23 ch	0	154	02 01
54	Moshiutkin, Vasilii	—	—	29	1567, 01 07 vt	—	—	—
55	Nashchokin, Dmitrii, *Dionisii, in.	92	01 08	33	1567, 02 03 pon	+26	159	02 28
56	Nashchokin, Fedor Alfer'ev	48	02 19	33	1567, 02 03 pon	−16	160	02 28

A	B: Commemorated person	C	D	E	F: Date	G	H	I
57	Nevezhin, Arsenii, *Akinf, in.	23	01 16	30v	1567, 01 18 sub	+02	—	—
58	Nevezhin, Andrei, *Arsenii, in.	23	01 16	30v	1567, 01 18 sub	+02	219	01 16
59	Pleshcheev, Nikita Grigor'ev	272	09 15	5v	1566, 09 17 vt	+02	165	09 15
60	Polev, Ivan Ivanov	180	02 24	12v	1566, 11 07 ch	#	170	02 24
61	Polev, Ivan Vasil'ev	180	02 24	8v	1566, 10 08 vt	#	170	02 24
62	Polev, Vasilii Fedorov	180	04 12	8v	1566, 10 08 vt	#	174	01 24
63	Poleva, Anna, *Anisiia, in., zhena Ivana Poleva	180	02 03	31v-32	1567, 01 28 vt	-06	167	02 24
64	Poleva, Kseniia, zhena Vasiliia Poleva	180	01 24	30v	1567, 01 21 vt	-03	171	01 20
65	Rakitin, Fedor Grigor'ev	173	09 30	7	1566, 09 24 vt	-06	—	—
~	Rakitin, Fedor Grigor'ev	173	09 30	30	1567, 01 16 ch	+08 §	182	01 08
66	Rakitin, Grigorii, *Gerontii, in.	173	09 30	7	1566, 09 24 vt	-06	181	09 30
67	Rakitin, Ivan, *Ignatii, in.	47	01 08	30	1567, 01 16 ch	+08	179	01 08
68	Rakitin, *Gurii, in., Ivanov syn	197	01 30	7	1566, 09 24 vt	#	—	—
~	Rakitin, *Gurii, in., Ivanov syn	197	01 30	30	1567, 01 16 ch	-14	—	—
69	Rakitin, *Vassian, in., brat Petra R.	248	01 16	30v	1567, 01 16 ch	+05	—	—
70	Rakitin, Petr Ivanov	248	01 16	30v	1567, 01 21 vt	+05	180	01 08
71	Riabchikov, Feodor Andreev, *Feodosij, in.	128	04 26	29v	1567, 01 11 sub	#	184	08 11
~	Riabchikov, Feodor Andreev, *Feodosii, in.	128	08 11	30	1567, 01 14 vt	#	184	08 11
72	Riabchikov, Ivan Zhikhor Andreev	97	01 25 / 01 07	32v	1567, 01 30 ch (crossed out)	(+05)	185	01 25
73	Riabchikova, *Marfa, in., mat' Feodora i Ivana Riabchikova	128	08 11	30	1567, 01 14 vt	#	186	08 11
~	Riabchikova, *Marfa, in., mat' Feodora i Ivana Riabchikova	97	01 25 / 04 17	32v	1567, 01 30 ch	+05	186	08 11

A	B: Commemorated person	C	D	E	F: Date	G	H	I
74	Rugotin, Grigorij, arkhiep. *Gurij kazanskii	279	12 06	25v	1566, 12 12 ch	+06	191	12 06
75	Sanin, *igumen Iosif Volotskii	—	—	4	1566, 09 09 pon	—	194	09 09
76	Sheremetev, Ivan Vasil'ev men'shoi	231	02 24	17v	1567, 03 02 ned korm zazdravnyi	+06	—	—
77	Sheremetev, Nikita Vasil'ev	237	09 12	5v	1566, 09 17 vt	+05	198	09 15
78	Sheremetev, Semen Vasil'ev, *Stefan, in.	222	10 08	11v	1566, 10 31 ch	+22	199	10 08
79	Sinitsyn, *Iona, in.	—	—	31	1567, 01 24 piat	+14	200	01 10
80	Sinitsyn, Ivan Iur'ev, *Iev, in.	50	01 10	31	1567, 01 24 piat	+49 §	211	02 26
81	Stupishin, arkhimandrit *Aleksii Simonova mon.	169	den' smerti	24v	1567, 04 16 sr			
82	Stupishin, arkhiep.*Trifon Polotskii	168	den' smerti	6	1566, 09 19 ch	−01 §	213	09 20
83	Stupishina, Anastiia, *Antonida, in.	168	01 20	31	1567, 01 20 pon	0	212	01 20
84	Ul'ianin, David, *Daniil, in.	34	09 04	6v	1566, 09 21 sub	+14	216	09 15
85	Voronin, Nikola, *Nil, in.	32	11 14	13	1566, 11 12 vt	−02	217	10 29
86	Zabolotskii, Grigorii, ep. *Gurii smolenskii	210	11 15	14	1566, 11 16 sub	+01	218	11 15
87	Zvorykin, Tikhon	95	?	7	1566, 09 26 ch	—	—	—

Regarding the Good Order of the Monastery: The *Tipik Solovetskago* and the Integration of the Spiritual with the Temporal in the Early Seventeenth Century

Jennifer B. Spock

General Introduction

The desire to live a right life in order to attain salvation is best known in the medieval Christian tradition, both East and West, in the form of its monastic life. Ideally, a hermit alone in the wilderness or a monk engaged in the activity of a cloister led an ascetic, contemplative life of prayer, fasting, labor, and observance. It has been argued that in Russia the influence of the monastics began to wane in the 16th century, increasing the importance of the parish clergy and resulting in an Orthodoxy that looked less toward monastic spiritual fathers for moral guidance and more toward homiletic texts.[1] Yet monasticism remained a strong thread in the pre-Petrine Russian religious experience. Monastic leaders played a significant role in the conversion of the eastern Slavs and in the maintenance of Orthodox society and Orthodox praxis in pre-Petrine Russia. Well into the 17th century elite and non-elite alike continued to send gifts and cash to monastic houses so that the monks would pray for the souls of the dead. Monks were perceived as leading an "angelic" life which rendered their prayers more pleasing to God and thus more efficacious.

Research for this article was supported in part by a grant from the International Research & Exchanges Board (IREX), with funds provided by the National Endowment for the Humanities, the United States Information Agency, and the U. S. Department of State. Also contributing was a grant from the Joint Committee on the Soviet Union and its Successor States of the Social Science Research Council and the American Council of Learned Societies with funds provided by the State Department under the Russian, Eurasian, and East European Training Program (Title VIII). None of these organizations is responsible for the views expressed. Other funding was provided by: the Henry Rice Scholarship, Center for International and Area Studies, Yale University; John F. Enders Research Assistance Grant, Yale University; Hilandar Research Library and the Resource Center for Medieval Slavic Studies, The Ohio State University; University Research Committee Grant, Eastern Kentucky University.

[1] Paul Bushkovitch, *Religion and Society in Russia: The Sixteenth and Seventeenth Centuries* (New York: Oxford University Press, 1992).

Rude & Barbarous Kingdom Revisited: Essays in Russian History and Culture in Honor of Robert O. Crummey. Chester S. L. Dunning, Russell E. Martin, and Daniel Rowland, eds. Bloomington, IN: Slavica Publishers, 2008, 251–67.

One of the largest of Russia's religious houses was the Monastery of the Transfiguration of the Savior and the Dormition of the Mother of God, commonly known as the Solovki Monastery. Solovki was founded around 1430 on an island of the same name in the middle of the White Sea, and had become a substantial house by the 1560s, including no less than 200 monks and 300 servants.[2] Solovki was somewhat unusual as an example of cloistered living, for its monks were less confined than in many other monasteries. The brothers were both wealthy and impoverished men from the settlements, villages, and towns of the north, along with some men from Moscow and other central towns. Hailing from the northern forests and villages of the White Sea region, most of the monks came to tonsure after a life lived in the wilderness—a life of trading, trapping, fishing, salt-production, or artisanal activity.[3] These men turned their occupations to the service of the monastery even as they took on the mantle, and so as monks they often continued to move freely about northern Russia engaged in trapping, fishing, salt-production, or trade. In their turn, northern trappers, traders, and peasants engaged in business daily entered Solovki's portals in addition to pilgrims who came to venerate Solovki's patron saints, Zosima and Savatii. Although interaction with the laity was not unusual for a monastic community, Solovki monks engaged in business with regions hundreds of miles from the cloister, from the eastern lands beyond the White Sea to as far south as Moscow.

The Solovki community aspired, nonetheless, to integrate the ideal forms of the monastic life into its daily routines. Like many other Russian monasteries it was neither completely cenobitic (communal), nor purely idiorrhythmic (a form of monasticism in which hermits lived in separate cells but came together for worship). Instead, it merged the communal life of a cloister in which the monks labored, prayed, ate, and worshiped together, with a strict cell regimen of prayer and contemplation. By the 17th century, Solovki had both a dormitory and a system of cells,[4] and had developed a guide for the community, the *Tipik Solovetskago*, that focused on church observances but

---

[2] "Gramaty sviatago Filippa, mitropolita moskovskago i vseia Rossii, v Solovetskuiu obitel'," *Dushepoleznoe chtenie* 3: 10 (1861): 192–206.

[3] Jennifer B. Spock, "The Solovki Monastery 1640–1645: Piety and Patronage in the Early Modern Russian North" (Ph.D. diss., Yale University, 1999), 183. Entries in the commemorative donation books (*vkladnye knigi*) of Solovki list a hometown or native region for half of the monks whose names appear in the lists. Of those whose native region was recorded, 75 percent were from the far northern regions of the former Novgorod lands or their outposts. Insitute of Russian History, St. Petersburg (hereafter IRI), Coll. 2, MS 125 and MS 152.

[4] Cells were small rooms of one to four people that could be "purchased" by making a donation to the monastery. Those monks who did not purchase space in a cell were instructed to live in the treasury dormitory: "*a kotorye ne kupiat i oni v kazennykh zhivut.*" *Tipik Solovetskago*, Russian National Library, Division of Manuscripts (hereafter RNB, OR) f. 717, MS 1059/1168, fol. 94.

also included admonitions about communal and cell life.[5] At Solovki, the unknown writers of this regulatory text incorporated changes in Orthodox monastic tradition such as services to the Mother of God and care of the dead that reflected the concerns and the realities of both the monastic community and its surrounding society.

None understood better than the church and its monastic leaders that monks were, first and foremost, human. The act of tonsure did not create an ideal soul, and in many cases, it intensified temptation, as can be seen in the lives of many monastic saints. What tonsure effected was to allow an individual the right to live a life of poverty, humility, chastity, and worship which, if followed correctly, would lead the soul to salvation. Representing the "angelic life," monks were nevertheless human and in need of guidance; the "angelic life" was difficult to achieve and few actually reached its highest level, the *schema*.[6] Monastic leaders and founders anticipated temptations, and from the early years of communal monasticism created regulations to help male and female monastics lead lives that their societies considered worthy of God. However, not all monastic communities faced the same problems.

In the Byzantine Orthodox tradition, of which Russia was a part, a cloister might change and alter its rules in order to accommodate the climactic or social concerns of the surrounding society. Church leaders expected monks, clergy, and laity to adhere to general precepts of Orthodoxy, yet the idea, often expressed in the past, that Eastern Orthodoxy (and by association Russian Orthodoxy) entrenched itself in stagnant tradition is misleading. Scholars of the church have long recognized the organic quality of Orthodoxy that allowed it to develop its traditions in reciprocation with a worshipful community. In formulating its liturgy and in crafting instructions for the monastic life, Orthodox leaders incorporated new hymns, developed nuanced understandings of the meaning of the liturgy, and addressed regional concerns from language to eating habits as it tailored monastic texts to local conditions.[7] Orthodox monasteries remained vital communities because they

---

[5] The manuscript book which contains the *Tipik Solovetskago* dates from the first third of the 17th century.

[6] *Schema* was both the highest level of monastic observance, characterized by a life of solitary contemplation, and the name of the headgear worn by those who had achieved it.

[7] Mikhail Skaballanovich, *Tolkovyi tipikon: Ob"iasnitel'noe islozhenie Tipikona s istoricheskim vvedeniem*, vol. 3 (Kiev: Imperial University of St. Vladimir, 1908). Skaballanovich provided a detailed study of the development of the liturgy and its *tipiki*. More recent works that illustrate the evolving nature of Orthodox practice are Hans-Joachim Schulz, *The Byzantine Liturgy: Symbolic Structure and Faith Expression*, trans. Matthew O'Connell (New York: Pueblo Publishing Co., 1986); and Robert F. Taft, *Liturgy in Byzantium and Beyond* (Aldershot, UK: Variorum, 1995). A discussion of the ways in which Orthodox monastic praxis could be carefully altered to suit the concerns of the community can be found, as one example, in Iosif Volotskii's discourse on drunken-

addressed spiritual concerns that were inextricably entwined with lay experience. The *Tipik Solovetskogo* is an example of the adaptive quality of Orthodoxy.

Byzantine Monastic Instructions

Russia's monastic life was built on the traditions of Byzantine Orthodoxy, in which many texts were vital to the instruction of souls, the proper observance of church services and the liturgy, and the smooth operation of a monastery. In order to inform praxis, the officers and inhabitants of a cloister utilized instructions for the liturgy, communal life, cell life, customary prayers, books of the Hours, Psalters, saints' lives, and homiletic works. Praxis could not be severed from right belief in the Orthodox world, and so the accepted practice of a cloister provided some insight into its spiritual life.[8] The most visible regulatory text of a monastery was often its "rule." However, the use of this term can be misleading.

Three types of Byzantine and Russian Orthodox documents are often translated into English as "rule" in reference to the cloistered life: *typikon* (Russian—*tipik*), *hypotheposis* (Russian—*ustav*), and *diatyposis* (Russian—*zavishchenie*).[9] None of these forms were fixed or standardized through the early modern period. In fact, Nikon of the Black Mountain (circa 1025–88) wrote:

> I came upon and collected different *typika*, of Stoudios and of Jerusalem, and one did not agree with the other, neither Studite with another Studite one, nor Jerusalem ones with Jerusalem ones. And, greatly perplexed by this, I interrogated the wise ones and the ancients, and those having knowledge of these matters and seasoned in things pertaining to the office of ecclesiarch and the rest, of the holy monastery of our holy father Sabas in Jerusalem…"[10]

Nikon's confusion was understandable but standardization was not necessarily expected in medieval Orthodox communities and most recognized that they followed a style of monastic life in keeping with Orthodox principles, while not always emulating exactly the practices of their predecessors.

---

ness and the need for Russian monks to eschew wine, despite its presence in Byzantine monasteries. *The Monastic Rule of Iosif Volotsky*, ed. and trans. David M. Goldfrank, rev. ed. (Kalamazoo, MI: Cistercian Publications, 2000), 155–57.

[8] Schulz, *Byzantine Liturgy*, xvii.

[9] Robert F. Taft, "Mount Athos: A Late Chapter in the History of the Byzantine Rite," in Taft, *Liturgy in Byzantium and Beyond*, 183.

[10] V. N. Beneshevich, ed., *Taktikon Nikona Chernogorca: Grecheskii tekst po rukopisi No. 441 Sinaiskago monastyria sv. Ekateriny*, Zapiski Ist.-Filol. Fakul'teta Petrogradskago Universiteta, vypusk 1, chast' 139 (Petrograd, 1917), 9, quoted in Taft, "Mount Athos," 179.

The *typikon* (*tipik*) guided the hegumen, officers (the treasurer and cellarer among others), and priests through the complexities of the liturgical year. It directed the use of the texts that were actually used during the services by reconciling the directions of the ordinary books (such as the *horologion* or Book of Hours), which did not vary according to the day, week, or year, with those texts that were "proper" (such as Psalters), which varied according to the needs of the feasts as they fell in the calendar year. The *typikon* was an ordinal or customary book that helped to resolve conflicts among the "propers."[11] The *hypotheposis* (*ustav*) focused upon the non-liturgical daily routines of a cloister, such as meals, clothing, and the role and the duties of the officers. A further instructional document used in Orthodox cloisters was the *diatyposis* (*zavishchenie*) or "testament" in which a father superior transmitted to his flock his concerns and directions for the proper disposition of the community.[12]

The most influential "rules" in Byzantine Orthodoxy were the *typikon* of St. Sabba of Jerusalem (often with the chapters of St. Mark appended), the Short and Long Rules of St. Basil the Great (which were in the form of a *hypotheposis*), the Testament of St. Theodore of Studios, and the Studite *typikon* developed by Patriarch Alexis of Studios, and now extant only in Slavonic.[13] The *typikon* of St. Sabbas included with its chapters on the proper observance of church services additional chapters that moved in the direction of a *diapothesis*, giving instructions for the proper order of meals and other daily concerns. The Long and Short Rules of St. Basil the Great incorporated Basil's thoughts on, and justifications for, regulations that dealt with everything from the wisdom of consulting doctors to proper procedures for reintegrating a runaway back into the community. The testament of St. Theodore of Studios, on the other hand, was less specific, beginning with a testament of faith and then offering general guidelines, primarily for the father superior or ab-

---

[11] Taft, "Mount Athos," 180. Taft provides a short, clear description of the relation among the various texts.

[12] A *diatyposis*, because it often was in the form of a last testament, does differ from the other two types of monastic instructions. Nonetheless, it was an important reference for a proper life in many monasteries and often provided specific guidelines on behavior. Two of the best known are that of Theodore of Studios (Byzantine) and Iosif Volotskii (Russian).

[13] See M. Monica Wagner, trans., *The Fathers of the Church: St. Basil* (Boston: Daughters of St. Paul, 1950); "Theodore Studites: 'Testament' of Theodore the Studite for the Monastery of St. John Stoudios in Constantinople," trans. Timothy Miller, in *Byzantine Monastic Foundation Documents: A Complete Translation of the Surviving Founders' 'Typika' and Testaments*, ed. John Thomas and Angela Constantinides Hero (Washington, DC: Dumbarton Oaks Research Library and Collection, 2000), 67–83. For an Old Church Slavonic copy of the *typikon* of Patriarch Alexis, see A. M. Pentkovskii, *Tipikon Patriarkha Aleksiia studita v Vizantii i na Rusi* (Moscow: Moskovskii patriarkhat, 2001). On the *typikon* of Patriarch Alexis, see Taft, "Mount Athos," 184.

bot (*igumen* or *hegumen*), on proper governance and role-modeling. The *typika* were indispensable to monastic life, and when available so were the *hypotheposis* and the *diatyposis* texts. All three models of monastic rule were employed by monastic leaders in Muscovy. In fact, most large monastic libraries contained copies of one or more of these and over time collected *typikon, hypotheposis,* and *diatyposis* texts. Eventually their equivalents, the *tipiki, ustavy,* and *zavishcheniia* written by Russia's monastic leaders were also gathered, yet there are few of these texts authored in pre-Petrine Russia that are extant and can rightly be called rules.

Pre-Petrine Russian Monastic Rules

Over time, Russian priests, hierarchs, and monks contributed a vast body of religious literature in the forms of sermons, commentaries, testaments, saints' lives, miracle stories, and letters that augmented the Byzantine religious texts. Standardization of text, form, and praxis did not begin until the late 17th century, so the variety of monastic experience in Orthodox Russia manifested the Orthodox practice of adapting appropriately to the needs of the community. The earliest known *ustav* to originate in pre-Petrine Russia is that of Efrosin of Pskov (d. 1479), whose instructions consisted of 19 relatively brief chapters on monastic life followed by seven brief chapters on how to conduct affairs with the outer world.[14] Efrosin's rule has been overshadowed in the historiography of pre-Petrine monasticism, however, by the more extensive texts of Iosif Volotskii (1439/40–1515), founder of the Volokolamsk Monastery.

The "Brief Rule" of Iosif was actually a set of discourses for Iosif's flock while the "Extended Rule" was his Testament, which added specific instructions for the proper conduct of the monastic life.[15] In both texts Iosif explained the precepts and traditions of a right life and exhorted the brothers to live that life with zeal.

Such testaments were not necessarily hard and fast rules, but advice, observations, and recommendations, intended to act as daily guides, but also open to interpretation and even change by their own authors. Iosif grounded his advice and precepts in Byzantine tradition, but urged his followers to turn to Russian spiritual figures for guidance by examining the lives of major monastic saints for inspiration on right behavior.[16] Thus, the Volokolamsk Monastery set a precedent for incorporating Russian practices and customs into an evolving monastic tradition.

---

[14] "Prepodobnogo Efrosina Pskovskogo chudotvortsa izlozhenie obshchezhitel'nogo predaniia," in *Drevnerusskie inocheskie ustavy: Ustavy rossiiskikh monastyrenachal'nikov,* comp. T. V. Suzdal'tseva, Russkii tipik (Moscow: Severnyi palomnik, 2001), 38–57. This volume reproduces part of an early 19th-century publication by Bishop Amvrosii (Ornatskii), but contains annotations and insertions by the compiler.

[15] *Rule of Iosif Volotsky,* 51–61.

[16] *Rule of Iosif Volotsky,* 227.

Other monastic instructions have come down to us, but except for that of Nil Sorskii, founder of one of Russia's most famous skit communities, they have received little attention.[17] Iosif's works refer to a rule composed by Kirill of Belozersk, but no extant text exists so its nature is unknown.[18] In the category of formal monastic rules, this leaves the *Tipik Solovetskago*, which was consciously crafted to mimic the style of the St. Sabbas *typikon* but tailored its chapters to the needs of the Solovki cloister.

Tipik Solovetskago

In the early 17th century Solovki's library housed a large collection of volumes that contained the wisdom and pronouncements of a host of Orthodox leaders. There were a number of copies of the *Typikon* of St. Sabbas with the chapters of St. Mark as well as works of St. Basil, St. John Chrysostom, and many others.[19] It is impossible to ascertain which of these tomes most frequently informed Solovki's leaders. No *ustav* or testament was crafted by a leader of Solovki, but in the early 17th century Solovki did produce the *Tipik Solovetskago* which was patterned after the *typikon* of St. Sabbas.[20] In fact, Solovki's *tipik* is unique in the known pre-Petrine Russian tradition of monastic rules in that it had no individual authorship but was created by the community as a whole.[21] It has none of the explanations and apologies (in the

---

[17] See *Nila Sorskago predanie i ustav*, with an article by M. S. Borovkova-Maikova, Pamiatniki Drevnei pis'mennosti i iskusstva, vol. 179 (St. Petersburg, 1912); and Fairy von Lilienfeld, *Nil sorskij und seine Schriften: Die Krise der Tradition im Rußland Ivans III* (Berlin: Evangelische Verlagsanstalt, 1963).

[18] *Rule of Iosif Volotsky*, 229–30.

[19] On the library of Solovki, see M. V. Kukushkina "Biblioteka solovetskogo monastyria v XVI v.," parts 1 and 2, *Arkheograficheskii ezhegodnik za 1970 god* (Moscow: Nauka, 1971): 357–71; *Arkheograficheskii ezhegodnik za 1971 god* (Moscow: Nauka, 1972): 341–55. See also *Opisanie rukopisei Solovetskogo monastyria, nakhodiashchikhsia v biblioteke Kazanskoi dukhovnoi akademii*, 3 vols. (Kazan: Kazanskaia dukhovnaia akademiia, 1881–98); S. A. Belokurov, "Biblioteka i arkhiv solovetskago monastyria posle osady (1676 goda)," *Chtenie v Obshchestve istorii i drevnostei rossiiskikh*, bk. 1 (1887): 1–80; N. N. Rozov, "Solovetskaia biblioteka i ee osnovatel' igumen Dosifei," *Trudy otdela drevnerusskoi literatury* 18 (1962): 294–304.

[20] One possible exception is a brief text on monastic garments purportedly written by Filipp Kolychev, hegumen of Solovki (1546–66) and subsequently metropolitan of Moscow (1566–68). I. A. Lobakova, "Mitropolit Filipp Kolychev i solovetskii monastyr'," in *Monastyrskaia kul'tura: Vostok i zapad*, comp. E. G. Vodolazkin (St. Petersburg: Rossiiskaia akademiia nauk, Institut russkoi literatury [Pushkinskii dom], 1999), 187–90. Lobakova refers to RNB, OR f. 717, MS 1127/1236, which she asserts is an *ustav* of Filipp Kolychev, despite its exclusive focus on garments. Although it provides evidence that monastic guidelines were altered to suit local and individual needs, it does not compare in scope with the *Tipik solovetskago*.

[21] There is a note in an 18th-century hand on the first folio of the manuscript book which reads: "Ustav i tipik prepodobnykh otsov nashikh Zosimy i Savvatiia Solovet-

classical sense) that can be observed, for example, in the testament of Iosif of Volokolamsk. This document reflects not only many of the liturgical and pious norms that were in practice throughout Russia, but also the variations which this northern community had developed to uphold its spiritual ideal and solve the practical problems created by its large size and its location in the White Sea region. The monastic life of Solovki combined the cell life of idiorrhythmic monasticism with the communal life of church services, the refectory, and shared labor, resulting in a semi-cenobitic monastic life that became common throughout pre-Petrine Russia. Solovki's *tipik* appears to have been part of that development by altering earlier customs to fit the needs of its community, while maintaining the precepts of Orthodoxy. Parts of the *Tipik*, such as the *panagiia* service, became a model for future observances.[22]

Why Solovki produced its own *tipik* is unclear. Georg Michels has uncovered evidence that during the reign of Tsar Michael Romanov, Patriarch Filaret chastised the monks for changing the customs at Solovki, but the text does not appear to mention exactly how he felt the monks had changed the cloister's traditions.[23] Filaret's strictures may have resulted from a perceived laxity in the new *tipik*, or Solovki may have written its *tipik* to counter the charges made by the patriarch. Whichever is the case, administrative texts from the 16th century contain evidence of practices that were clearly articulated in the 17th-century *Tipik*, suggesting that at least in part, the *Tipik* turned custom into code.

The *Tipik Solovetskago* has 35 chapters, 24 of which address the observance of the Hours and the Liturgy and their integration with the feasts of the church calendar. Like the St. Sabbas *typikon*, this rule added chapters on the proper ordering of the refectory meals, fasts, travels of the hegumen, and other concerns related to the good order of a large monastic house. In itself, the integration of liturgical life, cell life, and communal life was not unlike what was encountered elsewhere and in other *tipiki*. What made the Solovki *tipik* both Orthodox and innovative were its modest alterations of a number of traditions to fit the needs of the monastery. Two examples that illustrate how the size of this northern cloister and its local conditions served to influence the monastery are the changes it made to the *panagiia* ritual and its expansion of the care of the dead. The *Tipik's* elaboration of the *panagiia* service in praise

---

skikh chiudotvortsev derzhat' u Filippa mitropolita Moskovskogo v bolnitse ustavshchiku bezvynosu." However, based upon other texts in the Solovki library and archives there is no way to verify this assertion. Even if the *tipik* were indeed "kept" by Filipp (hegumen of Solovki 1546–66) there is no evidence that he wrote the text. No earlier versions of the *Tipik* are known to exist.

[22] On this and other aspects of the *panagiia* ritual, see Skaballanovich, *Tolkovyi tipikon*, 50–71.

[23] Georg Michels, "The Solovki Uprising: Religion and Revolt in Northern Russia," *Russian Review* 51: 1 (January 1992): 7.

of the icon of the Mother of God (*Bogoroditsa*) evolved, it seems, as a function of the size of the cloister, which both enabled and called for more elaborate ceremonial and more complex instructions. As seen in the instructions for the care of the dead, Solovki monks were allowed to keep personal possessions in their cells, which were transferred to the treasury upon the death of a monk. Solovki even tolerated cash in monastic cells without mentioning the permission of the superior—a most atypical concession to worldly concerns—and an indication that Solovki did in fact tailor its rules to the reality of Muscovy's northern socio-economic conditions.[24] Moreover, unlike other cloisters, Solovki's *tipik* made provision for commemoration of its lay servants and laborers as well as lay visitors, giving some indication of their importance to the cloister. Solovki provides an excellent overview of both the religious rituals that were observed in a large monastic house during the early Romanov years, and the important spiritual role it played in the White Sea territories.

The *Panagiia* Ritual

The *panagiia* ritual [25] is first found in manuscripts of the 14th to 15th centuries and is unique to the Christian Orthodox world.[26] Dedicated to the image of

---

[24] Iosif Volotskii conceded that monks were able to keep coins and other personal items in their cells but only with the permission of the hegumen (*Rule of Iosif Volotsky*, 193).

[25] The word *panagiia* (all holy) has three meanings: 1) the bread that is set aside for the Mother of God during the Eucharist, 2) a special medallion worn by a bishop that has an icon of the Mother of God on one side and often a small receptacle for a relic, and 3) the specific ritual discussed here. Skaballanovich described the steps of the ceremony as it was performed in the late 19th century. He followed each step during the first meal of the day and then discussed the basic forms that it took from its inception until the 19th century. Skaballanovich attempted to link the ceremony directly to the Old Testament and to explain its Christian origin with a 16th-century tale of the Dormition. He attributed the division of the blessed bread (*prosfora*) and the setting aside of the *panagiia* portion to the events described in this legend. However, the division of the loaf is from the first centuries of Christianity and probably has little bearing on the doctrine of the Dormition of the Mother of God. Skaballanovich focused on the most elaborate forms of the service to the exclusion of the earlier simpler versions. He referred to any ritual cutting of bread during the post-liturgical meal as a *panagiia* ceremony. However, it could be argued that the observance can only be called the *panagiia* at the point where it specifically involved the bread of the Mother of God. See Skaballanovich, *Tolkovyi tipikon*, 50–71. Other texts that mention the *panagiia* ritual are Jacobus Goar, *Euchologion Sive: Rituale Graecorum* (n.d.; repr., Graz: Akademische druck-U. Verlagsanstalt, 1960), 680–84; and John Glen King, *The Rites and Ceremonies of the Greek Church in Russia: Containing an Account of Its Doctrine, Worship, and Discipline* (1772; repr., New York: AMS Press Inc., 1970), 380.

[26] The precursor to the *panagiia* ceremony is first found in a manuscript *typikon* of the Patriarch Alexius of the Studios Monastery of Constantinople. The ritual laid out there was described by Skaballanovich as the earliest Slavonic *panagiia* rite (because Alexius

the Mother of God, the Russian *panagiia* ritual links the liturgical life of a cloister with the communal life of the refectory by a procession that moved directly from the close of the liturgy to the first meal of the day. The ritual centers on that portion of bread from the communion loaf or loaves that is set aside during the liturgy to honor the Mother of God. Depending upon the format used, a monk, priest, or abbot carried the bread from the church directly to the refectory in procession, where it was ritually eaten at the first meal of the monastic day.

The ceremony developed in Russia beginning in the early 15th century. It increased in complexity through the 17th century and may have been a Slavic insertion into the monastic instruction books.[27] The ceremony of the *panagiia* highlighted the piety of a select individual and the piety of the community as it shared a meal. After the benediction, the officiating priest or a monk whose performance and deeds were exceptional carried the *panagiia* bread on a special plate (*panagiar*) at the head of a procession from the church to the refectory. The monks followed behind in pairs. In early versions the bearer could be paired with another monk or proceed alone, and as the ceremony developed, the officiating priest or the hegumen walked with the bearer.[28] Special significance was attached to the leader of a procession, a not unusual circumstance, and special significance attached to the individual who walked alone: "he who does not pair up on the path [of the procession], that one holds the piece of bread."[29] In all cases, the *panagiia* was at the front of the procession and was carried by an individual who was either a sanctified member of the priesthood or was particularly pious.

Descriptions of the *panagiia* ritual vary, but according to all versions, from the moment the procession began, the monks chanted Psalm 144[30] ("Exalt God, Exalt the King") and timed its recitation so that it would end at the precise moment that the procession entered the refectory.[31] The two icons that

---

eventually ended up on Mt. Athos), and yet the bread of the Mother of God does not figure in it. For a published version of the *typikon* of Patriarch Alexius, see A. M. Pentkovskii, *Tipikon patriarkha Aleksiia Studita v Vizantii i na Rusi* (Moscow: Moskovskii patriarkhat, 2001).

[27] Skaballanovich maintained that there were no Greek copies of the St. Sabbas of Jerusalem *typikon* which contain the *panagiia* ritual, while a number of Slavonic instructions that were based on the St. Sabbas type of rule did contain the ceremony (*Tolkovyi tipikon*, 63).

[28] *Sbornik bogosluzhebnyi*, GIM/JVM, Eparkh. MS 299 (401), fol. 161; *Psaltyr s vossledovanniiam*, GIM/JVM, Eparkh. MS 103, fol. 240v; *Tipik solovetskago*, RNB, OR f. 717, MS 1059/1168, fol. 42v; Skaballanovich, *Tolkovyi tipikon*, 52.

[29] GIM/JVM Eparkh. MS 103, fol. 240v.

[30] The Eastern and Western churches numbered the Psalms differently. Psalm 144 in the Slavonic Old Testament is Psalm 145 in the King James Version of the Bible

[31] Skaballanovich, *Tolkovyi tipikon*, 51–52.

were most important to the meal and the *panagiia* were the Trinity and the Most Pure Mother of God. Once in the refectory, the first order of the day was to sit down in the right place "without argument or speaking."[32] The reading of the day took place either before or during the meal, which had a strict order.

Variations in the performance of the *panagiia* revolved around the treatment of the *panagiia* and in the number of church officers involved in its veneration. In some instances the bread was immediately divided and eaten, while in others it rested in a place of honor until the end of the meal and was then eaten as the final element of the service and the meal. In the early versions of the ritual (15th century) which appear to be intended for the needs of smaller cloisters, the monk who carried the *panagiia* loaf to the refectory distributed it among the brothers, who each took a piece with their own hands. A priest, or if there was no priest, that same monk, then held a piece of the bread by the thumb and pinky of the right hand. Shielding the little piece of bread with the middle three fingers and asking God for mercy, he made the sign of the cross. Then everyone ate the bread and proceeded with the meal as usual.[33] Both of these earlier Russian versions were available at Volokolamsk Monastery, a relatively young community. In the description from Solovki, however, the two forms were brought together so that part of the bread was eaten before the meal and part after.[34]

Differences in the versions of the *panagiia* appear to be the result of the size of a cloister rather than the time period.[35] In a later version (16th century) from Volokolamsk that was tailored to the needs of a larger institution (possibly Volokolamsk itself, in which the number of monks was approximately 40), the one who carried the bread and the priests (the plural is clear) all made the sign of the cross while holding the bread and then the community partook of the bread simultaneously.[36] By the late 16th century the rite lost the simplicity of its earlier composition.

As monasteries became more intricate communities, the *panagiia* ritual in Russia became increasingly complex. Solovki, which maintained hundreds of

---

[32] Ibid., 60.

[33] Ibid., 55; *Sbornik bogosluzhebnyi*, fols. 161–163v.

[34] *Tipik solovetskago*, fols. 42v–48.

[35] For example, in two separate Russian manuscripts from the 16th century one appeared tailored to a large community that had a cellarer and many priests. See Hilandar Research Library, Ohio State University (hereafter HRL), Fekula Collection, MS VI, *Tipikon ("Tserkovnoe Oko")*, fols. 155v–157v (hereafter Fekula VI) from the second quarter of the 15th century. Another assumed fewer participants and the need to adapt to circumstances. See HRL, State Historical Museum in Moscow, collection of the Joseph-Volokolamsk Monastery (hereafter GIM/JVM, Eparkh.), MS 299 (401), *Sbornik bogosluzhebnyi*, fols. 161–163v from the second half of the 15th century.

[36] HRL, GIM/JVM, Eparkh. MS 103 (166), *Psaltyr s vossledovanniiam*, fols. 240v.

monks by the mid-16th century and continued to grow into the 17th century, outlined in its *tipik* a highly formal ceremony that show-cased the hegumen and the officers of the monastery and the refectory (*trapeza*), but diminished the role of individual monks.[37] Rather than simply assigning roles to the abbot, the priest, and a particularly pious monk, as can be seen in earlier versions, Solovki incorporated roles for the cellarer, deacons, the *stolniki*[38] and the *budilnik* (waker). At Solovki the officiating priest became the bearer of the special loaf while the hegumen walked with him, or just behind. In the Solovki version the process of cutting the loaf set the hegumen apart from the rest of the flock. Additionally, the priests and deacons served the food as the meal progressed.[39] With an increase in numbers came specialization of tasks and the division of roles. The elevation of the *panagiia* stressed the authority of the hegumen, cellarer, and clergy.

The evolution of the *panagiia*, at Solovki at least, coincided with the need to incorporate into its ceremony an expanding hierarchy within a growing religious community and its already established services. Solovki's innovation became part of the later standardization of the ritual and bears close resemblance to the ceremony as it was performed in the 19th century.[40] The elaborate structure developed in the late 16th and early 17th centuries probably lasted because it accommodated a much larger community and helped to support the strict ceremonial and spiritual hierarchy within the community.

In the Solovki *Tipik*, the officiating priest carried the *panagiia* bread in procession accompanied by the cellarer. These two preceded the hegumen who followed next walking alone.[41] The hegumen then took the *panagiia* and intoned the *tropar* "Today begins our salvation" (*Dnes spaseniiu nashemu nachatok*). The priests all chanted with him and then he laid the loaf on the tray and stood in silence as the reading began and/or the drink was poured. Then the hegumen cut the loaf and took one piece for himself. Parts of the bread he gave to the cellarer and the reader, and then to the priest and brothers who each took a part.[42] Instructions for the meal and its dishes are detailed, including the bows, prayers, supplications, and description of how the food was to be passed out and collected. Unlike the Volokolamsk monastery, all the monks, officers, and hegumen received the same food. This was the first meal of the day, and the partaking of the *panagiia* was the last portion of the meal, accompanied by prayers to the Mother of God. At the end of the meal a

---

[37] *Tipik solovetskago*, fols. 42v–48.

[38] A *stolnik* is an officer whose role pertains to food service, and, it appears, assisting the cellarer.

[39] Skaballanovich, *Tolkovyi tipikon*, 52–54, 60. *Tipik solovetskago*, fols. 43–46v.

[40] The 19th-century *panagiia* service is described in Skaballanovich, *Tolkovyi tipikon*, 51–56.

[41] *Tipik solovetskago*, fol. 42v.

[42] *Tipik solovetskago*, fols. 43–43v.

deacon and the hegumen made the sign of the cross over the bread with prayers to the Mother of God asking for help and intercession. The hegumen "then cuts the holy bread and participates in the first [piece] himself." He then gave bread to the cellarer. The deacon carried the bread with the priest and distributed pieces to all the brothers with his own hand (note that the brothers no longer took the bread themselves). The holy plate was then placed on the table on another silver plate and all the brothers moved to their places. The meal finished, the dishes were removed, and the hegumen performed the final prayer, the brothers said, "Amen," the hegumen bowed to the ground, and each removed to his cell in silence.[43]

The instructions contained many similarities to those described by Skaballanovich for the 19th century. Based on the nature of the *Tipik Solovetskago*, a hegumen in collaboration with the council elders most likely developed the new ceremonial roles in the *panagiia* to produce a format that became the standard for later centuries. The *Tipik* provides evidence of Solovki's influence on the development of Russian Orthodox liturgical tradition and of its commitment to the maintenance of a communal life that connected to the life of worship.

Cell Life and the Care of the Dead

The Solovki *Tipik* also meshed the world of church observance with that of the cell. Although church rituals were distinct from cell life, the two influenced and informed one another to some extent. In the area of customary and proper cell rituals the *Tipik* indicated that the church calendar dictated the bows made before, during, and after cell prayers at Solovki. Moreover, the care of the dead and the church observance of commemoration was also linked to cell life at Solovki just as it was at other semi-cenobitic monasteries such as Volokolamsk. The changes that Solovki made in the *Tipik* for the commemoration of monks were linked both to the life of the cell and to its role as a spiritual and trading center in northern Russia. They attest to the role that regional differences played in the establishment of Orthodox tradition as late as the late 16th and 17th centuries. Many works on the care of the dead and commemorative practice have been published in recent years.[44] Solovki, how-

---

[43] *Tipik solovetskago*, fols. 42v–43, 46v–47v.

[44] Some of the most important are Ludwig Steindorff, *Memoria in Altrußland: Untersuchunen zu den Formen christlicher Totensorge*, Quellen und Studien zur Geschichte des östlichen Europa, vol. 38 (Stuttgart: Steiner, 1994); idem, "Commemoration and Administrative Techniques in Muscovite Monasteries," *Russian History/Histoire Russe* 22: 4 (1995): 433–54; Russell E. Martin, "Gifts for the Dead: Kinship and Commemoration in Muscovy (The Case of the Mstislavskii Princes)," *Russian History/Histoire Russe* 26: 2 (Summer 1999): 171–202; David Miller, "Motives for Donations to the Trinity-Sergius Monastery, 1392–1605: Gender Matters," *Essays in Medieval Studies* 14 (1998): 91–106; Spock, "Solovki Monastery," chaps. 1–4. A good discussion of the care of the dead in

ever, tinkered with the care of its own tonsured members as part of the sale of cells, and as part of the monastery's built-in charity even gave to servants and visitors the exact same gift of commemorative prayers that it gave to its own monks. Automatic memorials for laity, whether servants or otherwise, are not addressed in the St. Sabbas rule, the Studite rule, or the Volokolamsk rule. That fact alone speaks to the integration of lay and religious life on the island, and presents another indication of the adaptability of the *tipik* as a guide to the monastic life.

Regarding the death of monks, basic tradition remained intact, but the customs evolved. St. Sabbas, in the 43rd chapter of the *typikon* of the Jerusalem cenobium, indicated that after the death of a monk, a priest should offer the third-day, ninth-day, fortieth-day and *godishchnyia* (annual) services. The "Testament" of Iosif Volotsky gives no instructions regarding the death of monks because these instructions were present in the *obikhod*, which ordered the community to commemorate a monk from the Monastery for three years automatically (for more if he had given a gift). The monks recorded the name in the *vseletnykh spisok,* the *povsiadnevnyi spisok* up to three years, and the *sorokoustnyi spisok* and the manner of these services.[45] The *vseletnykh spisok* was used to read out the names of the dead on the anniversary of their deaths, and at Solovki cost a nominal sum of 5 *altyny* or 5/33 of a ruble and lasted in perpetuity. The *povsiadnevnyi spisok* recorded those names whose prayers should be read in the daily *lit'ia* service which also commemorated the dead. Entry in this list required a donation of a ruble for each year of prayer. The *sorokoustnyi spisok* commemorated the dead 40 days after death, and at Solovki cost 20 *altyny*. Thus, the total cost of Solovki's charity to both monks and laity was 3 rubles and 25 altyny: close to 4 rubles per person.

As part of the liturgical life of Solovki, and in keeping with Orthodox tradition, the names of deceased monks of Solovki were listed in the *sinodik* (often called *senanik*—"necrology") that was used for annual remembrance prayers. For administrative purposes, deceased who qualified for daily prayers were entered into the *vkladnye knigi* (donation books). At Solovki, however, instructions in the early 17th-century *Tipik* added that not just monks, but all those who died while in residence at the cloister or on its production lands, whether servants, invalids, or pilgrims, would automatically receive three years of daily prayer in addition to eternal entry in the *sinodik* even if they gave no donation for such prayers. All brothers and lay persons who died in the cloister or in the monastery's service were to be written into the

---

pre-Petrine Russia can be found in Daniel H. Kaiser, "Death and Dying in Early Modern Russia," in *Major Problems in Early Modern Russian History*, ed. Nancy Shields Kollmann (New York: Garland Publishing, 1992), 217–57.

[45] Steindorff, "Commemoration and Administrative Techniques," 436.

great *sinodik* for eternity.[46] This speaks in part to Solovki's regional role as a major center of pilgrimage. The cults of Solovki's two founders, saints Zosima and Savatii, attracted large numbers of pilgrims who deposited coins into vessels on the saints' tombs. By the late 16th and early 17th centuries this activity resulted in hundreds of visitors that donated hundreds of rubles of cash on a yearly basis.[47] The pilgrims in the north were not by and large the wealthy elite; they were fishermen, trappers, traders, and even women, who came from hundreds of miles away through swamps and forests to venerate the saints. Moreover, Solovki contained a hospital, so many northern inhabitants came to the cloister to receive medical care, or to die and receive last rites, including the tonsure.

In providing for three years of daily prayers, Solovki fulfilled an important charitable role for the surrounding community, attesting to the close ties that it formed with the laity. No other Russian Orthodox *tipiki* up to this time had provisions for the care of laity who had worked for a monastery or were visiting monastic lands for any reason. Given the extensive nature of Solovki's production lands and the large number of servants and pilgrims, this provision was extraordinary and expensive. The instructions were similar to the instructions of the *obikhod* of the Volokolamsk monastery, but included lay people under the umbrella of the monastery's charity and even allowed for limited personal property to be disposed of as the monk desired.

If a deceased monk had items remaining in his cell, such as icons or books or money or garments that belonged to him and not the treasury, or if he had a *mesto* (a place in a cell), the treasury received these items as a *vklad* (donation); the monk's name would then be commemorated in the daily services for as many years beyond the three-year minimum as the number of rubles that his belongings were worth.[48] Finally, if a brother had left anything to his spiritual father or to a brother that was not of the monastery, it could not be taken away.[49]

---

[46] "Ashche toia obiteli postrizhennik ili prikhozhei byl brat ashche malo ili mnogo zhil v monastyre sitse tvoriat neizmenno. A v bol'shoi senanik pishut vo veki vsiu bratiiu i mirian, kto pristavitsia vo obiteli ili gde na sluzhbe monastyrskoi." *Tipik Solovetskago*, RNB, OR f. 717, MS 1059/1168, fol. 94v.

[47] For a listing of the hundreds of rubles of cash deposited by the faithful at the tombs of Zosima and Savatii, see Spock, "Solovki Monastery," 448–50.

[48] "A u kotorogo brata chto ostanetsia obrazov ili knig ili deneg ili plat'ia chto u nego bylo svoe a ne kazenie, ili mesto kuplenoe to vse emliut v kaznu vkladom. A za to ego pominaiut po godu za rubl v liteinike. A bude soberetsia vsego ego vkladu na 50 rublev togo pominaiut v liteinike vo veki." *Tipik Solovetskago*, RNB, OR f. 717, MS 1059/1168, fol. 94v.

[49] "A kto chto prikazhet posle sebia na pogrebenie ili ottsu dukhovnomu ili bratu ko emu svoe a ne monastyrskoe i togo u nikh ne otnimaiut." *Tipik Solovetskago*, RNB, OR f. 717, MS 1059/1168, fols. 94v–95.

In connection with the care of the dead, the Solovki *tipik* stated that a monk must pay for cell space, and that the payment would go toward the commemoration of the deceased brother whom the new owner replaced. Thus, the *Tipik* codified the payment for cell space and connected it to the *sinodik* and the *liteinik*. A monk who paid for a cell not only cared for the soul of another brother, but was assured that he too would receive commemoration when another replaced him.

Thanks to the *Tipik*, which indicated that monks were allowed to retain some personal items in their cells, books, cash, and clothing could augment a monk's gift to Solovki and thereby increase the years of daily prayers on his behalf. Inscriptions within many of the books of Solovki and Volokolamsk indicated that monks were able to have books in their cells. At Volokolamsk it was not clear whether such books were considered private or communal property but at Solovki, books and other items including cash were clearly considered personal items and were duly entered into the donation books as *post mortem* gifts to the cloister.[50]

Solovki clearly altered and elaborated upon earlier monastic traditions to allow the monks, many of whom traveled far and wide beyond the monastery walls on monastery business, more leeway in the disbursement of their property. Cash was an integral part of life in the northern trading climate and even within the northern monastic life, so cash and personal items had to be accommodated at the cloister. What was astounding was that there is no indication in the *Tipik* that a monk's cell contents were in any way monitored by monastic officers. Solovki also built charitable donations of prayer into its monastic rule in order to care for not only the monks, which was customary, but also the laity. At Solovki monks and laity were from the same towns, engaged in the same trades, interacted frequently along the waterways, at fishing weirs, and within the monastery compound, and thus were to some extent part of the same northern community of laborers and souls, even though some were tonsured and others not. The automatic three years of prayer for deceased lay persons was a regional contribution to both the spiritual health of the north and to the development of a Russian monastic *tipik*. It was in keeping with Orthodox piety, but extended the role of the monastery as a charitable institution in new ways to automatically care for the souls of the laity, just as the hospital cared for their bodies.

Conclusion

The *Tipik Solovetskago* provides a few examples, two of which have been explored above, regarding Russian Orthodox praxis in the late 16th and early 17th centuries. It testifies to the monastery's adjustments to regional conditions and to its integration of the three elements of liturgical, communal, and cell life. Iosif Volotsky had already illustrated for Russia that regional con-

---

[50] *Rule of Iosif Volotsky*, 105.

cerns informed the structure and precepts of the Orthodox monastic life, but in the modern age of standardization, the importance of this fact can too easily be ignored. It has long been accepted that Orthodox monasticism, having no orders as in the Catholic West, shared a foundation of forms and could pick and choose from a range of traditions and adapt their choices to environmental conditions. This is true, but the traditions were built on solid foundations that were incontestable: the Church Fathers, the rules of the Byzantine houses, the precedents of acknowledged monastic spiritual leaders, and the exemplar of saints. Yet, with all the tradition, it is important to understand the extent to which local nuances shaped monastic, and therefore, Orthodox culture. Solovki Monastery projected two seemingly incompatible ideals of spiritual experience. In the first instance, as expressed in the *panagiia* service, Solovki not only maintained but exalted the role of hierarchy and status within the Orthodox clergy, thereby reflecting the incontestable hierarchy of heaven and the understanding of the monks as obedient servants of Christ. When it came to the matter of memorials, however, the cloister cared for the laity at the same level as tonsured monastics by providing them with the same commemorative benefits no matter how long or short their sojourn at the monastery had been. In part, this is probably the result of the familiarity of the monks with the lay population of the north. Since 75 percent of the monks came from northern towns and villages, the visitors to the monastery and its servants would have been well-known to the inhabitants of the cloister, and often members of the monks' immediate or extended families. In addition, the wealth of Solovki made this charitable arrangement possible.

The *Tipik Solovetskago* illustrated Solovki's commitment to both religious and lay community, understanding that the religious community had primacy. The ideals of the monastery had placed all Orthodox believers who had selected Solovki as a destination on an equal footing to begin their journey into the afterlife. In doing this, Solovki added one additional element to its integration of liturgical, community, and contemplative forms of life: it recognized the importance of the laity to the life of Solovki. Without the laity, Solovki's existence would have been far more difficult, for the laity contributed to the monastery's wealth and the glory of its saints. From the point of view of the faithful, the Mother of God interceded on behalf of Solovki and its supporters. In return, Solovki cared for her children, and sent them into the afterlife with the prayers of its monks, made efficacious by the "angelic life" that was governed by the *Tipik*.

Ivan Neronov: A Priest Who Lost His Mind?

Georg Michels

On January 31, 1632, Patriarch Filaret, the ruler of the Russian Orthodox Church, gave orders to arrest Ivan Neronov, parish priest of the Resurrection Church in Nizhnii Novgorod on the Volga River. Now accused of having "lost his mind and … not [being] in complete control of his thinking" (*v istuplenii uma byst'… i ne v sovershennom razume*), Neronov had previously enjoyed the enthusiastic support of the patriarch; in fact, he had been one of Patriarch Filaret's protégés since the early 1620s. Filaret had ordained Neronov and then assigned him to important parish positions in the patriarchal eparchy.[1] Filaret had also invited Neronov to the Kremlin and introduced him to Tsar Mikhail Romanov (who was Filaret's son), as well as to Muscovy's most powerful boyars. For nearly ten years, Filaret had sung Neronov's praises for teaching peasants the religious and moral principals of Russian Orthodoxy, and had endorsed him in all his endeavors. Why, then, did the patriarch suddenly withdraw his support in 1632 and declare Neronov insane?[2]

This episode was only one in a series of confrontations between Neronov and Muscovy's upper clergy that continued for more than 50 years of Neronov's long life and led to his repeated arrest and exile. Only in 1667, when Neronov was raised to the rank of archimandrite at the age of 73, did he finally make his peace with the church hierarchy. As I will demonstrate, Neronov was supported by Patriarch Filaret—and later patriarchs—because they wanted him to spread the basic tenets of Russian Orthodoxy to ordinary Muscovites. But Neronov's preaching turned in other directions with explo-

---

[1] The towns of Lyskovo and Nizhnii Novgorod, where Neronov acted as parish priest, figured prominently among the 55 towns that belonged to the patriarchal see under Filaret. The village of Sobolevo (also known as Nikol'skoe Sobolevo) was located near Iurevets, another important patriarchal town, and most likely was also under direct patriarchal jurisdiction. Cf. Ivan I. Shimko, *Patriarshii kazennyi prikaz: Ego vneshniaia istoriia i deiatel'nost'* (Moscow: Tipo-litografiia T-va I. N. Kushnerev i Ko., 1894), 113, 115, 117, 119–21; Pavel F. Nikolaevskii, *Patriarshaia oblast' i russkie eparkhii v XVII v.* (St. Petersburg: Tip. F. Eleonskogo, 1888), 3–6, 17, 22–23.

[2] *Akty, sobrannye v bibliotekakh i arkhivakh Rossiiskoi imperii Arkheograficheskoiu ekspeditsieiu Imperatorskoi Akademii nauk*, 4 vols. (St. Petersburg: V Tip. 2. otdeleniia Sobstvennoi E. I. V. Kantseliarii, 1836) (hereafter *AAE*), 3: 284–85.

Rude & Barbarous Kingdom Revisited: Essays in Russian History and Culture in Honor of Robert O. Crummey. Chester S. L. Dunning, Russell E. Martin, and Daniel Rowland, eds. Bloomington, IN: Slavica Publishers, 2008, 269–85.

sive consequences, and his behavior could be neither controlled nor predicted by the church.

When Neronov first came to the attention of Patriarch Filaret in the early 1620s, his actions seemed to conform entirely to Filaret's own stated ideals of religious reform and discipline.[3] As a psalmist (*psalmopevets*) and church reader in the village of Sobolevo near Iurevets on the Volga River, Neronov was then engaged in a vicious conflict with the parish priest and with a number of other unofficial priests who had found shelter in the village after becoming widowed, losing episcopal ordination charters, or suffering expulsion from their home parishes.[4] These unemployed priests were not much interested in performing the liturgy, and spent their time quarreling with each other and with the parish priest over the spoils of the parish. Since they had little to do, they were often drunk and got involved in all kinds of "illegal acts" (*bezzakonnye deianiia*) and "unruly behavior" (*bezchinstvo*). When Neronov accused these priests of "not living according to their calling" and of neglecting their divine duties, all hell broke lose and Neronov narrowly escaped a mob attack.[5]

Neronov fled the village to seek refuge at the Trinity Monastery, where his religious fervor brought him to the attention of the reform-oriented Archimandrite Dionisii, one of Patriarch Filaret's closest associates.[6] At Dionisii's

---

[3] Cf. "Pouchenie velikogo gospodina sviateishego Filareta patriarkha Moskovskogo i vseia Rusi, na postavlenie mitropolitom, i arkhiepiskom, i episkopom," in Filaret Gumilevskii, *Obzor russkoi dukhovnoi literatury* (St. Petersburg: Izd. knigoprodavtsa I. L. Tuzova, 1884), no. 220; "Pouchenie na postavleniia arkhimandritam, igumenam, i sviashchennikam," in Archimandrite Savva, *Ukazatel' dlia obozreniia Moskovskoi Patriarshei (nyne Sinodal'noi) riznitsy i biblioteki* (Moscow: V Universitetskaia tipografiia, 1858), no. 258. See also *AAE*, 3: 257–60, 283–84.

[4] On the central importance of the recitation and chanting of psalms in the Orthodox liturgy, see "Gradualpsalmen," "Psalmodie," "Stundengebet," "Stundengottesdienst," in Konrad Onasch, *Lexikon Liturgie und Kunst der Ostkirche unter Berücksichtigung der Alten Kirche* (Berlin: Buchverlag Union, 1993), 150–51, 323–24, 348–50.

[5] "Zhitie Grigoriia Neronova, sostavlennoe posle ego smerti," in *Materialy dlia istorii raskola za pervoe vremia ego sushchestvovaniia*, ed. Nikolai I. Subbotin, 9 vols. (Moscow: Izd. "Bratskoe Slovo," 1875–94), 1: 243–305, here 250–54 (hereafter "Zhitie Neronova"). The complete *Vita* survives only in one manuscript copy from the early 18th century, in Rossiiskii gosudarstvennyi arkhiv drevnikh aktov (RGADA) f. 381, Biblioteka Moskovskoi Sinodal'noi tipografii, op. 1, no. 420, fols. 150–77. Unlike the *Vita* of Avvakum, which became one of the most frequently copied texts of the Old Belief tradition, the *Vita* of Neronov has entered Old Believer manuscripts only in short fragments. Cf. Arkhimandrit Leonid, *Sistematicheskoe opisanie slaviano-rossiiskikh rukopisei sobraniia grafa A. S. Uvarova*, 2 pts. (Moscow: Tip. A. I. Mamontova, 1893–94), 1: 579–80.

[6] Dionisii had been appointed archimandrite of the Trinity Monastery by Patriarch Germogen but he had fallen from grace after Germogen's death in 1612. Upon his return from Poland in 1619 Filaret had him released from prison and restored to his

request, Filaret interceded in the Sobolevo conflict on behalf of Neronov. Filaret first ordained Neronov as a deacon, and then appointed him the parish priest of Sobolevo. One can imagine the consternation of the village clergy and peasants when the runaway psalmist returned with a patriarchal order demanding submission to his authority.[7]

Neronov was now a powerful man with the backing of the highest Muscovite authority, and the priests' days of drinking, stealing, and quarreling were soon over. Neronov had the priests' belongings and money confiscated, put them into chains, and threw them into a dungeon. He then started a campaign against drunkenness that targeted not only priests, but everyone in the parish. Filaret could not have been more pleased with the success of Neronov's anti-drunkenness campaign. The Sobolevo peasants, however, were furious and "could not endure the virtues ... of this true servant of God."[8]

A few years later, peasants and priests together managed to expel Neronov. Patriarch Filaret quickly reassigned him to the parish of Lyskovo in the patriarchal eparchy near Nizhnii Novgorod. There, he began a campaign against gambling and popular carnivals. When the peasants became angered, Patriarch Filaret again intervened on Neronov's behalf and gave him a parish position in Nizhnii Novgorod.[9]

But at some point after 1630, things began to go very wrong for Neronov. To begin with, Neronov directed his wrath against the voevoda of Nizhnii Novgorod, Boyar Fedor Ivanovich Sheremet'ev. In fervent sermons held in the markets of Nizhnii Novgorod, Neronov denounced Sheremet'ev "for being cruel ... and merciless towards all human beings and a taker of bribes." Sheremet'ev promptly had Neronov arrested and thrown into a dungeon

---

former position. Cf. Dmitrii Skvortsov, *Dionisii Zobninovskii, arkhimandrit Troitskogo-Sergieva monastyria (nyne Lavry)* (Tver': Tip. gub. pravleniia, 1890), 281, 285–86. Dionisii had a strong modeling effect on later church reformers and has not yet received much attention from modern scholars. His *Vita* was written by Simon Azarin and completed by Ivan Nasedka, two important church reformers in their own right. Cf. Simon Azarin, *Zhitie i podvizi prepodobnogo ottsa nashego arkhimandrita Dionisiia* (Moscow, 1834).

[7] According to Neronov's *Vita*, the embattled psalmist wrote himself to Patriarch Filaret. This scenario, however, is very unlikely because access to the patriarchal court during this period was not easily obtained by ordinary Muscovites ("Zhitie Neronova," 251, 254–55). Cf. Georg B. Michels, *At War with the Church: Religious Dissent in Seventeenth-Century Russia* (Stanford, CA: Stanford University Press, 1999), 31.

[8] "Zhitie Neronova," 255.

[9] Ibid., 255–56. Neronov's assignment to Lyskovo must have been a particularly difficult one. On the unruly Lyskovo peasants, who participated in the Stepan Razin revolt and continued to celebrate pagan festivals long after Neronov left the parish, see Andrei A. Titov, *Troitskii Zheltovodskii monastyr' starogo Makariia* (Moscow: Izd. A. N. D'iachkova, 1887), 38–41.

from which he only escaped several weeks later through the intercession of Patriarch Filaret.[10]

Another altercation occurred shortly after Neronov's release from prison. He went to Moscow and began a preaching campaign against the boyars who were in the habit of cutting their beards and "adopting foreign, barbarian customs."[11] According to Neronov, clean-shaven boyars should not be allowed to enter church buildings because they desecrated the holy Orthodox faith with their presence. Neronov also demanded that Filaret forbid minstrels at the courts of the tsar and patriarch. Members of the Boyar Duma responded by repeatedly beating Neronov and dragging him along the ground by his beard. Only when Filaret undertook to change the boyars' habits, did Neronov stop preaching against them.[12]

Neronov returned to Nizhnii Novgorod and became embroiled in yet another altercation, this time with the archpriest of the cathedral church, who resented Neronov's sermons about the local clergy's laziness and overindulgence in drink. The archpriest had Neronov thrown into a dungeon and chained with his neck to the wall. An unexpected (and unexplained) turn of events, which Neronov's biographer attributed to "the mercy of God" (*miloserdie Bozhie*), resulted in his release.[13] But interestingly, Patriarch Filaret did not intercede on Neronov's behalf in this last altercation. Instead, he had Neronov arrested again on the grounds that Neronov had gone mad and had given public sermons without the patriarch's blessing. In particular, Neronov was accused of preaching with "pride and much haughtiness," and falsely denouncing local priests as heretics. For these offenses, Neronov was to be exiled to the St. Nicholas Monastery in Karelia and kept in chains until further notice.[14]

What motivated the patriarch's dramatic change of heart? Why, after siding with Neronov in a number of previous altercations, did he suddenly turn against Neronov? I believe we may find an answer to these questions by looking at the individuals who came under Neronov's vitriolic attack. Sheremet'ev was a powerful member of the Boyar Duma and had become one of

---

[10] "Zhitie Neronova," 262.

[11] The cutting of beards had been banned repeatedly by the Russian Orthodox Church but these prohibitions apparently did not keep early 17th-century boyars from shaving themselves. For a good introduction to the problem, see Petr S. Smirnov, "Bradobritie," in *Pravoslavnaia bogoslovskaia entsiklopediia*, ed. Aleksandr P. Lopukhin and Nikolai N. Glubokovskii, 12 vols. (Petrograd: [s. n.], 1900–10), 1: 1005–22.

[12] "Zhitie Neronova," 263–64.

[13] Ibid., 266.

[14] *AAE*, 3: 284. On the St. Nicholas Monastery, which was located on the White Sea littoral, see A. A. Pavlovskii, comp., *Vseobshchii illiustrirovannyi putevoditel' po monastyriam i sviatym mestam Rossiiskoi imperii i sv. g. Afonu* (Nizhnii Novgorod: Izd. t-va I. M. Mashistova, 1907), 30–31.

Russia's wealthiest landowners thanks to Filaret's support.[15] The archpriest of the cathedral church in Nizhnii Novgorod was not only the region's most powerful churchman (in the absence of a bishop), but also the patriarchal eparchy's main tax collector.[16] Could it be that Filaret applauded Neronov's moral crusades as long as they were directed at ordinary Muscovites and the lower clergy, but that he did not sanction attacks on powerful boyars or church hierarchs?

Filaret seems to have expected that Neronov would soon die or commit suicide in his remote Karelian exile, but if so, he was greatly mistaken.[17] The chained prisoner endured his daily privations with stoicism. Instead of complaining, Neronov launched a preaching campaign against Abbot Sergei and his monks at the St. Nicholas Monastery. He accused them "incessantly" (*neprestanno*) of drunkenness and ignorance in religious matters: they paid no attention to their monastic rule, did not know the liturgy, and committed all kinds of transgressions against Christian morality. Unable to endure Neronov's tirades any longer, the monks conspired to murder him by overheating and smoking out his monastic cell. When this did not work, they tried other means of ridding themselves of their unpleasant prisoner. Neronov would undoubtedly have met an early grave at the hands of the St. Nicholas monks and their abbot, but he was saved by the sudden death of Patriarch Filaret on October 1, 1633.[18]

Restored to favor by Filaret's successor, the avid reformer Patriarch Ioasaf I (1634–40), Neronov was reassigned to his old parish church in Nizhnii Novgorod. Before going home, Neronov stopped at the Kremlin to meet with the new patriarch. It appears that Patriarch Ioasaf was in agreement with Neronov on the issue of popular religious reform, and Neronov was given free

---

[15] Robert O. Crummey, *Aristocrats and Servitors: The Boyar Elite in Russia, 1613–1689* (Princeton, NJ: Princeton University Press, 1983), 119, 179.

[16] The collection of fines (*pennye den'gi*), marriage fees (*venechnye poshliny*), and a tithe (*desiatil'nichie den'gi*) in the Nizhnii Novgorod region is documented in fragmentary financial records from early 1652, in RGADA f. 235, Patriarshii kazennyi prikaz, op. 2, no. 30, Prikhodnaia kniga 160 goda, fols. 488–500 (Arzamas district). The archpriests of Nizhnii Novgorod lost their formidable powers only after the creation of a new eparchy in 1672. Cf. Archimandrite Makarii, *Istoriia Nizhegorodskoi ierarkhii, soderzhavshaia v sebe skazanie o nizhegorodskikh ierarkhakh s 1672 do 1850 goda* (St. Petersburg: Izd. N. G. Ovsiannikova, 1857), 1–9.

[17] In a charter addressed to Abbot Sergei, the patriarch anticipated that Neronov would soon die or that he might try to commit suicide, in *AAE*, 3: 284 ("*a togo b este veleli berech' na krepko, chtob on ... durna nad soboiu nikotorogo ne uchinil*").

[18] The *Vita* implies that Neronov somehow managed to escape. This is, however, very unlikely because he was kept in chains and under constant supervision. Cf. "Zhitie Neronova," 269–70.

reign in Nizhnii Novgorod.[19] Once there, Neronov launched a crusade against folk festivals, often attacking minstrels and their bears with clubs. He closed down taverns, and railed against gambling. When Neronov was not battling the pagan practices and impiety of his parishioners, he was exhorting them to attend church services and go to confession. He also organized poor relief, and then took advantage of his captive audience to read stories from the gospels in order to bring "the word of God" closer to the people.[20]

The commercial and religious elite of Nizhnii Novgorod supported Neronov's efforts by contributing funds to establish a school for poor children and a convent for the many dislocated nuns (*staritsy*) who had previously lived in shacks around Neronov's parish church. They also provided money to build a new stone church to replace the dilapidated wooden building that Neronov had occupied under Patriarch Filaret. The archpriest, under instructions from the Kremlin, also supported Neronov. And the most powerful prelate in town, Archimandrite Rafail of the Pecherskii Monastery, tolerated Neronov, possibly because the preacher had interrupted the popular pagan festivals during which townspeople dressed as monks and proceeded to mock the archimandrite's authority.[21]

The absence of any visible conflict with church authority during the remainder of the 1630s may, in large part, be due to Patriarch Ioasaf's strong support of Neronov. One must, however, also consider the fragmentary nature of the evidence during these years. Should we assume that Neronov had, for the moment, silenced his acerbic criticism of church hierarchs because there is little trace of such conflicts? Or did the records simply not survive?

More complete documentation about Neronov's activities reappears in the late 1640s, after his promotion to the rank of archpriest and his transfer to Kazan' Cathedral on Red Square. Here again we find him ranting and raving against the church hierarchy. There is indirect evidence that Neronov's Mos-

---

[19] The current state of research on Patriarch Ioasaf's reform agenda is summarized in A. P. Bogdanov, *Russkie patriarkhi 1589–1700* (Moscow: Izdatel'stvo "Respublica," 1999), 1: 362–70; Wolfgang Heller, *Die Moskauer "Eiferer für die Frömmigkeit" zwischen Staat und Kirche (1642–1652)* (Wiesbaden: Otto Harassowitz, 1988), 11–12, 30–33.

[20] See especially a 1636 petition signed by Neronov and other Nizhnii Novgorod priests, in N. V. Rozhdestvenskii, ed., "K istorii bor'by s tserkovnymi bezporiadkami ... v russkom bytu XVII veka (chelobitnaia nizhegorodskikh sviashchennikov 1636 goda)," *Chteniia v Obshchestve istorii i drevnostei rossiiskikh pri Moskovskom universitete* (1902), bk. 2, smes', 1–31, esp. 18–31. See also "Zhitie Neronova," 259–63.

[21] On Neronov's interference with pagan festivals (which included mocking of the upper clergy) that took place in the immediate vicinity of the Pecherskii Monastery, see Rozhdestvenskii, "K istorii bor'by," 26–28. On popular ridiculing of Muscovy's monastic clergy, see evidence cited in Nikolai F. Kapterev, *Patriarkh Nikon i ego protivniki v dele ispravleniia tserkovnykh obriadov: Vremia patriarshestva Iosifa* (Sergiev Posad: Izd. M. S. Elova, 1913), 171 ("*igrishcha raznyia i merzkiia ..., na koikh sviatykh naritsaiut, i monastyri delaiut, i arkhimandrita, i kelaria i startsev naritsaiut....*").

cow sermons even went so far as to accuse the newly appointed Patriarch Iosif (1642–52) of corruption.[22] In a letter to Tsar Aleksei Mikhailovich (dated February 11, 1649), the patriarch complained bitterly about the tsar's confessor (and Neronov's patron), Stefan Vonifat'ev: "[He pretends] that there is no church in the Muscovite state and has called me, your pious servant, a wolf and not a pastor. He has also rebuked your pious metropolitans, archbishops, and bishops with swear words, and called them wolves and torturers (*gubiteli*)." Neronov was not present when Vonifat'ev rose during the 1649 Church Council and denounced the patriarch as a ruthless careerist, unworthy of his office. However, Neronov was among those whom Patriarch Iosif condemned at the 1651 Church Council for being slanderers (*klevetniki*) and false prophets and "beating ... and wounding him."[23] Again, the timely death of the patriarch in April 1652 may have saved Neronov from serious repercussions.

On the eve of Patriarch Iosif's death, rumors were circulating in Moscow that Neronov was an enemy of the true Russian religion because he wanted to change the church liturgy and do away with icons. These rumors which became known to the German traveler Olearius had little grounding in reality.[24] We only know for a fact that Neronov gave fervent sermons against the widespread use of *mnogoglasie*, that is the practice of chanting litanies, prayers, and psalms simultaneously or "in many voices" (*mnogoglasno*) which usually resulted in cacophony and chaos. This deeply-engrained custom, which existed not only in rural parishes but in most Moscow churches, considerably shortened church services and—according to Neronov—reflected a shocking ignorance of liturgical traditions. He denounced the resulting babble of voice which made the liturgical text and its medium, the Church Slavonic language, unintelligible and insisted that each segment of the liturgy had to be recited separately and "in one voice" (*edinoglasno*) so that congregations would be confronted with the full beauty of the Russian Orthodox tradition.[25]

[22] On the prevalence of corruption and venality in Patriarch Iosif's court, see Sergei M. Solov'ev, *Istoriia Rossii s drevneishikh vremen*, 15 vols. (Moscow: Izd. sotsial'no-ekonomicheskoi literatury, 1960–66), 6: 208–09.

[23] Kapterev, *Patriarkh Nikon*, 163–64, 172–73; N. A. Gibbenet, *Istoricheskoe issledovanie dela patriarkha Nikona*, 2 vols. (St. Petersburg: Tip. Ministerstva vnutrennikh del, 1882–84), 2: 471.

[24] Neronov was a strong supporter of icon worship and decorated his parish church in Nizhnii Novgorod with many holy images donated by wealthy patrons ("Zhitie Neronova," 271). Similar rumors circulated about Archipriest Loggin of Murom. The evidence suggests that they were planted by powerful enemies of the archpriest who felt threatened by his sermons against moral corruption. See Michels, *At War with the Church*, 52–53.

[25] "Rasprosnye rechi o edinoglasii (1651 goda)," in *Zapiski Otdeleniia russkoi i slavianskoi arkheologii Imperatorskogo russkogo arkheologicheskogo obshchestva*, 13 vols. (St. Petersburg, 1851–1918), 2: 394–97; RGADA f. 27, Tainyi prikaz, d. 68; Sergei A. Belokurov, *Iz dukhovnoi zhizni i moskovskogo obshchestva XVII veka* (Moscow, 1902), 48–49; Samuel H.

It was not until Nikon's patriarchate (1652–58) that liturgical reforms were widely achieved. Historians have often viewed Neronov as the mouthpiece for liturgical opposition to Patriarch Nikon, but in fact, as I have just indicated, Neronov was not entirely opposed to such reforms. He was a close observer of the book corrections and bought a number of revised Service Books from the Patriarchal Printing Press. However, unlike early Old Believers he did not denounce the *ispravlenie knig* (revision of books) in his writings and he certainly did not assemble detailed critiques of the new books as the Old Believer priests Lazar' and Nikita Dobrynin.[26] His letters written in the immediate aftermath of the 1654 Church Council, which declared the *ispravlenie knig* official church policy, do not dwell much on the issue. While they speak about the dangers of hasty changes in the liturgies—and even the potentially disastrous effects of abandoning ancient tradition—they nevertheless do not dispute the importance of liturgical reforms. The principal focus of these letters, however, was on the moral shortcomings and secular priorities of Patriarch Nikon and his minions.[27] Not surprisingly, unlike the Old Believers Avvakum and Deacon Fedor, Neronov never polemicized against the *Skrizhal'* (Tablet), a long theological treatise printed in June 1656 that introduced and justified the three-fingered sign of the cross (*troeperstie*).[28] While there is evidence that Neronov used the old liturgical books at the Ignat'eva Hermitage (*Ignat'eva pustyn'*) (see below), it is also clear that he did not insist on their use. In fact, Archbishop Simon of Vologda, one of Neronov's strongest enemies, testified that Neronov also used new liturgical books and never raised "any accusations against the current Service Books" (*viny ... na nyneshnye sluzhebniki nikakie ne skazal*).[29] It appears that Neronov was altogether less interested in liturgical issues than in moral ones; he got into trouble not be-

Baron, trans. and ed., *The Travels of Olearius in Seventeenth-Century Russia* (Stanford, CA: Stanford University Press, 1967), 257. On the *edinoglasie* reform and Neronov's involvement in its execution, see also Heller, *Die Moskauer "Eiferer für die Frömmigkeit,"* 53–55, 108–10.

[26] RGADA f. 1182, Prikaz knigopechatnogo dela, op. 1, bk. 50, Raskhodnaia kniga 7060 goda, fols. 260v, 521v, 539v, 636v; "Rospis' vkrattse novovvodnym tserkovnym razdorom," in Subbotin, *Materialy*, 4: 179–206; "Suzdal'skogo sobornogo popa Nikity Konstantinova Dobrynina chelobitnaia tsariu Alekseiu Mikhalovichu na knigu Skrizhal' i na novoispravlennye knigi," ibid., 1–130.

[27] Subbotin, *Materialy*, 1: 34–123, esp. 54–59.

[28] Ibid., 1: 147–48, 156, 338 ("Otpiska Grigoriia Neronova za evo rukoiu, chto on veruet Skrizhali"). Among their many objections against the *Skrizhal'*, early Old Believers pointed to the fact that the Greek original of the text had been printed in Venice. As Deacon Fedor put it, "there are heretical books in use among us that have come from Rome, Paris, and Venice...." (Subbotin, *Materialy*, 6: 30).

[29] Ibid., 157, 196.

cause he opposed Nikon's liturgical reforms, but because he accused the patriarch of moral corruption.[30]

In August 1653, Nikon had Neronov arrested and exiled to the Spaso-Kamennyi Monastery in Vologda. From his exile, Neronov wrote a series of letters to Tsar Aleksei Mikhailovich and Stefan Vonifat'ev in which he condemned Nikon's arrest and the torture of many other clerics.[31] These clerics, who led campaigns against moral vices such as drunkenness and promiscuity, were replaced by Nikon's own clients, whom Neronov considered to be criminals and sycophants.[32] Pleading that he could not remain silent in response to the patriarch's behavior, Neronov wrote: "Nikon gives powerful positions to those who execute his will, not the will of God. Sire, what good has ever come from those who were selected by the patriarch to hold office?"[33] Drawing on the letters of St. Paul and the writings of the church father John Chrysostomos, Neronov argued that the Russian church had been hijacked by "Christ-murdering bishops" (*khristoubiitsy arkhierei*) and "pseudo-spiritual powers" (*mniashshiesia dukhovnye vlasti*).[34] Unless Nikon were immediately removed from power, Neronov concluded, all hopes for a

---

[30] I have developed this argument in more detail in Georg B. Michels, "O deiatel'nosti Ivana Neronova v pervye gody Nikonovskoi reformy," in *Russkoe obshchestvo i literatura pozdnego feodalizma: sbornik nauchnykh trudov* [=vol. 17 of *Arkheografiia i istochnikovedenie v Sibiri*], ed. Nikolai N. Pokrovskii (Novosibirsk: Sibirskii Khronograf, 1996), 23–36. It is also noteworthy that the Old Believers themselves did not consider Ivan Neronov one of their own. His *Vita* is remarkably absent from Semen Denisov's early 18th-century collection of Old Belief hagiographies. Cf. Semen Denisov, *Vinograd Rossiiskii ili opisanie postradavshikh v Rossii za drevletserkovnoe blagochestie* (Moscow: Tip. G. Lissnera i D. Sovko, 1906). For additional information, see nn. 4, 5, and 33.

[31] Subbotin, *Materialy*, 1: 34–123. The distribution of alms to "the orphaned children of priests who died in prison" suggests that Neronov was fortunate to survive his own imprisonment under Patriarch Nikon. Cf. RGADA f. 235, Patriarshii kazennyi prikaz, op. 2, no. 41, Raskhodnaia kniga 165 goda, fols. 250 (28 January 1657).

[32] Subbotin, *Materialy*, 1: 36, 44, 47–48, 67–68. Patriarch Nikon's systematic replacement of parish priests and other clerics appointed by his predecessor, Patriarch Iosif, is documented in Gosudarstvennyi istoricheskii muzei (GIM) no. 424, Zapis' stavlennykh gramot 1645–1666 gg.

[33] Subbotin, *Materialy*, 1: 68 (letter to Tsar Aleksei Mikhailovich dated 27 February 1654). Unlike the letters of Avvakum and other Old Believers, Neronov's letters survive mostly in autograph copies from the dates when they were written. Cf. V. G. Druzhinin, *Pisaniia russkikh staroobriadtsev: Perechen' spiskov, sostavlennyi po pechatnym opisaniiam rukopisnykh sobranii* (St. Petersburg: Tip. M. A. Aleksandrova, 1912), 210–13.

[34] See, for example, Neronov's letter to Stefan Vonifat'ev dated July 13, 1654, in Subbotin, *Materialy*, 1: 94–108, esp. 97–98. Cf. a similar letter to Mariia Il'ichnichna, the tsar's wife, dated May 2, 1654 (ibid., 78–83) in which Neronov expressed joy in his own suffering at the hands of corrupt church hierarchs: "Nam bo viash'chaia chest', ezhe blagochestiia radi stradati" (83).

genuine moral reform of the Russian clergy and laity would be destroyed. This diatribe was clearly not directed at Nikon alone, but also at the leading hierarchs of the Russian church. An anonymous supporter, who wrote Neronov's *Vita* in the 1670s, insisted that these hierarchs "conspired against [Neronov] because they hated his teaching for its zealous emphasis on proper Christian conduct [*blagochinie*].... [Neronov] denounced ... especially those powerful clerics who did not behave according to their calling."[35]

Within a few days of his arrival at the Spaso-Kamennyi Monastery in Vologda, Neronov had accused Archimandrite Aleksandr of greatly neglecting his religious duties. Church services at the monastery were meaningless performances, Neronov claimed, because many monks did not show up and others fell asleep, while the rest shouted and quarreled about money and other trivial matters. During Mass, the archimandrite provided a bad moral example because he never taught the monks about the lives of the apostles and saints, and joked instead with the priests and deacons. Neronov found that life at the monastery was not guided by a strict moral code: the monks did not fast, and they often drank themselves into a stupor. And finally, Neronov observed that the archimandrite had no regard for the monastery's serfs because he forced them to work on Sundays and allowed his drunken retainers to descend upon the villages and wreak havoc.[36]

The archimandrite's initial respect for Neronov quickly turned to frustration and dismay.[37] When Neronov accused Aleksandr of neglecting prayer and edifying readings during the fasting period, Aleksandr could no longer control his rage. He grabbed Neronov by the hair and dragged him through the refectory. Convinced that Neronov had gone mad, Aleksandr began to slap him on both cheeks "for a considerable amount of time" (*vremia dovol'no*). Aleksandr finally fled his own monastery. When he returned after three weeks and found Neronov still spouting venom, he locked Neronov out of the church building, then had the troublesome archpriest thrown into solitary confinement, and finally threatened him with brute force. A supporter of Neronov's wrote a letter to the Kremlin expressing fear that the archimandrite and his monks were planning to murder Neronov.[38]

---

[35] "Zhitie Neronova," 282.

[36] Subbotin, *Materialy*, 1: 115–16.

[37] Surprisingly, Aleksandr had initially welcomed Neronov as someone sent to him by God, and instead of imprisoning him, Aleksandr had provided him with a furnished cell, extra food and drink, and a servant (ibid., 112–13).

[38] Abbot Feoktist to Stefan Vonifat'ev, 13 July 1654, in *Materialy*, 1: 109–19, esp. 115–18. The cellarer of the monastery was beaten and put into solitary confinement after sympathizing with Neronov (ibid., 117–18). For more information about Archimandrite Aleksandr, who soon afterwards became bishop of Kolomna, see Michels, *At War with the Church*, 79–85.

Aleksandr managed to have Neronov transferred to the Kandalashskii Monastery on the Kola Peninsula nearly 1,000 miles to the north of Vologda. Neronov, by now 60 years old, managed to escape this captivity in a daring flight across the stormy White Sea in April 1655. By the fall of 1655, he was back in Moscow, living in hiding, "constantly changing his clothes and running from place to place."[39]

Historians have primarily focused on Neronov's conflicts with Nikon, which left numerous traces in documentary sources, and ignored Neronov's stormy relationships with other church hierarchs.[40] Some of the most vicious conflicts of Neronov's career were fought from his native village of Lom, where he went into hiding in January 1656. Having had himself shorn a monk—and adopting the monastic name Grigorii—at some point after his escape from the Kola Peninsula, Neronov soon became the de facto leader of the Ignat'eva Hermitage.[41] He then became embroiled in conflict with the three church lords who had been disputing local jurisdiction since his childhood: the patriarch, the archbishop of Vologda, and the metropolitan of Rostov. These hierarchs quarreled over the rich fishing grounds of the River Sara and Lake Rostov (both near Neronov's native village of Lom), the right to tax prosperous local peasants, and the lands and fisheries owned by the affluent Ignat'eva Hermitage.[42]

In early 1656, agents of Patriarch Nikon invaded Lom and arrested most of the hermitage's monks.[43] Neronov was hidden by local peasants, even

---

[39] G. Murkos, trans. and ed., *Puteshestvie antiokhiiskogo patriarkha Makariia v Rossiiu v polovine XVII veka, opisannoe ego synom arkhidiakonom Pavlom Aleppskim*, 5 vols. (Moscow, 1896–1900; repr. Moscow: Ob-vo sokhraneniia literaturnogo naslediia, 2005), 4: 178.

[40] Nikolai F. Kapterev, *Patriarkh Nikon i tsar' Aleksei Mikhailovich*, 2 vols. (Sergiev Posad: Tip. Sviato-Troiskoi Sergievoi Lavry, 1909–12), 1: 432–90; Vera S. Rumiantseva, *Narodnoe antitserkovnoe dvizhenie v Rossii v XVII veke* (Moscow: Nauka, 1986), 93–106; Sergei Zenkovskii, *Russkoe staroobriadchestvo: Dukhovnye dvizheniia semnadtsatogo veka* (Munich: W. Fink Verlag, 1970), 62–70, 74–82; Nicholas Lupinin, *Religious Revolt in the Seventeenth Century: The Schism of the Russian Church* (Princeton, NJ: Kingston Press, 1984), passim.

[41] Neronov's sojourn at the Ignat'eva Hermitage lasted for almost ten years even though he often traveled to Vologda and Moscow, sometimes staying away for months at a time. Cf. "Zapiski zhizni Neronova," in Subbotin, *Materialy*, 1: 134–66, esp. 143, 158, 163, 165.

[42] Amvrosii, *Istoriia rossiiskoi ierarkhii*, 6 vols. (Moscow: Sinodal'naia tipografiia, 1807–15), 6: 958–59, 1022. "Delo po isvetam Neronova na Ionu mitropolita rostovskogo i Simona arkhiepiskopa vologodskogo," in Subbotin, *Materialy*, 1: 192–98.

[43] These agents were accompanied by musketeers. They received money from the Patriarch Finance Office and hired local peasants to transport the prisoners to Vologda. Cf. RGADA f. 235, Patriarshii kazennyi prikaz, op. 2, no. 38, Raskhodnaia kniga 164 goda, fols. 609, 612, 614r-v.

though they were subjected to "much misfortune" (*mnogu bedu*) for doing so. According to one report, numerous peasants were rounded up, taken to a dungeon in Moscow, and apparently tortured for failing to reveal Neronov's whereabouts. In August 1656, Metropolitan Iona of Rostov sent troops to join the search for Neronov, but they were not successful in locating him. The metropolitan then extended his search to the neighboring Velikii Ustiug region where Neronov had apparently been sighted. He gave orders to the local archpriest and Archimandrite Ignatii of the Arkhangel'skii Monastery to have Neronov arrested and immediately put into chains.[44] The metropolitan and the patriarch vowed "to cut him off from the Holy Church like a withered arm."[45] Patriarch Nikon's abdication in July 1658 appears to have saved Neronov's life.[46]

It is hard to reconstruct how many months, if not years, Neronov spent in episcopal torture chambers and monastic dungeons during the ten years following Nikon's abdication.[47] His tribulations came to an end only because Tsar Aleksei Mikhailovich took pity on him. In the summer of 1667, Neronov appealed to the tsar for help. He approached Tsar Aleksei Mikhailovich in person while the latter was on a pilgrimage at the Trinity Monastery. The tsar

[44] "Gramota rostovskogo mitropolita Iony k velikoustiuzhskomu arkhimandritu Ignatiiu i sobornomu protopopu Vladimiru o razyskanii ... beglogo startsa, chto byl v mire protopop Ivan Neronov," in *Akty kholmogorskoi i ustiuzhskoi eparkhii*, pts. 1–3 (St. Petersburg: Izd. Imperatorskoi Arkheograficheskoi komissii, 1890–1908) [=vols. 12, 14, 25 of *Russkaia istoricheskaia biblioteka*], 1: 292–94. Archimandrite Ignatii was a client of Patriarch Nikon who fell from power in 1658 (after the resignation of his patron). Cf. Pavel M. Stroev, *Spiski ierarkhov i nastoiatelei monastyrei Rossiiskiia tserkvi* (St. Petersburg: Tip. V. S. Balasheva, 1877); reprinted in vol. 35 of *Bausteine zur Geschichte der Literatur bei den Slaven*, ed. Fedor B. Poliakov (Cologne and Vienna: Böhlau Verlag, 1990), 740.

[45] "Sobornoe deianie na protopopa Ivana Neronova, v inochestve startsa Grigoriia, 1656 goda," in Subbotin, *Materialy*, 1: 124–33, esp. 130–31; GIM, Sinodal'noe sobranie svitkov, no. 1098.

[46] There are indications that Neronov used his personal connections with other high-ranking hierarchs (such as Metropolitan Pitirim of Krutitsy who had been excommunicated by Nikon) to win support in the Kremlin. See "Zapiski zhizni Neronova," 166.

[47] Subbotin, *Materialy*, 1: 203–08, 216–21, 224–29, 238–39; GIM, Sinodal'noe sobranie svitkov, nos. 1101, 1103. Neronov's principal persecutor was Archbishop Simon of Vologda, who had him beaten, chained, and immured in the Spaso-Prilutskii Monastery. Neronov considered Metropolitan Pavel of Krutitsy, *locum tenens* of the patriarchal see (1665–67), to be his worst tormentor ("*nyne paki nacha gnati mia i muchiti pache Nikona*"; 239). He accused Pavel of covering up the crimes of Archbishop Simon. And while imprisoned in the Iosifo-Volokolamsk monastery, Neronov suffered great indignities at the hands of Archimandrite Savvatii after the monks had revolted against their prisoner's moralizing sermons (217–19). Neronov's spirit remained unbroken by his jailers: "i smert' primu, no ne budy molchat' i vpred' budu emu velikomu gosudariu izveshchat'" (239).

immediately recognized Neronov as a protégé of his grandfather, Patriarch Filaret, and as a holy man who had suffered greatly for his beliefs. After asking Neronov to bless his wife and children, the tsar vowed to protect him from his enemies in the church.[48]

This encounter greatly transformed Neronov's life. With the support of Tsar Aleksei Mikhailovich, Neronov was elevated to the rank of archimandrite of the Danilov Monastery in Pereslavl'-Zalesskii, (where he had been a prisoner only a few months earlier). This sudden reversal of Neronov's tragic fate may not have occurred without the tsar's personal intervention but one wonders if his promotion to high ecclesiastical rank was not also a conscious move to put pressure on church hierarchs who had been affiliated with Patriarch Nikon (whose deposition and exile coincided with Neronov's elevation). We know, for example, that Neronov's strongest supporters in the hierarchy were bitter enemies of the former patriarch: Archimandrite Ioasaf of the Trinity Monastery (who became Nikon's successor as Patriarch Ioasaf II, 1667–72), Metropolitan Pitirim of Krutitsy (who became Patriarch Pitirim, 1672–73), and Archbishop Ilarion of Riazan (who became Metropolitan Ilarion in 1669).[49] Neronov's elevation coincided with these hierarchs' seizure of power at the patriarchal court and their efforts to remove die-hard supporters of Nikon from church positions.[50]

The dramatic promotion into the upper strata of the church hierarchy does not imply that Neronov made peace with the dismal realities of Russian church life. Rather, it gave him one last chance to impose his strict moral

---

[48] "Zhitie Neronova," 295–96.

[49] *Delo o patriarkhe Nikone po dokumentam Moskovskoi Sinodal'noi (byvshei Patriarshei) biblioteki* (St. Petersburg: Izd. Arkheograficheskoi Komissii, 1897), 20–22, 33, 54, 62–65, 72, 109, 111; Stroev, *Spiski ierarkhov*, 7, 36–37, 415, 1036; Subbotin, *Materialy*, 1: 153, 159, 166.

[50] Support for avid reformers like Neronov appears to have served the purpose of undermining the Nikonian careerists' prestige at the Kremlin and within the church hierarchy. Few of these reformers ever rose to high rank. Another notable exception was Abbot Ilarion of the Florishcheva Hermitage, who succeeded Archbishop Stefan of Suzdal', one of the most notoriously corrupt clients of Patriarch Nikon. Like Neronov, whom he knew very well, Ilarion was an avid critic of the hierarchy's moral behavior. His sermons against fornication, religious indifference, and popular heterodoxy were closely followed by the church elite. It is noteworthy, however, that it took almost 15 years before Stefan was deposed; Ilarion first became archbishop of Suzdal' (1681–82) and was quickly promoted to the rank of metropolitan (1682–1707). Cf. V. T. Georgievskii, *Florishcheva pustyn': Istoriko-arkheologicheskoe opisanie s risunkami* (Viazniki: Izd. Arkhimandrita Antoniia, 1896), 23; Georg B. Michels, "The Rise and Fall of Archbishop Stefan: Church Power, Local Society, and the Kremlin during the Seventeenth Century," in *Von Moskau nach St. Petersburg. Das russische Reich im 17. Jahrhundert*, ed. Hans-Joachim Torke (Wiesbaden: Harrasowitz Verlag, 2000) [=vol. 56 of *Forschungen zur osteuropäischen Geschichte*], 203–26; Stroev, *Spiski ierarkhov*, 657, 710.

ideals on unruly monks, priests, and peasants. For the remaining three years of his life, Neronov focused on disciplining the laymen and clerics under his immediate authority: he strictly forbade any drinking of alcohol, ordered everyone to attend church services, forced village priests to perform the liturgy (including all-night vigils) even on weekdays, put monks on fasting rations, and disciplined the slightest sign of misbehavior (such as falling asleep during his sermons). Towards the end of his life Neronov proudly claimed the complete eradication of drunkenness in the monastery. His successes were less noticeable in the monastery's hinterlands: in 1669, one year before Neronov's death, peasants and priests rose against him in revolt. "They cursed him with all kinds of indecent swearwords and beat him out of the Church of God." Unlike in the recent past, however, Neronov enjoyed protection from powerful members of the church hierarchy and, probably most significantly, from the royal court in the Kremlin. Tsar Aleksei Mikhailovich immediately dispatched emissaries of boyar rank to protect Neronov and had the troublemakers arrested.[51]

Thus at the end of his life, Neronov was again in the privileged position he had enjoyed under Patriarch Filaret nearly 50 years earlier. He had regained the power to impose his austere vision of Christian morality on rank-and-file Muscovites, and he used this power in Pereslavl'-Zalesskii as he had earlier in Sobolevo and Nizhnii Novgorod. But even now, Neronov walked a thin line with his disciplinary measures. Patriarch Ioasaf II had warned him not to give sermons against church leaders, and it appears that Neronov heeded the patriarch's advice. When Neronov died in January 1670, he was buried with honors and lauded as one of the great reformers of the Russian church.[52]

Although there were a few moments of noteworthy success, the story of Neronov's life ultimately reveals the futility of his efforts. Driven by a seemingly inexhaustible idealism, he almost always courted violence and disaster. The seeds of Neronov's zealotry appear to have been planted during his youth in the village of Lom. He grew up hearing his parents' stories about the legendary Ignatii, an ascetic monk who had withdrawn to Lom from a larger monastery during the middle of the 16th century and founded the Ignat'eva

---

[51] A. I. Svirelin, "Svedeniia o zhizni arkhimandrita Pereslavskogo Danilova monastyria Grigoriia Neronova," *Trudy Vladimirskoi uchenoi kommissii*, bk. 6 (1904), 1–47, esp. 45 ("*uchinili miatezh i evo arkhimandrita branili vsiakoiu nepodobnoiu braniiu i iz tserkvi Bozhiei von vybili…*"); "Zhitie Neronova," 298–302.

[52] "'Grigorii! Prestani priu imeti s arkhierei.' Grigorii zhe, otveshchav, reche: 'Vladyko sviatyi! Ashche i smert' priiati, gotov esm' pravdy radi, ne postyzhdusia glagolati pred tsari i vladyki'" ("Zhitie Neronova," 295). Cf. Svirelin, "Svedeniia," 47; "Zhitie Neronova," 304–05.

Hermitage.[53] Neronov was powerfully affected by the religious ideals and moral purity of his native village's saint that provided such a dramatic contrast to his impressions of church agents from Vologda, Rostov, and Moscow. These church agents descended on Lom whenever it was possible to extract taxes and fees (e.g., for baptisms, marriages, and burials), but otherwise demonstrated little concern for the well-being of the villagers.[54]

Neronov's first clash over the religious indifference of church agents occurred long before his encounter with Patriarch Filaret in the 1620s. In December 1612, Neronov set off for the nearby town of Vologda during the Christmastide carnival celebrations (*sviatki*). He was unpleasantly surprised upon his arrival at the archbishop's palace to find crowds of drunken episcopal retainers, among them priests and other clerics from the cathedral staff, dancing in the streets and shrieking like crazed demons. They had disguised themselves as ghosts with frightening masks and other "demonic paraphernalia" (*podobiia demonskie*). Outraged, the young Neronov berated the mummers for behaving like sinners and bad Christians. Most of his repugnance, however, was reserved for Archbishop Sil'vestr (1611–13) who was doing nothing to prevent the pandemonium. "How could this be the house of a bishop [*dom arkhiereev*]?" Neronov screamed at the crowd. Were bishops not supposed to teach ordinary people "to refrain from every evil" and to shun demons? Within minutes, as one eyewitness recalled, the infuriated members of the bishop's household threw themselves upon Neronov "like wild ani-

---

[53] By the time of Neronov's childhood, the Ignat'eva Hermitage had become the focus of a popular miracle cult. On display in the hermitage's church were the heavy chains that Ignatii had once wound around his body to mortify the flesh and the wooden plank on which he had slept. Icons depicting Ignatii as a helper of the poor, a healer of the sick, and a consoler of the despondent could be found in every peasant hut. The popularity of Ignatii among local peasants can be reconstructed on the basis of later evidence; see "Delo po izvetam Neronova na Simona arkhiepiskopa vologodskogo," in Subbotin, *Materialy*, 1: 201–13, esp. 204–07, and "Zhitie Neronova," 280–81. In a marginal note the editor of Neronov's *Vita* praised Neronov for his affiliation with the Ignat'eva Hermitage, in RGADA f. 381, Biblioteka Moskovskoi Sinodal'noi tipografii, op. 1, no. 420, fol. 169v ("*obitel', iuzhe tshchaniem svoim sobra*").

[54] The violence and corruption of Vologda church agents are amply documented for the period of Neronov's youth, in Sankt-Peterburgskii filial Instituta rossiiskoi istorii Rossiiskoi Akademii nauk (SPbFIRI) f. 117, Kollektsiia P. I. Savvaitova, nos. 20–21, 23, 31, 46, 48, 56, 62, 84. On the aggressive attempts of the Vologda bishops to expand their land holdings and tax incomes during this same period, see ibid., nos. 19, 25, 50, 57, 61, 72, 91. These realities of Russian church life were wryly and insightfully depicted in the film *Happiness* by Alexander Medvedkin, considered by Sergei Eisenstein to be the best Soviet film of 1934. Cf. Ronald Bergan, *Sergei Eisenstein: A Life in Conflict* (Woodstock, NY: The Overlook Press, 1999), 262–63.

mals" and beat him to a pulp. Neronov continued his vituperations until he lost consciousness and was left for dead in the gutter.[55]

This pattern was repeated throughout Neronov's life. Despite his determination to conform the behavior of his contemporaries to his moral ideals, he was never really successful in these efforts. One reason may have been that the cooperation of the upper clergy, upon whom real reform depended, was highly conditional. On several occasions he received a mandate to discipline peasants, townsmen, and lower-ranking clerics. But as soon as he targeted the corrupt and immoral behavior of Russia's ruling elites (both church and secular), his authority was quickly retracted and he was either exiled or imprisoned.

A look at the turbulent life of Ivan Neronov, and in particular, at his changing and often ambiguous relationship with Russia's church leaders, helps us to understand the dramatic failure of church reform during the 17th century.[56] It was Neronov's central contention that reform-oriented texts and ideas, widely produced and disseminated since the time of Patriarch Filaret, did not guide the actual behavior of Russia's ecclesiastical elite.[57] According to Neronov, if the church's principal representatives only lent lip service to reform ideals and did not apply them toward their own behavior, the church would not be able to reform itself.[58] He thus identified one of the central dilemmas of early modern Russian church history: How could church leaders "who did not live according to their calling" (as Neronov never ceased to emphasize), expect ordinary Russians to assimilate new disciplinary models of religious and moral behavior? This dilemma was not resolved during the 17th century and led to the deep and long-standing rift between church elite and ordinary Russians described by a leading Russian church historian as "one of the most ominous (*verhängnisvollste*) phenomena of Russian church

---

[55] "Zhitie Neronova," 246–48.

[56] This failure has been noted by several historians. Cf. Igor Smolitsch, *Russisches Mönchtum: Entstehung, Entwicklung und Wesen, 988–1917* (Würzburg: Augustiner-Verlag, 1953), vols. 10–11 of *Das Östliche Christentum*, N. F., 383–413, esp. 383, and more recently, Cathy J. Potter, *The Russian Church and the Politics of Reform in the Second Half of the Seventeenth Century*, 2 vols. (Ph.D. diss., Yale University, 1993), 2: 507–17, esp. 514.

[57] This was also the opinion of the Old Believers with whom Neronov shared a strong sense of moral urgency. In another essay, I argue on the basis of documentary evidence that Neronov did not exaggerate his claims (even though I also demonstrate that some bishops were genuinely guided by principles of moral reform). See Georg B. Michels, "Ruling Without Mercy: Seventeenth-Century Russian Bishops and their Officials," *Kritika: Explorations in Russian and Eurasian History* 4: 3 (2003): 1–29.

[58] For a powerful summary of Neronov's principal ideas about the spiritual mission of Orthodox church hierarchs, see two petitions to Tsar Aleksei Mikhailovich dating from 1660 and 1664, in Subbotin, *Materialy*, 1: 167–92.

life."[59] Neronov was among the first to see the pastoral failure of Russia's church elite, and he suffered greatly for his unremitting courage in fighting for genuine reforms that would bring even powerful office holders into harmony with moral virtues.[60]

---

[59] Igor Smolitsch, *Geschichte der Russischen Kirche 1700–1917*, vol. 1 (Leiden: E. J. Brill, 1964), 406 ("Diese Kluft, diese Abtrennung der Bischöfe von ihrer Herde, war eine der verhängnisvollsten Erscheinungen des russischen kirchlichen Lebens"). Cf. similar observations, ibid., 405 ("....eine erhabene kirchenfürstliche Distanz"), and 406 ("Die Memoiren des 18. Jahrhunderts berichten immer wieder vom Hochmut, von der Härte und der Unnahbarkeit der Bischöfe").

[60] Neronov's confrontations with the Russian church hierarchy anticipated the struggles of the 19th-century priest Ivan Belliustin, whom only "the personal intervention of the emperor [Alexander II]" saved from being thrown into a dungeon at the Solovki Monastery. Cf. Gregory L. Freeze, ed., *I. S. Belliustin's Description of the Clergy in Rural Russia: The Memoir of a Nineteenth-Century Parish Priest* (Ithaca, NY: Cornell University Press: 1985), 46–47.

Old Believers and the Soviet State in Riga, 1945–55

Roy R. Robson

In the past few years, our understanding of popular religious life in the Soviet Union has undergone a significant change. Once only the interest of émigré believers or militant atheists, Orthodoxy after 1917 is finally receiving sophisticated analysis by professional historians. The resultant picture is quite nuanced. Believers were persecuted, even martyred by the Soviet authorities. The communist state nationalized religious property, razed thousands of churches, and relegated religious servitors to the level of social parasites, the last to receive rations when food was scarce. However, religious life did continue: sometimes in exile, sometimes covertly, and sometimes quite openly. Often, belief and atheism existed on a continuum, with believers and Soviet authorities jockeying for control. The believers themselves developed strategies to use the Soviet system to their own advantage, pursuing legal recognition in the USSR.[1]

The next step in understanding the phenomenon of religion in the USSR is the analysis of religious communities in detail.[2] How did they respond to changing conditions in the USSR? How did they interact with the Soviet bureaucracy? What tactics did they use? Were there differences between Orthodox and Old Believer experiences under Soviet rule? This essay attempts to expand the research on local communities to that of the Old Belief. It will focus on the relationship between religion and communism on a local level by

---

[1] See William B. Husband, "Soviet Atheism and Russian Orthodox Strategies of Resistance, 1917–32," *Journal of Modern History* 70 (1998): 74–107. Even wider ranging is William B. Husband, *'Godless Communists': Atheism and Society in Soviet Russia, 1917–1932* (DeKalb: Northern Illinois University Press, 2000). Also see Edward E. Roslof, *Red Priests: Renovating Russian Orthodoxy and Revolution, 1905–1946* (Bloomington: Indiana University Press, 2002); and T. A. Chumachenko and Edward E. Roslof, *Church and State in Soviet Russia: Russian Orthodoxy from World War II to the Khrushchev Years* (Armonk, NY: M. E. Sharpe, 2002).

[2] There are some articles focused on one region or parish in the Orthodox church. See Chris J. Chulos, "Peasants' Attempts to Reopen Their Church, 1929–1936," *Russian History/Histoire Russe* 24: 1 (1997): 203–13; and Daniel Peris, "'God is Now on Our Side:' The Religious Revival on Unoccupied Soviet Territory during World War II'" *Kritika: Explorations in Russian and Eurasian History* 1: 1 (2000): 97–118.

Rude & Barbarous Kingdom Revisited: Essays in Russian History and Culture in Honor of Robert O. Crummey. Chester S. L. Dunning, Russell E. Martin, and Daniel Rowland, eds. Bloomington, IN: Slavica Publishers, 2008, 287–99.

studying the Riga Grebenshchikovskaia Old Believer Community (RGSO) in the period 1945–55.

Riga Old Believers and Secular Authority

Founded in 1760, the Grebenshchikovskaia Community was one of the most highly developed Old Ritualist groups in former Imperial lands. As the largest of the Baltic Old Believer communities, the Grebenshchikovskaia Obshchina was the de facto leader of the Old Belief in the Baltics. The magnificent church with its mammoth iconostasis, its school, charitable activities, printing press, and library all served tens of thousands of Old Believers in the region.[3] Except for closure during the mid-19th-century repression of Nicholas I, the community had experienced notably good relations with the Imperial government.

Latvian Old Believers offered little formal response to the atheist regime that had taken over Russia in 1917. For example, published minutes of the first Spiritual Council of Old Believer Preceptors, held in 1922, never mentioned the Bolshevik revolution. Instead, the community leaders promised to lead a more general "struggle with unbelief and sectarianism."[4] Unofficially, though, some Old Believer leaders were anxious about the threat of communism. M. A. Vlasov, both preceptor (*nastavnik*) of the Grebenshchikovskaia community and president of the Latvian Old Believer Spiritual Commission, kept copious notes from works by Marx, Lunacharskii, and related authors. He laboriously copied out quotes from a number of publications: *Nauka i tekhnika, Kommunizm i religiia, Izvestiia VTsIKa, Kapital, Antireligioznik, Religiia i sotsializm*, and others. Though he may not have spoken publicly about the threat of communism (no sermons on that topic have been found at the RGSO archive), Vlasov lamented that "in our time, we live in all but complete breakdown of our religious-moral life. And therefore, we may not have time to think about how to hold back ourselves and other infirm Christian brothers

---

[3] For histories of the Grebenshchikovskaia Obshchina, see I. N. Zavoloko, *Staroobriadtsy g. Rigi* (Riga: Izdanie Rizhskogo Kruzkhka Revnitelei Stariny pri O-ve "Grebenshchikovskoe Uchilishche," 1933), Aleksij Zhilko and Eduard Mekshs, "Staroobriadchestvo v Latvii: Vchera i segodnia," *Revue des études slaves* 69: 1–2 (1997): 73–88. See also V. V. Preobrazhenskii, *Russkie v Latvii* (Riga: Izd. Kom. po ustroistvu "D.R.K.," 1933); and T. Feigmane, *Russkie obshchestva v Latvii, 1920–1940 gg.: Uchebnoe posobie* (Riga: Latviiskii universitet, 1992). B. Infant'ev, *Russkie v Latvii: Istoriia i sovremennost'* (Riga: Lad, 1992) has a good bibliography. More general studies of ethnicity and religion in Latvia can be found in the all-Baltic number of *Religion, State, and Society* 27: 2 (1999). See also Pål Kolstø et al., *Nation Building and Ethnic Integration in Post-Soviet Societies* (Boulder, CO: Westview Press, 2000).

[4] "Protokol 1-go dukhovnogo s"ezda staroobriadcheskikh nastavnikov i nachetchikov Latvii ot 21 marta 1922 goda," *Staroobriadcheskii kalendar' na 1927 god* (Riga: Sovet Rizhskoi Grebenshchikovskoi Staroobriadcheskoi Obshchiny, 1927), 68.

from this deathly abyss, on the edge of which we stand."[5] Similarly, I. N. Zavoloko (editor of the Riga Old Believer journal *Rodnaia starina*) wrote that "contemporary humanity presents an extremely sad picture. The world is enveloped with satanic authority, destroying the religious-moral foundations of government and personal life."[6]

Enjoying the freedom afforded in independent Latvia after 1917, the Old Believers continued to develop the educational and philanthropic enterprises that had long augmented its liturgical life. The leadership of the RGSO consistently sought to publicize legal and political issues that related to the Old Believers. The *Staroobriadcheskii kalendar' na 1927 god*, for example, published information on registration of communities with the Latvian government.[7] Relations between the national Latvian government and the Old Believers culminated in a 1934 law on Old Believers.[8] For their part, the Old Believers seemed intent on being good Latvian citizens. To this end, the *Staroobriadcheskii kalendar' na 1940 god*, for example, listed President Karlic Ulmanis's cabinet ministries, addresses of main government buildings in Riga, and the most significant state holidays as set out by Latvian laws of 1920, 1921, and 1934.[9] What's more, the *Kalendar'* even noted Lutheran and Catholic holidays in Latvian (rather than Russian): "Lielā Lūdzamā Diena—den pokaiania liuteran (prepistuplennyi den')."[10]

The Old Believers in Latvia, however, did separate themselves from Latvian society in some important ways—few learned to speak fluent Latvian and all education was conducted in Russian (with Old Believers being the majority of Russians in Riga until the Soviet period). Likewise, Old Believers

---

[5] "Doklad" (n.p., n.d.), archive of the RGSO, Nastavnik Vlasov file.

[6] "Bratie-khristiane!" *Rodnaia starina*, no. 1 (24 October/6 November 1927), reprinted in *Rodnaia starina: Sbornik, posviashchennyi voprosam religiozno-nravstvennogo i natsional'-nogo prosveshcheniia* (Moscow: Izdatel'skii Dom Tretii Rim, 1997), 2. For an essay on Zavoloko's accomplishments, see Roy R. Robson, "Between Scholarship and Piety: I. N. Zavoloko and the Promise of the Old Belief," *Modern Greek Studies Yearbook* 18/19 (2002–03): 95–104.

[7] "Zakon o registratsii aktov grazhdanskogo sostoianiia," *Staroobriadcheskii kalendar' na 1927 god*, 81–88. Registration of Old Believer communities with secular authorities had been a divisive issue in Russia before the 1917 revolutions. By 1927, however, there seemed to be little division regarding the matter among Latvian Old Believers. For the situation from 1905–17, see Roy R. Robson, *Old Believers in Modern Russia* (DeKalb: Northern Illinois University Press, 1995).

[8] A recent paper by T. Feigmane, "Staroobriadchestvo: Opyt politicheskoi integratsii v gody pervoi respubliki," will be published in an upcoming *Staroobriadcheskii tserkovnyi kalendar'*.

[9] *Staroobriadcheskii kalendar' na 1940 god* (Riga: Sovet Rizhskoi Grebenshchikovskoi Staroobriadcheskoi Obshchiny, 1940), 4 ff.

[10] Ibid., 13. *Staroobriadcheskii kalendar' na 1927 god*, 68.

tended to live in the region surrounding the Grebenshchikovskaia compound, especially the aged and infirm, who found homes in the large poor-houses run by the community for needy Old Believers. In all, however, the history of Riga Old Believers during the early 20th century was notable for its successes—a large number of faithful, significant real estate holdings, active cultural and social organizations, and substantial philanthropy.[11]

Grebenshchikovskaia and the Soviet State

Like all religious institutions, however, Grebenshchikovskaia suffered during the years of World War II. When the USSR annexed Latvia in 1940, it nationalized the community's churches and other buildings, persecuted believers, and even exiled many to the northern forests and Siberian camps. (The most notable of those arrested was I. N. Zavoloko, who spent some 16 years in the Gulag.) Even the charitable poor house run by the Old Believers was "liquidated" in 1941 and given to the city, though apparently Old Believers continued to live in the establishment.[12] The situation worsened during the German occupation of Latvia, when Grebenshchikovskaia's large poor house was taken over and "the most feeble were violently evacuated to various places in the provinces, freeing the premises for so-called refugee Germans."[13] The Germans likewise raided the Grebenshchikovskaia buildings, taking glass from the windows for use in other locations.[14] The community sat next to the Jewish ghetto and suffered from that proximity too—Old Believers regularly had their houses taken by Nazi authorities.

Suffering—during both the Soviet and Nazi periods—encapsulates the most widely disseminated view of Old Believer history in the Soviet period. Aleksij Zhilko and Eduard Mekshs claim that "Repression gained steam in Latvia and many Old Ritualists performed their Way of the Cross in Siberia. All property of the Old Ritualist Church was nationalized, temples were neglected and their upkeep was barely supported."[15] The archival record, however, shows a more complex relationship between Old Believers and the state than Zhilko and Mekshs portray. There was no public anti-Soviet sentiment by the Old Believers, perhaps because its most vocal anti-communist, N. I. Zavoloko, was still in the Gulag. In fact, after the war the

---

[11] An introduction to this period through the lens of education reform can be found in Roy R. Robson, "Old Believer Education and Identity in Early Twentieth-Century Latvia," in *Culture and Identity in Eastern Christian History: Papers of the First Biennial Conference of the Association for the Study of Eastern Christian History and Culture*, vol. 7 *Ohio Slavic Studies*, ed. Russell Martin and Jennifer Spock (Columbus: The Ohio State University), forthcoming 2007.

[12] Latvias Valsts Arkhiv (LVA) f. 1448, op. 1., d. 47, fol. 58.

[13] LVA f. 1448, op. 1, d. 85, fol. 7.

[14] Ibid., fol. 26.

[15] Zhilko and Mekshs, "Staroobriadchestvo v Latvii," 83–84.

Grebenshchikovskaia community began to rebuild its premises and revive its institutions.[16] In 1945–46, the community asked the state for support in reconstruction of the charitable house on its grounds,[17] material aid "at the state's pleasure" for restoration of the Old Believer cemetery,[18] telephone service to aid in its care for the indigent,[19] and a state loan for the redevelopment of the economy after the war.[20]

Though it did not receive all of its demands (the request for telephone service, for example, was marked "not returned"), the community developed a pattern of favorable relations with communist authorities. In fact, Old Believer leaders across Latvia were considered far less of a threat to Soviet power than the pastorate of Catholic, Lutheran, or Evangelical faiths. In a secret file created shortly after the war by the Ministry of Religious Affairs of the Latvian SSR, some 24 of 33 Lutheran pastors, 39 of 48 Catholic priests, and 5 of 14 Evangelical Baptist ministers were marked for their anti-governmental activities. Only 3 of 22 Old Believer *nastavniki*, however, were listed as suspect of such activities, none of whom were then serving in Riga.[21]

Warming relations between the Grebenshchikovskaia community and the Soviet state began to pay off significantly for the Old Believers in 1946. On 15 February, the government took a dramatic step in proclaiming that "all real estate at Krasta ulitsa No. 73, city of Riga, is denationalized and returned to the Riga [Old Believer] community. All real estate situated in the city of Riga at Krasta ul. 73, is naturalized and returned to the Riga Grebenshchikovskaia Old Believer Community." This included the 722 square-meter church, poorhouse dormitories, and extensive offices, chapels, kitchens, and out-buildings in the walled enclosure at that address.[22] From that point onward, Grebenshchikovskaia was able to restore many of its traditional activities—by 1947,

---

[16] The *ustav* of Grebenshchikovskaia described the formal structure of Old Believer communities in Latvia: A council (*sovet*) of all Latvian Old Believers was headed by a president and met regularly in a conference; under the council was a spiritual court (*dukhovnyi sud*); next came the council (*sovet*) of each local community, including the *nastavniki* and other members. Under Soviet law, each community had to have a group of 20 lay members who acted as the legal guardians of the parish. See LVA f. 1448, op. 1, d. 88, fols. 13–24. On 8 February 1947, for example, Latvian Old Believers asked permission to convene both the council and spiritual court of a "religious-church and canonical character" for religious discipline. LVA f. 1448, op. 1, d. 46, fol. 28.

[17] Ibid., fol. 6

[18] Ibid., fol. 2.

[19] Ibid., fol. 3.

[20] Ibid., fol. 28.

[21] LVA f. 1448, op. 1, d. 36.

[22] LVA f. 1448, op. 1, d. 85, fol. 4; and LVA f. 1448, op. 1, d. 46, fol. 15. Though other communities may have had their churches denationalized, I could not find any such documentation.

some 91 people were registered to live at 73 Krasta ulitsa.[23] Moreover, the community leadership gained substantial power over its own activities by holding legal right to its property.

For their part, the Old Believers offered signs of becoming integrated into the new political system. A subtle indication came in late 1946, when the editors of *Sovetskaia Latviia* received a letter from the community boasting of its important book collection and correcting mistakes written about the community by the magazine in an earlier issue.[24] By July 1947, the Ministry of Religious Affairs claimed that all Latvian Old Believer communities had been successfully registered with the authorities.[25] Likewise, the Ministry had registered *nastavniki* across Latvia and regularly gave them *propiski* for travel among Old Believer communities in Latvia and Lithuania.

Perhaps the most significant nexus between state and church came, however, in public prayers for Soviet power. The question of praying for the secular leadership had a long and tortured history among Old Believers. Indeed, one of the most significant splits among the priestless concords occurred in the 18th century over prayers for the tsar, who had, in the minds of many Old Believers, become tainted with the power of Antichrist. Over the next hundred years, the Riga community slowly moved away from the Fedoseevtsy, their original concord, toward the Pomortsy tradition, which stressed the availability of canonical marriage and propriety of prayers for secular power. In short, the Pomortsy were the most likely Old Believers to "give Caesar his due" through prayers for the tsar. Additionally, the longstanding tradition of cooperation with secular authority (both Imperial and Latvian) had set over a century of precedent.

When the Soviet Union was victorious over Nazi Germany, perhaps it was natural for the Old Believers to pray for the well-being of that government. On 7 November 1946, the Grebenshchikovskaia community sent a telegram to the Minister of Religious Affairs, offering congratulations for "the joyful day of 29 years of the October Socialist Revolution," noting that it had held a prayer service in remembrance of the date.[26] This telegram was to be a template for similar greetings for the next 40 years.

Although Old Believers tended to take their cues from Riga, the first Baltic Old Believers to formalize their position on Soviet power were Lithuanian. Riga's Old Believer leadership, however, signaled its approval of the Lithuanian decision by publishing its decision in the 1949 calendar.

---

[23] LVA f. 1448, op. 1, d. 47, fols. 199–201.

[24] Ibid., fol. 62.

[25] Ibid., fol. 68. Though such a claim cannot be verified (since there may have been secret, unregistered groups), it does point to the ease with which Old Believers outwardly conformed to Soviet norms.

[26] Ibid., fol. 63. Similarly, the community sent the Minister of Religious Affairs a New Year's telegram every year, using the same language from year to year.

In 1948, the spiritual court of the Lithuanian Old Believers had heard a lecture—delivered by its president—entitled "On the Attitude of the Old-Orthodox Old Ritualist Church toward the Supreme Soviet Power."[27] In it, *nastavnik* F. S. Kuznetsov outlined the reasons for accepting and praying for secular power. Basing his comments on the New Testament, Kuznetsov notably refrained from mentioning the special problem of praying for an avowedly atheist power. The Lithuanian Old Believers also "declared and recognized Soviet power as divinely established." On "days of state holidays, in old ritualist prayer temples, prayers should be fulfilled for Soviet power. We pray canons to the savior or to the cross."[28] Most specifically, the Lithuanian group published slightly reworded versions of well-known *tropari*.

1. Lord save Thy people and bless thine inheritance, granting Russian power and its army (*voinstvo*) victory over its enemies and preserve the people by Thy cross.
2. You are the creator of all creatures and every earthly power lies in your realm and favor. Bless always the Russian power, keeping her government, army, cities, and all your people in peace and prosperity, according to your great mercy.[29]

In 1949, the Grebenshchikovskaia community proclaimed its own position regarding Soviet power. A meeting of the community's *sovet* took up the following issues:

1. A short historical path of the Old Believer church;
2. On the freedom of the Old Believer churches under Soviet rule;
3. The consolidation of the Stalin Constitution law on the freedom to take part in religious rites;
4. The situation of life of the Old Believer church in present times; freedom to fulfill divine services in the church; freedom of entrance to all believers to the temple.[30]

The ritual messages offered by these pronouncements were complex. On the one hand, Old Believers clearly realized a necessity to recognize Soviet authority. On the other hand, their prayers commemorated *Russian* rule in the Baltics, which had long precedent in the region. In addition, the acceptance of "Soviet power as divinely established" was less than a ringing endorsement—

---

[27] "Ob otnoshenii drevle-pravoslavnoi staroobriadcheskoi tserkvi k verkhovnoi sovetskoi vlasti," *Staroobriadcheskii tserkovnyi kalendar' na 1949 god* (Riga: Sovet Rizhskoi Grebenshchikovskoi Staroobriadcheskoi Obshchiny, 1949): 77–78.

[28] Ibid., 78.

[29] Ibid.

[30] LVA f. 1448, op. 1, d. 46, fols. 51–56.

the language of the prayers made it clear that *all* secular authority derived ultimately from God, whether it be pleasing to Him or not. Finally, the Pomortsy believed that all society had been tainted by the powers of Antichrist. If it had been possible to pray for the tsar (who had persecuted Old Believers), then it was conceivable to pray for the Soviet Union (which had, after all, liberated Latvia from the Nazis).[31]

The community itself was willing to play on its patriotism as necessary. In 1954, for example, Grebenshchikovskaia petitioned to open a seminary. The appeal noted the Old Believers' activity in peace efforts and their role in the Great Patriotic War. Pulling out all stops, the petition claimed that "The Old Believer church is dedicated to Soviet power just as is the Orthodox Church, and the *nastavniki* and the believers of the Old Believer church, being led by the Old Believer Soviet in the Latvian SSR, strongly love our homeland—the Soviet Union—our government, and its army and always pray that God will be with our fortunate *Rodina*, blessing the government...."[32] In other words, the Old Believers deserved the same educational institutions as the Russian Orthodox Church, not because of their religion but rather because of their equivalent service to the Soviet army and patriotic fervor.

A "Struggle for Power"[33] in the Riga Community

There were those who actively courted the Soviet system rather than passively accepting it. Father I. U. Vakon'ia, the self-styled "progressive"[34] rector of the Grebenshchikovskaia community, developed a long-standing and (apparently) cordial relationship with the ministers of religious affairs in the Latvian SSR.[35] Much of the archival material for the present study comes from

---

[31] There may have been organized opposition to prayers for the Soviet state. One archival file notes the development of a new Old Believer concord with views similar to the Filipovtsy, which had broken from the Pomortsy on the issue of prayers for the tsar. It seems more likely from the scant evidence, though, that the Old Believers in question were revisiting the problem of priestless marriage rather than prayers for secular rule. See LVA f. 1448, op. 1, d. 90, fols. 3–6.

[32] LVA f. 1448, op. 1, d. 92, fols. 24–25. For a description of this tactic used among Orthodox parishes, see Peris, "'God is Now on Our Side,'" 106 ff.

[33] In a report marked "secret" by the Ministry of Religious Affairs, a member of the community claimed that the differences between conservatives and progressives was mostly a "struggle for power" in the community. LVA f. 1448, op. 1, d. 91, fol. 80.

[34] The terms "progressive" and "conservative" were used by the Old Believers themselves. LVA f. 1448, op. 1, d. 92, fols. 60–61.

[35] On at least one occasion, being a progressive *nastavnik* paid off for Vakon'ia. In 1954, at the height of his struggle with opposition *nastavniki*, Vakon'ia's daughter applied to work at an institute for experimental medicine. Before accepting her as a student, the director pointedly inquired whether or not Vakon'ia was one of the "progressive servitors" of his cult. Vakon'ia furnished the requisite biography—including his work with the patriarch's peace initiatives of the mid-1950s. LVA f. 1448, op. 1, d. 92, fol. 60–60ob.

his copious and frequent reports to the ministry. During his tenure as rector, Vakon'ia sent letters as frequently as every day or two, though most reports arrived less regularly. Vakon'ia did not shrink from describing conflicts or other "trifles" in everyday administration.[36] Moreover, he claimed to view the long-serving Minister of Religious Affairs Juri Frantsevich Rostbert as "our person."[37]

Aligned against Vakon'ia and the other progressives were the conservative *nastavniki*, led by P. F. Fadeev and A. V. Volkov. These men were elder leaders (Fadeev had served as rector), particularly popular among the women of the community. In the community's complex of buildings, each *nastavnik* had his own "cell" that served as a meeting place, chapel, and physical symbol of his authority. These *nastavniki*—along with the choir director and financial manager—constituted the core of power in the community. The main struggle for control of the Grebenshchikovskaia Obshchina occurred within this small circle.

From about 1951 onward, the conservative and progressive factions argued about financial matters and bickered over wording of a congratulatory telegram to Stalin, but they did not fight openly.[38] In 1952, however, the conservatives lost the majority on "the twenty," which legally represented the community and served as a quasi-vestry board. In response, Fr. Fadeev led a faction claiming that the new board included people somehow incapable of serving the community. Fadeev's group, according to Vakon'ia's account, then tried to create a new board of 20 of their own choosing. The council voted 7-1 to discipline Fadeev for trying to wrest power for himself and for seeking personal gain rather than spiritual profit. As a protest, Fadeev began to gather up icons to take away from the church. His supporters created such a ruckus that the September 1953 meeting had to be closed down for lack of order. A second vote of the council against Fadeev's "terror," however, passed 8-0.[39] Vakon'ia had, he believed, thwarted a "putsch attempt."[40]

With Fr. Fadeev chastised, Fr. A. V. Volkov took up leadership of the conservative cause. Volkov had been born in Belorussia, had lost two sons in

---

[36] In a note sounding a little falsely modest, Vakon'ia apologized for "poorly informing" the government of the community's affairs, but hoped that he was right to include even the "trifles." LVA f. 1448, op. 1, d. 93, fol. 22.

[37] LVA f. 1448, op. 1, d. 90, fol. 3.

[38] For the financial disagreements, see LVA f. 1448, op. 1, d. 90, fol. 9. For the description of the telegram to Stalin, see LVA f. 1448, op. 1, d. 90, fol. 61: Vakon'ia reported that "Ekimov sent a telegram to Stalin in the name of all Old Believer communities. In the text he wished [Stalin] health and many years and emphasizes the word 'peace.' We read it and no one said anything, but I said 'not bad.'" Fadeev grumbled only, "it's late!"

[39] LVA f. 1448, op. 1, d. 91, fol. 79–79ob.

[40] LVA f. 1448, op. 1, d. 92, fol. 56.

World War II, and had served as a *nastavnik* since 1943. He was one of the few
Old Believer leaders to appear on the 1948 secret list of religious leaders involved in "anti-governmental activity." After the Fadeev affair, Volkov
"coarsely" opposed the progressives. Vakon'ia wrote that

> Volkov groups around himself all of the conservative elements.
> Rusak is now no longer afraid. He says: we now know that [Soviet]
> leadership does not get into our internal affairs, we are the complete
> masters.... O!!! They are friends in conservatism and in the struggle
> against progress. But Volkov wants ... to put together their block,
> with himself at the head.[41]

This was the first written indication that the struggle between conservatives
and progressives was related to Soviet authority. Vakon'ia went so far as to
call one of his opponents an "anarchist." Volkov, however, remained the central problem—he was "openly an enemy of Soviet power"—and the rest were
"held around him, as around a centrifugal power."[42]

The two groups used Old Believer traditions and rituals as weapons in
their dispute. On one occasion, Vakon'ia squabbled with *nastavnik* K. I. Voldaenko about a ritual ban placed on a church member and his family, who were
prohibited from singing in the choir. Vakon'ia supported the disciplinary action but Voldaenko did not, asking "From where came this smart-alec dictator? It's a shame that we [had been without] this smart-alec, that up to now
we didn't have such a smartie."[43]

In another situation, the conservatives fought to have the community
make its own candles, rather than buying them from the priestly Old Believer
archdiocese in Moscow. Candles could be produced more cheaply in Riga
than in Moscow, they argued, and would also be more ritually pure if made
at the community. Vakon'ia, however, preferred to buy candles from Moscow, apparently not wanting to make waves in Moscow or with the Ministry
of Religious Affairs. This was no small matter: Grebenshchikovskaia bought
some 33,000 candles in March, 1954 but thereafter received permission to buy
paraffin and beeswax directly to make candles at their own workshop.[44]
Moreover, the purity of ritual sacrifices was important to Old Believers.
Making their own candles proclaimed their spiritual purity in contrast to their
priestly counterparts in Moscow.

---

[41] Ibid., fol. 2.

[42] Ibid.

[43] Ibid., fol. 9.

[44] Ibid., fol. 19. Candle-making and sales were among the most lucrative sources of in-
come for parishes in the post-war USSR. For more on the subject, see Edward Roslof,
"A. A. Trushin: Communist Over-Procurator for Moscow, 1943–1984," *Modern Greek
Studies Yearbook* 18/19 (2002–03): 115–16.

The Fadeev affair was also fought in the ritual sphere. During Paschal celebrations in 1954, Fr. Fadeev met in a conference with a number of parishioners. Vakon'ia believed that Fadeev had organized a meeting—probably with liturgical services—in his own cell as an alternative to those in the main church. Fadeev signed a letter claiming that he had simply received parishioners in his cell who had come to inquire about his health. Volkov concurred, noting that it was correct to close the cell door in such situations. Unable to decide if Fadeev had acted inappropriately, the council instructed him not to have meetings there in the future.[45]

This did not fix the problem. Instead, a member of the board of twenty (Anastasia Alekseevna Kliment'ev-Eremeeva) decided to hold a collective intercessory service (*sbornyi moleben*) to St. Nicholas in honor of Fr. Fadeev. Kliment'ev-Eremeeva sought donations for Fr. Fadeev in the market and in factories.[46] Fr. Vakon'ia was so incensed—this was the most public ritual act of disobedience to his progressive leadership—that he quickly reported it to the Ministry of Religious Affairs by phone instead of his regular written report.

Having made his report, Vakon'ia confronted Fadeev in the latter's cell. On 24 June, the council voted 6-3 *not* to end sanctions against Fadeev (there were five pro-Vakon'ia, one neutral, and three pro-Fadeev). And yet, in rebellion, some 68 women gathered in Fadeev's cell, offering a *sbornyi moleben* "for his salvation and against his enemies," an obvious rebuff to the progressive leaders. Fr. Fadeev was flanked in his cell by another *nastavnik*, Fr. Gusev. They, in turn, had a large group of women standing around them, ready to defend their leaders. When the council of the Old Believer community tried to meet, the women allowed only Fadeev to speak, "as if he were the rector" rather than Vakon'ia. When Fr. L. A. Rys', a ranking member of the council, tried to disagree with Fadeev, the women began

> shouting (as if on command), absolutely not letting the member of the council and rector of the audit committee, L. A. Rys', speak, drowning out his shouting…. This is how the women were shouting: "These are not our affairs. If [Fadeev] drinks, [he'll] answer for it." Another assented, "It is no trouble that the drinker goes home to drink in the

---

[45] LVA f. 1448, op. 1, d. 92, fol. 43.

[46] There was precedent for this liturgical service. One Fevron'ia Iudovna Egorova (another member of the board of twenty) reminded Vakon'ia that when the chorister E. E. Timofeev was sent to prison, the community had sung a *moleben* that God might free Timofeev through an amnesty (ibid., 42). Old Believer custom made it clear that the service might be sung for any number of reasons: "Each Christian worshipper celebrates the *moleben* according to his own will and the election of prayers to be decided are subject to his own diligence and will." *Staroobriadcheskii kalendar' na 1931 god* (Riga: Sovet Rizhskoi Grebenshchikovskoi Staroobriadcheskoi Obshchiny, 1931), 90.

evening." A tall brunette named Obchinnikova shouted with them that "If one nastavnik is a drinker, then the other is a fraud."[47]

The committee had to stop its meeting, since no business could be conducted through the shouting back and forth.

The conflict between Vakon'ia and the progressives (on one side) and Fadeev, Volkov, and the conservatives (on the other) continued through the 1950s without resolution. While the community's public face paid homage to Soviet rhetoric (in the peace movement, for example),[48] the struggle for conservative versus progressive agendas never died out completely. To a large extent, this was a function of a community of believers existing inside a communist state. But in other ways, the differences of opinion at Grebenshchikovskaia Obshchina mirrored issues that had bedeviled Old Believer communities throughout their history — the role of the state in their affairs, the correct relationship between believers and outsiders, and the use of religious rituals to settle ideological differences.

The progressives, led by Valkon'ia, argued for integration into the political and social life of the USSR. In general, they tended to accept Soviet power as a *fait accompli* and wished to make the community prosper within the constraints created by the Soviet system. Neither did the conservatives openly want to disown Soviet power. Rather, they hoped to ignore it — continuing to live as traditionally as possible — unless they saw some advantage to using the system. Fr. Fadeev, for example, wrote one formal report to the Ministry of Religious Affairs, complaining that Fr. Vakon'ia had been falsifying the minutes of committee meetings. He did not know, apparently, that Vakon'ia had been sending far more detailed reports than the minutes to the Ministry.[49] Fadeev also traveled to peace conferences, though he seemed to have little interest in them, in contrast to Vakon'ia's enthusiasm.

More broadly, the period 1945–55 illustrated how Riga's largest Old Believer community struggled with new political situations. To the outside world, the RGSO continued its long tradition of acquiescence to secular authority, whether that be Imperial, Latvian, or Soviet. Pomortsy tradition (which had been generally accepted in Latvia by the 20th century) walked the line between liturgical recognition of secular power and ritual condemnation

---

[47] This scene is recounted in LVA f. 1448, op. 1, d. 92, fols. 56–58.

[48] On occasion, the RGSO leadership loudly echoed the rhetoric originating in Moscow. In a Paschal statement for 1952, the high council of Old Believers called for "peace in the world," spoke out against alleged "bacteriological warfare" in Korea and worried about the bloodletting "every day," not just "in Korea, but also in Mali, Vietnam, and Greece. This new idol-worshipping American-Anglo imperialism and its idol — gold — leads to death and the grief of mankind." LVA f. 1448, op. 1, d. 90, fol. 26.

[49] Ibid., fol. 55.

of the antichristian world. Following this strategy seemed to work for the Grebenshchikovskaia Obshchina.

Internally, however, the struggles for leadership in the community were linked directly to the problem of Soviet authority. The rector actively participated in the communist power structure—not least as an informant. In this way he hoped to bring the Grebenshchikovskaia community into line with the state-dominated Russian Orthodox Church. His motives were unclear— personal fame and heightened profile for the community probably played a role. The conservative leaders of the community, on the other hand, were willing to use the traditional means at their disposal—especially in the ritual and liturgical spheres—to undermine the authority of their progressive counterparts and to diminish the influence of Soviet authority.

In the end, neither camp won a decisive victory. Vakon'ia helped to set the RGSO on a path of engagement with the Soviet government, which continued throughout the Krushchev period of religious repression and well into the 1970s–80s. The *nastavnik*'s desire to make the RGSO a model of progressive religion, however, never materialized. Old Believers prized both tradition and ritual purity so highly that the Riga community remained at least partially set apart and suspect of Soviet authority for the next generation.

Rude & Barbarous Kingdom

The Richest Place in the World: An Early 17th-Century English Description and Military Assessment of Solovetskii Monastery

Chester S. L. Dunning

In The British National Archives at Kew is a curious, undated and unsigned document containing a unique and valuable description and military assessment of "the richest place this daie in the worlde," the fortress-like Solovetskii (or Solovki) Monastery of the Transfiguration located in Russia's far north on a small group of islands in the White Sea.[1] The document, written in English and dating from the early 17th century, has been known to scholars for about 100 years; it has been published twice and continues to be mined as a useful source by historians interested in Solovki and in Russian military and diplomatic history. For example, in 1999 Jennifer Spock completed a fine dissertation about the Solovetskii Monastery in which she made extensive use of the Solovki document and ably demonstrated the remarkable accuracy of much of its unique information.[2] Nevertheless, in spite of the attention the Solovki document has so far received, there is still no accurate transcription of the original text in print. Nor has anyone attempted to date the document precisely, identify its author, or carefully examine the context in which it was written. Furthermore, several errors have crept into scholarship as a result of flawed efforts to use the document as a historical source. This essay, dedicated to my friend and mentor Bob Crummey, will attempt to correct these problems.

Professor Vasilii N. Aleksandrenko was the first scholar to study the Solovki document, and his transcription of it was published in 1911.[3] But Aleksandrenko made a serious mistake at the outset that has greatly complicated use of the document ever since. He rashly concluded that a pencil inscription ("Russia Eliz.")[4] written on the back of an otherwise blank sheet of paper which served as the document's cover proved that the description of

[1] The National Archives of the United Kingdom: Public Record Office, State Papers Foreign [hereafter cited as S.P.] 91 [Russia], pt. 1, fol. 250–250v.

[2] Jennifer Baylee Spock, "The Solovki Monastery 1460–1645: Piety and Patronage in the Early Modern Russian North" (Ph.D. diss., Yale University, 1999). See esp. 37, 49, 106, and 156.

[3] V. N. Aleksandrenko, ed., "Zapiska neizvestnago avtora o Solovetskom monastyre," *Starina i novizna* 14 (1911): 193–95.

[4] S.P. 91, pt. 1, fol. 251v.

Rude & Barbarous Kingdom Revisited: Essays in Russian History and Culture in Honor of Robert O. Crummey. Chester S. L. Dunning, Russell E. Martin, and Daniel Rowland, eds. Bloomington, IN: Slavica Publishers, 2008, 309–25.

Solovetskii monastery dated from the reign of Elizabeth I (r. 1558–1603).[5] That led some historians to erroneously conclude that Queen Elizabeth had pursued cordial relations with the tsars while simultaneously plotting to plunder north Russia. In fact, the incorrect pencil notation was written by a naïve archivist sometime after the document was added to the Conway Papers but before the renowned family's archive was donated to the British government in 1857.[6] Internal evidence makes it clear that the Solovki document dates from the reign of James I (r. 1603–25) and that it was connected to the king's half-baked plan to intervene in Russia's Time of Troubles (1598–1613).[7] But as 20th-century scholars explored King James's pipedream of empire in northern Russia, they generally ignored the Solovki document because of Aleksandrov's conclusion that it dated from no later than 1603.[8] To their credit, a few historians suspected that there was a connection between the Solovki document and the English plan for intervention in Russia, but they were hesitant to say any more than that and failed to examine the document carefully.[9]

Another serious problem facing scholars making use of Aleksandrenko's transcription of the Solovki document was the poor job he did deciphering early modern English handwriting.[10] In preparing the document for publication, Aleksandrenko made many mistakes. For example, he wrote "guestes"

---

[5] Aleksandrenko, "Zapiska," 193n.

[6] British government archivists who inventoried the Conway Papers and distributed them (by 1858) to their proper new locations ignored the pencil notation "Eliz." on S.P. 91, pt. 1, fol. 251v, and placed the Solovki document among official state papers from the reign of James I.

[7] On the aborted English plan to annex Arkhangel'sk and other parts of northern Russia, see "Proekt vziatiia Moskovskago gosudarstva pod pokrovitel'stvo Anglii, predlozhennyi angliiskim rezidentom Dzhonom Merikom," *Chteniia v obshchestve istorii i drevnosti rossiiskikh pri Moskovskom universitete* (1874), bk. 3, sec. 4, pt. 1, 75–83; I. Liubimenko, "Angliiskii proekt 1612 goda o podchinenii russkogo severa protektoratu korolia Iakova I," *Nauchnyi istoricheskii zhurnal* 2: 5 (1914): 1–16; idem, "A Project for the Acquisition of Russia by James I," *The English Historical Review* 29 (1914): 246–56; V. Virginskii, "Proekty prevrashcheniia Severovostochnoi Rossii v angliiskuiu koloniiu v XVII veke," *Istoricheskii zhurnal*, no. 11 (November 1940): 91–95; Chester Dunning, "James I, the Russia Company, and the Plan to Establish a Protectorate over North Russia," *Albion* 21: 2 (1989): 206–26.

[8] See, for example, G. G. Frumenkov, *Solovetskii monastyr' i oborona Belomor'ia v XVI – XVII vv.* (Arkhangel'sk: Severo-Zapadnoe knizhnoe izdatel'stvo, 1975), 49.

[9] Inna Lubimenko, *Les relations commerciales et politiques de l'Angleterre avec la Russie avant Pierre le Grand* (Paris: Honoré Champion, 1933), 141; Virginskii, "Proekty," 94; A. N. Nasonov, ed., *Ocherki istorii SSSR: Period feodalizma. Konets XV v. – nachalo XVII v.* (Moscow: Akademiia nauk SSSR, 1955), 588; Dunning, "James I," 222.

[10] On this problem with Aleksandrenko's scholarship, see Chester Dunning, "A Remarkable English Source concerning Ivan Bolotnikov and the Rebel Siege of Moscow in 1606," *Forschungen zur osteuropäischen Geschichte* 58 (2001): 265.

for "guiftes" (gifts); "grieft" for "guift" (gift); "wishes" for "riches"; "Loghs-mille" for "Loghswilly" (Lough Swilly); "loard house" for "Ward howse" (Wardhouse or Vardøhus). Aleksandrenko also inadvertently left out several words, resulting in garbled sentences; and he omitted one entire line ("…be to paie for it, then in England. They maie have bere their lykwyse for readie mony…"), rendering the surrounding text unintelligible. Scholars using Aleksandrenko's version of the Solovki document perpetuated his errors and not infrequently failed to comprehend some of the document's unique information. Without doubt, the most seriously misunderstood passage in the Solovki document is this one:

> This Abbaie hath also contineuall guiftes from all ptes of that Empire from everie riche man at his deathe for the obtayning of theise Commendatorie Billetes to their Sainct, everie on being confident, according to the measure of his guift to this howse to receave his preferrment in heaven.

In transcribing the passage, Aleksandrenko wrote the wrong word "guestes" for "guiftes" (gifts) and the wrong word "grieft" for "guift" (gift). The result is not just inaccurate; it completely distorts the meaning of the original text and has confused historians using Aleksnadrenko's transcription.[11] No steady stream of guests went to Solovetskii Monastery, and no measure of their grief was assessed by the monks. Instead, as Jennifer Spock has demonstrated, gifts large and small poured into the monastery almost nonstop, and—if we are to believe the Solovki document—the value of a donor's gift may have affected his or her chances of getting into heaven.

In 2004, Roy Robson published a very interesting book, *Solovki: The Story of Russia Told Through Its Most Remarkable Islands*, in which he provided a new transcription of the Solovki document and placed it in its correct context, James I's plan to intervene in northern Russia. Nevertheless, Robson underestimated the king's enthusiasm for the plan and mistakenly declared that the main reason for English interest in Solovki was because the islands threatened the plan for intervention "since they could be used as a stronghold from which to harass English vessels in the White Sea."[12] I have argued elsewhere against recent scholarship attempting to cast doubt on James's active and continuing interest in the protectorate scheme,[13] and it is clear that English interest in Solovki had more to do with its reputation as the richest place in

---

[11] See, for example, Aleksandrenko, "Zapiska," 193n; Spock, "The Solovki Monastery," 156.

[12] Roy R. Robson, *Solovki: The Story of Russia Told Through Its Most Memorable Islands* (New Haven: Yale University Press, 2004), 63–67.

[13] Chester Dunning, "A 'Singular Affection' for Russia: Why King James Offered to Intervene in the Time of Troubles," *Russian History* 34, nos. 1–4 (2007): 277–302.

the world. Close examination of the evidence reveals that James was extremely enthusiastic about the possibility of intervening in north Russia and may have continued to pursue the project even after learning of Mikhail Romanov's election as tsar.[14] A more significant problem with Robson's work is that his transcription of the Solovki document is less reliable than Aleksandrenko's and contains many errors.[15] Thus, there is still a need for an accurate transcription of the Solovki document and a careful evaluation of the context in which it was written.

Solovetskii Monastery, founded in 1429 by the monks Savvatii and Zosima, occupies a strategic location near the mouths of several important rivers. Solovki grew rapidly into an important regional spiritual, economic, and administrative center, but the monastery's reputation and wealth rose meteorically during the reign of Ivan the Terrible (1547–84). In 1547, Metropolitan Makarii crowned Tsar Ivan IV and presided over the blessing of Savvatii and Zosima as miracle workers, which added immeasurably to Solovki's prestige and fame. From the beginning of his reign, Tsar Ivan proved to be an enthusiastic supporter of the monastery, lavishing money, land, and lucrative privileges on it. According to Jennifer Spock, Ivan became Solovetskii Monastery's "greatest patron."[16] Many large gifts also flowed to Solovki from the tsar's wealthy courtiers, and Ivan's immediate successors continued his extraordinary generosity.[17] By the late 16th century Solovki was renowned as one of the wealthiest monasteries in Russia.[18] As its status, power and

---

[14] Chester Dunning, "A Letter to James I concerning the English Plan for Military Intervention in Russia," *The Slavonic and East European Review* 67: 1 (1989): 94–108.

[15] Using both Aleksandrenko's transcription and the original document, Robson (*Solovki*, 65–66, 270n19) wrongly wrote "guestes" for "guiftes" (gifts); "grieft" for "guift" (gift); "mats" for "majesty"; "theme" for "thence"; "Loghsmille" for "Loghswilly" (Lough Swilly); "loard howse" for "Ward howse" (Wardhouse or Vardøhus); "does ryse sundrie fountaines" for "do ryse from sundrie fountaines"; "migt drawe no more water those" for "must drawe no more water then those." Robson also left out several words and omitted one entire line ("…be to paie for it, then in England. They maie have bere their lykwyse for readie mony…"), rendering the surrounding text unintelligible.

[16] Dmitrii S. Likhachev, "Solovki v istorii russkoi kul'tury," in *Arkhitekturno-khudozhestvennye pamiatniki Solovetskikh ostrovov*, ed. Likhachev (Moscow: Iskusstvo, 1980), 19; Timothy Ware, *The Orthodox Church* (New York: Penguin Books, 1964), 114–17; Spock, "The Solovki Monastery," 53, 68, 71–75.

[17] William C. Brumfield, "Tradition and Innovation in the Sixteenth-Century Architecture of Solovetskii Transfiguration Monastery," *The Russian Review* 62: 3 (July 2003): 357–59; Spock, "The Solovki Monastery," 77, 88–91.

[18] *Letopisets Solovetskii na chetyre stoletiia ot osnovaniia Solovetskago monastyria do nastoiashchago vremeni, to est' s 1429 po 1847 god* (Moscow: Tip. V. Kirilov,1847), 46; *Polnoe sobranie russkikh letopisei*, 40 vols. (St. Petersburg/Leningrad and Moscow:

architectural splendor grew, so too did stories about the great wealth accumu-
lating within its walls. It was even rumored that Ivan the Terrible stored his
personal treasure chest in Solovetskii Monastery just in case the paranoid tsar
needed to make a quick getaway to England.[19] During the late 16th century,
Solovki became well known to Western merchants visiting the White Sea, and
it started appearing on maps printed as far away as Italy.[20] Not surprisingly,
the monastery's fame and legends of its wealth eventually attracted unwanted attention from Russia's western neighbors.

Solovki's security problems began during Tsar Ivan's long and unsuccessful Livonian War (1558–83). In 1571, a fleet of Swedish and Dutch ships
appeared in the White Sea and leisurely reconnoitered Solovki, which at that
time had no walls or cannon, only some small-caliber gunpowder weapons.
Although the Westerners did not land on the islands, the monastery's abbot
immediately reported the incident to the tsar, along with reports that the
Swedes were continuing their plans to seize the monastery's wealth. Tsar
Ivan was initially distracted by other problems, but the government began to
take notice of strategically located Solovki's vulnerability.[21] Throughout the
Livonian War Swedish military forces also menaced Russian towns and vil-
lages on the western and southwestern shores of the White Sea and the Kola
(Murmansk) Peninsula, eventually forcing Moscow to react.[22] Since many of
those border area settlements already owed sometimes onerous obligations to
Solovetskii Monastery, it was only logical for the tsar to put Solovki in charge
of supervising the defense of the region.[23]

Arkheograficheskiia komissiia, Nauka, and Arkheograficheskii tsentr, 1843–1995), 14:
44; Frumenkov, *Solovetskii monastyr'*, 30; Spock, "The Solovki Monastery," 106.

[19] S. Yakobson, "Early Anglo-Russian Relations (1553–1613)," *Slavonic and East European Review* 13 (1934–35): 608.

[20] See, for example, the map of "Moscoviae Imperium" drawn by Giovanni Antonio
Magini (1555–1617) and published in *Geographiae universae tum veteris, tum novae
absolutissimum opus ...* (Venice, 1596).

[21] *Istoriia pervoklassnago stavropigial'nago Solovetskago monastyria* (St. Petersburg: E.
Evdokimov, 1899) [hereafter cited as *ISM*], 55; M. I. Belov and Ia. Ia. Gakkelia, *Arti-
cheskoe moreplavanie s drevneishikh vremen do seredinu XIX veka*, vol. 1 of *Istoriia otkrytiia i
osvoeniia Severnogo morskogo puti* (Moscow: Izdatel'stvo Morskoi transport, 1956), 88–
90; Frumenkov, *Solovetskii monastyr'*, 18.

[22] Frumenkov, *Solovetskii monastyr'*, 27–28; *ISM*, 56.

[23] Brumfield, "Tradition and Innovation," 357–59; Frumenkov, *Solovetskii monastyr'*, 34;
Spock, "The Solovki Monastery," 74. See also A. M. Borisov, *Khoziaistvo Solovetskogo
monastyria i bor'ba krest'ian s severnymi monastyriami v XVI–XVII vekakh* (Petrozavodsk:
Karel'skoe knizhnoe izd-vo, 1966); A. A. Savich, *Solovetskaia votchina XV – XVII vv.
(Opyt izucheniia khoziaistva i sotsial'nykh otnoshenii na krainem russkom severe v drevnei
Rusi)* (Perm': Permskii gosudarstvennyi universitet, 1927); I. Z. Liberzon, ed., *Akty
Solovetskogo monastyria, 1479–1571* (Leningrad: Nauka, 1988); idem, *Akty Solovetskogo
monastyria, 1572–1584 gg.* (Leningrad: Nauka, 1990).

Tsar Ivan began the fortification of Solovki in 1578, ordering construction of a log wall around the monastery.[24] A contingent of 100 well-armed and supplied *strel'tsy* was also stationed there permanently, along with four cannon.[25] Starting in 1579, Solovki-based military forces periodically engaged in combat against Swedish troops maneuvering on the mainland.[26] The loss of Narva to the Swedes in 1581 forced Moscow to pay even more attention to protecting its now vital White Sea trade route and Solovki. With north Russia under almost constant pressure from Sweden during the final years of the Livonian War and during the reign of Tsar Fedor (r. 1584–98), Russia's central government eventually invested heavily in Solovki's fortifications. Tsar Fedor's regent and brother-in-law, Boris Godunov, was an energetic builder and deserves most of the credit for supervising and mobilizing resources for Russia's late 16th-century burst of fortress construction, including Solovki's upgrade. Tsar Fedor sent more artillery and soldiers to the monastery and ordered the construction of stone walls around it.[27] The tsar also continued to shower Solovki with money, land and privileges, but the wealthy monastery was also forced to pay some of the costs of building its own defenses. Hundreds of additional workers were brought to Solovki to help in the mammoth task of constructing the stone fortifications.[28] The Russo-Swedish War of 1590–93 threatened Solovki seriously enough to push wall construction into high gear. By the end of Tsar Fedor's reign Solovki had been transformed into an impressive, well-defended nerve center for the entire region's defenses. Solovki supervised and helped pay for the fortification of its neighboring towns, including Kem', Keret, Kola, Soroka, and Sumskii posad. With reason

---

[24] Likhachev, "Solovki v istorii russkoi kul'tury," 22.

[25] Frumenkov, *Solovetskii monastyr'*, 19.

[26] *ISM*, 56–57; Likhachev, "Solovki v istorii russkoi kul'tury," 23–24.

[27] Daniel Rowland, "Architecture and Dynasty: Boris Godunov's Uses of Architecture, 1584–1605," in James Cracraft and Daniel Rowland, *Architectures of Russian Identity 1500 to the Present* (Ithaca, NY: Cornell University Press, 2003), 36–37; *Letopisets Solovetskii*, 45–46; Spock, "The Solovki Monastery," 77; Frumenkov, *Solovetskii monastyr'*, 20–25, 29–30; O. D. Savitskaia, "Arkhitektura Solovetskogo monastyria," in Likhachev, *Arkhitekturno-khudozhestvennye pamiatniki Solovetskikh ostrovov*, 77–83; V. V. Kostochkin, "Novye dannye o stenakh i bashniakh Solovetskogo monastyria," *Arkhitekturnoe sledstvo* 20 (1972): 33–38.

[28] V. A. Burov and V. V. Skopin, "O vremeni stroitel'stva kreposti Solovetskogo monastyria i ee zodchem monakhe Trifone," in *Pamiatniki russkoi arkhitektury i monumental'nogo iskusstva*, ed. V. P. Vygolov (Moscow: Nauka, 1985), 52, 58–70; Frumenkov, *Solovetskii monastyr'*, 24, 29; V. V. Skopin and L. A. Shchennikova, *Arkhitekturno-khudozhestvennyi ansambl' Solovetskogo monastyria* (Moscow: Iskusstvo, 1982), 52; Likhachev, "Solovki," 23–24.

the Swedes came to view the abbot of Solovetskii Monastery as the tsar's principal voevoda of north Russia and Solovki as the region's main bulwark.[29]

Solovki's massive granite fieldstone and boulder walls were more or less completed during Boris Godunov's reign (1598–1605); the result was a pentagonal fortress protected by a thick wall approximately a kilometer in circumference and punctuated by six enormous watchtowers that were up to ten meters high and up to seven meters thick at the base. Although Russian fortress design lagged behind that of Western Europe, according to William Brumfield the construction of Solovki's walls was truly "one of the most remarkable achievements of fortification engineering in Europe."[30] The number of *strel'tsy* stationed at Solovki fluctuated from 100 to 200, depending upon the strategic situation; and many other people employed in fortification construction or other tasks at the monastery were available to defend it if necessary.[31] If things got truly desperate, there were enough weapons stored at Solovki to arm everyone, including the monks. During the Time of Troubles things got nearly that desperate.

At the heart of the Time of Troubles was Russia's first civil war, which occurred in two phases (1604–05 and 1606–12). The bitter and protracted civil war fought in the name of Ivan the Terrible's youngest son Dmitrii nearly destroyed the country and prompted Polish and Swedish military intervention.[32] Ostensibly to challenge Polish intervention, starting in 1609 Sweden's King Karl IX ordered his army to probe north Russia's defenses, including Solovki and the mainland towns under its sway. Karl made grandiose plans to conquer the entire White Sea area, including Solovki and Arkhangel'sk.[33]

---

[29] *Akty sobrannye v bibliotekakh i arkhivakh Rossiiskoi imperii Arkheograficheskoiu ekspeditsieiu Imp. Akademii nauk*, 4 vols. and index (St. Petersburg, 1836–38) [hereafter cited as *AAE*], 2: 210; Frumenkov, *Solovetskii monastyr'*, 8, 27, 34; Brumfield, "Tradition and Innovation," 357, 359; N. A. Golubtsov, ed., *Pamiatnaia knizhka Arkhangel'skoi gubernii na 1913 god* (Arkhangel'sk: Gubernskaia tip., 1913), 13.

[30] Savitskaia, "Arkhitektura Solovetskogo monastyria," 77–83; Kostochkin, "Novye dannye," 33–38; *Letopisets Solovetskii*, 45–46, 49; Frumenkov, *Solovetskii monastyr'*, 21–22, 32–33; Brumfield, "Tradition and Innovation," 356–58; Robson, *Solovki*, 56–60.

[31] *Letopisets Solovetskii*, 45–46, 49–50; Frumenkov, *Solovetskii monastyr'*, 20–25; Vasilii Krestinin, *Kratkaia istoriia o gorode Arkhangel'skom* (St. Petersburg: Imp. Akademiia nauk, 1792), 3–4, 97–98; *ISM*, 56–59.

[32] Chester S. L. Dunning, *Russia's First Civil War: The Time of Troubles and the Founding of the Romanov Dynasty* (University Park: Pennsylvania State University Press, 2001), chap. 22.

[33] V. Lileev, "Shvedskaia interventsiia nachala XVII veka," *Istoricheskii zhurnal*, no. 1 (1940): 110–15; V. Pegov, *Pol'sko-shvedskaia interventsiia v Karelii v nachale XVII v.* (Petrozavodsk: Kargosizdat, 1939); I. Shaskol'skii, *Shvedskaia interventsiia v Karelii v nachale XVII v.* (Petrozavodsk: Gos. Izd-vo Karelo-Finskoi SSR, 1950); George Vernadsky, *The Tsardom of Moscow, 1547–1682*, 2 vols. (New Haven: Yale University Press, 1969), 1:

He intended to close Russia's northern ports to all Westerners, forcing them to sail to Swedish ports in the Baltic Sea to gain access to Russian markets and trade goods.[34]

Off and on from 1609 to 1611, Swedish officials attempted to negotiate with Solovki's abbot, periodically demanding the surrender of towns within the monastery's jurisdiction and even urging the monks to support Karl's son, Karl Filip, as a candidate for tsar. Not surprisingly, Solovki's answer was a defiant refusal to cooperate with the Swedes or to support a foreign tsar.[35] That defiance eventually pushed Karl to issue a stark ultimatum to Solovki and to send two military forces into the region—one by land and the other by sea. Swedish land forces quickly got bogged down as they met increasingly fierce resistance and an uncooperative native population.[36] During the summer of 1611, however, Swedish ships once again approached Solovki and stayed in its vicinity for several days. Then, for unknown reasons, the ships turned away and disappeared—just as they had done in 1571. To the monks of Solovki, this was nothing less than a miracle brought about by the intervention of saints Savvatii and Zosima.[37]

News of the "miraculous" defense of Solovetskii Monastery spread like wildfire. English merchants of the Russia Company (or Muscovy Company) undoubtedly heard about it. The English, who had established commercial and diplomatic relations with Russia in the 1550s, had long known about Solovki. Russia Company merchants first visited Solovetskii Monastery in 1566.[38] By the early 17th century Solovki's great wealth and mighty fortifications were well known to the English, who also tracked Swedish military intervention in the region. Extremely displeased with Swedish efforts to conquer north Russia and close the White Sea, Russia Company officials began

---

245; Artur Attman, *The Struggle for Baltic Markets: Powers in Conflict, 1558–1618* (Göteborg: Vetenskaps- o. vittechets-samhället, 1979), 176–77.

[34] Michael Roberts, *The Early Vasas: A History of Sweden, 1523–1611* (Cambridge: Cambridge University Press, 1968), 267–79, 450; Attman, *Struggle for Baltic Markets*, 193–94, 200; Frumenkov, *Solovetskii monastyr'*, 54.

[35] *AAE*, 2: 295, 308; *Letopisets Solovetskii*, 52; *ISM*, 65–66; Spock, "The Solovki Monastery," 208–09; Golubtsov, *Pamiatnaia knizhka*, 44; Frumenkov, *Solovetskii monastyr'*, 36–38, 45–47; Savich, *Solovetskaia votchina*, 68, 214; Shaskol'skii, *Shvedskaia interventsiia*, 90.

[36] Frumenkov, *Solovetskii monastyr'*, 10, 39–43; Vernadsky, *Tsardom*, 1: 263; *ISM*, 66–68; *AAE*, 2: nos. 129, 195–96; *Letopisets Solovetskii*, 52; Robson, *Solovki*, 63; Golubtsov, *Pamiatnaia knizhka*, 45; V. Shunkov, "Narodnaia bor'ba protiv pol'skikh i shvedskikh okkupantov v nachale XVII veka," *Istoricheskii zhurnal*, nos. 1–2 (1945): 3–8.

[37] *Letopisets Solovetskii*, 52–53; Frumenkov, *Solovetskii monastyr'*, 43–44, 53–56; Spock, "The Solovki Monastery," 208–09; Robson, *Solovki*, 63.

[38] Thomas Southam, "Voyage to Solovetsky," in *Early Voyages and Travels to Russia and Persia by Anthony Jenkinson and Other Englishmen*, ed. E. Delmar Morgan and C. H. Coote, 2 vols. (London: Hakluyt Society, 1886), 1: 193–94.

planning how to prevent that worst-case scenario from occurring. Out of those deliberations emerged James I's strange plan to intervene in north Russia and to seize the port of Arkhangel'sk and other profitable places in the region, apparently including Solovki.[39] In the spring of 1613, when the Russians were informed by Swedish agents and others about the audacious English plan to seize Arkhangel'sk, they were also told that the predatory Britons had designs on Solovki.[40]

During the summer of 1612, John Merrick, chief agent of the Russia Company, held conversations with prominent Russians about the possibility of English intervention in north Russia to prevent Sweden from conquering the region. Merrick returned to England filled with enthusiasm about the possibility of putting north Russia under the protection of King James, and during the winter of 1612–13 Russia Company officials and their allies produced a sketchy plan for English diplomatic and military intervention in Russia which was presented to James and discussed by his Privy Council in the spring of 1613. Support for the scheme came from three influential and overlapping groups: major investors in Sir Thomas Smith's joint-stock companies who dreamed of profits that might flow from dominating Russian markets and the Volga trade route, radical Protestants who supported intervention in Russia to stop Catholic Poland from conquering the country, and the remnant of the old Essex party who had long championed a robustly Protestant foreign policy and the further development of Anglo-Russian trade.[41] Near the center of the groups pushing for intervention in Russia stood George Abbot, Archbishop of Canterbury and a major investor in Smith's various money-making enterprises.[42]

---

[39] Lubimenko, *Les relations*, 141; Virginskii, "Proekty," 94; Frumenkov, *Solovetskii monastyr'*, 51–52; Attman, *Struggle for Baltic Markets*, 186, 191–96; Robson, *Solovki*, 64.

[40] Givi Zhordaniia, *Ocherki iz istorii franko-russkikh otnoshenii kontsa XVI i pervoi poloviny XVII v.*, 2 vols. (Tbilisi: Akademiia nauk Gruzinskoi SSR, 1959), 1: 353, 363–68, 378–78; *Akty istoricheskie, sobrannye i izdannye Arkheograficheskoiu komissieiu*, 5 vols. (St. Petersburg, 1841–42), 3: 4–5.

[41] Dunning, "'A Singular Affection' for Russia," 277–302; John Chamberlain, *The Letters of John Chamberlain*, 2 vols. (Philadelphia: American Philosophical Society, 1939), 1: 393–98, 402–06, 451–52; S. L. Adams, "The Protestant Cause: Religious Alliance with West European Calvinist Communities as a Political Issue in England, 1558–1630" (D. Phil. diss., Oxford University, 1973), 198–99, 228–30; T. S. Willan, *The Early History of the Russia Company, 1553–1603* (Manchester: Manchester University Press, 1956), 257–58.

[42] Chester Dunning, "The Fall of Sir Thomas Overbury and the Embassy to Russia in 1613," *The Sixteenth Century Journal* 22: 4 (1991): 695–704; idem, "King James," 219–20; Adams, "Protestant Cause," 198–99, 230, 240; Kenneth Fincham, *Prelate as Pastor: The Episcopate of James I* (Oxford: Clarendon Press, 1990), 46–47, 268–69; Chamberlain, *Letters*, 1: 393–95, 402–06, 443; Alastair Bellamy, *The Politics of Court Scandal in Early*

Backers of the plan for intervention in Russia never tired of dangling the prospect of great wealth before the king, who was desperate for new sources of revenue at the time. James became extremely interested in the project, and in May 1613 he dispatched Merrick to Arkhangel'sk to pursue the plan if conditions were right and if Russian officials were still receptive to the idea.[43] As it turned out, the election of Tsar Mikhail had dramatically changed the strategic situation in Russia, putting an end to James's fleeting dream of a northern empire. Nevertheless, during the spring and early summer of 1613 James was receptive to plans for military operations in the White Sea, especially if they could block Swedish intervention and tap Russia's wealth simultaneously. The Solovki document, with its emphasis on the great riches of the monastery and the need for expensive siege forces to overcome its defenses, was closely connected to the king's larger plan to establish an English protectorate over north Russia.

The Solovki document was probably written in the spring or early summer of 1613. It was not addressed to the acting secretary of state at the time, but was penned instead as a private request directed to a very high-ranking individual sympathetic to the intervention scheme. The name of that person is not given in the document; he is referred to simply as "yor Grace." In the early 17th century that title was reserved for dukes and the archbishop of Canterbury, in this case almost certainly George Abbot.[44] The author of the Solovki document was himself a fairly high-ranking military officer (or former officer) with good connections and access to excellent intelligence about Solovki. Nevertheless, the combination of his naïve description of the geography of Solovki (referring to it as a peninsula) and his exaggeration of the size of the fortress-monastery (claiming it to be twice the size of the Tower of London when it is about the same size) and the strength of its garrison (claiming it had 1,500 soldiers when there were never more than a few hundred) indicate that he had probably never visited north Russia. It is possible, therefore, that he was one of the dozen or so English and Scottish officers who had served in Russia as commanders of the mercenary forces raised by the king of Sweden to help Tsar Vasilii Shuiskii resist Polish military intervention. Many of those officers entered Russia via the Baltic Sea and eventually left by the same route; they knew something about Russia and Russian military affairs but would probably have made the same kinds of mistakes the author of the Solovki document did. It may not be possible to identify the author, but

---

Modern England: News Culture and the Overbury Affair, 1603–1660 (Cambridge: Cambridge University Press, 2002), 37–39, 43–44, 50–51.

[43] Geraldine Phipps, *Sir John Merrick: English Merchant-Diplomat in Seventeenth Century Russia* (Newtonville, MA: Oriental Research Partners, 1983), chap. 3; Liubimenko, "Angliiskii proekt 1612," 1–16; idem, "A Project," 246–56; Dunning, "James I," 206–26.

[44] J. A. Simpson and E. S. C. Weiner, eds., *Oxford English Dictionary*, 2nd ed., 20 vols. (Oxford: Clarendon Press, 1989), 6: 720.

the list of Britons whose military service in Russia fits the necessary profile is at least relatively short.[45] One likely candidate, Thomas Chamberlayne (author of the Russia Company's formal proposal to King James to establish a protectorate over north Russia), fits the profile but should probably be excluded because in the spring of 1613 he was scheduled to accompany John Merrick on his sensitive diplomatic mission to Arkhangel'sk.[46]

It is quite possible that the author of the Solovki document, as well informed about the Solovetskii Monastery as he was, had never been to Russia but was simply keen to go after learning about Solovki's wealth and the evolving English plan to establish a protectorate over north Russia. He could have gathered intelligence about Solovki from Russia Company merchants and soldiers returning from Russia. If that was the case, a closer look at the history of the Solovki document itself may help to identify its author. As noted earlier, the document was part of the Conway Papers donated to the British government in 1857. The bulk of the Conway Papers date from the early 17th century and had been the property of Edward Conway, first Viscount of Conway and first Viscount of Killultagh (1564–1632).[47]

The son of a Welsh knight, Edward Conway started his career as a soldier. He commanded an infantry regiment during the two-month siege (and sacking) of Cadiz in 1596. Immediately after the siege, for his courage in battle he was knighted by his commander-in-chief, Robert Devereux, the Earl of Essex. As the new Lord Conway of Ragley, Edward demonstrated a flair for administration and diplomacy, for which he was rewarded with the governorship of Brill in the Netherlands, a post he held until the town was returned to the Dutch in 1616. Conway's loyal service to King James eventually netted him the post of secretary of state (1623–28). King Charles I made him president of the Privy Council, a position Edward held until his death in 1632.[48] Like other early modern English secretaries of state, Viscount Conway regarded government documents in his possession as his personal property. For that reason, papers related to his official duties remained in the hands of the

---

[45] For English and Scottish military officers with experience in Russia who could have written the Solovki document, see Geraldine Phipps, "Britons in Seventeenth-Century Russia: A Study in the Origins of Modernization" (Ph.D. diss., University of Pennsylvania, 1971); and Sonia E. Howe, ed., *The False Dmitri: A Russian Romance and Tragedy Described by British Eye-Witnesses, 1604–1612* (London: Williams and Norgate, 1916).

[46] H. C. G. Matthew and Brian Harrison, eds., *New Oxford Dictionary of National Biography*, 61 vols. (Oxford: Oxford University Press, 2004) [hereafter cited as *DNB*], 10: 968–69; Lubimenko, "A Project," 246–47; S. Konovalov, "Thomas Chamberlayne's Description of Russia, 1631," *Oxford Slavonic Papers* 5 (1954): 107–16.

[47] *Calendar of State Papers, domestic series, of the reign of Charles I, 1625–1649*, vol. 23 [Addendum (1625–1649)] (London: HMSO, 1897).

[48] *DNB* 13: 43-44; Charles R. Mayes, "The Early Stuarts and the Irish Peerage," *The English Historical Review* 73: 287 (April 1958): 227–51.

family until shortly after the Crimean War. Since the Solovki document was found among Viscount Conway's papers, it is remotely possible that Edward Conway was himself the author of the Solovki document. He may have become bored with his job as governor of Brill and learned about the plan to intervene in north Russia from Sir Ralph Winwood, the English ambassador to the Dutch Republic, who was well informed about the project.[49] Conway fits the profile of the most active supporters of the protectorate scheme. Like others in that group (with whom he had some interesting associations), he was an ardent Puritan committed to a vigorously Protestant foreign policy, an investor in the enterprises of Sir Thomas Smith, and an admirer of the late earl of Essex.[50] Nevertheless, a closer examination of the history and content of the Solovki document reveals an even more likely candidate for its authorship—Viscount Conway's well known brother, Sir Fulke Conway (c. 1565–1626).

When government archivists inventoried the Conway Papers, official documents that had belonged to Secretary of State Conway were forwarded to the State Paper Office where the bulk of them were placed in State Papers 14, containing the archives of secretaries of state during the reign of James I.[51] But something unusual about the Solovki document caught the attention of a sharp-eyed archivist. It is possible that his interest was stirred by the memory of a then-recent event, the bombardment of Solovki by a British warship in 1854.[52] In any case, the archivist noticed that the Solovki document was not addressed to the secretary of state, but was instead a private request. Private or not, however, the document clearly concerned matters of state and, for that reason, was not sent to the British Museum along with the rest of the Conway family's private papers. Since the Solovki document's cover sheet had that misleading pencil notation "Russia Eliz." but was obviously not from the reign of Elizabeth (for example, the document mentions the king), the archivist wisely placed it in State Papers Foreign 91 among official documents from the reign of James I that concerned Russia. Indeed, the Solovki document ended up very near other documents concerning the protectorate

---

[49] Historical Manuscript Commission, *Report on the Manuscripts of the Duke of Buccleuth and Queensberry* (London: HMSO, 1899), 1: 124–25, 136–37; Adams, "Protestant Cause," 198–99, 223–25, 227–30, 232, 236, 238-40.

[50] Vivian Larminie, "The Jacobean Diplomatic Fraternity and the Protestant Cause: Sir Isaac Wake and the View from Savoy," *The English Historical Review* 121: 494 (2006): 1300–26; *DNB* 51: 469–71; Theodore K. Rabb, *Enterprise and Empire: Merchant and Gentry Investment in the Expansion of England, 1575–1630* (Cambridge, MA: Harvard University Press, 1967), 269; Dunning, "'A Singular Affection' for Russia," 282–86; Chamberlain, *Letters,*1: 393–98, 402–06, 451–52.

[51] S. C. Lomas, "The State Papers of the Early Stuarts and the Interregnum," *Transactions of the Royal Historical Society*, n.s., 16 (1902): 97–132.

[52] Robson, *Solovki*, 155–63, 193.

scheme.[53] Nevertheless, as will be demonstrated below, the Solovki document was likely originally located in the private papers of Sir Fulke Conway, papers which upon his death in 1626 came into the possession of his brother, Viscount Edward Conway.

Like his brother, Fulke Conway began his career as a soldier. During the Nine Years' War (1594–1603), he served as an infantry captain under the command of the Lord Lieutenant of Ireland, Robert Devereux, the Earl of Essex. Fulke proved to be an energetic and successful officer and was knighted by Essex in 1600.[54] For his excellent service, first in 1600 and again in 1609 (after the "flight of the earls" in 1607 and the ruthless suppression of the subsequent O'Doherty rebellion), Sir Fulke Conway received from King James one of the largest and most prestigious land grants in northern Ireland, a fine estate and castle that had been confiscated from Hugh O'Neill, the Earl of Tyrone. Specifically, Fulke received the bulk of the highly prized Manor of Killultagh. (By the time Viscount Conway took over the sprawling estate in 1626 it had grown to approximately 70,000 acres.)[55] This information is relevant to our search for the author of the Solovki document. Whoever wrote that document identified two places in northern Ireland well suited for concentrating men and military supplies and secretly harboring ships bound for the White Sea: Lough Swilly (a former haunt of the O'Neills and the point of departure for the "flight of the earls") and "Caelbegges" ("Calebeg," "Corran Callebeg," or Killybegs). Both of those places had been used surreptitiously by Irish rebels during and after the Nine Years' War, and both locations were well known to Sir Fulke Conway who had been posted in the same region during the war. In fact, each of these relatively obscure "havens" was located within one day's ride from Conway's Killultagh estate.[56]

---

[53] Thomas Chamberlayne's "Proposition of the Muscovites to render them subiects to the King of England" (composed during the winter of 1612–13) is located in S.P. 91, pt. 1, fols. 228–30.

[54] Richard Bagwell, *Ireland under the Stuarts and during the Interregnum*, 3 vols. (London: Holland Press, 1963), 3: 269; William Arthur Shaw, *The Knights of England: A Complete Record from the Earliest Time to the Present Day* (London: Sherrot and Hughes, 1906), 97.

[55] R. F. Williams *The Court and Times of Charles the First*, 2 vols. (London: H. Colburn, 1848), 1: 209.

[56] The famous map maker John Norden labeled both Lough Swilly and Calebeg as "havens" on his early 17th–century map of Ireland. I wish to thank Dr. David Hudson for his help in navigating the historical geography of the northern Irish coastline. See Bagwell, *Ireland under the Stuarts*, 1: 37, 106–07; Fynes Moryson, *An History of Ireland, from the year 1599, to 1603*, in Henry Morley, ed., *Ireland under Elizabeth and James the First* (London: G. Routledge, 1890); John H. Andrews, "John Norden's Map of Ireland," *Proceedings of the Royal Irish Academy* 100C (December 2000): 188; idem, *John Norden's Maps of Ireland* (Dublin: Royal Irish Academy, 2000). A copy of Norden's map of Ireland may also be found in Philip O'Sullivan-Beare, *A History of Ireland under*

Sir Fulke Conway was not only one of the first of King James's military "servitors" to be rewarded for "lengthened and useful services" with land confiscated from disgraced Irish lords; he was also among the very first of them to be encouraged by the king to undertake the "project of the plantation of Tyrone."[57] Thus, Fulke Conway became a pioneer in the Plantation of Ulster along with Sir Arthur Chichester, Baron of Belfast and Lord Deputy of Ireland, the man who had advised the king to reward Conway with the Manor of Killultagh. Sir Fulke's early participation in the Ulster Plantation alongside the notorious Lord Deputy Chichester made Conway a very wealthy man. Starting in 1609, Sir Fulke began transplanting Welsh and English Protestants to his Irish estates, built a planned community for them (Lisnegarvey, later known as Lisburn), and was reported to be a very popular landlord.[58]

Significantly, the Solovki document contains an insider's knowledgeable discussion of how to raise and outfit 5,000 soldiers in Ireland and then quietly deploy them for service in north Russia. Whoever he was, the author was undoubtedly aware that during the initial phase of the Plantation of Ulster thousands of Irish "swordsmen" had been enticed or dragooned into military service in Russia, ending up in the mercenary forces raised by the Swedes to help Tsar Vasilii Shuiskii fight against Polish interventionists.[59] It is entirely possible that the author of the Solovki document had been involved in the recruitment of those soldiers. In any case, Lord Deputy Chichester had taken the lead in ruthlessly removing Irish Catholics from the path of Protestant settlers by harsh measures ranging from "extermination" to deportation (known as "transportation").[60] Chichester actually boasted that he had deported as many as 6,000 "bad and disloyal" Irishmen to Sweden;[61] and in

---

Elizabeth: Chapters toward a History of Ireland in the Reign of Elizabeth (Dublin: Sealy, Bryers and Walker, 1903).

[57] George Hill, *An Historical Account of the Plantation in Ulster at the Commencement of the Seventeenth Century, 1608–1620* (Shannon: Irish University Press, 1877), 76; *Calendar of State Papers, relating to Ireland, of the Reign of James I, 1603–1625. Preserved in Her Majesty's Public Record Office,* 5 vols. (London: HMSO, 1872–80), 3 [1608–1610]: 275–77.

[58] James Godkin, *The Land War in Ireland: A History for the Times* (London: Macmillan, 1870), 109.

[59] Maija Jansson, Paul Bushkovitch, and Nikolai Rogozhin, eds., *England and the North: The Russian Embassy of 1613–1614* (Philadelphia: American Philosophical Society, 1994), 49–50, 58–59.

[60] *DNB* 11: 397–402; Thomas Gainsford, *The true exemplary, and remarkable history of the Earle of Tirone* (London: G. P., 1619); Cyril B. Falls, *Birth of Ulster* (London: Methuen, 1936), 67; John McCavitt, *Sir Arthur Chichester, Lord Deputy of Ireland, 1605–1616* (Belfast: Queen's University of Belfast, 1998), 45–46; Raymond Gillespie, *Seventeenth-Century Ireland: Making Ireland Modern* (Dublin: Gill and Macmillan, 2006), 44–48.

[61] *Calendar of State Papers, relating to Ireland, of the Reign of James I,* 4 [1611–1614]: 479–80; McCavitt, *Sir Arthur Chichester,* 154.

1610, he specifically recommended that untrustworthy surplus Irishmen be shipped off for military service in Russia.[62] Sir Fulke Conway, as one of the principal organizers of the "plantation of Tyrone," almost certainly shared the Lord Deputy's sentiments and would probably have looked with favor upon any opportunity to get rid of surplus Irishmen and turn a profit at the same time. It is noteworthy that the author of the Solovki document discusses how to separate the soldiers signing up for Russian service from much of their pay—by selling them beer in the harbors and on the ships "for readie mony" before setting sail to north Russia. Whether he was planning to sell the beer himself or to split the profits with a local concessionaire, the author was certainly a sharp businessman.

It is entirely possible that Sir Fulke Conway learned about the developing project to establish a protectorate over north Russia and saw it as a potentially lucrative business opportunity as well as a chance to advance his career. He may have heard about the protectorate scheme from Lord Deputy Chichester. It is very likely that Chichester learned about the king's plan; he was a well informed official with very good connections who corresponded with Archbishop Abbot in this period about the problem of surplus Irishmen. The Lord Deputy was also mentioned in a memorandum written by a member of the Privy Council concerning its discussion of the "project touching Muscovia."[63] Chichester would undoubtedly have approved of the protectorate scheme and may have encouraged Conway to request Archbishop Abbot's support for a related scheme that would "transport" several thousand more Irish soldiers to Russia. As a trusted "servitor" of the king with highly relevant experience and credentials, Sir Fulke Conway would have been a natural choice to command an expeditionary force launched to "compass" and capture Solovetskii Monastery. Taking all these things into consideration, my conclusion is that Sir Fulke Conway wrote the memorandum about Solovki in the spring or early summer of 1613 and that a copy of the document remained among his personal papers until they were added to Viscount Edward Conway's archive sometime after Fulke's death in 1626.

დ ⴢ

Transcription of S. P. 91/1, folio 250–250v

[fol. 250] The Abbaie of Solofskie or Sollavescie is scituat within the Whyte Sea upon the terretorie of Russia, upon a Peninsula or neck of land, stretchinge into the same sea some good distance from the bodie of the main continent of Russia. It is sometimes in the nature of an Island by reason of a

---

[62] *Calendar of State Papers, relating to Ireland, of the Reign of James I*, 3 [1608–1610]: 371.

[63] Gillespie, *Seventeenth-Century Ireland*, 45; British Library, Lansdowne Manuscripts 142, fol. 395, memorandum of Sir Julius Caesar, 14 April 1613. I wish to thank Dr. David Hudson for his help in deciphering Sir Julius Caesar's difficult handwriting.

smale brooke crossinge the neck theirof which with the meltinge of the snowe for that time becomes a sea, & is not to be passed other then by boates to that pt where the Abbaie stands.

This Abbaie or howse of monkes hathe the reputacon to be the richest place this daie in the worlde. The veines from whence theise springes of Treasor sholde flowe doe ryse from sundrie fountaines.

Their Emperors owte of an anncient grounded opinion held of the hollines of this place, have ever used at their deathe to send most rich presentes & much Treasor to it, becawse they maie from the cheif of their Covent receave a Commendatorie billet or scrowle to St. Nicolas the Russ his patron in heaven, shewinge the bountie of their Emperor to his principall howse uppon earthe St. Solofskie.

This Abbaie hath also contineuall guiftes from all ptes of that Empire from everie riche man at his deathe for the obtayninge of theise Commenda-torie Billetes to their Sainct, everie on beinge confident, according to the measure of his guift to this howse to receave his preferrment in heaven.

They have also a great contribucon yearlie from 30 other riche Abbaies over whom this howse havinge a kynde of a Metrapollitan Superintendancie swaiethe, & unto whom they doe yearlie paie most rich & lardge stipendes.

They have by manie other Conduicts great store of presentes & monies which dailie comes to them from all ptes of that lardge Empire. And on thinge is speciallie noted of them that whatsoever Treasor comes into their howse, it never sees the light abroad more, unless sometimes uppon extraordinarie occacon of warr, they send their Emperor monies which uppon the shuttinge up or end of the same is dulie repaied again.

But of this place, & of the riches their the Russian merchantes are able to discorse at lardge, & so can others besyds the merchants.

How the same is to be compassd, if the kings majesty by yor Grace his procurement wilbe at the chardge of men & shippes, with gods helpe I will contryve if it be comitted to my trust.

[f. 250v] The howse or Abbaie is in circuite twyce as lardge as the Tower. It is of late within theise 12 yeares fortefied with Bulworkes & good store of great ordinance, it had a garnison of 1500 soldiers. I dare not saie good ones the Russes beinge a most cowardlie nacon. It is not good to atempt it with a lesse number of soldiers then 5000.

The shippes for that place must drawe no more water then those which the Muscovie companie weare wont to send for those seas. It wilbe best & with the least suspicon to set forthe the voyadge from the harbors of Cael-begges & Loghswilly in the north of Ireland which harbors doe open uppon the broad sea the occean even over gainst the north Cape of Norwaie by which or shippes must passe on their voyadge, their waie lyinge from thence by the Ward howse, & thence longst the coast of Lapland untill they turne into the Whyte Sea.

The soldiers maie be raisd in Ireland pt of the companies, & the rest of other men. The pretext maie be for some exployt to be done uppon the westerne Isles.

For victualles their maie be butter pork & bisquit pvyded in Ireland & for beof duringe the time the armie shalbe at the water syde & in harbor, & for on month after, but for the rest of the voyadge it wilbe best to pvyde english beof. The victualles their wilbe beter cheape if readie mony be to paie for it, then in England. They maie have bere their lykwyse for readie mony whylst the shippes lie in harbor, but for no longer time.

It wilbe necessarie to victuall for vj monthes, thowghe I hope the voyadg maie be performd in 3 or 4 monthes.

Their must be canon, demy canon & culverin for batterie, if otherwyse wee cannot prevaile by scalladoe, & Pettarres. Their must alsoe be some myners if neede be, & municon powder, match & lead with store of great shott.

Icon-Painting in the Russian North:
Evidence from the Antonievo-Siiskii Monastery*

Ann M. Kleimola

Foreigners entering the "rude and barbarous kingdom" of Muscovy along the great river road of the Northern Dvina passed within a few miles of the Antonievo-Siiskii Monastery, a remarkable cultural center of the Russian North that remained largely invisible to outside eyes. The community was founded in 1520 by the monk Antonii and four followers who settled beside a lake in the forests near the confluence of the Siia River and the Northern Dvina, about 50 miles upstream from Kholmogory. The settlement's prosperity began shortly thereafter with a grant of land from Vasilii III. By the end of the 16th century the monastery was a substantial second-tier regional church institution (the Solovetskii Monastery far overshadowed all of the other Pomor'e monasteries), with income from landholdings, coastal saltworks in Nenoksa and Una, fishing rights including a share in the use of the Varzuga river on the Kola Peninsula, and warehouses in Vologda and Kholmogory, as well as donations from churchmen, local residents, and pilgrims.[1] Despite suffering three major fires in the 16th and 17th centuries, the monastery was rebuilt each time and continued to grow. Its Trinity Cathedral, completed in 1607, was one of the first masonry structures in the region. The Annunciation "winter church" and the gate-church dedicated to St. Sergii of Radonezh also were rebuilt and additional facilities, including a bell tower and cells, were constructed. The community numbered 50 monks by the 1540s, about 80 in

* For assistance that made completion of this paper possible, I wish to express my gratitude to the Center for Russian, East European, and Eurasian Studies, University of Illinois at Urbana-Champaign; Helen Sullivan and the staff of the Slavic Reference Service, University of Illinois Libraries; Professors Shirley Glade, Gail Lenhoff, and Daniel Kaiser.

[1] A. A. Kizevetter, *Russkii Sever: Rol' severnogo kraia Evropy: Rossiia v istorii russkogo gosudarstva* (Vologda: Tipografiia Soiuza Severnykh Kooperativnykh Soiuzov, 1919), 36, 43; M. M. Bogoslovskii, *Zemskoe samoupravlenie na russkom severe v XVII v.* (Moscow: Izd-vo Imperatorskago Obshchestva istorii i drevnostei rossiiskikh, 1909), 1: 68–71; M. V. Kukushkina, *Monastyrskie biblioteki Russkogo Severa: Ocherki po istorii knizhnoi kul'tury XVI–XVII vekov* (Leningrad: Nauka, 1977), 25–29; Vladimir Bulatov, *Russkii Sever: Kniga tret'ia. Pomor'e (XVI–nachalo XVIII v.)* (Arkhangel'sk: Izd-vo Pomorskogo gosudarstvennogo universiteta imeni M. V. Lomonosova, 1999), 77, 93.

Rude & Barbarous Kingdom Revisited: Essays in Russian History and Culture in Honor of Robert O. Crummey. Chester S. L. Dunning, Russell E. Martin, and Daniel Rowland, eds. Bloomington, IN: Slavica Publishers, 2008, 327–39.

1588, but had grown to 184 monks and 183 lay residents (*mirian vsiakikh chinov*) by 1658.[2] (See fig. 9 following p. 72.)

Antonii himself set the monastery's focus on cultural activity. Book culture flourished at Siiskii. When Antonii died in 1556 the monasterial library already had 66 manuscripts. Later abbots, particularly Feodosii (1643–52 and 1662–87) and Nikodim (1692–1721), were bibliophiles whose personal cell libraries became part of the monasterial holdings. Nikodim alone donated 28 manuscripts. By 1701 the inventory of monastic property listed 387 manuscripts and 364 printed books.[3] Antonii also launched the monastery's tradition of icon-painting. A native of the Dvina hamlet Kekhta, he learned the art in his youth, as attested in a memorial inscription on a stone in the monastery refectory: "A zealous seeker after virtue and chastity from childhood, he was skilled in reading and icon-painting from the age of seven."[4] According to tradition, as he was traveling toward the White Sea he painted icons for several village churches along the Onega, including the dedicatory icon of the Annunciation church in Turchasovo and that of the church of St. Nicholas the Wonder-Worker in the settlement attached to the Vaimuzha parish.[5] His Life (*zhitie*) records that he himself painted the dedicatory icon that adorned his Trinity church. As Antonii mentioned in a 1540 petition to the grand prince requesting that an abandoned settlement nearby be granted to the monastery, the icon had already performed many miracles.[6] A few years later the churches of the monastery burned down, but Antonii's Trinity icon survived.[7]

---

[2] Kukushkina, *Monastyrskie biblioteki*, 26, 30; Bogoslovskii, *Zemskoe samoupravlenie*, 1: 68. Illustration 1, from K. K. Sluchevskii, *Po Severo-zapadu Rossii, Tom 1: "Po Severu Rossii"* (St. Petersburg, 1897), 212, provides an overview of the monastery complex. The division of the Arkhangel'sk library specializing in the Russian North commemorated the 440th anniversary of Antonii's death with an exhibition featuring works about the saint and his monastery; see *"Troiskii Antonievo-Siiskii Monastyr'": Katalog knizhno-illiustrativnoi vystavki*, comp. Z. V. Istomina, M. A. Smirnova, and O. A. Solov'eva (Arkhangel'sk: Arkhangel'skaia oblastnaia nauchnaia biblioteka, 1996).

[3] Kukushkina, *Monastyrskie biblioteki*, 28, 44, 199. On literary activity at the monastery, see E. A. Ryzhova, "Literaturnoe tvorchestvo knizhnikov Antonievo-Siiskogo monastyria XVI–XVIII vv.," in *Severnorusskie monastyri*, ed. S. A. Semiachko (St. Petersburg: Dmitrii Bulanin, 2001), 218–64.

[4] Kukushkina, *Monastyrskie biblioteki*, 25.

[5] T. M. Kol'tsova, *Ikony severnogo poonezh'ia* (Moscow: Severnyi Palomnik, 2005), 22; T. M. Kol'tsova, *Severnye ikonopistsy: Opyt biobibliograficheskogo slovaria* (Arkhangel'sk: Severo-Zapadnoe knizhnoe izdatel'stvo, 1998), 36–37.

[6] V. V. Bryzgalov, "Chelobitnaia Antoniia Siiskogo 1540 g.," *Arkheograficheskii ezhegodnik za 1978 god* (Moscow: Nauka, 1979), 309–10.

[7] *Zhitie prepodobnogo Antoniia, Siiskogo chudotvortsa* (Sviato-Troitskii Antonievo-Siiskii monastyr', 1999), 16–17; Makarii, Bishop of Arkhangel'sk and Kholmogory, "Istoricheskiia svedeniia ob Antonievom Siiskom Monastyre," *Chteniia v Imperatorskom obshchestve istorii i drevnostei rossiiskikh pri Moskovskom universitete*, bk. 3 (1878), 104–05. A

Antonii was buried on the right side near the altar in his church of the Trinity. An embroidered pall covered the sarcophagus, and the brethren adorned his grave with icons and candles. Two versions of his Life were written in 1578–79, one by Iona, a monk at the monastery, and the other by Ivan IV's son Ivan.[8] Antonii Siiskii was canonized at a church council in 1579. After the tsar accidentally killed his son in 1581, a manuscript with the tsarevich's service for Antonii Siiskii was sent to Abbot Pitirim in 1583.[9] Ivan IV himself sought the saint's intercession, as indicated by his donation in 1583/84 of 450 rubles and framed icons in memory of his son Ivan, including an icon depicting Antonii the Wonder-Worker painted by the sovereign's icon painter Maksim.[10] In 1584 the royal family again turned to Antonii Siiskii for heavenly aid: Ivan and his sons Fedor and Dmitrii sent 500 rubles (a marginal note corrects the sum to 1300 rubles) to the monastery for memorial prayers for the disgraced victims of the Oprichnina, along with ten framed icons and ten extra frames. Icons above Antonii's grave, perhaps including the royal gift, depicted the saint in prayer and the intercession of the Mother of God. By the late 16th or early 17th century a collection box for alms stood beside the tomb.[11]

Even after his death, Antonii Siiskii remained a patron of icon-painters, as reflected in the first posthumous miracle ascribed to the saint. Pitirim, who was abbot from 1577 to 1586 and again from 1592 to 1597, painted many new icons and restored old ones. He fell ill, had to leave his post, and eventually, believing death was near, prayed to the Trinity and St. Antonii. Pitirim fell asleep, and then "saw how a magnificent elder, adorned with gray hairs," was approaching him from the Saint's tomb, carrying a sack. "Do you wish to be well and finish what you have begun?" he asked. Pitirim replied that he wished to do so but could not. The elder told him: "The Holy Trinity heals you, do not grow faint in your work; I, the Abbot Anthony, have come to visit

---

1691 inventory of the church lists another icon by Antonii, an image of Nicholas the Wonder Worker in an engraved case; O. N. Mal'tseva, "Siiskii ikonopisnyi podlinnik: Novye materialy ob ikonopisnoi masterskoi Antonievo-Siiskogo monastyria XVII veka," in *Religiia v istorii kul'tury: Sbornik nauchnykh trudov* (St. Petersburg: Izdanie GMIRa, 1991), 29.

[8] On the literary history of the Life, see E. A. Ryzhova, *Antonievo-Siiskii monastyr': Zhitie Antoniia Siiskogo (Knizhnye tsentry Russkogo Severa)* (Syktyvkar: Izd-vo SyktGU, 2000).

[9] L. I. Denisov, comp., *Pravoslavnye monastyri Rossiiskoi imperii* (Moscow: Izdanie A. D. Slupina, 1908), 32–33. A book with the manuscript was still in the monasterial sacristy in 1908.

[10] A. F. Iziumov, "Vkladnyia knigi Antonieva Siiskago monastyria 1576–1604 (7084–7202) gg." *Chteniia v Obshchestve istorii i drevnostei rossiiskikh pri Moskovskom universitete*, bk. 2 (1917), 1, 8; Makarii, "Istoricheskiia svedeniia," 75.

[11] Iziumov, "Vkladnyia knigi," 2; A. G. Mel'nik, "Grobnitsa sviatogo v prostranstve russkogo khrama XVI–nachala XVII veka," *Vostochnokhristianskie relikvii*, ed. A. M. Lidov (Moscow: Progress-Traditsiia, 2003), 536–37, 542–45.

you in your affliction." After the wonder-worker touched the sick abbot, Piti-rim recovered and devoted himself with new enthusiasm to painting icons and making the monastery's churches more beautiful.[12]

Subsequent abbots built upon this foundation, and through a combina-tion of luck and diplomacy made the monastery a major cultural center in the North. The community's most prominent moment on the national stage came in 1599, when Tsar Boris Godunov exiled a political enemy, the boyar Fedor Nikitich Romanov, to the monastery with orders that he be made a monk. The situation was delicate, but Abbot Iona (1597–1634) managed to maintain a friendly relationship with the distinguished prisoner. After six years in the North, the monk Filaret Romanov returned to Moscow when Tsar Dmitrii gained the throne and eventually became head of the church during the reign of his son Mikhail, the first Romanov tsar. But his substantial donations—in-cluding icons of the Vladimir Mother of God, John the Baptist, the Deisus, the Annunciation, and others, a pall for Antonii's tomb, a chased silver frame and other adornments for the Trinity icon, a chandelier, and a censer—indicate that he remembered the monastery kindly, and the Romanov connection gave the representatives of Antonievo-Siiskii greater influence in Moscow.[13]

Abbot Iona apparently had high regard for the work of Istoma Savin, an icon-painter who was on the permanent staff of the Kremlin Armory Work-shop. In 1595 Iona donated three Deisus icons as well as an icon of the Mother of God "In Thee Rejoiceth" and a large icon depicting the Mother of God "The Queen Doth Stand," painted by Savin, for the local row of the iconostasis.[14] In 1604 another donor, the priest Kalistrat, gave the monastery an icon of the Old Testament Trinity painted by Savin.[15] A donation book entry under 1611 notes the gift of Savin's depiction of the wonder-worker Antonii, sent by the Moscow resident Zhdan Shapov, while in 1616 the monastery received more icons by Savin (an Old Testament Trinity, Annunciation, Mother of God "Tenderness" [Umilenie], Gerasim of the Jordan, a folding icon with depic-tions of Christ, the Mother of God, and John the Baptist with Sergii of Rado-nezh and Antonii Siiskii praying before them, and an icon of the Konev Mother of God), which were bequests from the estate of Abbot Isidor of the

---

[12] The Northern Thebaïd: Monastic Saints of the Russian North, comp. and trans. Fathers Seraphim (Rose) and Herman (Podmoshensky) of Platina (Forestville, CA: Fr. Sera-phim Rose Foundation, 1995), 161–62. The volume reproduces photographs, taken be-fore the 1917 Revolution, of Antonii's reliquary (p. 160) and two 17th-century icons painted at the monastery, one a church calendar for March, the other a depiction of the Evangelist Matthew (p. 160); see also pre-Revolutionary photographs of the monastery on p. 159.

[13] Kukushkina, Monastyrskie biblioteki, 27; Makarii, "Istoricheskiia svedeniia," 22, 67, 76, 105–07; Iziumov, "Vkladnyia knigi," 3, 24–25.

[14] Iziumov, "Vkladnyia knigi," 18.

[15] Ibid., 23.

Koriazhemskii Monastery.[16] The collection grew under Iona's successor, Feodosii, who began to gather Savin's work systematically. Feodosii ordered and acquired additional icons by Savin during trips to Moscow, and even when he was exiled to the distant Kozheozerskii Monastery Feodosii ordered 20 small icons from the Armory Workshop painter.[17]

Feodosii, abbot from 1643 to 1652 and from 1662 to 1687, son of a Kholmogory silversmith, became a monk at age 18, fleeing family pressure to take up his father's occupation. He was known for his love of books, reflected in his copying and collecting of manuscripts, and for his icon-painting, especially his 1645 donations to the monastery of images depicting Sophia the Holy Wisdom and Antonii Siiskii.[18] He was sent off for ten years to the Kozheozerskii Monastery because of church politics, but during that time he continued both branches of activity. Feodosii probably worked with the local painter Vasilii Mamontov on images for the iconostasis of the Resurrection church (1654) in the hamlet Piiala.[19] In 1658 he composed the "Tale of the Miraculous Icon" (*Povest' o chudotvornoi ikone* or *Chudo ot ikony*), an account of the Guiding (*Odigitriia*) Mother of God image that survived the fire of that year at the Antonievo-Siiskii Monastery, and after returning to Siiskii as abbot, Feodosii worked on preparing a new redaction of the Life and witnessed the opening of Antonii's relics.[20] In 1663 the abbot donated six icons to the Siiskii monastery, including an image of Antonii the Wonder-worker which was placed in a gilded, chased frame, one of the three frames for local-row icons that had been donated by Nikon, then the Novgorod metropolitan, when he visited the monastery in 1652 on his way to accompany the relics of Metropolitan Filipp from the Solovetskii Monastery to Moscow.[21] Feodosii probably prepared the artwork, 153 drawings reflecting everyday scenes from secular and monastic life, for the Illustrated Life of Antonii Siiskii (*Litsevoe*

---

[16] Ibid., 28–29; Makarii, "Istoricheskiia svedeniia," 77.

[17] O. N. Mal'tseva, "Ikonopisnaia masterskaia Antonievo-Siiskogo monastyria v XVII veke," *Sbornik materialov (sentiabr' 1994–iiun' 1995)*, vyp. 2 *"Pogibshie sviatyni,"* [4-aia Rossiiskaia nauchno-prakticheskaia konferentsiia, chast' 3], ed. A. K. Krylov and O. Ia. Krylova (St. Petersburg: Bibliopolis, 1996), 60; Kol'tsova, *Severnye ikonopistsy*, 119–20.

[18] Kukushkina, *Monastyrskie biblioteki*, 103; A. Kirillov, "Podvizhniki blagochestiia, pochivaiushchie v usypal'nitse Antonievo-Siiskogo monastyria," *Arkhangel'skie eparkhial'nye vedomosti*, no. 15 (1898): 399 n. 136; Kol'tsova, *Severnye ikonopistsy*, 119–120.

[19] Kol'tsova, *Ikony severnogo poonezh'ia*, 28. An icon depicting Antonii Siiskii, dating from the second half of the 17th century but as yet unattributed, was first published only recently in *Ikony Russkogo Severa: Shedevry drevnerusskoi zhivopisi Arkhangel'skogo muzeia izobrazitel'nykh iskusstv* (Moscow: Severnyi Palomnik, 2007), vol. 2, no. 132.

[20] I. A. Kochetkov, ed., *Slovar' russkikh ikonopistsev XI–XVII vekov*, (Moscow: Indrik, 2003), 723; Ryzhova, *Antonievo-Siiskii monastyr'*, 124–58.

[21] Iziumov, "Vkladnyia knigi," 45, 59; Makarii, "Istoricheskiia svedeniia," 78–79, 108. Nikon donated 150 rubles to pay for the frames.

zhitie Antoniia Siiskogo), which, according to the foreword, was created at the Siiskii Monastery under his "assiduous care."[22] Evidently he also supervised the production of another copy of the Life of Antonii, which he gave in 1682 "to the benefit of their souls" to the distinguished royal adviser Artamon Sergeevich Matveev and his son Andrei Artamonovich shortly before the elder Matveev was killed during a strel'tsy uprising in Moscow. The manuscript was adorned with a full-length miniature of Antonii Siiskii, ornamental vegetative designs, large capital letters in gold and black, and a red morocco binding.[23] Feodosii compiled anthologies of saints' lives of northern origin, generally featuring the founders of small monasteries or tales about icons,[24] and began to compile a collection of icon patterns in the library of the Siiskii Monastery, including not only those of local artisans but also designs of icon-painters from Moscow, Vologda, Velikii Ustiug, and Sol'vychegodsk.[25]

Nikodim (1692–1721), the abbot most often identified with the monastery's tradition of icon-painting, was born as Vasilii Mamontov in the village Shurenga on the Onega. Having studied in Kargopol' and Ustiug, he met his predecessor Feodosii at the Kozheozerskii Monastery, where Mamontov was beginning his education under the tutelage of his grandfather, Abbot Sergii.[26] The future abbot began to paint and restore icons for the Antonievo-Siiskii Monastery in the 1650s, and continued to paint after he took religious vows as the monk Nikodim in 1673. Later serving as the monastery's treasurer, librarian, and deputy administrator in Moscow, he became the first archimandrite in 1692.[27] As monasterial librarian, Nikodim directed the copying and illustration of books for the monastery's collection and wrote a Life of Abbot Feodosii. He had his own cell library, of both manuscripts and printed editions of lives of the saints, dictionaries, literary tales, translated literature, and books with engravings, and perhaps he learned engraving himself. He also continued Feodosii's efforts to gather examples of icon designs. For about half a century Nikodim collected icon patterns, both tracings (*prorisi*) and transfers (*perevody*), and in 1692 gathered them into a manuscript that came to be known as the Siiskii icon-painting pattern book (*Siiskii ikonopisnyi podlinnik*). Nikodim's collection included about 40 drawings by "Vasilii Mamontov" in addition to models by such noted Moscow and provincial artists as Simon

---

[22] Kukushkina, *Monastyrskie biblioteki*, 108–09.

[23] Ibid., 110.

[24] Ibid., 109.

[25] Kol'tsova, *Severnye ikonopistsy*, 119–20.

[26] Kukushkina, *Monastyrskie biblioteki*, 165. In the northern monasteries even educated bookmen, such as the Siiskii abbot Feodosii and archimandrite Nikodim, learned reading by working with an elder who had one or two pupils (Kukushkina, *Monastyrskie biblioteki*, 12).

[27] V. G. Briusova, *Russkaia zhivopis' 17 veka* (Moscow: Iskusstvo, 1984), 158; Kukushkina, *Monastyrskie biblioteki*, 111.

Ushakov, Prokopii Chirin, Ermolai Vologzhanin (Ermolai Sergeev from Vologda), Vasilii Kondakov from Sol'vychegodsk, Bogdan Zotikov, Fedor Zubov, and Semen Spiridonov. The book was part of his personal library until a few months before his death, when he donated it to the monastery library.[28]

The icon production of the Antonievo-Siiskii Monastery reached the height of its development in the 17th century, when abbots Feodosii and Nikodim not only painted icons themselves but supported the development of the monastery's substantial icon-painting workshop.[29] The Siiskii Monastery atelier employed the talents of lay artists as well as monks. Some were local craftsmen, while others, such as Fedor Zubov, Bogdan Zotikov, and the Sol'vychegodsk painter Vasilii Kondakov worked periodically at the monastery on special commissions.[30] Their icons, as well as the bulk of work done by painters employed regularly at the monastery's workshop, appear to have been ordered to fill particular needs of various churches, ranging from an entire iconostasis to a single commission for a dedicatory icon, and thus do not reflect the preferences of individuals. The latter are revealed, however, in the personal donations of individuals recorded in the monastery's donation

---

[28] Kukushkina, *Monastyrskie biblioteki*, 25, 44, 103, 108–10, 165–67; Briusova, *Russkaia zhivopis' 17 veka*, 140, 144, 150–51, 158; Kol'tsova, *Severnye ikonopistsy*, 24. On the Siiskii pattern book, see Gleb Markelov, *Kniga ikonnykh obraztsov: 500 podlinnykh prorisei i perevodov s russkikh ikon XV–XIX vekov/Russian Icon Designs: A Compendium of 500 Canonical Imprints and Transfers of the Fifteenth to Nineteenth Centuries*, 2 vols. (St. Petersburg: Izd-vo Ivana Limbakha, 2002), 1: 5–16, 22, 24, 27, 540; T. M. Kol'tsova, "Arkhimandrit Antoniev-Siiskogo Monastyria Nikodim i ego rekomendatsii po restavratsii ikon," in *Grabarevskie chteniia V* (Moscow: Skanrus, 2003), 104–06. N. V. Pokrovskii's publication describes 470 patterns in detail: N. V. Pokrovskii, *Siiskii ikonopisnyi podlinnik*, parts 1–4 (St. Petersburg: Tip. Glav. upravleniia udelov, 1895–98). On the definitions of tracings and transfers and the techniques for producing and using both, see Markelov, *Kniga ikonnykh obraztsov*, 1: 5–30.

[29] On the workshop's painters and activities, see Mal'tseva, "Siiskii ikonopisnyi podlinnik," 19–34, and "Ikonopisnaia masterskaia Antonievo-Siiskogo monastyria," 58–73.

[30] Kol'tsova, *Severnye ikonopistsy*, 24. To date art historians have identified about 50 painters who worked at the monastery: see Kol'tsova, *Ikony severnogo poonezh'ia*, 22, 27–28, 36; Kol'tsova, *Severnye ikonopistsy*, 36–37, 40, 46, 49–50, 57–59, 66, 69–72, 78, 87, 90–92, 94–95, 98, 105, 108, 111, 114–15, 117–20; *Slovar' russkikh ikonopistsev XI–XVII vekov*, 29, 59, 70, 103, 120–21, 141, 147, 160, 214–15, 222, 226, 228, 248, 305–06, 316, 348–50, 370, 376, 394, 418, 429, 431–32, 450–51, 458, 520, 568–69, 608, 618–20, 639, 654, 681, 700, 710, 720–21, 723, 735, 763, 785; O. V. Ovsiannikov, "Severnyi ikonopisnyi fond po pis'mennym istochnikam: Puti formirovaniia i sud'by v XVI–XIX vv.," *Chteniia po issledovaniiu i restavratsii pamiatnikov khudozhestvennoi kul'tury Severnoi Rusi, posviashchennye pamiati khudozhnika-restavratora Nikolaia Vasil'evicha Pertseva 1902–1981* (Arkhangel'sk: Pravda Severa, 1992), 49–51; Makarii, "Istoricheskiia svedeniia," 57–58; P. Ivanov, "Opis' Siiskago monastyria 1598 g. i letopisnyiia zametki," *Drevnosti: Trudy Arkheograficheskoi komissii Imperatorskago Moskovskago arkheologicheskago obshchestva* 2 (1902), col. 376.

books (*vkladnye knigi*).[31] Between 1585/86 and 1695 28 donors gave the monastery 89 icons specifically identified by image (other entries refer only to icons with no further designation). Perhaps it is not surprising that two-thirds (18) of the donors were churchmen, ranging over the entire hierarchy from Patriarch Filaret to local elders. Half of the secular donors were local, from monastic lands or from Kholmogory. The "outsiders" included three Moscow residents and two Vologda townsmen.

    Analysis of the iconographic themes favored by donors sheds additional light on a question raised by Daniel Kaiser in his examination of the daily life of Russian urban residents. In looking at the role that icons played in the religious practices of 18th-century Moscow townsmen, Kaiser identified the themes of the icons that ordinary Christians installed in their homes in order to determine whether certain images had a "special hold on the venerations of early modern Russians."[32] The icons in the 18th-century private collections analyzed in Kaiser's study fell into four categories. Those depicting Mary, the Mother of God, "occupied the dominant position"—they comprised "nearly half of all icons reported as personal property." Within this category, the cult of the Kazan' Mother of God was most popular, followed by that of the Vladimir Mother of God. Icons of the Saviour accounted for less than a fifth of the total, with "generic" identifications slightly outnumbering specifically "Resurrection" depictions, followed by the Mandylion and "Tenderness" images. Representations of church holidays other than the Resurrection were quite rare. Icons depicting various saints showed the greatest variation and "accounted for a bit more than one-third" of the items in the data set. St. Nicholas was "far and away the most usual," with John the Baptist as the next most common. M. V. Vorozhbitova's analysis of about 1100 icons from private property seized by the Confiscation Chancellery between 1730 and 1782, summarized in Kaiser's study, reveals similar distribution patterns.[33]

    Donors to the Antonievo-Siiskii Monastery similarly showed a marked preference for images depicting the Mother of God, who appeared on 24 (28 percent) of the donated icons. Nine of these are not further identified. The Kazan' Mother of God figured on three, the Vladimir Mother of God also on

---

[31] For texts, see Iziumov, "Vkladnyia knigi"; Ivanov, "Opis' Siiskago monastyria 1598 g."; Makarii, "Istoricheskiia svedeniia."

[32] Daniel H. Kaiser, "Icons and Private Devotion Among Eighteenth-Century Moscow Townsfolk" (manuscript in progress). I am grateful to Prof. Kaiser for providing me with a copy of this study.

[33] M. V. Vorozhbitova, "K kharakteristike religioznogo soznaniia moskovskikh obyvatelei XVIII v. (na osnove sostava domovykh ikon)," in *Stolichnye i periferiinye goroda Rusi i Rossii v srednie veka i rannee novoe vremia (XI–XVIII vv.): Doklady tret'ei nauchnoi konferentsii (Murom, 17–20 maia 2000 g.)*, ed. V. L. Ianin (Moscow: Drevnekhranilishche, 2003), 249–58.

three (but all from the same donor), with single instances of other variations.[34] Two depictions of the Annunciation and one of the Dormition increased Mary's representation. Representations of the Saviour took various forms: four images of the Resurrection, two of the Transfiguration, two of the Entrance into Jerusalem, one of the Presentation (*Sretenie*), two of the All-Merciful (*Vsemilostivyi Spas*) and one of the Never-Sleeping (*Nedremannoe Oko*) Christ. Three donors contributed images of the Trinity, perhaps for the cathedral, and two gave depictions of the Lord God Sabaoth. Among images of saints, the five depictions of the Solovetskii Wonder-workers barely topped the four of John the Baptist. But ten icons were specifically identified as Deisus images, depicting Christ, His Mother, and John the Baptist. St. Nicholas appeared on only three donated icons, as did Antonii Siiskii. Other donations depicted a substantial number of additional saints.[35]

The selections of subject matter probably reflected the preoccupations of the largely clerical pool of donors. Two of the three St. Nicholas icons came from urban settlement residents, who presumably would have had more need of St. Nicholas' intercession in matters of marriage, travel, and welfare of livestock. In one case the depiction of St. Nicholas accompanied by the Apostle Andrew and Matthew the Evangelist was probably the only icon Bogdan Naumov Telovykh of Kholmogory owned, since he left it to the monastery along with his clothing and shoes.[36] Saints from their own area apparently appealed to both lay and clerical donors. In addition to the monastery's founder Antonii, the Solovetskii Wonder-workers and Kirill Belozerskii were regional saints. One of the bequests of Abbot Isidor of the nearby Koriazhemskii Monastery included Deisus icons portraying Christ, His Mother, and John the Baptist accompanied by Antonii Siiskii and Sergii of Radonezh, thus linking the icon to both the monastery and its gate-church.[37] Karp Avtonomov Gorbun of Vologda sent an icon depicting his town's wonder-worker, St. Dmitrii Prilutskii.[38] Elder Evfimei Protopopov, a church lector (*kryloshanin*) from

---

[34] The Mother of God Incarnate (*Voploshchenie*), interceding with Christ in the company of saints and martyrs, Tenderness (*Umilenie*), of the Sign (*Znamen'e*), Guiding (*Odigitriia*), "The Queen Doth Stand" (*Predsta tsaritsa*), "In Thee Rejoiceth" (*O tebe raduetsia*), the Konev Monastery image, and in the vision of St. Sergius.

[35] The Apostle Peter, the Moscow Wonder-Workers, Andrew the First-Called, Gerasim on the Jordan, St. Anthony, Dmitrii Prilutskii, John Chrysostom, the Myrrh-Bearing Women, Kirill Belozerskii, Semyon the God-Receiver, John the Theologian, Metropolitan Aleksei, the Great Martyr Catherine, the Venerable Pavel Obnorskii the Wonder-Worker, and Paraskeva Piatnitsa.

[36] Iziumov, "Vkladnyia knigi," 55. The other St. Nicholas icons came from the former abbot Pavel in 1664 (Iziumov, "Vkladnyia knigi," 62) and from Karp Avtonomov Gorbun, Vologda trader and icon-painter, in 1669 (Iziumov, "Vkladnyia knigi," 68).

[37] Ibid., 28–29.

[38] Ibid., 68.

Ustiug Velikii, donated an icon of the Kazan' Mother of God with depictions of the Ustiug Wonder-workers Prokopii and Ivan in the side margins.[39] The former abbot Pavel presented the monastery with an icon portraying the Venerable Pavel Obnorskii the Wonder-worker.[40] For Ivan Uarov, a secretary (*d'iak*) of the Patriarch, the appropriate donation was an image of his own regional protectors, the Moscow metropolitans Petr, Aleksei, Iona, and Filipp.[41]

Not all bequests, however, came to the monastery as intended. In 1676 elder Paisii Siiskii, who had long served as cellarer (*kelar'*) of the Antonievo-Siiskii Monastery, was appointed treasurer (*kaznachei*) for the Moscow Patriarch. From 1683 on he made large donations to the monastery, especially books, but also icons.[42] When Paisii died in 1695 he was buried at the Antonievo-Siiskii Monastery, which was supposed to receive additional bequests, including an especially treasured icon of the Mother of God "with many miraculous holy relics" (*so mnogimi sviatykh chudotvornymi moshchami*). Patriarch Adrian, however, ordered that the icon be given instead to the Transfiguration Cathedral in Kholmogory. Kholmogory was the seat of a recently created Northern archbishopric, and the patriarch supported the efforts of the first Archbishop of Kholmogory, Afanasii (1682–1702), to make his cathedral altar a model for the entire region, in the same way that the Kremlin Dormition Cathedral served the capital and the realm. Undoubtedly the loss of this prized relic intensified the animosity already evident between Archimandrite Nikodim of the Siiskii Monastery and Archbishop Afanasii, who had supported his own candidate for the position of archimandrite at Siiskii.[43] After Nikodim's appointment, the two became increasingly competitive both in their building of libraries and in their sponsorship of icon-painting workshops.

Monks frequently made donations of icons periodically over the years, in much the same way that Archimandrite Nikodim at various times transferred manuscripts from his personal cell collection to the monastic library. Our clearest indication of the iconographic themes most prized by members of the monastic community, however, probably comes from the notations of the contents of individual monks' cells at the time of their death. When elder Lavrentii died on October 10, 1676, the monastery's treasury acquired his re-

---

[39] Ibid., 36.

[40] Ibid., 62.

[41] Ibid., 50.

[42] Kukushkina, *Monastyrskie biblioteki*, 30. In 1683 along with other items Paisii donated 17 icons with carved silver crowns and gilded silver frames. Unfortunately, the iconographic subjects of these works were listed in the sacristy registers, not in the donation book (Iziumov, "Vkladnyia knigi," 77).

[43] V. N. Bulatov, *Muzh slova i razuma: Afanasii—pervyi arkhiepiskop Kholmogorskii i Vazhskii* (Arkhangel'sk: Pomorskii gosudarstvennyi universitet imeni M. V. Lomonosova, 2002), 160; Kukushkina, *Monastyrskie biblioteki*, 116.

maining possessions, including a triptych in a carved and gilded silver cover, another triptych with a carved silver cover, ungilded, a diptych with a damascened silver cover, an icon of the Mother of God with a chased silver cover and carved gold crown, and two icons in gold depicting Zosima and Savatii of Solovki and Antip and Kirill.[44] According to an inventory of April 19, 1677, the deceased elder Makarii Grudtsyn Maslov had a number of icons among the possessions in his cell: Deisus icons in a chased gilded cover, the crowns set with stones and the Saviour holding an amber cross; St. Kirill of Beloozero, the Wonder-Worker, in a chased cover, with a carved crown and attached adornments, not gilded; the Wonder-Worker Antonii, in a chased cover, with a carved crown and attached adornments, not gilded; a triptych on copper, depicting the Resurrection and other feast days of the Lord, with a silver cover, not gilded; another triptych in silver, with the Saviour and saints in the middle and the Trinity and Resurrection on the two side panels, with a carved gilded silver cover inscribed on the edges; and a diptych on copper depicting the Presentation and the Entrance into Jerusalem, without a cover. In addition his possessions included a pair of leaves (*stvory*) with an image of the Guiding Mother of God and the Lord God Sabaoth with archangels above, with saints on the sides, without a cover.[45] When elder Rafailo died on 1 June 1692, his estate contained an icon of Mother of God with a crown and cover of gilded silver, and a matching icon of the holy martyr Paraskeva, without a cover but with a gilded silver crown.[46] The size and value of estates might vary widely, but perhaps not surprisingly, the image each kept to the end was that of the Mother of God. The donation book of the Trinity-Sergius Monastery records a few parallel cases that bear out this pattern. Between 1638 and 1667 five elders at death left a total of 15 icons to the monastery, 7 of which depicted the Mother of God—and all five elders had at least one. Similarly, eleven donors, secular and religious, sent icons either with the coffin of the deceased or to be placed at the grave site—and 9 out of 11 were images of the Mother of God.[47]

Icons from the Muscovite period remained among the most precious relics of the monastery until the end of Imperial Russia. In the late 19th century the wonder-working Trinity icon, mounted in the chased silver niello frame sent by Patriarch Filaret, held the place of honor in the iconostasis near Antonii's tomb, while the adjoining side-chapel displayed Antonii's icon of the Mother of God Tenderness along with the wonder-working icon of the Smolensk Mother of God that had miraculously survived the 1658 fire.[48] But for

---

[44] Iziumov, "Vkladnyia knigi," 70.

[45] Ibid., 70–71; Makarii, "Istoricheskiia svedeniia," 82–83.

[46] Iziumov, "Vkladnyia knigi," 78.

[47] E. N. Klitina, T. N. Manushina, and T. V. Nikolaeva, eds., *Vkladnaia kniga Troitse-Sergieva monastyria* (Moscow: Nauka, 1987), 187, 206, 207, 210, 211 (elders) and 103, 109, 110, 136, 246, 249, 277 (others).

[48] Makarii, "Istoricheskiia svedeniia," 21.

the most part the monastery retained few traces of the 16th or 17th centuries. Recounting his travels in the region in the 1880s, the poet K. K. Sluchevskii, contrasted the Old Russian beauty of the interior of the Stroganovs' cathedral at Sol'vychegodsk with the shiny, gilded, bright-green framework of the icon-ostasis in the Siiskii Monastery church and the new, elaborately ornamented canopy over Antonii's relics. Almost all of the monastery's old icons had been overpainted, and "in truth, you don't know what is worse: the shiny new Ital-ianate images in the iconostasis or these unrecognizable outlines of old icons masked in paint and varnish."[49] After the 1917 Revolution, unfortunately, the Siiskii Monastery's icons were scattered. In the 1920s and 1930s some icons were taken from the monastery to the Tret'iakov Gallery in Moscow and the Russian Museum in then-Leningrad, some sent to local museums, and others were stolen or destroyed. The location of many remains unknown. The icons now in the museums of Petersburg, Moscow, and Arkhangel'sk remain, for practical purposes, unavailable for study under their layers of later overpaint-ing and darkened olifa, and their place of origin has not been determined.[50] The collection of the Arkhangel'sk museum includes an icon of the Mother of God Tenderness which has an inscription noting that this icon, painted by Antonii, was renovated in 1882.[51] It awaits restoration. The Arkhangel'sk col-lection also has a 17th-century depiction of John the Baptist with an inscrip-tion on the back noting that "Abbot Feodosii of the Siiskii Monastery prays before this holy image."[52] This is probably the icon of John the Baptist that Feodosii donated to the Antonievo-Siiskii Monastery, along with five others, in 1663.[53] Additional early works from the Siiskii Monastery may well be un-covered as restorers continue to clean the roughly 80 percent of stored icons still awaiting attention.

From its origins up to the 18th century, Antonii Siiskii's monastery sup-ported and developed the cultural life of the Russian North. Antonii and his successors built a major library collection, painted icons, and sponsored workshops that both created new icons and restored older works. Nikodim's pattern book, with its collection of models ranging from ancient Greek exam-ples to the new styles of the Kremlin Armory Chamber and tracings of West European engravings, attests that contemporary trends in icon painting "were not limited to the narrow region of Moscow" and penetrated into the Russian North.[54] The manual not only provided a compendium of styles in use in the 17th century, however, but it also included a narrative section summarizing

[49] Sluchevskii, *Po severo-zapadu Rossii*, 1: 213.

[50] Mal'tseva, "Siiskii ikonopisnyi podlinik," 25.

[51] Kol'tsova, *Severnye ikonopistsy*, 36–37; *Slovar' russkikh ikonopistsev*, 619–20.

[52] Kol'tsova, *Severnye ikonopistsy*, 119–20; *Slovar' russkikh ikonopistsev*, 723.

[53] Iziumov, "Vkladnyia knigi," 59.

[54] Kukushkina, *Monastyrskie biblioteki*, 166–67.

Nikodim's advice on the preservation and restoration of holy images. Drawing upon his decades of experience, he outlined the necessary conditions of temperature and air circulation, described suitable tools for restoration work, and gave recipes for cleaning agents to be used on dirty icons, for those with darkened olifa, while explaining how to treat those with and without covers. His compilation is an important testament to the first stages of the science and practice of art restoration in Russia, and it had great influence on Russian icon-painting culture, despite being compiled by an icon-painter in a remote Northern monastery.[55] While the monastery was remote in distance from Russia's center, it was not isolated. As its pattern book reveals, the art at Siiskii embodied the nation's iconography of the 17th century.[56]

---

[55] Kol'tsova, "Arkhimandrit Antonievo-Siiskogo Monastyria Nikodim," 106–09.

[56] Kukushkina, *Monastyrskie biblioteki*, 166.

Die Strasse in der Alltagswahrnehmung russischer Bauern des 17. Jahrhunderts

Carsten Goehrke

Zum Bild des „Rude and barbarous kingdom", welches die westeuropäischen Reiseberichte vom Moskauer Reich der frühen Neuzeit entwerfen,[1] tragen ganz wesentlich die Modalitäten des Reisens[2] bei: Endlose Naturstrassen, auf

---

[1] Für das 16. Jahrhundert s. Rude and Barbarous Kingdom: Russia in the Accounts of Sixteenth-Century English Voyagers, ed. Lloyd E. Berry and Robert O. Crummey. Madison: University of Wisconsin Press, 1968. – Für das 17. Jahrhundert s. in zeitlicher Reihenfolge beispielsweise Dnevnik Mariny Mnishek. St. Peterburg: Dmitrii Bulanin, 1995 (aus dem Polnischen); Adam Olearius, Vermehrte Newe Beschreibung Der Muscowitischen und Persischen Reyse. Schleswig 1656; repr. Tübingen: Niemeyer, 1971; Andrej Rode, Opisanie vtorogo posol'stva v Rossiiu datskogo poslannika Gansa Ol'delanda v 1659 godu. In: Utverzhdenie dinastii. Moscow: RITA-Print, 1997, S. 9–42; Puteshestvie v Moskoviiu barona Avgustina Meierberga … k tsariu i velikomu kniaziu Alekseiu Mikhailovichu v 1661 godu, opisannoe samim baronom Meierbergom. In: Utverzhdenie dinastii. S. 43–184 (Übersetzung aus dem lateinischen Originaltext); Nicolaas Witsen, Moscovische Reyse 1664–1665. Journaal en aentekeningen. Uitgegeven door Th.J.G. Locher en P. de Buck. Deel 1–3. 's-Gravenhage: Martinus Nijhoff, 1966/67 (unzureichende russische Übersetzung: Nikolaas Vitsen, Puteshestvie v Moskoviiu 1664–1665. Dnevnik. Perevod so starogollandskogo V. G. Trisman [St. Peterburg: Symposium, 1996]); Posol'stvo Kunrada fan-Klenka k tsariam Alekseiu Mikhailovichu i Feodoru Alekseevichu. St. Peterburg, 1900 (holländischer Text und russische Übersetzung); J. G. Sparwenfeld's Diary of a Journey to Russia 1684–87, ed. and trans. Ulla Birgegård. Stockholm: Kungl. Vitterhets Historie och Antikvitets Akademien, 2002 (schwedischer Text und englische Übersetzung); Johann Georg Korb, Tagebuch der Reise nach Russland. Hg. und eingeleitet von Gerhard Korb. Graz: Akad. Druck- und Verlagsanstalt, 1968 (deutsche Übersetzung des lateinischen Originaltextes).

[2] Zum Strassenwesen, Postdienst und Reiseverkehr Russlands in der frühen Neuzeit: E. G. Istomina, Dorogi Rossii v XVIII – nachale XIX veka. In: Issledovaniia po istorii Rossii XVI–XVII vv. Sb. statei v chest' 70-letiiu Ia. E. Vodarskogo. Moscow: RAN, 2000, S. 181–208; L. M. Marasinova, Puti i sredstva soobshcheniia. In: Ocherki russkoi kul'tury XVIII veka, chast' pervaia. Moscow: Izd. Moskovskogo universiteta, 1985, S. 257–284; A. S. Kudriavtsev, Ocherki istorii dorozhnogo stroitel'stva v SSSR (dooktiabr'skii period). Moscow: Dorizdat., 1951, S. 78–132; A. N. Vigilev, Istoriia otechestvennoi pochty, 2-e izdanie, pererab. i dopoln. Moscow: Radio i sviaz', 1990; Frank Joyeux, Der Transitweg von Moskau nach Daurien: Sibirische Transport- und Verkehrsprobleme im 17. Jahrhundert. Phil. Diss. Universität Köln. Köln, 1981; O. N. Kationov,

Rude & Barbarous Kingdom Revisited: Essays in Russian History and Culture in Honor of Robert O. Crummey. Chester S. L. Dunning, Russell E. Martin, and Daniel Rowland, eds. Bloomington, IN: Slavica Publishers, 2008, 341–51.

denen man während der „Zeit der Wegelosigkeit" *(rasputitsa)* im Schlamm versank – wenn im Frühjahr der Schnee taute und im Herbst erste Fröste und erneutes Tauwetter sich abwechselten –, aber bei anhaltendem Regen auch des Sommers; auf sumpfigen Wegstrecken Knüppeldämme, welche den Wagen derart durchrüttelten, dass die armen Insassen vermeinten, alle Knochen zu brechen; trotz besseren Fortkommens auf schneebedeckten und gefrorenen Strassen im Winter auf abschüssigen Strecken umstürzende Schlitten oder Schneewehen, in welchen man stecken blieb.[3] Auch Bauern traten in das Blickfeld der Reisenden, insoweit sie Gespanndienste zu leisten hatten oder vor den Fremden Reiss aus nahmen. Dabei registrierten die Ausländer mit ihrem an eine andere Kultur angepassten Blick[4] sehr wohl, wie unpopulär die vom Staat erzwungenen Gespanndienste bei den Bauern waren und wie brutal sie von den Vertretern der Obrigkeit dabei behandelt wurden. Aber dies war die Perspektive des fremden Blicks, des Blicks von aussen. Wie die Bauern selber, aus ihrer Alltagsperspektive heraus die Strasse erlebten – als Bestandteil ihres Wirtschaftslebens, ihres Sprachhorizontes, als Element der gesellschaftlichen Kommunikation, als Last, aber auch als Chance zugleich – ist bislang kaum untersucht worden.[5] Diesen Fragen soll mein Essay gelten, ohne dass ich dabei einen Anspruch auf Vollständigkeit erheben möchte. Aus Platzgründen beschränke ich mich auf das 17. Jahrhundert.

Dass die dichter besiedelten Regionen des Moskauer Reiches von einem regelrechten Geäder aus Naturstrassen durchzogen waren, zeigen die Kartenskizzen *(chertezhi)*, die sich vor allem aus der zweiten Hälfte des 17. Jahrhunderts erhalten haben. Es sind dies in der Regel grobe, nicht massstabgerechte Faustzeichnungen, welche Besitzgrenzen oder die Grenzen von Dorfgemarkungen wiedergeben und sich der Strassen als Orientierungshilfen bedienen. Dass die Strassen dabei ein hierarchisches Gefüge gebildet haben, welches von den Haupt- oder Poststrassen bis hinunter zu reinen Zufahrtswegen zu Heuschlägen auf Waldlichtungen reicht (oft ehemalige Siedlungen, soge-

---

Moskovsko-Sibirskii trakt i ego zhiteli v XVII – XIX vv. Novosibirsk: Izd. NGPU, 2004. – Oberflächlich und schlecht recherchiert dem gegenüber die historisch-geographische Dissertation von Paul Shott, The Role of Highways and Land Carriage in Tsarist Russia. Ph.D. University of Oklahoma, Oklahoma. Ann Arbor, Mich.: University Microfilms International, 1985.

[3] Für die zweite Hälfte des 18. Jahrhunderts s. Rudolf Mumenthaler, Über Stock und Stauden. Reiseumstände in Russland nach Reiseberichten aus der zweiten Hälfte des 18. Jahrhunderts. In: Zwischen Adria und Jenissei. Reisen in die Vergangenheit. Werner G. Zimmermann zum 70. Geburtstag, ed. Nada Boskovska et al. Zürich: Rohr, 1995, S. 225–272.

[4] Näheres bei Gabriele Scheidegger, Perverses Abendland – barbarisches Russland. Begegnungen des 16. und 17. Jahrhunderts im Schatten kultureller Missverständnisse. Zürich: Chronos, 1993.

[5] Zu einzelnen Aspekten s. Christoph Schmidt, Strasse und Wald im Zarenreich. In: Archiv für Kulturgeschichte, 78 (1996), S. 303–323.

nannte Wüstungen, *pustoshi*), lässt sich nicht nur der unterschiedlichen Strichstärke der Karten entnehmen,[6] sondern auch der Terminologie: An der Spitze rangiert die „Grosse Strasse" *(doroga bol'shaia)*, gefolgt von der „Strasse" ohne Zusatzbezeichnung *(doroga)*, der Nebenstrasse *(doroga proselochnaia)*, dem Fahrweg *(doroga proezzhaja)* und dem Strässlein *(dorozhka)*. Von den 110 topografischen Bezeichnungen, welche V. S. Kusov auf den von ihm untersuchten 975 Kartenskizzen des 16. und 17. Jahrhunderts fixiert hat, rangieren die Strassen mit 1,44 Prozent auf dem neunten Platz.[7]

Alle diese Strassen – selbst die vom Staat unterhaltenen Heer- oder Poststrassen – präsentierten sich als Naturstrassen,[8] also eigentlich als blosse Pisten, die lediglich an sumpfigen Stellen durch Bohlenbeläge bzw. Knüppeldämme *(mosty)* unterfüttert waren. Für die Posttrakte, die radial von Moskau ausstrahlten,[9] schrieb das Gerichtsbuch *(sudebnik)* von 1589 bei Strassen und Brücken eine Mindestbreite von anderthalb Sashen' (3, 2 Meter) vor, die auch in Wäldern frei gehalten werden mussten.[10] Im 17. Jahrhundert wurde die Mindestbreite auf 3 Sashen' (6, 4 Meter) erweitert; sogar Nebenstrassen mussten mindestens 2 Sashen' breit sein.[11] In der Praxis sah dies jedoch oft so aus, dass die Kutscher ausgefahrene Pisten, wo dies möglich war, umgingen und sich einen noch jungfräulichen Parallelweg suchten. In waldarmem Gelände konnte eine „Grosse Strasse" daher aus zahlreichen parallel verlaufenden Karrenrinnen bestehen, so dass der Trakt sich leicht auf hundert Meter Breite ausweiten konnte.[12]

---

[6] V. S. Kusov, Chertezhi zemli russkoi XVI–XVII vv. Moscow: Russkii mir, 1993, *passim*; Einzelbeispiele: A. P. Gudzinskaia, N. G. Mikhailova, Graficheskie materialy kak istochnik po istorii arkhitektury pomeshchich'ei i krest'ianskoi usadeb v Rossii XVII veka. In: Istoriia SSSR 1971, 5, S. 214–227; B. N. Morozov, Chertezh kontsa XVII veka podmoskovnoi votchiny kniazei Vorotynskikh. In: Arkhiv russkoi istorii, vyp. 2. Moscow 1992, S. 185–192.

[7] Kusov, Chertezhi, S. 42/43. Toponyme nach Häufigkeit der Nennung auf den Kartenskizzen: 1. pustosh', 2. derevnia, 3. rechka, 4. selo, 5. reka, 6. gorod, 7. sel'tso, 8. monastyr', 9. doroga etc. (alle Strassen summiert), 10. ozero, 11. tserkov'.

[8] Zeitgenössische Zeichnungen aus westlicher Feder in: Al'bom Meierberga, Vidy i bytovyia kartiny Rossii XVII veka. St. Peterburg 1903, Nr. 7, 9, 10, 24, 31, 32, 34, 37, 38, 48–51.

[9] Karten bei Vigilev, Istoriia otechestvennoi pochty, S. 110, 154, 173; Kudriavtsev, Ocherki istorii dorozhnogo stroitel'stva, bei S. 80.

[10] Sudebniki XV–XVI vekov. Pod obshchei red. B. D. Grekova. Moscow-Leningrad: Izd. AN SSSR, 1952, S. 413, § 224.

[11] Kudriavtsev, Ocherki istorii dorozhnogo stroitel'stva, S. 97.

[12] Dies war noch zu Beginn des 20. Jahrhunderts verbreitete Praxis, cf. Sergej S. von Podolinsky, Russland vor der Revolution. Die agrarsoziale Lage und Reformen. Berlin: Berlin Verlag, 1971, S. 110–112.

Wenn man vom innersten Lebenskreis der Bauern ausgeht, dann dienten die dorfnahen Strassen und Wege in erster Linie landwirtschaftlichen Zwecken. Vom Dorf aus, dessen Durchgangsstrasse beim Ein- und Austritt gelegentlich durch einen Schlagbaum oder eine Tordurchfahrt gesichert war,[13] fuhren die Bauern auf ihre Felder, um zu pflügen, zu säen und zu ernten oder das Vieh auf die Brache und in den Wald zu treiben. Auch entlegene Wüstungen wurden „per Anfahrt" (*naezdom*) genutzt, meist als extensive Heuschläge, wobei die Zufahrt mühsam und auf den Kartenskizzen oft nur durch eine gerissene Linie markiert war.[14] Zum unmittelbaren Wirtschaftshorizont der Bauern gehörte auch die Funktion der Strassen als Orientierungshilfe bei der Festlegung oder Neufestlegung von Besitzgrenzen, beispielsweise wenn es darum ging, die eigene Gemarkung gegen Nachbardörfer abzugrenzen und den Grenzverlauf in Besitzdokumente oder Steuerbücher eintragen zu lassen.[15] Dabei wird gelegentlich zwischen einer (leichter fahrbaren) Winterund einer (schwerer fahrbaren) Sommerstrasse unterschieden.[16]

Vom Heimatdorf weiter weg führten die Gütertransporte, welche insbesondere Bauern der zarischen Hofverwaltung (*dvortsovye*), Guts- und Klosterbauern für ihre Herrschaften zu leisten hatten. Mehrmals jährlich mussten sie Getreide, Schlachtvieh, Geflügel, Eier, Wodka, Bau- und Brennholz an den Zarenhof in Moskau, an ihren Herrenhof in der Stadt oder an ihr Kloster liefern, die oft Hunderte von Kilometern entfernt lagen.[17] Für die weite Reise wurden die dazu abgeordneten Fuhrleute mit einer Wegzehrung ausgestattet, welche man sinnvoller Weise „für den Weg" (*na dorogu*) nannte.[18]

Vom Heimatdorf weiter weg führte der Weg aber auch den Gemeindeältesten oder Starosten, wenn er in Steuerangelegenheiten zum Wojewoden in der Provinzstadt zitiert wurde. Wie das Ausgabenbuch des „Vereidigten" des Gemeindebezirks Sov'e im Kreis Viatka, Timofei Zagrebin, für das Rechnungsjahr 1674/75 ausweist, musste er im Laufe des Rechnungsjahres fünfzigmal für insgesamt 140 Tage nach Chlynov oder Slobodskoi reisen, um sich für den schleppenden Steuereingang seiner Bauern zu verantworten, für sie am Pranger zu stehen oder im Gefängnis zu sitzen und durch Bestechung der staatlichen Amtsträger und ihrer Gehilfen Fristerstreckungen für die Steuerzahlung zu erwirken. In der Regel mietete er dafür auf Gemeindekosten ein

---

[13] Abbildungen in: Al'bom Meierberga, Nr. 13, 23, 33.

[14] Kusov, Chertezhi, S. 103, 110, 145.

[15] Cf. Pamiatniki delovoi pis'mennosti XVII veka. Vladimirskii krai (im Folgenden PDPVK). Moscow: Nauka, 1984, Nr. 4, 10, 11; Pamiatniki russkogo narodno-razgovornogo iazyka XVII stoletiia (Iz fonda A. I. Bezobrazova). Izdanie podgotovili S. I. Kotkov et al. (im Folgenden PRNRIa), Moscow: Nauka, 1965, Nr. 65.

[16] Delovaia pis'mennost' Vologodskogo kraia XVII–XVIII vv. (im Folgenden DPVK), Vologda: VGPI, 1979, S. 38/39.

[17] Cf. beispielsweise die Transportlisten in: PDPVK, Nr. 75, S. 73.

[18] Beispiele aus dem späten 17. Jahrhundert für Klostergüter in: Ibid., Nr. 75, 84–86.

Fuhrwerk mit einem Kutscher, „zur schnelleren Beförderung" (dlia skorogo dela oder dlia skorogo pospeshen'ia) oder zu Zeiten der Wegelosigkeit (dlia bezdorozhitsy, bezdorozhitsa bol'shaia).[19]

Chancen bot die Strasse einzelnen Bauern dort, wo es an ihr etwas zu verdienen gab. Diese Möglichkeit eröffnete sich vor allem an viel befahrenen Heer- oder Poststrassen. Als Goldgruben erwiesen sich vor allem jene Stellen, wo eine „Grosse Strasse" einen Fluss querte und dieser für einen Brückenschlag zu breit war. Dann kamen entweder Seilfähren zum Einsatz[20] oder – wenn diese nicht möglich waren – Fährprähme, die mit Langrudern gesteuert wurden.[21] Die Rechte für den Fährbetrieb (perevoz) musste man von den Grundbesitzern, auf deren Land die betreffenden Stellen lagen – sei dies ein Kloster, sei dies die zarische Hofverwaltung, na otkup pachten.[22] Von den Gebühren für den Fährbetrieb profitierten nicht nur die Pächter, sondern auch die Bauern, die als Gehilfen im Einsatz standen und damit zu Nebeneinnahmen kamen. Allerdings war die Arbeit auf den Fähren nicht ohne Tücken, zumal ausländische Reisende immer wieder die geringe Professionalität der Fährleute beklagten. Als die dänische Gesandtschaft Hans Oldelands Anfang Juni 1659 auf dem Rückweg von Moskau bei Volokolamsk die Lama auf einem Floss von schlechter Qualität überquerte, kam durch die Ungeschicklichkeit der Fährleute einer der begleitenden Strelitzen fast zu Tode.[23] Als Marina Mniszech im Frühjahr 1606 auf dem Weg von Polen nach Moskau, wo sie den ersten falschen Zaren Demetrius ehelichen sollte, mit ihrem gewaltigen Tross den Dnepr überquerte, ertranken sogar mehrere Leute, weil der Fährprahm völlig überladen war.[24] Die Einnahmen aus Fährstellen waren offensichtlich so lukrativ, dass gelegentlich Nachbarbauern versuchten, Strasse und Überfahrt gewaltsam auf ihr eigenes Territorium zu verlegen. 1645 erhoben beispielsweise Bauern des Moskauer Voznesenskii-Klosters beim Zaren Anklage gegen Bauern des Patriarchen, weil diese die Zugfähre über die Nerl' im Kreis Vladimir, welche die Klosterbauern gepachtet hatten, mitsamt der Strassenzufahrt auf ihr Gemeindegebiet verlegt, die vorhandenen Fähreinrichtungen zerstört, den Prahm vom Zugseil gelöst und die

---

[19] A. A. Preobrazhenskii, Raskhodnaia kniga zemskogo tseloval'nika Sov'evskoi volosti Viatskogo uezda 1674–1675 goda. In: Arkheograficheskii ezhegodnik za 1966 god. Moscow: Nauka, 1968, S. 407–424.

[20] Abbildungen in: Al'bom Meierberga, Nr. 26, 35, 36.

[21] Ibid., Nr. 14.

[22] PDPVK, Nr. 87, S. 115; A. V. Topychkanov, Povsednevnaia zhizn' dvortsovogo sela Izmailova v dokumentakh prikaznoi izby poslednei chetverti XVII veka. Moscow: OAO Moskovskie uchebniki i Kartolitografiia, 2004, S. 80.

[23] Utverzhdenie dinastii, S. 41/42.

[24] Dnevnik Mariny Mnishek, S. 37.

Arbeiter vertrieben hätten.[25] Dieser Missbrauch dürfte gar nicht selten vorgekommen sein, denn das Gesetzbuch von 1649 widmete ihm sogar zwei
Paragraphen.[26]

Die Strassen waren schon im 17. Jahrhundert die Lebens- und Kommuni-
kationsadern Russlands – im Guten wie im Schlechten. Auf ihnen – und dort
wo es ging, auch auf den Flüssen – wickelten sich nicht nur die Last- und
Personentransporte ab, jagten die staatlichen Kuriere dahin, wälzten sich die
Truppen durchs Land. Sie dienten auch den Bauern, die mit oder ohne Pass
ihres Herrn auf Arbeitssuche unterwegs waren, zum raschen Vorankommen,
aber auch den Unmassen von Läuflingen, die sich der Bindung an die Scholle
durch Flucht zu entziehen suchten.[27] Das wussten natürlich auch die staatlichen Häscher *(syshchiki)*, welche die Spuren der entlaufenen Bauern aufzu-
nehmen und ihrer wieder habhaft zu werden suchten.[28]

Die Strasse zog aber ebenfalls all jene an, die meinten, man müsse sich an
geeigneter Stelle nur auf die Lauer legen und all das abschöpfen, was da an
Verlockungen vorüber zog. Die Akten des 17. Jahrhunderts sind voll von
Klagen über Raubüberfälle auf öffentlichen Verkehrswegen, sogar am hellen
Tage. Dabei ging es nicht einmal nur um schlichte Räuberbanden, die von
diesem Gewerbe lebten.[29] Sehr häufig handelte es sich nach dem Motto „Gelegenheit macht Diebe" um einen „Nebenerwerb" ganz normaler Menschen,
die eigentlich ihren Lebensunterhalt als Bauern verdienten. Häufig waren es
ganze Dörfer, deren Männer sich zusammentaten, um Strassentransporte zu
plündern – nicht selten auf Anstiften oder unter Führung ihres Herrn oder
seines Gutsverwalters.[30] Aber es brauchte nicht einmal wertvolle Waren, um

[25] Krest'ianskie chelobitnye XVII v. Iz sobranii Gosudarstvennogo Istoricheskogo
muzeia (im Folgenden KCh). Moscow: Nauka, 1994, Nr. 180, S. 145.

[26] Sobornoe ulozhenie 1649 goda. Tekst. Kommentarii. Rukoviditel' avtorskogo kol-
lektiva A. G. Man'kov. Leningrad: Nauka, 1987, Kap. IX, § 9, 19, S. 29/30; deutsch-
sprachige Ausgabe: Christian Meiske, Das Sobornoe Ulozhenie von 1649, Teil 1–2.
Halle/Saale 1985, Teil 1, S. 82, 85.

[27] I. V. Stepanov, Guliashchie – rabotnye liudi v Povolzh'e v XVII v. In: Istoricheskie
zapiski 36 (1951), S. 142–164.

[28] Näher dazu: Carsten Goehrke, Die Wüstungen in der Moskauer Rus'. Studien zur
Siedlungs-, Bevölkerungs- und Sozialgeschichte. Wiesbaden: Steiner, 1968, S. 180–200,
223–225.

[29] Beispiele dazu: S. I. Kotkov, N. P. Pankratova, Istochniki po istorii russkogo
narodno-razgovornogo iazyka XVII – nachala XVIII veka. Moscow: Nauka, 1964, S.
245, Nr. 43, 44; PRNRIa, S. 90, Nr. 162; S. 132, Nr. 9; S. 129, Nr. 2; PDP, Nr. 185.

[30] 1629 überfiel Fürst Ivan Meshtscherskii mit den Leuten seines Gutsdorfes einen
Bauern, der auf zwei Pferdeschlitten Mehlsäcke transportierte und nahm ihm die
Waren, die Pferde, die Kleider und das Geld ab, welches er als Pachtgebühr für
Heuschläge zu Gunsten der zarischen Hofverwaltung einkassiert hatte, s. KCh, Nr.
262; cf. ebenfalls Nr. 90 (1619). – Ganz ähnlich verhielt es sich auch mit der

sich einem Überfall auszusetzen: Als 1683 eine Kolonne von 108 Bauern der zarischen Hofverwaltung auf dem Weg zu weit entfernten Heuschlägen am Rand der Strasse eine Zwischenübernachtung einlegen musste, fiel in der Dunkelheit ein Gutsherr aus der Nähe mit seinen Knechten und Bauern über sie her, nahm ihnen Kleider und das bisschen Geld ab, das sie mit sich führten, und schlug zwei von ihnen halb tot.[31] Wenn zwei Nachbardörfer, die zu verschiedenen Herren gehörten und deren Äcker teilweise im Gemenge lagen, sich gegenseitig befehdeten, gehörte es zu den Standardmitteln der Einschüchterung, die Felder der anderen Seite zu überweiden, die gegnerischen Bauern auf der Strasse anzuhalten, zu verprügeln, auszurauben und ihnen den Weg zu versperren.[32]

Die Land-, sogar die Stadtstrassen blieben das ganze 17. Jahrhundert hindurch höchst unsicher.[33] Noch 1735 erliess die Regierung einen Ukaz, welcher vorschrieb, an den Stellen, wo der Posttrakt von Petersburg nach Moskau durch Wald führte, die Strassenschneise auf 30 Sashen' (ca. 64 Meter) zu verbreitern, um Raubüberfälle auf Reisende zu erschweren.[34]

Schwerer allerdings als die Unsicherheit auf den Strassen drückten die Lasten, welche der Staat den Bauern in Zusammenhang mit den Strassen aufbürdete: die Pflicht des Strassen- und Brückenunterhalts und die Anspannpflicht. Beides lastete zunächst auf allen steuerpflichtigen Bauern, wurde aber 1615 auf diejenigen Landgemeinden eingeschränkt, welche im Umfeld von Post- und Kurierstrassen lagen.[35] Die wichtigsten waren im 17. Jahrhundert die Poststrassen von Moskau über Rostov Veliki und Jaroslavl' nach Vologda (und Archangel'sk), von Moskau über Tver', Gross-Novgorod und Pskov nach Livland, von Moskau über Smolensk nach Wilna und schliesslich in südlicher Richtung von Moskau nach Kiev, nach Belgorod und nach Valuiki.[36] Dem Staat ging es vor allem darum, den Unterhalt von Strassen, Brücken und Fähren sicherzustellen, für staatliche Kuriere, für Dienstleute und Ausländer, welche mit staatlichen Pässen reisten, sowie für durchziehende Truppenteile die unentgeltliche Benutzung gebührenpflichtiger Passagen durchzusetzen

---

Flusspiraterie: 1688 plünderten die Männer eines Dorfes unter Führung ihres Gutsverwalters zwei Lastflösse auf der Suda, s. DPVK, S. 14/15.

[31] KCh, Nr. 267. – Ähnlich 1668 ein Überfall von Bauern auf andere Bauern und Bäuerinnen, die auf einer Wüstung einen Heuschlag mähten, s. DPVK, S. 53–55.

[32] PRNRIa, Nr. 5, S. 131.

[33] Zu den Regierungsmassnahmen gegen das Räuberunwesen cf. John L. H. Keep, Bandits and the Law in Muscovy. In: Ders., Power and the People: Essays on Russian History. Boulder-New York: Columbia University Press, 1995, S. 87–107 (= East European Monographs, No. CDXV).

[34] Schmidt, Strasse und Wald, S. 303.

[35] Kudriavtsev, Ocherki istorii dorozhnogo stroitel'stva, S. 97.

[36] Streckenkarten bei Vigilev, Istoriia otechestvennoi pochty, S. 90, 110.

und Missbräuche zu verhindern. Diesen Fragen galt im Gesetzbuch von 1649 das 9. Kapitel mit 20 Paragraphen.[37]

In jedem Frühjahr hatten die Bauerngemeinden, welche für den Strassenunterhalt zuständig waren, die Strassen wieder instand zu stellen und durch den Eisgang beschädigte Brücken zu reparieren. Besondere Arbeit machten dabei die Knüppeldämme, mit deren Hilfe sumpfige Strassenabschnitte passierbar gemacht werden sollten und die im Russischen wie die Brücken die Bezeichnung *mosty* trugen. Wie ein solcher Knüppeldamm auf der am stärksten befahrenen Poststrasse zwischen Moskau und Petersburg beschaffen war, beschreibt der Engländer William Coxe, der im letzten Viertel des 18. Jahrhunderts Osteuropa bereiste: „Die Strasse ist allenthalben gleich breit, und auf folgende Art angelegt: queer über dieselbe liegen in gleichlaufenden Reihen Baumstrünke, die in der Mitte und an beyden Enden durch lange Stangen und hölzerne Pflöcke an die Erde befestiget sind. Diese Baumstrünke sind mit Ästen belegt, und diese sind obenauf mit Sand oder Erde überstreut. So lange die Strasse neu ist, ist sie ganz gut zu befahren; wenn aber die Baumstämme tiefer in den Boden einsinken, und wenn der Sand oder die Erde davon abgerieben oder durch Regen weggespühlt worden, wie das oft mehrere Meilen hintereinander der Fall ist: dann hat die Strasse beynahe nichts anders als eine ununterbrochene Reihe von Furchen, und die Bewegung des Wagens ein unaufhörliches Stossen, und diess viel heftiger, als ich es je auf dem rauhesten Pflaster empfunden habe."[38] Man hat berechnet, dass für 150 Werst Unterbau dieser Art 2,1 Millionen Baumstämme erforderlich waren.[39] Ein Reisender des 17. Jahrhunderts zählte allein auf der Poststrasse zwischen Moskau und Smolensk 533 derartiger Knüppeldämme.[40] Da kann man ermessen, welche Mühsal sich vor den unglücklichen Bauern auftürmte, denen die Instandhaltung dieser Strasse oblag. Und das Ergebnis sah nach kurzer Zeit doch wieder so aus, dass noch die Reisenden des ausgehenden 18. Jahrhunderts trotz neuer Wagentypen ihr blaues Wunder erlebten.[41] Dies betraf

---

[37] Sobornoe ulozhenie 1649 goda, Kap. IX „O mytach, i o perevozech, i o mostach", S. 28–30; deutsche Übersetzung bei Meiske (1985), S. 80–85 („Von Zöllen, Fähren und Brücken").

[38] Wilhelm Coxe, Reise durch Polen, Russland, Schweden und Dänemark. Mit historischen Nachrichten und politischen Bemerkungen begleitet. Aus dem Englischen von J. Pezzl. Bd. 1–3, Zürich 1785–1792, hier Bd. 1 (1785), S. 318/19. – Englische Originalausgabe: William Coxe, Travels in Poland and Russia. Three volumes in one. Reprint New York: Arno Press and The New York Times, 1970.

[39] Carsten Goehrke, Russischer Alltag. Eine Geschichte in neun Zeitbildern vom Frühmittelalter bis zur Gegenwart. Bd. 1–3, Zürich: Chronos, 2003–2005, hier Bd. 2 (2003), S. 52.

[40] Vigilev, Istoriia otechestvennoi pochty, S. 79.

[41] Zum verfügbaren Sortiment an Fuhrwerken und zu den Reiseumständen im 18. Jahrhundert: Mumenthaler, Über Stock und Stauden...

insbesondere die am stärksten befahrenen Poststrassen: Zwischen Moskau und Jaroslavl' an der Wolga waren im 17. Jahrhundert täglich bis zu 700 oder 800 Lasttransporte gleichzeitig unterwegs,[42] und die häufigen ausländischen Gesandtschaften führten allein schon um des Prestiges Willen einen grossen Tross mit. Marina Mniszech als künftige Zarin brachte im Frühjahr 1606 auf ihrem Weg von Polen nach Moskau ein offizielles Gefolge von 1.969 Personen nebst 1.991 Pferden mit; hinzu kamen als Moskauer Eskorte weitere 300 Personen zu Pferde. In kluger Voraussicht hatten die Russen zuvor die Brücken und Knüppeldämme extra ausgebessert, doch trotzdem versanken kurz vor Smolensk viele Fuhrwerke wegen des Strassenzustands im Morast.[43]

Wenn die Reparaturarbeiten an Strassen und Brücken aufwändig und schwer, aber zeitlich kalkulierbar waren, da sie im Frühjahr stattfanden, verhielt es sich mit den Anspanndiensten völlig anders. Mit ihnen musste man das ganze Jahr hindurch rechnen, und oft kamen sie in einem für die Bauern ungünstigen Moment – etwa während man mit Erntearbeiten beschäftigt war. Mit den Anspanndiensten verhielt es sich so: Für den regulären Post- und Kurierdienst standen Staatspferde zur Verfügung, die an den Poststationen (iamy) gewechselt wurden. Wenn jedoch der gerade verfügbare Bestand an Staatspferden nicht ausreichte, weil Transportleistungen ausser der Reihe zu erbringen waren oder ausländische Reisende mit grossen Trossen durchpassierten, dann wurden Bauern mit ihren Rossen aufgeboten. Dass sie diese Aufgebote unwillig befolgten und sie nach Kräften zu sabotieren suchten, lässt sich gut nachvollziehen. Doch die Vertreter der Staatsmacht waren nicht zimperlich, um Säumigen Beine zu machen. Der polnische Verfasser des sogenannten „Tagebuches Marina Mniszechs", der seine Herrin nach der Ermordung des ersten falschen Demetrius in die Internierung begleitet hatte, berichtet, was er am 26. Juni 1608 an einer Poststation auf der Strasse von Jaroslavl' nach Vologda anlässlich eines Aufgebotes an Hunderten von Bauerngespannen beobachten konnte: „Dies geschieht mit einer ausserordentlicher Grausamkeit, mit welcher sie die Leute behandeln, denn wenn diese sich verspäten, dann bestrafen sie sie auf folgende Weise: Sie stellen alle Muzhiki in einer Reihe auf und – am einen Ende beginnend – schlagen drei Mann mit einer Peitsche jeder einen Muzhik dreimal auf die Beine. Und wenn sie die Runde beendet haben, fangen sie wieder von vorne an, so lange, bis die Fuhrwerke vollzählig sind."[44] In fast jedem ausländischen Reisebericht können wir lesen, dass es zu Verzögerungen kam, weil die Bauern unterwegs bei erster sich bietender Gelegenheit mitsamt ihren Pferden verschwanden.[45]

---

[42] Kudriavtsev, Ocherki istorii dorozhnogo stroitel'stva, S. 80.

[43] Dnevnik Mariny Mnishek, S. 36.

[44] Ibid., S. 116. – Der Beobachter beschreibt hier offensichtlich die Praxis des *pravezh*, bei welcher die Delinquenten mit Stöcken auf die Schienbeine geschlagen wurden.

[45] Posol'stvo Kunrada fan-Klenka, S. 370; Witsen, Moscovische Reyse; holländischer Text (Teil 2), S. 239.

Wen die Verfolger wieder schnappten, wurde „dapper geslaagen", wie Witsen auf Holländisch schreibt.[46]

Da nimmt es nicht Wunder, dass viele Dörfer an Poststrassen leer waren, wenn eine ausländische Reisegruppe mit grossem Tross sich näherte.[47] Als die holsteinische Gesandtschaft, als deren Sekretär Adam Olearius amtete, 1634 zwischen Gross Novgorod und Torzhok unterwegs war, liessen die Bauern eines Dorfes sogar einen Bienenschwarm los, um die ungebetenen Gäste so schnell wie möglich zu verscheuchen.[48] Wie die Heuschreckenplage müssen die ausländischen Gesandtschaftstrosse den russischen Bauern vorgekommen sein, zumal wenn sie sich auch noch zur Rast auf den frisch bestellten Äckern breit machten. Als 1676 die holländische Gesandtschaft Koenraad van Klenks auf der Rückreise von Moskau nach Archangel'sk zwischen dem Troitsa-Sergiev-Kloster und Aleksandrov auf einem Feld neben der Heerstrasse rastete, zeigten sich schon bald Horden mit Knüppeln bewaffneter Bauern unter Führung ihres Gutsherrn, die Anstalten machten, die ungebetenen Gäste davonzuprügeln. Erst als sich herausstellte, mit welch hochrangigen Persönlichkeiten man es zu tun hatte, lenkte der Dienstadlige ein und versöhnte sich mit dem holländischen Gesandten bei einem guten Trunk Branntwein.[49]

Schwer lastete auf den Bauerndörfern und Städten entlang der Durchgangsstrassen auch die Einquartierungspflicht. Selbst im Frieden führten in Dörfern einquartierte russische Truppen sich auf, als ob sie feindliche Besatzer wären, nahmen den Bauern das Vieh weg und plünderten die Felder.[50] Johann Georg Korb, der mit der habsburgischen Gesandtschaft von 1698/99 in dem damaligen russischen Grenzstädtchen Dosoguvo westlich Smolensk übernachten musste, erkundete gemeinsam mit dem lokalen Starosten Einquartierungsmöglichkeiten. Als dieser sich für das beste Haus am Ort entschied, bezog er vom entnervten Hausbesitzer, der wohl ständig molestiert wurde, eine kräftige Tracht Prügel.[51]

Aber selbst ausserhalb dieser „normalen" Unzuträglichkeiten war ein Bauer, der sich auf einer Staatsstrasse bewegte oder in deren Nähe seinen Verrichtungen nachging, vor unangenehmen Überraschungen nie sicher. Immer wieder kam es vor, dass ein staatlicher Eilkurier (gonets), dessen Reittier erschöpft war, bevor er die nächste Poststation erreicht hatte, einem Bauern einfach das Arbeitspferd ausspannte und damit auf Nimmerwie-

---

[46] Ibid.

[47] Olearius, Vermehrte Newe Beschreibung, S. 23, 26.

[48] Ibid., S. 26.

[49] Posol'stvo Kunrada fan-Klenka, S. 551.

[50] PRNRIa, Nr. 156, S. 88.

[51] Korb, Tagebuch der Reise nach Russland, S. 44.

dersehen davon jagte.[52] Das konnte für den betroffenen Landwirt zu doppeltem Schaden führen: Als in einem solchen Fall der wütende Bauer, der mit seinen Produkten gerade zum Markt in Moskau unterwegs war, den Kurier verfolgte und ihm das entwendete Ross wieder abzunehmen versuchte, fielen in der Zwischenzeit andere Bauern über seinen verlassenen Karren her und plünderten ihn aus.[53]

Alles in Allem wird man wohl annehmen dürfen, dass vor allem für die Bauern, die in der Nähe von Poststrassen lebten, die Alltagswahrnehmung der Strasse eher negativ besetzt war. Die Strasse musste ihnen als ein Teil des Zwangssystems erscheinen, in welches sie eingebunden waren und das ihnen in Gestalt von Machtträgern – Kurieren, Vorstehern von Poststationen, Offizieren und Pristawen, welche ausländischen Gesandtschaften als Chefs der Begleiteskorten beigegeben wurden – immer nur fordernd entgegentrat und seine Forderungen mit Rücksichtslosigkeit und Gewalt durchsetzte. Wehren konnte man sich dagegen nur bedingt: durch kollektive Verweigerungs- und Verzögerungsmanöver, wo dies gewisse Aussichten auf Erfolg bot, durch Widerstand, wenn man sich im Bunde mit dem eigenen Herrn wusste, und am ehesten durch Flucht. Den Rechtsweg zu beschreiten durch Bitt- und Klageschriften war langwierig, unsicher und hatte allenfalls Aussicht auf Erfolg, wenn die eigenen Herren mitzogen.

So erscheinen die Strassen des Moskauer Reiches im 17. Jahrhundert als eine Art Brennglas, in welchem sich viele der Probleme widerspiegeln, die den Alltag der bäuerlichen Gesellschaft jener Zeit geprägt haben – die öffentliche Unsicherheit, die weitgehende Rechtlosigkeit der Bevölkerung, die Solidarität der Dorfgemeinschaft im Guten wie im Schlechten, die Versuchung zur Selbstbereicherung, wenn sich eine Gelegenheit dazu bot, und schliesslich das Mittel der Gewaltanwendung sowohl von oben nach unten als auch von unten nach oben und sogar der Bauern untereinander.

---

[52] Moskovskaia delovaia i bytovaia pis'mennost' XVII veka. Izd. podgotovili S. I. Kotkov et al. Moscow: Nauka, 1968, Nr. 55, S. 70/71 (aus dem Jahr 1658).

[53] KCh, Nr. 95, S. 94 (Ende des 17. Jahrhunderts).

The King "Should Be but Imaginary": The Commonwealth of Poland-Lithuania in the Eyes of an English Diplomat, 1598

Nancy S. Kollmann

Many of us were introduced to Robert Crummey's work when we read Giles Fletcher and other English travelers in that memorably titled book, *Rude and Barbarous Kingdom*. Amidst his prodigious scholarship—ranging widely from boyar culture to Old Believer communities to the spirituality of Old Belief— Bob's publication of early English travelers to Russia has been particularly influential. Like many other publications at the time,[1] it responded to America's Cold War fascination with Russia; subsequently, as the waves of "culture wars," deconstructionism, and a "linguistic turn" moved through historical studies, *Rude and Barbarous Kingdom* provided students a fertile field of political incorrectness that they could submit to ever more sophisticated critique. While appreciative of the factual knowledge these travelers provided, even Crummey noted judiciously in 1968 that to place "considerable reliance on the information provided by European travelers ... is a treacherous, although necessary, undertaking."[2] Since the publication of Marshall Poe's and Larry Wolff's studies of tropes about Eastern Europe and Russia in European travel literature,[3] we are all the more sensitive to the subjectivity of sources that dare to call another culture "barbarous." What prompted Bob to disseminate the English accounts, and what keeps us all coming back to them, of course, is the optimistic hope that historians can cull something of real historical insight from sources so deeply imbricated with presuppositions, judgments, and comparisons. Some of these authors were, after all, eyewitnesses.

---

[1] On travel accounts alone, see the Arno Press series "Russia Observed," with over 25 titles published in 1970–71, and also Harry W. Nerhood, *To Russia and Return: An Annotated Bibliography of Travelers' English-Language Accounts of Russia from the Ninth Century to the Present* (Columbus: Ohio State University Press, 1968).

[2] Lloyd E. Berry and Robert O. Crummey, eds., *Rude and Barbarous Kingdom. Russia in the Accounts of Sixteenth-Century English Voyagers* (Madison: University of Wisconsin Press, 1968), xiv.

[3] Marshall T. Poe, *"A People Born to Slavery": Russia in Early Modern European Ethnography, 1476–1748* (Ithaca, NY: Cornell University Press, 2000); Larry Wolff, *Inventing Eastern Europe: The Map of Civilization on the Mind of the Enlightenment* (Stanford, CA: Stanford University Press, 1994).

Rude & Barbarous Kingdom Revisited: Essays in Russian History and Culture in Honor of Robert O. Crummey. Chester S. L. Dunning, Russell E. Martin, and Daniel Rowland, eds. Bloomington, IN: Slavica Publishers, 2008, 353–66.

Giles Fletcher certainly was, and he was also a product of Eton and Cambridge University. His "Of the Russe Commonwealth" is perhaps the most influential among those published by Crummey. I for one have studied and analyzed it over many years. Therefore I was fascinated while teaching East European history to discover (on the recommendation of my colleague Frank Sysyn) a travel account that complements Fletcher in striking ways. Soon after Fletcher's 1591 account of Muscovy, in 1598 another English diplomat, George Carew, penned a description of the Commonwealth of Poland-Lithuania.[4] Carew was a university-educated lawyer, MP, and highly placed Chancery official, author of a highly-regarded manual of bureaucratic procedures. As a diplomat he was sent on sojourns to Poland in 1598 and France in 1605, ending life in 1612 with a knighthood, powerful patrons, and a modest fortune.[5]

Carew was also a scholar, if not by profession, then by avocation. He wrote a great deal, employing a research method of eye-witness observation, personal interviews, and secondary reading. In addition to the diplomatic dispatches written in Latin that Carew sent to the Queen in 1598, which focus on Baltic issues,[6] Carew in that year or soon thereafter wrote a comprehensive survey of the entire Commonwealth. After his diplomatic service in France in 1605–09, he wrote a similar "Relation" about French society, politics, and geopolitics. But neither work—both apparently submitted to his monarch and both extant in manuscript in royal collections—was published in his lifetime. His "Relation of the State of France" was published in 1749,[7] and his account of Poland-Lithuania saw the light of day in full publication only in 1965.[8]

In writing such learned treatises, Carew was probably influenced by the example of his elder brother Robert, a professional historian. But that he did not publish them has contributed to debates on the authorship of his Polish book, whose manuscript identifies no author. The eminent Polish historian

[4] Carolus H. Talbot, ed., "Relation of the State of Polonia and the United Provinces of that Crown Anno 1598," *Elementa ad Fontium Editiones* 13 (Rome, 1965).

[5] W. J. Jones, "Carew, Sir George (ca. 1556–1612)," *Oxford Dictionary of National Biography* (2004).

[6] "Res Polonicae Elisabetha I Angliae Regnante Conscriptae...," *Elementa ad Fontium Editiones* 4 (Rome, 1961), no. 153.

[7] Carew's French account is included in Thomas Birch, ed., *An Historical View of the Negotiations Between the Courts of England, France, and Brussels, from the Year 1592 to 1617...* (London, 1749).

[8] "Relation." Before that, Siegfried Mews published a complete summary of Carew's text, with extensive quotations translated into German: *Ein englischer Gesandtschaftsbericht über den polnischen Staat zu Ende des 16. Jahrhunderts* (Leipzig: S. Hirzel, 1936). Long excerpts regarding religion have been published in Elida Maria Szarota, ed., *Die gelehrte Welt des 17. Jahrhunderts über Polen* (Vienna: Europaverlag, 1972), 44–52; and in Stanislas Lubieniecki, *History of the Polish Reformation and Nine Related Documents*, ed. George Huntston Williams (Minneapolis: Fortress Press, 1995), 390–98.

Stanisław Kot attributed it to William Bruce (a jurist who taught at Jan Zamoyski's academy in Poland in the late 1590s) on the strength of his Polish experience and his authorship of works about the Turks and Tatars.[9] But recent authors have argued convincingly for Carew, citing his superior skills in English (Bruce, a Scot, admitted to being unskilled in English), his Protestant sympathies (Bruce's Catholicism clashes with the text's hostility to the Papacy and Jesuits), his similar book on France, and evidence that the French historian Jacques-Auguste de Thou used Carew's dispatches on Poland in his own history.[10]

George Carew was like Giles Fletcher in many ways—university educated, fluent in Latin and Elizabethan English, a devoted diplomat and civil servant to Elizabeth I, a Protestant. Since the Polish-Lithuanian Commonwealth at the end of the 16th century was so different from Muscovy, Carew drew rather different conclusions than did Fletcher. But the sensibility in the two accounts is the same. They represent the genre of what Poe calls "state descriptive" literature. Both authors had first-hand, eyewitness experience and also scholarly knowledge based on study of published travelogues and histories. Fletcher went to Russia as an envoy of Elizabeth I in 1588–89 and penned an account that so outraged proponents of trade with Muscovy that they had it banned; needless to say, it was also banned in Russia until its first full publication in the revolutionary year of 1905. Nevertheless, in England Fletcher's work went through several (often bowdlerized) editions,[11] since it

---

[9] "Bruce (Bruse, Brussius) William," *Polski słownik biograficzny* (Cracow) 3 (1937): 3–4.

[10] Talbot argues for Carew in "Introductio," in "Relation," xiii–xiv. Sebastian Sobecki makes so strong an argument for Carew that his cautionary conclusion ("one cannot argue for Carew's authorship with the same certainty with which William Bruce can be excluded"—p. 176) seems unwarranted. Sobecki, "The Authorship of *A Relation of The State of Polonia, 1598*," *The Seventeenth Century* 18, no. 2 (2003): 172–79. Jones says that de Thou used the "Relation" in Book 121 of his "Universal History," while Talbot says de Thou used the dispatches (Jones, "Carew" vs. Talbot, "Introductio," xiii). Comparison of Carew's Latin dispatches ("Res Polonicae," nos. 152 and 153) and his "Relation" with de Thou's text suggests Talbot is correct. In addition, it is known that de Thou and Carew were personal friends and de Thou himself praised Carew as (in a later French translation) "jeune homme qui avait autant de sagesse que de courage." See Jacques-Auguste de Thou, *Histoire universelle...* (London/Paris, 1734), 13, bk. 121, p. 316 and passim.

[11] On editions, see Marshall Poe, *Foreign Descriptions of Muscovy: An Analytic Bibliography of Primary and Secondary Sources* (Columbus, OH: Slavica Publishers, 1995), 124; and *Rude and Barbarous Kingdom*, 108. On its reception in England and Russia, see *Rude and Barbarous Kingdom*, 107–08; and Giles Fletcher, *Of the Russe Commonwealth by Giles Fletcher: 1591*, ed. Richard Pipes (Cambridge, MA: Harvard University Press, 1966), 26.

spoke to the English fascination with things Russian in the 16th and 17th centuries.[12]

Carew's account would not have pleased most Poles, had they known about it, but it would have confirmed some of what the literate English public in the late 16th century thought about points east. In their different ways Fletcher and Carew both exemplify contemporary tropes about Eastern Europe. Fletcher, for example, condemned Muscovite "tyranny" and lawlessness, decried the degradation of what he called Muscovy's "nobility" and condemned Russian Orthodoxy in terms a Protestant would use against Catholicism, reviling its superstition, ritual and clerical ignorance. As another student of "Of the Russe Commonwealth" has remarked, "what it says of Russia tells us indirectly what Fletcher thinks of England."[13]

One can say the same of Carew. Betraying, like Fletcher, a respect for rule of law, benevolent monarchy, a civically conscious nobility, and a thriving economy, Carew finds in the Polish-Lithuanian Commonwealth a king stripped of power, a narcissistic aristocracy, and a stifled economy. Carew's comments on Poland-Lithuania echo the ideas of popular theorists such as Sir Thomas Smith, who portrayed the "sovereignty" of England as a partnership of monarch and commons, represented not merely by Parliament and nobility but ultimately by a free citizenry from noble to yeoman (male, of course); Smith also, like Carew, emphasized the importance of a free peasant economy for progress.[14]

Let us first survey the "Relation" as the "state-description" that it presents itself as. For the modern reader, the text can present challenges. Not divided into thematic chapters as was Fletcher's work, Carew's text is only earmarked by topics in the margins. Although the language is a lively Elizabethan prose with many entertaining turns of phrase, the vocabulary can be hard going. Carew often slips into a macaronic combination of English and Latin, usually regarding legal and diplomatic topics, and he lards his English with now antiquated vocabulary (*bawres* for peasants, from the German *bauer*; *kmetones* for serfs; *fumalia* for tax)—all of this off-putting to 21st-century American undergraduates.

Reflecting England's lively interest in exotic peoples, Carew peppers his text with ethnic characterizations and stereotypes, for which the Common-

---

[12] Daryl W. Palmer, *Writing Russia in the Age of Shakespeare* (Aldershot, UK: Ashgate, 2004); Elena Shvarts, "Putting Russia on the Globe: The Matter of Muscovy in Early Modern English Travel Writing and Literature" (Ph.D. diss., Stanford University, 2004); Rima Greenhill, "From Russia with Love: A Case of *Love's Labour's Lost*," *The Oxfordian* 9 (2006): 9–32.

[13] Richard Pipes, introduction to Fletcher, *Of the Russe Commonwealth*, 26.

[14] See Anne McLaren's's account of the gender tensions in Smith's theory: "Reading Sir Thomas Smith's *De Republica Anglorum* as Protestant Apologetic," *The Historical Journal* 42: 4 (1999): 911–39.

wealth's diverse population provided many opportunities. On his first page he characterizes the Poles with details suggestive of personal experience: "they are large of body, tall, uprighte, and personable. The gentry full of ceremonies, civill and curteous in enterteinement, bountifull at table, costly in dyett, great gourmandes, and quaffers, not sleepy, nor heavy in theire dronkennesse, as the Dutche, but furious, and quarellsome, highe-mynded, and proude, but in a iollity, and not surly, as the Germans"(3). On people of the steppe, whom he did not visit, on the other hand, he relies on tropes. Like other travelers, he praised the Dnieper Cossacks for their bravery and hardiness and calls them "wonderfull skillfull in besetting the wayes, intercepting the enemy" (115), while he conforms to stereotype in calling the Crimean Tatars "a barbarous people of infamous lyfe ... all lyve idlely, they counting it base to trade, or use mechanicall artes" (155).[15]

While such ethnographic comments are interspersed in the text, Carew is mainly focused on the political. He wants to know who is in power, what the institutions are, who pays what tax to whom, and how they make money. For students of early modern Poland, his text is a rich resource—it describes not only the central institutions of the public sphere of the Commonwealth, but also the many pockets of social, regional, and confessional autonomies that abounded in that complex, typically early modern polity.

Carew is particularly assiduous in describing the economic resources and geopolitics of the Baltic coast, not surprisingly since he was sent by Queen Elizabeth to defend England's maritime interests in the Baltic against Spanish intrigues.[16] He provides fascinating detail on Pomerania and Ducal Prussia— semi-autonomous vassal states in Crown Poland, itself half of the newly formed (1569) "Commonwealth of Poland-Lithuania" (8–31). Carew describes the thriving metropolises of the Prussian lands—Koenigsburg with its university; the semi-autonomous bishopric of Warmia; the self-governing cities of Danzig and Elbing. Reflecting his economic philosophy, he praises this Baltic enclave: "the state of the people is much better then in Polonia; they may purchase mannors, are capable of honours, magistracies and spirituall prefermentes, and admitted to the Counsaile ... standing allwayes uppon theire Germane libertie would not leave theire owne lawes for those of Polonia ... which in tyme would have made the people slaves to the Nobilitie, and so have impoverished and ruined the countrey" (19).

Describing Crown Poland, Carew defines the provinces, palatinates, bishoprics, and other administrative centers of greater and lesser Poland and identifies vassal duchies and their special rights and obligations to the King (5–6). He expounds at length on the autonomies of the principality of

---

[15] See my essay on similar tropes in travel accounts to Ukraine: Kollmann, "The Deceitful Gaze: Ukraine Through the Eyes of Foreign Travelers," *Journal of Ukrainian Studies* (forthcoming).

[16] "Res Polonicae," no. 139.

Mazovia (6–7) and relates the history of Polish control of Galicia and Volhynia, calling it "Russia rubra" (7). Of Podolia in modern-day western
Ukraine, he remarks "It farr excells any place of Europe for grayne and pas-
ture" but notes that its "wonderfull fertilitie" is untapped because of constant
Tatar raids (7–8). He identifies the rivers and resources of Volhynia, pausing
to remark on the towering personality of the Duke of Ostrih/Ostrog, Constantine, Palatine of Kiev, "a greate souldioure, and of greate service for the
Crowne … but blunt and not so wise a Senatoure, according to the nature of
hys countrey" (31). He amplifies on that last comment: "The Inhabitantes of
Volhinia are the most valiant and warlike of all the Russians as continually
exercised with the incursions of the Tatars, which makes that bothe the
Princes, and Nobles are more feirce, rude and unlearned then the Polonians,
as bordering and so participating of the nature of those barbarous nations"
(32). Here Carew echoes tropes identified by Poe and Wolff, distinguishing
degrees of civility and barbarity across the Commonwealth.

Carew devotes extensive attention to the Grand Duchy (32–38), detailing
its rivers and resources, offices and bishoprics and casting a critical eye on
myths of the origins of the Lithuanian dynasty (34). Detailing the terms of the
Unions of Krewo (1385) and Lublin (1569), he accurately observes the tensions
between Poland and Lithuania in their dynastic relationship: "Notwithstanding thys union, the Lithuanians held theire state severall from the Crowne, accounting it but as a stricte confederacy, and themselves not obnoxious the
Maiestie of Polonia" (36). He again plays with barbarity and civility in describing the Lithuanians of Samogitia: "resting in their barbarousnes and not
desyring wealth, or troubling themselves with ambition, covetousnes, or
other cankers of mans mynde. Of body very large, tall, and stronge as growing from theire cradle in hardnes, and unacquainted with delightes, studies,
and exercises of the intellectuall facultie … lyke the Lithuanians in language
and in manners, but that they are more barbarous, and the Lithuanians made
mylder and civiller by a greater knowledge, and fixed profession of Christianity" (38).

Befitting his diplomatic mission, Carew is as informative on the Commonwealth's geopolitical situation as on its geography and regions. Advising
the Queen on diplomatic dealings with the Poles, he notes that no alliance
with the Polish king "dothe any waye bynde the Poles," since the Diet controls foreign policy (136). Because of the complex powers of king, Senate and
nobility, he declares that "the Poles must be handeled with greate dexterity"
(136). Carew runs through the principal diplomatic issues engaging Poland
with its neighbors: he devotes attention to the Pope's interest in Polish politics, primarily in securing an anti-Turkish league and spreading the Counter
Reformation (141–42); he pauses on Spain, England's key maritime rival, detailing its active trade with the Commonwealth in military provisions and
munitions (144). He devotes significant attention to Poland's southern strategy, engineered by one of his heroes, Chancellor Jan Zamojski. He labels

Zamojski's policy of cultivating Moldova, Transylvania, and Wallachia and keeping peace with the Turks wise, since, he declares, the Poles lack the ability to war effectively against the Turks: their border is not fortified, they would have to deal with the Crimean Tatars as well as the Ottoman army, they cannot afford the mercenary infantry they would need for such warfare (150).

Readers of Fletcher will be interested in Carew's account of the Commonwealth's interaction with Muscovy. He admires Tsar Boris Godunov (ruled 1598–1604) as "wise and civill beyond the nature of those rude nations" (160), but repeats clichéd and undoubtedly secondhand refrains about the Muscovite tsar in general: "hys authority as absolute as the Turkes, hys subiectes most obedient as slaves, and faithfull uppon opinion of the princes earthly divinity" (162). His account breaks off with an unflattering portrait of the King Sigismund Vasa: "the kinge hymselfe is not malitious, easy of nature, quiet, delighted with musick, gyven to mechanicalls, devote in hys profession, poore in Civill and military artes, beseeming so greate a potentate, and lastly altogeather an unfitt heade for suche a mighty and stirring body as Polonia is" (164).

An Anglican at a time when English monarchs were struggling to prevent the proliferation of Protestant sects as well as to establish a firm union of church and state, Carew found untold religious diversity in the Polish-Lithuanian Commonwealth. He alleges that not only can there be found in the Commonwealth several established religions, but also "borrowed superstitions" and "wonderfull nombers of heretikes, especially in the capitall article of the Trinity" (64). He describes the flourishing Protestant sects—Calvinist in Poland and Lutheran in Prussia and Livonia—their legal rights and Radziwill patrons. He sneers at the resurgence of Catholicism (calling it the "Papist" sect and "Romish" religion, 68–76), attributing it to Catholic King Sigismund's policy of appointing only Catholics to office and to "the dilligence of the Jesuites, whoe nestle themselves everywhere in that lande" (65). Citing the new Jesuit schools, he approvingly notes that "neither Zamoysky whoe doth not greatly fancy theise busybodies will committ hys universitie to them, nor the Schollers of Cracow by any meanes admitt them" (66).

Noting the dominance of Orthodox Christianity in "Russia alba, and for the most parte in Lithuania, Russia rubra, Volhinia, Podolia," he gives good evidence of Orthodoxy's late 16th-century struggle to survive: "The cheife prynce of thys religion is the olde Duke of Ostrog, Palatyne of Kiovia, whoe notwithstanding suffers hys twooe sonnes to follow the Romish." He further accurately notes that the Orthodox hierarchy, unlike the Catholic, was excluded from government: "they are not Senatours, neyther meddle they with any parte of the State." And he knows about the recent Union of Brest (1596): "so that now in the Polish State the Vladitians [Orthodox bishops] begynn to acknowledge the Popes Supremacy" (67).

Surveying yet more religious diversity, Carew calls the Christian Armenians "most skillful and riche marchantes"; notes that a small group of Muslims live near Vilnius, "priviledged with liberty of religion"; asserts that "those lawes, or priviledges more in favoure of the Jewes then Christians, were graunted by Boleslaus Duke of the Greater Polonia 1264"; and, finally, asserts that "those which retayne Polytheoticall Idolatry are the Pagans dwelling in Livonia, Samogitia, Lithuania and at Ceremissa on the borders of Russia, whoe worshipp severall creatures, and idolles, retayning still Ethnicall rites and sacrifices" (67–68).

Mindful of conflagrations in France and England, Carew is impressed with the religious tolerance in the Commonwealth: "For religion there is not in any contrey such variety, but that seemes better to mainteyne the common peace, then yf the lande were devided into twooe bodies of religion, as France is" (129). He notes that religious war has been avoided by the facts that religious minorities are so large and that Christians of various sects have been allowed to hold office. He argues that, while the Catholic clergy "blowe theise coles" of religious tension, the secular elite resists religious war. Again, he lauds Zamojski: "The cheife patron of thys liberty is the Chauncellor [Zamojski], whoe seeing the strength of the Common Wealthe to be devided into 3 mayne bodyes of greatest bulke, viz. Catholikes, Protestantes, and Greekish, knowes that yf by pursuite, or depression any parte should be mooved to take armes, ... there would follow the ruine of the State" (130).

As befitting a diplomat, Carew took great interest in the Commonwealth's military formations. He praises the "valoure" and discipline of the noble cavalry army with its "multitude of horsse," but he finds their vainglorious monopoly over arms the army's principal weakness. On the one hand, they resist the development of new formations using lower social classes, while on the other hand, the nobility does not serve well, especially the poor, who seek all means to escape military service (107–09). Furthermore, he condemns the complicated process whereby war is declared, requiring the Diet to vote funds and declare war, which it rarely is willing to do and certainly not promptly (109–11). To bolster their military preparedness, Carew offers several recommendations. He advises that public revenue be set aside for war and that immunities of privileged social classes be repealed, since these subjects "preferr theire particular before the common good" (124). He laments that if their infantry and navy equalled the cavalry, "the Poles needed not feare the power of any neighboure whatsoever. But they neglect them ... for feare of arming the Commons, or as thincking them superfluous" (120).

Finally, reflecting 16th-century Elizabethan preoccupations with legal controls on power, Carew focuses on government and laws (75–107). He is particularly informative on the multiplicity of legal systems in the realm—"Polish, Moschovitish, Russish, Lithuanish, Prussish, Silesian, Walakish and Dutche" (95). He enumerates the working of the king's courts for noblemen, the landlords' rights over their serfs, the towns' Dutch and German law, and the criminal and high appeals courts (94–107). The degree of detail here—on laws of inheritance of land succession, female rights to immoveable property and crime and punishment—is fascinating for modern readers. He provides a nearly complete list of the offices and names of the Senators in 1598—2 archbishops, 13 bishops, 29 major palatines and high dignities, 31 major castellans, 49 minor castellans, and 10 marshalls, chancellors, and treasurers (77–81). For most he identifies religion, and occasionally personal characteristics: Albert Laski is "learned, well languaged, famous for hys service against the Tatarians … too magnificall whereby he dissipated a greate patrimony, and disgraced hymselfe by dishonorable shiftes at home, and abroade"; Kristofer Radziwill is "very potent. Evangelicall"; a certain Leszczynski is "Evangelicall very zealous in hys profession" (77).

Sorting through the categories he knows from a good education in classics and contemporary political theory (he cites Jean Bodin, for example),[17] he struggles to characterize the Commonwealth. While Fletcher had easily labeled Muscovy a "tyranny," Carew finds no easy answer. He rejects "monarchy": "That it is no monarchy, it is too manifest, seeing that no parte of the soveraintie is in the prince alone, but eyther in hym and the Senate joyntly, or in the united states of the Parliament." He dismisses "aristocracy," since the Senate is too constrained by other political groups: "the Senate can doe nothing without the kinges consent, nor in matters of absolute Maiesty, without consent of the Parliament, swayde by the Authority of the Nobilitie, which sendes thither theire Nuncios whereby some would inferr that it is a Democracy, seeing the Summum Imperium is cheifly in the Nobility." But he is also dubious about "democracy," since the burghers are excluded from representative government. He ends up calling the government a mixture of all three—Monarchicall, Aristocraticall, and Democraticall (39–40)—reflecting the 16th-century theoretical focus on defining "mixed" constitutions by theorists such as Smith and Bodin.

Keenly aware of the complex politics of English succession in his own homeland, Carew derides Poland's elective monarchy, taking pains to contradict the conceit—popular since the political reforms of 1569 and 1572—that Poland's monarchy had always been elective. Rather, he shows dynastic succession until the late 14th century. And he expresses alarm at the juridical disorder of the election system, providing a cautionary tale for Englishmen: "the manner and order of the kinges election is not established by any lawe or statute, which makes that every change synce the fayling of the Jagelloes stocke hath ben daungerous for the kingdome, and might have ben fatall to it" (42). Providing a detailed summary of the interregna from 1572 to 1587 (43–54, 137–40), he amply demonstrates the pernicious effect of "turbulent heades, who soughte theire greatnes by plotts, practises and factions, which they

---

[17] References to Bodin on 45, 54, 62, 100. Classical references on 4, 86, 107, 155 (Tacitus, Ptolomy).

might make in the uncertaine election, and troubles of the kingdome" (43). He scorns the popular defense of the chaotic electoral practice—"that it were preiudiciall to the publike libertie to have the election circumscribed, and directed by lawes, affirming that the more the election were at random, the larger were the libertie"—demonstrating that elections were hardly "free" but rather typically dissolved into "open warre" (43).

Lamenting the ways in which the nobility has infringed on monarchical power through succession crises, he enumerates the powers the king has lost: "without the authority of the Senate, or Dyet, [he] can make no lawes, warre, peace, league, or truce, commaunde no tributes, or dispose of them being gathered, heare no Embassadours sent to the State, iudge no cause of any of the Nobility, create no gentelman ... cannot coyne or marry ... alienate or morgage any parte of the Domayne ... doe no publike acte" (54). He details other means by which the nobility has "clipt the eagles wynges" (60)—by disallowing the king to build fortifications, to import foreign nobles loyal to him and to confer any honors on foreigners. Carew ridicules the famous *pacta conventa* imposed since 1572 on kings at their election, which include such demands as that the king should agree to "lyve chastly and honestly," "take no bribes," and "lyve moderately." Rightly noting that "theise absurde articles, which of a father of the realme make the kinge a pupill," Carew concludes that the king "should be but Imaginary, depending uppon the Senate, and nobility" to the "manifest hurte and daunger of the whole body" (61–62).

Carew acknowledges that the nobility would desire this situation because under such a king "(the weaker the better) they may enioye the benefitts, dignities, and liberties of the lande." But he also argues that even they understand that they need to "retayne the shadowe of a Monarchy" because "the bare name of the kinge suppresseth the exorbitancies of factions...." (53). Nevertheless, Carew holds out hope for improvement. He details the king's continued rights and potential bases of power: "He bestoweth all magistracies, Dignities, offices, and benefices at hys pleasure, he disposeth of hys revenewe, ... he propoundes all matters in the Diet when and how he will, he iudgeth, and executes sentences arbitrarily" (55). Carew underscores that "The kinges revenew, if the realme were ordered in that poynte as the most moderate states in Europe, would be wonderfull, in regarde of the greatenes of the lande, the commodityes of great advauntage on which without oppressing hys subiectes he might raise mighty customes, and the opportunity of hys havens of Prussia and Livonia" (55).

He reviles those who would conspire and revolt against the rare king who might "be couragious, resolute, and one, which will not suffer suche insolencies, but restrayne them, and execute the lawes so farre as hys authority reacheth" (58–59). He singles out Stephan Batory (ruled 1575–86) for praise, applauding his decision to execute a rebellious nobleman: "whereas all men presumed he durst not doe it for feare of drawing the whole Nobility on hys necke, after that the heade was cutt off, the lande was more peaceable and the factions became more temperate, standing in awe of the kinge and the lawes. Such is the nature of the Poles, Hungarians, Transilvanians, Moldavians, and Wallachians, that by mildenes they growe insolent, and by roughe dealing more obseqious" (60). Demonstrating his regard for rule of law, he notes that such a national character would lead most rulers to become tyrants, but that tyranny was impossible in Poland because the king's ambitions are "tempered and restrayned by moderation of lawes, which suffer no prince how cruell so ever to prove a tyrante" (60).

Carew holds up Jan Zamoyski as a model citizen: a man of "learning, eloquence, deepe reache, iudgement, and other politicall vertues.... [H]e is the most absolute gentleman for Civill and military vertues, that ever that contrey bredd.... By profession he is a Catholike, but very moderate, secretly having correspondency with the Protestantes, and openly mainteyning liberty of religion for the publike peace, and security"(117–18). Thus, Carew finds potential for change in the Polish political system precisely because the foundation exists in law, institutions and civic consciousness among some to constrain the monarch so that he might rule for the public good. If only the nobility would play its role of servants of the state, as Zamojski did. Alas, it is this social class that Carew found to be the root of Poland's political—and economic—malaise, and it is this class that receives his most caustic critique. Neither do they rule in the interests of the greater good, nor do they foster productivity and economic progress. Rather, they legislate in their own self-interest and oppress their peasants.

He attributes much of the disease of the political system to the willfulness and self-indulgence of the magnates: "bothe the great Lordes, and private riche gentlemen keepe great traynes ... allso great guardes of Hayduckes, and Cosackes, so that it seemes the state standes uppon violence, the security being rather in eache mans ability to defende hymselfe, then in the publike protection of the lawe. Thys causeth great ryotes, and may in tyme devide the State" (83). He sees their power shored up by "the poore Nobility ... [of which] there is an huge multitude" (84). Carew is beside himself in condemning the profligacy of the Polish nobility, which he considers a constant threat to the body politic, as, for example, when the gentry selfishly refuses to pay for war: "the subiectes, though inriched by the spoyles of the Crowne are not thereby the more enabled to helpe the Common Wealthe, thys accesse servng allmost onely for the keeping of a greater state, and theire naturall emulation of pompe and prodigall spending, whereby the wealthe of the lande is broughte to be in horsses of great price, iewells, sylkes, and other exoticall wares for the backe and belly" (124).

Carew unleashes his venom on the Diet, finding it not a consensual organ of informed citizens like his ideal of the English Parliament, but a "tumultuous" assembly of armed men, who abuse the *liberum veto* (whereby individual delegates can "refuse to assent") for narrow self-interest: "Thys makes that commonly the good of the state, and necessary lawes are crossed, and the

Dyetts to the greate charge of the common wealthe protracted, without all-most effecting anything" (94). He finds true danger to the realm in the legal equality of nobles, given how many poor nobles were in the pay of magnates: "in Polonia, where the voyce of every poore servingman being a gentleman weighes as muche in all Conventes and elections as the greatest princes … in the Roman Common Wealthe thys was the common matter of seditions" (85).

He has little patience for the Polish defense of their anarchic ways as expressions of "freedom," offering up his own, characteristically Elizabethan, view on liberty: "This impunity [from the law] is one parte of the Polish liberty, which they thincke, that they onely of all people in Europe enioye, whereas yf we measure the liberty of the greatest parte of the State, we shall fynde that no civill Commonwealthe is so slavish, the commons not being in equall protection of the lawe. For questionles that State which is obnoxious to the violence of another is not free, as it is in Polonia, where iustice is not administred arithmetically to all. So that onely the Nobility seemes to be free, which not onely in Geometricall iustice enioyeth all exemptions, and hath the honors, and preferments, but allso tyrannise over the other." Carew declares "For seeing that true liberty consisteth specially in the security of oure lyves, goodes, and honors, they cannot be counted free which in them lye open to daunger and violence" (106).

For Carew, it all comes down to excess power for the nobility and servility for the working classes. Of the townsmen, he declares "The Plebian order … is most base, and contemptible, not onely barred from the State, but allso obnoxious to the wronges and insolencies of the gentry…." (88). The peasants "differ lyttle from slaves" (90), powerless before the law and burdened with manual labor on their landlord's domains. He calls the nobles "allmost … absolute lordes over theire possessions, and subiectes in so muche that no prynce in Europe hath so absolute power over hys subiectes as the gentlemen of Polonia have over theires"(63). In a fiery passage, he lays the blame for the Commonwealth's weaknesses at the feet of the nobility: "In the Nobility concurre all othlocraticall headines, perversenes, impotency, secession and other popular temptestes and outrages. From thys forme proceedes invalidity of the lawes, impunity, robbing of the Domayne, and publike state," concluding that "the tyranny of the Nobility … is most to be feared" (133).

How to fix this flawed body politic? Throughout Carew implicitly condemns the political system for its imbalance of monarch and nobility, but his specific prescriptions strike a mercantilist note: first, he urges that the Commonwealth conquer some neighboring territory, "which should remayne tributary for the ease of the publike charge, and not be admitted to the participation of the Polish immunities" (125). He urges gaining control of "the Sarmatian Sea" [the Baltic], and "getting the commaunde, or at least free trade of the Boristhenes [Dnieper], to be ioyned with the Duna [Western Dvina]" (128). Thus he argues for an aggressive foreign expansion to open up trade routes and monarchical income. Second, he argues that a Treasury should be amassed by taxing the nobles and clergy, collecting escheated inheritances, instituting a universal sales tax and a land tax, increasing the peasant obligation by one grosch and instituting a poll tax for all (125–26).

Further, he urges that the Commonwealth develop a wiser export policy. "It may seeme strange, how that kingedome should not be riche which besydes commodities of greate importance is the common granary and Arsenall of all Europe" (126). He advises that no raw materials be exported and that skilled artisans be imported (126–27). He urges curbing the nobility with "sumptuary lawes" and cultivating production: "For no state which is riotous and sumptuous, specially being neither well peopled, nor industriously manured, ... can above the maintenance of herselfe affourde sufficient for the buying of forreyne commodities, which shewes that in all states the industry of the people in mechanicall artes, and populousnes makes the foundation of inrytching any Contrey" (126). In one of his most charming metaphors, Carew pleads that the nobility should bolster the working people, not oppress them: "it being a most sure rule, that no state can be riche, where traders and Artisans are wronged, and troden on, they being the silke wormes whereupon all states grounde theire wealthe ... as on the other syde, the husbandmen are the antes for the bringing in of the harvest for sustenance, bothe which labouring for the common good, and necessity should be defended by the gentry, Champions of the State" (127).

Greatest "Champion of the State" should be, of course, the king. Carew suggests that he should shore up his power by "strengthening and raising the people, especially the Burgers in imitation of the Emperors of Germany. Thys must be don by securing them from insolency, inriching them by trade, and exempting them from the iurisdiction of the Nobility, so that in tyme they mighte growe in wealthe, able to bande themselves for the defence of theire liberty against the Nobility" (134). Cultivating the bourgeoisie—the silkworms and ants of the early modern economy—could do in Poland what it was seeming to do in England.

Assessing Carew's account in the light of Elizabethan politics, Carew emerges as a proponent of strong monarchy tempered by rule of law, not surprising for a man who made his living in the monarch's service. His recommendations for improving the Polish political economy might seem Polonophilic, but they also served English interests by bolstering Poland as a potentially pro-English bastion to balance the waxing power in the Baltic of France and Sweden.

Regarding Poland-Lithuania, one is struck by Carew's decent-mindedness: one can feel his moral outrage. In Carew's vision, the Commonwealth's peasants should be free to join the economy as productive citizens, townsmen should enjoy the benefits of property owning and trade, and noblemen should earn their political privileges by ruling in the interest of the common good. He may be idealizing his homeland—in late Elizabethan England, social inequities were rising and Parliament and monarchy had a long and turbulent century yet to go to establish the healthy, civic-minded balance that Carew wishes for Poland. Nevertheless, the reader is struck by Carew's even-handed, thoughtful critique.

Carew's thorough account prompts reflection on states and state building, since it demonstrates how early modern states worked in day to day practice. In so doing, it suggests the inadequacy of current paradigms such as "empire" and "national monarchy." As the extensive quotations cited here attest, the Commonwealth was not an empire, yet it was permeated with ethnic and religious diversity. Because of that diversity, it was not a typical "national monarchy" or "well-ordered police state": it could not centralize on the model of Tilly's and Brewer's rising early modern "national states."[18] Yet it was not a throw-back to "medieval" or "feudal" fragmentation; this parliamentary monarchy co-existed with vassal duchies and widespread personal immunities. It was a multi-confessional state that would never have survived a "confessionalization" movement. Students of state building will see in action multiple paths to modernity as they observe the Commonwealth's rulers and ruling elites confronting early modern challenges: funding a modernizing army; building an efficient bureaucracy; governing far-flung localities and policing officials; mobilizing social groups to serve the state; mobilizing natural resources; navigating the shoals of Reformation and Counter Reformation. Why the Polish-Lithuanian Commonwealth's parliamentary monarchy failed to succeed as well as that of England—the bellwether of modernization—is made a bit more clear by George Carew's engaging and astute critique.

---

[18] See Charles Tilly, ed., *The Formation of National States in Western Europe* (Princeton, NJ: Princeton University Press, 1975); and Charles Tilly, *Coercion, Capital, and European States, AD 990–1992* (Cambridge, MA: Blackwell, 1992), chaps. 2–6. On a later period, see John Brewer, *The Sinews of Power: War, Money and the English State, 1688–1783* (Cambridge, MA: Harvard University Press, 1988).

The Soviet Role in the Creation of Israel Reconsidered

Richard Hellie

> The "living spirit" of the Eastern support to Israel
> was Stalin himself.[1]

> It is doubtful whether Israel would have come
> into being had it not been for Soviet support.[2]

Certainly one of the most enigmatic events of the 20th century was the role of the Soviet Union in the creation of the state of Israel. It made little sense in 1947, and with six decades of hindsight, it seems to have been an even less wise move on the part of the USSR. No one doubts that Soviet support was absolutely vital for the creation of Israel out of the League of Nations mandate of Palestine. But there seems to be absolutely no concensus on why the Soviet leaders, Stalin, Malenkov, Beria, Kaganovich, Molotov, Vyshinskii, Khrushchev et al., all thoughtful and intelligent (if somewhat mentally disturbed) individuals, did what they did or why they thought it was either in their immediate or long-term best interest. One can only wonder why that group of intelligent men could not (or did not) foresee at least some of the negative consequences the creation of Israel would have for the Soviet Union/Russia. I have been hoping that some high-level discussions/communications/memoirs on the issue would come to light, but to date I am aware of nothing. The purpose of this essay is to examine these issues given the currently available data and see whether some sense can be made of them.

There are many hypotheses on why the Soviets pressed for the creation of Israel—the alleged motives of Stalin & Co.:

1. For decades one position was that the Soviets did it to annoy Britain ("to pull the British lion's tail"), to which Palestine had been mandated by the League of Nations after World War I and

---

[1] Voroshilov to Mikunis at Dmitrov's funeral, Sofia, July 1949, cited in Arnold Krammer, *The Forgotten Friendship: Israel and the Soviet Bloc, 1947–53* (Urbana: University of Illinois Press, 1974), 81.

[2] Yaacov Ro'i, *Journal of Israeli History* 22: 1 (Spring 2003): 21.

Rude & Barbarous Kingdom Revisited: Essays in Russian History and Culture in Honor of Robert O. Crummey. Chester S. L. Dunning, Russell E. Martin, and Daniel Rowland, eds. Bloomington, IN: Slavica Publishers, 2008, 367–87.

the collapse of the Ottoman Empire.[3] The problem with this thesis is that Britain was scheduled to pull out of Palestine even before Israel was created, as discussed below.[4]

2. The "logic" of the first point is aided by the fact that the British consistently hindered Jewish migration to Palestine, and the Soviets reasoned that the Zionists had no more love for the British than they did. The Soviets calculated that with a mutual adversary, friendship with Israel might be possible. The Soviet expectation was that Israel would be an anti-colonial and anti-West-European power.[5] History certainly did not work out this way, at least not for very long.

3. At least modestly convincing is the proposition that Stalin already in 1928 proposed exploiting contradictions between capitalist states. After 1945 he saw his chance. Relations between the United Kingdom and the United States became quite strained over the problem of Palestine.[6] Britain, in charge of the Palestine Mandate,

---

[3] Heller traditionally notes that Soviet aid stemmed from the wish to undermine British imperialism. Joseph Heller, *The Birth of Israel* (Gainesville: University Press of Florida, 2000), 62. See also Christopher Andrew and Vasili Mitrokhin, *The World Was Going Our Way: The KGB and the Battle for the Third World* (New York: Basic Books, 2005), 222; Paul Johnson, *A History of the Jews* (New York: Harper and Row, 1987), 527. Johnson has recently stated that in the years 1944–48, "Soviet policy was more pro-Israel than America's" (*The New York Times*, 3 August 2006). A variation on this was that Britain converted Lebanon into its "springboard to reach Russia's border," and the Soviets hoped to be able "to render it useless by intervening in the Palestine issue." *Documents on Israeli-Soviet Relations 1941–1953*, ed. Yaacov Ro'i (London: Frank Cass, 2000), 135. Before Gromyko's speech in 1947, getting the British out of the Middle East was a primary Soviet objective (*Documents on Israeli-Soviet Relations*, 174).

[4] Britain decided to pull out of Palestine in January–February of 1947 and turn it over to the United Nations. On December 4, 1947, the British definitively decided to leave on May 14, 1948. Ahron Bregman, *Israel's Wars 1947–93* (London: Routledge, 2000), 7, 9. See also Heller, *Birth of Israel*, 57, who stresses "early 1947" as the time the British gave up on Palestine. The critical date was Bevin's speech to the House of Commons on February 26, 1947. See also Michael J. Cohen, ed., *The British Decision to Evacuate Palestine, 1947–1948* (New York: Garland, 1987). Fraser observes that it was becoming obvious that British influence in world affairs was waning as that of the US rose. T. G. Fraser, *The Arab-Israeli Conflict* (New York: Palgrave Macmillan, 2004), 18.

[5] Pinkus makes the point that the Soviets lost faith in the ability of the Arabs to drive the UK out of the Middle East and came to believe that only the Jews were capable of removing the British from Palestine. Pinkus, *The Jews of the Soviet Union: The History of a National Minority* (New York: Cambridge University Press, 1988), 166. Heller also mentions that the Soviets gave up on the Arabs as an anti-imperialist force (*Birth of Israel*, 59).

[6] See the January 3, 1946 Beirut-to-Moscow dispatch: "The Palestine question is the key issue in Anglo-American differences on the eastern shore of the Mediterranean"

wanted zero Jewish immigration to placate the Arabs, whereas Truman and the US urged the British to permit 100,000 European refugees to emigrate to Palestine.[7] Inter-imperialist contradictions became a mantra of Molotov-era Soviet foreign relations.

4. Another proposition is that the Soviets wanted to annoy the oil barons and sheiks of the Middle East, and calculated that the existence of Israel would do that.[8] Undoubtedly the creation of Israel did do that, but the USSR almost immediately began to woo Egypt and other countries of the region. How the creation of Israel could have gained the U.S.S.R. any points in the Middle East is not clear, especially if the Muslims blamed the Russians for the creation of Israel. (Recently, February 2007, this has been one of the Muslim grievances in Chechnia against Russia.)

5. Another purported reason is that the Soviet leadership viewed the Arabs as allies of the Nazis in World War II and thus automatic enemies. By the same "logic," Jews desiring the creation of Israel, the enemy of the Arabs, and persecuted by the Nazis, should be supported by the Soviets.[9]

6. Yet a sixth hypothesis is that the creation of Israel would take Islamic pressure off the southern rim of the USSR. The idea seems to be that there was fear that the Muslim countries of the Middle East might try to proselytize in the Muslim republics of the USSR against Soviet persecution of Islam, against the Soviet promulgation of atheism and secularism. The logic is that, if the southern rim foreign countries were diverted to think about Israel, they would not have time for the Islamic republics of the USSR. This all makes good sense, but there is no evidence to support any of it—especially when one takes into consideration that the southern rim

---

(*Documents on Israeli-Soviet Relations*, 122). See also Krammer, *Forgotten Friendship*, 51–52.

[7] G. V. Kostyrchenko, *Tainaia politika Stalina: Vlast' i antisemitizm* (Moscow: Mezhdunarodnye otnosheniia, 2001), 400–01.

[8] Stalin is alleged to have said, "Let's agree to the establishment of Israel. This will be a pain in the ass for the Arab states and will make them turn their backs on the British. In the long run it will totally undermine British influence in Egypt, Syria, Turkey, and Iraq." Pavel Sudoplatov and Anatoli Sudoplatov, *Special Tasks: The Memoirs of an Unwanted Witness—a Soviet Spymaster* (Boston: Little, Brown, 1994), 296. Note that this supports the anti-British thesis, perhaps the thesis of taking pressure off the Soviet southern rim, and shows that Stalin was capable of thinking long-term.

[9] Pinkus, *Jews of the Soviet Union*, 166. Pinkus also makes the point that the Soviet Union hoped to be rid of the European refugee problem by opening Palestine to Jewish settlement, but there seems to be little evidence that the USSR was concerned about that. Heller terms it "stabilization of Eastern Europe by means of a mass Jewish exodus to Palestine" (*Birth of Israel*, 59).

neighbor countries themselves were not independent operators, but Western colonies.[10]

7. Yet another reason is that Soviet leaders saw the creators of Israel as radicals who might become their "socialist" allies in the Middle East.[11] The problem with this in general is that more people saw the Jews of Palestine, as well as international Jewry in general, as allies of the bankers on Wall Street than saw them as individuals collectively and effectively devoted to the cause of international socialism—in spite of the fact that socialist governments ran Israel for the first two decades of the country's existence.[12] Moreover, as Joseph Heller stresses, Zionists constantly sought Soviet support after the war, but the Soviets in general refused to talk with them.[13]

8. A 2005 Russian interpretation is that the Soviets after World War II revived the classical Russian security tactic of expanding the frontiers. For Russian-language readers the title of the book, *For What Reason Did Stalin Create Israel?*, alone should be an eye-opener. The creation of the Eastern bloc was the best example, but attempts to annex the Turkish Straits, Xinjiang, Iran, Tripolitania (= Libya), Greece, Finnish and Chinese naval bases, and even the Belgian

---

[10] Later, in November of 1949, a coalition of Arab states directed against the USSR was contemplated (Heller, *Birth of Israel*, 66). The Baghdad Pact, uniting Britain, Turkey, Iran, Pakistan, and Iraq against "Soviet expansionism," was formed on February 4, 1955. (Minus Iraq after 1959, it became CENTO.)

[11] Soviet chargé d'affaires in London Kukin in 1945 "reiterated that Soviet circles did not doubt that the Jews of Palestine were a progressive element" (*Documents on Israeli-Soviet Relations*, 110). The idea is that Zionism was "progressive," as some Soviets believed that Zionists were (Heller, *Birth of Israel*, 59). For more in the infinite variations on this theme, see Krammer, *Forgotten Friendship*, 47–50.

[12] Pinkus alleges that the Soviets hoped that the creation of Israel might win the support of world Jewry for the USSR (*Jews of the Soviet Union*, 167). His entire dilemma is squaring this with abuse of Jews within the USSR. He wonders about a "double policy, differing internally and externally" (ibid., 166). Heller has a good discussion about whether socialist Zionism shared a common ideology with the Soviet regime (*Birth of Israel*, 53). One of the Israeli communist parties, Mapam, allegedly had a plan to seize power "if a revolutionary situation developed" (ibid., 69). In Jerusalem, the League for Friendly Relations with the USSR in May of 1946 aroused the interest of the Mandate police (*Documents on Israeli-Soviet Relations*, 130).

[13] Heller, *Birth of Israel*, chap. 2. The Palestinian Zionists understood that the Soviets "did not want to turn them down, but were not in a position to accept" (*Documents on Israeli-Soviet Relations*, 111).

Congo were failed examples. Israel was yet another failed example.[14]

9. A new point is that Zionists from the Soviet sphere of influence met in Basel, Switzerland, and agreed that they would support the USSR in world affairs if the Soviet Union would support the creation of a Jewish homeland. This information comes from recently released British MI5 intelligence data. More will be said on this point below.

The topic of the origins of Israel has reached the point that the issue is so obfuscated that the role of the USSR in the creation of Israel often is not even mentioned.[15] For example, after the 1967 Six-Day War, when the 1945–53 (late Stalin) era was discussed, the creation of Israel was not even mentioned in Western historiography.

Even more astonishing, at least to me, is that the story is presented that in 1945–46 the situation of the Jews was more or less okay in the USSR, but already by January 1947, anti-Semitism in the Soviet Union was so intense that only extreme schizophrenics could have sponsored the creation of Israel. Long lists of causes for the rise of an implacable Soviet stance against Jews everywhere by January 1947 are presented. Most of these "reasons" would have had especial appeal to a paranoid such as Stalin. Thus, although Jews fought the Nazis nobly and vigorously and suffered immeasurably, they treasonously wanted to retain contacts with foreign Jews and others they met abroad or were separated from by the war. Soviet Jewish soldiers were suspected of having dual loyalties, to the USSR and to the survivors of the Holocaust abroad. Stalin again regarded any such activities as treasonous. Moreover, the annexations of the Baltic States and elsewhere resulting from the August 23, 1939 Hitler/Stalin (Molotov/Ribbentrop) pact and then the expansion of the Soviet bloc westward into Poland and elsewhere brought under Soviet hegemony as many as two million[16] additional Jews whose loyalty to the Soviet Union was automatically questionable. Their attempts to maintain contacts with relatives in the West were also regarded as treasonous. Moreover, Jews had been emigrating from the Russian Empire in large numbers since 1881 (over two million between 1881 and 1914) and had relatives

---

[14] Leonid Mlechin, *Zachem Stalin sozdal Izrail'?* (Moscow: Iauza. Eksmo, 2005), 100, 127–30. In the summer of 1946 Litvinov said: "Russia has returned to its former conception of security: expanding frontiers. The more territory you have, the more secure is your safety." Molotov is reported to have said: "My task is to expand the borders of the USSR. It seems that Stalin and I have done this" (ibid., 129–30). Mlechin also stresses that the Soviets wanted to force the British out of Palestine (ibid., 106).

[15] T. G. Fraser in his *The Arab-Israeli Conflict* never mentions the role of the Soviet Union in the creation of Israel.

[16] Pinkus, *Jews of the Soviet Union*, 345n95.

throughout the world. Those who survived the Holocaust in the Soviet Bloc began to try to re-establish contacts with their relatives both inside and outside the Bloc, and this was regarded with deep suspicion. Jews looking for their relatives were accused of "wandering around too much."[17]

Further suspicion fell on Soviet Jews once the Israeli War of Independence had begun. A number of Soviet Jews volunteered to go to Palestine to fight for the Israeli cause, which again aroused great suspicions among the Soviet paranoids.[18]

Yet in spite of all these facts, well known to the masters of the Kremlin, they ignored them and seemingly proceeded against what would appear to the logical mind to be against their own interests by pushing for the creation and recognition of Israel.

There is considerable dispute over whether Stalin himself was an anti-Semite, but there is no doubt that he was an anti-Zionist,[19] as was Soviet ideology in general (much of it created by Soviet Jews). Yet he proceeded to effect the Zionist platform, the creation of the Jewish state of Israel. This has never been satisfactorily explained.

A few words of background are in order here. The story of Zionism is available in many places and only tangential to our story, so will be glossed over here. Thus the story seems to begin with World War I and the collapse of the Ottoman Empire, of which Palestine was a part. A number of significant world leaders began to state for the record that world Jewry deserved a homeland in Palestine, whence the Jews had originated. The most notable was the Balfour Declaration of November 2, 1917, which stated that Britain "favored the establishment in Palestine of a national home for the Jewish people."[20] This was the intellectual forerunner of the League of Nations Mandate of July 24, 1922, according to which Britain was "responsible for placing the country under ... conditions [which would] secure the establishment of the Jewish national home."[21] How this was to be effected was not spelled out and was complicated by the fact that both Balfour and the League talked about protecting the rights of the indigenous Palestinians and the fact that the

---

[17] Ben Ami, *Between Hammer and Sickle* (Philadelphia: The Jewish Publication Society of America, 1967), 27–32.

[18] Mlechin, *Zachem Stalin sozdal Izrail'?* 185–88, 203.

[19] For a good, recent discussion by a man who cannot be considered a pro-Stalinist, see Donald Rayfield, *Stalin and His Hangmen: The Tyrant and Those Who Killed for Him* (New York: Random House, 2004), 435–41. In 1931 Stalin claimed anti-Semitism was "like cannibalism" and condemned it until he died (ibid., 435). On this issue, see Sudoplatov and Sudoplatov, *Special Tasks*, 295.

[20] Fraser, *Arab-Israeli Conflict*, 8. Arthur James (later Lord) Balfour wrote this in a letter to Lord Rothschild. He was responding to suggestions from "Russian" Zionists Chaim Weizmann and Nahum Sokolow, who lived in London.

[21] Ibid., 8–9.

British establishment typically was pro-Arab for policy reasons, especially as they all desired access to Middle/Near Eastern hydrocarbons. This was true for most British leaders through 1948.

The Gordian knot was cut by Oxford Professor Reginald Coupland in 1937. He acknowledged that it was impossible to give the Jews a "homeland" intermingled with the Arabs, and proposed that Palestine be *partitioned* [emphasis added—RH] into Jewish and Arabic sectors.[22] This was what was done in 1947.[23] Not accidentally, the Committee for Illegal Immigration to Palestine (the Mossad le'Aliyah Beth) was created in 1937.

The rise of Hitler, the outbreak of World War II, and the Nazi Goering-Heydrich directive of July 31, 1941 on the extermination of the Jews turned the issue of a Jewish state from a debate between Zionists and their supporters and the Arabs into a matter of life and death for millions of Jews in the Nazi path. The problem was aggravated by both British and American refusal to offer refuge to Jews fleeing extermination.[24]

In response to the unwillingness of the "free countries" (the United Kingdom and the United States) to do anything to help the Jews trying to avoid extermination, Zionists led by Chaim Weizmann and David Ben-Gurion (an admirer of Lenin—in 1923)[25] met at the Biltmore Hotel in New York and drafted a program (the Biltmore Program) on May 9, 1942 which called for an end to the British Mandate and insisted on Jewish control over immigration to Palestine to found a Jewish "Commonwealth." On the ground in the Middle East, Jews took matters into their own hands. The Jewish Agency for Palestine's guerilla arm (the underground defense force of the Yishuv, the Jewish community), the Haganah, began to collect arms to harass

---

[22] Fraser, *Arab-Israeli Conflict*, 12. Published on July 7, 1937, this partition document is usually attributed to Lord Peel (Bregman, *Israel's Wars*, 6, 9, 59).

[23] Fraser, *Arab-Israeli Conflict*, 12.

[24] There were so many acts of negligence and commission on this front that one could not possibly list them all in anything less than a long book. One notorious case, however, stands out and is worth repeating. In December 1941 the unseaworthy Rumanian cattle vessel the *SS Struma* with 769 Jewish refugees was bound for Haifa and it sank (exploded; was torpedoed by a Soviet submarine) in the Black Sea on February 24, 1942, drowning all on board, after the Turks denied its passengers asylum in Istanbul and the British denied it permission to sail to Palestine (Fraser, *Arab-Israeli Conflict*, 16). Ami Isseroff alleges that the Soviets sank the *Struma* as part of collaboration with the British in blocking massive immigration to Palestine (http://www.mideastweb.org).

[25] Heller, *Birth of Israel*, 51. It is alleged that Ben Gurion attended the First Communist International Conference in France with Mao Tse Tung and Ho Chi Minh, and that that may have given Stalin confidence in Ben Gurion (Paul Johnson, *History of the Jews*, 527).

the British in Palestine with the goal of facilitating the migration of Jews to Palestine.[26]

Arms are not just lying around, but have to be gotten somehow from someone. Here is where the Soviets saw their entry point. Providing the guerrillas with arms unquestionably harassed the British, who diverted 100,000 troops from the European theater to Palestine.[27] Britain and the USSR were allegedly allies in the war against Hitler, and so the diversion of British forces to combat the Haganah weakened them in Europe. I am not aware of any evidence detailing Soviet deliberations on such calculations, but am sure that they must have taken place. As will be shown below, Soviet military intelligence had long enjoyed good relations with some of the Zionists, so moving from information to materiel was not as difficult as one might imagine.

In 1942 League "V" for Friendship With the USSR was established in the Yishuv, which contributed to perceptions in the West that some Palestinian Zionists were pro-Soviet — which indeed they were.[28]

In February of 1944 the Jewish organization Irgun declared war on the British Mandate. Irgun's ideologist, Vladimir Jabotinsky (b. 1880, Odessa; d. 1940, New York) was a man with Eastern European credentials. He founded Haganah in 1920 and also the Zionist Revisionist (right) movement. He claimed that the Jews had a right to a homeland on both banks of the Jordan, thus "adding specifics" to Coupland's statements. Irgun's leader, Menahem Begin, had enjoyed relations with the Soviets for years. The role of the (Avraham) Stern (born in 1907 in Poland) Gang (Lehi/Leh'i) in driving the British out of the Palestine Mandate is contested,[29] but the point here is that the Stern Gang received help from the Soviets.[30] Already in December 1944 the Soviets in internal memos stated that they would support the creation of a Jewish homeland in Palestine if England and the USA would agree.[31]

As the war was ending, Stalin agreed privately with Roosevelt and Churchill at Yalta in February of 1945 that Palestine should be turned over to the Zionists for development as a national homeland. At the same time in London the Soviet delegate to the founding conference of the World Federation of Trade Unions, V. Kuznetsov, voted on behalf of the Soviet delegation

---

[26] The Jewish Agency for Palestine was created in 1928 in response to a 1923 British proposal. The Arabs were also offered an agency, but refused.

[27] Bregman, *Israel's Wars*, 6.

[28] On September 26, 1945, members of the V League said that they were "not afraid of being thought a Soviet 'agency'" (*Documents on Israeli-Soviet Relations*, 108).

[29] The underground organization was formally known as LEHI (Lochami Heruth Yisrael = Freedom Fighters of Israel). Bregman puts it that the Stern Gang "rendered the mandate unworkable" (*Israel's Wars*, 6).

[30] Sudoplatov and Sudoplatov, *Special Tasks*, 293.

[31] *Documents on Israeli-Soviet Relations*, 90–92.

that Jews should be permitted to continue building Palestine as a national home.[32]

Once the war in Europe was over and Britain made no moves on the Jewish homeland issue, on October 1, 1945, the Jewish Agency ordered the Haganah to begin an armed revolt.[33] Around May of 1946 Soviet Jews in the NKVD told Eliahu Dobkin, in charge of immigration for the Jewish Agency, that the USSR understood that the Yishuv was not a tool of American/British imperialism and that Jews needed a "territorial center."[34]

The Soviet efforts on behalf of the creation of the Jewish state in Palestine were numerous. Among their first and perhaps most important acts were military. There was a UN embargo against arms shipments to the Middle East, which was honored by the USA but routinely violated by the USSR. The embargo did not apply to the independent Arab countries.[35] Most of the military hardware employed by the Zionists in Palestine and then the new Jewish state was provided indirectly by the Soviet Union. Much of it initially was Nazi booty left over from World War II. Especially important were Nazi Messerschmidt Me-109s, still in their original crates, shipped from Czechoslovakia, where they had been manufactured by the Nazis after the Allied bombing of Germany became too ferocious. The Jewish Agency paid $44,000 apiece for the planes. At Soviet orders, the Czechs devoted an entire military air base (Zhatec) to transporting arms to Tel Aviv, the so-called "Balak flights." Soviet Secret Police (MGB) chief Lavrentii Beria was in charge, acting through Czech Communist party general secretary Rudolph Slansky, his deputy Bedrich Geminder, and General Bedrich Reicin, deputy minister of defense—all Jews.[36] The Soviets typically used other countries to do their arms provisioning. Captured Nazi small arms and antitank grenades were shipped by the Soviets from Rumania to Palestine.[37] The Soviets provided a clear path from Central Europe through Soviet Austria, Hungary, and Yugoslavia to the Mediterranean for the transit of the materiel. After Independence, the Israelis

---

[32] Pinkus, *Jews of the Soviet Union*, 164; Heller, *Birth of Israel*, 53.

[33] Fraser, *Arab-Israeli Conflict*, 27; *Documents on Israeli-Soviet Relations*, 118n2.

[34] Heller, *Birth of Israel*, 56.

[35] In January 1948 London agreed to sell $25 million worth of arms to the Arabs. Bruce J. Evensen, *Truman, Palestine, and the Press* (New York: Greenwood Press, 1992), 135, 147.

[36] Amy Knight, *Beria: Stalin's First Lieutenant* (Princeton, NJ: Princeton University Press, 1993), 169; Andrew and Mitrokhin, *The World Was Going Our Way*, 222. Also central was the fact that the Jewish Agency convinced the Soviets to order their Czech clients to cease selling arms to the Arabs (Mlechin, *Zachem Stalin sozdal Izrail'?* 151, 164–65). Krammer has additional details on the Czech arms sales and training of personnel (*Forgotten Friendship*, 58–82).

[37] Sudoplatov and Sudoplatov, *Special Tasks*, 293; Mlechin, *Zachem Stalin sozdal Izrail'?* 134.

still regarded the Soviets as their major arms supplier. Without Soviet aid, Israel would have been destroyed immediately by the Arab armies, which invaded the moment after the Israeli declaration of statehood. In October of 1948 the Israelis presented a long list of desired materiel, including 70 tanks, 680 artillery pieces, 50 fighters, and 24 light bombers.[38] Troops and others were also trained in Czechoslovakia. Soviet instructors read them lectures on political topics.

A trickle of Jewish migration to Palestine continued throughout the prewar period, primarily from Europe. Shaul Avigur (Saul Meyeroff, born 1889 in Latvia) was in charge of Mossad's illegal operations to smuggle Jews into Palestine in spite of the British Mandate prohibition.[39] The USSR continued to support the emigration of Jews to Palestine after the war from all the countries of Europe except the USSR.[40]

The Soviets in 1946 facilitated the movement of considerable numbers of Zionists from Poland through Czechoslovakia and Soviet Austria to Palestine. Berman, the Soviet-appointed head of the Polish secret police (see below), was a central figure in the transit of personnel south. The Soviets also facilitated the emigration to Palestine of Jews from other Soviet-occupied Eastern European countries after the war.[41] Moscow believed 200,000 Jews were on their way to Palestine beginning in Poland through Czechoslovakia and the Soviet zone of Austria in September 1946.[42] Population was the crucial issue for the Zionists, along with the right to buy land in Palestine.

Also important was military intelligence to inform the Israeli combatants of what their actual and potential enemies might be doing. The Soviets had intelligence agents throughout the Middle East, and their information was funneled to the Zionists/Israelis. Prime Minister Menahem Begin, for example, had well-established contacts with Soviet intelligence. Prior to that, he had been in a Soviet concentration camp and in exile after having been a Beitar leader in Poland in 1939. After his release, he was in the "new Polish army" headed by General Vladislav Anders. The Anders Army was under the

---

[38] Heller, *Birth of Israel*, 62. *Documents on Israeli-Soviet Relations* contains many examples of post-Independence Israelis trying to buy arms from the Soviets.

[39] For great detail on this issue, see Yehuda Bauer, *Flight and Rescue: BRICHAH* (New York: Random House, 1970).

[40] Pinkus, *Jews of the Soviet Union*, 167.

[41] See Bauer, *Flight and Rescue*, 152–53 and passim for examples of Soviet assistance to those desiring to emigrate to Palestine.

[42] *Documents on Israeli-Soviet Relations*, 142. The Soviets probably did not help (but also did not hinder) this particular migration. Rather late in the game, on September 17, 1946, Moscow warned its ambassadors and ministers in Poland, Rumania, Czechoslovakia, Bulgaria, and Hungary not to become involved with the departure of Jews for Palestine (ibid., 147). Obviously they had been involved in emigration matters before that.

control of the NKVD. Presumably he came to know the Soviet intelligence people in the camp, in exile, in the Anders Army, or in transit. He arrived in Palestine in 1943 and joined Irgun. MI5 concluded that Begin got financial assistance from the Soviets.

Legally, the most important Soviet activity was on the international scene, especially at the United Nations. Palestine was under the nominal control of the UN as successor to the League of Nations, which had removed Palestine from Ottoman control after World War I, and it was essential to convince the UN that Israel should be created by partitioning Palestine into Jewish and Arabic sectors.

Soviet Foreign Minister Andrei Andreevich Gromyko played a major role in that sphere with his address before the Seventy-Seventh Plenary Meeting of the UN General Assembly on May 14, 1947, "The Need for a Jewish State."[43] He noted that "The aims of the Mandate have not been achieved.... The aspirations of a considerable part of the Jewish people are linked with the problem of Palestine and of its future administration.... (It is time for the UN to help the survivors of Hitler by deeds.)" He convincingly stressed that "no Western European state was willing to provide adequate assistance for the Jewish people in defending its rights and very existence from the violence of the Hitlerites.... This explains the aspirations of the Jews to establish their own state.... It would be unjust to deny the right of the Jewish people to realize their aspirations.... Palestine must be *partitioned, if necessary* [emphasis added, RH—Gromyko had the Jewish-Arabic conflict in mind], into two

---

[43] *Documents on Israeli-Soviet Relations*, 189–96, no. 83. It is correctly alleged that Gromyko's speech was written by Boris Efimovich Shtein, an adviser/consultant to the Ministry of Foreign Affairs (MID) (Kostyrchenko, *Tainaia politika Stalina*, 400). The interesting point is Shtein's "nationality": Jews had been generally purged from the Soviet foreign policy establishment by this time. Moreover, it should be noted that in a Moscow memorandum of July 27, 1945, Maksim Litvinov made a number of the points that Gromyko made two years later, such as the fact that the British Mandate had not carried out the Balfour Declaration. He proposed that Palestine should be put under a temporary Soviet trusteeship. The British would not permit that, so Litvinov proposed a tri-partite UK-UN-Soviet trusteeship (*Documents on Israeli-Soviet Relations*, 104–05). In a long memo of March 6, 1947 to Andrei Vyshinskii, Shtein writing, on "The Palestine Question," concluded with "A Possible Position for the USSR," in which he makes many of the points that are in Gromyko's speech. Shtein observed that the USSR had not yet formulated its position, which should be: get the British out, give Palestine independence, have the UN institute a democratic constitution that would resolve Jewish-Arab antagonism (ibid., 171). Partition was not mentioned. This became the Soviet position (I. V. Samylovskii to Ia. A. Malik) on March 14 (ibid., 172). This remained so on April 12–15, 1947 (ibid., 174–75, 179–80). Vyshinskii was always a solid supporter of Israel. For examples, see Mlechin, *Zachem Stalin sozdal Izrail'?* 123, 211.

independent states, one Jewish and one Arab...."[44] Apparently Soviet policy
was in such a state of uncertainty at the moment that it was not certain until
May 12 that Gromyko would deliver the speech. Many reasons for Soviet uncertainty can be (and have been) cited, but it would be nice to know what
happened in the first couple of weeks of May that made the anti-Zionist Stalin
change his mind.[45]

People from the Jewish Agency for Palestine were astounded and remarked: "It's pure Zionism."[46] Zionists expressed their gratitude to the Soviets and contrasted the Soviets' helpfulness with "the anti-Jewish attitude of
both the British and Americans."[47] Stalin and the other high Soviet officials
consciously made their public stand coincide with that of the Agency.[48]

Gromyko's speech was followed by utterances in favor of partition by
Semen K. Tsarapkin, Minister of the Soviet Embassy in New York, on October
13, 1947, and again by Gromyko himself, and more strongly than before, on
November 26, 1947, in which he pointedly supported the Partition Plan, GA
181.[49] The Partition Resolution was passed on November 29, 1947. This followed the UN Special Committee on Palestine (UNSCOP, appointed in May
1947) report of September 1, 1947 calling for the partition of Palestine. On
September 30, 1947, V. M. Molotov, from Moscow, ordered Andrei
Vyshinskii, head of the Soviet delegation to the General Assembly, not "to
oppose the majority opinion on the issue of the partition of Palestine." He

---

[44] Heller stresses that Gromyko did not call for partition of Palestine (*Birth of Israel*,
58). After the speech, Mikhail S. Vavilov, the first secretary of the Soviet embassy in
Washington, was vague on Gromyko's meaning, but wanted to know how it had
played with American Jews (ibid., 59–60). Here Heller speculates that perhaps the Soviets wanted to split the British-US anti-Soviet front (ibid.). See point 3 above. A bit
later, on July 31, Vavilov is reported to have stated that: "The Soviet government
understands the Jewish desire, as well as the necessity for statehood." He also stated
that the Soviets believed that the *yishuv* was progressive and could "block anti-Soviet
intrigues, so easily hatched among the reactionary circles ruling the Arab countries at
present" (*Documents on Israeli-Soviet Relations*, 217). See point 4 above. On September
11 Vavilov talked about "the possible relations of the [sic] Jewish state with the USSR"
(ibid., 221), which would seem to imply the existence of Israel was a *fait accompli* in his
mind.

[45] Nikita Khrushchev observed that "the USSR voted for the creation of Israel in the
UN. We did so only under pressure and with grave reservations and with many con-
ditions." *Khrushchev Remembers: The Last Testament* (Boston: Little, Brown, 1974, 344).
One can only ask: "What pressure? What conditions?"

[46] Evensen, *Truman, Palestine, and the Press*, 61.

[47] *Documents on Israeli-Soviet Relations*, 196–97 (15 May 1947)

[48] Mlechin, *Zachem Stalin sozdal Izrail'?* 118–23 and passim.

[49] An internal Soviet memo (Bakulin to Vyshinskii, Moscow) of July 30, 1947 noted
that partition was a likely option (*Documents on Israeli-Soviet Relations*, 211). See also
Mlechin, *Zachem Stalin sozdal Izrail'?* 136–37.

observed that the Soviets were motivated by "tactical considerations" and did not want "to take the initiative in the creation of a Jewish state.... The creation of an independent Jewish state ... conveys our position."[50] On October 16 Molotov encouraged permitting 150,000 Jews to move to Palestine, which would help solve "the general problem of impoverished European Jews."[51] On October 26 Molotov informed Stalin of what had been happening, that these actions were in agreement with the Jewish Agency. Poskrebyshev reported that Stalin agreed.[52]

After the rhetoric, it was time for political action. The Soviets provided the necessary votes for Resolution 181 to create Israel out of a partitioned Palestine to pass in the General Assembly, 33 to 13 with 10 abstentions (November 29, 1947). (A two-thirds majority was required.) This was the product of the UNSCOP recommendation.

The Soviets provided not only their own three votes (USSR, Ukraine, and Belorussia), but also the votes of the "satellite" countries Poland and Czechoslovakia. Had they desired, at any of these junctures the Soviets could have changed their tune and the creation of Israel would not have occurred, at least not at that time.

In spite of its prior activities, the Soviet Union was only the second country to recognize the new state of Israel, created on May 14, 1948—the date of the Israeli declaration of independence and the date of the expiration of the British mandate. The United States was the first country *de facto* to recognize Israel,[53] on May 15, 11 minutes after David Ben-Gurion made the Israeli declaration. Soviet delegate Andrei Gromyko, who obviously had been reading the American press, claimed that Truman's recognition was "a policy devoid of principle."[54] (The Soviets allowed the weekend to pass and then, Molotov, at Stalin's order, in response to Israeli Minister of Foreign Affairs Moshe Shertok's request, recognized Israel on May 18. Soviet recognition was both *de jure* as well as *de facto*. The USA recognized Israel de jure only on January 31, 1949, after Truman's successful election.)[55]

There is considerable controversy over why President Truman jumped at the recognition opportunity, even though in his "Yom Kippur Statement" of

---

[50] *Documents on Israeli-Soviet Relations*, 226–27.

[51] Ibid., 228. This is the sole Soviet reference to the material condition of Jewish refugees I have found. In this context, one must remember that the condition of most Soviets was no better.

[52] Ibid., 236.

[53] The State Department currently claims that "the United States played a key supporting role" in Israel's creation (US Department of State, Bureau of Near Eastern Affairs, "Background Note: Israel," May 2006, 8).

[54] Evensen, *Truman, Palestine, and the Press*, 167.

[55] Truman's recognition of Israel is still a "hot topic." See the excerpt from Michael Beschloss's new book in *Newsweek*, 14 May 2007: 30–37.

October 4, 1946, he had announced his support for the partition of Palestine and recognition was just a logical consequence of partition. The four best explanations are (a) he was trying to save his presidency by decisive action after his administration had waffled on the partition issue and been roundly criticized for historically unprecedented ineptness.[56] Another explanation is (b) that he was just respecting diplomatic protocol: the UN had created Israel and therefore the USA should recognize the new state.[57] A third explanation (c) is that Truman had many Jewish friends. His initial business partner was a Jew. In 1945 his major adviser was David Niles, who was pro-Jewish and always had his eye on the "Jewish vote" in American elections. (Postmaster General Robert Hannegan on October 6, 1947, made a speech on Jewish contributors to the Democratic Party who expected that the USA would support the Jews in Palestine—according to Margaret Truman's memoirs.) Truman tried to admit Jewish refugees into the United States and was blocked by Congress. In August of 1945 he tried to get the British to admit 110,000 refugees to Palestine and was crudely rejected by the British, who limited immigration to 1,500 per month. Had this been permitted, the pressure by Zionists to create Israel would have been greatly diminished. A fourth explanation (d) is that the appropriate people in Washington were well aware of the activities of the USSR on the Palestinian question and the creation of Israel. They believed that if the US did not act, US inaction would cede the scene totally to the Soviets as Israel became a Soviet satellite.[58] Truman's White House counsel Clark Clifford stressed this last point on May 12, that Truman should act before the Soviets did.[59]

This last argument had two sides, however. The State Department and the CIA argued that partition was unworkable and that a Jewish state

---

[56] The details are presented in Evensen, *Truman, Palestine, and the Press*, 135 ff.

[57] This was crucial because Truman had been accused of "victimizing" the United Nations by waffling on the issue of the partition of Palestine and the creation of Israel in the winter of 1948. UN Secretary General Trygve Lie announced that he felt so personally betrayed that he considered resigning (ibid.,155,158).

[58] On March 21, 1948, Clifton Utley claimed on NBC radio that if the USA did not support the creation of Israel by partition of Palestine, the Soviets would move into the Middle East and immediately would capture Italy (ibid, 154). See Ian J. Bickerton, "President Truman's Recognition of Israel," *American Jewish Historical Quarterly* (December 1968): 173–239.

[59] Fraser, *Arab-Israeli Conflict*, 43. Joseph Harsch of the *Christian Science Monitor* alleged that "losing Palestine would mean Russia could strangle American interests not only in the Mediterranean but throughout the Western world" (CBS radio scripts from January 1948, cited in Evensen, *Truman, Palestine, and the Press*, 134, 147). Clifford is quoted in Evensen; restoring Truman's reputation was part of his reasoning (ibid., 165). George Marshall almost resigned as Secretary of State over the issue.

facilitated Soviet expansion. They noted the USSR support for the creation of Israel as evidence.[60]

This essay is not about the USA and the recognition of Israel, but the point must be stressed that the "American government" was by no means unanimously in favor of the creation of Israel. Moreover, the issue of the partition of Palestine intersected with the Soviet question and the beginnings of the Cold War. This was especially true at the Near East desk of the State Department, where the Arab (oil—Aramco) lobby was strong and there was fear that antagonizing the Arabs might lead to a cut-off of oil supplies. Moreover, defense planners feared that American meddling in Palestine would provoke civil war and encourage the Soviets to intervene.[61]

Gromyko spoke on behalf of partitioned Israel in the Security Council on July 7, 1948. Heller observed that "without the Soviets' unambiguous aid, ... the state [of Israel] might have been stillborn."[62]

The USSR also voted to admit Israel to the UN on May 11, 1949 (Resolution 273 [III]). Throughout this period, between Resolutions 181 and 273, the necessity for the partition of Palestine, the absurdity of proposals to put "the mature Israelis" under trusteeship, and the right of an independent Israel to

---

[60] In March of 1948 the State Department utilized the "war scare" of January–February 1948 "to reverse American policy on the partition of Palestine and to shatter the Zionist vision of a Jewish homeland on the eve of its realization" (Evensen, *Truman, Palestine, and the Press,* 50, 78, 124 141). On March 19 Truman allegedly abandoned support for partition. On March 20 he claimed that he had been double-crossed by the State Department into making it appear as though he had changed his position on partition (ibid.,153).

[61] See Peter L. Hahn, *Caught in the Middle East: U.S. Policy Toward the Arab-Israeli Conflict, 1945–1961* (Chapel Hill: University of North Carolina Press, 2004). Secretary of Defense James Forrestal especially was concerned about oil issues and, together with Loy Henderson, head of the State Department's Near East desk, initiated Truman's reconsideration of his partition policy and led the opposition to it (Fraser, *Arab-Israeli Conflict,* 38; Evensen, *Truman, Palestine, and the Press,* 130–31, 136). Drew Middleton fed the "Soviets are taking over" hysteria with comments such as on "the historical tendency of the Russian Empire to push southward" (*New York Times,* 9 and 10 January 1948, cited in Evensen, *Truman, Palestine, and the Press,* 133). This sentiment was strengthened by the Communist takeover of Czechoslovakia on February 25, 1948. Italy, France, Finland, and Palestine were seen as Moscow's next victims (ibid., 138–39, 143). Mlechin goes overboard when he writes that the entire U.S. government was against the Zionists (*Zachem Stalin sozdal Izrail'?* 73).

[62] Heller, *Birth of Israel,* 61. This involved the so-called Bernadotte plan (June 27, 1948) that would have made Israel part of a union of Transjordan and Palestine and subject to the Arabs.

acquire arms and defend itself were constants of Soviet rhetoric and practice.[63]

Related to all this is what might be called a numbers game, i.e., how many Jews were there in the USSR? This is relevant to our story because one of the ultimate costs of the recognition of Israel has been massive emigration, and it is important to know what that human capital cost has been. The figures given for the Soviet Jewish population between the end of World War II and the beginnings of the Brezhnev-era emigration have ranged from two to three and one-half million.[64] This itself is an exceedingly complex issue worthy of a separate essay, but here only a few of the elements will be mentioned. One fundamental problem is simply defining who was a Jew in the late Soviet context. Jewish law says that "ethnicity" passes through the mother, but that was not binding on the Soviets. For them, the crucial, quantifiable element was Line 5 ("nationality" — introduced in 1932) of the Soviet internal passport, which might read "Jew," "Russian," "Armenian," "Ukrainian," or more than 100 other possibilities. In the 1870s for Jews this would have been fairly clear, but after a century of urbanization, modernization, and intermarriage, the issue was no longer so clear. Internal passports were issued when and where a child was when he/she was 16, and apparently the 16-year-old could pick whichever nationality he/she desired.[65] Then there was the fact that at various times in Soviet history it was more or less advantageous to be known or counted as a Jew, and so it is generally assumed that the census numbers were sometimes arbitrary.

Given just these facts, it should not be too surprising that the counts of Jews varied quite widely. When foreigners got into the act of commenting on the census figures, additional variables were introduced. One was an allegation that the Soviets were embarrassed over the consequences of the Nazi-Soviet Nonaggression Pact, so they claimed that the Soviets over-reported the number of Jews. This in turn led to numbers around 2 million as the Western commentators reduced the Soviet numbers which were assumed to be inflated. Numbers as high as 3.5 million stem from assuming a Soviet undercount, and then trying to correct it upward. The current assumption is that

---

[63] V. V. Naumkin et al., eds., *Blizhnevostochnyi konflikt 1947–1956: Iz dokumentov Arkhiva vneshnei politiki Rossiiskoi Federatsii* (Moscow: Materik, 2003), 16–21, 24–33, 36–39, 42–60; Mlechin, *Zachem Stalin sozdal Izrail'?* 157–59. A good review of the post-independence pro-Israeli Soviet rhetoric can be found in Krammer, *Forgotten Friendship*, 30–31 and passim.

[64] Israel Miller, "Don't Forget Us!—the Three Million Jews of Russia," *Ave Maria* 106 (9 December 1967): 13–15; Joshua Rothenberg, "How Many Jews Are There in the Soviet Union?" *Jewish Social Studies* 29 (October 1967): 234–40. American Zionist J. Robinson claimed 2,000,000 in November 1946 (*Documents on Israeli-Soviet Relations*, 154).

[65] Boris Smolar, *Soviet Jewry Today and Tomorrow* (New York: Macmillan, 1971), 79.

there were about 2.3 million Jews in the entire USSR at the beginning of the Brezhnev era, in the mid-1960s.

While Brezhnev permitted the emigration of Soviet Jews, hundreds of thousands departed before he realized its costs and halted the flow. Gorbachev permitted the resumption of emigration and about a million emigrated to Israel from the territory of the USSR after 1989. Now there are only 200,000–400,000 Jews remaining in Russia. (Of course some Jews remain in Ukraine, Lithuania, and in other parts of the F.S.U.) About 40,000 Israelis have emigrated back to Russia. Brezhnev realized that this was costing the USSR huge sums, and tried to recoup those human capital investment costs by charging an emigration tax. This was alleged to be a violation of human rights, but it also gives a basis for calculating the enormous financial cost of Stalin's facilitating the creation and then his recognition of Israel.[66] As noted below, the USSR/Russia undoubtedly made one of the largest human capital transfers in history to Israel.

The writing of this essay has been motivated by two contemporary events. The first is the alleged demographic crisis in Russia and the government's response to it. The fact is that the population of Russia has been declining by about 800,000 per year. There are three major causes of this population decline: (1) very low birth rates, so that there are only about 1.2+ children per woman, far below reproduction rates; (2) very high prime-age male mortality rates; (3) emigration. Russian President Putin has declared that reversing the population collapse is one of his primary goals. Part of his program is inviting "home" Russian émigrés. The big question is whether Jews are included among the "Russian émigrés." While not excluding Jews explicitly, a long article in the June 30, 2006 issue of *Moscow News* made it fairly clear that the target population is the Russian colonists living in the former non-Russian republics of the USSR.[67] The question of interest to me is whether Stalin & Co. in any way anticipated that the creation of Israel might lead to the emigration of the Jews. If not, why not?

The second current event was a recent statement by Anatolii Ivanovich Utkin, director of the International Studies Center of the USA and Canada Institute of the Academy of Sciences. On July 20, 2006, he observed that

---

[66] From that sum one has to subtract the value of the property the emigrants were forced to leave behind as well as the pensions the leavers had to forego. The emigration had also enormous political costs for the USSR: those who stayed (including the non-Jews) wondered about the viability and desirability of the Soviet Union—which undoubtedly contributed to its collapse in 1991.

[67] See "Putin Calls for Russians to Return Home," *The Moscow News*, no. 24 (4228), 30 June 2006: 3. Russian *Life* for September/October 2006 has an article "Please Come Back: Russians Lured Home with Financial Incentives" that stresses "ethnic Russians." "Russian authorities are hoping to attract up to four million people with the monetary incentives, primarily from the former Soviet republics" (9–10).

"Russian capitalism has turned out to be weak, especially when it comes to brains."[68] Replacing "Russian capitalism" with "Soviet socialism," could not Stalin & Co. have anticipated that this might be a consequence of the creation of Israel? There are allegations that the Soviets in the 1940s did not discuss nationality in terms of talent, but that is blatantly false. The Soviet intelligence operative Pavel Sudoplatov in his memoir *Special Tasks* discusses an incident of 1943 when actor Solomon Mikhoels and poet Itzik Feffer were about to embark on a fundraising tour of the USA on behalf of the Jewish Antifascist Committee. Secret Police Chief Lavrentii Beria called them in and "instructed them to emphasize the great Jewish contribution to science and culture in the Soviet Union."[69] To imagine that this same Beria did not comprehend four years later the importance of Jewish brains for the USSR can only be described as ludicrous. It is hard to imagine that he did not discuss this when the matters of sending Gromyko to New York and the creation of Israel were being considered. Unintended consequences happen all the time, but it is difficult to imagine that no one thought of the issue of what the consequences of the creation of Israel might be for Russia's brainpower.[70]

The problem of this essay has been why the Soviet Union took the lead in sponsoring the creation of Israel. I still do not have all the answers, but will continue looking.[71] At the moment, some conclusions may be reached. The first point seems to be that Soviet support for the creation of Israel was linked to the widely discussed project of 1944–45 to turn the Crimea into a Jewish homeland. The Crimean Tatars had been expelled from the peninsula for allegedly collaborating with the Nazis, and the region was available for resettlement. Many Soviet leaders suggested turning it into a homeland for the Jews.[72] (Birobidzhan had been created to keep the Chinese out and flopped as a Jewish homeland project.) For unknown reasons, after the end of World War II Stalin dropped the idea of a Jewish republic in the Crimea. The

---

[68] *Rodnaia gazeta*, no. 27 (20 July 2006), quoted in *Johnson's Russia List* 2660, no. 167 (24 July 2006), item 2.

[69] Sudoplatov and Sudoplatov, *Special Tasks*, 188.

[70] Alexander Pumpyansky in "Sharon, Peres, and Russian-Israeli Capital" writes that "the one million Russian Jews in Israel [are] tremendous capital that Russia, perhaps not understanding or even wishing to, has invested in Israel" (*New Times*, July 2006).

[71] The prospects do not seem to be encouraging. Yaacov Ro'i, commenting on the volume of some 500 documents in the collection *Documents on Israeli-Soviet Relations*, notes that attempts to supplement the collection were futile. "The most blatant lacunae are the actual decisions taken by the Soviet leadership to support the establishment of a Jewish state in Palestine and input from the Soviet security apparatus regarding the danger represented by Soviet Jews' identification with and sympathy for Israel."

[72] Sudoplatov alleges that Stalin and Molotov came up with the Crimean Jewish homeland idea to aid their British allies by taking the focus off of Palestine and diverting world Jewish leaders (*Special Tasks*, 292).

Crimean discussion, however, launched the idea that a Jewish homeland would be desirable.

The problem of the Jewish survivors of the Holocaust remained. In November 1945[73] an Anglo-American Committee of Inquiry for Palestine was established which recommended in April 1946 admitting 100,000 displaced persons to Palestine, but rejected the proposal for the creation of a Jewish state.[74] The Committee ignored and thus snubbed the USSR. Soviet deputy ministers of foreign affairs Vladimir Georgievich Dekanozov and Andrei Ia. Vyshinskii pointed this out to Stalin and suggested that a public policy be formulated advocating a Jewish state in Palestine. Vyshinskii, with the consent of Molotov, published an article in the Soviet *New Times*[75] advocating the creation of a Jewish state in Palestine. Simultaneously Soviet agents were sent through Rumania to combat the British in Palestine. They were the ones who arranged the shipment of captured Nazi materiel to the Zionist guerrillas.[76]

The Soviets insisted that none of "their Jews" would desire to emigrate, perhaps part of the assimilationist delusion that will be discussed below. The fact was otherwise, however, and in late 1947 Stalin took advantage of this. A handful of carefully selected Jews were allowed to emigrate and intelligence agents Andrei Mikhailovich Otroshchenko and Aleksandr Mikhailovich Korotkov were in charge. One of their tasks was to make sure that a number of the emigrants were Soviet agents who were charged with countering American attempts to win Israel to its side and to "ensure that Israel became an ally of the Soviet Union."[77] From this one might conclude that Stalin and his entourage could see through the assimilationist delusion—which makes their persistent actions in support of the creation of Israel even more unintelligible.

This brings us to a summary: what was the purpose of the Soviet endeavor to create Israel? The Soviets hoped that they were going to gain a base (an outpost, a center of influence) in the Middle East. They knew it would not be under Soviet control to the extent captured Eastern Europe was, but they did not want to be left out of the region entirely.[78] They might not be able to replace the British completely, but at least they would not cede the region completely to the Americans. Surprisingly, the Soviets did not (sufficiently/ adequately) consider the potential long-term consequences (the Brezhnev-era

---

[73] "TimeLine of Palestinian Israeli History," http://www.mideastweb.org/timeline.htm (accessed 27 February 2007), 8.

[74] Fraser, *Arab-Israeli Conflict*, 29.

[75] The article was signed by K. Serezhin, "Problems of the Arab East," 1 February 1946. Subsequently Vyshinskii was always a strong supporter of Israel (Mlechin, *Zachem Stalin sozdal Izrail'?* 208–09).

[76] Sudoplatov and Sudoplatov, *Special Tasks*, 292–93.

[77] Andrew and Mitrokhin, *The World Was Going Our Way*, 222–23.

[78] Sudoplatov and Sudoplatov, *Special Tasks*, 291–93.

refusenik movement has not been mentioned here, only the emigration of the period), but were thinking relatively short-term and in international terms only.

The 22nd World Zionist Congress met in Basel/Basle on December 9, 1946.[79] That seems to provide the final clue for the reasons for the active, public Soviet role in the creation of Israel. After the World Congress in Basel, a number of pro-Soviet delegates remained in Basel in 1947. Among those individuals were Adolf Berman (from Poland; his brother was Jakub Berman, head of the Polish State Security Service), Abraham Suckewer (from Vilnius), Aharon Zisling (Ziesling; Cizling, born 1901 in Belarus; the first Israeli minister of agriculture), Meir Yaari (an Austrian), and Benzion Goldberg (an American journalist).[80] They agreed that they would serve as a "pro-Soviet lobby" in exchange for Soviet support of Israeli statehood.[81] This led Stalin to believe that the new nation would be socialist and hasten the decline of British influence in the Middle East and perhaps replace it with Soviet influence. Gromyko's speech and the other critical Soviet UN actions followed. Whether Stalin was double-crossed[82] is a separate issue, but the fact is that the Soviets gained almost nothing for their role in the creation of Israel and in fact lost a great deal.

Yet one more fact needs to be mentioned in trying to understand why Stalin & Co. could not (did not) look into the future to try to predict the consequences of their actions, especially emigration and dissent. Contemporary Americans believed that the Jews of the Soviet Union had been largely, if not entirely, assimilated.[83] I myself met such types in 1963–64 and later, so cannot be surprised that this may have been a nearly universally held view. The Soviets insisted early on that "their" Jews would not want to emigrate, inter alia,

---

[79] Gabriel Gorodetsky, *Soviet Foreign Policy, 1917–1991: A Retrospective* (Portland, OR: Frank Cass, 1994), 13; *Documents on Israeli-Soviet Relations*, 166.

[80] Of these five, only Zisling and Yaara are mentioned in Heller's *Birth of Israel.*.

[81] Sami Rozen, "Israel's Declaration of Independence Written by Moscow's Agent [Ahron Zisling]," *Axis Information and Analysis*, 22 May 2006 (www.axisglobe.com/article. asp? article = 872). Many of the delegates also took part in an organization called the League for Cooperation with Soviet Russia, no doubt a Soviet front organization like the Council for American-Soviet Friendship. After the Gromyko speech, Moshe Sneh (Kleinbaum; born in Poland in 1909), a senior figure in Mapam (sometimes termed a communist), demanded that the Yishuv shift its orientation to the Soviet Union; he was rebuffed by Ben-Gurion (Heller, *Birth of Israel*, 60). Sneh swore "that we shall never let the Soviet Union down" (Andrew and Mitrokhin, *The World Was Going Our Way*, 222). Thus, it appeared not only to many Americans, but to many Soviets that a newly created Israel would drift at least toward, if not into, the Soviet camp.

[82] The Hebrew University historian Joseph Heller uses the phrase "terrible ingratitude" (*Birth of Israel*, 66).

[83] This was even a theoretical point for Stalin (Rayfield, *Stalin and His Hangmen*, 439).

because the USSR was an advanced, socialist, non-discriminatory state.[84] In other words, although Line 5 of the passport said "Jew," many people may have felt that this was meaningless and, were it not for the absurdity of the Soviet nationalities policy, it should have read "Soviet." If that was true, this would explain the total, profound shock felt by the Soviet leadership when "their" Jews responded enthusiastically to the creation of Israel.[85] It was even "worse" when Israeli ambassador Golda Meir showed up at the Moscow synagogue on New Year's Day, October 16, 1948, and was mobbed by thousands of enthusiastic Jewish citizens.[86] Moreover, many Soviet Jews were extraordinarily positively impressed by the performance of the Israeli army in the war of independence over the Arabs trying to crush the new state. It convinced them that the words "Jew" and "victim" need not be synonymous. Other events frightening to Soviet authorities were mass demonstrations on Simchas Torah.[87] Had such sentiments been known before the Gromyko speech, the Soviet leadership might have been considerably more hesitant about participating so actively in the creation of Israel.

[84] The "definitive statement" on this issue was made by Il'ia Erenburg in *Pravda* on September 21, 1948. See Heller, *Birth of Israel*, 61–62, for more on the Soviet position on emigration. Post-Soviet evidence has come to light indicating that Erenburg was not the believing Soviet tool he appeared to be. He even went so far as to say that the main task of the Jewish Anti-Fascist Committee was to combat anti-Semitism in the USSR (Redlich, 414, no. 167). This obviously was a supreme heresy, for the official dogma proclaimed that there was and could be no anti-Semitism in the USSR. This issue for this topic is whether Stalin believed the rhetoric, which I am inclined to believe that he did.

[85] Shimon Redlich, *War, Holocaust and Stalinism: A Documented Study of the Jewish Anti-Fascist Committee in the USSR* (Luxemburg: Harwood Academic Publishers, 1995), passim. All the Jews of a place called Zhmerinka asked the Soviet government "to go to our homeland to create a large Jewish democratic state" (ibid., document no. 152).

[86] Salo W. Baron, *The Russian Jew under Tsars and Soviets* (New York: Macmillan, 1964), 318. See also Joseph B. Schechtman, "When the State of Israel Was Proclaimed," in Ronald I. Rubin, *The Unredeemed: Anti-Semitism in the Soviet Union* (Chicago: Quadrangle Books, 1968), 149–57; Ami, *Between Hammer and Sickle*, 31–32.

[87] Smolar, *Soviet Jewry Today and Tomorrow*, 114–25. Andrew and Mitrokhin term the Soviet reaction "alarm" (*The World Was Going Our Way*, 223).

Some Remarks on Russian Intellectual History and the Origins of Eurasianism

Nicholas V. Riasanovsky

I received my doctorate from Oxford. The last stage of that quest consisted in the public defense of my dissertation on the Slavophiles, challenged by two official opponents, faculty members with whom, according to the rules of the procedure, I had not done any previous work. Max Beloff began by expressing an interest in my study, but he wondered why it had been presented under the rubric of history and not philosophy. I explained that I came to Oxford from Harvard, where such investigations were in the domain of intellectual history. Beloff retorted: "Another meaningless American classification." I had a sinking feeling: "There goes..." But actually from that point on everything went well. Beloff liked my work, and so did the other examiner, Sergei Konovalov, who pleaded, rather disarmingly, that, difficult though this is, I should try to find more originality in Russian thought. So I received my doctorate and even added my defense to other fond memories of Oxford, such as the devoted guidance of my supervisor, B. H. Sumner, and the seemingly endless conversations with the other supervisor, Isaiah Berlin.

Still, Beloff's caustic comment deserves an answer, and indeed different answers are possible. For my part, I think of philosophy as a search for ultimate goals, truth, logical, perhaps even esthetic, perfection. Intellectual history, by contrast, deals with the impact of ideas on humanity. To take an extreme example, Nazism amounts to nothing for philosophy, but it is extremely important in intellectual history, because of the disaster it produced (or at least contributed very heavily to producing).

Or consider the intractable subject of the Soviet Union. Very much has been written about communist ideology. Authors have ranged from such splendid specialists as professors Leszek Kolakowski and Andrzej Walicki to almost any number of other scholars, journalists, diplomats, and even people of any other sort who had some contact with Soviet reality. And yet that ideology needs more rather than less emphasis. Failures to appreciate it in full range from suspicions of intellectual history as basic causation to the omnipresence of the official Soviet dogma and doctrine to the point that it appears as something obvious and natural rather than imposed. A very large number of misconceptions stems from substitution of the struggle of leaders for power, vanity, suspiciousness, pride, vengeance, conspiracies, etc., for Marxism-Leninism. Usually the error is simply mixing the levels of discourse. It is

Rude & Barbarous Kingdom Revisited: Essays in Russian History and Culture in Honor of Robert O. Crummey. Chester S. L. Dunning, Russell E. Martin, and Daniel Rowland, eds. Bloomington, IN: Slavica Publishers, 2008, 389–407.

not that Soviet protagonists were free from the above-mentioned vices and rivalries in all their forms. It is rather that their vices and rivalries took place within the basic framework of their ideology, by no means eliminating that ideology. A comprehensive ideology is of fundamental importance in the first place because that is how those who believe in it, whether they are aggressive or passive, honest or dishonest, vain or modest, see the world. And that is how the world was seen from the Kremlin from 1917 to 1991.

In fact, the Soviet leadership, from Lenin, to Stalin, to Khrushchev, to Brezhnev, to Andropov, to Chernenko, to Gorbachev, as well as their numerous associates and assistants, demonstrated a remarkable ideological consistency. Lenin, whose contributions extended Marxism to Marxism-Leninism, has often been accused of fanaticism, but not of unbelief. Stalin, whose almost entire intellectual, particularly theoretical, baggage was limited to Marxism, considered that, after Lenin, he became the true seer and leader. On a more naive and less murderous plane Khrushchev put his heart into the competition of his socialist fatherland with the capitalist world, especially the United States of America, and was still counting Soviet gains in the production of milk, meat, and eggs as he was dismissed from office. Brezhnev's long rule came to be known as a period of stagnation precisely because no fundamental changes took place, and the USSR continued on its established dogmatic course. Many observers noted a decline in enthusiasm for old beliefs and goals, but there was nothing to replace them. Nor did the leadership of Andropov and after him Chernenko transform the scene; besides, both died very shortly after attaining the highest position.

Even the last occupier of that position, the reformer who finally arrived, Gorbachev, was in his own way as much a Marxist-Leninist as Khrushchev. In addition to impeccable communist service prior to his elevation, he praised the Soviet system—for example, for having successfully solved the problem of nationalities just before that problem exploded—and spoke of the wonderful potentialities of the Party, to general amazement, even after being rescued from the putsch of the hard-liners. Gorbachev's authentic vision was that of a repaired, restored to its full glory, and dynamic Leninism. Fate willed otherwise.

Finally, after the collapse of the USSR and the new availability of primary sources, scholars find only further confirmation of the enormous role of ideology in Soviet Russia. In particular, at the highest Party and government level there seems to be no instance, no matter how private or secret, of a cynical use of Marxism to trick the unwary or mislead the masses. One confronts certainly a community of believers, although it is fair to speculate that with the passage of time that community contained fewer fanatics.

Yet, enormously significant as the Marxist-Leninist ideology was in the emergence and history of the Soviet Union, one should also be aware of the limitations of its role. For one thing, Marxism simply did not cover some important, even very important areas of state activity. Thus classical Marxism offered no manual on foreign policy after the revolution for the good reason that there was to be no such policy, but instead of division, diplomacy, and war, a united proletarian world. Lenin and his associates looked for that world in the Russian revolution itself and especially in revolutionary outbreaks in central and eastern Europe as well as in the invasion of Poland by the Red Army. But when the revolution failed to spread, they had to improvise, and improvise they did from the Treaty of Brest-Litovsk signed on the 3rd of March 1918, to the collapse of the Soviet Union in 1991. Bereft of comprehensive guidance, the Soviet leaders used their Marxism in specific instances including the creation and the entire activity of the Comintern and later the Cominform. It is also only with reference to Marxism that one can understand the Soviet expectations of a war between the United States and Great Britain (the new capitalism challenging the old capitalism) or the light treatment of the rise of Nazi power in Germany, which represented to them the last gasp of dying imperialism to be followed by a major struggle against the Social Democrats for the allegiance of the German people. (Western observers and even governments came to equally incorrect conclusions from different assumptions, such as the expectations that once in power the Nazis would acquire conservatism, moderation, and even good manners.)

Moreover, theory had to be translated into practice, and that almost inevitably means adaptation and change. A textbook example was provided by the First Five-Year Plan with its remarkable ups and downs, but essentially with its relentless drive to produce (or collectivize) as much as possible and even beyond the possible. The drive would stop only at the edge of the precipice and even beyond that edge as millions of peasants who perished during collectivization would testify if they could. But there were other and more subtle forms of adaptation. The end product, whether in economics, social policy, or culture, would be, of course, connected to the plan, but also greatly changed by Soviet reality.

Also, the dominant position of Soviet Marxism did not exclude some roles for certain subordinate, even contradictory teachings, such as nationalism and anti-Semitism, in the thirties but especially in connection with the Second World War and its aftermath in the Soviet Union and abroad.

It is also appropriate to ask what is meant by Soviet ideology. The discussion above referred only to the communist ruling group and its Party and government machines, and although that group made a stupendous effort to encompass the entire people in all of the people's activities, in retrospect the success of that endeavor seems doubtful, to say the least. And, to enlarge the issue, there were important historical reasons that brought communism to Russia, the Third Reich to Germany, or the New Deal to the United States of America. Those reasons were both of an "intellectual" and of a "non-intellectual" kind. Thus, apparently, both the great depression and Hitler's ranting, as well as much else, were needed to establish Nazism in Germany. Intellectual history is only one major aspect of history, but that does not make it unimportant. Unfortunately, in contrast to Marxist and some other historians, I know of no formula to arrange the aspects in their proper relationship and sequence. Rather, each case has to be examined separately and on its own with as much understanding and flexibility as possible.

What, then, are the requirements for studying, teaching, and writing in the field of intellectual history? I would put first a deep interest in ideas and at the same time in the particular historical circumstances in which these ideas appear, operate, and disappear. At a certain level of generalization or abstraction ideas belong entirely to philosophy. Uncounted pages of historical analysis, or literary criticism for that matter, have been wasted in trying to establish the nature of reality or the true character of human knowledge. Not that these issues are unimportant. Indeed they represent main lines of thought in our Western civilization. But they do not belong in book reviews. Not surprisingly, some intellectuals trained in philosophy, such as Alexandre Koyre or Andrzej Walicki, who were willing to practice the historian's nomi-nalistic craft, easily rank with the best in the profession. Certain others, such as my teacher Isaiah Berlin, educated primarily in philosophy and classical languages, kept denying that they were historians, until their standing in the discipline made denial impossible. Still others, for example Nicholas Ber-diaev, refused to adjust and thus remained bad historians, whatever their stature and importance in philosophy. It was demonstrated time and time again that it is possible to descend from Hegel to Hitler, but not to reverse the direction. However, and to repeat, historians of intellectual development need not occupy the highest levels of human thought, but they should be able to understand that thought as well as its fortunes at lower levels. One of their great advantages is that they have the world to select from.

Next to, or rather together with, competence to deal with intellectual top-ics, intellectual historians must know the language of their subjects. In my case and in those of many of my students Russian has been particularly im-portant, although it is difficult to imagine an intellectual historian who cannot use French and German. Indeed, I repeatedly quote to my graduate students from Griboedov, totally out of context but straight to the point, "что нам без немцев нет спасенья" (that there is no salvation for us without the Germans) and especially their omnipresent published doctoral dissertations. As to Rus-sian, no further urging may appear to be needed, except that the competence in the language required for Russian intellectual history is greater than that necessary for many other "Russian" subjects, much beyond what our witty colleague, Professor Maurice Friedberg, labels as "intermediate Russian." It is especially painful to see people study hard and at times still fail. I remember the bafflement of a student who had just returned from a period of instruction in Leningrad and wanted to know why the Soviet Union opposed marriage— his evidence for that was a huge sign in a factory to which he had been taken: "doloi brak" (in context, obviously "down with spoilage," not "down with marriage," although the two words are identical). Even more to the point, a

brave American specialist in Russian culture who lectured in Russian was up-
set by his reception. He began a lecture by stating that his approach to Russian history was entirely ironic and could immediately see his audience turn
against him. The next day a leading newspaper wrote of "nekii ironicheskii
istorik," a certain ironic historian, altogether negatively. What our lecturer
did not know was that whereas in certain high English-speaking circles to
which he belonged "ironic" had recently acquired also a positive meaning,
suggesting many-sidedness, complexity, a certain distance from the object,
perhaps ambivalence, as opposed to simple-mindedness, the Russian "ironicheskii" continued to designate, as of old, only something close to sarcastic or
satirical. To put it crudely, the lecturer had informed his listeners that he is
interested in Russian history solely to make fun of it.

There is yet another reason why students of Russian intellectual history
should know the Russian language very well. However one judges Tiutchev,
Dostoevsky, or Tolstoy as thinkers, they were unsurpassed writers with a fantastic power of expression. Tiutchev, one of the great poets of the world, did
not become a theoretician of Romanticism or a literary critic, but bits of his
poetry tell us more and better about the new intellectual climate than volumes by other authors. Witness:

Дума за думой, волна за волной —
Два проявленья стихии одной:

The English would read:

Thought after thought, wave after wave —
Two manifestations of one element: (or: the same element)![1]

Genius aside, Russian writers of every sort contributed much to Russian
intellectual history. Indeed it has been argued that in Russia literature acquired a truly sweeping range and resonance, often taking the place of philosophy, social criticism, or political debate. Whether ascribed to the Russian
character, the impact of the Orthodox Church, the tsarist and Soviet oppres-
sions, or still other decisive factors, the resulting picture seems valid, at least
to some considerable extent. And it means, among many other things, that
American students of Russian intellectual history overlap broadly with specialists in Russian language and literature, the academics least likely to be
satisfied with "intermediate Russian." Their criticism may even be excessive,
because occasionally it proved possible to state something relevant about
Russian thought while confusing gender and case endings.

---

[1] Fedor I. Tiutchev, *Polnoe sobranie sochinenii*, ed. Petr V. Bykov (St. Petersburg: Izd. T-
va A. F. Marks, 1913), 116.

Students of Russian intellectual history should make their own translations from Russian and from other languages when appropriate. The danger of relying on available translations is too great. My Harvard teacher Mikhail Karpovich learned that lesson once and for all, when assigning Kliuchevskii in English and noticing that a tribe was paying its tribute in cheese. A check with the Russian gave сырье, not сыр (raw materials, not cheese). My own experience has been mostly negative. I remember a wind bending branches instead of breaking trees and much else. In poetry especially a straight and clumsy prose translation may be preferable to artistic versions.[2]

Interested, able to deal with intellectual topics, and competent in Russian, we can turn to reading our material. Much has been written about reading recently, some of it useful. But the most important point was established long ago—probably by the first teacher—namely that each person reads the same passage differently. A crucial issue is whether and to what extent a given item should be read straight or whether one must allow for the hidden agenda. The contemporary reading public has become quite skeptical in that regard as evidenced by the equation of "I read it in the paper" with unsupported and

---

[2] Not to end on a negative note on translations, useful, even indispensable in our field, I would like to assert that occasional perfect translations even of poetry do exist, although they are usually not produced as translations. My favorite:

Mais elle etoit du monde, où les plus belles choses
Ont le pire destin
Et rose elle a vécu ce que vivent les roses,
L'espace d'un matin.   Francois de Malherbe (1555–1628)

And

Творец из лучшего эфира
Соткал живые струны их,
Они не созданы для мира,
И мир был создан не для них!   Mikhail Lermontov (1814–1841)

Both "Consolation à Monsieur du Perier" and "A Demon" are among the most famous poems in world literature. They are also the poems most indelibly connected with their illustrious authors. These authors, Malherbe and Lermontov, constituted significant moments, perhaps even stages, in the development of the languages and the literatures of their respective countries. More to the point, Lermontov knew French language and literature very well, while Malherbe was located in the mainstream of that literature. But here the parallels and especially possible connections cease. There is no entry under Malherbe in the *Lermontov Encyclopedia* (V. A. Manuilov, ed., *Lermontovskaia entsiklopediia*, 1981), nor have I been able to establish any meaningful connections on my own. Malherbe and Lermontov belonged to different ages, different stages in the development of European literature, different languages, different countries, and different milieus. Everything was different—except the four lines of verse quoted above. Nicholas V. Riasanovsky, "A Note on Perfect Translating," *Rus: Studia Literaria Slavica in Honorem Hugh McLean,* ed. Simon Karlinsky, James L. Rice, and Barry P. Scherr (Oakland, CA: Berkeley Slavic Specialties, 1995), 204–07.

probably incorrect information or the almost total refusal to consider politicians and political literature at face value, not to speak of the field and nature of advertising. Much of that skepticism is, of course, warranted. And yet some of the most numerous and worst mistakes in intellectual history come from not reading one's sources to the end and, if you will, "straight." There is a tremendous bias in having the subjects of research conform to the scholars' own views or their research agendas. It is quite appropriate and useful to discover ideas of the so-called Utopian socialists in Marxism and other later socialist doctrines. It is wrong to present them and their views simply in terms of the bits they contributed to subsequent socialist light. I wrote a book trying to expound Fourier's teaching straight, madness and all.[3]

There is a joke that Marx was penalized in the next world for not quoting Lenin in his works. We should, therefore, be careful to learn who could be quoted by our protagonists and, more broadly, what was the general intellectual scene at the time. From my first study of the Slavophiles I came across rather isolated treatments of the Russian thinkers in relation to such giants as Hegel and Schelling, sometimes with the additional claim that the Russians, because they were different from the German giant or giants in certain specific respects, were obviously original. Such an attitude meant simply leaving out most of the European intellectual world.

It is also important to find out as much as possible not only what the intellectuals who interest us read, or at least could have read, but how they read it. Again, a great danger is the substitution of the critic's own perception of the issues involved for that of the subject's. Thus Soviet scholars typically assigned deism, skepticism, and atheism to their "progressive" heroes on the grounds that the rational or scientific views and knowledge of the heroes clearly disagreed with religion. Those declarations were not very helpful for students researching not the Soviet intelligentsia, but, let us say, Lomonosov.

A persistent problem for scholars of modern Russian intellectual history has been its relationship to Europe as a whole. I agree that at least since Peter the Great Russian thought (not necessarily shared by the Russian masses or some Orthodox clergy) can be understood only as part of European thought. Yet in Russia—to be sure, not only in Russia—major adjustments had to be made. For example, while scholarship on the French Enlightenment has become entangled in a great debate on the role of the so-called third estate, in Russia there was simply no such thing. An insightful modern Russian intellectual history could be written by tracing in detail that continuous issue of identity with and allegiance to Western thought, yet the need to apply it to Russian conditions. Here I shall mention only one method, selectivity. The Age of Reason offered several major models of governance. But only one took firm root in Russia: enlightened despotism. As Plekhanov explained the mat-

---

[3] Nicholas V. Riasanovsky, *The Teaching of Charles Fourier* (Berkeley: University of California Press, 1969).

ter, with special reference to the dominant literary genre of the ode, glorifying in particular the rulers:

> Our ode writers flattered beyond all measure. This, unfortunately, cannot be denied. But, in the first place, flattery in an ode was demanded by the custom of the time. It was a disgusting custom, but the contemporary readers and listeners knew that the exaggerated plaudits, contained in odes, had to be accepted *cum grano salis*. And the most important thing—precisely what I want to point out to the readers—the ode writers were adorers of autocratic power not only from fear but also out of conviction. From it, and from it only, they expected the impulse for progressive development in Russia. How then they could fail to glorify it and sing it in their odes?[4]

Because thinking and communication is part of every human society, no matter how simple or how sophisticated, so is intellectual history. Our general unconcern with it is largely a result of taking it for granted. That is why at times a look at a radically different society makes its intellectual assumptions, and by contrast and comparison our own assumptions, stand in a sharp relief. I had that experience, for example, when reading Professor Frederick Wakeman's splendid study of Ming China. Like the first foreign language, the first foreign culture may put one's own into perspective and demonstrate that instead of being cabined and confined by absolute structures one is free to look for different ways to achieve the same or similar ends. Indeed one is tempted to put learning a different culture as another requirement for students of Russian intellectual history, although their knowledge of it would have to fall short, for practical reasons, of a mastery of Chinese, or Egyptian, hieroglyphics.

Intellectual history has many wonderful parts and problems. From childhood I have been fascinated by the doctrines of early Christian sects and of modern social, political, and economic prophets about whom I kept reading in the great Brockhaus-Efron encyclopedia and in other reference works in our home library. History is largely a tale of evolution and diffusion. Yet at times the intellectual historian is struck by something coming seemingly from nowhere and has to face the issue of originality and origins. That is how the teaching of Charles Fourier affected me, and why much later I wrote a book about it. As I indicated earlier in this paper, Fourier has to be read straight and entire—into the obvious insanity of the message. Then indeed Fourier's

---

[4] G. V. Plekhanov, *Istoriia russkoi obshchestvennoi mysli* (Moscow: Lit.-izd. otdel Nar. Kom. po prosveshcheniiu, 1919), 3: 32. For the broader picture, see "The Image of Peter the Great in Russian Enlightenment 1700–1826," in Nicholas V. Riasanovsky, *The Image of Peter the Great in Russian History and Thought* (New York: Oxford University Press, 1985), 3–85.

system will have unity, symmetry, meaning, and even a kind of grace. Or almost so—because the supreme mathematical formula which embodies Fourier's system does not really exist and, therefore, cannot be produced, understood, or reproduced. I spent no time on Fourier's famous, or notorious, cahier containing only numbers.

Fourier's teaching, or rather parts and bits of his teaching, have been used uncounted times and for a great variety of purposes ranging from an absolute critique of civilization to socialism of all sorts and more recently environmentalism. Far from objecting to these borrowings one has to recognize them as the best use of Fourier's writings, for the total system, to repeat, is beyond comprehension. While lost in Fourier's cosmology or numerology, one remembers such statements as: "The poor incessantly attempt to rob the rich on an individual basis, and the rich continually plunder the poor as a class."[5] Borrowing is fine, whether to benefit Marxism or any other doctrine. Only the borrowed part should not be presented as the essence of Fourierism while dismissing the rest of the teaching as inconsequential, an effort to attract attention or a display of humor. Fourier's staggering originality did not, of course, mean that he was not connected with the thought of his age, for that would be an impossibility. Indeed, I think that Fourierism can be best understood as one insane terminus of the Age of Reason. Fourier, fiercely independent, recognized one predecessor, Newton, and he considered it his task to extend Newton's limited but real achievement to social relations, humanity, as well as the entire cosmos.

As one more comment both on reading and on Fourier, I might mention what was probably my most memorable interview in the Soviet Union. At that time I was writing my book on Fourier and was briefly in Moscow for another reason, but decided also to seek out the best Soviet specialist on Fourier, Ioganson Isaakovich Zilberfarb. I found him easily at a historical institute of the Academy, and he received permission to have lunch with me. We went through the line in a nearby cafeteria and sat down at a table for two. Zilberfarb then got up from the table and brought me a big apple. The rapport was immediate, because Zilberfarb was a kindly, well-mannered, and soft-spoken Russian intellectual like many of the people with whom I had been brought up. I concentrated on the bibliography of our subject, which he probably had mastered better than anyone else in the world. I hurried, because I did not know how long we could be together. Still, when the apple was gone, I found time to ask Zilberfarb about his letter to a prominent periodical. That periodical had published a scholarly article about Fourier's anti-Semitism. Fourier had, in fact, been anti-Semitic along the lines common in his time, namely in believing that the Jews were always middlemen and did not themselves pro-

---

[5] Charles Fourier, *The Utopian Vision of Charles Fourier: Selected Texts on Work, Love, and Passionate Attraction*, trans. and ed. Jonathan Beecher and Richard Bienvenu (Boston: Beacon Press, 1971), 302.

duce anything of value to society. And then Zilberfarb exploded with a letter denouncing the author of the article for slandering Fourier, one of the brightest lights of humanity. I asked: "Ioganson Isaakovich, how could you, who know Fourier perhaps better than anyone else, state that he was not anti-Semitic?" He answered: "But, Nikolai Valentinovich, he did not want to exterminate us, did he?"

My next major concern with the issue of originality and origins came with my study of Eurasianism.[6] Eurasianism emerged quite formally and officially in the year 1921 when four young Russian intellectuals published a collective volume, *Iskhod k Vostoku*, that is *Exodus to the East*.[7] The four were Prince Nikolai Sergeevich Trubetskoi, to be famous as a linguistic scholar, Petr Nikolaevich Savitskii, an economist-geographer and specialist in many subjects, Petr Petrovich Suvchinskii, a gifted music critic and many-sided intellectual, and Georgii Vasilievich Florovskii, a theologian, intellectual historian, and also a person of numerous interests with a remarkable breadth of knowledge.

The introduction spoke of a world cataclysm—the year, to repeat, was 1921—of a catastrophic change of scenes, of a new age, of the dying of the West and the imminent rise of the East. It concluded: "Russians and those who belong to the peoples of 'the Russian world' are neither Europeans nor Asiatics. Merging with the native element of culture and life which surrounds us, we are not ashamed to declare ourselves *Eurasians*."[8]

Ten essays by the four authors followed. They ranged from Suvchinskii's "The Strength of the Weak" and Florovskii's "The Cunning of Reason" to Trubetskoi's fascinating "The Upper and the Lower Layers of Russian Culture (The Ethnic base of Russian Culture)" and Savitskii's "Continent-Ocean (Russia and the World Market)." The second Eurasian symposium came out as early as the following year, 1922, with two new authors joining the original four. Altogether, seven consecutively numbered symposia appeared, the last in 1931. Other Eurasian literary undertakings included a special joint volume directed against Roman Catholicism, *Rossiia i Latinstvo—Russia and Latinism*, published in 1923, *Eurasian Chronicle*, 12 volumes of which came out in the period from 1925 through 1937, as well as some books and many booklets and articles written by individual authors. Savitskii proved to be especially prolific. The Eurasians could even boast, although usually not for long, of weeklies, monthlies, or other periodicals in such centers of Russian emigration as Paris, Brussels, and Tallinn. To be sure, some adherents left the move-

---

[6] See Nicholas V. Riasanovsky, "The Emergence of Eurasianism," *California Slavic Studies* 4 (1967), 39–72.

[7] P. N. Savitskii, ed., *Iskhod k Vostoku: Predchustviia i sversheniia. Utverzhdeniia evraziitsev* (Sofia: Rossiisko-bolgarskoe kn-vo, 1921). It is now available in English: *Exodus to the East: Forebodings and Events. An Affirmation of the Eurasians*, ed. and trans. Ilya Vinkovetsky, with an afterword by Nicholas V. Riasanovsky (Idyllwild, CA: Charles Schlacks, 1996).

[8] Savitskii, *Iskhod k Vostoku*, vii. Italics in the original.

ment, and Florovskii even published a masterful critique of it.[9] Many others, however, arrived to replace them. A notable acquisition was Professor George Vernadsky, often described as the Eurasian historian, who during his many years of teaching and publishing at Yale, did much to acquaint the English-speaking world with the new ideology. Vernadsky stressed the decisive significance of the relation between the steppe and the forest societies on the enormous Eurasian plain, the ethnic and cultural complexities of Russia, and the major and organic contribution of eastern peoples, especially the Mongols, to Russian history. Eurasianism gained its main following among Russian students and other young Russian intellectuals in exile.

The thirties turned out to be disturbing for Eurasians as for many others. Politics came increasingly to occupy the center of their attention, supplementing and in part replacing the original emphasis on a spiritual revolution and the creation of a new *Weltanschauung*. The Eurasian "party" expected to supplant the Communist Party and lead a new Russia to a glorious future. It was their attitude or attitudes toward Soviet Russia—ambivalent and "dialectic" already in *Exodus to the East*—that both divided the Eurasians repeatedly among themselves and also accounted for the greatest hostility between them and other "White" Russians. There were claims of betrayal as well as some actual activity of Soviet agents in connection with the movement. Weakened by division and disappointed in its millennial hopes, what we may call classical Eurasianism came to its end with the Second World War, although a few writers, notably Professor Vernadsky, continued to enrich the Eurasian literature in the post-Second World War period. But Eurasianism had a fantastic revival in Russia in the years preceding and especially those following the collapse of communism. That new Eurasianism, or rather Eurasianisms, inchoate, contradictory and going in every direction, lies, however, outside this presentation.[10]

The great originality of classical Eurasianism consisted in the fact that it was the first Russian ideology to renounce the very concepts of "Russia" and "Russians" as well as any fundamental connections of the country and the

---

[9] G. V. Florovskii, "Evraziiskii soblazn," *Sovremennye Zapiski* 34 (1928): 312–46.

[10] As one historian wrote on the subject of the new Eurasianists: "They have rediscovered the post-revolutionary, émigré theories of Eurasianism and its heretofore suppressed late Soviet-era exponents such as L. N. Gumilev. As purveyed by Gumilev and his epigones, classic Eurasianism has been leavened with messianism, racism (including anti-Semitism), anti-Americanism, conspiracy theories, and cosmism. The resultant brew constitutes a veritable Russian New Age movement, noteworthy for its obscure and idiosyncratic ideology, which is not accessible to the general public. The ideology does have a following, a veritable cult has grown up around the posthumously published works of Gumilev—but has yet to become anything approaching a mass movement." John D. Klier, "The Dog That Didn't Bark: Anti-Semitism in Post-Communist Russia," in Geoffrey Hosking and Robert Service, eds., *Russian Nationalism Past and Present* (London: St. Martin's Press, 1997), 129–47, here 141.

people with the peoples both of Europe and of Asia. Russians and other "peoples of the Russian world" were neither Europeans nor Asiatics but a distinct breed of humanity described best as "Eurasians." It was the total break with Europe that proved especially stunning. To be sure there had been some Polish and other European intellectuals who had long suspected or even declared that Europe ended just past the Vistula, that Russians were Finnic or perhaps Mongol in ethnicity and that, in any case, they had no claim to membership in the European community. But these were hostile foreigners, never Russians. As for the latter, even in the deservedly famous comprehensive and sustained critique of the West by the Slavophiles, one of the main charges was that Russians were brothers and sisters of other Europeans but were not treated accordingly by them. Even in the extreme case of Danilevskii, who did separate himself and his country sharply from most European peoples, the entire hope, the entire future, resided in Slavdom, thus again pointing West rather than to any kind of Eurasia. The unprecedented assertion of the Eurasians could not even be understood, let alone accepted, by most Russian intellectuals. The most common academic criticism of the Eurasians came to be their alleged gross exaggeration of Asiatic influences in Russian history, the critics failing even to comprehend the larger Eurasian claims. As in the case of the readers of Fourier, they could not read straight and to the end. And these poor readers included such leading historians of Russia as Paul Miliukov.

Where did Eurasianism come from? As in the example of Fourier, the Eurasians had rich material to make their original construction. The former came at the end of the Enlightenment and had much else to use besides. The latter, in their turn, responded to the crucial, indeed catastrophic, events as well as the tangled thought of their time. The events included especially the First World War, the revolution or revolutions in Russia, and a broader development described by such phrases as the rise of colonial peoples, the decline of imperialism, or the gradual loss by the so-called white race of its dominant global position. Eurasianism certainly belongs with the post-First World War European ideologies distinguished by their bitter rejection of the past and their vague messianic hopes for the future.

As to imperialism and colonialism, only one work preceded directly *Exodus to the East*, Trubetskoi's *Europe and Mankind*, published a year earlier.[11] It was an out-and-out indictment of Western imperialism. Trubetskoi argued that the alleged universal civilization, progress, and higher values which the colonizers claimed to bestow upon the colonized were merely the chauvinism of Europe, made all the more dangerous by its larger claims, which had misled and seduced non-European intellectuals. If one condemned the narrow-minded and aggressive patriots of a given locality, of Prussia, or of Germany, why should one defer to the much more dangerous and far-ranging patriots

---

[11] Kn. N. S. Trubetskoi, *Evropa i chelovechestvo* (Sofia: Rossiisko-bolgarskoe kn-vo, 1920).

of Europe? Because of their different psychologies and own cultures, native peoples could never enter the civilization of Europe as equal partners and develop fully and creatively within its framework. In terms of European culture they would always be second-rate. Their own cultures, on the other hand, were in no sense inferior to European culture. They were simply different. The plotting of all cultures on a continuum with that of Europe at the summit represented one of the most pernicious intellectual errors of the age. Indeed, it was precisely this insidious ability of Europeans to make the exploited peoples, that is, the educated classes of these peoples, see things the European way which accounted in large part for the European domination of mankind. Therefore, in order to throw off the European yoke, the intellectuals of other societies, blinded by Europe, had first to recover their sight and to see the falsity as well as the evil of European claims and pretensions. Then they could lead their peoples in an irresistible bid for independence. Launched by Trubetskoi, imperialism and colonialism became a central issue or issues of the Eurasian doctrine.

There is no reason to doubt the sincerity of Trubetskoi and his associates or their devotion to their new faith. Still, Eurasianism can also be viewed as a determined defense of the Russian empire—and after it, of the Soviet Union, and still later of the projected and explicitly Eurasian ideal state of the future—in an age when empires crumbled. And indeed, if the Russian empire were a symphonic unity of peoples, more than that, if there were really no Russian empire at all but only one organic Eurasia, the dangers of separatism and breakup lost their meaning.

However, it was the Russian Revolution that mattered most to the Eurasians. All of the original Eurasians were young émigré Russian intellectuals, sometimes brilliant intellectuals, suddenly deprived of their country. Older migrants generally retained their established convictions while adjusting, well or ill, to life abroad. Younger generations, when not part of the new Soviet reality, joined fully Western societies and their beliefs. But for the future Eurasians, about to assume their rightful place in the intellectual and cultural evolution of their fatherland, nothing remained. "Russia vanished,"[12] or, to quote another pregnant statement "byt ischez" (the way of life vanished). In a sense, Eurasianism constituted a desperate bid to reestablish vanished Russia, to transmute a fragmented and rootless existence in a foreign society into an organic and creative life at home. The scope of the dream corresponded to that of the loss. As to the precise benefits and rewards to be distributed in the Eurasian Utopia, the evidence is incomplete and in part contradictory, because, for one thing, Eurasian views on the role of private property in the Russia of the future underwent change during the evolution of the movement. Yet one point at least remained clear: an ideocracy was to be ruled by ideocrats.

---

[12] Savitskii, *Iskhod k Vostoku*, 11.

Intellectual influences on the creators of Eurasianism were, of course, many. I shall consider briefly only two very important subjects: geopolitics, and the immediate cultural and intellectual background in Russia for the Eurasian movement. (In fact, Eurasianism combined two distinct concepts of Eurasia, a geopolitical and an ethnic-cultural one, perhaps reinforcing each other, but also quite separable.) The first can be considered a product of Savitskii's application of European, especially German, geopolitical theories to Russia. The very term "Eurasia" was apparently introduced by an Austrian geologist, Eduard Suess.[13] As a young student of the famous economist and intellectual Petr Struve, at the Polytechnic Institute in Petrograd, Savitskii was immersed at the time of the First World War in geopolitical literature. In formulating Eurasianism he created his own geopolitical doctrine. The step was a natural one to take both because the huge Eurasian land mass, one possible version of "the heartland," was bound to loom large in much geopolitical thinking, and because Savitskii had the added incentive of his close acquaintance as a scholar with his fatherland as well as of fervent patriotism.

The Russian and general European scholarly background for Eurasianism was rich and varied. For instance, it was only towards the end of the 19th century and the beginning of the 20th that Turkic and especially Finno-Ugric scholarship, developed by many scholars in a number of countries, had progressed sufficiently for Trubetskoi and Roman Jakobson to engage in their fascinating theorizing concerning the Eurasian association of languages. Perhaps even more immediately relevant for Eurasianism were studies detailing the rich cultural background of ancient Russia and linking elements of Russian and non-Russian cultures. In field after field, and topic after topic Russian scholars were discovering a new and largely "non-Western" richness in the Russian and "pre-Russian" past, and its connection with other civilizations. Archeology, history of art with its discovery of "the Scythian style," music, literature with its new links between Kievan epos and those of Persia and the Turkic peoples, investigations of folklore, history, and much else, all contributed to a fuller appreciation of Russia as a cultural and historical entity and suggested to some the need for a new scholarly synthesis.[14]

A remarkable example of the new approach can be found in the section of Kliuchevskii's lectures on Russian history where the historian discusses the relationship between the Great Russians and the Finnic tribes. Professor V. O. Kliuchevskii, it hardly needs recalling, taught until his death in 1911 at the

---

[13] Otto Böss, *Die Lehre der Eurasier: Ein Beitrag, zur russischen Ideengeschichte des 20. Jahrhunderts* (Wiesbaden: O. Harrassowitz, 1961), 25–33.

[14] The Eurasians themselves mention many of the relevant works. Long lists of them can be found in Vernadsky's bibliographies. In this connection, special attention should be paid to the development of Oriental studies in Russia. See especially V. Bartol'd, *Istoriia izucheniia Vostoka v Evrope i Rossii*, 2nd ed. (Leningrad: Leningradskii institut zhivykh vostochnykh iazykov, 1925).

University of Moscow, considered the leading Russian university. He was almost certainly the most popular historian of Russia on the eve of the Revolution. Kliuchevskii's analysis of the Finnic contribution to the emergence of the Great Russians occupies 20 pages of the fourth edition of his celebrated *Course of Russian History*.[15]

Finnic tribes had established themselves in the northern part of the great Russian plain before the Slavs. They were responsible for thousands of non-Russian place names in that vast area, for example, the names of the rivers ending on "va" including *"Moskva"* itself, "ua" meaning *water* in Finnic. When the Slavs came into the region, the meeting of the peoples had in general a peaceful character. Russian records and popular traditions preserve no memory of warfare; the Finnic tribes were according to all evidence an exceptionally quiet and peaceful people, while the Russians, mostly peasants, wanted to settle down in the enormous and largely virgin territory rather than engage in conquest. As a result, the two peoples found themselves scattered and intermingled in the vast area, a fact confirmed by the intermingling of Finnic and Russian geographic names. When the Great Russian type and society, differentiated from the Ukrainian and the White Russian, finally emerged in central and northern European Russia, they bore unmistakable evidences of a Finnic impact and indeed had incorporated Finnic elements within themselves. The very physical type of the Great Russian indicated Finnic influences: more pronounced facial bones and a darker pigmentation of skin and hair than in the case of other Slavs, as well as a different nose. Similarly, the Great Russian language was probably affected by its non-Russian and non-Slavic neighbors. "The ancient phonetics of Kievan Russia changed especially noticeably in the northeastern direction, that is, in the direction of Russian colonization which created the Great Russian people through an amalgamation of Russian population and Finnic. This leads to the supposition of a relation between the two processes."[16] Even more obviously, "popular beliefs and customs of the Great Russians preserve to our days clear indications of Finnic influences."[17] In particular, the religious beliefs of the two peoples became extremely closely intertwined as well as thoroughly confused, with the primitive deities of the poorly developed Finnic paganism generally becoming demons for the advancing Orthodox in the area. In a sense then, local population managed to adhere to some extent to both faiths. Finally, Finnic tribes contributed to the rural nature of the emerging Great Russian society, for they themselves were a rural, as well as a socially undifferentiated people.

---

[15] V. Kliuchevskii, *Kurs russkoi istorii,* 4th ed. (Moscow: Tip. Mosk. Gor. Arnol'do-Tret'iakovskago, 1911), pt. 1, 361–82.

[16] Ibid., 371.

[17] Ibid.

Indeed Trubetskoi's brilliant essay on "The Upper and the Lower Layers of Russian Culture (the Ethnic Base of Russian Culture)" could almost be considered an identical twin to Kliuchevskii's masterful lecture on the Great Russians and the Finnic tribes. There was only one crucial difference. Neither Kliuchevskii nor any of his predecessors in Russian intellectual history considered himself or herself Eurasian or was so considered by others. That creative spark, that *idée maitresse* of the new ideology had to come from elsewhere.

And it came, apparently, with the remarkable cultural renaissance, the so-called Silver Age, which dawned upon Russia at the very end of the 19th century and the first decades of the 20th. The new self-definition or self-definitions were expressed at about the same time by several writers or groups of writers, especially poets. For example, Velimir Khlebnikov, a leading futurist poet, declared in 1912: "I know about the mind of a continent, not at all similar to the mind of islanders. A son of proud Asia does not come to terms with the peninsular intellect of the Europeans."[18] He also castigated, for instance, Kant who "intending to determine the boundaries of human reason determined the boundaries of German reason. The absent-mindedness of a scholar..."[19] Professor Roman Jakobson, a most important witness and indeed participant, attached considerable significance to the futurist roots of the Eurasian revolt.[20] It is worth noting that at least one of the original four Eurasians, Suvchinskii, pointed to futurism as the cultural form of the coming organic and creative age.

Fascination with Asia and identification with Asiatic or quasi-Asiatic peoples developed especially among the so-called symbolists. In 1910–11, Andrei Belyi, one of the most important and prominent writers of the period, published *St. Petersburg*, a stunning tale of the capital city in 1905, of a gathering revolution, violence, and nightmare. "Asiatic" elements abounded in Belyi's novel, especially in its striking nightmare sequences. A mysterious Persian, a figure of delirium, materialized, or seemed to materialize at one point, a Mongol face glared from a wall, the horsemen of Jenghiz Khan again rode in the steppe. *St. Petersburg* may well be interpreted as a depiction of a fatal conflict between the city of Peter, a symbol of order, organization, rationality, and Westernization in Russia, and the seething, revolutionary, "Asiatic" masses.[21] "Asia," then, was inside Russia, not merely outside. But Belyi's identification with "Asia" went beyond this rather abstract general scheme, for the two

---

[18] Velimir Khlebnikov, *Sobranie proizvedenii* (Leningrad: Izd-vo pisatelei v Leningrade, 1933), 5: 179.

[19] Ibid., 183.

[20] Conversations with Professor R. O. Jakobson in the winter of 1961–62.

[21] Belyi's earlier novel, *The Silver Dove* (1908–09), contained in a weaker form some proto-Eurasian elements. The two novels were meant to constitute the first two parts of a trilogy, *East and West*, the third part of which was never written.

main protagonists of the tale, the Ableukhovs, father and son, the important bureaucrat and the undecided revolutionary, were explicitly of Mongol origin, and it was his own ancestors that came to the younger Ableukhov in his frenzied visions.

Even more memorable than Belyi's was a similar vision of the supreme poet of the age, Aleksandr Blok, which found its best expression in the poem entitled "The Scythians" and written on the 30th of January 1918:

> You are millions. We are hordes and hordes and hordes.
>   Just try, fight us!
> Yes, we are Scythians! Yes, we are Asiatics,
>   With slanting and greedy eyes!

And several stanzas later, always addressing the West:

> Russia is a Sphinx. Rejoicing and grieving,
> And bathed in black blood,
>   It looks, looks, looks at you
> With both hatred and love![22]

Blok's vision, like Belyi's, combined hatred and love, massacre and the coming of a new world, all-pervasive terror and a kind of exultation. As the epigraph for his poem Blok selected the words of Vladimir Solov'ev, the man who exercised in so many ways a dominant influence on Blok's age: "Panmongolism! Although the name is savage, still it caresses my ear." Behind Belyi and Blok a reader might see Vladimir Solovev's preoccupation with "the yellow peril," terror turned into identification and exultation. Again, as in the case of Belyi, who dealt quite explicitly with the revolutionary year of 1905, Blok wrote his poem in the wake of the October Revolution of 1917 and at the same time that he was writing his celebrated revolutionary poem "The Twelve." In terms of Eurasian ideology, Blok's formulation was more precise than Belyi's, for he presented his Russians-Scythians not simply as Asiatics, but rather as an independent third element between Europe and Asia, which had for centuries protected the West, had "held the shield between two hostile races, the Mongols and Europe!"[23]

Blok and Belyi were not alone. In 1916–18, there developed a movement known as "the Scythians," linked to the symbolist group and led by the critic R. Ivanov-Razumnik, which combined the new self-identification in opposition to Europe with a revolutionary and apocalyptic tone and messianic

---

[22] Aleksandr Blok, *O rodine* (Moscow: Gos. izd-vo khudozhestvennoi literatury, 1945), 88–91. For the circumstances of the writing of the poem, see K. Mochulskii, *Aleksandr Blok* (Paris: YMCA Press, 1948), 411–13.

[23] Blok, *O rodine*, 88.

hopes.[24] The stage was set for the flowering of a full-fledged and original new ideology. Trubetskoi could well write on the 28th of July 1921, the year of the formal inauguration of Eurasianism: "The new direction is being carried in the air," and cite in the first instance Blok and two other poets as evidence for his assertion.[25]

My book on Romanticism was, again, devoted to origins: *The Emergence of Romanticism* (Oxford University Press, 1992). The original spark, the Romantic creative vision apparently appeared first in poetry, in England and in Germany at the end of the 18th and the beginning of the 19th century. A deeply personal experience, it acquired, nevertheless, a set three-fold structure with the third stage consisting in a return to the first. Often the pattern has been described as union, separation, and reunion. Yet the third stage, reunion, usually did not mean the exact replay of the initial union, but, rather, a union made somehow richer through the experience and the overcoming of the period or stage of separation. In philosophical and historical terms the Romanticists frequently defined the third stage as a conscious union in contrast to the original unconscious one, as a fully understood and articulated and therefore stronger condition. Yet typically they themselves remained only at the entrance to the third stage, striving desperately from their hell to reach its almost tangible blessedness—sometimes, as in the case of Novalis, to the brink of madness.

However, with the help of German idealistic philosophy and certain other doctrines the obsessive Romantic formula could be moved from the individual to groups, classes, societies, and ages, as demonstrated, for example, by Ivan Aksakov, a spokesman for the premier Russian Romantic ideology, that of Slavophilism:

St. Petersburg as the embodiment of a negative moment of history cannot create anything positive in the Russian sense. According to a well-known dialectical law it is possible to return to the positive only

---

[24] *Skify*, 2 vols. (Petrograd: Knigoizd-vo "Skify," 1917–18).

[25] N. S. Trubetskoi's letter to R. O. Jakobson. I am very grateful to Professor Jakobson for letting me see and use Trubetskoi's then unpublished correspondence. "Eurasian" notes can be found also in the writings of some other authors of approximately the same period, such as V. Briusov, M. Tsvetaeva, B. Pilniak, and M. G. Rozanov. See Gleb Struve, *Russkaia literatura v izgnanii: Opyt istoricheskogo obzora zarubezhnoi literatury* (New York: Izd-vo im. Chekhova, 1956), 40–49. If Professor R. E. Steussy is to be believed, Pasternak's *Doktor Zhivago* constitutes the last major Eurasian contribution to Russian literature, with the mysterious Evgraf as the prime representative of Eurasia in contrast to the main protagonist's Westernism. If so, the novel certainly continues the Eurasian literary "tradition" of love and hatred, violence and terror, revolution and epochal changes. Steussy, "The Myth Behind *Doktor Zhivago*," *The Russian Review* 18 (July 1959): 184–98. Pasternak, although then quite young, did belong to the cultural renaissance, to the age of Belyi, Blok, etc.

through a negation of the negation itself, in other words through a negation of the St. Petersburg period, through a negation of St. Petersburg as a political principle which guided Russian life for almost two centuries. The result will be a Russian nation freed from exclusiveness, and called into the arena of world history. Is that clear?[26]

Ivan Aksakov himself turned to Panslavism apparently looking forward to the epochal confrontation of the Slav and the German, which would bring to the surface the deep meaning of Slavdom and usher in the third dialectical stage. Nor is there any shortage of the contributions of Romanticism to nationalisms and pan-movements as well as to other ideologies in numerous countries. But I have already exceeded my allotted space and time.

It may be quixotic to look for the first inspiration and try to trace it and its results in later years. Yet it is when dealing with original ideas or perceptions and genuine poetry that this approach appears at times to impose itself. It was Pasternak who wrote: "The clearest, the most memorable and the most important point in art is its emergence, and the greatest works of art of the world are, in fact, while narrating about most diverse things, telling of their own birth."[27] Still, if one disagrees with Pasternak, and even with the entire search for origins, there remain many fascinating problems in Russian intellectual history.

---

[26] Ivan Aksakov, *Sochineniia*, 7 vols. (Moscow, 1886–87), 5: 632.
[27] Boris Pasternak, *Proza, 1915–1958* (Ann Arbor: University of Michigan Press, 1961), 241.

Culture, Law, Women, and War

Near-Death Experiences

Eve Levin

Pre-modern Russian miracle cycles contain many accounts of what might be termed "near-death experiences." That is, they tell of situations where patients were "at the hour of death" (*pri smertnom chasu*), or "lay close to death" (*lezha u smerti*), or appeared "as though dying" (*iaki umershu*), or for whom "the soul was already not in [them]" (*iako uzhe i dukhu ego ne byti v nem*), or "despaired of [their] life" (*zhivota svoego otchaiavshusia*).[1] Then the patients received the miraculous intervention of a holy figure, who interacted with them, healed them, and returned them to life. Later they told of their experiences at the shrines of the saints, creating a historical record.[2]

However, "near-death experience" is a modern concept. It came into existence in the mid-1970s as a descriptor of visions of what purported to be continuing existence, glimpsed by individuals on the brink of death, usually from illness or accident. A substantial popular literature emerged, disseminating accounts of "true" experiences, and asserting a variety of explanations for them.[3] In their wake, scholars, too, have studied the phenomenon. For some persons who claimed near-death experiences (or NDE's, as cognoscenti call them) and for many of the promoters of their accounts, the NDE constitutes compelling testimony, backed by scientific evidence, of an afterlife. They as-

---

[1] These exact phrases are found in the miracle cycles of St. Sergei Radonezhskii (B. M. Kloss, *Zhitie Sergeia Radonezhskogo*, vol. 1 of *Izbrannye trudy* [Moscow: Iazyki russkoi kul'tury, 1998], 531); of Sergei Penezhskii (Russian State Archive of Ancient Acts [hereafter, RGADA], Rukopisnyi fond TsGALI, f. 187, op. 1, no. 57, fol. 25; of Aleksandr Svirskii (Hilandar Research Library [hereafter, HRL], Saratov State University Collection [SGU], no. 357, fol. 135; idem, fol. 89v); of Antonii Siiskii (RGADA f. 187, op. 1, no. 12, fol. 208).

[2] On the validity of miracle tales as historical sources, see Isolde Thyret, "Muscovite Miracle Stories as Sources for Gender-Specific Religious Experience," in *Religion and Culture in Early Modern Russia and Ukraine*, ed. Samuel H. Baron and Nancy Shields Kollmann (DeKalb: Northern Illinois University Press, 1997), 115–31.

[3] The existence of the volume *The Complete Idiot's Guide to Near-Death Experiences* by P. M. H. Atwater and David H. Morgan (Indianapolis: Alpha Books, 2000) demonstrates how thoroughly the near-death phenomenon has penetrated American culture. Two associations focusing on near-death experiences maintain websites; see http://www.nderf.org (Near Death Experience Research Foundation) and http:/iands.org (International Association for Near-Death Studies) (accessed 24 October 2005).

Rude & Barbarous Kingdom Revisited: Essays in Russian History and Culture in Honor of Robert O. Crummey. Chester S. L. Dunning, Russell E. Martin, and Daniel Rowland, eds. Bloomington, IN: Slavica Publishers, 2008, 411–25.

sert that NDE's share the same common characteristics, regardless of the culture of the experiencer, proving (they say) that the visions reflect an eternal reality. Skeptics, on the other hand, point to the cultural differences reflected in the accounts. They attribute similarities to cultural contamination in the modern world, or to physiological changes that occur in the brain when death is imminent.[4] A small number of religious skeptics attribute near-death experiences to Satan, who, they say, is trying to delude human beings concerning the path to salvation.[5]

Specialists in the study of near-death experiences have asssembled lists of the supposed "universal" features that all NDE'ers have. In one version, they are

1. Sense of separation from the body, often becoming a "spectator" to the death scene;

2. Journey through a tunnel or darkness or void;

3. Encounter with deceased relatives or friends, or with a "being of light";

4. Replay of life experiences;

5. Immersion in light and love, accompanied by a sense of understanding eternal truth;

6. Return to life in order to complete unfinished business;

7. Transformation of the outlook on life, with greater compassion and loss of fear of death.[6]

Of course, the lists of "universal" features vary.[7] A cross-cultural comparison of contemporary accounts indicates that no feature is found in every society.[8]

---

[4] For scholarly works on near death experiences, see Carol Zaleski, *Otherworld Journeys: Accounts of Near-Death Experiences in Medieval and Modern Times* (New York: Oxford University Press, 1987); idem, *The Life of the World to Come: Near-Death Experiences and Christian Hope* (New York: Oxford University Press, 1996); Allan Kellehear, *Experiences Near Death: Beyond Medicine and Religion* (New York: Oxford University Press, 1996); Mark Fox, *Religion, Spirituality and the Near-Death Experience* (London: Routledge, 2003).

[5] For examples, see David Ritchie, "The 'Near-Death Experience,'" http://www.orthodoxinfo.com/death/nde.aspx; "Near-Death Experience: Angel of Light?" http://www.watchman.org/na/anglight.htm (both accessed 25 October 2005). For a brief summary of this view, see Fox, *Religion, Spirituality and the Near-Death Experience*, 92–96; and Faith Wigzell, "Reading the Map of Heaven and Hell in Russian Popular Orthodoxy: Examining the Usefulness of the Concepts of *Dvoeverie* and Binary Oppositions," forthcoming. I am grateful to Dr. Wigzell for providing me with a copy of her paper in advance of publication.

[6] This summary is based on Zaleski, *Life of the World to Come*, 19; see also 31–32.

[7] See also the 15-point version in Fox, *Religion, Spirituality and the Near-Death Experience*, 16, and Zaleski, *Otherworld Journeys*, 102; the 6-point version in Kellehear, *Expe-*

As Carol Zaleski notes, "Between those [researchers] whose attention is captured by the discrepancies among different visions and those who are dazzled by their similarities, there is a temperamental distance, unlikely to be bridged by logical arbitration."[9]

Contemporary Russian accounts of near-death experiences, called *obmiranie*, share quite a few of the characteristics of the composite NDE. According to Faith Wigzell, who has pioneered research on *obmiranie* accounts, they often include visionaries leaving their bodies, going through a dark tunnel, being accompanied by a presence (a relative or an angel) shrouded in light, meeting deceased relatives, and feeling a sense of joy, just as in the Western norm. In contemporary Russian accounts, very often visionaries see the torments of Hell, and quite often the rewards of Heaven as well. Wigzell notes that Russian *obmiranie* accounts carry a strong moral message, in which the recipients of the vision—almost always women—warn others against the behaviors that they find most reprehensible. These behaviors include abortion, suicide, sorcery, drunkenness, and secular frivolity.[10] As we will see, premodern Russian accounts of near-death experiences diverge significantly from the contemporary models, both Russian and Western.[11]

While "near-death experience" may be a term of recent provenance, accounts of wondrous, pre-death tours of the afterworld date back to antiquity. Not all excursions to the afterworld occurred when the "traveler" was on the brink of death.[12] Quite a few, including the most famous Russian story in this genre, the "Journey of the Mother of God amongst the Torments," have no human witness to the trip.[13] However, when dying persons are the witnesses, they see an afterworld similar to that described in other texts of that culture.

This pattern suggests that visionaries who have near-death experiences enunciate them within the cultural tropes available to them. Of course, there can be no direct corroboration of the content of the vision. Recitation of any dream or vision, whether it occurs before death or in ordinary sleep, necessarily reflects the visionary's reconstruction rather than the dream itself.

riences Near Death, 3; and the 4-point version posted on the website of the International Association for Near-Death Studies (http://iands.org/nde_index.php).

[8] Kellehear, *Experiences Near Death*, 8–9, 32–34.

[9] Zaleski, *Otherworld Journeys*, 180.

[10] Faith Wigzell, "The Ethical Values of *Narodnoe Pravoslavie*: Traditional Near-Death Experiences and Fedotov," *Folklorica: Journal of the Slavic and East European Folklore Association* 8: 1 (Spring 2003): 54–70; and Wigzell, "Reading the Map of Heaven."

[11] I have examined two dozen accounts, most dating to the 17th century. All are recorded in cycles of miracles attached to saints' vitae.

[12] Zaleski, *Otherworld Journeys*, 26–42.

[13] "Khozhdenie bogoroditsy po mukam," in *Khrestomatiia po drevnei russkoi literature XI–XVII vekov*, ed. N. K. Gudzii (Moscow: Gos. uchebno-pedagogicheskoe izdatel'stvo, 1962), 92–98.

Dreamers create coherent tales out of imperfectly-remembered fragments, and knowledge acquired later can easily reshape their memory of the vision.[14] Furthermore, the versions of the accounts of near-death visions that reach the public record are many steps removed from the visionaries' original, private, experience. In the interim, numerous parties had a chance to reshape the visionary's account, to bring it into conformity with the norms that mark an "authentic" visionary experience. As Carol Zaleski noted concerning medieval Western European accounts of near-death experiences:

> [W]e cannot simply peel away the literary wrapper and put our hands on an unembellished event. Even when a vision actually did occur, it is likely to have been reworked many times before being recorded. The vision is a collaborative effort, produced by the interaction of the visionary with neighbors, counselors, the narrator, and other interested parties. One cannot point to the moment when the vision changed from a matter of personal confession into a public project; rather, it is built up in layers placed over one another like a series of transparencies. Though a bottom layer of actual experience may be present in some (but certainly not in all) vision stories, its contours are nearly indistinguishable from those of the superimposed images through which we discern it.[15]

The same holds true of premodern Russian accounts of near-death experiences. In the tale of the near-death experience of Tsar Feodor Ivanovich, we can see the steps in the construction and dissemination of a tale of the miraculous. According to the account, when Tsar Feodor was dying, he saw a "shining" figure, and told his attendants to make a space for the patriarch. When they told him that the patriarch had not yet arrived, Feodor told his attendants, "Do you see? A shining man in hierarch's garments is standing by my bed." Only Feodor saw the figure, but his attendants decided that "it was indeed an angel of God who came to him." When the real patriarch, Iov, arrived to hear the dying tsar's last confession, the attendants told him about the tsar's astral visitor. Iov implored Feodor, "do not hide this vision from me, your [spiritual] father, so that to my humble self all of God's love of humankind and of your imperial (tsarskoe) beneficence will be revealed." Feodor confirmed his vision, adding that the shining figure "told me to come with him." The patriarch interpreted the vision as a contemporary manifestation of God's favor to "ancient holy tsars" who were chosen to receive visions

---

[14] Iain R. Edgar, *Dreamwork, Anthropology and the Caring Professions* (Aldershot, UK: Avebury, 1995), 33–35, 111. Fox argues that NDE's are unlike dreams because 1) experiencers note a difference; and 2) they recount witnessing efforts to resuscitate them (*Religion, Spirituality and the Near-Death Experience*, 3).

[15] Zaleski, *Otherworld Journeys*, 86.

and angelic visitations." Although the patriarch then prayed fervently for the tsar's physical recovery, Feodor passed away soon after. Upon Feodor's death, the heavenly visitation, combined with the peaceful, shining appearance of his body, demonstrated his sanctity.[16]

It is unclear what, exactly, Feodor originally saw, but he himself took it to be the patriarch, an earthly rather than an astral figure. Through exchanges between Feodor and his attendants, the astral nature of the figure became clear. The attendants then briefed the real patriarch when he arrived, and the patriarch not only accepted Feodor's vision as real, but also defined it as angelic, a sign that the tsar shared God's favor with the most venerable monarchs of ancient days. Then the author of the account—who might well have been Patriarch Iov himself—used the vision to hint broadly at Feodor's own status as a saint. Finally, the entire text of Feodor's biography-as-hagiography entered the larger Russian chronicle tradition.[17]

Witnesses and authors, then, could decisively shape the retelling of the dying person's experience. A striking example of this phenomenon is found in the personal letters of Tsar Aleksei. Writing in 1652 to Metropolitan Nikon of Novgorod (whom he later appointed to the patriarchal throne), Aleksei described his experience at the bedside of the dying patriarch Iosif. He averred to Nikon that he "knew that he [Iosif] saw a vision." He continued, "I don't remember where I read [that] before the separation of the soul from the body, a person sees all his good and evil deeds." But when Aleksei asked the dying man's confessor whether Iosif had seen "any sort of vision," the confessor denied it. Aleksei retorted, "Watch and see what will happen. You yourself don't know what you are saying." The confessor then duly reported that the patriarch must be seeing something. They watched the dying Iosif then, and according to Aleksei, Iosif looked around at the ceiling and into a corner, shouted out, and flailed his arms, as if hitting someone.[18] However, Aleksei did not claim to know the content of Iosif's para-mortem experience, and Iosif himself did not regain consciousness and explain.

In contrast to Feodor's and Iosif's experiences, which were decisively shaped by witnesses and the author of the account, certain narratives show little reediting. The miracle tales recorded in the cycles of obscure provincial saints, featuring individuals of little social import, remain close to the recip-

---

[16] *Polnoe sobranie russkikh letopisei* (St. Petersburg: Tip. M. A. Aleksandrova, 1910), 14: 16–18.

[17] My thanks to Daniel Rowland for pointing out Iov's close connection to the text, which he discusses in his Ph.D. dissertation, "Muscovite Political Attitudes as Reflected in Early Seventeenth-Century Tales about the Time of Troubles," (Yale University, 1976), 16–24.

[18] "Povest' o prestavlenii patriarkha Iosifa," in *Moskoviia i Evropa*, ed. A. Liberman and S. Shokarev (Moscow: Fond Sergeia Dubova, 2000), 501.

ient's original testimony.[19] In a few cases, the written account preserved the visionary's first-person voice, suggesting minimum reediting took place.

One such account is preserved in the cycle of St. Petr, the Newly-Appeared Miracle Worker, whose relics lay in the Church of St. Nicholas in Cherevkovskaia *volost'*. In 1677, a woman named Agripina Grigorieva doch' told the priest at the shrine:

> Suffering entered my entire body, and for fifty weeks I could not control it or hold anything because of that disease… Then I had a vision in the night, and a handsome person in bright clothing came and I could not look at him. He said to me, "Woman, do not fear but only believe. Why do you not call upon the help of the newly-appeared miracle-worker Petr who is in Cherevkovskaia *volost'* in the chapel near the church of St. Nicholas the Miracle-Worker?" Then I awoke from that sleep, and I was healthy in all my being. My neighbors came, and they rejoiced at my health. And they said to me, "Agripina, a man came and told us to collect snow from three hills and warm it, and if you wash your hand, you will be completely healthy." And I did this. After I washed, then my body began to ache. That evil suffering was worse than before, and I was at the end of my life. But then I remembered my earlier vision that I had seen in the vision in the night. Then I began to pray to the newly-appeared miracle-worker Petr for forgiveness of my transgression, that I did not believe my vision and healing. Then I promised him, the miracle-worker, to recite the requiem, and to fulfill everything of my promise. And with my fulfillment at that time I became completely healthy.[20]

Little in Agripina's account matches the model of modern near-death experiences. She reported no separation from her body, no journey through a tunnel, no replay of her life, and no indescribable joy. She did not return to life because of unfinished business, and she did not find the experience to be transformative. In fact, her first action after the remarkable healing vision was to try the folk cure her neighbors had learned about from an itinerant healer—an action that in her society was marked as impious, not spiritual. The only feature Agripina's experience shared with the modern master list was a vision of a being shrouded in light.

Another woman, Anna Ioannova doch', reported a different sort of near-death encounter with St. Petr. As she lay "near death," she heard her neigh-

[19] Thyret, "Muscovite Miracle Stories," 116–20.

[20] Russian State Historical Archive, St. Petersburg [hereafter, RGIA], f. 796, op. 25, no. 723, fols. 356–57. This manuscript is a huge compendium of materials gathered in an investigation into cults in the 1740s. It includes many verbatim copies of earlier texts, such as this one.

bors talking about a possible pilgrimage, and in her vision, she visited the shrine. Although Anna saw herself from outside her body, her journey did not take place through darkness, or to the otherworld of Heaven (or Hell, for that matter). She did not meet the saint, or anyone at all. She did not see the deeds of her life replayed, she felt no immersion in love. She was not conscious of any need to return to this life; she simply woke up. And her life continued unchanged, except for her return to health.[21] In short, she experienced only one of the "universal" traits of the near-death experience.

Kiprian Mikheev syn Petanov had a near-death experience involving St. Nikodim Kozheozerskii, and in 1677, he provided this account to the Kozheozerskii abbot. After receiving chrysmation, Kiprian prayed to St. Nikodim. Then

> it was as though darkness came upon my eyes and suddenly two monks came into my house: one the reverend Nikodim, and the other shorter in height than the reverend. He had a white beard that was long down to his ribs. The monk asked the reverend, "Is this the one for whom your prayers were summoned?" The reverend Nikodim answered the monk, "This is the one." Then they became invisible. I asked my mother about the arrival of the monks. She said to me, "No, child, I did not see the monks you are asking about." From the time of the apparition of the reverend I soon became well, as you see me.[22]

Kiprian experienced darkness, and he met a spiritual figure, although Nikodim was not arrayed in light. On the contrary, Nikodim and his monastic companion looked so ordinary that Kiprian took them to be solid human beings. He made no mention of visiting heaven, or feeling great joy or peace, or choosing to return to earthly life; nor did his life change drastically, except for regaining his health.

The third-person accounts of near-death experiences show no more consistency with the "universal" characteristics. The only features that appear frequently are out-of-body experiences and visions of saintly figures, often (but not always) illuminated. Premodern Russians on the verge of death did not usually go through tunnels, see their lives flash before their eyes, meet deceased relatives, or take a tour of Hell, or Heaven.

Abbot Pitirim of the Siiskii monastery had an out-of-body experience. Lying on his deathbed, able to breathe only with great effort and pain, he "saw himself going to the church, as though to do prayers in his mind. And then suddenly he saw on the right side of the Church of the Life-Giving Trinity, from the tomb of the reverend Antonii, an unknown monk, going straight

---

[21] RGIA f. 796, op. 25, no. 723, fols. 355v–356.

[22] Russian National Library [hereafter, RNB], Solovetskoe sobranie, no. 182/182, fols. 76v–77.

to the cell where the abbot lay suffering in his illness."[23] Similarly, the ailing deacon Ioann Kitrikhnov saw himself going to the shrine of St. Feodosii Totemskii. As he stood there, the doors of the church opened, and the deacon found himself in the church, where one monk knelt in prayer in front of the icon of God Almighty while another lit a candle. The deacon asked the second monk who he was and who the kneeling monk was. The monk with the candle gave his name as Aleksandr, and identified the kneeling monk as his superior, Feodosii. When Feodosii arose, the deacon begged him for healing. Feodosii told him to visit the shrine, blessed him, and took his hand.[24]

Saints appear frequently in visions, as one might expect in a genre dedicated to documenting their post-mortem existence. The carpenter Iakov, suffering from an illness that caused severe pain in his throat, saw a vision of "a woman formed in light, who had a sea reed in her hand." She touched his throat with it, and directed him to the icon of the Mother of God at Chernaia Gora. When he awoke, his throat was healed.[25] Often, dying patients invoked the saints in prayer before seeing them in visions. Abbot Pitirim of the Siiskii monastery naturally called upon the institution's founder. When St. Antonii appeared, he was "adorned with angel-like gray hair," and Pitirim recognized him as a "saint of God" even before he identified himself. In order to ascertain that it was indeed the monastery's founder who visited him in his vision, when Abbot Pitirim awoke, "he summoned one of the monastic priests, namely Tit, and asked [him] … about our reverend father Antonii, what his height was, and what age, and what his appearance was like." From this description Pitirim was able to affirm that the figure who appeared in his deathbed vision was the same.[26] Or, to put it another way, Pitirim's memory of his dream merged with the priest Tit's description of St. Antonii as he remembered him, and the two became verification of authenticity for each other. When a layman named Feodor later had a deathbed vision of St. Antonii, his description, too, conformed to the model Pitirim and Tit had established.[27]

In a few cases, it was the prayers of relatives that brought the saint into the dying patient's vision. Mariia was dying in childbirth when her husband prayed for the intercession of St. Kirill Novoezerskii. Following her husband's prayers, Mariia received a vision in the form of "a certain monk, tall and handsome." The figure identified himself as St. Kirill, made the sign of the cross over her belly, and told her that she would give birth to a boy and that

---

[23] RGADA f. 187, op. 1, no. 12, fols. 208–208v; miracle tale dated after 1566.

[24] RGIA f. 796, op. 25, no. 723, fols. 295v–296v, dated 1697.

[25] RGADA, Rukopisnyi otdel MGAMID, f. 181, no. 905, fols. 20–20v, dated after 1584 and before 1608).

[26] RGADA f. 187, op. 1, no. 12, fols. 208–211v.

[27] RGADA f. 187, op. 1, no. 12, fol. 231v.

she would be healthy again.[28] The father of a young married girl prayed for St. Zosima's intercession when he found his daughter dying of self-inflicted knife wounds. The girl attempted suicide because she was unable to tolerate further abuse by her husband. The saint appeared to the girl and gave her a salve to heal the cuts, explaining that he could not disregard her parents' tears.[29]

A woman named Mariia from Moscow had a vision of saints that did not go exactly according to the established script. As her relatives surrounded her deathbed, Mariia invoked the Moscow miracle-working hierarchs Petr, Aleksei, Iona, and Filipp to heal her. But when they appeared to her in a vision, they were accompanied by a fifth saint, Sergei Radonezhskii. They discussed among themselves, "Who summoned her to die now? No; so she will be healthy." Then "one of them," as she recalled, "approached me, put his hand on my head and healed me; and which one of them healed me I could not figure out." After her recovery, Mariia carefully paid her respects to all five saints.[30]

The saints did not always identify themselves by name in these accounts. Although later readers are expected to recognize the saint upon first appearance in the tale, the accounts hint that the patients connected the apparition with a specific saint more slowly. For example, the demon-possessed laborer Filipp had run away from the Gur'ev monastery and was lying "as though dead of cold and hunger" when he had a vision. A monk "with a dry face, a long beard, and short hair, of middling height" lifted him up and showed him the path back to the monastery. Apparently it was only Filipp's parish priest who recognized that his spiritual son had encountered St. Gurii; he was the one who reported the miracle at the monastery.[31]

Similarly, the ailing peasant Moisei saw "a monk, like a wondrously-holy vision" (*starets sviatolepen videniem*), who told him to get out of bed and go home. When he asked the apparition, "Who are you, man of God?" the only reply he got was, "Do you not see that I am a monk?" It was only after Moisei awoke that he identified the figure in his vision as St. Feodosii Totemskii.[32] But another beneficiary of St. Feodosii's intercession, the scribe Grigorii Bolonin, recognized him at once. In Grigorii's vision, the saint stretched out his hand three times and sprinkled him with something "like sand."[33] Ivan, a lay servant of the Obnorskii monastery, had a sequence of three near-death vi-

---

[28] RNB, Kirillo-Belozerskoe sobranie, no. 38/1277, fols. 106–108v, dated after 1532 and before 1582.

[29] RGADA f. 181, no. 692, fols. 331v–334v.

[30] Kloss, *Zhitie Sergeia Radonezhskogo*, 531–32.

[31] RGIA f. 796, op. 25, no. 723, fols. 571v–572, dated 1706.

[32] RGADA, Biblioteka Sinodal'noi tipografii, f. 381, no. 260, fol. 47v, dated after 1655 and before 1689.

[33] RGADA f. 381, no. 260, fols. 47v–48, dated after 1655 and before 1689.

sions of St. Pavel, but recognized him only the third time. In an attack on the monastery, Tatar raiders had slashed Ivan's throat and left him for dead in the snow. Upon recovering consciousness, Ivan had dragged himself to a building, where "a person" (*chelovek*) called to him from the window advising him to use paper to bind his throat and then go home. On the way, Ivan despaired of surviving his wounds and the cold, when a "wondrously-holy monk" reassured him, "God has the power to resurrect the the dead and to effect existence from non-existence." Once Ivan arrived at his home, the monk came through the window to him in his sickbed. On this occasion, the monk wielded a knife, with which, as he explained, he cut the illness out of Ivan. Ivan saw his visitor leave through the window, and ascend through the air to the monastery. Only then did he recognize him as St. Pavel.[34]

In premodern Russian accounts, the saint was not always arrayed in light. St. Nikodim usually appeared in ordinary guise, as he did to Kiprian Petanov. In one account, he directed the woman patient to pray to God and the Mother of God; in another, he told the young man to seek healing from St. Nikodim. In a fourth account, the saint did not appear at all.[35] Evdokeia Gerasimova doch' saw an "unknown priest in a black shirt, a person of middling height, a round face and gray beard and hair." He gave her communion bread, and directed her to the tomb of St. Sergei Penezhskii.[36] Readers of the account understand, of course, that Evdokeia saw St. Sergei himself.

Encounters with dead relatives are strikingly absent from premodern Russian near-death experiences. Only Mariia, who experienced a vision of St. Aleksandr Svirskii, also saw a deceased relative. In her vision, the saint appeared accompanied by two monks, one of whom was her father, and the other a monk—apparently of her acquaintance—named "Pavel." But Mariia did not interact at all with her father in the vision, but only with St. Aleksandr. Aleksandr told Mariia that he had come to heal her at her father's behest, in gratitude for the generous alms he had donated to the monastery.[37] Thus, Mariia's account lacks the emotionally-affective reunion with family members that characterizes modern NDE's, both Western and Russian. Wigzell proposed that the emphasis on encounters with dead relatives in modern Russian *obmiranie* accounts reflects both the importance of commemoration of the dead in Russian Orthodoxy and a substratum of Slavic pagan ancestor

---

[34] A. S. Gerd, *Zhitiia Pavla Obnorskogo i Sergiia Nuromskogo: Teksty i slovoukazatel'* (St. Petersburg: Izd. S.-Peterburgskogo universiteta, 2005), 130–34, dated before 1536.

[35] RNB, Solovetskoe sobranie, no. 182/182, fols. 67v–68v, 76v–77, 78v–79v, 82–82v; first miracle after 1625 and before 1656; second dated 1677; third dated after 1688 and before 1716.

[36] RGADA f. 187, op. 57, fols. 19–20v, dated after 1585 and before 1652.

[37] HRL, SGU, no. 357, fols. 136v–137.

worship.[38] Yet the rarity of this element in premodern Russian NDE's complicates Wigzell's hypothesis.

Only a few of the persons who had near-death experiences in premodern Russia reported a specific decision to return to this world in order to complete unfinished business. Abbot Pitirim, for example, was taken ill while in the midst of renovating the monastery's church. When the apparition of the monastery's founder, St. Antonii Siiskii, asked him, "Do you wish to be healthy, so that you can complete this task, for which you have laid a good basis?" Pitirim responded, "Yes, I want to, Father, but I cannot eat because of this very serious illness, and so I can't involve myself in even the smallest matter." St. Antonii assured him that the Trinity would heal him, "only do not weaken in this task. I will be your helper in the accomplishment of this task."[39] Mariia, the daughter-in-law in an elite Novgorodian family, begged St. Aleksandr Svirskii to let her return to this world, promising large donations to his monastery in gratitude. She reminded the saint that she had an aged mother and young children who depended upon her.[40] Unlike in modern near-death experiences, neither Pitirim nor Mariia expressed any reluctance to return to this world, perhaps because they did not experience the fabled joys of Heaven.

The son of a priest returned not to complete his own work, but rather to remind his father of his obligations. The boy, lying near death, saw St. Sergei Penezhskii in the square outside the church. St. Sergei told the boy that he was suffering for his father's transgression. The priest had promised to build a chapel over the saint's tomb, but had failed to do so. The boy promised to prompt his father, and upon awaking, he did.[41]

Usually, premodern Russian patients who encountered near-death experiences settled back into their former life. A man named Foma, who encountered St. Antonii Siiskii in a near-death experience, received a stern lecture from the saint concerning his behavior: "The Lord has created this disease for the healing of your spiritual illnesses, so that you can know your transgressions, and race to God in repentence, so that you can receive release from your illness. Now, if you want to be healthy, then repent that you transgressed." But although the experience spurred Foma to go on pilgrimage to the Siiskii monastery, he does not appear to have altered his life course in any obvious way.[42] Another man, suffering from a withered arm, pledged to St. Pavel Obnorskii that he would provide labor to the monastery if he were healed, and then saw a "monk in the depth of old age" who poked him in the

---

[38] Wigzell, "Reading the Map of Heaven."

[39] RGADA f. 187, op. 1, no. 12, fols. 209–10.

[40] HRL, SGU, no. 357, fols. 134v–137.

[41] RGADA f. 187, op. 1, no. 57, fols. 23–29v, dated after 1585 and before 1652.

[42] RGADA f. 187, op. 1, no. 12, fols. 232v–235v.

ribs. Upon regaining partial health, the man journeyed to the monastery, where he received full healing and stayed to fulfill his promise.[43]

Other visionaries did not respond at all, even to obey the saint who appeared to heal them. The most striking case concerned Vasilii, a cattleherd. When Vasilii lay paralyzed and dying, he invoked St. Simon Volomskii. But in his vision, he did not see Heaven or the saint, but rather his own home, and three icons. One icon was of the Savior; the second, the Mother of God of Kazan, and the third of St. Simon. A voice came from the third icon directing Vasilii to the saint's shrine for healing. But like Agripina, who ignored the vision from St. Petr, Vasilii returned to his work as a cattleherd until his illness recurred. He then had a second vision, in which an unknown person came and reminded him to go to the Volomskii monastery. Again Vasilii promised, but yet again, once he regained his health, he forgot his pledge. In a third vision, a terrifying voice reproached him: "O cruelhearted and disobedient Vasilii! How dare you oppose God's power!" The voice ordered him again to St. Simon's shrine, on pain of more suffering and a "bitter death." Awaking from this frightening vision, Vasilii set out on his promised pilgrimage. But on the road he collapsed, and he experienced a fourth vision. St. Simon appeared and warned him not to reconsider his decision. Vasilii continued on the road, but the dark overcame him. As his body weakened and he felt himself entering his final illness, Vasilii cried in prayer to St. Simon. Through the saint's prayers, Vasilii came out of the dark place and found the Volomskii monastery.[44]

In a few cases, however, the experience led patients down a different subsequent path. The carpenter Iakov, whose throat was healed through a vision of the Mother of God, built a church to house the icon he credited with his recovery.[45] Antonina, the wife of a priest, experienced the greatest transformation in her life as a result of her near-death experience. As she lay dying, scarcely able to breathe, saw St. Kirill Novoezerskii dressed as a priest and holding a cross. He directed her to come on pilgrimage to his monastery. But when she told her husband about her experience, he doubted its veracity, and forbade her to go on pilgrimage. So subsequently, she reported another near-death encounter with the saint. This time the saint gave her berries to treat her illness, and instructions for her to convey to her husband, on how to read the prayer service to the Savior and to the Mother of God. He also "taught her from divine scripture":

> Child Antonina, direct your husband not to allow into the holy church fourth marriages or third marriages of either the male or the female sex. And whoever has a conflict with someone and does not

---

[43] *Zhitiia Pavla Obnorskogo*, 110–11, dated before 1536.

[44] RGIA f. 796, op. 25, no. 723, fols. 274v–276, dated 1682.

[45] RGADA f. 181, no. 905, fol. 20v.

apologize must not enter the church... Whoever ignores God's holy days, who does not fast on Wednesdays and Fridays, who does not honor the day of Christ's resurrection, who lives in a bestial manner like a swine wallowing in a slough of sin, if they do not repent and cease from their evil and lawless actions, there will be a great punishment from God upon the people.

Antonina experienced a degree of recovery, albeit not complete, from this second near-death experience. This time, she was able to prevail upon her husband to perform in the manner St. Kirill dictated.[46] By invoking her near-death vision of St. Kirill, Antonina gained power in her marriage; she came to dominate over her husband, telling him how to do his job.

Antonina's near-death experience shared the feature of moral judgment with the modern accounts Wigzell reported. However, Antonina's list of significant offenses, which focused on violations of marital canons, social discord, and non-observance of holidays, bears little resemblance to modern women's complaints.[47]

I have found only one account of a near-death experience from premodern Russia that resembles contemporary models. It is found in the vita of St. Aleksandr Svirskii, and it concerned Daniil, a wealthy merchant. The friends gathered around his sickbed decided that he had already died when Daniil "saw himself in the market, standing in a certain great and light place. He could not think how that had happened, how he had gone there." After this separation from his body, Daniil experienced other features of the model NDE. Two "angels of Christ," "bright youths with gold crowns on their heads ... shining like the sun," took him by the arms and carried him up into the air. But then a "voice from Heaven" directed the angels to take him back. But before they did, Daniil begged them to show him the residence in Heaven that was prepared for his beloved mentor Aleksandr, who was then still alive. The angels agreed, and they showed him "such a bright place, glorious and filled with every joy." The dwellings of the saints were located amongst "many diverse fruited and greatly flowering trees" where the "souls of the righteous" took their rest. Then they took him to a "fragrant place filled with every joy," a "paradise" that "neither human mind nor language can describe, nor the eye see." In that place was a "miraculous city," built of gold and precious stones. There he found Aleksandr, "sitting on a throne in great glory, and a gold crown was on his head. His face was shining like the sun, and his clothing was white like light." Daniil approached him and bowed, asking for his teacher's blessing. Aleksandr responded that God would bless him, but if he wanted to return to Heaven, first he needed to go and accomplish pious deeds. At that, the angels took Daniil to show him the specific deed Alek-

---

[46] RNB, Kirillo–Belozerskoe sobranie, no. 38/1277, fols. 112v–20v, dated 1613.

[47] Wigzell, "Ethical Values," 58–63.

sandr had in mind: the construction of a church. After that, Daniil found himself once again in his bed.[48] Daniil's account is exceptional in that it incorporates nearly all the features common to contemporary Western near-death experiences, except the supposedly most common one, the tunnel. Unlike contemporary Russian NDE's, Daniil's vision includes no explicit moral agenda, although it is clear that righteousness is rewarded. But the purpose of Daniil's account was not to reassure him that he would attain Heaven, but rather to affirm Aleksandr Svirskii's status as a living saint destined for Heaven.

Why is it that premodern Russian near-death experiences so rarely resemble contemporary ones? Of the "universal" traits, only one, the appearance of an astral being, sometimes arrayed in light, occurs with any frequency (although most of the traits are reported on rare occasion, suggesting that they had not been edited out). Despite what Tsar Aleksei "read somewhere," Russian accounts did not feature life reviews. Instead, premodern Russians' NDE's look exactly like other accounts of miraculous interaction with the saints. Many patients suffering from less serious illness or facing difficult circumstances also reported out-of-body experience and holy figures who appeared to them. Many patients with less critical illnesses also made pilgrimage to the shrine of the saint; some, too, used their status as recipients of miracles in order to preach, in the saint's name, their own version of proper morality.[49] The only characteristic that distinguishes "near-death" experiences from the other illness narratives found in miracle cycles is the passing reference to the patient being "near death."

In premodern Russia, then, no distinctive "near-death experience" existed. Premodern Russia did have a well-developed discourse of miraculous, healing encounters with holy figures. Thus, "near-death" patients needed to fit their actual experiences into a recognizable presentational form, namely the miracle tale. But the purpose of miracle tales was not, primarily, to record the subjective sensations of the patient, but rather to testify to the power of the saint. For that goal, it was sufficient for the saint to effect healing when recovery could not be expected. Patients did not need to experience any sort of vision, even of the saint, for their experiences to be recognized as legitimate. If they did report a vision, the expectations of listeners would be that they would report seeing the saint. Consequently, an apparition of the saint became a common feature of premodern Russian illness accounts, including those that occurred peri-mortem.

---

[48] HRL, SGU, no. 357, fols. 89–93v.

[49] For more on this subject, see my unpublished papers, "Imagining Illness and Envisioning Cures: Deliriums in Miracle Accounts," presented at the AAASS National Convention, St. Louis, 18–21 November 1999; and "Miracle Tales as Illness Narratives," invited lecture at Oxford University, 21 October 1999.

The purpose of modern Western NDE's is to provide compelling evidence of the reality of an afterlife. They claim to present scientific proof of continued sentient existence after death, appropriate for a society where science carries the highest evidentiary stature. Furthermore, the modern Western afterlife fits our conception of a heavenly milieu: a place democratically open to all, where everyone is fully accepted and loved, where dear friends and family are reunited. Unlike modern visionaries, premodern Russians did not have any pressing reason, most of the time, to describe the conditions of the afterlife. They lived in a culture where the existence of Heaven and Hell were givens, and they and everyone they knew would end up in one or the other, as God judged. In this context, it would be worthwhile to know what was pleasing and displeasing to God, and so visionaries reported messages from holy figures on how people should behave. But most of all, premodern Russian accounts intended to prove that even the most hopeless situations could be ameliorated through the intercession of God and the saints. Thus Russian accounts of "near-death experiences" are really about this world, and not the next.

Property among Elite Women in 17th-Century Russia

Daniel H. Kaiser

In his landmark study of the 17th-century Russian elite, Robert Crummey observed that the families of the boyar elite were organized around men whose ancestors had founded patrilines and begun the accumulation of properties with which to sustain these lineages. But despite this orientation, he continued, women played an important part in Muscovite society and politics. As mothers, women might aim to emulate the fecundity of the spouses of Aleksei Mikhailovich, regularly generating children in an age of high mortality and thereby guaranteeing the survival of the lineage. Secondly, as links to other clans, women "formed the cement that held the Russian high nobility together," establishing bonds among families anxious either to scale the social ladder or to hold onto advantageous positions already gained. Contributions like these, however, rarely found their way into official sources, with the result that few women appear in this narrative of elite political power; their part in the complicated politics of the age seems screened from view, reduced to the private rather than public sphere.[1]

Subsequently several scholars have attempted to identify and articulate the precise contributions that elite women made to Muscovite politics. Nancy Kollmann, for example, argued that, although

> Women's roles in Muscovite politics and society ... were not publicly acknowledged, ... women were nevertheless significant. Their seclusion enhanced their value as brides and mothers, and their ability to forge bonds between families allowed kin groups to function as units in political life. Their friendships with other women gave them the opportunity to influence marriage making and to supplement male communication networks. Women, however secluded, were integrated into the life of the elite.[2]

This insight derived from Edward Keenan's claim that in early modern Russia "the politics of betrothals and marriages was in fact the politics of power in

---

[1] Robert O. Crummey, *Aristocrats and Servitors: The Boyar Elite in Russia 1613–1698* (Princeton, NJ: Princeton University Press, 1983), 65–81, here 75.

[2] Nancy Shields Kollmann, "The Seclusion of Elite Muscovite Women," *Russian History/Histoire russe* vol. 10, pt. 2 (1983): 186.

Rude & Barbarous Kingdom Revisited: Essays in Russian History and Culture in Honor of Robert O. Crummey. Chester S. L. Dunning, Russell E. Martin, and Daniel Rowland, eds. Bloomington, IN: Slavica Publishers, 2008, 427–40.

the Kremlin."[3] In tracing weddings of the sovereigns, Russell Martin has shown exactly how marrying into the royal house depended upon calculation and court politics. But doing so did not mean that the women themselves were important actors; instead, these brides emerge as stand-ins for the patrilines from which they sprang. As Keenan famously put it, "it was the brothers, uncles, and fathers of the lucky brides who formed the innermost circle of power."[4]

Isolde Thyrêt, however, attempted to expose the contributions of elite women themselves, decoding the symbolic and ritual world of the Kremlin. Employing both literary and artistic texts, Thyrêt persuasively demonstrated that elite women deeply and powerfully influenced Muscovite politics, even if their roles were rarely made explicit in conventional political evidence.[5] Nada Boškovska, too, was not content to think of women as mere pawns in men's games. She aimed to explode the myth that "noble ladies were held like prisoners ... [who] whiled their time away with sewing and embroidering, and were not even allowed to manage their own household, which was run by stewards." Dissenting vigorously from this caricature, Boškovska affirmed women's "full legal capacity," and cited instances in which women contracted debts, owned, managed, and alienated large bodies of land. In this reading of the evidence, women in Muscovy—and not only elite women—exercised considerable power independent of their fathers, brothers, and husbands.[6] In her study of honor, Nancy Kollmann makes the same point, noting the apparent disconnect between the expression of patriarchal prejudice and the reality of women's real power: "Patriarchy existed as a cultural code affirming men's psychological sense of superiority, regardless of its economic or social instrumentality."[7]

I myself have argued that, although it would be unfair to characterize Muscovite women as brutalized victims, they were nevertheless far from free agents. In particular, even though there was evidence for change over the course of the century, 17th-century statutes severely constrained women's right to landed property in order to assuage the interests of patrilines: "Law

[3] Edward L. Keenan, "Muscovite Political Folkways," *Russian Review* 45 (1986): 144.

[4] Russell Edward Martin, "Dynastic Marriage in Muscovy, 1500–1729" (Ph.D. diss., Harvard University, 1996); Keenan, "Muscovite Political Folkways," 144.

[5] Isolde Thyrêt, *Between God and Tsar: Religious Symbolism and the Royal Women of Muscovite Russia* (DeKalb: Northern Illinois University Press, 2001).

[6] Nada Boškovska, "Muscovite Women During the Seventeenth Century: At the Peak of the Deprivation of their Rights or on the Road Towards a New Freedom?" in *Von Moskau nach St. Petersburg: Das russische Reich im 17. Jahrhundert*, ed. Hans-Joachim Torke (Wiesbaden: Harrassowitz Verlag, 2000), 47–62; and in more detail in Boškovska, *Die russische Frau im 17. Jahrhundert* (Cologne: Böhlau, 1998).

[7] Nancy Shields Kollmann, *By Honor Bound: State and Society in Early Modern Russia* (Ithaca, NY: Cornell University Press, 1999), 72.

guaranteed a man's relatives the opportunity to repurchase lands alienated from the control of a clan, restricted women's access to clan property, and in general treated women's rights as distinctly inferior to men's."[8] Even elite women, who had access to substantially more resources than did most women, lived within these limitations. Indeed, legislators may well have had elite women in mind in drawing up statutory limits upon control of property, because if women helped construct and secure power for elite families as Crummey has suggested, then these same women posed the most serious threat to the economic survival of patrilineal clans if they took clan property into their husbands' families.

The last wills and testaments of some prominent 17th-century women illustrate well, as Robert Crummey himself first noted, that men often played a decisive role in disposing of women's properties.[9] Careful study of these wills proves that, even though elite women exercised what Nada Boškovska calls "full legal capacity" and sometimes controlled imposing amounts of wealth, they nevertheless operated within a patriarchal system of property designed to serve elite patrilines.

☙ ❧

When Antonida Khvorostinina prepared her last will and testament in September 1617, she had many aims in mind.[10] Widowed since 1608, she was nevertheless accustomed to the circles of power, as her deceased husband, Fedor Ivanovich Khvorostinin, was named *okol'nichii* in 1585, and, since at least 1593, boyar.[11] Before his death, Fedor Ivanovich had been tonsured in the Trinity-St. Sergius Monastery, the same institution to which many of his kin had made donations in the 16th century (and continued to do in the 17th century). It comes as small surprise, therefore, that as she prepared her will, she enjoyed the company of a whole clutch of churchmen from the same monastery. Understandably mindful of burial and eternal salvation, Khvorostinina began by itemizing a long list of generous gifts to monastic executors—

---

[8] Daniel H. Kaiser, "Law, Gender and Kin in Seventeenth-Century Muscovy," *Russian History/Histoire russe* 34 (2007): 316.

[9] Crummey, *Aristocrats and Servitors*, 237.

[10] Russian State Archives of Ancient Acts (RGADA), Documents from the College of Economy f. 281, no. 14932. Another copy appears in the Russian State Library (RGB), Manuscript Section, Trinity-St. Sergius Monastery Collection f. 303, no. 541, fols. 295–97v.

[11] A. P. Pavlov, *Gosudarev dvor i politicheskaia bor'ba pri Borise Godunove (1584–1605 gg.)* (St. Petersburg: Nauka, 1992), 33, 52–53. See also *Russkii biograficheskii slovar'*, 27 vols. (St. Petersburg-Moscow: Izdatel'stvo Imperatorskogo istoricheskogo obshchestva, 1896–1918), 21: 291–92.

50 rubles all told—in exchange for Christian burial.[12] In addition, she provided 50 rubles for commemorative meals at the monastery and an icon of the Most Holy Mother of God in a silver-chase frame decorated with pearls and precious stones. Finally, adding to an earlier endowment of 100 rubles and estates in Bezhetsk (Baskakovo) and Gorodetsk districts, the dying princess donated the villages of Bogoroditskoe and Pavlovo in Pereiaslavl' and Rostov districts, respectively, awarding as well some outlying fields of Pavlovo to the Borisogleb monastery.[13] By her own evaluation, these properties were worth more than 1000 rubles, but by any calculus they were generous gifts, indicative as much of Khvorostinina's financial well-being as of her religious commitment. Her will continued by bequeathing yet another estate, Gorodishche in Iaroslavl' district, to her nephews, Iurii Dmitreevich and Ivan Andreevich Khvorostinin.

All these properties had occupied a significant place in the October 1602 testament of Fedor Ivanovich Khvorostinin, a document that reveals how dependent Antonida was upon her husband's control of property. Khvorostinin's will, although it identified a series of estates that totaled some 4000 chetverti, gave Antonida but one estate, Bogoroditskoe in Pereiaslavl' district.[14] Significantly, the testament provided her only with lifetime use, specifically prohibiting her from alienating the land. At her death the property was to go to their (only?) son, Grigorii, along with several other estates: Baskakovo in Bezhetskii Verkh, Pavlovo in Rostov district, and Romanovo in Kostroma district. Gorodishche in Kostroma district, which had come to Fedor as a result of a deal with his brothers and nephews, was to be divided: Grigorii was to receive one-third; Ivan and Iurii Dmitrievich Khvorostiniin were to divide their father's third; Andrei Khvorostinin and his son were to own the third share. Although the testament made other grants, Fedor Ivanovich intended that his son receive the bulk of his property; to Antonida, by contrast, Fedor Ivanovich gave only a widow's bench, additionally instructing her "to live together with my son Prince Grigorii, and possess the villages and livestock together"—apparently during the boy's minority.[15] In other words, Fedor Ivanovich foresaw Antonida fulfilling the traditional role for women in a patrilineal society: helping secure the next generation and not interfering in her husband's property.

---

[12] For a survey of the costs involved in 17th-century burials, see Richard Hellie, *The Economy and Material Culture of Russia, 1600–1725* (Chicago: University of Chicago Press, 1999), 507–10.

[13] E. N. Klitina, T. N. Manushina, and T. V. Nikolaeva, eds., *Vkladnaia kniga Troitse-Sergieva monastyria* (Moscow: Nauka, 1987), 46.

[14] Pavlov, *Gosudarev dvor*, 170.

[15] S. D. Sheremetev, "Dukhovnoe zaveshchanie kniazia F. I. Khvorostinina," *Russkii arkhiv*, bk. 1 (1896): 573–75.

When Antonida composed her testament in 1617 she showed herself responsive to her husband's wishes, even in the face of a severe problem: at the time she composed the testament, Grigorii Fedorovich was held captive in Lithuania.[16] Consequently, Antonida devised to the Trinity-St. Sergius monastery nearly all the properties her husband had intended for their son. In willing Gorodishche to her husband's nephews, instead of to her son, Antonida nevertheless responded to the precedent implied by her husband's testament, transmitting to Khvorostinin cousins a third of a property in which they had a share. In this way, at least the patriline would preserve title to the estate. But to address her husband's wishes, Khvorostinina specified that, "should God bring my son Prince Grigorii Fedorovich back from Lithuania, then all those estates pass to my son, Prince Grigorii."[17] In its conditional form, therefore, the bequest of Khvorostinin estates to Grigorii Fedorovich reproduced almost all her husband's wishes, preserving family property for the Khvorostinins, to whom she had been joined by marriage. Even the grants to the Trinity-St. Sergius monastery, something her husband's testament did not anticipate, at least joined clan property already donated there, providing a kind of virtual existence for the patriline, whose gifts funded on-going remembrance in the monastery.[18]

In her other awards, however, Khvorostinina made no concession to the clouded title of the property. For example, in a preface to the new grants, Khvorostinina recalled earlier gifts to the monastery: "And I myself earlier gave [to the Trinity-St. Sergius Monastery]," she writes, "a contribution of 100 rubles and my own estate (*otchinu svoiu*) Baskaki [Baskakovo] in Bezhetsk and Gorodetsk districts." In fact, the monastery donation book references the 100-ruble cash gift (along with some movables), but only Khvorostinina's testament confirms receipt of Baskaki, which her husband's will had described as *his*, and which he willed to his son, rather than to her.[19] She then continued:

---

[16] Because of his son's "treason," Khvorostinin had had several Kostroma estates confiscated. See Pavlov, *Gosudarev dvor*, 170.

[17] She reserved only the standing grain and reserve flour from two estates to pay her debts and the produce of a third estate to share with her slaves.

[18] *Vkladnaia kniga Troitse-Sergieva monastyria*, 46–47 ("Rod Khvorostininykh").

[19] Ibid., 46. Larissa Kirichenko's study of the monastery's landholding archive reports no separate gift charter for Baskaki, citing only Khvorostinina's testament. L. A. Kirichenko, *Aktovyi material Troitse-Sergieva monastyria 1584–1641 gg. kak istochnik po istorii zemlevladeniia i khoziaistva* (Moscow: Rossiiskii gosudarstvennyi gumanitarnyi universitet, 2006), 63, 189. The 1746 fire may have destroyed the relevant document. S. V. Nikolaeva, "Vklady i vkladchiki v Troitse-Sergiev monastyr' v XVI–XVII vekakh (po vkladnym knigam XVII veka)," in *Tserkov' v istorii Rossii*, sb. 2 (Moscow: Institut rossiiskoi istorii RAN, 1998), 81.

> And after my death give to the Lifegiving Trinity [Monastery] and to
> the Miracleworkers Sergei and Nikon my estate of Bogoroditskoe in
> Pereslavl' district and Pavlovo in Rostov district together with all the
> settlements around them in exchange for prayers for my soul and for
> my parents' [souls] [*po svoei dushe i po svoikh roditelekh*].

Her husband had, of course, given her lifetime possession of Bogoroditskoe,
but he had also prohibited her from alienating the property, insisting instead
that on her death she transfer it to their son. True, Grigorii was at that time far
away, and the odds of his returning safely were hard to calculate. But even
though she made the award conditional, honoring in the breach her husband's directive, Khvorostinina seems to have reckoned that she had some
independent claim to this property, and appropriated for her own and her
parents' souls all the prayers which the property might generate.[20]

So far as the record can tell, Khvorostinina never had any claim to Pavlovo, and Fedor Ivanovich had specifically bypassed her in awarding the land
to their son. Yet she seems to have worried not about the Khvorostinins
claiming the estate, but her own kin. "Whatever *kinsmen of my mother* [empha-
sis added—DK]," she wrote, "wish to redeem these estates must give to the
monastery of the Lifegiving Trinity and to the Miracleworkers Sergei and Nikon in memory of me and my parents 500 rubles for Bogoroditskoe and surrounding hamlets and 450 rubles for Pavlovo and its surrounding hamlets."
She went on to value her earlier bequest at another 400 rubles, making clear
that the land was sizable and valuable, and that she hoped to make redemption costly, if not impossible. In fact, between 1625 and 1628 the monastery accepted almost 1400 rubles from men who redeemed properties that Khvorostinina had willed to the Trinity-St. Sergius monastery, indicating that the
prices she affixed on these estates must have approximated actual values.[21]

So there can be no doubt that Khvorostinina was a rich woman, thanks to
the enormous estate that her husband had accumulated; that she chose finally

---

[20] Kirichenko points out that the sons of Dmitrii Buturlin had donated half this village
to the Trinity St.-Sergius Monastery in the 1570s, and that another half at that time remained in the hands of Ivan Grigor'evich Sobakin (*Aktovyi material*, 30). This history
suggests that Khvorostinin might have gained the village either as part of his wife's
dowry or by purchase.

[21] M. S. Cherkasova, *Krupnaia feodal'naia votchina v Rossii kontsa XVI–nachala XVII vv.*
(Moscow: Drevlekhranilishche, 2004), 91. On the gift to the Borisogleb monastery, see
S. V. Strel'nikov, "Rostovskii Borisoglebskii monastyr' i ego vkladchiki v XV–pervoi
treti XVII v. (po materialam vkladnykh knig)," in *Russkaia religioznost': Problemy izucheniia*, ed. A. I. Alekseev and A. S. Lavrov (St. Petersburg: Zhurnal Neva, 2000), 107–
08. Nikolaeva observes that 17th-century gifts to the monastery were less likely to
include land than had been true in the 16th century, and that gifts from the "feudal
clans" also fell off in comparison to an earlier time, even before publication of the 1649
Ulozhenie ("Vklady i vkladchiki," 99, 106).

to be buried beside her husband is therefore unsurprising.[22] In marrying Fedor Ivanovich Khvorostinin, she had attempted to fulfill the role expected of her: she had generated at least one son, and she may well have helped cement other connections for her husband.[23] Although in the main she had fulfilled the bulk of her dead husband's instructions, she was no simple puppet either, proving, in the face of her son's unlikely return, that she could act independently, with what some might even call "full legal capacity."

Evdokiia Fedorovna Odoevskaia was connected to two of the most influential families in 17th-century Muscovy. Daughter of Fedor Ivanovich Sheremetev, who represented one of the richest and most powerful families in the realm, and wife of the boyar Nikita Ivanovich Odoevskii, who occupied many important positions during the reign of Aleksei Mikhailovich (including chairing the commission that compiled the 1649 *Ulozhenie*), Evdokiia Fedorovna fulfilled many of the ambitions for women in Muscovy's elite. When she composed her last will and testament in September 1671, just three weeks prior to death, Odoevskaia possessed a sizable estate, so that, like Antonida Khvorostinina, she belied the image of imprisoned, oppressed women.

As with most Muscovite testators, Odoevskaia began by recalling her mortality and expressing a wish for eternal salvation. To help guarantee this result as well as to finance other forms of commemoration, Odoevskaia made substantial donations to five different church institutions. To the Novodevichii Convent, where Odoevskaia hoped not only to be buried, but also to take the monastic habit, was to go 500 rubles.[24] Four other monasteries—Voznesensk, Trinity-St. Sergius, Kirillov, and Chudov—were to receive 100 rubles each.[25] In other words, in church endowments alone, Odoevskaia dispensed

---

[22] *Spisok pogrebennykh v Troitskoi Sergievoi Lavre ot osnovaniia onoi do 1880 goda* (Moscow, 1880), 29. On the advantages and history of burials here, see David B. Miller, "Pogrebeniia riadom s Sergiem: Pogrebal'nye obychai v Troitse-Sergievom monastyre, 1392–1605 gg.," in *Troitse-Sergieva lavra v istorii, kul'ture i dukhovnoi zhizni Rossii. Materialy II Mezhdunarodnoi konferentsii 4–6 oktiabria 2000 g.* (Sergiev Posad: Sergievo-Posadskii gosudarstvennyi istoriko-khudozhestvennyi muzei-zapovednik, 2002), 74–89.

[23] Aleksei Mikhailovich L'vov was one of her executors, and among her debtors she counted Ivan Fedorovich Volkonskii and Mariia Teliatevskaia.

[24] The 1674–75 contribution book of the Novodevichii monastery confirms and details Odoevskaia's 500-ruble gift, which included a welter of gold, jewel-encrusted garments and other valuables. *Istochniki po sotsial'no-ekonomicheskoi istorii Rossii XVI–XVIII vv.: Iz arkhiva Moskovskogo Novodevich'ego monastyria* (Moscow: Akademiia nauk SSSR, Institut istorii SSSR, 1985), 164–66. She was in fact buried beneath the cathedral altar; see S. Kipnis, *Novodevichii memorial: Nekropol' monastyria i kladbishcha* (Moscow: Art-Biznes-Tsentr, 1998), 30.

[25] *Vkladnaia kniga Troitse-Sergieva monastyria*, 110.

900 rubles. Her confessor received 30 rubles and the patriarch 50, and both were to remember the dying woman's "sinful soul."

Generous gifts to church institutions and to churchmen did not exhaust Odoevskaia's property. Altogether, the testament invokes almost 50 heirs, expansive even among the most munificent estates of this age. Most heirs, however, received only token gifts from movable property. For example, Odoevskaia awarded icons (usually with expensive frames) to many kin—her son Iakov and his wife, along with their three children, for example; to another son Fedor, his wife, and her son, Vasilii, and Vasilii's wife; to another grandson, Iurii, and his wife, as well as to their three children, and so on. In the process, Odoevskaia made heirs out of members of the Vorotynskii, Kurakin, Troekurov, and Sheremetev families (reflecting perhaps the primary links, both biological and social, that she represented to her husband), and to each she awarded an icon, all of which were said to have silver frames.[26]

But to her son went the most prominent bequest, the Sheremetev estate of Borisoglebskoe in Kostroma guberniia. Odoevskaia had received this property through her father's testament, and, in an excellent example of what Michelle Marrese has called "gender tutelage," Sheremetev had directed that she pass the property on to her son, Iakov.[27] It is worth emphasizing that it was Sheremetev—not Odoevskii—land that she transmitted by testament, and that, furthermore, in making the award she was responding to her father's directive: "and I," she wrote, "in the fear of God and [in fulfillment of] the oath of my father, the boyar Fedor Ivanovich, award to my son after my death my Kostroma estate along with the adjacent lands (*pustoshi*) that I purchased."[28] Perhaps reflective of the confidence she had gained from purchasing these additional properties, Odoevskaia added an important condition to the bequest, stipulating that, should she survive her current illness and succeed in entering the convent, her son was not to interfere in this estate, the income from which was to maintain her so long as she lived. "And without my knowledge," she continued, my son "is to take nothing for himself, nor give away any slaves, nor transfer any peasants into other estates." In a final assertion of agency, Odoevskaia prohibited her son from selling, mortgaging, or

---

[26] Typically understood exclusively in religious terms, icons nevertheless also bore real market value, in addition to whatever sentimental value they might carry. See N. P. Chesnokova, "Vyvoz russkikh ikon na khristianskii vostok v XVII v.," in *Torgovlia, kupechestvo i tamozhennoe delo v Rossii v XVI–XVIII vv.: Sbornik materialov mezhdunarodnoi nauchnoi konferentsii (Sankt-Peterburg, 17–20 sentiabria 2001 g.)* (St. Petersburg: Izdatel'stvo Sankt-Peterburgskogo universiteta, 2001), 102.

[27] A. V. Barsukov, *Rod Sheremetevykh*, 8 vols. (St. Petersburg, 1881–1904), 3: 510–24; Michelle Lamarche Marrese, "The Enigma of Married Women's Control of Property in Eighteenth-Century Russia," *Russian Review* 58 (1999): 380–81.

[28] Barsukov, *Rod Sheremetevykh*, 7: 348.

exchanging the Kostroma estate, "because that estate is a service estate (*vysluzhenaia*) of my grandfather, the boyar Ivan Vasil'evich."[29]

Ivan Vasil'evich Sheremetev had first gained this enormous estate from Ivan IV in 1560, with the proviso that it pass to no one except a son.[30] Ivan transmitted the property to Fedor Ivanovich, who declared in his 1645 testament that he intended to transfer Borisoglebskoe to his two daughters, Ovdot'ia (Evdokiia) Odoevskia and her sister, the nun Aleksandra.[31] By June of 1649, events obliged Fedor Ivanovich to revise his plans. As the new testament explained, "because of the Sovereign's new statute in the Ulozhenie, prohibiting nuns from holding votchina land," the testator now gave the estate entirely over to Ovdot'ia, requiring in exchange that she provide half the food and income necessary to maintain Aleksandra. Furthermore, Sheremetev specified that Ovdot'ia was to transmit the property to her son at her death.[32]

What explains these decisions? Fedor Ivanovich Sheremetev was a very wealthy man, owning something like 3,000 peasant households and more than 30 estates, ancestral property constituting the essential core. With no male heirs, Fedor Ivanovich contemplated transferring much of his estate to his daughter's family, the Odoevskiis. To facilitate this result he first petitioned the tsar to allow him to convert granted estates into purchased property, thereby freeing him to give the property to whom he wished. In this Sheremetev succeeded, but he encountered resistance in his intention to alienate hereditary estates as well. His brother's sons, thinking themselves the only legitimate heirs of clan estates, "not only demanded them for themselves," the historian Iurii Arsen'ev wrote, but also "settled on various forceful actions aimed at their aged uncle." Although the nephews won their point, Fedor Ivanovich also won his, settling the greater part of his property—but not Sheremetev hereditary estates—upon his grandson through bequests to Odo-

---

[29] Ibid., 349. Estates awarded for exceptional service were converted service lands, which, although in practice they approximated patrimony, nevertheless were distinct from patrimonial and purchased estates. See Ann M. Kleimola, "'In Accordance with the Canons of the Holy Apostles': Muscovite Dowries and Women's Property Rights," *Russian Review* 51 (1992): 210, 217.

[30] A. V. Antonov and K. V. Baranov, eds., *Akty sluzhilykh zemlevladel'tsev XV–nachala XVII veka* [hereafter *ASZ*], 3 vols. (Moscow: Arkheograficheskii tsentr-Pamiatniki istoricheskoi mysli-Drevlekhranilishche, 1997–2002), vol. 3, no. 494.

[31] Barsukov, *Rod Sheremetevykh*, 3: 501.

[32] Ibid., 515. The 1649 law code attempted to restrict the growing land fund of church institutions by, among other things, prohibiting monks and nuns from owning estates. Instead, just as Sheremetev's testament prescribed, the law required that the lands be transferred to kin, who then had to provide the necessary financial support to the monk or nun. See L. I. Ivina, ed., *Sobornoe Ulozhenie 1649: Tekst, kommentarii* (Leningrad: Nauka, 1987), 90 (X.43–44).

evskaia and her husband, both of whom were instructed on their deaths to transmit their bequests to Iakov Nikitich Odoevskii.[33]

Consequently, although the Sheremetev clan rallied to sustain the principle of patriliny, Fedor Ivanovich was nevertheless able to dispose of much of his property as he chose. But whatever damage this decision did to the patriline, his daughter continued to fulfill her duty, at life's end transmitting property precisely as her father dictated. Even though this bequest meant that substantial property passed from the Sheremetev to Odoevskii clan, the dying woman's gift did not diminish the (considerable) Sheremetev patrimonial holdings. On the other hand, as Crummey has noted, the transfer of property significantly enhanced the Odoevskiis' situation, converting them into one of the country's wealthiest patrilines, whose youngest heir now enjoyed significant resources with which to defend his family's interests.[34] As a result, Odoevskaia had accomplished the major goals that the Muscovite patrilineal system had for in-marrying women. Even then, however, her affiliation with her husband's patriline was not secure.

Ludwig Steindorff has argued that Muscovite commemorative prayer lists took their basic organization from clans: "blood kinship took precedence over kinship by marriage," he observed, but "the spouse was treated as a member of the donor's family."[35] This point reinforces the view that commemorative gifts "reveal the range of kinship awareness of elite clans and the importance of horizontal links by marriage."[36] Indeed, Princess Efrosiniia, the name Odoevskaia took as a nun, appears with members of the Odoevskii clan in the 1705 sinodik of the Novodevichii monastery.[37] But Odoevskaia's choice of burial site indicates that, whatever her husband's kin may have thought,

[33] Crummey, *Aristocrats and Servitors*, 119–20; Iurii Arsen'ev, "Blizhnii boiarin kniaz' Nikita Ivanovich Odoevskii i ego perepiska s Galitskoiu votchinoi (1650–1684)," *Chteniia obshchestva istorii i drevnostei rossiiskikh pri Moskovskom universitete* (henceforth *ChOIDR*), no. 2 (1903): 24–26.

[34] Crummey, *Aristocrats and Servitors*, 119.

[35] Ludwig Steindorff, "Princess Maria Golenina: Perpetuating Identity Through 'Care for the Deceased,'" in *Culture and Identity in Muscovy, 1389–1584/Moskovskaia Rus' (1359–1584): Kul'tura i istoricheskoe samosoznanie*, ed. A. M. Kleimola and G. D. Lenhoff (Moscow: ITZ-Garant, 1997), 574. As Steindorff himself proves elsewhere, however, the women's names in general appear in commemoration lists more rarely than men's, and wives much less often than their husbands'. Liudvig Shtaindorff [Ludwig Steindorff], "Kto blizhnie moi? Individ i kul'tura pominoveniia v Rossii rannego novogo vremeni," in *Chelovek i ego blizkie na Zapade i Vostoke Evropy (do nachala novogo vremeni)*, ed. Iurii Bessmertnyi and Otto Gerhard Oexle (Moscow: RAN, Institut vseobshchei istorii, 2000), 212–20.

[36] Russell E. Martin, "Gifts for the Dead: Death, Kinship and Commemoration in Muscovy (The Case of the Mstislavskii Princes)," *Russian History/Histoire russe* 26: 2 (Summer 1999): 201, 202.

[37] *Istochniki po sotsial'no-ekonomicheskoi istorii Rossii*, 273.

she did not feel fully joined to her husband's clan. Unlike Antonida Khvorostinina, Odoevskaia did not wish to be buried beside her husband, and requested instead burial beside her sister, who had earlier taken vows in Novodevichii convent. This choice certainly reflected the woman's religious commitment, but also affirmed a lasting identification with her natal family.

∂⊱ ⊰∂

A similar perspective emerges from the 1625 last will and testament of Ol'ga Vasil'evna Godunova.[38] As a clan, the Godunovs were far from wealthy, especially as measured by other members of the elite, and over the 17th century their fortunes understandably waned.[39] Nevertheless, thanks to the Godunov government they scaled the appointments ladder, although this success may well have worked against them later. Matvei Mikhailovich Godunov, for example, achieved both *okol'nichii* (1598) and boyar (1603) status, and Nikita Vasilievich made it to *okol'nichii* (1598); the Trinity-St. Sergius donation book identifies as boyars several other Godunovs in the late 16th and early 17th century.[40]

The Ziuziny, for their part, occupied a more modest place in Muscovite society. Although their clan held hereditary estates even in early Muscovy, few members of their line succeeded to high office.[41] As Godunova's testament confirms, Aleksei Ivanovich Ziuzin reached *okol'nichii*, but he was already dead by 1618/19, and no other Ziuzin seems to have succeeded so well.[42] All the same, in devising her testament Godunova placed her trust and resources not upon her Godunov in-laws, but rather upon the men and women associated with the Ziuzins. Many of her heirs were descended from Ziuzin parents, but the most significant person in Godunova's will was the widow of *okol'nichii* Aleksei Ivanovich Ziuzin, Fedora Grigor'evna, and her two sons. Godunova made them executors and chief heirs to her estate.

Muscovite testaments of this age rarely named a woman as executor, and those few testators who did normally selected their wives (in the company of other executors). Consequently, even though Godunova also named as executors a group of churchmen and a nephew, in choosing a woman executor Godunova consciously followed an unusual course, presumably aware that it

---

[38] Arkhimandrit Grigorii, "Dukhovnaia zheny Alekseia Ivanovicha Godunova, Ol'gi Vasil'evny, rozhdennoi Ziuzinoi," *ChOIDR*, no. 4 (1868): 1.

[39] Crummey, *Aristocrats and Servitors*, 108; O. A. Shvatchenko, *Svetskie feodal'nye votchiny v Rossii vo vtoroi polovine XVII veka* (Moscow: RAN, Institut rossiiskoi istorii, 1996), 262. On the rise of the Godunovs' fortunes, see Pavlov, *Gosudarev dvor*, 186–88.

[40] Crummey, *Aristocrats and Servitors*, 179; *Vkladnaia kniga Troitse-Sergieva monastyria*, 121–22.

[41] Vasilii Grigor'evich Ziuzin appeared as *dumnyi dvorianin* by 1584 (Pavlov, *Gosudarev dvor*, 27).

[42] Crummey, *Aristocrats and Servitors*, 181.

would provoke notice. But Fedora Grigor'evna was no pushover. Only two years after her husband died, she managed to effect for her daughter Elena a very favorable marriage, betrothing her to the boyar, prince Dmitrii Mamstriukovich Cherkaskii, using her wealth to enrich the girl's dowry with a long list of movables and half of Khinskoe estate in the Moscow district.[43] Clearly Fedora Grigor'evna knew how to get things done, and the pluckiness and ambition she displayed in seeking a good match for her daughter betrayed no sign of her wilting before patriarchal authority. Making Ziuzina executor, Godunova testified to her own independence.

Further proof of Godunova's character emerges from the bequest she made to Fedora Ziuzina and her children—Godunova's dowry estate in Uglich district, the village of Spasskoe along with the hamlets of Torokanovo, Novoselki, and the outlying fields of Otvodnaia, Zmeeva, and Ovinnishcha, along with all the relevant forests and fields. Like the property that Fedor Sheremetev bequeathed his daughter, this estate did not spring from Ziuzin hereditary lands; instead, Godunova's father, Vasilii Grigor'evich Ziuzin, had purchased it from Petr Romanovich Pivovo in 1582/83.[44] Apparently no marriage contract or dowry gift charter survives to confirm the point, but Godunova described the estate as part of her dowry, and certainly acted with the authority of an owner. For example, in confirmation of her grant, Godunova remarked, "I have already given them, Fedora and her children, the deed (*krepostnaia zapis'*), so that they may henceforth possess my estate." In exchange, Godunova required of the heirs that they contribute a total of 110 rubles—50 to the Chudov monastery for commemoration, 15 for burial, another 25 for commemorative meals, 15 for those who took part in her burial service, three rubles each to two confessors, and five rubles each to three nieces (which totals 126 rubles, despite the total announced earlier).

In making her award, Godunova was aware of the potential for claims on the land from the Ziuzins, whom she warned against trying to redeem the property: "and henceforth, after my death, no one in my clan (*rod*) and the Ziuzin lineage (*plemia*) has any claim to this estate," she wrote, except the heirs she named. Godunova reminded would-be suitors that her father had *purchased* this land, which meant that she had every right to it. As the 1649 code put it, "widows have no claim on hereditary estates or those awarded for service, but only on purchased estates." Therefore, Godunova continued, "no one is to interfere in this, my dowry property which my father

---

[43] S. D. Sheremetev, "Riadnaia zapis' Eleny Alekseevny Ziuzinoi (zheny kniazia Dmitriia Mamstriukovicha Cherkaskago)," *Izvestiia russkogo genealogicheskogo obshchestva* 3 (1902): 97–99. Fedora evidently shared this property with her sister-in-law, Anna, in whose name Khinskoe village had been given to Trinity-St. Sergius monastery in 1612 (Cherkasova, *Krupnaia feodal'naia votchina*, 76).

[44] *ASZ*, 1, no. 94.

purchased."[45] In other words, Ziuzin kinsmen should know that Spasskoe was not a hereditary estate (*rodovaia votchina*), but purchased property to which she was fully entitled.

Should kinsmen try to redeem these lands, Godunova required that they pay Fedora and her children 700 rubles and give an additional 200 rubles to the Chudov monastery. These sums indicate that Godunova intended more than a fair price for her bequest: the deed which confirmed her father's purchase of this land reports the price of the land as 400 rubles (plus one horse).[46] Although the land value might well have risen since the 1580s, when a fierce depopulation of estates was underway, an increase of more than 100% seems hard to justify, except if the testator intended to scare away any interference. If this motive be credited, then Godunova was surely showing herself to be a cagey and assertive landowner, and not the stereotypical victim of gender oppression.

On the basis of her own evaluation, altogether Godunova handed out property worth in excess of 1200 rubles. Dealing with such grand sums did not prevent her from focusing upon the much smaller grants that she made to a long list of churchmen, slaves, and other relatives: 2 rubles to the priests and deacons for the 40-day commemoration and for entry in the sinodik; 0.25 rubles to the woman who baked the eucharist bread; 0.2 rubles for the ceremonial wine and incense; 0.2 rubles to sacristan and guard; 0.25 rubles to the church clerk, and so on. Her slave, Senka Vlasov, she emancipated, and gave him a horse and a cow; three other slaves, their wives and children she freed, assigning each a share of rye and wheat. Godunova also freed the four women who lived with her in the convent, and gave each a half-ruble and some grain.

Finally, Godunova remembered various relatives with token bequests. As noted above, she had made the primary heirs responsible for five-ruble legacies to three nieces: Afim'ia Afonas'evna, wife of Timofei Zagoslovskogo; Natal'ia Afanas'evna, wife of Kuzma Chelishchev; and Mar'ia Afanas'evna, wife of Prince Stepan Shakhovskoi. These three families occupy a modest place in the surviving records of Muscovy. To judge by the 17th-century cadasters, only the Shakhovskie held as much property as the Ziuziny and none of them had family members in powerful positions in government.[47] A nephew, Fedor Ivanovich Zuzin, received an icon of the Kazan' Mother of God, and another nephew, Kuz'ma Mikhailovich Chelishchev, received a mare. To two grandsons she awarded a mare and stallion each, while two granddaughters received a cow each.

---

[45] Ibid., 2; *Sobornoe Ulozhenie*, 83 (XVII.1).

[46] ASZ 1, no. 94.

[47] Shvatchenko, *Svetskie feodal'nye votchiny*, 282–83. See also N. A. Chelishchev, *Sbornik materialov dlia istorii roda Chelishchevykh* (St. Petersburg, 1893).

And so this woman of property closed out her accounts, dispensing land of enormous value, but which did not originate in her family's hereditary estates, to a restrictive list of heirs. At the same time, she was mindful of her humblest servants, making sure to shave off small sums and odd bits of live-stock with which to enrich their lives. Making heirs out of nephews and nieces, Godunova also assigned bits of property to children from these matches, proving that she was far from inattentive to relatives. Indeed, antici-pating claims that natal kin might make against her awards, Godunova at-tempted to forestall them, warning relatives away. At the same time, she was seemingly oblivious of her husband's kin. So far as her testament can confirm, in death Ol'ga Vasil'evna anticipated no communion with the Godunovs, which may explain why she sought burial in the Chudov monastery, "near the Miracleworker Aleksei, with my father, Vasilii Grigor'evich [Ziuzin] ... and with my brothers, Larion and Iakov."

আ ৰ

As their testaments reveal, these three women cannot fairly be described as victims. Each possessed an estate rich in cash and land, the equal of some of Muscovy's wealthiest men, and they proved themselves very capable man-agers. At the same time, they operated within the constraints of a patriarchal society oriented around patrilines. Dowered off with purchased properties, these brides forsook their own families to join their husbands' lineages, there to give birth to new generations and, so far as they could, nourish these heirs into adulthood. Along the way, they might come into possession of consider-able resources, although they proved themselves responsive to husbands and fathers in disposing of this property. As a result, at death they seemed ambiv-alent about the extent to which they had successfully joined their husbands' patrilines. Hardly battered victims, these women were also far from inde-pendent agents.

In writing about the 17th-century provincial gentry, Valerie Kivelson has argued that "the female line of inheritance frequently received consideration and protection in contested cases.... Direct descent rather than patriliny or lineage rated top marks from the courts."[48] But, as these three women show, among elite families with hereditary estates, lineage certainly mattered.

[48] Valerie A. Kivelson, "The Effects of Partible Inheritance: Gentry Families and the State in Muscovy," *Russian Review* 53 (1994): 206, 207.

Registering Land Titles in Muscovy

George G. Weickhardt

The concept that there should be some public record of the transfer of land titles is an ancient one. In the book of Genesis, it is stated that Abraham purchased land from Ephron the Hittite for 400 shekels, and that the land was "deeded to Abraham as his property in the presence of all the Hittites who had come to the gate of the city."[1] The purpose of proclaiming the transfer to the Hittites at the city gates was obviously to secure clarity and notoriety as to who owned the land and perhaps even to give other claimants to it an opportunity to challenge the transaction. These purposes of clarity and notoriety of title are achieved today by recording or registering one's deed, which involves depositing the deed with a governmental authority, which maintains it and other similarly deposited deeds in a permanent record. The recorded deeds usually contain a description of the boundaries of the property, or reference a survey from which they can be determined.

In the Middle Ages in Europe the Church and its monasteries acted as repositories of various documents of legal importance, including records of births, deaths, marriage and sometimes conveyances of property.[2] By the late Middle Ages, many of the Hanse cities also recorded similar documents.[3] The first modern national recording system was established by the English Parliament in 1535, when it enacted the so-called Statute of Enrollments.[4]

By the middle of the 17th century Muscovy had also developed a comprehensive system for recording land titles. Through this system landowners enjoyed substantial security in title and protection from invalid claims. Indeed the system of title recording in the Muscovite tsardom was as advanced as those in some of the nations of Western Europe. The party whose title was recorded with the Service Land Chancellery (*Pomestnyi prikaz*) would be rec-

---

[1] Genesis 23:18 (New International Version). The King James Version reads "made sure unto Abraham for a possession in the presence of the children of Heth before all that went in at the gate of his city."

[2] Hans Hattenhauer, *Die Entdeckung der Verfügungsmacht* (Kiel: Hansischer Gildenverlag, Joachim Heitman & Co., 1969).

[3] Paul Rehme, *Lübecker Ober–Stadtbuch* (Hannover: Helwingshe Verlagsbuchhandlung, 1895), passim.

[4] *Statutes of the Realm*, 11 vols. (London: The Record Commission, 1810–28), 3: 549 (the official citation of this statute is 27 H.8 c. 16).

Rude & Barbarous Kingdom Revisited: Essays in Russian History and Culture in Honor of Robert O. Crummey. Chester S. L. Dunning, Russell E. Martin, and Daniel Rowland, eds. Bloomington, IN: Slavica Publishers, 2008, 441–57.

ognized by the Chancellery courts as the legal owner of the property. The boundaries to property could likewise be determined from cadastral surveys on file in the same chancellery. In other words, recording one's title with the chancellery became the means for gaining legal recognition by the tsardom that one owned the land in question. Priority of title was given to the first to record his deed. This system of recording titles had slowly developed over the preceding four centuries, but it was revamped and perfected in the second quarter of the 17th century. This study shall address the origins of this system, and, in particular, whether a foreign model was used.

No previous study has addressed the recording of deeds in Muscovy, although there has been some attention to related subjects. Much attention has been devoted in the literature to the history of land cadasters (*pistsovye knigi*) and surveys and to the history of the Service Land Chancellery, which eventually became the registry of deeds.[5] No attention, however, has been directed to how the Chancellery and the cadasters and other records it maintained were transformed into a system for resolving disputes between private parties over who held title to property.

The origins of the Muscovite recording system can only be understood in relation to the development of land cadasters. The Mongols had conducted three censuses in the 13th century. Nothing remains of these records, which were probably little more than headcounts for purposes of taxation and army recruiting. Local princes eventually assumed responsibility for collecting the Horde's tribute, which was levied on the basis of a half *grivna* per *sokha*. *Sokha*, of course, literally meant the wooden plow commonly used in Rus', but for tax purposes it probably meant some standard unit of area that may have varied depending on the locality and productivity of a farmstead. By the 15th century the *sokha* had become a more complex unit of assessment that took account of the number of peasants, animals, beehives, fishtraps, and other productive assets.[6]

The oldest surviving cadasters and *sokha* registers (*soshnye pis'ma*) were compiled in the mid- to late-1490s in five localities in Novgorod. These cadasters were compiled as part of Ivan III's redistribution of Novgorod land as service lands (*pomest'e*) to his military servitors.[7]

[5] See, for example, A. V. Chernov, "K istorii pomestnogo prikaza," *Trudy Moskovskogo gosudarstvennogo istoriko–arkhivnogo instituta* 9 (1957): 195–250; Aleksei Konstantinovich Leont'ev, *Obrazovanie prikaznoi sistemy upravlenii v russkom gosudarstve: Iz istorii sozdaniia tsentralizovannogo apparata v kontse XV–pervoi polovine XVII v.* (Moscow: Izd-vo Moskovskogo universiteta, 1961); Peter B. Brown, "The Service Land Chancellery Clerks of Seventeenth-Century Russia: Their Regime, Salaries, and Economic Survival," *Jahrbücher für Geschichte Osteuropas* 52 (2004): 33–69.

[6] Henry L. Eaton, "Cadasters and Censuses of Muscovy," *Slavic Review* 26: 1 (March 1967): 55–56.

[7] Ibid., 56–57.

The first national or at least multiregional cadasters were compiled in the mid-16th century. Separate cadasters were compiled in 1537–46, 1561–69, and 1581–92.

The last of these became an important record of the residence of peasants for purposes of binding that population to the land. Starting in mid-century the cadastral surveys became the responsibility of the Service Land Chancellery, which maintained the vast amount of documentation compiled.[8]

The process of compiling cadasters has been well described by Veselovskii. The first priority was to measure the area of the land of each settlement. The officials usually surveyed the fallow areas and assumed that they represented one-third of the total tilled area. The results of such surveys would, however, be refined by obtaining information from the peasantry. The surveyors also collected information on the number of homesteads, forests, pastures, gardens, beehives, fisheries, mills and other assets from which the ability of the peasants to bear taxes could be judged.[9]

Although the cadasters referenced the owners of the settlements and their boundaries, the cadastral officials did not at first collect deeds for recordation. Written deeds had been used since at least the 14th century, when we begin to see substantial numbers of written private deeds, most of them deeds of gift to monasteries, although there are some deeds of sale as well. Besides private gift or purchase, the other way to acquire title to land was by a grant from the grand prince in the form of an immunity charter. Most of the early immunity charters involve grants of land to monasteries. The monasteries eventually acquired vast amounts of land (by some estimates as much as one-third of the total tillable acreage) by deeds of gift and by immunity charters from princes. The immunity charters typically exempted the land from taxation and gave the monastery legal jurisdiction over those residing on the land, except for serious felonies like murder and robbery.[10]

Another way to acquire title to land was by will. Monasteries played an important role in the development of wills in Russia. Monks often assisted lay persons in drafting their wills, and the monasteries were frequently beneficiaries of wills.

---

[8] Ibid., "Cadasters," 57–58, 60.

[9] For a detailed history of the compilation of cadasters, see Stepan Borisovich Veselovskii, *Soshnoe pis'mo: Izsledovanie po istorii kadastra i pososhnogo oblozheniia*, 2 vols. (Moscow, 1915–16), passim.

[10] See, for example, documents collected in *Akty sotsial'no–ekonomicheskeskoi istorii severo–vostochnoi Rusi kontsa XIV–nachala XVI v.*, ed. Boris Dmitrievich Grekov, 3 vols. (hereafter, *ASEI*) (Moscow: Izd-vo AN SSSR, 1952–64); Lev Vladimirovich Cherepnin, *Akty feodal'nogo zemlevladeniia i khoziaistva XIV–XVI vekov* (hereafter, *AFZKh*), 3 vols. (Moscow: Izd-vo AN SSSR, 1951–56). See also Marc D. Zlotnick, "Immunity Charters and the Centralization of the Muscovite State" (Ph.D. diss., University of Chicago, 1976).

In order to protect their vast landholdings from competing claims, the monasteries maintained files of the deeds, wills, and immunity charters on which their titles were based. These files, many of which are extant today, contain not only the deeds of the property to the monastery, but often other documents in the chain of title. Because the monasteries usually held hundreds of separate parcels, these files were voluminous. Thus, rather than relying on recording their deeds with the tsar, the monasteries maintained their own files of deeds.[11]

How would a landowner protect his property from competing claims by neighbors, trespassers, or others in the late 15th and early 16th century, before there were comprehensive nationwide cadasters or recording of private deeds? The landowner would simply file a lawsuit against the competing claimant with the grand prince or some local prince. In the surviving judgment charters from this period, one of the parties is usually a monastery. This is due in part to the fact that most of the surviving judgment charters come from monasterial archives, but also because the monasteries were substantial landholders and seasoned litigants.

The monasteries used their files of deeds, wills and immunity charters to good effect in litigation concerning the ownership of hereditary estates. The clergy at this time had a near monopoly on literacy, and thus enjoyed an advantage in the presentation and interpretation of written records. Typically the monastery's adversary was a lay person who based his claim on the testimony of long-term residents of the locality (*starozhil'tsy*). The monastery's claim, on the other hand, was based not only on such testimony, but also on deeds, immunity charters, or other legal documents. In most such cases the monastery won. [12]

While it is not the purpose of this study to analyze all the published judgment charters systematically, several implicit principles or rules can be observed in a representative sample of them.[13] One commonly accepted legal principle that can be distilled out of these cases is that the courts would usually honor a deed or charter, as long as it appeared to be authentic and supported by testimony of long-term residents. There were, however, cases involving allegedly forged or extorted deeds, which the judges would not honor if credible evidence of forgery or extortion was produced.[14] One of the most unforgivable tactics was to testify that one had a deed but fail to pro-

---

[11] *ASEI*, passim; *AFZKh*, passim.

[12] For an excellent collection of translated judgment charters, see Horace Dewey and Ann M. Kleimola, *Russian Private Law XIV–XVII Centuries*, Michigan Slavic Materials 9 (Ann Arbor: University of Michigan Dept. of Slavic Languages and Literatures, 1966). See in particular documents 36, 45, and 46.

[13] Ibid. This collection contains examples of virtually all of the typical situations that gave rise to litigation.

[14] Ibid., documents 49, 51, and 55.

duce it.[15] In other cases, deeds or claims based on deeds were not honored because the lay adversary or adversaries had been in adverse possession for many years.[16] Other cases might involve no deed or charter and would be disposed of on the basis of testimony only.[17] Interestingly there are some early cases where a boundary dispute was resolved by reference to some previous privately conducted survey.[18]

While the above discussion does not represent a systematic analysis of all the available judgment charters, a reading of the available charters indicates that in general judges resolved cases on the basis of credible evidence. An authentic deed was considered credible evidence, especially if possession was corroborated by longterm residents. It is also noteworthy that the judgment charters available up through the mid-16th century concern disputes over hereditary estates (*votchina*, the most unconditional type of tenure) versus service land (*pomest'e*). While the results in these judgment charters seem fair, this system of protecting property rights had two main weaknesses.

First, there was no central registry of deeds, and many claimants to property did not even have written deeds. Many (but not all) of the disputes could have been resolved more simply by reviewing deeds as recorded. While the results of the reported litigation were fair, one would actually have to go through a trial to protect his claim to land.

Second, what is also interesting about the judgment charters from the late 14th through early 16th centuries is that they hardly ever cite any governing law as the basis of the decision. The judges, who could be the tsar, a boyar or other servitor, appear to apply a rough sense of justice: the party with the best evidence or the better credibility prevails.

The lack of citation to governing law is understandable because there was very little published law concerning hereditary estates. The Rus' Law (*Russkaia Pravda*) contained some rules on inheritance, such as the rule that upon the death of the father, the sons would divide the property among themselves. Daughters, for whom there was a moral if not legal obligation to provide a dowry, would inherit only in the absence of sons, and the wife would receive a portion as a life estate only. There were also prohibitions on destroying boundary markers.[19] These provisions were continued in the *Sudebniki* of 1497 and 1550, the latter code also codifying the right of clan members to

---

[15] Ibid., documents 33, 35, and 45.

[16] Ibid., documents 38, 40, and 43.

[17] Ibid., document 41.

[18] Ibid., documents 29, 30, and 32.

[19] Expanded Redaction, Articles 70–73, 90–95. Serafim Vladimirovich Iushkov and Lev Vladirmirovich Cherepnin, eds., *Pamiatniki russkogo prava* (hereafter, *PRP*), 8 vols. (Moscow: Gosudarstvennoe izd-vo iuridicheskoi literatury, 1952–63), 1: 132–35; Daniel H. Kaiser, ed. and trans., *The Laws of Rus': Tenth to Fifteenth Centuries* (Salt Lake City: Chas. Schlacks, Jr., 1992), 28, 30–31.

redeem hereditary estates (*votchina*) that had been sold outside the clan. The *Sudebniki* also contained statutes of limitation on land litigation.[20] Other than these few rules, there was little law to govern disputes over the title to property.

As indicated above, the published judgment charters almost exclusively concern hereditary estates. Service land was subject to a separate system of regulation. The first substantial use of service land grants was in the newly conquered Novgorod lands in the late 15th century. Such lands were conferred by a grant from the grand prince/tsar. A recent study of early service land grant charters from the late 15th to the mid-16th century indicates that such lands could be transferred to one's son or kinsman but only with the permission of the grand prince. (Interestingly, the early grant charters did not mention an obligation of service.)[21] The Service Land Chancellery, as its name implies, eventually became responsible for keeping track of grants and handling petitions for transfers of service land. The chancellery thus in effect became a registry of titles to service land. In other words, titles were de facto registered with the Service Land Chancellery in connection with the requirement that transfers of service land be approved. The rules for transferability, however, were not published until the promulgation of the Conciliar Law Code (*Sobornoe Ulozhenie*) in 1649.

A similar system for registering transfers of hereditary estates did not exist in the 16th century. The first known decrees governing rights in hereditary estates appear in the reign of Ivan IV. For example, a 1551 decree prohibited the purchase of land by monasteries without the approval of the tsar. Another 1551 decree clarified the redemption rights of clan members as to lands previously bequeathed to monasteries. Decrees of 1562 and 1572 prohibited service princes from selling, mortgaging or exchanging their hereditary estates or giving them in dowry or by will to daughters without the tsar's consent.[22] These decrees, while they diminished the alienability of hereditary estates, would not provide much guidance for most litigation over the ownership of property. There are no known decrees from this period on the transferability of, or other issues relating to, service lands.

That disputes about title, ownership, and boundaries might be resolved by reference to the cadasters first appears clearly in a judgment charter from 1584. The defendant, Andrei Sherefedinov, claimed a hereditary estate in the Riazan' village of Shilovo by virtue of a mortgage note purchased by his son-in-law. The plaintiff, Timofei Shilovskoi, alleged that the defendant had him arrested and brought in chains to Moscow where the deed was extorted from

---

[20] *PRP*, 3: 346–73 and 4: 356–70.

[21] Donald Ostrowski, "Early Pomest'e Grants as a Historical Source," *Oxford Slavonic Papers* 33 (2000): 36–63. It remains to be demonstrated how common transfers of service land to the grantee's son were during this period.

[22] *PRP*, 4: 521–32.

him by torture. The plaintiff requested both an inquest and an investigation of the cadastral records of the Service Land Chancellery to resolve the dispute, as well as testimony from witnesses to the deed in question. The case was eventually decided by then Prince (later tsar) Vasilii Shuiskii, who ordered an extract of the cadastral records from the Service Land Chancellery as to whether and how much of the land was hereditary estate versus service land and in whose name it was registered. The Chancellery responded with a detailed memorandum that stated that the cadasters from 1562/3 showed that one-half of Shilovo, described with particularity as to metes and bounds, was held as a hereditary estate by the son of Timofei and his kinsmen. The tax records of 1574 showed that Shilovo was held by Timofei and his brother through the will of their uncle Danilo. But patrimonial estate cadasters of 1576/7, however, showed that Timofei had sold his interest and that of his brother to Andrei's son-in-law, as Andrei had contended. Although these cadastral records supported the defendant, Shuiskii nonetheless concluded on the basis of other evidence (testimony of the witnesses to these deeds) that the deed to Andrei's son-in-law was forged.[23] Thus, while the case of Timofei versus Andrei was ultimately decided on the basis of other evidence, it indicates that the Service Land Chancellery was maintaining detailed records of conveyances of hereditary estates.

That the 1562/3 and 1576/7 cadasters and the 1574 tax records should provide information as to transfers of title to hereditary estates is understandable in view of the promulgation of the Decree on Service (*Ulozhenie po sluzhbe*) in 1556.[24] Under this decree holders of all land, both hereditary estates and service land, had to provide to the tsar one mounted soldier per 100 chetverts of land. In essence the service obligation imposed on hereditary estates and service land became identical. It thus became important for the Service Land Chancellery to keep and maintain records of ownership of both service land and hereditary estates.

Another judgment charter from the late 16th century indicates greater reliance on the documentary evidence than earlier charters. In a 1597 case, the Service Land Chancellery considered the claims of two widows to maintenance allotments from their husband's service land. The claim was decided on the basis of a careful review of the various previous grants of the same lands in the chancellery's records. This is not only the first judgment charter the author has been able to locate dealing with service land, but also the first decision of the Service Land Chancellery on a contested matter.[25]

---

[23] Dewey, *Private Law*, document 58.

[24] *Polnoe sobranie russkikh letopisei*, 41 vols. (Moscow-St. Petersburg: Tip. I. N. Skorokhodova, 1846–1995), 13 (1904): 268–69.

[25] *Akty sluzhilykh zemlevladel'tsev XV–nachala XVII veka* (hereafter, *ASZ*), 3 vols. (Moscow: Izd. "Arkheograficheskii tsentr," 1997 [vol. 1]; "Pamiatniki istoricheskoi mysli," 1998 [vol. 2]; "Drevlekhranilishche," 2002 [vol. 3]), 3: 521.

The disruptions and disorder in the period of the Oprichnina and the Time of Troubles created many new issues about the validity of titles to land. Many estates were confiscated during the Oprichnina. At the conclusion of the Oprichnina, the former owners still asserted claims to these lands. Later, during the Time of Troubles, False Dmitrii II distributed many lands to those loyal to him, and the validity of these titles was called into question after the installation of the Romanov dynasty. There were also questions raised about titles given to those for "sitting out the siege" of Moscow (*za Moskovskoe osadnoe sidenie*) during the reign of Vasilii Shuiskii and during the campaign of the Polish Crown Prince Wladyslaw.[26]

The regime of Tsar Mikhail Fedorovich and his father, Patriarch Filaret, addressed and resolved nearly all of these uncertainties systematically and with alacrity. While we do not have the Statute Book of the Service Land Chancellery prior to 1613, we do have a comprehensive set of decrees promulgated after 1613 designed to address the above problems.[27] These decrees, assembled as the statute book of the Service Land Chancellery, later became the basis for Chapter XVI of the 1649 Law Code.[28] They will be summarized here chronologically.

In general, the policy of the regime was to confirm titles that had been granted or otherwise obtained in politically or legally ambiguous circumstances. For example, decrees of 1613 and 1623 confirmed titles that had been granted by False Dmitrii II.[29] These decrees later became Articles 25 and 26 of Chapter XVII of the 1649 Law Code. A decree of 1620 confirmed titles to excess lands—beyond the boundaries indicated in cadastral surveys—occupied and tilled for many years by holders of hereditary estates.[30] This decree later became Article 18 of Chapter XVII. Decrees of 1620 and 1627 confirmed titles granted for "sitting out the siege of Muscow."[31] These decrees later became Articles 16, 17, 19, 20, and 49, of Chapter XVII. A 1628 decree confirmed title to empty lands sold as hereditary estates by Ivan IV under a decree of 1572/3.[32] This became Article 45. A 1631 decree resolved the title to lands that had been left to wives and daughters in violation of Ivan IV's rules of

---

[26] For the decrees later addressing these problems, see the *Ustavnaia kniga* of the Service Land Chancellery, published in *PRP*, 5: 430–531.

[27] Ibid.

[28] *PRP*, 6: 22–448; Richard M. Hellie, *The Muscovite Law Code: The Ulozhenie of 1649* (Irvine, CA: Chas. Schlacks, 1988). Chapters of this code will be subsequently cited by Roman numerals and articles by Arabic numerals. All terminology and partial translations will follow the Hellie edition.

[29] *PRP*, 5: 436, 437.

[30] Ibid., 445–46.

[31] Ibid., 446, 450, 461.

[32] Ibid., 461.

inheritance. Such lands were granted to the women who held them as life estates, and on their death were to pass to male clan relatives.[33]

In addition to these decrees dealing with particular situations that had created uncertainty of title, the Filaret regime promulgated decrees in 1627 setting forth the general rules for inheritance of hereditary estates in some detail.[34] In general these rules required that clan hereditary estates and hereditary estates awarded for service would pass to male offspring, and only in the absence of male offspring to daughters, but that wives could succeed to purchased hereditary estates and lands given as their dowry. These rules have been described in greater detail elsewhere, and will thus not be further elaborated here.[35]

While the law relating to hereditary estates was set forth in some detail, the statute book of the Service Land Chancellery contains very few decrees on service land. A decree of 1644 deals with the requirement of obtaining permission to exchange service lands.[36] Another decree of the same year deals with maintenance allotments for widows to be granted out of service lands.[37] Otherwise, as far as extant records are concerned, the publication of detailed regulations relating to service land would have to wait until the 1649 Law Code.

Chapter XVI of the 1649 Code deals with service land and contains 69 articles, most of which concern when a transfer of service land will be registered or recorded (*rospiska,* noun; *rospisati,* verb),[38] presumably by the Service Land Chancellery, although that organ is only infrequently mentioned in Chapter XVI.[39] The consistent pattern or principle of these provisions is that a transfer of service land was void unless it was accepted for registration. Chapter XVI enumerates in some detail the types of transactions that can be registered. For example, sons' petitions to succeed to their father's service lands would be granted as long as they had not concealed any unregistered holdings (Articles 24–26). In general service lands would be divided evenly between the children of the servitors to whom the land was registered (Article 34). Articles 3–8 deal with exchanges and provide that exchanges would be registered if service landholders exchanged their land with each other, with

[33] Ibid., 466–68.

[34] Ibid., 452–99.

[35] George G. Weickhardt, "The Pre-Petrine Law of Property," *Slavic Review* 52: 4 (Winter 1993): 663–79.

[36] *PRP,* 5: 480.

[37] *PRP,* 5: 481.

[38] What was registered was not a deed (*gramota*) or entitlement (*oklad*) but "service land" (*pomest'e*). It is not clear from the language of the Code whether a document or a deed was received and filed.

[39] The Service Land Chancellery is also referenced in Chapter XVII, Article 34, quoted below.

monasteries, or with holders of hereditary estates.[40] Article 6 provided, however, that such exchanges would be invalid if not registered. Article 12 in fact specified that unregistered holdings in general would be confiscated. If holdings were unregistered, they could be registered if there were no petitions pending against the holders regarding their right to possession (Article 27). As to competing claims for the same service landholding, Article 64 provided that one had to register a transfer of service land within three months, and that if the grantee or transferee delayed in doing so beyond three months, and if someone else had previously registered a claim to the same service land, the first to petition for registration would prevail. This of course gave holders of service land a substantial incentive to register transfers as soon as possible. Article 63 provided that the boundaries to service land were to be determined by the cadastral books, even if there were testimony to the contrary.

Chapter XVI of the 1649 Law Code dealt almost exclusively with service land, except for Article 51, which provided that anyone claiming to hold lands as *hereditary estates* had to deposit hereditary estate documents with cadastral officials for their claim to be recognized as a hereditary estate. Almost all the remaining provisions on hereditary estates appear in Chapter XVII. The principle of giving priority to the first to register that we saw in Chapter XVI, Article 64, may also be seen in Chapter XVII, Article 34, which provides that if a holder of a hereditary estate sells it and gives the purchaser a deed, but then feloniously sells the same land to another purchaser, the first purchaser to register it is recognized as the owner. The other purchaser could seek his money back from the seller, but had no claim to the land. It is worth quoting this provision in full, because it represented a true innovation:

> If someone sells his own clan, or service, or purchased hereditary estate to someone, and takes the money, and gives a purchase document; but does not register that hereditary estate in the books in the Service Land Chancellery as the property of the purchaser; and subsequently he feloniously sells that same hereditary estate of his to someone else, and takes the money, and registers that hereditary estate in the books of the Service Land Chancellery as the property of the latter purchaser: that person for whom that hereditary estate is registered in the books in the Service Land Chancellery shall own that hereditary estate. Order this first purchaser not to own this hereditary estate because he, having purchased that hereditary estate, did not register it as his own in the books of the Service Land Chancellery.

---

[40] These provisions making service land alienable and inheritable were an important milestone in the process by which service land became equivalent to hereditary estates, finally effected by Peter the Great.

In sum, a deed to a hereditary estate had to be recorded with cadastral of-ficials before it could be recognized as valid, and the first to record would be given priority. What if a deed were forged or extorted, as happened in some of the judgment charters from the 16th century? Article 35 provided that if it was established that a person registered a forged deed, he was to be beaten with the knout and the land returned to its rightful owner.

The general principle running through these provisions on both service land and hereditary estates is that, in the absence of forgery or extortion, the registered owner held legally valid title to the property. Theoretically, then the Service Land Chancellery was to be the registration office for all land transfers, and absent proof of forgery or extortion, its records as to ownership were conclusive. At the same time, it maintained cadastral surveys of all properties, indicating their metes and bounds. Thus to establish who owned a piece of property and its boundaries, one, at least in theory, simply had to refer to the records of the Service Land Chancellery. In this respect the Muscovite system of recording deeds and maintaining surveys is almost equivalent to modern recording systems. Such a system cannot eliminate litigation about land titles and boundaries, but it can certainly reduce the scope of potential disputes. The lawsuits of the 15th and 16th centuries, where often one party had a deed and the other only the testimony of long-term residents, could not arise under this system, at least in theory. If one had no recorded deed, he had no legal claim to the property.

Indeed, the surviving records of post-1649 lawsuits reveal that disputes focused on narrower and simpler issues of applying the provisions of the 1649 Law Code and referring to the records of the Service Land Chancellery. For example, a case decided in 1658 involved a dispute over the amount owed on a mortgage. The mortgagee produced a document stating that the property could be redeemed only by the payment of 900 rubles. The note on record with the Service Land Chancellery was only for 70 rubles, so the document on record was deemed conclusive and the document produced by the mortgagee was determined to have been fraudulently altered.[41]

In a case decided in 1676 a childless widow had inherited her husband's purchased hereditary estate and a maintenance allotment from his service land. She petitioned for his inherited hereditary estates, which had escheated. The petition was properly denied under the provisions of the 1649 Law Code.[42]

In 1696 a dispute between a monastery and lay person over empty lands was decided in accordance with Chapter XVI, Article 63 of the 1649 Law Code. This provision, discussed above, provided that the cadastral books were to determine the right to service land, even if there was testimony to the

---

[41] *Akty otnosiashchiesia do grazhdanskoi raspravy drevnei Rossii* (hereafter, *AGR*), 2 vols. (Kiev: Tip. I. A. Davidenko, 1860–84), vol. 2, no. 121, 196–202.

[42] *AGR*, vol. 2, no. 139, 366–82.

contrary. There were also a number of later decrees involved, but the dispute was decided by reference to the cadastral books from 1581/2.[43]

To summarize the above history of the Muscovite system of registering titles, the principle was established early in the history of service land that the permission of the tsar was required to transfer service land, even if it were from a father to a son. The original concept was not so much that one had merely to record the transfer; rather one had to obtain the tsar's consent. The Service Land Chancellery eventually became the repository of all such records. The promulgation of the Decree on Service in 1556 created a need for additional central records of who owned hereditary estates.

Chapters XVI and XVII of the 1649 Law Code represent a further step in the process: they provided that a transfer of land was not valid unless it was registered and that the first to register prevailed over a subsequent registration. What was originally a regime where the holder of service land had to obtain the tsar's permission to transfer it, became a regime where the Law Code expressly stated what type of transfers were allowed and the holder merely had to register the transfer. The requirement of registration was later applied to hereditary estates as well.

In modern parlance, the first-to-register rule is called a "race" system: whoever wins the race to the recording office would have priority of title. Using a "race" system to resolve claims between private litigants was definitely a new departure in the 1649 Code. Unfortunately, none of the standard works on the origin of these provisions in the 1649 Code provide the origin of this concept. While the need to maintain accurate records of land ownership for purposes of service and tax obligations can explain the requirement of recording in general, giving priority to the first to register was not strictly necessary for purposes of tax and service obligations. It also appears to have no precedent prior to the 1649 Code.

Muscovy's race concept bears a distinct resemblance to the first modern recording statute in Western Europe, the English Statute of Enrollments of 1535, referenced above. This statute provided that no title to land

> shall pass, alter or change from one to another … except the same bargain and sale be made by writing indented and sealed and enrolled in one of the King's Courts of Record at Westminster … and the same enrollment to be had and made within six months next after the date the same writing indented.[44]

In other words, for title to pass the parties had to record a written deed with the central courts in London within six months. This provision was

---

[43] *AGR,* vol. 2, no. 180, 774–83.

[44] See full citation in n. 4 above. The spelling in the original has been updated by the author.

interpreted by English courts to mean that the first to enroll his deed would prevail, even over a deed executed earlier. While the background and history of the Statute of Enrollments is complex (and beyond the scope of this study) suffice it to say that one of the principal motivations of Henry VIII and Parliament in the requirement that a deed had to be "enrolled" to be valid was to protect and secure tax revenues from the land. The crown of course had to know who owned land in order to tax it.[45]

While clever English lawyers soon developed devices for evading the Statute of Enrollments, it was still in place in the 17th century. A strong defense of the statute published by one Fabian Phillipps in 1662 asserted that it provided a clear record of titles. In other words, Phillipps argued that the great virtue and advantage of the Statute was not protection of the royal revenue, but protection of private titles to land from competing, invalid claims. The deeds, once recorded, were stored in the Tower of London, and were available for inspection if the deeds in the lands of the parties were lost or destroyed.[46]

The Muscovite system of resolving the priorities of competing claims was remarkably similar. Whoever recorded first was prior in right, even if he had purchased the property later than a competing purchaser who had not recorded. While Phillipps argued that this was a highly reasonable rule, there are obviously other perhaps more reasonable rules for resolving priority between competing claimants who have purchased the same property. (The rule in most American states today is that the person recording a deed will secure priority over an earlier but unrecorded deed only if he or she is without actual notice of the competing claim.) Without arguing the relative merits of the two systems, suffice it to say that the Statute of Enrollments and the 1649 Law Code both adopted the same, distinctive rule: whoever records first is accorded priority. Each statute, indeed, even gave the purchaser or grantee of land a certain grace period—three months in the Muscovite statute on service land and six months in the English statute—to complete registration before the rule giving priority to the first to register took effect. This grace period was necessary because in both nations the registry was maintained in the capital and it would take a certain amount of time to register purchases or other transfers transacted in distant provinces.

---

[45] John H. Scheid, "Down Labyrinthine Ways: A Recording Acts Guide for First-Year Law Students," *University of Detroit Mercy Law Review* 80 (Fall 2002): 97–101.

[46] Fabian Phillipps, *The Reforming Registry, or, A representation of the very many mischiefs and inconveniences which will unavoidably happen by the needless, chargeable, and destructive way of registries proposed to be erected in every county of England and Wales, for the recording of all deeds, evidences, bonds, bills, and other encumbrances; written in the Year 1656 when Oliver and the Levelling–party made it their design to ruin monarchy* (London: Tho. Newcomb, 1662), 12–49.

The resemblance of the Muscovite rule to the English rule of course raises the possibility of borrowing or influence, either direct or indirect. There is, however, no direct evidence of such borrowing or influence. The author knows of no copies or summaries of the Statute of Enrollments in the Muscovite archives and no direct evidence that the Muscovites were aware of the English system. At the same time, however, the author has not located any nation or jurisdiction, other than England and Muscovy, that used the "race" system in the 17th century. The idea that Muscovy would borrow or copy an English statute seems farfetched at first blush because their legal systems were so different. Nevertheless, the following circumstantial evidence at least permits an inference of borrowing or influence.

First, the Muscovite tsardom and England developed cordial, intense and frequent commercial and diplomatic contacts starting in the reign of Ivan IV. The White Sea trade route in fact became the principal avenue of Muscovy's foreign trade. Trade with England through the White Sea flourished during the years 1554–1600, and during the last three decades of this period an average of approximately ten English ships per year arrived in the White Sea. English merchants were allowed to travel and trade within Russia, as well as set up both a rope factory and shipyard there. The Russia Company also maintained a permanent trading post in Moscow staffed by a Chief Agent, and regional trading posts in Vologda, Kholmogory, Yaroslavl', and Arkhangel'sk.[47]

The English sent frequent embassies to the tsar that were led by well-educated and commercially well-informed men: Richard Chancellor (1553–54), Anthony Jenkinson (1561–64, 1566, 1571–72), Thomas Randolph (1568–69), Daniel Sylvester (1575), Jerome Bowes (1583–84), Jerome Horsey (1580–84, 1586–87, 1589–91), Giles Fletcher (1588–89), and John Merrick (1595–97).[48] Although these embassies' primary function was to negotiate commercial arrangements, most of the men were probably well informed enough to be able to explain the English system of registering deeds. That the Russians would ask these English agents for information and assistance on non-commercial matters is demonstrated by the future Patriarch Filaret's request to Horsey that he compose a Latin grammar "in the Slavonian character."[49] Horsey also supplies a rambling and discursive account of a Church council called by Ivan IV in 1580 to coerce or persuade the monasteries not to accept any further gifts or bequests of land from lay persons. He states that Ivan at least got the monasteries to supply him with an inventory of all towns, lands, and reve-

---

[47] Thomas Stuart Willan, *The Early History of the Russia Company, 1533–1603* (Manchester: Manchester University Press, 1968), 1–50.

[48] Ibid., 50–51, 117–18, 163–64, 169–71, 172–77, 189, 224, 218–20, 241.

[49] Jerome Horsey, "Travels," in *Rude & Barbarous Kingdom: Russia in the Accounts of Sixteenth Century English Voyagers*, ed. Lloyd E. Berry and Robert O. Crummey (Madison: University of Wisconsin Press, 1968), 368.

nues in their possession.[50] Horsey does not indicate why he was invited to this council, but his account may suggest at least the possibility that Ivan sought advice on how to keep track of the ownership of land.

The tsar also sent embassies to England: Osip Nepeia Grigor'ev (called Nepea in the English sources, 1556),[51] four merchants in 1568,[52] G. A. Savin (1568),[53] F. A. Pissemskii (1582–83), Reynold Beckman (1584), G. I. Melkin (1600–01),[54] and A. I. Ziuzin (1613–14).[55] These embassies unsuccessfully sought a military alliance against the Poles and Swedes, a refuge for the tsar in England in the event he was deposed or expelled, military supplies, and credit. They successfully sought reciprocal trade agreements and artisans and experts. Among the English artisans and experts that actually came to Russia were doctors, shipwrights, rope makers, miners, architects and apothecaries. Although their number was probably not sufficient to have a major impact on the Muscovite economy, the importation of these craftsmen indicates that Ivan recognized that he was dealing with an advanced nation from which he and Muscovy had much to learn. Boris Godunov even sent four youths to study in England, although they never returned.[56]

After 1600 the English were supplanted by the Dutch as the most important trading partner using the northern route, but the English continued to send several ships a year.[57] Diplomatic contacts between the English and Russia, however, intensified in the first two decades of the 17th century. These contacts were dominated by Sir John Merrick, who served as ambassador to Russia in 1602, 1613, 1614–17, and 1620–21. Merrick also mediated the Stolbovo treaty between Russia and Sweden in 1617, earning great respect and gratitude from the tsar for his skillful and indefatigable efforts. The economic gains for the Muscovy Company were, however, not as great as anticipated. Russia, as before, desired a political and military alliance with England, and England the right to pursue trade with Persia through the Volga-Caspian route. Neither side was willing to give the other what it wanted. Merrick was,

---

[50] Ibid., 281–85.

[51] For an interesting account of Nepea and his embassy, see Samuel H. Baron, "Osip Nepea and the Opening of Anglo–Russian Commercial Relations," *Oxford Slavonic Papers*, New Series, 11 (1978): 42–63.

[52] Willan, *The Early History of the Russia Company*, 16–17.

[53] Ibid., 110.

[54] Ibid., 160–62, 167–68, 236–38.

[55] See Maija Jansson and Nikolai Rogozhin, eds., *England and the North: The Russian Embassy of 1613–1614*, trans. Paul Bushkovitch (Philadelphia: American Philosophical Society, 1994), which contains a translation of the instructions and report given to Ziuzin.

[56] Jansson, *England*, 130–31.

[57] Paul Bushkovitch, *The Merchants of Moscow, 1580–1650* (Cambridge: Cambridge University Press, 1980), 44–45.

however, able to negotiate the right to explore for iron ore, grow flax in the Vologda area, and engage in whaling. Merrick also served as the host for numerous Russian embassies to England, including those of S. I. Volinskii and M. I. Pozdeev (1617–18), I. S. Pogozevo (1621–22), and V. Esipov (1628). The Muscovy Company thereafter began to face severe financial difficulties. Approximately 90 years of cordial relations came to an end in 1649 when the tsar terminated the Company's privileges in Russia, largely in reaction to the execution of Charles I.[58] Prior to this, however, England was the Western nation with which Russia had the most contact and the most cordial relationship, with the possible exception of the Netherlands.

Second, 17th-century Muscovy demonstrated keen interest in the laws and legal institutions of Europe. A recent study by the author suggests that the Muscovites were aware of and borrowed from Western Europe certain sophisticated concepts of criminal procedure. In particular, the Muscovite system of criminal procedure bears such striking resemblances to the code known as the *Constitutio Criminalis Carolina* promulgated by the Hapsburg Emperor Charles V in 1532, that we can conclude that it probably had a strong influence on Muscovite procedure.[59] The Muscovites also translated the third Lithuanian Statute of 1588 into Russian, and it was thereafter frequently consulted as a source and in fact became the source for many provisions in the 1649 Law Code. The Ambassadorial Chancellery also kept good track of political news in general from Western Europe. The translators of the chancellery translated news and documents from the West, principally Germany, the Netherlands, England, and Sweden. These translations were compiled in collections for reading to the tsar and the boyars. In short, the chancellery made it its business to keep the tsar well informed on what was happening in Western Europe.[60]

Third, while mere similarity of legal institutions or rules does not compel an inference of borrowing, most legal historians would conclude that there was borrowing of legal rules or institutions where an unusual or highly

---

[58] Geraldine M. Phipps, *Sir John Merrick, English Merchant-Diplomat in Seventeenth-Century Russia* (Newtonville, MA: Oriental Research Partners, 1983), 1, 117–128, 136, 165, 182.

[59] George G. Weickhardt, "Probable Western Origins of Muscovite Criminal Procedure," *Russian Review* 66 (January 2007): 1, 55–72.

[60] Ingrid Maier and Wouter Pilger, "Second Hand Translation for Tsar Aleksej Mixajlovič: A Glimpse into the 'Newspaper Workshop' at *Posol'skii Prikaz* (1648)," *Russian Linguistics* 25 (2001): 209–42. The *kuranty* for 1600–1639 are published as Nina Ivanova Tarabasova et al., *Vesti–kuranty, 1600–1639 gg.* (Moscow: Izd-vo Nauka, 1972). For *kuranty* on England, see E. I. Kobzareva, "Izvestiia o sobytiiakkh v Zapadnoi Evrope v dokumentakh Posol'skogo prikaza XVII veka." (Kandidatskaia dissertatsiia, Moscow State University, 1988), where chap. 4 is entitled "Vesti ob Anglii (1642–1688 gg.)." The author, who has not seen this unpublished dissertation, is indebted to Daniel Waugh for the reference.

advanced procedure appears in a second country shortly after its introduction in the originating country, particularly where there is no domestic precedent for the procedure in the borrowing country. As far as the author can determine, the Statute of Enrollments was the first national system of recording land titles in Europe and the first to employ the "race" concept. It was thus an unusual if not unique and highly advanced statute, and, as far as the author has been able to determine, Muscovy was the only nation other than England to introduce the "race" system. While Muscovy had developed national cadasters on its own and kept records of who owned land in the Service Land Chancellery, the use of these records to resolve claims between private litigants and the adoption of a "race" recording system had no precedent in Muscovy.

When Robert Crummey published *Rude and Barbarous Kingdom* in 1968, the author suspects that he hardly anticipated that anyone would claim that English embassies to Moscow might be an avenue for the transmission of ideas about how to design a rule for priority of title based on recording deeds. But there is sufficient circumstantial evidence to suggest that this was at least a distinct possibility. Despite this evidence, the lack of any direct evidence makes it difficult to contend that it is more probable than not that the Statute of Enrollments influenced Muscovite recording practice.

Let us suppose, on the other hand, that Muscovy's race recording system was devised independently by the Muscovites shortly after its introduction in England. While this seems to the author to be a somewhat unlikely coincidence, one should nonetheless recognize that the concept of recording was homegrown, and it may have been a short step to move from keeping records relating to the ownership of land to the concept that the first to record his title had priority.

Whatever its source, this innovation put Muscovy at the forefront in Europe in its development of an advanced system for guaranteeing security of title. It provided a simple and reasonable method for notoriety and clarity of land ownership, for providing a grantee or purchaser with protection from a seller who subsequently attempts to sell the same property to someone else, and for determining priority between successive grantees. Whatever its origins, the Muscovite recording system demonstrated keen interest in security of private titles. The above account of the history of Muscovite land records shows a developing and continuing awareness of the need to eliminate uncertainty and ambiguity in land titles. This interest stemmed not only from fiscal needs, but also from the necessity of keeping track of the members of the service class who owed a duty of military service. To keep the system of taxation and military service running smoothly it was of course important not only to keep track of who owned what land, but also to provide a simple and definitive formula for resolving claims to the same land.

What Was *Chernoknizhestvo*? Black Books, Foreign Writing, and Literacy in Muscovite Magic

Valerie A. Kivelson

On April 17, 1635, two brothers, the priest Druzhin and the priest Kondratii, sat in conversation at a social gathering, drinking brew (*braga*) at Cossack Khorlamka Mastiskov's house. Having drunk themselves to the point of intoxication, as their neighbors testified they did on a regular basis, the two got into a fight, also a routine occurrence between them, and began exchanging insults. In the heat of the drunken brawl, Priest Druzhin shouted at his brother: "You ate sixteen pigs at my house, and you're a heretic too! You keep heretical black books at your house!"[1]

Aside from reducing the modern reader to fits of incredulous laughter (or at least, that's its consistent effect on me), this passage raises some puzzling questions. What is the association among these various charges? What did each of these accusations mean to the accuser, the accused, the assembled witnesses, and the court authorities who eventually heard the case? What did Priest Druzhin have in mind when he added "heretical black books" to the list of his brother's offenses? And finally, and most to the point of this article, what did these inebriated priests or any of their contemporaries think "black books" were?

The brief answer to the last question is that we really don't know. "Black books" (*chernye knigi*) and the related terms of "black book magic" (*chernoknizhestvo*) and "black book magicians" (*chernoknizhniki, chernoknizhtsy*) appear with some regularity in the official texts condemning magical practice from the beginning of the 16th century on. David Goldfrank identifies perhaps the earliest usage of the term in Iosif Volotskii's introduction to his *Prosvetitel'*, written around 1502–04. Here Iosif condemns the seductions of astrology, magic (*charodeistvo*), and black book magic as leading the credulous astray.[2]

---

[1] RGADA (Rossiiskii Gosudarstvennyi Arkhiv Drevnikh Aktov, Moscow) f. 210, stolbtsy razriadnykh stolov, Prikaznyi stol, stlb. 91, fols. 293–302.

[2] I am deeply grateful to David Goldfrank for this reference. *Skazanie i novoiavivshesia eresi novogorodskikh eretikov,* as quoted in N. A. Kazakova and Ia. S. Lur'e, *Antifeodal'nye ereticheskie dvizheniia na Rusi XIV–nachala XVI veka* (Moscow-Leningrad: AN SSSR, 1955), 471: "Toliko zhe dr'znovenie togda imeiakhu k derzhavnomu protopop Aleksei i Fedor Kuritsyn, iako nikto in. Zvezdozakoniiu bo prelezhakhu, i mnogym basno-

Rude & Barbarous Kingdom Revisited: Essays in Russian History and Culture in Honor of Robert O. Crummey. Chester S. L. Dunning, Russell E. Martin, and Daniel Rowland, eds. Bloomington, IN: Slavica Publishers, 2008, 459–72.

Will F. Ryan cites another early use of the term in the condemnations of Maksim Grek in 1525 and 1531, when he was charged with "employing sorcery against the Grand Prince, of heresy, judaizing, and practicing Hellenic and Jewish book magic [black book magic] and witchcraft."[3] These early appearances were followed swiftly by the condemnation in the *Domostroi*, a 16th-century household handbook, of "black book magic" (*chernoknizhie*), along with the use of spells, "sorcery and witchcraft as propounded in *Rafli* and almanacs [and other astrological and prognostic texts], censured books, *The Seraph*, ... and any other Devil-inspired art."[4] "Black books" make an appearance again in Grigorii Kotoshikhin's account of legal practice in Muscovy in the 1660s.

In law, the "black book magic" terminology appeared again in Peter the Great's Military Statute of 1716. Known as a path-breaking piece of Europeanizing legislation, in the area of *chernoknizhestvo*, the law perpetuated rather than altered the general set of associations with dangerous, heretical, book-based magic. It also maintained the traditional Muscovite vagueness of definition. Assuming we know what it is talking about, the new law opens by addressing a general category: "*Whoever is a CHERNOKNIZHNIK OR IDOL-WORSHIPPER.*" In its lengthy explanatory introduction, the first article of the code explains that it is the duty of a Christian subject to serve the Sovereign and Fatherland. Consequently, "because all blessing, victory and good fortune originates with the one all-powerful God," any deviation from the path of Christian righteousness threatens to undermine the blessed condition of the Fatherland. In other words, dealing with the forces of evil, as presumably *chernoknizhniki* and idol worshippers did, jeopardized Russia's good standing in the scales of divine justice, and would have immediate ramifications on the battlefield. The whiff of treason that had long characterized Muscovite ideas of *chernoknizhestvo* was now made more explicit. "For this reason," Peter's exposition continues, "all icon-worship and magic [*charodeistvo*] are strictly forbidden. And if such a one is found who engages in these or in similar superstitious or blasphemous activity, in accordance with their standing, they should be cruelly locked up in irons and whipped with a cat-o'-nine-tails or

---

tvoreniem' i astrology i charodeistvu i *chernoknizhiiu*. Sego radi mnozi k nim uklonishasia, i pograizosha vo glubine otstupleniia."

[3] W. F. Ryan, *The Bathhouse at Midnight: An Historical Survey of Magic and Divination in Russia*, Magic in History (University Park: Pennsylvania State University Press, 1999). The records of Maksim Grek's trials are published in N. N. Pokrovskii, *Sudnye spiski Maksima Greka i Isaka Sobaki* (Moscow: Glav. arkhivnoe upravlenie, 1971).

[4] *The Domostroi: Rules for Russian Households in the Time of Ivan the Terrible*, ed. and trans. Carolyn Johnson Pouncy (Ithaca, NY: Cornell University Press, 1994), 112–13. See discussion in Ryan, *Bathhouse at Midnight*, 21, 84, 226–27. Embodying Muscovite ambivalence about magic, late copies of the *Domostroi* include as appendices various magical handbooks of healing, of the sort specifically proscribed in the text. See *Domostroi* (St. Petersburg: Nauka, Peterburgskoe otdelenie, 1994).

burned altogether." Still unsatisfied with the clarity of his explanation, Peter provided yet more elaboration, this time in a section labeled "Explanation":

> The punishment of burning is the usual form of execution for *cherno-knizhtsy*, and also for those who effect harm on others through poison or through writings or words, defile the name of God, or turn from him.[5]

As all of these prohibitions illustrate, unsanctioned books, particularly the imported writings of ancient or foreign traditions of astrology and high magic, were critical pieces in a Muscovite notion of what defined black-book magic and made it uniquely terrifying. But, as we will see, not only suspicious books of high learning but also any act of writing outside of officially authorized venues aroused such fears. *Chernoknizhestvo* drew together in its terrifying ambit these most dreaded behaviors conceivable in a Muscovite imagination: heresy, that is, renouncing the Orthodox God and Jesus in pursuit of other, darker powers; treason, in its direct threat to the interests of the state and more indirect threats to the state's agents and the overall social order; and unsanctioned writing, which held an uncontainable potential to unleash all the furies of heresy, treason, and lawlessness. The notion that the very worst forms of magic involved uncontrolled uses of literacy surfaces in uses of the term *chernoknizhestvo* in a broad range of contexts. It was expressed by churchmen and lawmakers in council and decree, and by soldiers, priests, and peasants in situations like the one just described, involving plenty of alcohol, which so frequently accompanied the exchange of such charges.

Black book magic was a charge so heinous that few would articulate the words and even fewer had the guts to carry through on an accusation in court. The term, though frequently condemned in ecclesiastical texts and law codes, enters the transcripts of actual trials rather rarely. Of 250 17th-century trials for magic and witchcraft that I have examined, a grand total of 6 involve charges of keeping black books. Three of the cases were initiated not against the purported holder of black books, but in their defense, with charges of slander against those who had invoked the terms in the first place. In October 1674, *zhilets* Andrei Ivanov syn Bezobrazov submitted a petition in the governor's office in Torzhok, complaining that his first cousin, Vasilii Mikhailov syn Bezobrazov, had slandered Andrei's stepbrother, Ivan Tulubeev, by calling Tulubeev "a *chernoknizhets* and heretic." The machinery of state immediately cranked into motion. The local governor, following orders sent from Moscow, investigated more fully and eked out the full story. All concerned parties admitted that they had gotten into a fight in the governor's office, a

---

[5] *Zakonodatel'nye akty Petra I: Pervaia chetvert' XVIII v.*, Pamiatniki russkogo prava, vyp. 8, ed. K. A. Sofronenko (Moscow: Gosudarstvennoe izdatel'stvo iuridicheskoi literatury, 1961), 321, 485.

fight provoked by a feud over property within the extended Bezobrazov-
Tulubeev family. Vasilii Bezobrazov admitted that he had called Ivan Tulubeev a heretic in the heat of the moment, even though, in actuality, he knew
of no heretical leanings on Ivan's part. "And in this he freely admits his guilt
before the sovereign." "But," Vasilii insisted, "he, Vasilii, did *not* call Ivan
Tulubeev a *chernoknizhets*, and with that Andrei Bezobrazov slanders him
with no basis"[6]

Vasilii's reluctance to admit to having added *chernoknizhets* to the list of
aspersions, slanderous and otherwise, is odd, given that he not only freely admitted to libeling his cousin with the label of "heretic," but also cheerfully
added to his charges the information that his uncle's stepson was a "known
criminal." Moreover, Vasilii was not shy about venting his personal animosity
against Tulubeev in the court of law. Describing the infamous fight with his
relatives in the governor's office, he testified:

> in that argument I, your slave, called … Ivan Tulubeev a heretic with-
> out any malice of purpose [*bez khitrosti*], because he, Ivan Tulubeev
> told my uncle Ivan and his son Andrei to destroy me, your slave, ut-
> terly and [he] took my little *pomest'e* and little peasants and little
> house and held them for five years or more.[7]

But, presumably because the term evoked such unspeakable evil, he dug in
his heels at confessing to calling his arch-foe a *chernoknizhets*. Even when
faced with torture, he insisted that he had not used that word.

The next case involves a completely different cast of characters but reads
remarkably similarly, even including charges of keeping "black books" purportedly made and denied between brothers, and an elusive connection to the
period of urban and regimental rebellions of 1662. According to a denunciation submitted to the Military Chancellery in Moscow, Ivan Iakovlev syn
Alekhanov had participated in looting the home of the prominent merchant
Vasilii Shorin during the Moscow riots of 1662, or at least he had in his possession several items—a woman's headdress and a kaftan of azure damask
linen—which had been stolen from Shorin's house at that time. The denunciation also charged Ivan with keeping "black books" in his house. The accusation was submitted in the name of Ivan's brother, *razriadnyi sytnik* Maksim
Iakovlev syn Alekhanov. When questioned, Ivan denied all charges, including possession of black books, and further, maintained that the handwriting

---

[6] RGADA f. 210, Belgorodskii stol, stlb. 768, fols. 57–68, 93–95; quotes on fols. 93–94.
The third case where black books are brought up in a slander suit brought against the
person who mentioned black books in the first place is RGADA f. 210, Prikaznyi stol,
stlb. 2630, 70 fols. (continued in stolbtsy 2640 and 2646).

[7] RGADA f. 210, Belgorodskii stol, stlb. 768, fol. 56.

on the petition was not his brother's, although he could not identify whose it was. Interestingly, when the brother was questioned, he supported this story.

> On November 4, 1672, Maksim and Ivan Alekhanovy appeared in the Military Chancellery. And Maksim's petition against his brother Ivan was read aloud and shown [to him], and Maksimko was questioned about whether he had submitted that petition to the Sovereign. Maksimko, having heard and seen the petition, said in questioning that he did not write it and did not submit it to the sovereign. He doesn't know who wrote it and submitted it. And he knows of no such criminality associated with his brother Ivan.[8]

When the brothers' houses in their village in Iaroslavl' Province were searched, investigators discovered neither the stolen goods nor any trace of black books. The case appears to be another odd instance of slander, with no one taking responsibility for having raised the specter of black books.

A black-book charge apparently bumped a case up to a higher level of seriousness, perhaps because of its redolence of both heresy and treason. In a legal culture where accuser was as likely as accused to end up in the torture chamber, dangling from the strappado as burning hot pincers were applied to the body and the knout exercised its persuasion, few accusers were bold or committed enough to stand behind such a charge. In the following case as well, the tip-off about black books and magic serving patently treasonous ends came from an anonymous source whose identity was never established. In 1694, an anonymous denunciation reached the authorities, charging cellarer Nikifor of the Kirillov monastery in Beloozero of living in sin with a woman named Kat'ia and doing "disgusting things" with her and with other monks. Proceeding to the heart of the matter, the denunciation informed the young co-rulers, Ivan Alekseevich and Peter Alekseevich that "they want to bewitch Tsar Peter Alekseevich and your tsaritsa and your children to death using roots and grasses…. And they have black books."[9] Black books in this case remain unspecified, undefined, but they are clearly implicated in lethal, treasonous magic. The context suggests that black books contain malefic spells with which to work harm, or with which to bewitch the other suspicious ingredients—roots and grasses—involved in the case.

Another deadly serious charge of keeping back books comes from Vologda, from the year 1677. This is finally an instance that offers us a clear picture of what 17th-century Muscovites had in mind when they threw about charges of keeping "black books." In this snowballing case, which drew ever increasing numbers of suspects into its maw, accusations were at first exchanged among the clerks, serfs, and slaves of *stol'nik* Fedor Tikhonov syn

---

[8] RGADA f. 210, Prikaznyi stol, stlb. 672, fols. 54–128; quotes from fols. 64, 70, 70ob.

[9] RGADA f. 210, Prikaznyi stol, stlb.1677, 58 fols.; quote from fols. 17–18.

Zykov but quickly escalated to higher levels of society. Ultimately, the drag-
net swept a number of clerks of the Moscow chancelleries into its net and
even pointed toward a man at the very pinnacle of Kremlin power, boyar
Artamon Sergeevich Matveev, until very recently top advisor to the tsar. The
story is complex, but many of the details are important. In 1677, according to
the court records, Zykov's peasant Vaska Alekseev ran away from his landlord's estate, carrying with him a counterfeit manumission document that he
himself had copied from a template in his master's household and signed by
forging his master's signature. "Fedor Zykov questioned people in his household about that emancipation document, using force to make them speak. His
slave Vaska Tatarinov said that, while cleaning out the bailiff's documents, he
wrote out a manumission document for himself and forged Fedor's signature
on it." Tatarinov attested that another of Fedor's men, Mishka Svashevskoi,
possessed another such counterfeit manumission. In addition, Vaska Tatarinov told his master, "Mishka Svashevskoi has *black books*, and Mishka copied
them from books that belonged to Boyar Artemon Sergeevich Matveev. And
he, Fedor, did not question his people more but ordered all of them clapped
in irons and informed the boyars about it." Mishka Svashevskoi and the two
Vaskas, Vaska Alekseev and Vaska Tatarinov, were carted to Moscow and
interrogated.

Questioned before the assembled boyars in the Golden Hall in the Moscow Kremlin, Miskha Svashevskoi said: "Vaska has a notebook hidden in the
floor of the porch of Fedor's house, written in his own hand. *And in it is written a renunciation of Christ God.*" Vaska reversed the charges, saying:

> Mishka has *black books*, and he knows that he does because three
> weeks or so ago Mishka showed him a notebook with his own hands
> at Fedor's house on the porch, and that notebook was written in
> Mishka's hand.

Like witnesses in the previous cases, Vaska noted that Mishka had boasted to
him of his black books "while drunk," but unlike the witnesses in the previous cases, Vaska maintained that the charge was absolutely true. "Mishka
was drunk, but those letters lie in Mishka's storeroom, in the ground.... And
Vaska saw a renunciation of Christ God written out in that notebook. Mishka
told Vaska that he kept that book and he would look at it, but he hadn't read
it. If he would start to read it without knowing what he was doing, he would
never rid himself of demons [*besy*]."[10]

Checking into the veracity of the story, the boyar court dispatched a high-
ranking State Secretary to investigate. In Mishka Svashevskoi's storeroom, a
box with letters was taken out of the ground. "And in the box was a notebook

---

[10] RGADA f. 210, Prikaznyi stol, stlb. 749, 385 fols.; and stlb. 734, fols. 115–203; quotes
from stlb. 734, fols. 115–17.

with twelve pages, and of those, 5 were written on…. On the first page was a spell about the cooling of a husband and wife (i.e., failure of sexual relations). On that same page … and onto the next page was written a spell for withstanding torture. On that same page in two lines and on the following four pages was written a renunciation of faith and of the Lord God himself, and a spell for calling demons [*besy*] and for seducing the female sex…."[11]

This case provides exactly the evidence we need to figure out the puzzle of "black books." Black books, in this case, are precisely what one might expect: books of maleficent magic, involving both renunciation of God and the summoning of demons or devils to one's aid. Christine Worobec's formulation looks pretty close to summing up the whole story: a *chernoknizhnik*, she says, is "a person who plies his trade with the aid of a black book." A black book, as we have just seen, is a book of dark magic spells, probably one that includes an explicit renunciation of the Christian god and therefore inherently heretical. The anecdotal evidence of our handful of cases also suggests that books might earn the label of "black" when they or their users bore some mark of treason, whether through overt participation in a riot or conspiracy to assassinate the tsar or less blatant but equally treasonous small scale actions, like forging emancipation documents that would undermine the laws of the realm and the authority of both tsar and master.[12]

Lest the picture look too clear, however, it is worth noting that not all the spells in the Mishka Svashevskoi's "black" notebook were demonic. Some called upon the protection of the saints or reworked popular prayers: "And in that notebook on the last page was drawn a cross in a circle and on the cross and around it was written: *God's holy saints …. Immortal saints have mercy on us.*" Along with the spell about the cooling of husband and wife were also found a copy of "The Dream of the Virgin," one of the most popular apocryphal prayers used in magical incantation, and a prayer about Paraskeva Piatnitsa.[13]

---

[11] RGADA f. 210, Prikaznyi stol, stlb. 749; and stlb. 734, fols. 115–203; quotes from stlb. 734, fols. 117–18.

[12] Christine Worobec, "Witchcraft Beliefs and Practices in Prerevolutionary Russian and Ukrainian Villages," *Russian Review* 54: 2 (1995): 165–87, here 169. Ryan dismisses Worobec's definition as "an over-literal guess" (*Bathhouse at Midnight*, 258n89).

[13] RGADA f. 210, Prikaznyi stol, stlb. 734, fol. 118. On Paraskeva Piatnitsa, see Joanna Hubbs, *Mother Russia: The Feminine Myth in Russian Culture* (Bloomington: Indiana University Press, 1988), chap. 4, "The Coming of Christianity: Mary and Paraskeva-Piatnitsa," 87–123; Eve Levin, "The Christian Sources of the Cult of St Paraskeva," in *Letters from Heaven: Popular Religion in Russia and Ukraine*, ed. John-Paul Himka and Andriy Zayarnyuk (Toronto: University of Toronto, 2006), 126–45. On "The Dream of the Virgin," see Ryan, *Bathhouse at Midnight*, 298–300; *Sny Bogoroditsy: Issledovaniia po antropologii religii*, ed. Zh. V. Kormina, A. A. Panchenko, and S. A. Shtyrkov, Studia ethnologica, vyp. 3 (St. Petersburg: Evropeiskii un-t v Sankt-Peterburge, 2006).

As evident in the small number of cases in which the term "black book" occurs, the use of this powerful label was a risky business, and not surprisingly was quite rare. Other formulations referring to magical texts were employed far more frequently than "black books" or its derivatives in both decrees against magic and in the accusations and trial testimony of the 17th century. Fortunetelling or divination books, prognostic texts, spell books, notebooks, or simply letters/writings (*pis'ma*) play a role in 49 of the 225 cases I have examined, and their content is often similar to that of Mishka Svashevskoi's black books, though usually without the renunciation of Christ or God, and without identifiably treasonous intent. Mikishka Ondreev, a transient hunter-trapper, was arrested in the fortress town of Ilimsk in Siberia for carrying a whole library of "magical" or "witchcraft letters" (*vorozhebnye pis'ma*). His "letters" included:

> in Mikishka Ondreev's hand "the Dream of the Mother of God," and a prayer to St. Catherine, martyr of God; and a prayer about the dream of the Lord's Vicar Jesus, written out in Mikishka's hand. And among those letters they found a prayer of Christ's martyr St. Catherine, in Mikishka's hand. And another letter had suns [drawn on it] and a cross drawn in his, Mikishka's, hand. And the third letter had spells for hunting wild animals. The fourth letter had spells for moving cleanly (?), not in Mikishka's handwriting. The fifth was a spell to seduce women. The sixth letter had other spells. Also: a prayer to the Mother of God and to the Son; a written spell against impotence; a spell to cure hernias and toothache and against various misfortunes; a spell to make peasants fear him, Mikishka; and a spell to catch fish....
>
> And among those same letters were found a prayer in an unknown language, not Russian, but written in Russian [letters].[14]

These "letters" are not labeled "black books" in this case, or in dozens like it, but the population and the authorities were sufficiently suspicious of this kind of unauthorized writing, even with apparently benign content (such as prayers) and apparently benign intent (such as catching fish), to arrest, interrogate, torture, and punish those who copied or kept them. The inclusion, in poor Mikishka's case, of a text "in an unknown language, not Russian, but written in Russian letters," undoubtedly made his situation all the worse. An unfortunate Armenian mercenary found himself under fierce interrogation and subject to merciless rounds of torture when his Muscovite comrades dis-

---

[14] RGADA f. 214, stlb. 586, ll. 7–15; quote on fols. 11–13. On supplicatory prayers as part of magical ritual, see Eve Levin, "Supplicatory Prayers as a Source for Popular Religious Culture in Muscovite Russia," in *Religion and Culture in Early Modern Russia and Ukraine*, ed. Samuel H. Baron and Nancy Shields Kollmann (DeKalb: Northern University Press, 1997), 96–114.

covered that he had words in a strange and unknown language tattooed on his back. Logically enough the "strange and unknown language" turned out to be Armenian, and the text a nostalgic paean to his distant homeland, but the Muscovites were hard to dissuade from their idée fixe that with foreign letters on his back, he must have some kind of nefarious magic up his sleeve.[15]

When found in combination with a suspicious root, a book in a foreign language added up to such a potent symbol of magical power that a vagrant monk and a stable hand paired up and made quite a nice living for a while in the 1690s by conning people into paying for their feigned fortunetelling. After the stableman's father-in-law gave them a book in some foreign language, supposedly meant for telling fortunes, the two decided "to claim that they knew how to tell fortunes [*vorozhit'*], so they would be able to collect money." They "went among the monks and among all ranks of Kolomna residents to their houses with that book, and, not having any idea what they were doing, looked purposely as if they were reading that book, and told fortunes. Pouring water into vessels, they would look in that water and pretend to tell fortunes, and pretend to drive out unclean spirits." As their business took off, they added to their repertory roots for curing stomach pain. "As part of a thorough investigation, that book was shown to those people who know the languages of other lands so that someone could read it, but such a person did not appear in Kolomna."[16] Equipped with roots and mysterious writing, the men walked a fine line between harmless healing and dangerous witchcraft, but since their business never verged on the treasonous and their counterfeit magic never touched on the demonic, no one thought to label their mysterious foreign book a "black book." Foreign magical texts, especially in conjunction with roots and herbs, drew the suspicion of neighbors and the ire of the authorities, but did not quite suffice to earn the terrible name of black book magic.

A common feature that unites these cases, whether or not they involved black books, points to a third important and dangerous aspect of magic involving forbidden texts in 17th-century Muscovy: magic was most sharply feared when it involved not only heresy and treason, but also the possession and creation of texts in unsupervised venues by unauthorized individuals. Muscovites were obsessed with control and regulation, with eliminating disorderly spontaneity and with retaining a monopoly on all avenues of power and control for those officially invested with the authority of church and state. With its general ability to empower the self-seeking, disruptive elements of

---

[15] RGADA f. 210, Prikaznyi stol, stlb. 152, fols. 57–78, 79–83.

[16] RGADA f. 210, Prikaznyi stol, stlb. 2565, fols. 286–95, 458–61, quotes from fols. 286–88. On the magical significance of foreign words, see A. S. Lavrov, *Koldovstvo i religiia v Rossii, 1700–1740 gg.* (Moscow: Drevlekhranilishche, 2000), 131.

society, the pen posed a clear and present danger when wielded by the wrong people.

In a clear illustration of the anxiety incurred by undisciplined literacy, an anonymous and decidedly suspicious set of papers found on the stairs of the governor's office in Beloozero in 1694 precipitated an investigation at the highest level, focused entirely on the act of writing. Heading up the stairs to work early one morning, a guard discovered a kerchief tied with a thread. Untying it, he discovered some kind of official-looking document, sealed with an official seal, and several papers with writing. Terrified by his discovery, he rushed directly to the governor's home, presumably waking him up, so he could hand over the incriminating papers. The governor too was appalled by the horror that had landed in his lap: the forged official document was sealed over his own name, thereby implicating him in the seditious act of abusing the sovereigns' names (an act formally defined as treason in the 1649 law code). Claiming that he hadn't dared read the other papers, he sent them directly to the co-tsars, Ivan and Peter Alekseevich, and boyars in the Chancellery of the Great Palace in Moscow. There, having viewed the texts in question and having found them to be a perplexing list of numbers, the sovereigns determined the case to be one of "criminality and sorcery and evil intention." The high-ranking official dispatched to investigate carried explicit orders to round up and torture anyone identified as suspiciously literate.

> You should search around the monastery to find out whose handwriting is on those letters and who composed them and wrote them and threw them [on the steps] anonymously, and show them to as many people as possible…. to find out if they know whose handwriting it is. If no one recognizes the handwriting…. then investigate to find out whether there are … people of any rank or prisoners sent from Moscow who might engage in such criminal plots or from among upstanding people or servants or servitors in the settlements outside of the monastery or people of any rank whatsoever, men or women, widows or girls, who might themselves know how to read and write, because anonymous letters can sometimes turn out to be from women.

Once the suspects were locked up in chains, the orders specified that they should not under any circumstances be given those controlled substances: pen or ink. Along with a large number of guards, the investigating official brought along an executioner from Moscow to carry out the multiple rounds of torture and ultimate execution of those convicted in this flagrant abuse of literacy, with its direct connotations of sorcery, heresy, and treason.[17]

---

[17] RGADA f. 210, Belgorodskii stol, stlb. 1032, fols. 11–13, 165–183.

Writing itself carried weighty and ambivalent potential, powerfully effective when wielded in appropriate ways; dangerous and unpredictable when uncontrolled. Some of the perceived potency of the materiality of the written word is evident in a pattern of punishment for possession or copying of magical texts. In a cruel mirroring of the offenses committed, the sentence issued to one of the men implicated along with Mishka Sashevskoi for copying and keeping books of spells read "he should be beaten with the knout and *all those spells should be burned on his back*, and he should be exiled with his wife and children to Siberia and registered as an agricultural peasant."[18] The texts themselves were evidently not problematic enough to merit suppression, since they were to be officially inscribed on his flesh; it was the unauthorized act of writing that was actionable.

The focus on the act of writing surfaces again in another case, typical of many. In April 1647, Iurii Shestakov, a clerk of the Zemskii prikaz, informed against Garasimko Kostiantinov, a servant of the New Savior Monastery in Kozlov on the grounds that he, Iurii had witnessed that servant reading some kind of "untoward" document (*neistovye pis'ma*). Iurii tore the document out of the servitor's hands, and immediately turned it in to the authorities under seal. The authorities—a highly placed lot including boyars and other men of duma rank—viewed this blatant act of spontaneous reading and writing (understood as "criminality") of unidentifiable documents (called "heretical notebooks," without reference to content) as seriously as did the clerk Iurii. The boyars questioned Garasimko closely about the origins and nature and explanation of his literacy. On April 30th, the very day after receiving Iurii's denunciation, they interrogated Garaskimko:

> about whether those heretical notebooks (*ereticheskie tetratki*) were his and whether he wrote them and who taught him such criminality (*vorovstvo*) and from whom he copied them.
>
> And the servitor Garasimko in questioning said that he learned to write from the same master as the clerk Iurii Shestakov, but afterwards, during his wanderings, he forgot how to write, and he learned to write again from Iurii Shestakov and Iurii gave him many letters in his own hand to copy. And for the sake of learning, he copied those letters, but whether he copied out the notebooks or not, he doesn't remember.

Now that Iurii himself had been incriminated, he too was called upon to testify. He admitted that he and Garasimko had indeed learned to write from the same master, and in fact they had been close friends and lived together for

---

[18] RGADA f. 210, Prikaznyi stol, stlb. 734, fol. 198. Other cases of spells being burned onto the backs of their owners: ibid., fols. 115–203. See also stlb. 749; stlb. 567, fols. 202–06.

many years. Nonetheless, he protested rather unconvincingly, Garasimko hadn't returned from his wanderings to study with him, and moreover Garaskimko couldn't possibly have learned to write from him, because Garasimko was years older than he, Iurii. As a defense against Garasimko's innuendos, Iurii protested that he had served the sovereign faithfully by informing against his criminal friend with the unfettered literacy. Equating Garasimko's possession of the peculiar writing with *murder*, Iurii protested that "in your sovereign decrees and in the *Ulozhenie* law code it says that if someone truthfully informs in murder cases [*dushegubnye dela*] and worthily informs you, sovereign, and leads truthfully to identifying criminals, and if the criminals speak against them during torture because of hostility, then by your sovereign decree it is ordered *not* to believe their denunciations."

On the first day of the trial, the notebooks themselves were produced in evidence. The record laconically remarks "in those same notebooks according to the investigation was written over and over again in many places: *slave of God, Garasim.*" The harmless content did nothing to allay the court's fears. In fact, they ignored the content entirely and focused monomaniacally on the handwriting and the act of writing. Presiding Boyar Ivan Morozov insisted that Garasimko should write out those same words in the presence of the court, so that his writing could be compared with the incriminating document. "And the notebooks were shown to Garaskimko. And having looked at the notebooks, Garasimko said: It is possible that writing is his writing, but honestly, he can't identify it because he wrote a lot during the course of his studies."

Garasimko's testimony and defense also focused on the act of writing, which he attempted to diffuse as an issue by arguing that he had no deliberate plans or intentions in mind while copying out texts. Repeatedly harping on his simplicity and lack of forethought or intent, he explained that when he was a boy, in Voronezh Province,

> walking along the road, I found some writing—two notebooks with spells against gunshot wounds. And being stupid from birth, not knowing how to write, I started to copy out one of the notebooks and it was my first attempt at writing.... I found those writings and copied one of the notebooks from stupidity, not knowingly, from simplicity. And now I, unfortunate one, lie under guard. I am oozing pus from the wounds resulting from torture. Wretched and in great deprivation, I am perishing and dying of hunger.

Garasimko was lucky; his disclaimers proved effective. For his dreadful crime of copying out a few words, he was "tortured harshly and raised twice on the strappado, and given 42 blows, and his head was shaved, and water was poured on his head, and he was burned hard," but in the end, he was released on surety.[19]

Texts belonged in the sanctioned venues and in the hands of authorized clerics and officials, not in the pockets of wandering hunters, stablemen, or lowly monastic servants. When writing escaped the corridors of power and floated free among the population, serfs and slaves might forge emancipation documents, in effect stealing the power of official words for their own lawless ends. Anonymous writers might undermine the integrity of the sovereigns' officials and laws, and unscrupulous swindlers might use the aura of foreign writing to cozen the credulous out of their hard-earned cash. That the mysterious power of the pen could effect such inversions of established hierarchies gave compelling support to the assumption that unchecked literacy and magic were linked in some perilous fashion. Even when deployed by clerks like Vaska Andreev and Mishka Svashevskoi, whose jobs involved their writing skills, writing outside the safe confines of those official functions—for pleasure, in pursuit of private goals, or just for the sake of writing—incurred suspicion and carried a degree of risk.[20]

At a practical level, Muscovites' anxieties about magical texts reveal an underlying suspicion of the written word and appreciation of its awesome power. Writing of any kind exercises a magical power to conjure forth images, ideas, out of thin air, to record distant events and to keep track of people, goods, and movement across time and space. Words can even summon the non-existent into being. In a culture profoundly shaped by Christianity's emphasis on Jesus as the Word incarnate, as Claudio Ingerflom has pointed out, words, whether in textual or oral incarnation, exercised a strong magic even within the sanctioned rites of the Church.[21] When they escaped the confines of the church, even perfectly ordinary prayers could take on disruptive, atomistic power. And when those words were incomprehensible ones, be-

---

[19] RGADA f. 210, Prikaznyi stol, stlb. 565, fols. 6–21.

[20] On the isomorphism between the fear of magic and the suspicion of private goals, see Andrei L'vovich Toporkov, "Gramota No. 521: Zagovor ili liubovnaia zapiska?" in *Slovo i kul'tura*, vol. 2, ed. T. A. Agapkina et al. (Moscow: Indrik, 1998), 230–41.

[21] Claudio Sergio Ingerflom, "How Old Magic Does the Trick for Modern Politics," paper presented at the AAASS, Washington, DC, November 2006. Words, whether written or oral, are imbued with magical power in many (most?) cultures, but in Christian cultures, that magic may be expressed within a particularly Christian context. See, for instance, Ryan's chapters on "Texts as Amulets" and "Magic of Letter and Number," *Bathhouse at Midnight*, 293–337. On meaning in writing in non-Christian cultures, the literature is vast, but see for instance, Gülru Necipoğlu, *The Topkapı Scroll: Geometry and Ornament in Islamic Architecture. Topkapı Palace Museum Library MS H. 1956; with an essay on the geometry of the muqarnas by Mohammad al-Asad* (Santa Monica, CA: Getty Center for the History of Art and the Humanities, 1995); Christian de Pee, *The Writing of Weddings in Middle-Period China: Text and Ritual Practice in the Eighth through Fourteenth Centuries* (Albany: State University of New York Press, 2007).

cause they were foreign, because they were muttered or whispered as was the norm for Russian sorcerers or fortunetellers (*sheptuny*—"whisperers"), or because they were written down in a largely illiterate society, their mystery and their magical might increased all the more.

In the lived context of everyday name-calling and drunken brawls, Muscovites appear to have applied a definition of black books and black-book magic that cleaved fairly closely to the meanings attributed to the terms in official texts. Charges of black books remained rare and were often denied under pressure, suggesting a degree of fear and awe that lingered around these particular terms because of their association with specifically heretical, treasonous leanings and foreign, unchristian learning. However, the particular dread of black books drew on a broader suspicion evident in Muscovite society. The horror of *chernoknizhestvo* displayed in intensified form a far more generalized fear of literacy run amuck, of illicit copying and circulation of texts, and of the capacity of writing to serve the disruptive ends of subversive individuals instead of the authorized goals of sanctioned hierarchy.

Women and the Russian Military, 1650–1730: A Preliminary Survey

Carol B. Stevens

"Soldiers alone do not make an army."[1] As military historians have long acknowledged, there is far more to an army than the combatants themselves; logistics, training, finances, propaganda, and recruitment are among the many topics that have received specialized study. A field that remains somewhat less well studied is that of women and war, even though, during the early modern period in Europe, and perhaps elsewhere, "at no time were so many women engaged in warfare."[2] This engagement included a particularly broad variety of occupations and activities, and it provides a glimpse, albeit fleeting, into the lives of women at a time when their voices are rarely heard outside of elite circles.

In the early modern era, women's involvement in military life was largely informal and supportive; nonetheless, it had an important, indirect relationship to the military establishments of a variety of European countries. To explain: As a prolific school of historiography testifies, the role of governments in controlling and appropriating social violence, and then in raising, fielding, and supporting armies and navies, underwent significant changes between the 15th and 18th centuries. By the late 19th century, most European states mustered armies and navies staffed largely by their nationals. These armies and navies were military establishments supported by complex public systems of finance, recruitment, food, and military supply. There was every expectation, politically and socially, that governments were responsible for the creation and maintenance of such military systems. In preceding centuries, however, few of these statements would have been true. First of all, violence and the use of force had not been exclusively harnessed to governmental entities. Further, many European armies and navies relied upon the semi-private recruitment of combatants such as mercenaries and privateers.

---

[1] Holly A. Mayer, *Belonging to the Army* (Columbia: University of South Carolina Press, 1996), 1. My thanks to Philip Uninsky, as always, for his editorial comments and to Brian Davies for his recommendations.

[2] Brian Crim, "Silent Partners: Women and Warfare in Early Modern Europe," in *A Soldier and A Woman: Sexual Interaction in the Military*, ed. Gerard J. De Groot and Corinna Peniston-Bird (New York: Pearson Education, 2000), 27, with specific reference to the period 1500–1650.

Rude & Barbarous Kingdom Revisited: Essays in Russian History and Culture in Honor of Robert O. Crummey. Chester S. L. Dunning, Russell E. Martin, and Daniel Rowland, eds. Bloomington, IN: Slavica Publishers, 2008, 473–90.

Perhaps even more noticeably, military support systems were not the exclusive province of government. Off the field of battle, taxes were collected by tax farmers; provisions were mustered by contractors and requisitioned by combatants themselves, and so on. Closer to the troops themselves, military support systems were also sustained by impromptu and unacknowledged, as well as quasi-governmental, actors. Sutlers, gunsmiths, military advisors, laundresses, nurses, cooks, prostitutes, tailors, local foragers, and many others supported the daily rounds of military men on and off the battlefield. As many as half of the non-combatants that followed an army could be women. [3] Many had personal connections to the troops as well as working for and with them. Military families contributed not only labor, but a sense of community vital to the combatants' well-being and military abilities. In these and other ways, then, women in the early modern period played a critical role in sustaining European troops on and off the battlefield; their private actions helped sustain rudimentary and developing military support systems and in many respects made possible the functioning of early modern armies and navies. Although such contributions were sometimes vital, military establishments reacted to informal support in a variety of ways, attempting with mixed success to acknowledge, transform, control, or even ban it. [4]

Russian armies of the early modern period differed in a variety of ways from their counterparts further west. They had larger proportions of cavalry, for example, and in the 17th century many troops served for a single season or campaign at a time. [5] Despite such differences, one is prompted to wonder about Russian equivalents to the informal, private, or semi-official military support systems that were so important further west. Some elements of this question, such as the recruitment and role of mercenaries in the 17th-century army, have received some research attention. [6] However, there has been little

---

[3] Barton C. Hacker and Margaret Vining, "The World of Camp and Train: Women's Changing Roles in Early Modern Armies," http://www.assostoria.it/Armisovrano/Hacker-Vining.pdf (accessed April 2008), 3–4.

[4] For West European armies, it is particularly noticeable that attempts to ban camp-followers intensified in the early 19th century. Cf. Barton C. Hacker, "Women and Military Institutions in Early Modern Europe: A Reconnaissance," *Signs* 6: 4 (1981): 643–71.

[5] See Robert Frost, *The Northern Wars: War, State, and Society in Northeastern Europe* (New York: Longman, 2000), for some contrasts. Peter Perdue, "Military Mobilization in Seventeenth- and Eighteenth-Century China, Russia, and Mongolia," *Modern Asian Studies* 30 (1996): 757–93, contrasts Russian military support systems with those of China.

[6] For example, William M. Reger, IV, "Baptizing Mars: The Conversion to Russian Orthodoxy of European Mercenaries during the Mid-Seventeenth Century," in *The Military and Society in Muscovy, 1450–1917*, ed. Eric Lohr and Marshall Poe (Leiden: Brill, 2002); and Reger, "In the Service of the Tsar : European Mercenary Officers and the

discussion of Russian non-combatants, whether they were officially recognized by the Crown or not. Women's participation in such support systems has received practically no attention, although some related research has centered on the impact that the growing military establishment and its institutions had on women's lives in the late and post-Petrine period.[7] This paper offers a very preliminary survey of the more informal support systems of the Russian military with a particular focus on women within them. It demonstrates that women did in fact play a role in the Russian military: a few as combatants and campfollowers, and others as the basis of military communities on and off the battlefield.

There were, of course, women combatants—in Russia, as in North America and in Europe. Those women anywhere who abandoned more supportive roles to carry ammunition, load cannon, evacuate the wounded, and exhort the troops on the battlefield are sometimes numbered among these. In Russia, Nadezhda Durova's actions as a Hussar officer fighting against Napoleon are perhaps best known, thanks to Mary Zirin's translation of her memoir. Durova's enrollment in the military followed an apparently failed marriage; she saw active service in 1807 and again 1812–15.[8] She is not a solitary example. There were others, such as "Katia," a woman who fought with Muscovite troops during the Livonian War (1558–82); she reputedly participated in four battles before her death, as noted by a chronicler.[9] Women's major military contributions were not usually in active combat, however, and women like these, who fought alongside men on the battlefield, are not the topic of this paper.

Western European armies, in the early modern period as now, depended on a variety of non-combatants to sustain them. Some of these non-combatants were government functionaries or were at least acknowledged in government records. Particularly toward the end of the early modern period, this group came to include military advisors, quartermasters in charge of food supply, baggage train officers, and sutlers licensed by the army. But this was far from all, as European governments grappled with the organizational, fiscal, and economic implications of supplying increasingly large armies; unofficial and semi-official sellers of information, tailors, peddlers, messen-

---

Reception of Military Reform in Russia, 1654–67" (Ph.D. diss., University of Illinois at Urbana-Champaign, 1997).

[7] See, for example, P. P. Shcherbinin, *Voennyi faktor v povsednevnoi zhizni Russkoi zhenshchiny v XVIII – nachale XX v.* (Tambov: Iulius, 2004); Elise Kimerling Wirtschafter, *Social Identity in Imperial Russia* (De Kalb: Northern Illinois University Press, 1997), among others.

[8] Nadezhda A. Durova, *The Cavalry Maiden: Journals of a Russian Army Officer in the Napoleonic Wars*, trans. Mary F. Zirin (Bloomington: Indiana University Press, 1988).

[9] Johannes Renner, *Livonian History, 1556–1561*, trans. J. S. Smith and William Urban (Lewiston, NY: Edwin Mellen Press, 1997), 43.

gers, nurses, cooks, laundresses, prostitutes, servants, and military families provided unofficial, private substitutes for services that governments could not offer. This latter group included many women. For many of them, following the army was a financial necessity—the death of a man or his departure through recruitment or conscription having disrupted a precarious household economy. They (like the men following the army) became petty entrepreneurs, selling a variety of goods and services. In addition to filling important gaps in army support, they made a meager living for themselves or augmented soldiers' pay to sustain their families. A relative few, more privileged, played more exclusively domestic or social roles.[10]

As one can easily imagine, this company of non-combatant and unofficial individuals trailing an early modern European army could easily equal if not surpass the number of actual combatants. In the latter part of the 16th century, for example, some Europeans assumed that at least 2,000–4,000 non-combatants would trail an army of 3000 men. Well into the 18th century, military commanders recognized the benefits conferred by such support, even as they deplored the complications posed by its presence. The Spanish army of Flanders, for example, based its logistical calculations on the number of mouths (*bocas*) it had to feed not on the size of its combatant force, thus recognizing both the presence of and the need for the "long tail" of the army baggage train. The size of that "tail" could be astounding. In 1577, 5300 Spanish soldiers with their 2000 lackeys officially counted as 20,000 mouths—including an additional 12,000 informal and official non-combatants. Similarly, during the Thirty Years' War according to an eyewitness, two-thirds of the people in General Aldringer's army marching to relieve Constance were non-combatants.[11]

For Russian armies, by contrast, little is known about almost any non-combatant support. The present state of research—as well as a variety of other factors to be discussed below—makes it difficult to imagine Russian armies attended by any precise equivalent to the Spanish situation. The most is known about non-combatants who were formally recognized, even official, elements of the Russian army. For example, the Kolomna military register of 1577 records the presence of 184 baggage-train slaves for 230 servicemen; they were presumably charged with duties not dissimilar to batsmen or lackeys in other armies. Nearly half the *zhiltsy* and three-quarters of the Moscow *dvoriane* went to war attended by such slaves in 1632; these slaves were joined in

---

[10] Hacker, "Women and Military Institutions," esp. 646–54; Geoffrey Parker, *The Army of Flanders and the Spanish Road* (Cambridge: Cambridge University Press, 1972), 86–87, 288–89; Catherine Wendy Bracewell, *Uskoks of Senj: Piracy, Banditry and Holy War in the Sixteenth-Century Adriatic* (Ithaca, NY: Cornell University Press, 1992), 101.

[11] Parker, *Army of Flanders*, 86–87, 288–89; Geoffrey Mortimer, *Eyewitness Accounts of the Thirty Years' War, 1618–1648* (Houndsmills, UK: Palgrave-MacMillan, 2002), 33, quoting Sebastian Bürster.

the baggage train by trumpeters and drummers. The huge baggage trains accompanying the Muscovite armies dispatched to fight the Khanate of Crimea in 1687 and 1689 were not entirely composed of carts and supplies, but included drivers, servants, and others.[12] Medical personnel enjoyed official non-combatant status in the latter part of the 17th century; quartermasters, officers in charge of military camps, clean-up, and other such activities also joined the official military rosters.[13]

Women and men who do not appear in the formal military records, those who may have been equivalent to the campfollowers in West European baggage trains and army encampments, have gone almost entirely undiscussed by historians of the Russian army. There are good reasons for this, since several factors suggest that characteristic West European army followers, who provided supplemental services and a community for army life, might not have been entirely appropriate to the Russian context. One reason has to do with the configuration of the Muscovite army before 1700. Muscovy had both campaign and garrison forces. The latter generally lived near the Muscovite fortresses in which they served; except for emergency supplies, their support systems were almost entirely personal and will not be discussed here. More relevant to this discussion is the campaign army, which was seasonally active. When called up or conscripted, men typically mustered in the late spring for a campaign and disbanded again in the fall, with the men returning home before winter set in. There were exceptions, such as a prolonged siege, the requirement to garrison a newly conquered fortress, or perhaps the avoidance of law and service obligations, but these were not characteristic.[14] These conditions make it very probable that a Muscovite life following the drum was also less than a full-time occupation, barring unusual circumstances. Thus, the campfollower who ended the Thirty Years' War saying, "I was born in war, I have no home, no country, and no friends; war is all my wealth and now

---

[12] Richard Hellie, *Slavery in Russia, 1450–1725* (Chicago: University of Chicago Press, 1982), 468–69, 471; Carol B. Stevens, "Why Muscovite Campaigns against Crimea Fell Short of What Counted," *Russian History/Histoire russe* 19: 1–4 (1992): 487–504; Stevens, *Soldiers on the Steppe: Army Reform and Social Change in Early Modern Russia* (De Kalb: Northern Illinois University Press, 1995), 113. Chinese armies in the 17th century also included non-combatant civilians and attracted merchant-sutlers. Nicola De Cosmo, trans. and ed., *The Diary of a Manchu Soldier in Seventeenth-Century China*, (London: Routledge, 2006), 36–37.

[13] See, for example, N. Novombergskii, *Materialy po istorii meditsiny v Rossii*, 5 vols. (St. Petersburg: M. M. Stasiulevich, 1905–10), 1: 18, 25–27, 42–43, *inter alia*; Russian State Military History Archive (hereafter RGVIA) f. 489, op. 1, ed. khr. 2451; RGVIA f. 490, op. 2, d. 4, fols. 15–55; and other Petrine regimental records that list quartermasters, baggage train officers, medics, scribes, and *profosy* (clean-up officers) on the regimental rosters.

[14] See the summary in Carol B. Stevens, *Russia's Wars of Emergence, 1460–1730* (New York: Pearson-Longman, 2007), 160–68; Stevens, *Soldiers*, 21–22.

whither shall I go," seems most unlikely to have had Russian counterparts of the same era, male or female.[15] Until after the Petrine reforms had made army life a year-round, indeed a life-long, commitment, it seems logical that informal, auxiliary support for the Muscovite army might easily have taken a different shape than for more permanent armies. Finally, serfdom and other assigned socio-legal categories in the 17th century formally tied much of the taxpaying population to its villages and towns; the agglomeration of Muscovite categories into the broader and more rigid Petrine ones (*sostoianie*) resoundingly reinforced this in the 18th century. This situation helped embed women (and men to a lesser degree) securely in family and community structures and limited the number of those who were free and had economic incentives to follow the army.[16]

These constraints notwithstanding, several groups of Russians did support the army in an unofficial capacity throughout the early modern period. Among these, military contractors (*markatanty, podriadchiki*), who delivered and sold food and other supplies to the army, were the most openly acknowledged. Although relatively rare in Russia's less commercial economy, they did operate near the army when it was on the march even before 1700. Early in the 18th century, they received a kind of semi-official status. Peter's Military Regulations (*Voinskii ustav*, 1716), for example, both acknowledged their presence and tried to contain their activities. They were to follow the army (separately) on campaign, and they were to pursue their trades in rows set aside for that purpose when military encampments were established.[17] This offers little information about the source, permanence, or gender of military contractors, although one researcher believes that women very rarely became contractors (*markatantki*) in the 18th century.[18]

Others who provided services to the army on the march were much less openly acknowledged and are consequently more difficult to find in the

---

[15] Hacker and Vining, "World," 9, citing H. G. Koenigsberger, "Thirty Years' War," in *The Age of Expansion*, ed. H. Trevor-Roper (New York: McGraw-Hill 1968), 44. Even during the disbanding of armies during the Thirty Years' War, wives and other camp-followers might perforce stay with mercenary regiments as they sought another 'post.'

[16] Valerie A. Kivelson makes a similar point in "Through the Prism of Witchcraft," in *Russia's Women: Accommodation, Resistance, Transformation*, ed. Barbara Evans Clements, Barbara Alpern Engel, and Christine D. Worobec (Berkeley: University of California Press, 1990), 84.

[17] For example, N. Novombergskii, *Ocherki vnutrenniago upravleniia v moskovskoi Rusi XVII stoletiia: Prodovol'stvennoe stroenie. Materialy* (Tomsk: Tip. Sibirskago T-va Pechatnago Dela, 1914), vol. 1, doc. no. 361; Stevens, *Soldiers*, 95; *Polnoe sobranie zakonov Rossiiskoi Imperii, 1649–1913*, Series 1, 45 vols. (St. Petersburg: Tip. II Otdeleniia Sobstvennoi Ego Imperatorskago Velichestva Kantseliarii, 1830–1916) [hereafter *PSZ*], doc. no. 3006, esp. pp. 270, 280; no. 3035.

[18] Shcherbinin, *Voennyi faktor*, 411.

historical record. Prohibitions on activity in and near army camps nonetheless strongly suggest that the Russian army had its "hangers-on," both male and female. There are 17th-century orders to set guards on military baggage trains and to eliminate spying, as well as decrees forbidding the presence of prostitutes and illegal vendors of alcohol, tobacco, and grain among the troops. Some such prohibitions continued on into the early Petrine period.[19] However, a great deal remains to be learned about these individuals and their connection to the army. Given the social conditions already mentioned, it seems logical to suppose that many of them lived nearby and were only temporary adherents. They would also be most likely to appear when Russian armies overwintered near settled populations, which did not happen very often prior to 1700. Others attached to the army, however, were neither temporary nor voluntary; military prisoners and captives—among whom surprised observers identified many women and children—burdened the Russian army on the move, although again, little is known about their activities. Still others were deliberately summoned. In the early 1700s, for example, Peter's own correspondence from the front requested that women be sent to launder and mend clothing.[20] In short, the presence of campfollowers can be deduced for 17th- and early 18th-century armies in Russia, rather along Western European patterns. Paintings of military scenes suggest that their presence persisted into the early 19th century.[21] However, given the current state of research, is it unclear how numerous the Russian campfollowers were, whether the women among them (laundresses, prostitutes, and wives) generally traveled with the troops, or if they were captured or collected around army encampments.

Russian armies enjoyed another, rather different category of informal military support from those just cited, however. Particularly prior to 1665, military wives could provide an unusual kind of distant support to the men in the campaign army. For example, while their spouses served in the campaign army, the wives of landholding servicemen remained on the land, in

---

[19] *Akty moskovskago gosudarstva*, 3 vols. (St. Petersburg, 1890–91), vol. 2, doc. nos. 660, 706, 534–37, 739; *PSZ*, doc. nos. 165, 166, 2036, 3006. M. Kuznetsov, *Prostitutsiia i sifilis v Rossii: Istoriko-statisticheskie issledovaniia* (St. Petersburg: Tip. T. S. Balasheva, 1871), 56–58.

[20] *PSZ*, doc. no. 3006; G. V. Esipov, "Zhizneopisanie kniazia Menshikova," *Russkii arkhiv*, bk. 2 (1875): 240–41; N. G. Ustrialov, *Istoriia tsarstvovaniia Petra velikogo*, 6 vols. (St. Petersburg: Tip. II otdeleniia Sobstvennoi Ego Imperatorskago Velichestva Kantseliarii, 1858–69), vol. 4, pt. 1., 125–26; Michele Bianchi et al., *Trumpas pasakojimas apie Lietuvos ir Lenkijos kara su Maskva XVII a.* (Vilnius: Lietuvos dailes muziejus, 2004), 141; Brian Davies, personal communication. (My thanks to Igor Spacenko, Colgate '09, for research assistance particularly here in Lithuanian.)

[21] See the painting by Fedotov entitled "Ustanovka ofitserskoi palatki (1843)," in Dmitrii Sarabianov, *Pavel Andreevich Fedotov* (Leningrad: Khudozhnik RSFSR, 1985); and A. Orlowskii's painting "Na Biwaku," in Muzeum Narodowe w Warszawie, *Aleksander Orlowski, 1777–1832* (Warsaw: Arkady, 1957), n.n.

their families and communities, supervising the agricultural production upon which their domestic solvency and community status relied.[22] Presumably, for the same period, the wives and community of peasant recruits also worked to sustain the necessities upon which their families' economies depended. But where there was seasonal military service, that situation was neither permanent nor even necessarily prolonged, despite the intensification of service demands during the Thirteen Years' War. Over the years between their call-ups, men might be absent for a sequence of several summer months. In such circumstances, some shortcomings of official supply might be disregarded, and other informal support might reasonably be deferred. Meanwhile those domestic activities that took place while men were away had an immediate impact on their fall return (and winter sustenance). Servitors' attachment to families and estate economies is clear. Men who served significantly longer than expected were not slow to complain. Others requested leave from the cavalry forces to deal with family emergencies at home. The wives of landholders even occasionally visited the troops during the campaign season, sometimes bringing their families with them.[23] This latter variety of social and morale-building visits by elite women continued into the 18th century, even as the army became more permanent and its campaigns much longer and more drawn out. One of the more spectacular early examples is Catherine I herself. She not only accompanied her imperial spouse on the campaign against the Ottomans at Pruth but thereafter she frequently traveled with him and the troops, up to and including the Persian campaigns at the end of his reign. Although she was certainly not typical, Catherine was also not alone in such military expeditions. Furthermore, Peter borrowed her relatively richly provided entourage to provide a suitable setting for his meetings with foreign dignitaries.[24]

---

[22] Valerie A. Kivelson, *Autocracy in the Provinces* (Stanford, CA: Stanford University Press, 1996), 98. In the first part of the 17th century, the length of an active duty season was also limited (Kivelson, *Autocracy,* 45). Service *skazki* of the Petrine and pre-Petrine eras are likely sources for further, if scattered, information here. Examples are to be found in RGVIA f. 490, op. 2.

[23] Shcherbinin, *Voennyi faktor,* 409–10, citing inter alia, E. N. Shchepkin, "Zhenskaia lichnost' v istorii Rossii," *Istoricheskii vestnik,* no. 7 (1913): 163–65. A particularly poignant complaint is *Dopolneniia k Aktam istoricheskim,* comp. and ed. Arkheograficheskaia komissiia, 12 vols. (St. Petersburg: V Tip. II Otdeleniia Sobstvennoi Ego Imperatorskago Velichestva Kantseliarii, 1846–72), vol. 4, no. 146, also cited in John H. L. Keep, *Soldiers of the Tsar* (Oxford: Clarendon Press, 1985), 85. An escalation of campaigns lasting more than a season during the Thirteen Years' War should be noted.

[24] Lindsey Hughes, "Catherine I, Consort to Peter," in C. C. Orr, *Queenship in Europe* (Cambridge: Cambridge University Press, 2004), 144; *Russian Women, 1698–1917,* ed. Robin Bisha et al. (Bloomington: Indiana University Press, 2002), 216; N. I. Pavlenko, *Ekaterina I* (Moscow: Molodaia gvardiia, 2004), 19; *Zakonodatel'nye akty Petra I,* comp. N. A. Voskresenskii (Moscow and Leningrad: AN SSSR, 1945), 1: 179–80.

For Muscovy's permanent troops, these 'distant' informal support systems worked only slightly differently from those available to landholding servitors and peasant conscripts in the 17th century. Year-round, salaried troops were a minority in the army, including musketeers (strel'tsy), founded in the mid-16th century, and the new formation select infantry regiments (vybornye soldaty), established nearly a century later. Permanent military service carried distinctive social identification for these men and their wives. Thus, for example, terms for the wives of new formation infantry (soldatka, soldatskie zheny) came into use with the introduction of that category of troops in the 1630s.[25] As is well known, musketeers lived in assigned neighborhoods or quarters in towns and near garrison fortresses (sloboda). The select infantry regiments had similarly assigned living space, and foreign officers in Moscow formed a part of the "Foreigners Quarter" (nemetskaia sloboda). (Billeting such military families on civilians was a temporary alternative.)[26] The residents of these suburbs usually received their lands collectively, and they saw themselves and were treated by the Muscovite administration as unified military communities. Despite their permanent status, these troops served in seasonal campaigns and were accustomed to return to home and family after several months' service. Thus, one of the objections proffered by Moscow-based musketeers in 1697, as they were dispatched straight from one military assignment to another, was that they would be unable to return to their families and neighborhoods in their accustomed way. And, when mutinous musketeers (strel'tsy) were sent from Moscow to permanently garrison southern cities in 1683 and Azov after 1698, they did not go alone. Not only their immediate families, but in the latter case retirees, widows, and other members of their Moscow suburb were sent with them.[27]

The role of these particular military wives in supporting army life was slightly different than for landholding and serf families. Men in the permanent forces occasionally served within easy distance of their homes in urban neighborhoods. Musketeers (strel'tsy) in particular served as police, sentries, and honor guards, and in other local offices. In addition to seasonal service with the campaign army, troops like the select infantry regiments were called upon to garrison distant and recently captured fortresses, or bolster siege troops, and these assignments resulted in more prolonged absences that might last a year or more.[28] In the latter part of the 17th century, however, the

[25] Shcherbinin, Voennyi faktor, 26.

[26] S. V. Karpushchenko, ed., Byt Russkoi armii XVIII–nachala XX v. (Moscow: Voennoe izd-vo, 1999), 16–17. Garrison cossacks also held collective grants, but they applied to agricultural land.

[27] PSZ, doc. nos. 1690, 1746, 1836; Akty Arkheograficheskoi ekspeditsii, vol. 4, doc. no. 280, esp. sections 7–10, 23; Keep, Soldiers, 99.

[28] Garrison duty beyond the borders lasted for a year or more (Stevens, Soldiers, 104–05).

Muscovite government acknowledged an obligation to pay and support the select infantry regiments, even as it had formerly paid the musketeers. Nonetheless, wives and families functioned much as their rural counterparts did, sustaining themselves and maintaining their places in their neighborhoods as they awaited the return of absent servicemen. However, these women were supplementing whatever military pay they received with sales, artisanal, and other urban earnings. Occasionally, there were reports of wives who did not remain in their urban quarters but were present with their spouses on the site of the army's encampments. For example, several wives of foreign officers lived for an extended period in the Russian siege camp at Smolensk in the 1630s, even crossing over to the Polish side in the immediate aftermath of the siege.[29] It is not known whether these women had followed the army or joined their spouses later at the front.

Thus far, this very preliminary survey has indicated that there were campfollowers and other non-combatants near the Russian army on campaign in the 17th and 18th centuries; among these individuals, women were present in some, at this point indeterminate, numbers. At the same time, the seasonal and episodic nature of most military service prior to the Northern War (1700–21) suggests that military wives played a much greater role in supporting military activity from home than one might have otherwise predicted.

It is logical to conclude, therefore, that the effort to enforce regular, permanent military service during the Northern War would have had a considerable impact on the army's informal support systems. As the Petrine military establishment moved toward larger, permanent, year-round forces, there was initially considerable confusion about the implications of this transition for wives, families, and their roles in the new military configurations. During the first Petrine levies, some servicemen took an optimistic view, turning up at their place of service with their wives, as well as their servants.[30] More commonly, there were attempts to separate men in the army from their wives and families. As landholders realized that conscription now meant losing the labor of their serf recruits permanently, they attempted to limit the associated losses to their labor force by petitioning, with some initial success, to retain control over the departing soldiers' wives and children.[31] The early Petrine

---

[29] The record also suggests that at least one ordinary soldier's wife was sent home from the Livonian front. Russian State Archive of Ancient Acts (hereafter RGADA) f. 371, op. 2, d. 153, chast' 1 (1684); Shcherbinin, *Voennyi faktor*, 410, citing Shchepkin, "Zhenskaia lichnost'," 163–65; I. R. Sokolovskii, *Sluzhilye inozemtsy v Sibiri XVII veka* (Novosibirsk: RAN II, Sibirskoe otdelenie, 2004), 79–81.

[30] Shcherbinin, *Voennyi faktor*, 36, cites *Stoletie voennogo ministerstva, 1802–1902: Glavnyi stab. Istoricheskii ocherk* (St. Petersburg, 1902), chast' 1, kn. 1, 33–44.

[31] *PSZ*, doc. no. 1820; Shcherbinin, *Voennyi faktor*, 36. Landholders' initial success was later overturned. On the other hand, slaves enrolling in the army under Peter had the right to claim their wives and children as early as 1700 (Hellie, *Slavery*, 702).

military establishment was barely able to keep pace with the demands of raising, training, and supplying an increasingly permanent military; the needs of attached wives and families were ignored, no matter how useful their contributions might have been. For example, finding quarters—even on the way to the front—just for the thousands upon thousands of men posed immense difficulties. By 1705, state decrees urged recruiters to resolve any problem with soldiers' families by taking only 15- to 20-year-old bachelors. They were to be quartered in groups in existing (civilian) housing and carefully supervised by their sergeants; the suggested norm was three men to a bed. Given the army's constant need for recruits as the Northern War dragged on, however, the prohibition on conscripting married men was withdrawn within two years. As permanent service and longer campaigns became the norm, the probability of seasonal or occasional involvement in military life by wives at home obviously decreased rapidly. Consequently, few military men saw their wives and families with any frequency. The bombardiers of Schlusselberg, for example, petitioned to see their families after eight years' absence. Even officers reported few home leaves over the course of the Northern War.[32] Military support directly from home and family had clearly become negligible. On the other hand, the Petrine state did continue to recognize its obligation to pay support to some soldiers' wives and children, even when it was unable to fulfill it.

But the Russian government did not always disregard soldiers' families and their informal military contributions. The status of the lower ranks in the Russian army stabilized as a free, non-taxpaying category of the population (*soldaty*). Those whose status depended on the *soldaty*—soldiers' wives (*soldatskie zheny, soldatki*) and children (*soldatskie deti*)—were also often defined as free and non-taxpaying before the end of Peter's reign.[33] This categorization freed them from the demands and supervision of landlords, if they so desired, but theirs was an ambiguous condition at best. Only a relatively small percentage of wives and families shared the peacetime accommodation of a regiment in billets and in barracks, as they were formally permitted to do. Although hardly well or humanely treated, these women continued to be acknowledged in the payment of soldiers' food allowances and in the norms for their allocation of living space. By the mid-18th century, resident wives were actively urged to work as regimental laundresses, seamstresses and even

---

[32] RGVIA f. 490, op. 2, d. 32, fol. 33ob, and d. 49, fol. 113ob, for example; Shcherbinin, *Voennyi faktor*, 37; Karpushchenko, *Byt*, 17–27.

[33] For example Elise Kimerling (Wirtschafter), "Soldiers' Children, 1719–1856," *Forschungen zur osteuropäischen Geschichte* 30 (1982): 61–136; Kimerling (Wirtschafter), "Social Misfits," *Journal of Military History* 59: 2 (1997): 227–32; Shcherbinin, *Voennyi faktor*, 26–29.

food-sellers.[34] Except in the case of settled garrison troops, however, these contributions to regimental life are assumed to have been periodic, since regiments on active duty could be absent for prolonged periods. While it is generally assumed that wives did not follow active-duty troops, 18th- and 19th-century memoirs suggest that perhaps they occasionally did.[35] Women who did not follow their spouses to the barracks clearly made no contribution whatsoever to the support of the regiments. Indeed, the separation between these wives and their soldier-husbands was often total; they might not even know of a spouse's death, for example.[36] The isolation and impoverishment that could characterize the lives of rural *soldatki*, whether they remained in the countryside or eked out a precarious existence in the towns, have been ably documented; information about their status and experience is more generally available for the later 18th and 19th centuries.[37]

The conditions in which soldiers' wives (*soldatki*) lived, and the contributions that they made to military life, were neither as uniform nor consistent in the Petrine period as the preceding paragraph may sound. For example, despite the general upheaval in the military establishment after 1700, the urban military neighborhoods (*sloboda*) of the *strel'tsy* and select infantry regiments persisted. The oldest of these infantry regiments were founded and settled after 1642; others (the Preobrazhenskii and Semenovskii regiments) were Guards units created in the 1690s by Peter.[38] The Preobrazhenskii chancellery, perhaps best known for its special investigatory activities, also ran the Guards regiments and recruitment, so that the 'suburbs' of the select and Guards units were transferred to or created under its direct purview. Its records include a variety of military and secret investigations files, alongside a profusion of more prosaic complaints filed by soldiers and their wives; a sampling

[34] Elise Kimerling Wirtschafter, *From Serf to Russian Soldier* (Princeton, NJ: Princeton University Press, 1990), 35–40; Karpushchenko, *Byt*, 29; Shcherbinin, *Voennyi faktor*, 36–37; *PSZ*, doc. nos. 2034, 2036.

[35] Durova, *Cavalry Maiden*, 83; C. H. von Manstein, *A Contemporary Memoir of Russia* (New York: DaCapo Press, 1968), 137–38.

[36] Shcherbinin, *Voennyi faktor*, 37; others inaccurately assumed a spouse's death. For example, RGADA f. 22, op. 1, d. 20.

[37] Kimerling Wirtschafter, "Social Misfits"; idem, *From Serf to Russian Soldier*; idem, *Social Identity*; and idem, "Soldiers' Children, 1719–1856." Also see Shcherbinin, *Voennyi faktor*; Karpushchenko, *Byt*; Beatrice Farnsworth, "The *Soldatka*: Folklore and Court Record," *Slavic Review* 49: 1 (1990): 58–73.

[38] M. D. Rabinovich, *Polki Petrovskoi armii, 1689–1725: Kratkii spravochnik* (Moscow: Sovetskaia Rossiia, 1977); I have not yet seen A. V. Malov, *Moskovskie vybornye polki soldatskogo stroia v nachal'nyi period svoei istorii, 1656–1671* (Moscow: Drevnekhranilishche, 2006), although a translation of Malov, "The Sovereign's Moscow Select Regiments of the *Soldatskii* Discipline: Commanders," *Tseikhgauz* 14 (2001), 2–7, and others are available on the web at http://marksrussianmilitaryhistory.info (accessed April 2008).

of these latter offer an early, close look at the roles of *soldatki* in community military life even as the Petrine reforms took shape.

These regimental neighborhoods appear to have been populated by a relatively unchanging group of military families in the early 18th century. Within these parameters, the community's men were predictably more mobile than the women; soldiers departed on active service assignments without much fanfare, to return only when their tours of duty were complete. Early 18th-century military responsibilities were unending; even retired army men were mobilized for tasks such as escorting new recruits to their destinations.[39] Not all service took place at a distance. When men were present, the modern reader of these documents sees them occupied with a variety of nearby military tasks—guarding prisoners, discharging sentry and guard duties; in a later case, one was a commissar in charge of local postal wagons.[40] Both servicemen and the occasional woman who left the suburb expected to return to their homes; they often left a neighbor or friend in charge of their belongings until they came back again.[41] In the Preobrazhenskii petitions examined, relatively few permanent departures or new arrivals were indicated. One man did leave because of assignment to a different regiment, apparently leaving his family behind; another, already retired, possessed himself of the regiment's carpentry tools and departed, leaving his wife to explain.[42]

The soldiers' wives lived in tightly knit, predominantly military communities. Given irregular patterns of arrival and departure by different contingents of soldiers, the neighborhoods may have been predominantly female at given moments, but they certainly were not exclusively so. Even in their spouses' absence, women remained in their own homes or quarters. Some wives described themselves as remaining "after him" (after a husband had left) in their own place "in his regiment" (in his regimental neighborhood).[43] Unlike the rural *soldatki* later in the century, these soldiers' wives were far from isolated. Their neighborhoods were originally organized by regiment, and apparently retained much of that basic organization into the 18th century. It comes as no surprise, therefore, that the social networks and daily interactions that sustained them were comprised of other military men and

---

[39] RGADA f. 371, op. 2, d. 743 (1714); d. 4903 (1705); N. Ia. Novombergskii, *Slovo i delo gosudarevy* (Moscow: Iazyki Slavianskoi kul'tury, 2004), vol. 2, doc. no. 3 (1707; *strel'tsy*).

[40] For example, RGADA, Dela Preobrazhenskogo Prikaza i Tainoi Kantseliarii, f. 7, d. 173 (1723); f. 371 op. 2, d. 2312 (1725).

[41] RGADA f. 371, op. 1, d. 14284 (1703); f. 371, op.1, d. 14990 (1701); f. 371, op. 2, d. 9940 (1714).

[42] RGADA f. 371, op. 1, d. 14983 (1701); Novombergskii, *Slovo*, 1: #72 (1641; *strel'tsy*).

[43] RGADA f. 371, op. 2, d. 743 (1714).

women, usually of their own rank or standing, often of the same regiment. [44] Natal'ia, Provtorokh's daughter, married a member of the Lefortovskii regiment, as did her daughter, and her neighbor, Matrena.[45] Semen Turganikov was a soldier in the Semenovskii regiment, and his sister married another member of the same regiment.[46] Frequently, but by no means exclusively, women's interactions were with other women. Thus, the wives of soldiers in the same regiment went about town together. There were other combinations, however. Family groups, such as a brother and sister, or groups of women with a male escort appeared.[47] Women's networks, like men's, moved comfortably beyond the confines of their regimental suburbs. When they met those from outside their own neighborhoods, regimental men and women both tended to interact with other military men and women. When a soldier in the Preobrazhenskii regiment filed a complaint, for example, he supported it with witnesses from a surprising variety of other military backgrounds; a dragoon, a military medic, a lieutenant, the wife of a foreign colonel, and others had congregated in the streets of a military neighborhood, even though most of them were not affiliated with the resident infantry regiment.[48] Similarly, women quarrelling about household belongings called witnesses of different military affiliations; in one case, these included the wife of a sailor and the wives of two soldiers in the Semenovskii regiment. A woman with one regimental affiliation launched an accusation against a woman married into a different regiment.[49]

Although soldiers' wives from regimental neighborhoods interacted predominantly with other local military people, this was not the extent of their social networks. *Soldatki* also dealt with members of the urban communities (*posadskie liudi*) near whom they lived. On occasion, they apparently stuck together against outsiders; in such cases, their most frequent non-military interlocutors were those same nearby urban residents, for reasons described below.[50] Individual *soldatki* had friends and connections outside their own towns: a mother-in-law living in Moscow was plausibly cited as the source of dangerous political gossip; other women visited their friends from other towns.[51]

---

[44] Nancy Shields Kollmann, *By Honor Bound: State and Society in Early Modern Russia* (Ithaca, NY: Cornell University Press, 1999), 96, reports comparable results.

[45] RGADA f. 371, op. 2, d. 2312.

[46] RGADA f. 371, op. 2, d. 3797 (1702).

[47] RGADA f. 371, op. 2, d. 4798 (1702); op. 1, d. 14287 (1703), op. 1, d. 14818–19 (1697).

[48] RGADA f. 371, op. 2, d. 3992 (1702).

[49] RGADA f. 371, op. 2, d. 9940 (1714); op. 1, d. 14822 (1697).

[50] RGADA f. 371, op. 2, d. 3792; op. 2, d. 3997 (1702); op. 2, d. 9705; op. 2, d. 9884 (1715); op. 1, d. 14287 (1703).

[51] RGADA f. 371, op. 2, d. 2312 (1725); f. 7, d. 173 (1723).

The close quarters and persistent interactions of a military neighborhood did not breed perfect amity; petty disagreements escalated easily.[52] Women often complained about other military wives and widows living nearby. Longstanding feuds within a regiment erupted into accusations before the authorities. A woman complained that her neighbor had stolen a pan and her hat; the neighbor retaliated with the allegation that illegal alcohol was manufactured and sold next door. The first then stormed into the chancellery offices to report that her neighbor harbored illegal religious books. This was a significant escalation and led to the imprisonment of the accused who, when last heard of, was "dying a hungry death" in prison.[53]

Neighbors, usually those of similar standing and rank, traded recriminations and insults. Like their social betters, *soldatki* and those around them furiously resented verbal abuse and libelous name-calling and frequently brought their complaints about such matters before the authorities.[54] These included unspecified exchanges in the street, mutual recriminations between soldiers' wives, among military men and women, or with outsiders. While some complaints were lodged by a man on behalf of a member of his family—a sister or his wife, women also lodged complaints and otherwise spoke up on their own behalf.[55] Some of the insults leveled at men were related to their military profession and activities; one was accused of deserting his regiment, others were cursed at for their manner of carrying out their duties. Men did not take kindly to being called a robber or a thief. Men and women complained that others were impugning the honor and sexual conduct of soldiers' wives; a girl and her father were sent to Siberia for spreading gossip about a major's wife who lived with a man to whom she was not married.[56]

Nor was physical aggression involving women far from the surface. Domestic violence and street brawls appear to have been relatively commonplace, though weapons were rarely used. There were reports of women being beaten up by their husbands and women being threatened in the street. One woman was threatened with violence for frightening a horse; she escaped un-

[52] For further discussion of this point, see Nancy Shields Kollmann's discussion of communities, honor, insult, and violence in *By Honor Bound*, chap. 3.

[53] RGADA f. 371, op. 2, d. 743 (1714).

[54] Kollmann, *By Honor Bound*, 96.

[55] RGADA f. 371, op. 1, d. 14960 (1701); op. 1, d. 14859 (1698); op. 1, d. 14847 (1689); op. 1, d. 14818–19 (1697); op. 1, d. 14421 (1726), op. 1, d. 14399 (1721); op. 1, d. 14342 (1718); op. 2, d. 9883 (1715); op. 2, d. 3992 (1702); op. 2, d. 3797 (1702); op. 2, d. 495 (1705); f. 7, d. 357 (1733).

[56] For example, RGADA f. 371, op. 2, d. 3797 (1702); f. 22, op. 1, d. 17 (1745); f. 371, op. 1, d. 14791 (1696); op. 1, d. 14960 (1701); op. 1, d. 14959; op. 1, d. 14847; op. 1, d. 14399 (1721); op. 1, d. 14342 (1718); f. 7, op. 1, d. 427 (1735); f. 7, op. 1, d. 357.

harmed only because her brother defended her.[57] Women also fought one another.[58] In a particularly dramatic case, a sword was used, albeit in a somewhat unconventional manner. A drunken postman (*iamshchik*) was frustrated in his attempt to reclaim the horses he needed for his postal carts from the soldier standing guard. The guard's wife, who was apparently keeping her husband company while he was on duty, became the target of the postman's anger, and he attacked her with a long stick from the cart traces (the traces are the two sticks connecting the cart to the horse's harness). Although the postman's swing missed the guard's wife, he hit the infant in her arms a solid blow. The attacker then turned on the guard himself, first with the stick and then with a shovel. The guard tried to defend himself with a sword; his wife grabbed it from him and pushed the sword broadside against the postman's chest forcing him out of the courtyard into the street; she claimed that no blood was drawn. In the street, however, the furious postman, bloodied perhaps by a fall outside the gates, knocked the guard's eleven-year-old daughter into the mud before the child was rescued by the most effective belligerent in the mêlée—her mother.[59]

The soldiers' wives who lived in these tightly knit military communities appear by and large to have shared a limited but not impoverished existence. When their men were around, women's daily activities seem often to have revolved around them. The postal guard noted above, as well as other guards, even prisoners had their wives at their sides during some of the day. A soldier on sentry duty appears to have spent his time running errands through town in the company of his comrades' spouses. In addition, a number of women in the military suburb were involved in small sales and even petty manufacturing. It was alleged that some made and sold illicit alcohol; others reported stopping to consume a cup of wine with a friend. A number undertook small sales from their own or even a neighbor's house, or perhaps even ran a small stall (*lavka*). Trade in red currants, household goods, isolated silk items, and a variety of other objects are mentioned. Direct sales competition with townswomen seems the probable explanation for some of the frequent disputes between *soldatki* and their urban neighbors. Other women sold minor services to augment their incomes. A soldier's widow did laundry and cooking for prisoners in the local jail. Other soldiers' wives stored or held personal and household belongings for later collection by soldiers' families. In the mid-17th century, an officer's household evidently let rooms to, or at any

---

[57] RGADA f. 371, op 2, d. 743; op. 2, d. 3797; op 2, d. 9702—this one about wounds sustained in a fight with a drunk; f. 371, op. 1, d. 14287; op. 1, d. 14898; op. 1, d. 14859; op. 1, d.15001.

[58] RGADA f. 371, op. 2, d. 3792; op. 2, d. 9884; f. 371, op. 1, d. 14951–52, op. 1, d. 14955–59.

[59] RGADA f. 22, op. 1, d. 17.

rate housed, a retired soldier and his wife.[60] Few of these occupations individually would have yielded much cash or useable goods; realistically, they probably supplemented each other and additional sources of income. Only a few could realistically be described as significant financial contributions.

In this context, disputes about property ownership were common. Some of the disputed items were ordinary enough—clothing, such as shirts and a winter coat (*shuba*), and household items like cooking pots and pans.[61] Debts (including past due taxes) were a persistent problem.[62] Yet occasional items suggest that substantial sums were occasionally available to these soldiers' households. Among the domestic belongings of some *soldatki*, reputedly left with friends in their absence, were those that have the ring of somewhat greater prosperity: caftans with taffeta trim and special buttons, silk and black velvet items, small gems, or golden clasps for clothing, for example.[63] The most significant property disputes focused on real estate, especially living space. That housing was highly prized is hardly surprising, since soldiers and other military personnel often lived in billets. In Preobrazhenskii village, for example, there was a house belonging to a soldier who was languishing in Turkish captivity. The captive's wife lived in the house until her death; at that point, however, the property was hotly disputed between a clerk in the Preobrazhenskii chancellery and the captive's brother. Another such case seems to reveal clearly some of the normal limits of *soldatka* prosperity. A woman whose husband had recently purchased a house in the suburb returned to it only to be confronted with a fellow *soldatka* who had been billeted on her as the new owner of the house. An altercation arose, and the new owner threw the billetee and her belongings into the street. As a result, she was excoriated as "a rich woman" and accused of improper behavior toward soldiers' wives. Any significant rural holding was the focus of immense interest and machinations, many of them very unpleasant.[64]

In short, these soldiers' wives of the early 18th century, most of whom lived in the suburbs of Russia's elite infantry regiments, were members of tight-knit and predominantly military communities. Even as spouses and neighbors departed on possibly prolonged service assignments, the women themselves were supported by an extensive and quite stable network of family and fellow soldiers and their wives. Surprisingly perhaps, these neighborhoods were composed in such a way that the departure of particular companies or battalions did not denude the settlements of men. Some were left

---

[60] Novombergskii, *Slovo*, vol. 1, doc. no. 210; RGADA f. 371, op. 2, d. 743; op. 2, d. 4903; op. 2, d. 2312.

[61] RGADA f. 7, op. 1, d. 435; f. 371, op. 2, d. 743; op. 1, d.14284; op. 1, d. 14822; op. 1, d. 14916; op. 1, d.14973; op. 1, d.15001.

[62] RGADA f.173, op. 1, d.14320; op. 1, d. 14421; op. 1, d. 14999.

[63] RGADA f. 371, op. 2, d. 9940.

[64] Novombergskii, *Slovo*, vol. 2, doc. no. 43 (1725).

behind, not only members of other companies, but also retirees and those with local military assignments. These soldiers' wives apparently suffered neither from the rejection and isolation that plagued the wives of serf conscripts later in the century, nor from extreme poverty. Women augmented military salaries with petty sales and service, often out of their homes. These activities suggest marginal, but on the whole successful, domestic economies. Some of their belongings even suggest occasional windfalls.

The role that these soldiers' wives played in supporting military life at the front is less clear. It seems likely that little was left of the immediate contact and support they might have provided to their particular spouses when campaigns were seasonal and generally shorter. The unusual stability of their communities, however, provided a very different background for these infantrymen than the more typical rootlessness of barracks for the men and rural isolation for their wives.

This brief survey explores the variety of informal support that sustained the Russian army in the 17th and 18th centuries, and the role that women played therein. Some of their activities resembled West European responses to similar problems. Elsewhere, however, unusual characteristics of Russian military organization produced unusual answers to the questions of informal military support for the troops. For the moment, however, much work remains to be done before detailed discussions of these options are possible.[65]

---

[65] All-male soldiers' cooperatives (*artely*) may eventually have offered part of a solution. John Bushnell, "The Russian Soldiers' Artel', 1700–1900," in *Land, Commune, and Peasant Community in Russia*, ed. Roger Bartlett (New York: St. Martin's Press, 1900), 376–95.

News Sensations from the Front: Reportage in Late Muscovy concerning the Ottoman Wars

Daniel C. Waugh

This essay concerns the ways that awareness of the larger world may be shaped by news about current events and by retrospective historical memory. My inspiration is some Muscovite texts, by themselves probably insignificant, whose study raises broader issues about early modern cultural history. There is growing interest in how the emergence of the modern press helped create in Europe a sense of "contemporaneity" as one of the hallmarks of the transition to "modernity." That is, through growing access to regular foreign news, people were able to situate themselves in an expanded world of human action, in the process moving away from providential interpretation of events to a more "rational" understanding of the world.[1] The validity of this interpretation of the impact from new media and communications depends to a considerable degree on what one can document about readers and their responses, subjects which to date are still considerably under-studied. Even if assumptions about the growing sense of "contemporaneity" are valid for Western Europe—and to a degree I question that argument—to expect to find synchronous developments in Russia may be unreasonable. Apart from the issue of contemporary responses to current news, it is of interest to examine how the news stories of one era might look to later generations. It is very easy to read back a significance not felt at the time; similarly the emphasis of the earlier story might change if it is invoked as a part of contemporary political discourse.

---

[1] This was the subject of a conference in Bremen, "Time and Space on the Way to Modernity: The Emergence of Contemporaneity in European Culture," 15–16 December 2006. Important books which support this idea are: Holger Böning, *Welteroberung durch ein neues Publikum: Die deutsche Presse und der Weg zur Aufklärung. Hamburg und Altona als Beispiel* ([Bremen:] Edition lumière, 2002); and Wolfgang Behringer, *Im Zeichen des Merkur. Reichspost und Kommunikationsrevolution in der Frühen Neuzeit* (Göttingen: Vandenhoeck & Ruprecht, 2003). The paper which I co-presented with Ingrid Maier at Bremen questioned this emphasis. See also my *"We Have Never Been Modern": Approaches to the Study of Russia in the Age of Peter the Great," Jahrbücher für Geschichte Osteuropas* 49 (2001): 321–345; and idem (in Russian, D. K. Uo), *Istoriia odnoi knigi: Viatka i "ne-sovremennost'" v russkoi kul'ture Petrovskogo vremeni* (St. Petersburg: Dmitrii Bulanin, 2003), esp. chap. 7.

Rude & Barbarous Kingdom Revisited: Essays in Russian History and Culture in Honor of Robert O. Crummey. Chester S. L. Dunning, Russell E. Martin, and Daniel Rowland, eds. Bloomington, IN: Slavica Publishers, 2008, 491–506.

My specific subject is reports about the late 17th-century European wars against the Ottoman Turks, a topic which first occupied me as a graduate student, when I had the temerity to ask Bob Crummey for a copy of his *Rude and Barbarous Kingdome*.[2] The importance of the Ottomans for early modern Europe is undoubtedly still underestimated, despite the nearly continuous wars against the Turks and large volume of contemporary publications regarding them. The Ottomans were often central to the concerns of the Muscovite government even if, until well into the 17th century, it had largely resisted being drawn into fighting them. Muscovite priorities lay elsewhere, and there was a distinct lack of empathy for the plight of the sultan's Orthodox subjects.[3] It is somewhat ironic, therefore, that when Muscovy finally plunged into the Turkish wars in the 1670s, its ambassadors were unable to elicit much support, since the major Western powers then had other concerns.[4] What ultimately would bring together a coalition of Christian states was the Ottoman siege of Vienna in 1683. The dramatic defense of the city was followed by a rolling back of Ottoman control in southeastern Europe, a process that ended only in the 20th century.[5]

Reports about the Turkish Wars continually appeared in regularly published newspapers and in hundreds of separately published pamphlets whose impact as sources of news still merits study.[6] Understandably, the Turkish

---

[2] This work resulted in a dissertation on Muscovite *turcica* and a monograph, *The Great Turkes Defiance: On the History of the Apocryphal Correspondence of the Ottoman Sultan in Its Muscovite and Russian Variants*, with a foreword by Academician Dmitrii Sergeevich Likhachev (Columbus, OH: Slavica Publishers, 1978).

[3] See, for example, Nikolai F. Kapterev, *Kharakter otnoshenii Rossii k pravoslavnomu Vostoku v XVI i XVII stoletiiakh* (Sergiev Posad: M. S. Elov, 1914).

[4] Notably the embassies of Andrei Vinius and Pavel Menezii. See N. A. Kazakova, "A. A. Vinius i stateinyi spisok ego posol'stva v Angliiu, Frantsiiu i Ispaniiu v 1672–1674 gg.," *Trudy Otdela drevnerusskoi literatury* 39 (1985): 348–64; N. V. Charykov, *Posol'stvo v Rim i sluzhba v Moskve Pavla Meneziia* (St. Petersburg: A. S. Suvorin, 1906).

[5] Contemporaries appreciated the significance of the Ottoman defeat in the 1683–99 war. See the substantial book marking the signing of the Treaty of Karlowitz in 1699: *Der siegreich geendigte Römisch-Käyserliche, Pohlnische, Muscowitische und Venetianische XV. Jahrige Türcken-Krieg ...* (Hamburg: von Wiering, 1699).

[6] Regarding this latter point, see Mario Infelise, "The War, the News and the Curious: Military Gazettes in Italy," in *The Politics of Information in Early Modern Europe*, ed. Brendan Dooley and Sabrina A. Baron (London: Routledge, 2001), 216–36. Infelise emphasizes that, unlike other important centers for distribution of news in Europe, Venice relied on media other than regularly published newspapers. Even though Böning recognizes that pamphlets and broadsides were a significant supplement to the newspapers, it seems wrong to suggest that the pamphlet literature was somehow inferior to the newspapers because it appeared only with some delay, which was certainly not always the case. Cf. Böning, *Welteroberung*, 72–73; Jutta Schumann, "Das politisch-militärische Flugblatt in der zweiten Hälfte des 17. Jahrhunderts als

material is also abundant in the Muscovite news translations and summaries known as the *kuranty*, which were compiled on a regular basis in the Diplomatic Chancery starting when Muscovy joined the European postal network in the 1660s.[7] The publication and study of the *kuranty* continues, with the results so far not giving us any reason to revise drastically what we have long known about the very limited Muscovite awareness of the outside world and current events in it.[8] That said, it is nonetheless of interest to see what events were reported and how they were recorded.

One of the longstanding confrontations of the Turkish wars pitted the Venetians against the Ottomans in the Eastern Mediterranean in battles often reported in the *kuranty*.[9] A few Western engravings of the Venetian-Turkish war for Crete in the 1660s have been found as well in the library of Andrei Vinius, the Muscovite translator of Dutch extraction who would head his government's postal service to the West in the last quarter of the 17th century.[10] In 1687, during campaigns in the Morea, the Venetians and some Habsburg military contingents besieged Turkish-held Athens.[11] There on the night of

---

Nachrichtenmedium und Propagandamittel," in *Das Illustrierte Flugblatt in der Kultur der Frühen Neuzeit*, ed. Wolfgang Harms and Michael Schilling, Microkosmos: Beiträge zur Literaturwissenschaft und Bedeutungsforschung 50 (Frankfurt am Main: Peter Lang, 1998), 226–58.

[7] The still standard work on the Muscovite post is I. P. Kozlovskii, *Pervye pochty i pervye pochtmeistery v Moskovskom gosudarstve*, 2 vols. (Warsaw, 1913). Five volumes of the *kuranty* have so far been published, with a sixth forthcoming.

[8] Recent work on the *kuranty* includes Stepan Mikhailovich Shamin, "Kuranty vremeni pravleniia Fedora Alekseevicha: K probleme zainteresovannosti Moskovskogo pravitel'stva v operativnoi informatsii o evropeiskikh sobytiiakh 1670–80-kh gg." (Avtoreferat diss. na soiskanie uchenoi stepeni kandidata istoricheskikh nauk, Moscow, 2003); and two monographs on the language of the texts and many articles by Ingrid Maier, the editor of the forthcoming foreign source volume in the *kuranty* series. The present article is part of a book about Muscovite acquisition of foreign news which I am writing with Prof. Maier. Her suggestions for this article have been invaluable.

[9] For the Morea campaigns of the 1680s, see *Venezia e la guerra di Morea: Guerra, politica e cultura alla fine del '600*, ed. Mario Infelise and Anastasia Stouraiti (Milano: Franco Angeli, 2005); and Laura Marasso and Anastasia Stouraiti, *Immagini dal mito: La conquista veneziana della Morea (1684–1690)* (Venezia: Fondazione Scientifica Querini Stampalia, 2001). I am indebted to Prof. Infelise for sending me copies of these books and his notes from materials in Venetian collections. For reports in Muscovy, see, e.g., *Vesti-Kuranty 1651–1652 gg., 1654–1656 gg., 1658–1660 gg.* (Moscow: "Nauka," 1996), 20–21, 44, 61, 65–66, 97, etc.

[10] See N. Levinson, "Al'bom 'Kniga Viniusa' — pamiatnik khudozhestvennogo sobiratel'stva v Moskve XVII veka," *Ezhegodnik Gosudarstvennogo istoricheskogo muzeia 1961 god* (Moscow, 1962): 72–98.

[11] On the campaign, see K. M. Setton, "The Venetians in Greece (1684–1688): Francesco Morosini and the Destruction of the Parthenon," in *Papers Read at a Joint Meeting of the*

September 26, as an English translation of a serial Venetian diary of the war laconically reported, "they began to play with their Bombs upon the Fortress; one of which fell among their Ammunition, and fir'd a great part of it, to the great terror of the Besieged, whose Defences began to fail them, their Parapets being ruin'd, and their great Guns dismounted."[12] The German newspapers at the time, equally laconic, added one significant detail: "Denn 26 fiel eine Bombe in den berühmdten Tempel Minerve, welches das Haupt Magazyn war."[13] And so the Parthenon was left in ruins (see fig. 1 following p. 72).

One of the commanders at the siege, Count Königsmark, noted how "eine Bomme [*sic*] in den sehr berühmten Tempel Minerva, welcher Seither so vielen hundert Jahren respectiret worden, fiel," with the result being: "Das Getümmel, so durch Entzundung aller dieser Munition entstand, war greul- ich, zumahl dadurch mehr also 200 Weiber und Kinder zusambt dieser so berühmten Antiquität in die Lufte flohen."[14] His report was a source for news printed in the *Europaeische Zeitung* (Hanau). That text, or one very similar to it, received in Moscow via the Riga post on December 12 (O.S.), in turn was the source for an account of the event in the Russian *kuranty*:

Из Венеции ноября в 8 день.

Из Афина турского города нам подтвержают, что тот город стоит на высокой каменной горе и у того города одне врата да три стены а в нем 40 пушек а ратных людей 400 человек салдатов, и под тот город наши войска сентября в 20 день приступ чинили, и проведав господин граф Кениксмарк, что того города в кирхе богини Минерфа, турки все свои всякие воинские запасы сохранили, велел своим гранатчиком бросать в ту кирху огнестрельные гранаты, и 24-го дня сентября ту кирху со всеми запасы сожгли и верхней замок города того от того зажжения разрушился. Однако ж турки з городовых стен нам крепкой отпор дали, и от того города отбили, и увидя, что наши в тот город непрестанно стреляют и огненные гранаты пускают, и сентября 26-го числа несколько человек знатных турок для договору к нам вышли. И нам объявили, что они тот город здати нам хотят, не для воинского нашего разорения но для того, что у них в кирхе все воинские запасы згорели. И били

Royal Society and the American Philosophical Society 3 (Philadelphia: The American Philo- sophical Society, 1987), 1–85.

[12] *A Journal of the Venetian Campaigne, A. D. 1687. Under the Conduct of the Capt. General Morosini... Translated from the Italian Original, sent from Venice...* (London: H. C. Taylor, 1688), 38.

[13] *Die Europäische Relation* (Altona), 1687, no. 91 (datelined Athens, 11 October): 732. Cf. *Leipziger Post- und Ordinar-Zeitung*, 1687, no. 45/4 (datelined Venice, 7 November): 718.

[14] *Relations-Courier* (Hamburg), 1687, no. 178: [2–3].

челом, чтоб им в той здаче дать несколько дней сроку, и дано им на шесть дней сроку, на которой срочной день 1500 человек мужеска и женскаго полу ис того города вывесть. И даны им до города Смирна карабли и провожатые.

Ныне войско наше стоит под Афином, а конница назад пошла под город Коринфо.[15]

The approach to "translation" in this case was quite typical of what we find in the *kuranty* once the postal system had been established, the flow of news regularized, and the quantities of news received thereby far exceeded Muscovite needs. Summaries were the order of the day. The texts had to be quickly processed and then read to the tsar and boyars, in the given instance, on December 16, four days after the news had been received.

The Western accounts of the event convey the sense that the loss of one of the great monuments of antiquity was deemed incidental to the capture of Athens from the Turks. The responses in Venice were perhaps the most complex, given the singular attention which was lavished there on the re-conquest of the Morea and the controversies over the decision to abandon Athens only a few months after it had been taken.[16] One of the earliest short news pamphlets reporting its capture merely told readers that a bomb had hit a powder magazine and that subsequently the Turks surrendered.[17] The Venetian publisher of the serial diary of the campaign lavishly reviewed the glorious

---

[15] Russian State Archive of Ancient Acts (hereafter, RGADA), Kuranty: Translations of Foreign News, f. 155, op. 1, 1687, no. 6, pt. 3, pt. 2, fols. 253–54 (copy kindly provided to me by Stepan Shamin). An identical copy, removed from its Muscovite archival environment in the beginning of the 20th century, is in the Library of the Russian Academy of Sciences (BAN), St. Petersburg, MS 34.14.12, fols. 76, 17, 18. The immediately preceding entry, datelined Vienna, October 13, contained other news on the Turkish/Tatar wars. This particular section of the *kuranty* is specified as being from "Tsesarskie" (i.e., German) printed sources. Compare the Russian text with the article under the heading "Venedig den 17. Novembris st. n.," *Europaeische Zeitung* (Hanau), 1687, no. 90, 8 November: [2]. Note that dates in the headings generally are those of the source for any given report even if the calendar in the city where the newspaper was published was different. This explains the apparent contradiction of events occurring after the publication date or cases where it seems the news traveled impossibly fast. The Gregorian (N.S.) calendar was ten days ahead of the Julian (O.S.).

[16] Regarding the debate, see Léon de Laborde, *Athènes aux XVe, XVIe et XVIIe siècles*, 2 vols. (Paris: J. Renouard, 1854), 2: 191 ff. Laborde was appalled by the Venetian commander Francesco Morosini's bungled attempt to cart off some of the sculptures which had survived and even more incensed by the fact that he seriously considered the complete destruction of the Acropolis before abandoning the city.

[17] *Nuova, e Distinta Relatione Dell'Acquisto della Città, e Fortezza d'Athene Fatto dall'armi della Sereniss. Rep. di Venetia Sotto la Ualorosa Direttione dell'Illustriss. & Eccelentiss. Sig. Francesco Morosini...* (Venice and Ferrara: Filoni, 1687), [3].

history and ancient ruins of Athens, as Mario Infelise has put it, "due not so much to the importance of the military episode as to the suggestiveness of the place." In a subsequent number the campaign diary finally lamented what had happened to the Parthenon ("the most beautiful antiquity of the world has been destroyed, a memorial that had never yielded to the injuries of time…"). A separate account published in Venice later that year included an accurate description of the Parthenon and what was left of the Temple of Minerva.[18] Giacomo Filippi even composed verses "Per la bomba che nell'assedio d'Atene felicemente intrapresa da Sua Serenità rovinò il tempio di Minerva."[19]

It should not surprise us that the cultural significance of the site would find echoes in Baroque Venice. Furthermore, the besieging troops obviously included at least some officers who had an appreciation of Classical antiquity.[20] An anonymous eyewitness diary by a Swedish officer laments at length the destruction of the temple and describes the building in great detail.[21] The Imperial general who shared some of the responsibility for the explosion recognized that the temple was famous. Of course what those who lamented the loss failed to appreciate is that the Parthenon in 1687, severely damaged in a fire in late antiquity and defaced first by conversion into a Christian church and later into a mosque, was hardly an unsullied monument to the age of Pericles.[22] Even in Venice, the episode occupied a relatively small place in the outpouring of material on the Turkish Wars. Elsewhere in Europe the explosion of the Parthenon as a news story seems not to have had very

---

[18] Infelise, "The War," 218, 223–24, and 218–19. The Venetian archives contain a military engineer's drawings dramatizing the explosion (Fig. 1). Engravings from them are in Laborde, *Athènes*, 2, following pp. 150, 172.

[19] Giorgios I. Pilidis, "La bomba arrogante e la poesia servile: celebrazioni poetiche," in *Venezia e la guerra*, 276.

[20] Laborde, *Athènes*, devotes vol. 1 and the first part of his vol. 2 to demonstrating how by the second half of the 17th century there was a substantial European interest in Athens and its antiquities. Thus the destruction of the Parthenon cannot be excused as "medieval" ignorance (177–78).

[21] See L. Dietrichson, "Zum zweihundertjährigen Gedächtnis der Zerstörung des Parthenon," *Zeitschrift für bildende Kunst* 22 (September 1887): 367–76. Accounts by other officers involved in the siege are largely matter-of-fact. See Léon Laborde, *Documents Inédits ou Peu Connus Sur L'Histoire et Les Antiquités d'Athenes, tirés des Archives de L'Italie, de la France, de L'Allemagne, etc.* (Paris: J. Renouard, 1854), 148–54. For an account by the well-educated Anna Agriconia Akerhjelm, an attendant to Königsmark's wife, see Laborde, *Athènes*, 2: esp. 276–79.

[22] See Robert Ousterhout, "'Bestride the Very Peak of Heaven': The Parthenon after Antiquity," chap. 9 in *The Parthenon: From Antiquity to the Present*, ed. Jenifer Neils (Cambridge: Cambridge University Press, 2005), 293–329.

long legs.[23] Once reported, it became simply one more of the war stories which followed in rapid succession as campaigns unfolded, battles were won and lost. There is *as yet* no evidence that the event made any impression whatsoever in Muscovy. Arguably, no one there had ever before heard of the Parthenon, and few individuals would have been able to locate Athens on a map.[24]

A decade after the Parthenon blew up, there was another noteworthy event in the Turkish wars. On September 11, 1697, at Zenta (Senta) on the Tisza River in what is now northern Serbia, the Habsburg army under Prince Eugene of Savoy destroyed the Ottoman army, killing the Grand Vizier and sending the Sultan fleeing for his life. News of the victory quickly made the papers, and reports about the battle, the consequent celebrations and the military follow-up continued to be published for several weeks.[25] The *Leipziger Post- und Ordinar-Zeitung* indicated in a report from Vienna, "It is

[23] In fact, it was not even reported immediately in all the newspapers. As Laborde notes (*Athènes*, 2: 148–49 n), Theophraste Renaudot cryptically mentioned the event in his important *Gazette* only on December 27.

[24] Athens was not prominent enough to be listed in "Opisanie razstoianie stolits narochitykh gradov, slavnykh gosudarstv i zemel ... po rozmeru knigi, imenuemyia Vodnyi mir," compiled in 1667, apparently by Andrei Vinius from a Dutch sea atlas and known in at least ten pre-19th-century manuscript copies. See V. A. Petrov, "Geograficheskie spravochniki XVII v. 'Poverstnaia kniga' i 'Opisanie rasstoianiiu stolits, narochitykh gradov slavnykh gosudarstv i zemel'... ot grada Moskvy,'" *Istoricheskii arkhiv* 5 (Moscow-Leningrad: Izd-vo AN SSSR, 1950): 150. Stepan Shamin attempts to demonstrate the geographic knowledge at the Muscovite court by tabulating which cities in the headings of *kuranty* texts were glossed by the clerks in the Diplomatic Chancery. His assumption is that those not glossed were well known to the listeners when the *kuranty* were being read aloud. There is apparently no mention of Athens in the *kuranty* for 1676–82. See S. M. Shamin, "Politiko-geograficheskii krugozor chlenov pravitel'stva tsaria Fedora Alekseevicha," *Drevniaia Rus': Voprosy medievistiki* 1(15) (March 2004): 21–22. In fact Athens was known in Muscovy. As Sergei Bogatyrev has pointed out in a posting to H-EarlySlavic (April 15, 2007), the *Povest' o sozdanii i plenenii Troiskom*, known in 16th-century copies, mentions the city and describes sites in Ancient Greece (but not the Parthenon) which a Muscovite miniaturist even decorated with semi-nude statues when illustrating this passage. A search through the Muscovite translations of Western cosmographies may turn up additional material on Athens, if not on the Parthenon. Individuals like Nikolai Spafarii-Milescu and the Likhud brothers could be expected to have known about Athens, at least from Classical sources.

[25] The most complete collection of early German newspapers, at the Deutsche Presseforschung in Bremen, includes the following with Zenta-related news: *Die Europäische Relation* (Altona), 1697, nos. 73, 75; *Relations-Courier* (Altona), 1697, nos. 145, 147, 149; *Hamburger Relations-Courier*, 1697, no. 146; *Relation aus dem Parnasso* (Hamburg), 1697, nos. 75, 76; *Leipziger Post- und Ordinar-Zeitung*, 1697, nos. 37/1, 37/2 and supplement, 37/4; nos. 38/1, 38/2, 38/4; *Stralsundischer Relations-Courier* 1697, nos. 76-80.

certain that this is the most important action in this entire war in that the enemy has never suffered such a great loss of its best manpower with so little loss on our side."[26] An Imperial commander, Prince Charles of Vaudemont, had trumpeted the news in the streets of Vienna on his way to the Imperial Palace;[27] a few days later the arrival of Count von Dietrichstein with trophies must have created a public sensation. Turkish banners and horse-tail standards (*Ross-Schweiffe*) were displayed in the Cathedral of St. Stephen during the solemn mass celebrating the victory. Additional news articles tabulated the numbers killed and wounded on both sides, the wagons and treasure captured, and painted a gruesome picture of a river so full of corpses that one could walk across on them as though on a bridge. In the days following the battle, the stench of rotting bodies was such as to overwhelm even premodern noses accustomed to foul odors.[28] Reports in the regularly published newspapers were supplemented simultaneously by the publication of separate pamphlets.[29]

Tsar Peter I learned about the Habsburg victory at Zenta in Amsterdam, where he had arrived some two weeks before the battle. During this unprecedented first visit of a Russian ruler to Western Europe, the tsar and his entourage had, of course, ample opportunity to access Western news sources first-hand and send translations of them back to Moscow.[30] Apart from what he could learn from the press, it is clear that the Habsburg court was keeping him well informed about the battle. The Habsburg affairs files contain several

---

[26] *Leipziger Post- und Ordinar-Zeitung*, 1697, no. 38/1, lead article datelined Vienna, 21 September: 597, my translation. For a contemporary English translation of a typical newspaper account of the battle, see *A Full and True Account of a Total Victory over the Turks with an Account of the Coronation of the King of Poland* (n.p. [1697]).

[27] *Leipziger Post- und Ordinar-Zeitung*, 1697, no. 37/1: 584.

[28] "Aus dem Kayserl. Feld-Lager bey Klein-Canischa vom 18. Sept.," *Stralsundischer Relations-Courier*, 1697, no. 80, Vom 1. Wein-Monaht: [4].

[29] See the advertisements in *Hamburger Relations-Courier*, 1697, no. 146, 38/1 (Montagis.), 20 September: 8; *Stralsundischer Relations-Courier*, 1697, no. 82, Vom 8. Wein-Monaht: 8. Of particular interest for its detail and statistics of the Imperial losses is *Relations-Diarium Der Grossen Zwischen denen Käyserlichen und Türckischen Armeen den 11. September 1697...* (Vienna: Anno 1697, den 18. September; several other nearly identical editions). For additional Zenta pamplets, see notes below.

[30] For examples of Dutch newspapers with Russian annotations of their having been translated in the Netherlands while Peter was there, see Ingrid Maier, "Niederländische Zeitungen ('Couranten') des 17. Jahrhunderts im Russischen Staatsarchiv für alte Akten (RGADA), Moskau," *Gutenberg-Jahrbuch 2004*: 196; idem, "Presseberichte am Zarenhof im 17. Jahrhundert: Ein Beitrag zur Vorgeschichte der gedruckten Zeitung in Russland," *Jahrbuch für Kommunikations-Geschichte 2004*: 109. I have not searched Dutch newspapers for accounts about Zenta.

originals and translations of accounts about it which still await analysis.[31] Of significance is the fact that at least three of the Russian accounts about Zenta are known in manuscripts that circulated in Muscovy outside of the chancery milieu.

Arguably the most interesting of these Russian texts about Zenta is the longest, known from a single copy in a Pogodin Collection miscellany of historical texts from the late 17th–early 18th century.[32] The immediate "convoy" of the Zenta pamphlet includes a widely known fictional account of a 16th-century Muscovite embassy, the translation of an inscription on the grave of Constantine the Great, and a copy of the indictment against the rebellious *strel'tsy* in 1698. The text about Zenta seems to be a complete translation of a separately published German pamphlet and is distinguished for its substantial detail about the military operations over a period of about three weeks leading up to the battle.[33] The material undoubtedly comes from eyewitness description, which the publisher then combined with material from shorter newspaper articles.[34] In particular he drew upon the widely distributed account about the arrival of Count Dietrichstein in Vienna, the planned celebration of the *Te Deum Laudamus* ("и завтрешнего дни образ пресветлые Богородицы понесен будет в костел Святаго Стефана и тамо пета будет «Тебе Бога хвалим» для полученной над турком победы"), and the statistics of casualties and booty.

The second Russian account is little more than a statistical tabulation of losses and booty. Like the Pogodin text, it is known in one manuscript, a miscellany compiled from separate quires in the Solovki Monastery.[35] The

---

[31] In particular, it will be necessary to analyze the material in the files in RGADA, Relations of Russia with Austria, f. 32, 1697, op. 1, no. 13, pts. 1 and 2, of which so far I have seen only a listing of headings. Also, there is at least one short newspaper account in the *kuranty* files, RGADA f. 155, 1697, op. 1, no. 12, fol. 61. The latter text does not coincide with any of the Western newspaper accounts I have so far located, nor with the three Russian texts which circulated outside the chanceries in Muscovy. I am grateful to Prof. Maier for references to this material in RGADA and to Stepan Shamin for sending me the text from f. 155.

[32] For a description of the manuscript, Russian National Library (hereafter RNB), Collection of M. P. Pogodin, no. 1561, see A. F. Bychkov, *Opisanie tserkovno-slavianskikh i russkikh rukopisnykh sbornikov Imperatorskoi Publichnoi Biblioteki* (St. Petersburg, 1882), 116–18. I am grateful to Nataliia Pak for providing me with a transcription of this text.

[33] The text corresponds to *Ausführliche Relation, Dessen Was sich seit den 22. Augusti bis den 13. September in Ungarn zwischen der Christlichen und Türckischen Armee zugetragen. Aus dem Feld-Lager bey Zenta den 13. September Ao. 1697* (n. p.). Other German pamphlets about Zenta have similar titles but different texts.

[34] Thus, cf. RNB, Pogodin, no. 1561, fol. 128v, and *Relations-Diarium* (Vienna, 1697): [8], and fols. 128v–129v with *Leipziger Post- und Ordinar-Zeitung*, 1697, no. 38/2: 601.

[35] The manuscript is RNB, Collection of the Solovki Monastery, no. 862/972. What I assume is that one of our three Zenta texts, possibly this one, is also known in a copy

literary context for this short account is fairly typical for texts which originated in government chanceries in the late 17th century but somehow made their way into broader circulation. In this case the "convoy" is other news items: an account about the Astrakhan rebellion in 1706 and a printed copy of the Petrine *Vedomosti* from 1723. The quire containing the Zenta text is arguably the oldest part of the book, possibly a copy dating from soon after the battle.

The Solovki text is prefaced by a heading "Почта," by which we probably should understand the foreign post, the main source providing the newspapers translated in Moscow. It is not uncommon for headings in *kuranty* translations to mention specifically the receipt of the sources through the post. While the title of the text which follows is not identical with the title in the Pogodin account, the two overlap sufficiently to argue that Solovki borrowed from Pogodin or its immediate source.

<table>
<tr><td>RNB, Pogodin No. 1561</td><td>RNB, Solovki No. 862/972</td></tr>
<tr><td>

Подлинное обявление, что с августа ж 22-го по 13 сентября меж християнским войском учинилось. Писано из обозу при Центе сентября 13-го числа 1697-го году.

</td><td>

206-го сентября 1 числа меж христианском и турском учинилось. Писано из обозу при Ценке сентября 13-го числа лета 1698 [*sic*].

</td></tr>
</table>

The Solovki text contains the old-style date for the battle, in place of the dates in the longer pamphlet title encompassed by its long narrative. In the absence of such a specific narrative text in the Solovki copy, the ubiquity of the statistics it contains makes determination of its source difficult.[36] Allowing for some distortion by editing or copying, much that is in it *could* be from the Pogodin text or its immediate source.[37] However, the final phrases seem to argue that the Solovki text is an independent one.[38]

---

from the archive of a north Russian family of peasant merchants, the Shangins. See S. M. Shamin, "K voprosu o chastnom interese russkikh liudei k inostrannoi presse v Rossii XVII stoletiia," *Drevniaia Rus': Voprosy medievistiki* 2(28) (June 2001): 42–59, here 57, citing the discovery by B. N. Morozov.

[36] For the Russian text, see Uo, *Istoriia odnoi knigi,* app. 6b, 301–02.

[37] Cf., for example, *Relations-Diarium* (Vienna, 1697), [8], which contains some of the exact numbers: the total of wounded cavalrymen is 327, of infantrymen 1114, of dead and wounded horses 825, and of lost horses 112.

[38] The mention of the French ambassador is a problem here, although his presence in the vicinity at the time was reported: *Relations-Diarium* (Vienna, 1697), [2], and *Continuation Der erfreulichen Zeitung von der Remarqvablen Victoria Welche die allergerechtesten Käyserlichen Waffen über den Erb-Feind den Türcken in Ungarn bey Zenta erhalten haben* (Vienna, 21 September 1697), [3].

The third Russian account of Zenta is known from a copy which, like that in the Solovki manuscript, was preserved in one of the remote parts of the Russian state far from the capital and its diplomatic translators. We will call this the Khlynov text, since it was in the library of a sacristan in Khlynov (later re-named Viatka) by approximately 1700.[39] The text claims a Latin source, which is not impossible, since the court in Vienna was communicating with Peter in Latin. At its outset, the rhetorical style of the Khlynov text distinguishes it from any of the other accounts so far discovered:

> Хотя в начале дело показалось зело худо, а потом Бог милостивой на нас презрил на Тиссе реке близ места именуемаго Сента, иде же Бог преизобильно даровал победу превеликую.... Правил и наставил нашего войска некоторый князь имянем Евгений принсонт Сабалдивский, которой имеет всякую доблесть, верность и всякия добродетели в себе, которых подобает имети всякому господину.

Although it moves on to a more factual recitation of statistics (which overlap but do not exactly coincide with those in other accounts), the first part of the text concludes in a way that could point to a possible clerical author. It relates the arrest of several Jews including one "well-known" Apekgan, under suspicion of their having aided the enemy.[40] Then in a different hand the manuscript contains a second and partially repetitive set of statistics from a report erroneously datelined Vienna 21 October (instead of September) and apparently drawn from a different source. In style and content we can easily recognize here one of the ubiquitous newspaper reports on the battle. We are left with the unanswered question of where and by whom the two parts of the Khlynov text were spliced together.

Having more than one text about Zenta in contemporary Russian translations should not surprise us, given the centrality of the event for

---

[39] The manuscript is in the State Library of Uzbekistan, MS PI 9250. For details, see Uo, *Istoriia odnoi knigi*, passim; the text is in app. 6a, 300–01. The Khlynov sacristan, Semen Popov, collected other late Muscovite *turcica* and copies made from the published Petrine *Vedomosti*, in which the subject in the first instance was the Great Northern War.

[40] There is a sentence on detention of Jews in an article datelined Vienna, September 22, in the *Stralsundischer Relations-Courier*, 1697, no. 79, Vom 27. Herbst-Monaht: [4]. Nothing there connects their arrest with suspicion of possible relations with the Turks. Sermons preached about the battle were being published, although it is difficult to imagine one of them was a source here. See Christoph Wegleiter, *Christliche Danck-Predigt für den am 1. (11.) Herbst-Monat dieses 1697. Heil-Jahrs unweit Zenta an der Theys herrlich bestrittenen Sieg …* ([Altdorf]: Meyer, 1697); *Festivitas Gloriosa, Das ist Glor- und Sigreiches Lob- und Danck-Fest Welches Den 13. October 1697 in der Hohen Thumb-Stiffts-Kirchen zu Passau wegen der den 11. September wider den Erb-Feind der Türcken in Hungarn bey Zenta erworbenen hochansehnlichen Victori, Solenniter gehalten …* (Passau: Höller, 1697).

Russian-Habsburg relations and the substantial Russian interest in news about the Turkish wars. Such reports often accompany items such as descriptions of Peter the Great's capture of Azov or the apocryphal correspondence of the sultan.[41] Similarly, we should not be surprised by the circulation of such materials outside of the chancery milieu. While for most of the 17th century foreign news in Russia was considered a state secret, occasionally the government disseminated news about successes of Russian allies. Moreover, chancery clerks began to take home copies of texts.[42] It seems unlikely though that enough of this material circulated so that many Muscovites became aware of the contemporary larger world in the same way that a good many individuals in cosmopolitan cities in the West could become informed by purchasing a newspaper or hearing it read aloud in a tavern.

Nonetheless, we might venture here that even in the decade between the report about the Parthenon and that about Zenta, the doors were opening just a bit for the broader dissemination of news, thanks to a desire on the part of Peter's young regime to spread that information. Pamphlets were published in the West about the siege and taking of Azov.[43] The German and Dutch newspapers reported what they learned from Peter's embassy regarding continuing successes of Muscovite armies against the Tatars as well as the fact that those victories were being celebrated in various Russian cities.[44] The idea of public display with appropriate Baroque fanfare to celebrate military victories was becoming part of Russian culture, at least in the capital.

Of course we cannot know what readers in Russia may have thought of the reports about Zenta.[45] It is unlikely that anyone there at the time knew who Prince Eugene was or would have much cared. After all, only thanks to that battle did his name become a household commodity in Vienna. And surely, unlike Azov, whose memory Peter and later generations took pains to preserve, Zenta was quickly forgotten. It was not a Russian battle or a Russian hero.

If such accounts of the Turkish Wars would then largely have fallen on deaf ears in Muscovy, what aspects of contemporaneity might have had

---

[41] For details, see Waugh, *The Great Turkes Defiance*.

[42] For a good overview of evidence about the circulation of news texts outside of the chanceries, see Shamin, "K voprosu."

[43] An example is *Nuova, e Distinta Relatione Della Presa della Famosa Fortezza di Assac Fatta dalli Moscoviti...* (Venice and Rome: Domenico Antonio Ercole, 1696).

[44] For example, *Leipziger Post- und Ordinar-Zeitung*, 1697, no. 27/2: 588.

[45] Peter and his entourage are quite a different matter, given the fact that Zenta paved the way for the Habsburg Emperor to sign a separate peace and abandon his Russian ally. For the consequent Russian negotiations with the Habsburgs, see Iskra Schwarz, "K voprosu o sud'be Sviashchennoi Ligi v sviazi s prebyvaniem Velikogo Posol'stva v Vene," in *Reflections on Russia in the Eighteenth Century*, ed. Joachim Klein et al. (Cologne: Böhlau Verlag, 2001), 126–37.

greater resonance? Among the *kuranty* of the 1660s is a set of translated reports about the false Messiah, Shabbetai Zvi, whose appearance in the Ottoman Empire interested Jew and gentile throughout Europe.[46] These accounts occupy disproportionate space among the news being translated in Muscovy at the time, probably due to the fact that contemporary Muscovites, including the tsar and the members of his court who might be privy to the news, had been touched by widespread eschatological expectations. The events of the church schism were in play, which could only have heightened the contempory relevance of this news. Even though there is no evidence that the accounts in the *kuranty* were disseminated outside the chanceries, a book written as an anti-Jewish polemic by the Ukrainian Orthodox cleric Ioannikii Galiatovskyi included similar Western pamphlet material about Shabbetai. Copies of Galiatovskyi's *Mesia pravdyvyi* circulated in Muscovy, which means that this contemporary pamplet literature reached more people than would otherwise have been the case. All in the name, of course, of religious polemic defending the True Faith.

A second example is a series of accounts containing prophecies of the coming Judgment, the first of which seems to have appeared in Muscovy in the 1660s, and the last around 1730.[47] While not many copies are known, the Russian texts are probably successive translations of pamphlets which kept appearing outside of Muscovy. These pamphlets clearly appealed to religious sentiment, and for that reason, when found in the hands of religious dissenters whom the Muscovite authorities chose to condemn in the same breath with the "Old Believers," they and their owners were punished. Yet here was material of contemporary interest for the Muscovites who would dare to possess and disseminate such texts.

One might conclude from these examples that a focus on such contemporary issues in Muscovy simply proves the old point about Russian cultural backwardness vis-à-vis the West. After all, modern newspaper historians emphasize how a rational and secular age was dawning, as evidenced by a very low percentage of 17th-century newspaper articles devoted to wonder tales

---

[46] For the first discussion of this material in the *kuranty*, see my "News of the False Messiah: Reports on Shabbetai Zevi in Ukraine and Muscovy," *Jewish Social Studies* 41 (1979): 301–22. This has now been superseded by Ingrid Maier's articles: "Polnische Fabelzeitung über Sabbatai Zwi übersetzt für den russischen Zaren (1666)," *Zeitschrift für slavische Philologie* 62 (2003): 1–39; idem, "Acht anonyme deutsche und polnische Sabetha Sebi-Drucke aus dem Jahre 1666. Auf der Spur nach dem Drucker," *Gutenberg-Jahrbuch* 83 (2008): 141–60.

[47] See Uo, *Istoriia odnoi knigi*, 48–53, the work by Michels and Lavrov cited there, and two articles by S. L. Shamin, "V ozhidanii kontsa sveta v Rossii (konets XVII–nachalo XVIII v.)," *Voprosy istorii*, no. 6 (2002): 134–38; idem, "Chudesa v kurantakh vremen pravleniia Fedora Alekseevicha (1676–1682 g.)," *Drevniaia Rus': Voprosy medievistiki* 4 (6), December 2001: 99–110.

and their providential interpretations.[48] The modernizing European mind was abandoning medieval superstition and a religious interpretation of the otherwise inexplicable. Yet by themselves statistics derived from such content analysis are of limited value. The same newspaper publishers who were reporting on Zenta and advertising separate pamphlets on the battle were hawking as well new editions of what they claimed were famous almanacs with astrological prognostications.[49] In fact, in Europe as in Muscovy, the popular mind was still little touched by what we today call the "scientific revolution." Even leading exponents of the latter were still very much into astrology, and most individuals believed in a providential interpretation of history.

Even if Galiatovskyi's writings or these translated eschatological pamphlets reached but a small audience, was there other contemporary news which might have had broader resonance in Muscovy? One possible answer involves the spread of belief in miracle-working relics and icons. The 17th century in Muscovy was a time when veneration of relics and what were understood to be wonder-working icons proliferated. Indeed, alarmed by how such phenomena seemed to be getting out of hand, the Church (backed by the State) attempted, unsuccessfully, to bring the cults under control. Peter the Great's Synod attacked these popular cults with a vengeance, and with an equal lack of success.[50] Yet Muscovites were not alone in such beliefs and veneration, as any number of shrines and cults in the West (with new ones emerging all the time) would illustrate.[51] Even if the spread of news about some new miracle or cure was largely by word of mouth, the news reached a great many people. One might reasonably suppose that they remembered such news much longer than any number of reports connected with an obscure foreign battle, even against the "arch-enemy" of Christendom. To assess the impact of foreign news on early modern European minds requires that we take into account the widest range of other impacts on those same minds, including the legacies of deeply rooted cultural convictions which people would not lightly abandon.

---

[48] See, for example, Böning, *Welteroberung*, 132–35; Johannes Weber, "Strassburg, 1605: The Origins of the Newspaper in Europe," *German History* 24 (2006): 408–09.

[49] For example, in *Stralsundischer Relations-Courier*, 1697, no. 79, Vom 27. HerbstMonath: [8].

[50] For an example, see my "Religion and Regional Identities: The Case of Viatka and the Miracle-Working Icon of St. Nicholas Velikoretskii," *Forschungen zur osteuropäischen Geschichte* 63 (2004): 259–78.

[51] An example in the *kuranty* for 1646 concerns a holy spring at the German city of Hornhausen. See *Vesti-kuranty 1645–1646, 1648 gg.* (Moscow: Nauka, 1980), 136–42. 244–51. As Ingrid Maier shows in a forthcoming study, the Muscovite translation of the long list of those miraculously cured is based on a published German pamphlet, which appeared in more than one edition.

In conclusion, let us examine the afterlife of the news about these events in the Turkish wars. What happened to the Parthenon in 1687 now may seem to be of less interest than a later episode in its history.[52] We have grown accustomed to seeing the building that is emblematic of Athenian culture as a glorious ruin, even if the computer allows us to see a reconstruction in all its original glory. Indeed its iconic status for Greek nationalism and for others' perceptions of the glories of ancient Greece is really an invention of the 19th century. Léon de Laborde's book published in Paris in 1854 was, as Mario Infelise has put it, "inspired by a ferocious anti-Venetian sentiment."[53] But who today would similarly castigate the Venetians, who, after all, share with many of us a common cultural heritage? The news story about the Parthenon which attracts more attention concerns the removal of its sculptures to England by Thomas Bruce, Seventh Earl of Elgin, an event which provoked an immediate and vitriolic response by Lord Byron. In today's post-imperial world where claims about repatriating stolen treasures are a cornerstone of assertive national identity, the story of the Elgin marbles has been elevated to the level of scripture. The plundering of the Parthenon by the Earl of Elgin is emblematic, analogous to how the destruction of the Bamiyan Buddhas by the Taliban and the World Trade Center by al-Qaida are emblematic. However, one can imagine a situation where the focus on news about the Parthenon might again shift, for example in the hands of those who would use the incident to condemn the Turks as they seek to become part of the European Union. It is easy to imagine a discourse: "How could they possibly have thought of using the building as a powder magazine? They don't share European values."

What about the subsequent history of Zenta, which, unlike Athens and the Parthenon, is hardly a household name today? Here too we can see how news in earlier times may remain alive, if for divergent purposes. The great imperial capitals are full of emblems of past glories, which may still retain some meaning to those once ruled (or ruling) from the imperial palaces. In Budapest, a 19th-century statue to Prince Eugene commemorates the victory at Zenta, a major step in the liberation of Hungary from Ottoman rule. It is clear though that Hungarians saw the restoration of Habsburg rule throughout Hungary as a mixed blessing (the most striking evidence being the rebellion of Ferenc Rákóczi II a few years later). Even on the 300th anniversary of the battle, the joint Hungarian-Austrian exhibition commemorating

---

[52] On the history of responses to the Parthenon, see Mary Beard, *The Parthenon* (London: Profile Books, 2002); also, *The Parthenon*, ed. Jenifer Neils, esp. chaps. 10, 11.

[53] Infelise, "The War," 233n4. Note Laborde's dedication in vol. 2 of his *Athénes*: "Aux vandales, mutilateurs, spoliateurs, restaurateurs, de tous les pas, hommage d'une profonde indignation" ([iii]).

the event focused far more on its consequences for Habsburg-Hungarian relations than on the ousting of the Turks.[54]

Zenta made Prince Eugene a hero in the Habsburg Empire. His lustre grew from his continuing military success during the wars of the first decades of the eighteenth century.[55] If the Westernizing nobility of Peter's time were looking for a model to emulate, Prince Eugene ("которой имеет всякую доблесь, верность и всякия добродетели в себе, которых подобает имети всякому господину") could have served them well, as our Khlynov text so nicely suggests. Who could not but be impressed by his lovely Belvedere palace occupying one of the choicest pieces of real estate in Vienna and decorated with statuary proclaiming the apotheosis of its owner? The foreign visitor to Vienna today surely will note the statue to Eugene outside the Hofburg, even if it may take busy thumbing through the Lonely Planet guide to learn who he is. The road from Zenta leads as well to the Military History Museum in Vienna, where displays glorifying Austrian military history give pride of place to the sieges of Vienna. Zenta is there too, with the display of the gold signet ring which is mentioned in so many of the contemporary news reports as having been around the Grand Vizier's neck when he died in the battle (fig. 2). Just a few steps away are the banners and catafalque for Prince Eugene's state funeral and burial in 1736 in a separate chapel in the Cathedral of St. Stephen, where Zenta had been celebrated with a solemn Te Deum. Perhaps more than ever in a world where Vienna no longer rules an empire and Austrian military power is an artifact of memory, Austrian national identity requires the cult of Prince Eugene. Yet in witnessing, as I did in 2004, the use of the Military History Museum as a venue for ceremonies involving the current Austrian military and attempts there to interest Austrian schoolchildren in their past by showing them displays of old weaponry, I cannot but wonder whether Eugene and the Turkish wars have much of a future. Perhaps a defeat, like that at Kosovo for the Serbs, could better serve the purposes of national identity. Maybe it would be good simply to forget a battle whose reports, in the fashion of the day, routinely branded the Turks "The Archenemy." In the parts of Europe where Zenta has been most celebrated, such epithets just might be resurrected as part of a modern xenophobic and racist nationalism in response to, say, Turkish immigrants. Then we might well wish that the battle had been as quickly forgotten in Central Europe as it was in Muscovy.

---

[54] See *Zenta 1697. Neubeginn für Ungarn und Österreich. Austellung anlässlich des 300. Jahrestages der Schlacht bei Zenta*, ed. Lajos Cecséenyi (Vienna-Budapest, 1997). I am grateful to Prof. Andreas Kappeler for sending me a copy of this difficult-to-obtain booklet.

[55] One can sense the beginning of this adulation in contemporary texts. Verses at the end of one of the pamphlets begin: "Steh stille, Sonne steh! hier ist dein Josua, d. Savoyens tapffrer Prinz ..." (*Continuation Der erfreulichen Zeitung*, [4]).

In the Crossfire of the Cold War:
A Personal Note

Samuel H. Baron

Thanks to a fellowship at Harvard University, by late 1958 I had almost completed research for the full-length biography I intended to produce on G. V. Plekhanov. In drafting the first few chapters, I found myself lacking some data on my subject's early life, so I wrote to the administration of Dom Plekhanova requesting answers to a number of specific questions. At about the same time I expressed to Charles Gredler (then Chief of the Slavic Section of Widener Library) my hope to do first-hand research in Dom Plekhanova. On October 7, he obligingly wrote to V. Barashchenkov, director of the Saltykov-Shchedrin Library, with whom he had a working relationship, inquiring whether I might have access to Dom Plekhanova—which was then, as now, an affiliate of that library.[1] In a letter dated October 30, 1958, from T. K. Ukhmylova (then the head of Dom Plekhanova), I received very helpful answers to the questions I had posed. And, in a letter to Gredler dated November 14, Barashchenkov pledged that both published and manuscript materials at Dom Plekhanova would be available to me.[2] On January 16, 1959, Mme. Ukhmylova graciously wrote to me saying that she "would be pleased to see you within the walls" of the archive.[3] Unspeakably elated, I immediately applied to the Social Science Research Council and was awarded a research grant to enable me to take advantage of this exciting opportunity.

I was inexpressibly shocked, therefore, to receive another letter from Ukhmylova, dated February 25, 1959, declaring "as an addendum" to her previous communication that it would be unwise to plan a trip to Leningrad.[4] Lest there be any misunderstanding, she sent another letter, dated March 30, stating unequivocally that no materials could be put at my disposal. A new edition of Plekhanov's *Sochineniia* was being prepared, she explained, so that manuscripts and other materials would not be available.[5] Rather than acting

---

[1] C. Gredler to V. Barashchenkov, 7 October 1958. Of course the Saltykov-Shchedrin Library was renamed the Russian National Library in 1992.

[2] V. Barashchenkov to C. Gredler, 14 November 1958.

[3] T. K. Ukhmylova to S. Baron, 16 January 1959.

[4] T. K. Ukhmylova to S. Baron, 25 February 1959.

[5] T. K. Ukhmylova to S. Baron, 30 March 1959.

Rude & Barbarous Kingdom Revisited: Essays in Russian History and Culture in Honor of Robert O. Crummey. Chester S. L. Dunning, Russell E. Martin, and Daniel Rowland, eds. Bloomington, IN: Slavica Publishers, 2008, 507–10.

on her own, she was undoubtedly following an order given by Barashchen-kov, her superior.

It was impossible to believe the reason given me. What, then, could have been the real reason for the about-face? A close look at the chronology and the context of what occurred may demonstrate that I had been caught in the crossfire of the Cold War—specifically, the ideological combat between the propagandist Communist Information Bureau (Cominform) and the aggres-sively anticommunist Congress for Cultural Freedom. Allow me to elaborate.

An article of mine entitled "Plekhanov's Russia: The Impact of the West upon an 'Oriental' Society" had appeared in the June 1958 issue of *The Journal of the History of Ideas*.[6] In that piece, I cited major thinkers such as Montes-quieu, Hegel, Marx and Engels, and Max Weber who had characterized old Russia, along with China, Egypt, India, and Persia, as oriental despotisms. I also called attention to Karl Wittfogel, whose magnum opus *Oriental Despot-ism: A Comparative Study of Total Power* had recently been published.[7] In that work Wittfogel too identified Russia as an example of the phenomenon he had studied.[8] Wittfogel actually devoted a great deal of attention to ideas on the subject advanced by Marx and Engels and by Lenin. But he obviously knew little about the central role that the concept played in Plekhanov's thought, which I spelled out on the basis of my study of Plekhanov's writings from the 1880s and 1890s. (I had not yet read his subsequently published, multivolume *History of Russian Social Thought*.) Plekhanov had gone far be-yond Marx and Engels in the development of this idea, I asserted, and in many ways had anticipated Wittfogel.

To illustrate Plekhanov's conception succinctly, I cited the following pas-sage: "Old Muscovite Russia was distinguished by its completely Asiatic character. Its social life, its administration, the psychology of its inhabitants—everything in it was alien to Europe and very closely related to China, Persia, and ancient Egypt."[9] He credited Peter the Great's reforms, especially the eco-nomic reforms, with initiating the transformation of old (Muscovite) Russia. The process had continued since Peter's time, ultimately bringing about what Plekhanov called the Europeanization of the economy; and this fundamental change foreshadowed, he believed, the Europeanization of Russian social life via the overthrow of the tsarist regime. The last lines of my article read in part: "In 1917 there came an upheaval ... utterly different from that which Plekhanov had predicted.... [It] installed in power a regime that became, at

---

[6] Samuel H. Baron, "Plekhanov's Russia: The Impact of the West upon an 'Oriental' Society," *The Journal of the History of Ideas* 19: 3 (June 1958): 388–404.
[7] Karl Wittfogel, *Oriental Despotism: A Comparative Study of Total Power* (New Haven: Yale University Press, 1957).
[8] Russia figures prominently in Wittfogel's *Oriental Despotism*; see especially chap. 9 and pp. 427–42.
[9] Baron, "Plekhanov's Russia," 400.

least in the opinion of some, a modern version of the oriental despotism that Plekhanov believed to be dead and buried in Russia's past."[10] In a footnote, I commented: "Professor Wittfogel is a conspicuous exponent of this view."

My article would in all likelihood not have attracted attention outside a narrow circle of scholars but for its connection to Wittfogel. Karl Wittfogel (1890–1988) was a notable German historian and Sinologist who had been an active member of the German Communist Party. In 1934, he escaped from Nazi Germany and moved to the United States, where he became a professor at the University of Washington.[11] At some point, he became a virulent anti-communist and testified against American communists before Congressional committees. I did not share his overall outlook; indeed, in a review I had written of his *Oriental Despotism*, I found the work illuminating and suggestive, but I also criticized the polemical tone in what was ostensibly a scholarly work.[12] Nevertheless, when I sent an offprint of my article to Wittfogel, he responded enthusiastically. He inquired whether I could send reprints that he wished to distribute to a dozen persons—he named them—whom he thought would find my article of interest.[13]

On October 17, 1958, Wittfogel informed me that Boris Souvarine, who edited a Paris-based journal called *Le Contrât Social*, wished to publish a French translation of my article. I was pleasantly surprised and readily agreed. Later I learned that Souvarine was a Russian who had emigrated to France, had served as a leader of the Communist International, and was a conspicuous figure in the French Communist Party. When he became critical of Stalin, he was expelled from the Party (1924), but he remained politically active and in time became a fierce anti-communist. In 1935, he published what was probably the most significant biography of Stalin up to that time.[14]

There were obvious parallels between the lives of Wittfogel and Souvarine. They were among the types—liberals, former communists, and non-communist leftists—who were mobilized by the Congress for Cultural Freedom (created in 1950, and presently headquartered in Paris) to engage in ideological combat with the Soviet Union and international communism. The organization was spearheaded in the United States by ex-communist Sidney Hook, a professor of philosophy at New York University, and supported by leading intellectuals such as John Dewey, Arthur Schlesinger, Jr., Bertrand

---

[10] Ibid., 404.

[11] A hagiographic study of Wittfogel's thought is G. L. Ulmen, *The Science of Society: Toward an Understanding of the Life and Work of Karl August Wittfogel* (The Hague: Mouton, 1978).

[12] *The Journal of Politics* 20, no. 1 (1958): 220–22.

[13] K. Wittfogel to S. Baron, 3 September 1958.

[14] Boris Souvarine, *Staline: Aperçu historique du bolchévisme* (Paris: Plon, 1935). An English edition was published a few years later: *Stalin: A Critical Survey of Bolshevism*, trans. C. L. R. James (New York: Longmans, Green and Co., 1939).

Russell, Arthur Koestler, Raymond Aron, and Ignazio Silone. The Congress for Cultural Freedom sponsored many international conferences and established numerous publications to carry on its work. Among these was *Encounter*, based in England, and *Le Contrât Social* in Paris. Only in 1967, many years after the Congress for Cultural Freedom's creation, did it become known that the organization and its publications were covertly funded by the CIA.[15]

My article appeared in the January 1959 issue of *Le Contrât Social*. I feel certain that its appearance triggered the disappointing letters from Dom Plekhanova that I received in late February and March. This proposition assumes that my article became known to officials in the USSR—perhaps they were employed in the Saltykov-Shchedrin Library—who carefully tracked the activities of ideological foes, including the publications of the Congress for Cultural Freedom. My article would have been anathema to Soviet authorities on several scores, but most immediately because of its apparent association with Wittfogel and Souvarine and its link to the Congress for Cultural Freedom.

I was only a small fry and by no means a militant Cold Warrior, but—like countless others of that era—I suffered the consequences of being caught in the crossfire between two resolute antagonists. This misfortune, however, was not fatal to my project. Research in the huge amount of printed material available enabled me four years later to complete *Plekhanov: The Father of Russian Marxism*.[16] And 35 years later, in a remarkable reversal made possible by the collapse of the Soviet Union, a Russian edition of the book was published as a collaborative effort of Dom Plekhanova and the former Saltykov-Shchedrin (now the Russian National) Library.[17]

---

[15] A relevant useful work is Frances Stonor Saunders, *The Cultural Cold War: The CIA and the World of Arts and Letters* (New York: New Press, 2000).

[16] Samuel H. Baron, *Plekhanov: The Father of Russian Marxism* (Stanford, CA: Stanford University Press, 1963).

[17] Samuel H. Baron, *G. V. Plekhanov, osnovopolozhnik russkogo marksizma* (St. Petersburg: Izd-vo Rossiiskoi natsional'noi biblioteki, 1998).

Contributors

Samuel H. Baron, Distinguished Professor Emeritus, University of North Carolina, Chapel Hill, shbaron@email.unc.edu

Jay Bergman, Professor of History, Central Connecticut State University, bergmanj@mail.ccsu.edu

Paul Bushkovitch, Professor of History, Yale University, paul.bushkovitch@yale.edu

Chester S. L. Dunning, Professor of History, Texas A&M University, c-dunning@tamu.edu

Carsten Goehrke, Professor of History Emeritus, University of Zurich, goehrke@ggaweb.ch

David M. Goldfrank, Professor of History, Georgetown University, goldfrad@georgetown.edu

Charles J. Halperin, Independent scholar, chalperi@indiana.edu

Richard Hellie, Thomas E. Donnelly Professor of History, University of Chicago, hell@uchicago.edu

Daniel H. Kaiser, Professor of History and Joseph F. Rosenfield Professor of Social Studies, Grinnell College, KAISER@grinnell.edu

Edward L. Keenan, Andrew W. Mellon Professor of History, Harvard University, keenan@fas.harvard.edu

Valerie Kivelson, Professor of History, University of Michigan, vkivelso@umich.edu

Ann M. Kleimola, Professor of History, University of Nebraska, Lincoln, rintintin996@yahoo.com

Rude & Barbarous Kingdom Revisited: Essays in Russian History and Culture in Honor of Robert O. Crummey. Chester S. L. Dunning, Russell E. Martin, and Daniel Rowland, eds. Bloomington, IN: Slavica Publishers, 2008, 511–12.

Nancy Shields Kollmann, William H. Bonsall Professor of History and Director of the Center for Russian, East European and Eurasian Studies, Stanford University, kollmann@stanford.edu

Ol'ga E. Kosheleva, Senior Fellow, Russian Academy of Education, Moscow

Eve Levin, Professor of History, University of Kansas, evelevin@ku.edu

Russell E. Martin, Associate Professor of History, Westminster College, New Wilmington, PA, martinre@westminster.edu

Georg B. Michels, Professor of History, University of California, Riverside, georg.michels@ucr.edu

David B. Miller, Professor of History Emeritus, Roosevelt University, dbmjjm@rcn.com

Boris N. Morozov, Senior Fellow, Archeographical Commission, Moscow, bmorozov@mtu-net.ru

Donald Ostrowski, Lecturer in Extension, Harvard University, don@wjh.harvard.edu

Alexis Pogorelskin, Professor of History, University of Minnesota, Duluth, apogorel@d.umn.edu

Nicholas V. Riasanovsky, Sidney Hellman Professor of European History Emeritus, University of California, Berkeley

Roy R. Robson, Professor of History, University of the Sciences in Philadelphia, r.robson@usp.edu

Daniel Rowland, Associate Professor of History and Director Emeritus of the Gaines Center for the Humanities, University of Kentucky, hisdan@uky.edu

Jennifer B. Spock, Associate Professor of History, Eastern Kentucky University, Jennifer.Spock@EKU.EDU

Ludwig Steindorff, Professor of History, Christian-Albrechts-Universität zu Kiel, lsteindorff@oeg.uni-kiel.de

Carol B. Stevens, Professor of History, Colgate University, kstevens@mail.colgate.edu

Isolde Thyrêt, Associate Professor of History, Kent State University, ithyret@kent.edu

Daniel C. Waugh, Professor of History Emeritus, University of Washington, dwaugh@u.washington.edu

George G. Weickhardt, Independent scholar engaged in private practice of the law in San Francisco, CA, GWeickhardt@Ropers.com